INTERNATIONAL
HANDBOOK
OF
NATIONAL PARKS
AND
NATURE RESERVES

INTERNATIONAL HANDBOOK OF NATIONAL PARKS AND NATURE RESERVES

Edited by CRAIG W. ALLIN

GREENWOOD PRESS

New York • Westport, Connecticut • London

Library of Congress Cataloging-in-Publication Data

International handbook of national parks and nature reserves / edited
   by Craig W. Allin.
      p. cm.
   ISBN 0-313-24902–4 (lib. bdg. : alk. paper)
      1. National parks and reserves—Handbooks, manuals, etc.
   I. Allin, Craig W. (Craig Willard)
   SB481.I565   1990
   338.78—dc20   89-26039

British Library Cataloguing in Publication Data is available.

Library of Congress Catalog Card Number: 89-26039
ISBN: 0-313-24902-4

First published in 1990

Greenwood Press, 88 Post Road West, Westport, Connecticut 06881
An imprint of Greenwood Publishing Group, Inc.

Printed in the United States of America

The paper used in this book complies with the
Permanent Paper Standard issued by the National
Information Standards Organization (Z39.48-1984).

10 9 8 7 6 5 4 3 2 1

CONTENTS

FIGURES AND TABLES

FIGURES

TABLES

PREFACE

Like a diner in a poor restaurant, a reader seeking to learn something of the state of preservation worldwide is likely to become overfilled yet remain unsatisfied.

Although scientists will argue persuasively that one cannot have too much science and that many of the features and phenomena of national parks around the world remain unstudied or understudied, the world is awash with thousands, if not hundreds of thousands, of scientific monographs dealing with various aspects of the geology, archaeology, ecology, flora, or fauna of one or more national parks. This literature is valuable for its contribution to our understanding of the natural world, but being written by scientists for scientists, it is rarely scintillating.

If the scientific monograph has a polar opposite in the national parks literature, it must surely be the travel brochure, as glossy and glib as the monograph is slow and scholarly. Written by admen to snare tourist dollars, the travel brochure describes parks that may be more illusion than reality.

Between the monograph and the travel brochure, there is, thankfully, a significant literature of parks and reserves, the work of scientists, journalists, historians, and others. At its best, this literature captivates the imagination with reality, not fiction. It deals most often with a particular park or a particular species, less frequently with a nation or a continent. Some parks, like Yellowstone or Kruger, and some species, like the African elephant or the Asian tiger, receive widespread attention; others go virtually ignored. Still, given enough time and the resources of a first-rate library, a thirst for global parks awareness might well be satiated here. Certainly it would be an enlightening effort.

National parks literature with a more general perspective or a comparative focus is more difficult to find. For a decade beginning in 1976 there was good reading in the international journal *Parks*, but it has fallen on financial hard times and ceased publication. Today, the proceedings of the decennial world conferences on national parks and the publications of the International Union for the Conservation of Nature (IUCN) may provide the only readily available sources for a comparative exploration of global parks preservation. Both have enormous value, but the former are infrequent and the latter primarily statistical.

The *International Handbook of National Parks and Nature Reserves* was conceived to fill an important gap in the national parks literature. Before discussing what this volume is, let me attempt to clarify what it is not.

The handbook is not exhaustive. There is far more to be said about the parks and reserves of each nation represented here. A major task as editor was to rein in the enthusiasm for prose on the part of contributors who might have preferred to write a book rather than a chapter. To be exhaustive of the subjects covered would require a library rather than a single volume, and it would contradict the image of practicality conjured up by the term *handbook*. In the end, to be exhaustive would be exhausting.

The handbook is not comprehensive. Approximately 120 nations have established national parks or similar reserves. About one in four are represented here. To attempt to survey them all would reduce this volume to a statistical summary. As such it would be a poor imitation of IUCN's ambitious efforts at global record keeping.

Although neither exhaustive nor comprehensive, the *International Handbook of National Parks and Nature Reserves* is representative, comparative, distinguished and political. Each of these characteristics is a virtue.

The handbook is representative. The chapters that follow describe and evaluate national parks and nature reserves in twenty-five nations and one regional and linguistic cluster. The nations selected represent the regional diversity to be found within each of six continents: Africa, Asia, Australia, Europe, North and South America, as well a range of Pacific island nations. The collection includes some of the wealthiest and most technologically developed nations on earth and some of the least. It includes former colonial powers and former colonies. It includes nations with long histories of park preservation and nations that have only recently undertaken this mission. It includes nations with diverse cultures and varying heritage of religion and language. If there is any systematic bias in the collection, it is probably to overrepresent nations with fairly active national park and reserve programs at the expense of those less active. Nevertheless, the chapters that follow describe an enormous diversity of experience, allow the reader to form an impression of the state of global park preservation, and suggest how much remains unknown about successful management of national parks and nature reserves and how much one nation might learn from the experience of another.

The handbook is explicitly comparative. Each of the chapters is written to a common outline. Each author addresses the history of park preservation, the natural values associated with parks and reserves, and the legal and administrative structures charged with park protection and management. Although the diverse experiences of the various countries here represented guarantee differing degrees of emphasis for each of these major themes and differing approaches to their articulation, these common topics provide the reader with an unusual opportunity for comparative study.

The handbook is distinguished because its contributors are. Efforts to identify and recruit them spanned almost three years and required extensive correspondence with participants in world park conferences, national park managers, and college and university faculty in many countries. Each of the authors is an expert in the area of his or her assignment, and many will be familiar to knowledgeable readers. Most are natives of the countries about which they write. Most have been involved as managers or consultants with the national park systems they describe. Contributors have been asked to evaluate as well. Evaluations are subjective, of course; they can be expected to reflect personal values and training. This subjectivity is inevitable; it is the price we pay for expertise. With expertise comes identification—with the country, the culture, the parks and reserves, and the individuals and agencies striving to preserve and protect them, often against insuperable odds. What is offered here, therefore, is most often an insider's view of the parks and their management. Whatever their respective affiliations, past or present, the contributors speak for themselves.

The handbook is political. An ecologist might have organized a survey of the world's parks and reserves according to some principle of biogeography. If the purpose is to determine how effectively the world's parks preserve samples of the world's ecosystems, nothing could be more appropriate. In fact, that is exactly how the third world conference on national parks was organized. This handbook, however, is organized according to political boundaries. To the world's fauna, flora, and gea, political boundaries are perfectly irrelevant, but to humans political boundaries are often the most important things in the world. The gods may have created nature, but it is the nation-state, a sovereign political entity, that creates, maintains, and manages national parks and reserves. By focusing on nations, we may better understand the impetus to preservation within each jurisdiction, and we will certainly better understand the legal protections, political pressures, and administrative arrangements that influence park protection.

The arrangement of the handbook is straightforward. An introduction sets the stage discussing the national park concept and its historical implementation first in individual nations and later by means of international agreements and institutions. Twenty-seven numbered chapters follow. Twenty-four deal comprehensively with the parks and reserves of a single nation. In deference to the pivotal role the United States has played in the global history of national parks development and to the exceptionally rich and diverse systems of nature preservation that have been established here, two chapters were allocated to the United States. One focuses on the traditional national parks, the other on the more recently established wilderness areas. The other exception amounts to a consolidation rather than a division. I accepted the opportunity to have the nine nations of French-speaking West Africa described in a single chapter.

Within each of the numbered chapters three broad themes are addressed. A section on history describes the major events associated with park preservation. A section on the parks and reserves themselves describes, as appropriate, the geological, historical, archaeological, biological, ecological, aesthetic, or recreational values designated for protection. A section on administration describes the agencies charged with park and reserve management, the threats with which they must cope, and the philosophies and resources with which they respond. Chapters also include notes and/or bibliography, which should be helpful to users who would like to read further. An effort has been made to emphasize titles available in English.

These numbered chapters are presented in alphabetical order by each country's popular name. Where a single popular name is claimed by more than one modern state—which is true of China and Germany in this volume—the full legal names are used in the chapter titles without affecting their alphabetical order. The consolidated chapter appears alphabetically as West Africa.

Completion of a task such as this has a way of reminding one of a lifetime of debts: to my parents, Willard and Beverly Allin; to the teachers who most influenced and guided my intellectual development, James Magee and Harold Fletcher at Grinnell College and Duane Lockard at Princeton University; to Kathleen Armstrong, who encouraged me to follow my heart and explore the politics of public lands; and especially to Elizabeth Sparks, who willingly tolerates both my presence and my absence on a daily basis.

There are, of course, more specific debts associated with this volume: to the late Thomas Lucke of the National Park Service for his valuable advice and continuous goodwill; to Dean William Heywood, Dean Dennis Moore, and President David Marker of Cornell College for moral and financial support; to Harold Eidsvik for expert commentary on the introduction; to Jeffrey Cardon, Paul Garvin, and David Lyon, each of whom was happy to loan me a combination of expertise in natural science and a language other than English; to Sally Clute, Allison Howard, Carol Salazar, and Carlos Wendorff for help with translation from the Spanish; to Charles Connell, Sue Lifson, David Loebszck, and David Weddle for useful advice in their areas of expertise; to Carol Brokel, Diane Harrington, Lori Reihle, and Beth Wangen for timely and accurate typing; to Carol Brokel, Janice Ilg, Sonia Johnson, Beth Lewin, Janene Panfil, Tamra Thompson, Fleur Updegraft, Beth Wangen, and Christina Willemsen for administrative assistance with different parts of the project; to Juanita Lewis, Margaret Maybury, Loomis Mayer, Penny Sippel, and Mary Sive of Greenwood Press for their patience and skill; and most of all to forty contributors whose expertise and diligence are reflected throughout this volume.

Craig W. Allin

ABBREVIATIONS

ACT	Australian Capital Territory
ANILCA	Alaska National Interest Lands Conservation Act
AOF	Afrique Occidentale Française
APN	Administración de Parques Nacionales (Argentina)
ASI	Archaeological Survey of India
BLM	Bureau of Land Management (United States)
CITES	Convention on International Trade in Endangered Species
COHDEFOR	Corporación Hondurena de Desarrollo Forestal
CONAF	Corporación Nacional Forestal (Chile)
CONCOM	Council of Nature Conservation Ministers (Australia)
CONICET	Consejo Nacional de Investigaciones Científicas y Técnicas (Argentina)
CONSUPLANE	Consejo Superior de Planificación Economica (Honduras)
CPA	Construction and Planning Administration (China)
EEC	European Economic Community
FAO	Food and Agriculture Organization (United Nations)
GAO	General Accounting Office (United States)
HEA	Honduran Ecological Association
IBP	International Biological Program (Australia)
ICBP	International Council for Bird Protection
IFAN	Institut Français d'Afrique Noir
INDERENA	Instituto Nacional de los Recursos Naturales Renovables y del Ambiente (Colombia)

INPARQUES	Instituto Nacional de Parques (Venezuela)
IUCN	International Union for the Conservation of Nature and Natural Resources
IUPN	International Union for the Protection of Nature (renamed as IUCN)
LAC	limits of acceptable change (United States)
MAB	Man and the Biosphere Program (United Nations)
NACS	Natural Areas of Canadian Significance
NGO	nongovernmental organization
NPCA	National Parks and Conservation Association (United States)
NPPC	National Parks and Primitive Areas Council (Australia)
NRPP	Natural Resource Protection Program (United States)
NWPS	National Wilderness Preservation System (United States)
OECD	Organization for Economic Cooperation and Development
PHPA	Direktorat Jenderal Perlindungan Hutan dan Pelestarian Alam (Indonesia)
PNA	protected natural areas
RENARE	Dirección General de Recursos Naturales Renovables (Honduras)
RITS	Resource Information Tracking System (United States)
SRP	Significant Resource Problems (program revised as NRPP)
UNDP	United Nations Development Programme
UNEP	United Nations Environmental Programme
Unesco	United Nations Educational, Scientific, and Cultural Organization
VNIIPRIRODA	All-Union Research Institute of Nature Conservation and Reserves (USSR)
WWF	World Wide Fund for Nature (previously the World Wildlife Fund)

INTERNATIONAL
HANDBOOK
OF
NATIONAL PARKS
AND
NATURE RESERVES

INTRODUCTION: NATIONAL PARKS AND NATURE RESERVES IN GLOBAL PERSPECTIVE

Craig W. Allin

The national park movement was born in the United States, but it has developed and matured around the world. In the course of that development there has been substantial evolution—hopefully substantial maturation—in the philosophy which supports park preservation.

Early preservationists viewed national parks as isolated islands of naturalness distinct from civilization or human culture. In their view preservation was enough, and in the nineteenth century perhaps it was. In the twentieth century, however, population growth and economic and technological development have conspired to produce a global interdependence characterized by significant environmental problems. National boundaries present no obstacle to the unpleasant effects of ozone depletion or global warming, but they present a significant obstacle to the international cooperation that will be required to achieve global remedies.

The boundaries of national parks and reserves are equally permeable, and there is a growing appreciation that what goes on within the boundaries of national parks and what goes on beyond those boundaries is inextricably linked. Today a growing international conservation community regards national parks and reserves not as isolated islands of naturalness but as integral components in a global system of nature conservation, the success or failure of which will profoundly affect all the residents of Planet Earth.

In this volume chapters 1 through 27 elaborate the contributions of specific countries to the goal of global conservation. This introduction sets the stage by developing the conceptual, historical, and organizational context that the subsequent chapters all share. The terms ''national park'' and ''nature reserve'' are defined both in terms of the internationally accepted norms and also in the more general terms in which they are employed in this volume. The early history of the modern national park movement in the United States is briefly explored, as is the export of the national park concept to countries worldwide. Efforts to organize internationally on behalf of national parks and nature reserves are recounted, with particular emphasis on the era since World War II. It is in this most recent period that international conservation seems to have come of age, spawning important international organizations, setting rudimentary international standards, and providing formal international recognition and support for the preservation efforts of national governments. The chapter concludes with some observations about national parks preservation in the 1990s and beyond.

NATIONAL PARKS AND NATURE RESERVES

Today the terms "national park" and "nature reserve" have reasonably distinct meanings assigned by the International Union for the Conservation of Nature (IUCN) and generally recognized by the scientific and academic community around the world.

In November of 1969 the Tenth General Assembly of the IUCN meeting in New Delhi, India, recommended a uniform definition for national parks. Three years later this definition was endorsed by the Second World Conference on National Parks. The General Assembly proposed that

all governments agree to reserve the term "National Park" to areas answering the following characteristics and to ensure that their local authorities and private organizations wishing to set aside nature reserves do the same.

A National Park is a relatively large area:

1. where one or several ecosystems are not materially altered by human exploitation and occupation, where plant and animal species, geomorphological sites and habitats are of special scientific, educative, and recreative interest or which contains a natural landscape of great beauty; and

2. where the highest competent authority of the country has taken steps to prevent or eliminate as soon as possible exploitation or occupation in the whole area and to enforce effectively the respect of ecological, geomorphological or aesthetic features which have led to its establishment; and

3. where visitors are allowed to enter, under special conditions, for inspirational, educative, cultural and recreative purposes.[1]

The London Convention of 1933, the Washington Convention of 1940, and the African Convention of 1968 impose additional restrictions designed for the protection of fauna and flora, and the IUCN has adopted three supplementary standards requiring (a) strict statutory protection, (b) a certain minimum area, and (c) effective protection in terms of staffing and budget.

The IUCN has similarly defined nature reserves as areas "set aside for protection of nature and for scientific research."[2] This category is subdivided into "strict nature reserves," which are kept entirely free from human disturbance except for the minimal facilities required for scientific research, and "managed nature reserves," which differ from strict nature reserves in that "active management to protect particular species or biotic communities takes place within them."[3]

In 1978 a committee on nomenclature within the IUCN's Commission on National Parks and Protected Areas created a typology of protected areas based on the objectives for which the areas are established and managed. The typology recognized ten categories of protected areas, of which national parks, strict nature reserves, and managed nature reserves are three. The first eight categories denote a continuum of protection from Category 1 (Scientific Reserve/Strict Nature Reserve) to Category 8 (Multiple-Use Management Area/Managed Resource Area). Categories 9 and 10 stand outside the continuum, denoting areas recognized internationally as Biosphere Reserves and World [Natural] Heritage Sites.

At the request of the United Nations and consistent with the definitions stated above, the IUCN maintains a formal list of areas qualifying as "National Parks and Equivalent Reserves." The U.N. list provides the most definitive catalog of protected natural areas worldwide, and by 1985 the number of such areas had swelled to more than 3,000. However, as Raymond F. Dasmann has noted, "The concept of a national park which emerges from [the IUCN's] requirements and restrictions is sufficiently exclusive that a high percentage of the world's natural reserves actually included in the U.N. list would not be included if these criteria were strictly applied."[4]

Strict application of any international conservation standards is a two-edged sword. The desire to be included on the international rosters may motivate national leaders to higher standards of protection for their parks and reserves. Such a response would appear to serve the cause of international conservation. On the other hand, if areas that engender significant national pride are denied international recognition by the application of strict standards, national leaders may be inclined to reduce rather than to enhance their conservation efforts.

In this volume no effort has been made to set or enforce a standard that exceeds that of the IUCN. If anything, a somewhat more relaxed standard serves as the organizing principle for the chapters that follow. For our purposes the phrase "national parks and nature reserves" may be regarded as a generic term denoting any system of land tenure or zoning designed primarily to protect biogeographical or ecological resources of national or international importance and to preserve them in, or restore them to, a regime characterized by minimal human interference with natural processes. As the following chapters indicate, the standard of "national significance" varies widely as one moves from small, densely populated countries, where biogeographic features have been extensively modified by extended human occupation, to large, sparsely populated countries where extensive areas still show little sign of human modification.

Areas meeting the definition of "national parks and nature reserves" set forth in the previous paragraph are within the scope of this volume whether or not they are called ''national parks'' or ''nature reserves'' by their respective governments and whether or not the governments with primary responsibility for their creation or maintenance are in fact national.

Examples of areas administered primarily as natural reserves by national governments but not officially designated ''national parks'' include some nature monuments in Chile, aesthetic forests in Greece, wilderness areas and some national monuments and national wildlife refuges in the United States, and safari areas in Zimbabwe. Examples of areas with national or international significance that are administered by regional governments can be found in nations with federal forms of government, including Australia, Canada, the Federal Republic of Germany, and the United States.

In contrast, areas that have been designated as ''national parks'' or ''nature reserves'' by their respective governments will fall outside the scope of this volume if the primary purpose of their preservation is cultural or historical. A prominent example is Mesa Verde National Park in the United States, which protects primarily the cliff dwellings and other archaeological remains of the area's pre-Columbian residents.

HISTORICAL ORIGINS

The historical origins of parks preservation are lost in antiquity. Members of aboriginal hunting cultures often worshipped the animals among which they lived and upon which they depended for food. Elaborate taboos governed behavior, ensuring respect for the quarry and success for the hunters. In Siberia and North America the bear was described in honorific terms, and hunters often attempted to atone for their efforts by making peace with the fallen quarry. Viktor A. Shnirelman reports a Lapp legend in which a sacred reindeer offers its own life that men may live but warns the hunters ''to spare the females and the leaders of the herd in autumn,'' or else the hunting would cease.[5] Taboos like these preserved the quarry and, by doing so, preserved the hunters as well.

The step from a temporal taboo to a spatial one is not so great, and there are records of reserves dating back more than a thousand years. Undoubtedly many early reserves served religious purposes, but the protection of wildlife was also common. The State of Venice established reserves for deer and wild boar prior to the city's founding in 726, and wildlife reserves of various sorts were established in Europe from the fifteenth century forward. By far the most common was the seignorial game preserve where hunting was generally prohibited—not for the sake of the game, but to preserve its plentitude and with it the lord's pleasure. Similar reserves were established by African and Aztec monarchs. In China, centuries ago, parks were established for the propagation and display of hoofed animals, and in India the ''deer park of Sarnath'' was the setting for the first sermon of Gautama Buddha.

Although reserves of various sorts have a long history, the concept of a "national park" presupposes the existence of nations in the modern sense, sovereign nation-states. This condition was fulfilled in the middle of the seventeenth century. The rise of a "national parks movement" required two centuries more until a fusion of science and technology produced an industrial revolution and set humankind upon a course that altered natural landscapes at a prodigious rate. It was probably inevitable that this wholesale and unprecedented transformation of the land from natural to artificial environments should provoke a call for the preservation of what was being so rapidly lost, and it is not surprising that the first such calls should emanate from nations undergoing rapid industrialization. B. H. Green detects such a call in the words of the poet William Wordsworth, who wrote in 1810 that "persons of pure taste" deem the Lake District in northern England "a sort of national property, in which every man has a right and interest who has an eye to perceive and a heart to enjoy."[6]

In the United States early calls for preservation were equally unfocused. They came, by and large, from intellectuals along the Atlantic Coast and from European visitors like Alexis de Tocqueville, who recorded his observations of the American frontiersman in 1831. "[L]iving in the wilds, he only prizes the works of man. . . . [T]hat one should appreciate great trees and the beauties of solitude, that possibility completely passes him by."[7]

In contrast to the American frontiersmen, Tocqueville appreciated the aesthetic possibilities of undeveloped country; a year later George Catlin contemplated its preservation. In 1832 Catlin wrote of "the probable extinction of buffaloes and Indians."[8]

Many are the rudenesses and wilds in Nature's works, which are destined to fall before the deadly axe and desolating hands of cultivating man. . . . Such of nature's works are always worthy of our preservation and protection; and the further we become separated (and the face of the country) from that pristine wildness and beauty, the more pleasure does the mind of enlightened man feel in recurring to those scenes, when he can have them preserved for his eyes and mind to dwell upon.[9]

To Catlin, the solution was a national park: "What a splendid contemplation . . . [that both Indians and buffalo] might in future be seen (by some great protecting policy of government) preserved in their pristine beauty and wildness, in a magnificent park. . . . A nation's Park, containing man and beast."[10] Catlin's contemplations are hardly great literature, but they preview several themes central to the national park concept.

1. Catlin rejected the axiom, dominant in the Western world, that natural resources have value only as economic objects, as well as its corollary, that economic development is *ipso facto* good.

2. He argued that the marginal value of any resource, even an aesthetic resource, is likely to increase as a function of its perceived scarcity.

3. He foresaw the possibility of government as the agency of preservation.

4. He emphasized wildlife preservation, focusing, as have most of his successors, on a relative handful of large mammals, in this case the buffalo.

5. He emphasized the preservation of indigenous peoples and indigenous cultures, a concern that has only recently become common among park proponents.

Echoing Catlin, but surpassing him in eloquence, Henry David Thoreau made the case for national park preservation in an article entitled "Chesuncook" published in the *Atlantic Monthly* of August 1858.

Why should not we . . . have our national preserves . . . in which the bear and panther, and even some of the hunter race, may still exist, and not be "civilized off the face of the earth"—our forests . . . not for idle sport or food, but for inspiration and our own true recreation?[11]

THE FIRST NATIONAL PARKS

By the time Thoreau penned these words, the United States had already established its first natural reserve. In 1832 Congress had set aside the Hot Springs Reservation in Arkansas. In the nineteenth century the waters were believed to be medicinal; they are still considered therapeutic. Steven Mather, first director of the U.S. National Park Service, managed to have the reservation declared a national park in 1921, but John Ise, historian of the American parks, dismisses the designation as an aberration. "The springs . . . were located . . . in a fair-sized town, and a national park in a town seems something of a misnomer."[12] The 1832 Hot Springs Reservation demonstrated the government's commitment to preventing private exploitation, but no one has been eager to proclaim Hot Springs the world's first national park.

Within six years of the publication of "Chesuncook" the U.S. Congress had acted to create a great *natural*—if not immediately *national*—park. On June 24, 1864, President Abraham Lincoln signed into law a bill ceding the Yosemite Valley and the Mariposa Big Tree Grove to the state of California "upon the express conditions that the premises shall be held for public use, resort and recreation; [and] shall be held inalienable for all time."[13]

Hans Huth has argued persuasively that these events establish Yosemite as the world's first national park. Although the park was to be administered by California, it was the government of the United States that had acted to reserve the area and to specify the conditions of its occupation and use. Huth describes this as a "completely new idea" and credits Frederick Law Olmsted as the "driving force" behind it.[14]

Just as there can be no doubt the national government had acted, there can be none that the Yosemite Valley contained aesthetic and recreational resources of national or international significance. Granite peaks and domes rise high above an exquisite valley in the heart of the Sierra Nevada. Flora include a plethora of wildflowers and the giant sequoia. The valley boasts a number of impressive waterfalls, one of which is the highest in the United States. Lafayette H. Bunnell, the first American to describe the valley in print, was overwhelmed by the sight. "As I looked," he wrote, "a peculiar exalted sensation seemed to fill my whole being, and I found myself in tears with emotion."[15] Contemporary visitors share Bunnell's awe, and overcrowding is a serious concern during the summer months.

Huth's arguments notwithstanding, lack of administration by the national government has prevented most park historians from recognizing Yosemite as the world's first national park. That honor is reserved for Yellowstone, an area of 898,000 hectares (2.2 million acres) featuring high mountain meadows, lodgepole pine forests, spectacular canyons and waterfalls, numerous large mammals, and the earth's largest concentration of geysers and hot springs. Located primarily in the state of Wyoming in the Rocky Mountain Range, Yellowstone National Park was designated a Biosphere Reserve in 1976 and a World Heritage Site in 1978.

Popular histories of American national parks trace the birth of Yellowstone National Park to a campfire discussion, September 19, 1870, at Madison Junction, the confluence of the Firehole and Gibbon rivers. According to Nathaniel P. Langford, members of the Washburn expedition were discussing the commercial prospects associated with attempting to get title to land surrounding the various wonders when Cornelius Hedges interjected that there should be no private ownership at all and that the whole area should be set aside as a national park.

This makes for a romantic story, but the truth of it will never be known. Several others have plausible claims to be the originator of the Yellowstone Park idea. What follows is certain. Langford and Hedges were among those who agitated for the creation of a park. A subsequent expedition brought back photographs, and public interest was kindled. In a remarkably brief period of time, a bill was introduced, debated, passed, and signed by President Ulysses S. Grant. The Yellowstone Act of March 1, 1872, was the work of many hands, but the influence of the 1864 Yosemite Grant is apparent at several points in the text, including the critical passage reserving the Yellowstone area "as a public park or pleasuring ground for the benefit and enjoyment of the people."[16]

THE SPREAD OF THE NATIONAL PARK CONCEPT

In the half-century subsequent to the establishment of Yellowstone, the national park concept spread quickly in the United States and somewhat more slowly elsewhere.

In the United States Sequoia and Yosemite national parks were established in California's Sierra Nevada Range (1890). Yosemite National Park was originally a doughnut-shaped reserve surrounding the Yosemite Valley. In 1905 California returned the valley to national control, and the modern version of Yosemite National Park was born. Both Sequoia and Yosemite have achieved international recognition. Sequoia was designated a Biosphere Reserve in 1976, and Yosemite was listed as a World Heritage Site in 1984.

Other notable early additions to the system of national parks in the United States included Mount Rainier in Washington (1899); Crater Lake in Oregon (1902); Glacier in Montana (1919); Rocky Mountain in Colorado (1915); Mount McKinley—renamed Denali in 1980—in Alaska (1917); and Grand Canyon in Arizona (1919). Glacier was authorized as part of Waterton-Glacier International Peace Park in 1932, and Glacier, Rocky Mountain, and Denali were all designated Biosphere Reserves in 1976. Three years later Grand Canyon was listed as a World Heritage Site. With their present boundaries these nine reservations comprise 44,000 square kilometers (11 million acres). They form the core of the national park system in the United States and remain among the most precious of what have so often been called "America's crown jewels."

In nearby Canada an 1885 order-in-council reserved 26 square kilometers (10 square miles) around the Banff Hot Springs to prevent their private exploitation. Two years later the Rocky Mountain Park Act enlarged the reservation to 670 square kilometers (260 square miles) and, in language reminiscent of the 1864 Yosemite Grant and the 1872 Yellowstone Act, proclaimed it "a public park and pleasure ground for the benefit, advantage and enjoyment of the people."[17]

Other nations of the English-speaking world were relatively quick to adopt similar measures. Australia, New Zealand, and South Africa had established national parks by the end of the nineteenth century, and India followed in the first decade of the twentieth century.

In Europe, the governments of Germany, Russia, Sweden, and Switzerland had all established some sort of national parks prior to World War I. In Great Britain and the Netherlands national parks had been established by private rather than governmental initiative.

The development of national parks in both Europe and Africa was influenced by Belgium's Prince Albert, who was reportedly inspired during a visit to American parks in 1919. Upon his return to Belgium, the Herzogenwald or Duke's Forest was converted from a private preserve to a public park, and in 1925 an Albert National Park—now Virunga National Park—was established in the Belgian Congo. The Dutch government followed the American example in establishing the Udjun Kulon Reserve in Java early in the twentieth century, and the American influence has been cited by those responsible for national park development in England, Japan, Sweden, Switzerland, and elsewhere.

The United States may have provided some negative examples as well. In Canada, reports of the mismanagement of the Hot Springs Reserve in Arkansas seem to have influenced early park policy. In the USSR, protected parks and forests were established soon after the 1917 revolution, in part to make the point that nature destruction was capitalistic and the new Soviet regime was not.

EARLY HISTORY OF INTERNATIONAL PRESERVATION

International concern for the establishment and protection of parks is of somewhat more recent vintage. Roderick Nash has argued that the preservation of wild nature in national parks and wilderness areas has always involved a kind of commerce between areas with differing needs.[18] Appreciation of an untamed nature increases with the relative scarcity of the resource and the relative affluence of the appreciator. Just as the stimulus for preservation of American wilderness most often came from the affluent residents of the relatively more urbanized East Coast or of Europe, so too the stimulus for preservation of natural resources in less developed countries came most often from foreign elites: colonial administrators, scientists, businessmen, and affluent leisure seekers. During their era of hegemony, colonial powers were able to impose a variety of parks and reserves on indigenous peoples and cultures around the world. With the end of the colonial era following World War II, many former colonies adopted these parks and reserves as their own, frequently with a clear understanding that reserve maintenance encourages science, tourism, and the concomitant flows of hard currencies into these economically less developed countries.

Just as wholesale slaughter of the American buffalo inspired George Catlin's vision of a nation's park, rapid reductions of specific species inspired the first international efforts at nature conservation. Berlin hosted a convention on salmon fishing in the Rhine in 1885. In 1900 an agreement was drafted in London concerning African mammals, but it was never ratified. In Europe the demands of fashion decimated bird populations, and there were calls for international control. Meetings were held late in the nineteenth century, and in 1902 at a Paris conference sixteen signatories adopted a treaty for the protection of birds useful to agriculture. Seven years later the First International Congress for the Protection of Landscapes convened, also in Paris.

The migratory habits of birds and salmon are readily apparent, and these early conservation conferences demonstrate a dawning awareness that effective conservation must of necessity be international conservation. That lesson may be dawning still. In July of 1989 the heads of state of the world's major industrial democracies met in Paris. They acknowledged the importance of global environmental problems like ozone depletion and global warming but failed to articulate any specific program or commit any resources to their solution.

THE DEVELOPMENT OF INTERNATIONAL ORGANIZATION

Swiss conservationist Paul Sarasin deserves much of the credit for establishing the first intergovernmental organization devoted to nature preservation. As a result of his efforts, a protocol creating the Consultative Commission for the International Protection of Nature was signed by the representatives of seventeen European countries at Berne in 1913. Unfortunately, the advent of World War I ended the Consultative Commission's work before it had begun. An effort was made to reconstitute the commission in 1923, but it too foundered in a sea of international tensions.

In general, intergovernmental developments were few prior to World War II. In 1916 the United States and Canada agreed to a Migratory Bird Treaty designed primarily to perpetuate the ducks and geese popular with sport hunters. In 1933 a convention for the protection of the fauna and flora of Africa was promulgated in London, and a similar convention in Washington in 1940 addressed nature protection and wildlife preservation in the Western Hemisphere.

Perhaps more important in the interwar years was the rise of nongovernmental organizations (NGOs) committed to nature conservation: the International Council (originally Committee) for Bird Protection (ICBP) (1922); the Office International de Documentation et de Corrélation pour la Protection de la Nature (1928); and the American Committee for International Wild Life Protection (1930). These organizations and the Society for the Protection of the Fauna of the Empire were important in drafting the 1933 Convention for the Protection of the Fauna and Flora of Africa. The American Committee became singularly important as the true international bodies were sundered by World War II.

INTERNATIONAL UNION FOR THE CONSERVATION OF NATURE

Following the war, there was a widespread desire for a resumption of international cooperation in nature preservation, especially in Switzerland, the Netherlands, Britain, and the United States. Alternative forms of organization and possible relationships with the United Nations were debated in the U.N. Educational, Scientific, and Cultural Organization (Unesco), the various national governments, and the existing NGOs.

Under the leadership of its president, Dr. Charles Bernard, the Swiss League for the Protection of Nature organized conferences in Basel and Brunnen, the latter proclaiming a Provisional International Union for the Protection of Nature and calling upon Unesco to convene a conference to adopt a constitution. A number of individuals and organizations apparently wanted credit for the forthcoming conference, with the result that Unesco and the government of France issued joint invitations to governments while the Swiss League invited nongovernmental organizations.

The conference assembled in Fontainebleau, France, where on October 5, 1948, delegates representing 18 governments, 108 institutions and associations, and 7 international organizations formally constituted the International Union for the Protection of Nature (IUPN)—renamed the International Union for the Conservation of Nature and Natural Resources (IUCN) in 1956. The preamble to its constitution defined nature protection as "the preservation of the entire world biotic community, or man's natural environment, which includes the earth's renewable natural resources of which it is composed, and on which rests the foundation of human civilisation."[19]

As the first director-general of Unesco, Sir Julian Huxley had played an important role in events leading to establishment of the IUPN. He made an even greater contribution to the IUPN's emergence as a significant conservation force. By the time of the Fontainebleau conference, plans were well underway for a

U.N. Scientific Conference on the Conservation and Utilization of Resources (UNSCCUR) to be held in the autumn of 1949 at the U.N.'s temporary headquarters in Lake Success, New York. Under Huxley's leadership, Unesco joined forces with the new IUPN to organize an International Technical Conference on the Protection of Nature to follow immediately on the heels of UNSCCUR. Now generally denominated "Lake Success," this technical meeting constituted a kind of coming out party for the new IUPN and laid the foundation for much of the international conservation work of the subsequent decade.

The IUCN has achieved the status of a major participant in international environmental affairs even as it has tottered on the brink of bankruptcy. In 1961 sixteen prominent scientists and business leaders met at IUCN headquarters in Morges, Switzerland, and founded the World Wildlife Fund (WWF) as a fund-raising partner to IUCN. A recent change of name to World Wide Fund for Nature (WWF) suggests the breadth of its current interests. WWF has been a major success, but the resources of international organizations devoted to conservation remain severely limited in comparison with the task.

In 1988, as it celebrated the fortieth anniversary of its establishment, the IUCN counted among its assets the membership of 61 states, 128 governmental agencies, 33 international and 383 national nongovernmental organizations. Among the members were scientific bodies such as the Royal Geographical Society and Smithsonian Institution and advocacy organizations such as Greenpeace, the Australian Conservation Foundation, and the Sierra Club. IUCN membership also embraced a multitude of zoological societies, natural history societies, educational institutions, and organizations of indigenous peoples. The organization boasted a secretariat in Switzerland; several commissions of which the international Commission on National Parks and Protected Areas is most relevant to this volume; two international repositories for specialized information, the World Conservation Monitoring Centre and the Environmental Law Center; an operational staff of almost sixty, most of whom were posted to regional offices in Africa, Central America and Asia; and a budget of almost US$7 million.

In international conservation affairs, Robert Boardman describes the IUCN as the central actor but not the leader. It competes to a degree with the WWF; with the ICBP, which continues to concern itself primarily with bird preservation; and with the International Waterfowl Research Bureau, an offshoot of the ICBP and leader in preparation of the Ramsar [Iran] Convention of 1971, whose secretariat is now housed in the IUCN. Unesco, the U.N.'s Food and Agriculture Organization (FAO), and various national groups have been competitors or allies as issues and contexts have shifted, but in recent years an Ecosystem Conservation Group, consisting of UNEP, Unesco, FAO, and IUCN, has become more effective in coordinating international conservatism efforts.

WORLD CONFERENCES ON NATIONAL PARKS

Following World War II there were regular conferences on various aspects of nature conservation held primarily under the auspices of the IUCN, Unesco, and

FAO. Discussion of national parks and nature reserves was commonplace, and there was an increasing interest in convening a world conference devoted solely to protected areas. The IUCN's Commission on National Parks and Protected Areas was proposed during the parent body's Sixth General Assembly in Athens in 1958 and established in Warsaw in 1961. Under the leadership of Harold J. Coolidge the commission began organizing a world conference on national parks.

The first of what have become decennial world conferences met in Seattle, Washington, in the summer of 1962 with Harold Coolidge presiding. This meeting served to summarize the state of global knowledge on national parks and protected areas, establish important international linkages, and set the stage for a dramatic increase in national park establishment in ensuing years. Conference advocacy of marine parks helped establish the concept, but the number of such reserves remains small compared to the need.

The Second World Conference met in Yellowstone and Grand Teton national parks during September of Yellowstone's centennial year, 1972. It was a banner year for international environmental cooperation. The First U.N. Conference on the Human Environment met in Stockholm, Sweden, in June. The Stockholm Conference prepared a Declaration on the Human Environment and called for new institutional and financial arrangements to facilitate international cooperation in environmental conservation. In December the U.N. General Assembly responded by establishing the United Nations Environmental Programme (UNEP). UNEP's Third Governing Council, meeting in Nairobi, resolved to give greater attention to the maintenance of ecosystems including parks and reserves, endangered species and wildlife, genetic and other biological resources, and it has since sponsored a series of regional conferences on marine national parks and reserves culminating in a world conference in Tokyo in May 1975.

With one hundred years of park history and the new environmental initiatives to celebrate, the Second World Conference met in a period of unusual optimism, and conference recommendations for more new parks, more biogeographically representative parks, and better-managed parks and protected areas fell on receptive ears. Within two months Unesco had adopted the World Heritage Convention, and in the following decade national parks and nature reserves grew at an unprecedented rate. The number of protected areas increased 47 percent, from 1,823 to 2,671. The total area under protection increased 82 percent, from 217 to 396 million hectares (536 to 979 million acres).

Although the 1982 conference was officially advertised as the World Congress on National Parks, this assembly of representatives from sixty-eight nations was understood to be the direct successor to the 1962 and 1972 conferences. The World Congress met in Bali, Indonesia, in October 1982. It was the first national parks conference to meet in a developing nation and the first to give priority to the relationship between protected areas and socioeconomic development. In contrast to the previous world conferences, the posture of park advocates in Bali appeared defensive.

Just as the 1972 World Conference had been influenced by the Stockholm

Conference, the 1982 congress was influenced by publication, in 1980, of a *World Conservation Strategy* jointly authored by the IUCN, WWF, and UNEP with the support of FAO and Unesco. In response to increasing pressures for economic and resource development and in an effort to establish the continuing relevance of conservation in a shrinking world, the authors set forth three objectives linking conservation and sustainable development:

a. to maintain essential ecological processes and life support systems;

b. to preserve genetic diversity; [and]

c. to ensure the sustainable utilization of species and ecosystems.[20]

The dominant influence of the *World Conservation Strategy* was apparent in the congress's remarkably instrumental theme, "Parks for Sustainable Development"; in the frequency with which the strategy was invoked by speakers; and in the formal title of the proceedings, which were published in 1984, *National Parks, Conservation, and Development: The Role of Protected Areas in Sustaining Society*.

Participants endorsed a "Bali Declaration," which set forth the global task in these words:

The earth is the only place in the universe known to sustain life, yet as species are lost and ecosystems degraded its capacity to do so is rapidly reduced, because of rising populations, excessive consumption and misuse of natural resources, pollution, careless development, and failure to establish an appropriate economic order among people and among states. The benefits of nature and living resources that will be enjoyed by future generations will be determined by the decision of today. Ours may be the last generation able to choose large natural areas to protect.[21]

The World Congress also endorsed a list of twenty recommendations for expansion and improved management of the world's parks and reserves. The extent to which they will be heeded remains to be seen. Certainly the early indications are not completely encouraging. The congress recommended that the excellent international parks journal, *Parks*, resume publishing in Spanish and French as well as in English. Instead, within three years a lack of financial support from the international community had brought about the journal's effective collapse.

INTERNATIONAL RECOGNITION FOR NATIONAL EFFORTS

In recent decades the international conservation community has established systems for recognizing and stimulating the conservation of natural areas by individual nations. In principle, international recognition draws attention to the designated areas, increases both the breadth and depth of public support for them, and increases the probability that individual national governments and international NGOs will make a greater commitment to their protection.

This approach was pioneered by the Council of Europe, an association of twenty-one European nations with headquarters at Strasbourg, France. In 1965 the council established the "European Diploma," an award that attests both to the international importance of the designated site and to its effective protection. In the first fifteen years of this program forty sites were nominated by their respective governments, and nineteen sites, in thirteen different countries, were approved.

In the years that followed, Unesco was central to the establishment of two potentially global systems of international recognition for protected areas: the International Biosphere Reserve Program and the Convention Relating to the Protection of the World Cultural and Natural Heritage.

Biosphere Reserve Program

The Man and the Biosphere (MAB) Program was launched by Unesco in 1971. It aimed to improve the relationship between human beings and their environment by increasing knowledge of the earth's ecosystems and the human impact that alters them. Supervision of the program was entrusted to an International Co-ordinating Council made up of scientists from thirty nations. Unesco provided the international secretariat, and each of the participating nations established a national committee. By 1989 national MAB committees had been established in more than 100 countries.

A pivotal part of the MAB Program was Project No. 8, "Conservation of Natural Areas and the Genetic Material They Contain." The goal was a world-wide system of representative ecological areas, called "biosphere reserves," established to preserve genetic diversity while serving as laboratories and class-rooms for ecological research, monitoring, training, and education. The emphasis was on preserving entire ecosystems rather than single species, and a global system of biogeographic regions was developed as a guide to the representa-tiveness of the biosphere reserve system.

Three general categories of biosphere reserves have been defined: "(1) natural areas representative of biomes, their main subdivisions, and transition zones; (2) unique areas or areas with particular natural features of exceptional interest; and (3) man-modified landscapes." To facilitate comparative research, each reserve is to have a core zone preserved in its natural state and a buffer zone in which manipulative research may be performed. Alternatively, a strictly protected area like a national park or strict nature reserve may be paired with a biologically similar experimental area to form a single biosphere reserve. According to Napier Shelton, "It is this combination of both preservation and experimentation that makes biosphere reserves unique."[22]

By 1985 there were 243 reserves established in 65 countries. Most had been set aside previously as national parks or strict nature reserves, so it is difficult to say whether the Man and the Biosphere program has stimulated much new conservation. The program has stimulated important research including a number of projects that involve significant international cooperation.

World Heritage Convention

The Convention Concerning the Protection of the World Cultural and Natural Heritage was adopted by the General Conference of Unesco, November 16, 1972, and became effective on September 25, 1975, when Switzerland became the twentieth country to ratify. By combining natural and cultural preservation in one document, Unesco emphasized that each type of preservation is an important component of life quality, that transboundary phenomena like global pollution and international poaching threaten both natural and cultural resources, and that both natural and cultural resources are threatened by the lack of resources for protection in developing nations. Signatories to the convention recognize that the primary responsibility for preserving natural and cultural heritage within their borders falls on their own governments but also that the areas recognized are of international interest and importance and can benefit from international cooperation.

The convention defines "natural heritage" to be

- natural features consisting of physical and biological formations or groups of such formations which are of outstanding universal value from the aesthetic or scientific point of view,
- natural sites or precisely delineated natural areas of outstanding universal value from the point of view of science, conservation or natural beauty.[23]

The convention provides for a World Heritage Committee of nations elected by and from among the signatories and a World Heritage Fund to finance international cooperation. Upon nomination by individual nations, and with the advice of the IUCN regarding natural areas, the committee formulates the "World Heritage List" and the "List of World Heritage in Danger." Although the convention combines interest in natural and cultural heritage, individual areas are classified as natural, cultural, or mixed in the process of listing.

Operational guidelines for listing areas were established by the World Heritage Committee at its first meeting in June 1977. Natural properties must exhibit ecological integrity and meet at least one of the following criteria:

1. be outstanding examples representing the major stages of the earth's evolutionary history. . . .
2. be outstanding examples representing significant on-going geological processes, biological evolution and man's interaction with his natural environment. . . .
3. contain unique, rare or superlative natural phenomena, formations or features or areas of exceptional natural beauty. . . .

4. be habitats where populations of rare or endangered species of plants and animals still survive.[24]

A year later the World Heritage Committee officially established the World Heritage List, approving eight cultural and four natural properties. The charter entries on the natural heritage list were the Galapagos Islands off the coast of Ecuador, first brought to the world's attention by Charles Darwin; Nahanni National Park, a vast wilderness in northwestern Canada; Simien National Park, Ethiopia, an area of rugged topography and rare wildlife suffering serious incompatible human use; and Yellowstone National Park, U.S.A., home to rare, threatened, and endangered species and to the world's largest concentration of geysers.

By June 1989, 111 countries had subscribed to the World Heritage Convention, making it the world's most widely ratified conservation agreement. Of the 288 properties listed in 1988, however, only 68 were natural, and 9 were mixed natural and cultural. This relative imbalance reflects Unesco's longer association with cultural preservation and the domination of the World Heritage Committee by experts in cultural rather than natural heritage.

Notwithstanding the significant imbalance in natural and cultural properties listed, the World Heritage Committee and the World Heritage List have proven more successful than the World Heritage Fund. Subscribing states are assessed an amount equal to 1 percent of their share of the regular Unesco budget. As a practical matter, national governments meet their financial obligations to the fund when it suits them, and frequently other purposes seem more pressing. In 1988 the fund's budget was a meager US$2.7 million for all activities worldwide. At this rate of expenditure it would take two centuries to consume the funds the U.S. government proposes to spend on each of 132 B–2 ("Stealth") bombers.

A recent assessment of the state of the world's parks by Gary E. Machlis and David L. Tichnell concluded that parks formally recognized as biosphere reserves or world heritage sites do not differ significantly from other national parks in terms of reported threats to park resources.[25] One is tempted to infer that these designations have had little practical impact on national parks management, but Harold K. Eidsvik reports that the results of listing have been significant in some cases.[26]

INTERNATIONAL DIVERSITY AND GLOBAL REQUIREMENTS: LESSONS FROM THE CHAPTERS THAT FOLLOW

Biosphere People and the Illusion of National Sovereignty

Raymond F. Dasmann has coined the term "biosphere people" to remind us of the fundamental change in the global order brought about by the revolutions in industrialization, urbanization, communication, and transportation.[27] Until recently the earth was populated by "ecosystem people," who lived in relatively small communities or in rural areas and who depended for their existence on their stewardship of the ecosystem of which each individual was a part. Because ecosystem people had to live with the results of their actions, there were obvious disincentives to action that would disrupt the natural balance.

Most of us, by contrast, are biosphere people. Resources are mobilized on a global scale—from the entire biosphere—to provide for our food, shelter, comfort, or amusement. The resulting environmental problems—ozone depletion, loss of genetic diversity, deforestation, desertification, global warming, etc.— are increasingly global as well. Biosphere people live in a state of global interdependence, a condition in which national sovereignty is rapidly becoming an anachronism.

Despite all the evidence to the contrary, nation-states continue to behave as if they were sovereign and as if protecting that sovereignty were the most important thing on earth. For better or worse, for the foreseeable future, environmentally sensitive policies in general and parks and reserves in particular will be established or maintained when they appear to serve the interests of the states involved. National governments may be anachronistic, but they remain the dominant players in the world of national parks and nature reserves. International organizations play a subordinate role.

The Linkage of Conservation and Development

In an obvious sense national parks and nature reserves worldwide are threatened by economic development. Development has often meant the substitution of artificial (technology-dominated) environments for natural (biology-dominated) ones. Such substitution threatens national parks, which are established to protect and preserve the biological diversity and the opportunities for recreation and science that only natural environments can provide.

However, the absence of economic development may be a greater threat than is its presence. Poverty and overpopulation will drive nations to destroy their parks far more readily than will prosperity, which is generally associated with population stability. Ultimately, preserving national parks of global importance for future generations will require addressing the social and economic problems of the caretaker nations. Machlis and Tichnell put the case concisely:

We must always remember that national parks, for all their seeming wildness and the apparent dominance of Nature are partly social creations. They are conceived, established, maintained, and in turn threatened by society. Lost in the philosophical debates between "environmental protection" and "resource development" is the fact that the perpetuation of national parks does not depend upon one or the other; it depends on both.[28]

Taking a Long-Term View

Without in any way diminishing the point that effective long-term conservation depends on effective socioeconomic development, well-wishers of national park preservation—and, for that matter, well-wishers of human survival—must reject the subtly different argument that, in this era of fierce competition for resources, "parks must pay their own way."

Parks do pay their own way, of course, in aesthetics, in inspiration, in recreation, in science, in the opportunity for future choice, and in the preservation of genetic diversity. They always have. Unfortunately, appreciation of the benefits provided by parks requires a long-term view, and the two primary institutions that humans have evolved for decision making—economics and politics—are both notoriously short-sighted.

Economic theory systematically discounts the future, and corporate decision-makers are generally motivated by near-term consequences. In a perfect world this economic short-sightedness would be balanced by a political system that reflects the long-term interests of society, a system capable of representing noneconomic values and unborn generations. Too frequently, however, the political choice is as short-sighted as the economic one. Just as the business manager must show a healthy profit for each quarterly report, the politician must court the quick fix and show results before the next election.

If economic and political leaders will not do so, the burden falls on scientists and conservationists to make the case for a long-term view. In the long term, development is futile unless it is sustainable. National parks and nature reserves have already played an important role in sustaining society. As the twenty-first century approaches, the importance of their role can only increase.

Perhaps this volume will encourage its readers to embrace the lesson expressed so elegantly more than a century ago by Henry David Thoreau: "In Wildness is the preservation of the World."

NOTES

1. IUCN, Commission on National Parks, *U.N. List of National Parks and Equivalent Reserves*, 2nd ed. (Brussels, Belgium: Hayez, 1971), p. 13; and IUCN, *World Directory of National Parks and Other Protected Areas* (Morges, Switzerland: IUCN, 1975), p. P.8.1.

2. IUCN, *World Directory*, p. P.4.1.

3. Ibid.

4. Raymond F. Dasmann, "Development of a Classification System for Protected Natural and Cultural Areas," in *Second World Conference on National Parks*, ed. Sir Hugh Elliott (Morges, Switzerland: IUCN, 1974), p. 389.

5. Viktor A. Shnirelman, "Grandfather Bear," *Unesco Bulletin* (February 1988): 9.

6. B. H. Green in chapter 8 of this volume; quotation from William Wordsworth, *Guide to the Lakes* (London: Henry Frowde, 1906), p. 92.

7. Alexis de Tocqueville, *Journey to America* (New Haven: Yale University Press, 1960), p. 335.

8. George Catlin, *North American Indians*, 2 vols. (Philadelphia: Leary, Stewart, and Co., 1913), 1:ix.

9. Ibid., 1:293–94.

10. Ibid., 1:294–95.

11. Henry David Thoreau, "Chesuncook," *Atlantic Monthly* 2 (August 1858): 317.

12. John Ise, *Our National Park Policy: A Critical History* (Baltimore: Resources for the Future, 1961), pp. 244–45.

13. *United States Statutes at Large*, vol. 13, p. 325.

14. Hans Huth, *Nature and the American* (Lincoln: University of Nebraska Press, 1972), p. 149.

15. Lafayette H. Bunnell, *Discovery of the Yosemite* (Los Angeles: Gerlicher, 1911), p. 63.

16. *United States Statutes at Large*, vol. 17, p. 32.

17. Quoted by Roderick Nash, "The American Invention of National Parks," *American Quarterly* (Fall 1970): 734.

18. Roderick Nash, "The Exporting and Importing of Nature," in *Earthcare: Global Protection of Natural Areas*, ed. Edmund A. Schofield (Boulder, Colo.: Westview Press, 1978), pp. 599–615.

19. Quoted in Robert Boardman, *International Organization and the Conservation of Nature* (Bloomington: Indiana University Press, 1981), pp. 43–44.

20. IUCN, *World Conservation Strategy* (Gland, Switzerland: IUCN, 1980), p. vi.

21. Quoted in Jean R. Packard, "Bali Parks Congress Asks Worldwide Action Plan," *Parks* 7 (October-December 1982): 1.

22. Napier Shelton, "U.S. Biosphere Reserves Go to Work," *Parks* 3 (January-March 1979): 11.

23. Quoted in Howard Brabyn, "Protection of the World Heritage," *Parks* 1 (April-June 1976): 12.

24. Quoted in Peter H. Bennett, "Operational Guidelines for the World Heritage Convention," *Parks* 2 (October-December 1977): 6.

25. Gary E. Machlis and David L. Tichnell, *The State of the World's Parks: An International Assessment for Resource Management, Policy and Research* (Boulder, Colo.: Westview Press, 1985), p. 87.

26. Harold K. Eidsvik, Chairman, IUCN Commission on National Parks and Protected Areas, to Craig W. Allin, September 14, 1989.

27. Raymond F. Dasmann, "Life-Styles and Nature Conservation," *Oryx* 13, no. 3 (1976): 281–86.

28. Machlis and Tichnell, *The State of the World's Parks*, p. 95.

BIBLIOGRAPHY

Adams, Alexander B., ed. *First World Conference on National Parks*. Washington, D.C.: U.S. Department of the Interior, National Parks Service, 1962.

Allin, Craig W. *Politics of Wilderness Preservation*. Westport, Conn.: Greenwood Press, 1982.

Burnett, G. Wesley, and Lisa M. Butler. "National Parks in the Third World and Associated National Characteristics." *Leisure Sciences* 9 (1987): 41–51.

Carrington, Richard. *Great National Parks of the World*. New York: Random House, 1967.

Curry-Lindahl, Kai, and Jean-Paul Harroy. *National Parks of the World*. 2 vols. New York: Golden Press, 1967.

Douglass, David. "Unesco's World Heritage Program." *National Parks* 56 (November-December 1982): 5–8.

Eidsvik, Harold. "International Defense." *National Parks* 61 (September-October 1987): 12–13.

Elliott, Sir Hugh, ed. *Second World Conference on National Parks*. Morges, Switzerland: IUCN, 1974.

Forster, Richard R. *Planning for Man and Nature in National Parks: Reconciling Perpetuation and Use*. Morges: IUCN, 1973.

Huth, Hans. "Yosemite: the Story of an Idea." *Sierra Club Bulletin* 33, no. 3 (1948): 47–78.

IUCN Bulletin, vols. 15–21 (1984–1989).

Langford, Nathaniel P. *Diary of the Washburn Expedition to the Yellowstone and Firehole Rivers in the Year 1870*. St. Paul: F. J. Haynes, 1905.

McCloskey, Michael. "World Parks," *Sierra* 69 (November-December 1984): 36–42.

McNeely, Jeffrey A. "Protected Areas." In *The Future of the Environment*, edited by David C. Pitt. London: Routledge, 1988, pp. 126–44.

McNeely, Jeffrey A., and Kenton R. Miller, eds. *National Parks, Conservation, and Development: The Role of Protected Areas in Sustaining Society*. Washington, D.C.: Smithsonian Institution Press, 1984.

Magraw, Daniel Barstow. "International Law and External Threats to National Parks." In *External Development Affecting the National Parks: Preserving "The Best Idea We Ever Had."* Boulder: University of Colorado, Natural Resources Law Center, 1986.

Nelson, J. G., R. D. Needham, and D. L. Mann, eds. *International Experience with National Parks and Related Reserves*. (Department of Geography Publication Series No. 12.) Waterloo, Ontario: University of Waterloo, 1978.

Nelson, J. G., and R. C. Scace, eds. *The Canadian National Parks: Today and Tomorrow*. 2 vols. Calgary, Alberta: University of Calgary, 1969.

Osten, R. V., ed. *World National Parks: Progress and Opportunities*. Brussels: Hayez, 1972.

Parks, vols. 1–9 (1976–1985).

Runte, Alfred. "The National Park Idea: Historical Misconceptions and Ecological Realities." In *External Development Affecting the National Parks: Preserving "The Best Idea We Ever Had."* Boulder: University of Colorado, Natural Resources Law Center, 1986.

Schofield, Edmund A., ed. *Earthcare: Global Protection of Natural Areas*. Boulder, Colo.: Westview Press, 1978.

Shelton, Napier. "Parks and Sustainable Development." *National Parks* 57 (May-June 1983): 17–21.

U.S. Congress, Office of Technology Assessment Task Force. "Maintaining Biological Diversity Internationally." *Technologies to Maintain Biological Diversity*. Philadelphia: J. B. Lippincott, 1988, pp. 251–81.

ARGENTINA 1

Susan Calafate Boyle and Terence P. Boyle

Argentina is the second largest country in South America (2,776,650 square kilometers, 1,072,176 square miles), ranging in latitude between 21° and 55° south. It has the lowest point, 35 meters (115 feet) below sea level, as well as the highest point, 6,959 meters (22,831 feet), in the continent, and a great diversity of biogeographical zones. It was the third nation in the Western Hemisphere, after the United States and Canada, to develop a system of national parks. Despite serious political and economic problems that have affected the country through most of this century, Argentina has managed to develop, maintain, and enlarge a sophisticated network of parks and preserves. The beauty, uniqueness, and wide range of natural resources preserved in these areas deserve international attention.

HISTORY

The Argentine Park System dates from November 1903, when Dr. Francisco P. Moreno donated to the nation 3 square leagues (about 7,500 hectares, or 27 square miles) of land in the territories of Neuquén and Río Negro. Moreno's goal was to create a natural public park to preserve an area representative of the andino-patagonian forest where the fauna, flora, hydrographic systems, geomorphological features, and aesthetic values would be equally protected for the enjoyment of future generations.

The government accepted the gift and by 1907 added 43,000 hectares (106,000 acres) to the reserve. In 1922 Argentine Presidente Hipólito Yrigoyen officially decreed the creation of the National Park of the South, increasing its size to 785,000 hectares (1,940,000 acres). By 1934 the Argentine Congress enacted the first law that officially established the Argentine park system, Administración de Parques Nacionales (APN). It also renamed the first park Nahuel Huapí and added a second park to the emerging system. Located in the extreme northeast border of the country, Iguazú National Park incorporated the famous falls and also protected 55,000 hectares (136,000 acres) of *selva misionera*, one of the most complex biohabitats in the world.

Four new parks were created in 1937: Lanín, Los Alerces, Perito Moreno, and Los Glaciares. The first three units provide prime examples of various forms of andino-patagonian forests, including Southern Hemisphere beeches like *roble pellín (Nothofagus obliqua)* and *raulí (Nothofagus nervosa)*; the araucarian pine *(Araucaria araucana)*; *alerces (Fitzroya cupressoides)*, a type of cypress; *lingue (Persea lingue)*, a species of laurel; and other endemics such as *tique (Aextoxicon punctatum)* and *tepú (Tepualia stipularis)*. In the fourth one, Los Glaciares, protection extended to unique orographic features, such as continental ice fields and different types of glaciers.

The 1930s also witnessed the construction of the majority of the infrastructure that exists in the parks: roads, docks, ranger quarters, superintendents' offices, and hotels. APN also constructed public buildings such as schools, churches, hospitals, and railroad stations in the main towns within the parks' boundaries.

More than 85 percent of the present park surface was already under APN control before 1940. Park creation, however, has continued steadily since that time. National Park Laguna Blanca, established in 1940, is located in the Patagonian steppe and protects a sizable population of black-necked swans *(Cygnus melancoryphus)*. Eight years later APN added close to 45,000 hectares (111,000 acres) to the national heritage with El Rey National Park, designed to preserve the *selva tucumano-oranense*, one of the divisions of tropical forest of northern Argentina.

Río Pilcomayo National Park was established in 1951. It includes 55,000 hectares (136,000 acres) of aquatic environments such as *cañadas, esteros, madrejones, selvas ribereñas* and *bosques* (woodlands) and *pastizales* (grasslands). Soon after, in 1954, Chaco National Park became a member of the national network. Relatively small, it is representative of all the typical thorn-forest vegetation types of the *Chaqueño oriental* district. The same year saw the creation of the first Bosques Petrificados Natural Monument. This park protects the largest petrified araucarian forest in the world. Some of the trunks are 30 meters (100 feet) long and 2 meters (6 feet) in diameter. Another Patagonian park was created in 1960—Tierra del Fuego. It preserves the southernmost extension of the andino-patagonian forest, the coastal fauna, and *turberas* (Sphagnum bogs).

In 1966, 8,500 hectares (21,000 acres) were set aside to protect the *palmera (Syagrus yatay)*, a kind of palm tree. The new park, El Palmar, hosts the only protected and best surviving examples of this species. Formosa National Reserve was established two years later. Its object was to restore the fauna and the flora of what used to be the most productive zone of the semi-arid Chaco.

Both Baritú (1974) and Calilegua (1979) national parks, located in the northwest of Argentina, exhibit examples of different kinds of subtropical vegetation. Baritú, because of its inaccessibility, is endowed with rich fauna and flora practically undisturbed by man. In 1977, APN added Lihuel Calel National Park, which includes representative fauna and flora of a kind of shrub land, the *monte*.

The two latest additions to the national system are Laguna de Pozuelos Natural Monument and Los Cardones National Park. Laguna de Pozuelos preserves critical wintering habitat for aquatic avifauna, migrating from the Northern Hemisphere, mostly Wilson's phalarope (*Phalaropus tricolor*), and three species of flamingos, numbering about 25,000 birds, which are permanent residents of the monument. In addition, there are numerous endemic species like Puna teal (*Anas puna*), horned coot (*Fulica cornuta*), giant coot (*Fulica gigantea*), and Andean avocet (*Recurvirostra andina*). Los Cardones, officially inaugurated in November 1986, covers 76,000 hectares (190,000 acres). Its average altitude is almost 12,000 feet and is surrounded by even higher mountains.

In 1987 the Argentina Park System encompassed twenty units covering more than 2.5 million hectares (Table 1.1, Figure 1.1). But growth has not stopped. Two additional parks are presently being prepared for admission to the system, El Impenetrable and Iberá, and several others are being formally considered for future inclusion.

The legal status of the Argentine reserves has not undergone much change since their creation. The law of 1934 creating national parks operated until 1970. Modifications were then incorporated into a bill that, among other things, classified the areas protected and administered by the national government into national parks, natural monuments, and national reserves. These categories became parts of the 1981 law that is currently in force.

The national government has not been the only institution concerned with preservation in Argentina. The provinces also began in the 1930s to set aside areas as parks or reserves. Until 1965 the number of provincial units was small, and so was their size; eighteen parks covered 86,490 hectares (214,000 acres). Since then growth has increased greatly, and today ninety such areas encompass 7,779,364 hectares (19.2 million acres). See Table 1.2. There are also a few municipal, university-owned, and private reserves. Two of the latter belong to Fundación Vida Silvestre Argentina (Wildlife Foundation), one of the most prominent nongovernmental conservation organizations in Argentina. The creation of these reserves speaks of a growing and widespread ethic among the Argentine people for the protection of the natural heritage of the nation. It is true that in many of these areas the implementation of measures for management and control is weak due to lack of information and resources. Nevertheless, some of the provinces, like Chubut, have made considerable progress toward the establishment, protection, and management of a modern system of reserves.

In Chubut the province's conservation program is administered by the subsecretary of Public Information and Tourism. The first provincial laws regarding conservation date from 1957, but it was not until 1967 that a bill was presented before the provincial legislature creating provincial parks and reserves. The

Table 1.1
National Park System of Argentina

NAME	DATE ESTABLISHED	AREA (hectares)	PROVINCE
Nahuel Huapi	1922	758,000	Río Negro Neuquén
Iguazú	1934	55,500	Misiones
Los Glaciares	1937	600,000	Santa Cruz
P. Moreno	1937	115,000	Santa Cruz
Los Alerces	1937	263,000	Chubut
Lanín	1937	379,000	Neuquén
Lago Puelo	1937	23,000	Chubut
Laguna Blanca	1940	11,250	Neuquén
El Rey	1948	44,162	Salta
Río Pilcomayo	1951	47,000	Formosa
Chaco	1954	15,000	Chaco
Bosques Petrificados	1954	10,000	Santa Cruz
Tierra del Fuego	1960	63,000	Tierra del Fuego
El Palmar	1966	8,500	Entre Ríos
Formosa	1968	10,000	Formosa
Baritú	1974	72,439	Salta
Lihuel Calel	1977	9,911	La Pampa
Calilegua	1979	76,306	Jujuy
Laguna de los Pozuelos	1981	16,245	Jujuy
Los Cardones	1986	76,000	Salta

province began to develop a system that today includes eleven natural tourist reserves located mostly on the Atlantic Coast and in central Patagonia. Each one protects a special ecosystem or a natural feature with special aesthetic or resource value. They include extensive bird-nesting grounds, the only continental breeding station for the southern elephant seal (*Mirounga leonina*), permanent extensive colonies of sea lions (*Otaria flavescens*), Magellanic penguin (*Spheniscus magellanicus*) colonies, and petrified forests. By 1980 Chubut had already put into effect a sophisticated management plan and had established an excellent interpretive center at the entrance to Península Valdés, where many of the reserves

Figure 1.1
National Parks and Selected Provincial Preserves of Argentina

1. Iguazú National Park
2. Río Pilcomayo National Park
3. Formosa National Reserve
4. Baritú National Park
5. El Rey National Park
6. Chaco National Park
7. El Palmar National Park
8. Lihuel Calel National Park
9. Laguna Blanca National Park
10. Lanín National Park
11. Nahuel Huapi National Park
12. Lago Puelo National Park
13. Los Alerces National Park
14. Perito Moreno National Park
15. Los Glaciares National Park
16. Bosques Petrificados Natural Monument
17. Tierra del Fuego National Park
18. Calilegua National Park
19. Laguna de los Pozuelos Natural Monument
20. Talampaya Provincial Reserve
21. Ñacuñán Biosphere Reserve
22. Laguna Blanca Biosphere Reserve
23. Parque Costero del Sur Biosphere Reserve
24. San Guillermo Biosphere Reserve
25. Lobería Punta Bermeja
26. Península Valdez Provincial Reserve
27. Punta Loma Provincial Reserve
28. Punta Tombo Provincial Reserve
29. Dos Bahías Provincial Reserve
30. Ischigualasto Provincial Reserve
31. Campo del Tuyú Provincial Reserve
32. Los Cardones National Park

New Parks

a. Iberá
b. Impenetrable

Table 1.2
Natural Protected Areas of Argentina Other than National Parks

NAME	ADMINIS-TRATION[a]	AREA (hectares)	DATE ESTABLISHED
Buenos Aires			
Montes naturales: talares	P	-	1937
Pereyra Iraola	P	2,146	1949
Laguna Salada Grande	P	40	1949
Corral Laguna de los Padres	P	96	1957
Punta Lara	P	31	1958
Isla Botija	P	730	1958
Río Barca Grande	P	-	1958
Sierra de la Ventana	P	6,679	1958
Isla Laguna Alsina	P	46	1960
Estancia La Corona	E	70	1968
Isla Martin García	P	180	1969
Sierra del Tigre	M	140	1972
Campos del Tuyú	E	7,500	1978
Coast of the bay of Samborombón	P	9,380	1982
Ribera Norte	M	14	1983
Elsa Shaw de Pearson	E	1,500	-
Parque Costero del Sur	BR	30,000	1986
Catamarca			
Laguna Blanca	BR	770,000	1979
Chaco			
Isla del Cerrito	P	12,000	1970
(Strip 1,000 meters long parallel to the coast)	P	17,000	1970
Pampa del Indio	P	7,500	1978
La Pirámide	P	11,619	-
Fuerte Esperanza	P	28,447	-
Chubut			
Punta Loma	P	1,707	1967
Cabo Dos Bahías	P	1,183	1973
Punta Tombo	P	210	1979
Península Valdés	P	360,000	1983
Petrified wood "José Ormaechea"	P	24	1983
Cordoba			
Cerro Colorado	P	445	1957
Banados del Río Dulce	P	50,000	1966
Los Pocitos	P	4,920	1966
Monte de las Barrancas	P	7,656	1974
Corrientes			
Iberá	P	1,200,000	1982
Entre Ríos			
Isla Curuzú Chalí	P	16,000	1968
Isla del Pillo	P	100,000	1968
Laguna del Pescado	P	20,200	1968
Formosa			
Puerto Dalmacia	P	-	1967
Arroyo Ramírez	P	-	1967

Table 1.2 (continued)

NAME	ADMINIS- TRATION[a]	AREA (hectares)	DATE ESTABLISHED
Jujuy			
Olaroz-Caucharí	P	180,000	1981
La Pampa			
Parque Luro	P	7,608	1965
La Reforma	U	9,950	1973
Limay Mahuida	P	5,000	1974
La Reforma	P	5,000	1974
La Humada	P	5,000	1974
Salitral Levalle	P	9,501	1974
Chacharramendi	P	2,500	1974
Pichi Mahuida	P	4,119	1974
La Rioja			
Guasamayo	P	9,000	1963
Talampaya	P	215,000	1975
Laguna Brava	P	405,000	1980
Mendoza			
Divisadero	P	19,560	1961
Ñacuñán	BR	12,282	1961
Laguna de Llancanelo	P	40,000	1980
El Payén	P	450,000	1982
Divisadero Largo	P	492	1983
Parque Aconcagua	P	71,000	1983
Telteca	P	20,400	1984
Misiones			
General Belgrano	P	87,000	1977
San Pedro	P	9,500	1977
Guaraní	P	41,000	1977
Cainguas	P	17,000	1977
Corpus	P	-	1979
Caraguatay	P	-	1979
Islas Malvinas	P	10,036	1982
Neuquén			
Batea Mahuida	P	1,286	1968
Chañy	P	2,058	1968
El Tromen	P	-	1971
Epu Lauquén	P	7,450	1973
Colonia Maipú	P	100	1977
Bosque Nacional de Araucaria	P	1,000	1978
Río Negro			
Lobería Punta Bermeja	P	200	1971
Complejo Islote Lobos	P	800	1971
Salta			
Valle de Acambuco	P	8,266	1979
Los Palmares	P	6,000	1979
Los Andes	P	1,440,000	1980
San Juan			
Valle Fértil	P	800,000	1971
Ischigualasto	P	62,916	1971
San Guillermo	BR	981,460	1972

Table 1.2 (continued)

NAME	ADMINIS-TRATION[a]	AREA (hectares)	DATE ESTABLISHED
San Luis			
Quebracho de la Legua	P	2,300	1979
Santa Cruz			
Bahía Laura	P	-	1977
Río Puerto Deseado	P	10,000	1977
Cabo Blanco	P	-	1977
Los Escarchados	E	100	1978
Santa Fe			
Virá Pitá	P	3,555	1963
La Loca	P	2,000	1964
El Rico	P	2,500	1968
Cayastá	P	300	1970
Santiago Del Estero			
Copo	P	118,000	1968
Tucumán			
La Florida	P	2,882	1936
Los Sosa	P	890	1940
Santa Ana	P	18,500	1951
Sierra de San Javier	U	14,026	1973
Aguas Chiquitas	P	740	1982

Notes:
[a] P = Provincial Reserves
   M = Municipal Reserves
   U = University Reserves
   E = Private Reserves
   BR = Biosphere Reserves

Source: Susana Merino de Cuezzo. Areas Naturales Protegidas de la Argentina. Secretaria dé Agricultura y Ganaderia, Direccion Nacional de Fauna Silvestre. Unpublished manuscript, 1985.

are located. The land is privately owned and managed by cooperative agreement with the province of Chubut for the purposes of conservation and tourism.

Four of Argentina's reserves, three provincial and one private, are included in the Man and the Biosphere Program launched by the United Nations Educational, Scientific, and Cultural Organization (Unesco) in 1971. They are Reserva Provincial (Provincial Reserve) San Guillermo, Reserva Natural de Vida Silvestre (Natural and Wildlife Reserve) Laguna Blanca, Parque Costero del Sur (Coastal Park of the South), and Reserva Ecológica (Ecological Reserve) de Ñacuñán (Figure 1.1). Including more than 2 million hectares (5 million acres), these areas became biosphere reserves in the 1980s. They represent important ecological zones in which conservation is combined with ecological research, monitoring, education, training, and traditional land use.

PARKS AND RESERVES

The early national parks were created mostly to preserve the scenic beauty of certain areas and to protect portions of different biogeographic zones. Fostering tourism was one of the major goals of early directors of APN as they built roads, hotels, inns, and established systems of lake transportation. Preservation of the native fauna and flora was initially a primary goal. The concept of artificially enhancing nature was widely accepted, and APN originally supported the introduction and dissemination of exotic animals and plants.

As the APN system grew and matured, emphasis shifted to the protection of vegetation as in Chaco National Park, which preserves fine specimens of one of the most attractive species of Argentina's forest types—the *quebracho* (*Schinopsis* spp. and *Aspidosperma* spp.), a hardwood whose name literally translates as break ax. Attention also focused on the protection of wildlife, as in National Park Laguna Blanca, which was established as a refuge for black-necked swan.

The present policy of APN is not to preserve everything against the vagaries of man and nature. The agency aims to include diverse stages of ecosystem developments, of evolutionary levels, of the highest number possible of habitats compatible with the conservation of maximum (or optimum) floral and faunal diversity. The fundamental goal in the creation of new parks is to include those national ecosystems that are not present in the existing park system. At the moment it is calculated that only 40 percent of the biogeographic zones of Argentina are represented in the national parks. Major zones missing are *esteros*, a type of marsh (Iberá), the Paraná delta, the high Andes, the *Chaco seco*, the *Chaco austral*, and the *Chaco serrano*. The pampa is not included, nor are the shrub lands, *espinal* and *monte*, properly represented. There are no national parks in the arid or semi-arid Patagonia nor on the Patagonian coast.

Some of Argentina's parks, particularly those in Patagonia like Nahuel Huapí, Lanín, Los Alerces, but also some in the north like Calilegua, were created with the purpose of protecting river basins and ensuring the preservation of the area's most precious commodity—water.

Recreational use was another important consideration in park creation. A philosophy evolved that tourism, properly controlled, could greatly benefit the reserves. Some provincial parks like those in Chubut were established to attract tourists to the region. The protection accorded to this province's natural tourist reserves allows individuals to come in contact with the natural environment and to be educated by the experience. Chubut's programs aim to permit the enjoyment of the natural heritage, but at the same time they intend to guide and instruct visitors, so that from the contact between man and nature, the former will emerge educated and environmentally aware, and the latter will not suffer any deterioration.

Most private and some provincial parks were established to protect a species, like the *vicuña* (*Lama vicugna*), the *ciervo de las pampas* or European red deer (*Odocoiles bezoarticus*), the *macá tobiano*, and grebe (*Podiceps gallardoi*). Some, like Ischigualasto in San Juan, include extraordinarily rich paleontological deposits of therapsid reptiles. Others, like Talampaya in La Rioja, contain extensive archaeological remains. Unfortunately, many sites, including caves with rock art, are not protected because they are within private property. In most cases, however, the principal objective of park creation has been the general preservation of all the natural resources of a certain area.

Argentina's parks include important cultural resources. Living cultures are represented by two Indian tribes who reside at Curruhuinca and Rucachoroi within the boundaries of Lanín National Reserve. These communities make a living mostly through the raising of cattle, the sale of wood, some subsistence farming, and the occasional sale of their traditional weavings. They supplement their diet seasonally with the nutritious seeds (*piñones*) of the araucarian pines. Descendants of the Pehuenches, who acted as mediators between the Mapuches and the Tehuelches, these groups still maintain some of the customs, beliefs, and animism of their ancestors. APN is seriously concerned about the future of these aboriginal communities, which are on the verge of disappearance.

Archaeological sites are found throughout the parks. Several are currently being excavated in Nahuel Huapí National Park through an agreement with the University of Buenos Aires. Other academic institutions in Argentina and abroad support the APN's Museum of the Patagonia, located in Nahuel Huapí National Park. While there is no legal structure within APN to handle cultural resources, there is a growing awareness among the present park administration of the need to develop programs in this direction.

Growing concern for the protection of cultural resources is evident in the work of the National Commission of Museums, Monuments, and Historic Places. With an ambitious agenda and strong leadership, this group is trying to move beyond the restoration of old buildings. In an effort to raise the consciousness of the Argentine people regarding the importance of their cultural legacy, it is planning a variety of programs including a series of brief courses on techniques of building inventory, research projects in small towns of historical interest with architectural remains, and surveys and inventories of national monuments.

The APN and the National Commission are preparing a project on cultural preservation in the Calchaquí valleys in the northwest of the country. With the support of the National Secretary of Science and Technology they have begun systematic inventories of significant historic sites in the provinces of Salta, Tucumán, La Rioja, and Entre Ríos.

In cooperation with APN the National Commission is also developing the concept that the natural landscape is a part of the cultural heritage. For example, the commission plans a survey of park caves that contain pictographs. It hopes as well to go in depth in two or three of these sites to assess what types of conservation measures are necessary. Both organizations, APN and the National Commission, plan to join the National Secretary of Tourism to work on a series of objectives and activities, such as restoring La Candelaria, a Jesuit mission (*estancia*) in the province of Córdoba that will become a country hotel.

ADMINISTRATION

The APN is the government agency charged with the management of national parks, reserves, and natural monuments. It is administered by a directorate composed of a president, a vice-president, and four members. The president, vice-president, and one member are nominated by the secretary of agriculture, one member by the secretary of defense, another by the secretary of the interior, and the fourth by the secretary of social welfare, subsecretary of tourism.

The present park administration, following the policy of the president of the nation, is trying to promote greater participation from the provinces. It is trying to divest from the federal government some of the overwhelming power it has exercised in the past in a process of decentralization.

Historically, the centralized management of the agency, although established by federal law, has caused tension between APN and the provincial and municipal governments. APN's elitist image in the past has greatly hindered its ability to get support for its programs at the local level, resulting in lack of rapport and consultation between those groups with interest in the parks. APN has failed to participate in the drafting of either a local or a national policy regarding tourism.

APN has presently submitted a bill to Congress to reorganize the administration and management of Argentina's parks. The proposed legislation stresses the concept that a park is located within a particular social system that influences and is influenced by the park. According to the new law, the people themselves, especially those in the provinces, will participate in determining the future of the parks. APN is trying to give all Argentines the opportunity to have a say in the decision-making process and to make them responsible for their decisions.

To implement the democratization of the management process, APN has included in its current proposed legislation the creation of a Federal Council of Protected Natural Areas comprising one representative from each province and territory and one from APN. This council would make recommendations to APN in the formulation of national policy regarding natural protected areas. It would also try to harmonize and coordinate national and provincial policies regarding protection and the management of provincial reserves as well as study the feasibility of developing a national system of natural protected areas integrated both by national and provincial units.

This bill supports the creation of Honorary Counseling Commissions for each national park designed to strengthen the rapport between APN and the local communities. These commissions would be composed of six individuals representing the area under the jurisdiction or influence of the park and would act as liaison between the private sector and the park administration.

The present level of protection accorded to an area by APN varies with its classification as national reserve, national park, or natural monument. National reserves are set aside to preserve and protect ecological systems either within an adjacent national park or as independent units. Promotion and development of human settlements in such areas are approved only if they are compatible with the preservation of the region. Within this zone, human settlement, either in private or state lands, is supervised by the APN, and any building plans must be previously approved by APN. Introducing exotic species, mining, and commercial fishing are forbidden. Agricultural activities, cattle raising, hunting, and fishing are allowed in the reserves but regulated by APN. Logging and reforestation plans also need the approval of APN.

National parks encompass natural areas that represent and protect a biogeographic region. They aim to protect nature, encourage scientific investigation, educate, and provide aesthetic enjoyment. They are maintained with no other alterations except those necessary to ensure their proper management and the handling of visitors. No economic activities are allowed except for those associated with tourism. Unless absolutely necessary, the infrastructure required to handle tourism is located in adjacent national reserves. Where this is impossible, the infrastructure built in the parks is limited to only that which is absolutely necessary.

Natural monuments are regions, objects, wildlife, or plants of aesthetic, historical, or scientific value that receive absolute protection. The only activities allowed in such areas are closely supervised visits and duly authorized scientific work.

The proposed bill before Congress would modify this classification system. It would leave untouched the category of natural monuments, but would change the other two categories, national parks and national reserves, and would create two new areas, multiple-use reserves and natural-cultural reserves, within areas currently administered as reserves.

Multiple-use reserves would include areas where regulated exploitation of natural resources will be permitted. The APN could prohibit and restrict the use of these reserves and establish incentives to preserve certain species and communities. The administration and management of multiple-use reserves would allow a sustained exploitation of the native fauna and flora while preserving certain native species and communities. The percentage of the land devoted to development and human settlement would be held to the smallest possible area. There is wording in the proposed law to provide for other zones that would be developed depending upon the amount of modification to natural processes produced in them. The bill also encourages the creation of similar reserves by provincial governments in cooperation with APN. The national agency would furnish some of the necessary assistance for the management of these units.

Natural-cultural reserves are those areas with settled aboriginal communities intent in preserving their own cultural practices. The new law provides for and helps to develop the harmonious relationship of the aboriginal peoples with their environment. To facilitate the administration of such areas, APN intends to foster agreements with national and provincial institutions specialized in the protection and the maintenance of the native American cultures. APN would control the management of the natural resources in these reserves and include the aboriginal communities in planning and implementing management plans. APN would encourage programs of economic development based on the use of natural resources and the establishment of cooperatives and other forms of community organization.

Proposed changes in the management of national reserves are small, but they are significant, for they indicate a trend toward greater exploitation of the natural resources currently protected in the park system. The new law would allow economic activities in the reserves that claim to enhance the preservation or recuperation of ecosystems.

The category of national parks would also be modified. Two new zones are identified within parks—intangible and restricted. Intangible zones are the equivalent of wilderness areas in which scientific work will be given priority. Restricted zones resemble the present category of national parks, but the new bill adds a provision giving the federal government first rights to purchase any private land up for sale within the parks.

APN has limited research capabilities. A small group of scientists including five or six biologists is centered in Buenos Aires and is in charge of the entire national system. There are two other small groups, one in Nahuel Huapí National Park and another in Lanín National Park. Research projects at Nahuel Huapí include development of detailed vegetation maps, a study of the distribution of the river otter, *huillín (Lutra provocax)*, the impact of cattle on the upper Manso River basin, the impact of the exotic deer, *ciervo colorado (Cervus elaphus)*, on the various ecological zones present in the park, a survey of native and exotic fish, and a study of the *huemul (Hippocamelus bisulcus)*, a native deer.

Aware that research is essential to the proper management of the national areas, APN has established agreements with several universities and private organizations to carry out those analyses that are considered crucial. For example, Nahuel Huapí National Park has an agreement with the University of Comahue in Neuquén to make an extensive study of the watershed of lakes and rivers where fishing is prohibited and to do an ecological resources survey. The Argentine Research Council (Consejo Nacional de Investigaciones Científicas y

Técnicas or CONICET) has also funded a three-year study of the impact of exotic large herbivores, like the red deer, on the andino-patagonian forest.

APN needs additional budgetary support to be able to carry out the scientific studies that would allow a more appropriate and efficient management of the areas under government protection. The existing research groups are carrying out an impressive number of studies, but the diversity of the biogeographic systems represented in the Argentine Park System requires broader and more numerous analyses to ensure a proper scientific information base for management.

Some of this research finds expression in several kinds of APN's publications. Casual communications, discussions, and forums routinely appear in the periodical *Parques*. Scientific articles and lengthier monographs appear in the occasional *Anales de Parques Nacionales* as well as in guides on natural history such as Claes C. Olrog's *Las aves argentinas*.

Only 150 park rangers monitor the extensive territory administered by APN. Argentine rangers are well-trained, highly competent professionals. Most are graduates of the Center for the Training of Park Rangers, which was established in 1968 in Nahuel Huapí National Park. Rangers are responsible for making parks accessible to the people, but lack of support personnel forces many rangers to work as handymen, painting buildings, repairing cars, and clearing roads. So much of their time is taken up with these activities that some rangers feel that their technical expertise and their personal, professional development is starting to suffer. Lack of sufficient personnel results in insufficient supervision and inadequate education of visitors to the national lands. Low pay also affects the morale of the ranger corps. In some areas their wages are insufficient for them to provide for the basic needs of their families. Despite poor pay and insufficient funds to discharge their jobs adequately, Argentine park rangers are a key component to the success of both the national and the provincial park systems.

The importance of their contribution is evident throughout. Even provincial rangers display a great sense of professionalism and are ready to form groups to push for conservation measures. The Asociación de Guardafauna-Chubut is an excellent example. This association of wildlife rangers is trying to do as much as possible to improve, energize, and maintain the wildlife reserve system of the province of Chubut. With the support of Fundación Vida Silvestre Argentina, the association managed to stop a proposed plan for oil exploration and exploitation in Península Valdés Provincial Reserve.

One of the most serious threats to the protected natural values of Argentina is the country's present economic crisis. Lack of funds prevents the adequate maintenance of existing facilities and hampers the development of the necessary infrastructure in parks that have been created since 1940. Many parks lack basic services for tourists. Only five have visitor centers, only two have museums, most do not offer accommodations, and some are unable to provide visitors with any type of printed, interpretive information on the park. APN is planning to place additional emphasis on park development in the northwestern part of the country and has begun work on the implementation of a plan that would provide greater support to other areas besides the andino-patagonian region, which has historically been the most heavily endowed.

Argentina's present economic crisis is closely related to another crucial threat the agency faces. Certain provincial and municipal governments as well as private groups want a park system more open to economic development. Some provinces are challenging the authority of APN and are trying to get back some of the territory under national control. It is not likely that they will succeed. However, APN's management plans, particularly as presented in their proposed legislation, place too much emphasis on the economic development of the resources protected by the present park system. It is politically necessary to change the image of APN among the provinces and in the private sector and to encourage their support for APN's policies. The agency needs to listen to those individuals and organizations strongly associated with the national park system. Fostering rampant development of the limited resources within the parks will not measurably help the country's economic situation, and it will surely cause irreparable damage to Argentina's valuable natural environments.

The presence of settlers in some of the parks poses additional problems. Settlers raise cattle, sheep, and goats, which have produced considerable devastation in certain areas of the andino-patagonian region. APN has conducted studies that show the seriousness of the impact of overgrazing, particularly in Lanín and Nahuel Huapí national parks. In an effort to maintain good relations with the local populations, the current park administration is trying a two-pronged approach to solve this problem. They offer settlers the opportunity to relocate within nearby communities, subsidizing their move and their new housing. If this alternative is not acceptable, they allow settlers to remain within the park but encourage them to change economic activities, from cattle raising to some employment associated with tourism. It is not clear how successful this policy has been so far.

In spite of the current economic crisis, Argentina is a rich country endowed with abundant natural resources and settled with an intelligent, well-educated people. A strong conservation ethic is emerging that will hopefully foster continued protection and eventual expansion of the national and provincial system of parks, monuments, and reserves that are truly world resources.

BIBLIOGRAPHY

Cabrera, Angel L., and Abraham Wilink. *Biogeografía de America Latina*. Washington, D.C.: Organization of American States, 1980.

Dimitri, Milán Jorge. "Pequeña flora ilustrada de los parques nacionales andino-patagónoicos." *Anales de Parques Nacionales* 12 (1974): 1–22.

Echechurri, Héctor A. *Conservación y medio ambiente*. Buenos Aires: Administración de Parques Nacionales, 1984.

———. "Aspectos salientes de la planificación de los Parques." *Parques* 3 (February 1986): 5–6.

Erize, Francisco, Marcelo Canevari, Pablo Canevari, Gustavo Costa, and Mauricio Rumboll. *Los Parques nacionales de la Argentina y otras de sus áreas naturales.* Madrid: Instituto de la Caza Fotográfica y Ciencias de la Naturaleza, 1981.

Giúdice, Luis. "Conservación y federalismo." *Parques* 1 (February 1985): 8.

———. "Conservación y federalismo." *Parques* 2 (June 1985): 2–3.

———. "Documento sobre el sistema nacional de areas naturales protegidas." Unpublished manuscript, Administración de Parques Nacionales.

Gutman, Pablo. *¿Qué conservación, qué desarrollo?* Buenos Aires: Administración de Parques Nacionales, 1985.

Koolen, Ricardo. "La reforma legal en parques." *Parques* 2 (June 1985): 8.

Luti, Ricardo. "They Survive under the Southern Winds: Wildlife Protection in Northern Coastal Patagonia." In *National Parks, Conservation, and Development: The Role of Protected Areas in Sustaining Society*, edited by Jeffrey A. McNeely and Kenton R. Miller. Washington, D.C.: Smithsonian Institution, 1984, pp. 561–64.

Marchetti, Beatriz, and Rodolfo Burkart. "Evaluación del uso actual de las reservas y parques nacionales." *Parques* 3 (February 1986): 2–3, 9.

Marín, Angel Castillo. "Una sola estrategia." *Parques* 3 (February 1986): 7.

Martínez, Victor. "Naturaleza, moral y derecho: Opiniones de un político y estadista." *Parques* 3 (February 1986): 12.

Merino de Cuezzo, Susana. *Areas naturales Protegidas de la Argentina.* Secretaria dé Agricultura y Ganaderia, Direccion Nacional de Fauna Silvestre. Unpublished manuscript, 1985.

Morello, Jorge H. "La ecología y el medio ambiente." *Parques* 1 (February 1985): 2.

———. "La ecología y el medio ambiente." *Parques* 2 (June 1986): 3.

Morello, Jorge H., Luis A. Giúdice, H. A. Echechurri, and Julián Gil. *Planificación y gestión de los Parques Nacionales.* Buenos Aires: Administración de Parques Nacionales, 1984.

Monaglio, E. N. "Parques nacionales argentinos: Referencias históricas y biogeográficas." *Revista de la Sociedad Central de Arquitectos* 135 (December 1985): 38–43.

Natenzón, Claudia, and María T. Ruiz. "Creación de parques nuevos." *Revista de la Sociedad Central de Arquitectos* 135 (December 1985): 70–71.

———. "Política de Parques." *Parques* 1 (February 1985): 2–3.

Olrog, Claes Chr. *Las aves argentinas.* Buenos Aires, Argentina: Administración de Parques Nacionales, 1984.

Olrog, C. C., and M. M. Lucero. *Guía de los Mamíferos Argentinos.* San Miguel de Tucumán, Argentina: Instituto Miguel Lillo, 1981.

Reca, Alfredo, and Juan Carlos Pujalte. "Ideas para el relevamiento ecológico de los parques." *Parques* 2 (June 1985): 6.

Torrejón, Antonio. "Las areas naturales y el turismo en la provincia del Chubut, Argentina." *World Travel* 181 (November-December 1984): 83–84.

———. "Plan de manejo del sistema provincial de conservación del patrimonio turístico." Secretaría de Información Pública y Turismo, Provincia del Chubut, Argentina.

AUSTRALIA 2

J. Geoffrey Mosley

Australia's still expanding national parks and nature preserve systems are important internationally because of the opportunity they present to discover and enjoy the natural scenery and biota of what is, with the exception of Antarctica, the world's most isolated and least known continent. They protect a fascinating assembly of endemic plants and animals in an environment in which the impact of Western civilization is nowhere more than 200 years old and in many areas less than 100 years.

HISTORY

1866–1900: The First Parks

The concept of national preservation of important natural areas and natural phenomena had its beginnings in the early nineteenth century with colonial administrators who reserved from occupation or use aesthetically pleasing sections of river banks near the first settlements, and its continuation through the middle of the century by government land surveyors who recommended the establishment of public reserves over caves, waterfalls, and clifftop lookouts.

The first legislative mention of scenic area protection was in Tasmania in 1863, but the main early reservations in remote areas were in New South Wales, where a 2,025-hectare (5,000-acre) reserve was established at Jenolan Caves (Southern Blue Mountains) in 1866, and a reserve for public recreation and water supply was set aside in 1872 at Bungonia Gorge, then known as "The Great Canyon." In Victoria a public park at the extinct volcanic crater at Tower Hill was also set aside in 1866.

The major development in the nineteenth-century evolution of the concept

came with the gazettal of a series of more popular recreation reserves incorporating natural country near the capital cities of several of the colonies. The first
was a 175-hectare (432-acre) reserve at Mount Eliza (later Kings Park) gazetted
in 1872. Far more influential was the dedication on April 26, 1879, of 8,600
hectares (21,242 acres) of Crown land near Port Hacking, 23 kilometers (16
miles) south of Sydney. This appears to have been the first time anywhere in
the world that a conservation reserve was officially named a "national park"
and set aside "for the purpose of a National Park."[1]

National Park, as it was known until 1955 when it became Royal National
Park, was reserved under Crown lands legislation on the initiative of Sir John
Robertson in response to a citizen movement for better public parks. The action
was facilitated by the availability of lands reserved a few years earlier for the
Sydney to Illawarra railway. There is no evidence of a connection between the
dedication of National Park and the American reserve at Yellowstone set aside
in 1872 as a "public park or pleasuring ground."

Critics described the new national park as "inaccessible" and "a mere wilderness,"[2] and for several decades the acclimatization of exotic fauna and flora
and military exercises were considered appropriate uses. Nevertheless, the area,
which was mainly in a natural condition, was placed under the control of an
influential and well-funded board of management, and gradually over a period
of eighty years the conservation objective became more important.

Within two decades the other colonies had moved to establish national parks,
including South Australia's "National Park" at Belair (1891), Western Australia's Bannister River Fauna and Flora Reserve (1894–1907) of 65,000 hectares
(160,550 acres), and Victoria's "National Park" at Wilson's Promontory (temporarily reserved for this purpose in 1898).

The possibility of effective management of individual parks was increased
with the passage of legislation—in New South Wales in 1894 and Western
Australia in 1895—providing for special trusts or boards for the management of
reserves.

In 1893 the Australian Association for the Advancement of Science produced
a short list of areas most suitable for the purpose of national parks, including Fraser Island and Freycinet Peninsula. This was the first suggestion of an
Australia-wide system of parks.

1901–1955: Completing the Foundation Stones

By the turn of the century Australia had a number of individual parks and
reserves either managed by special boards or under the nominal control of lands
and surveys departments. The seeds of expansion were already sown in the form
of citizen movements for full-scale national parks at such places as Freycinet
and Mount Field in Tasmania, and Wilson's Promontory and Mount Buffalo in
Victoria. If systems of parks were going to be developed, they would be on a
regional basis because in 1901, when the self-governing colonies federated to

become the six states of the Commonwealth of Australia, they retained complete control of land and water resources. The six states and the self-governing Northern Territory have their own legislatures and most of Australia's national parks and other nature conservation reserves are controlled under state or Northern Territory Acts and by the agencies of these governments. The Australian Capital Territory (ACT), in which the national capital Canberra is located, has been controlled by federal government ordinances, but self-government was introduced in 1989. The Australian External Territories include the Australian Antarctic Territory, which is only slightly smaller than the remainder of Australia.

Only four national parks (two in the Northern Territory and two in External Territories) are established under federal legislation and managed by the Australian National Parks and Wildlife Service. However, the High Court (Australia's highest judicial body) has upheld the validity of the federal World Heritage Properties Conservation Act, and the federal government therefore has the power to intervene to protect existing and proposed world heritage areas within the states and the Northern Territory.

In 1906 the passage of the Queensland State Forests and National Parks Act paved the way for the establishment of the first statewide system of parks under the control of a central agency—the Forestry Department. The initial reserves, Witches Falls and Bunya Mountains national parks, were both established in 1908.

The 19,035-hectare (47,000-acre) Lamington National Park, a rain forest–covered plateau in Southern Queensland, was declared in 1915 in the face of competition from agricultural and logging interests. It was the first of a new breed of national parks, set aside more for their nature conservation values than their proximity to centers of population.

In 1915 Tasmania introduced the Scenery Preservation Act, which made comprehensive provision for the establishment of a system of scenic reserves administered by a special nature conservation authority—the Scenery Preservation Board. Among the scenic reserves established under the act were "The National Park" (Mount Field) and Freycinet National Park, both in 1916. The former had been the subject of a strong campaign by the National Park Association, but the government also saw it benefiting the tourist industry and a railway recently opened in the vicinity.

The legislative initiatives of Queensland and Tasmania were not followed by the other states, and between 1916 and the mid–1950s the number of parks and reserves expanded steadily with few changes in legislation.[3] In New South Wales a network of parks and reserves was developed largely as a result of the work of Myles Dunphy and the National Parks and Primitive Areas Council (NPPC) formed in 1932, but the parks remained under the overall control of the lands department.

Dunphy designed many park proposals in a systematic way and also pioneered the wilderness area concept in Australia. In 1931, being concerned about the threat of roads in national parks and learning about the progress of wilderness conservation on U.S. Forest Service lands, Dunphy was encouraged to press for a separate wilderness category in New South Wales. In 1934 Tallowa and Garawarra Primitive Parks became the first wilderness reservations in Australia.

Myles Dunphy submitted proposals for a Greater Blue Mountains National Park in 1932 and a Snowy-Indi National Park in 1943. These proposals became the bases for the two largest park aggregations in Eastern Australia.

The scope of the Blue Mountains scheme was staggering, but by the late 1970s a group of three parks—Blue Mountains (1959), Kanangra-Boyd (1969), and Wollemi (1985)—had been proclaimed, covering 738,000 hectares (1,823,800 acres), an area even larger than Dunphy's splendid vision.

The Snowy-Indi proposal bore fruit much more rapidly when the state government decided to protect the catchment of a major potential water impoundment project: the Snowy Mountain scheme. The Kosciusko State Park Act of 1944 created a 526,500-hectare (1,300,000-acre) reserve in this area. Summer grazing was allowed to continue for a time, but provision was made for 10 percent to be set aside as a "primitive area." In fact, the primitive area was not selected until 1962—when it was used to block a hydroelectric power scheme—because of an intense difference of opinion between Dunphy and the NPPC, both of whom favored the American concept of wilderness as an area available for unconfined recreation, and scientific groups plus some open-air enthusiasts, who preferred the model of a strict nature reserve open only to scientists.

The demands of scientists and fauna groups for closed reserves free from the recreational pressures of the national parks resulted in the Fauna Protection Act of 1948, which provided for a modern system of separate faunal reserves under the control of the chief guardian of fauna, Allen Strom, a strong advocate of this type of reserve. There was more emphasis in these reserves on the scientific values and on habitat protection than in the earlier sanctuaries established under the Animals and Birds Protection acts of South Australia (1919) and Tasmania (1938).

In South Australia as well, a Flora and Fauna Advisory Committee, created in 1937, was given responsibility for a series of new mallee-broombush reserves created on the Eyre and Lincoln peninsulas. The nature reserve system began to take shape in Western Australia with the appointment in 1952 of a Fauna Protection Advisory Committee to administer fauna reserves.

1956–1974: Consolidation and Systems

In spite of the early moves in Queensland and Tasmania to introduce a central system for the control of the parks, the general picture until the mid–1950s was marked by lack of central coordination; the public knew the reserves as single units rather than part of statewide systems. The change for national parks came with Victoria's National Parks Act of 1956, which established a National Parks Authority with immediate control over thirteen areas. Ten years later South Australia established a National Parks Commission, which by 1972 controlled over ninety parks. In this year the act was amended to establish categories of "national park," "conservation park," and "recreation park."

Having led with the dedication of the first national park, it is not surprising that New South Wales was the first to establish a national parks and wildlife service. Following public criticism of parks policy, the comprehensive National Parks and Wildlife Act of 1967 was introduced by Tom Lewis, lands minister and later premier. It amalgamated national parks and nature reserves (the former faunal reserves) under a National Parks and Wildlife Service and provided for the first time for zoning of wilderness areas. This agency became the model for joint services in Tasmania (1971), South Australia (1972), Queensland (1975), the Commonwealth (1975), the Northern Territory (1980), and Victoria (1986).

In most regions such changes were introduced in a calm atmosphere, but in Tasmania the replacement of the Scenery Preservation Board by the National Parks and Wildlife Service resulted from intense public protest against the proposed flooding in 1967 of a large section of Lake Pedder National Park. Another result was the establishment of the South West National Park, later extended to 442,200 hectares (1,092,200 acres).

The establishment of the Queensland National Parks and Wildlife Service can also be seen as the result of enhanced public interest in conservation, which was manifest in this case during the 1969–1974 controversy over plans to extract mineral sands from the Cooloola Sand Mass. In the aftermath of this episode, the first stage of the Cooloola National Park was proclaimed in 1976.

A Great Sandy National Park was established in 1971–1973 at the northern end of Fraser Island, but boundaries were carefully drawn to avoid conflict with logging and mining. In the mid–1970s, as controversy erupted over the sand-mass parks, the state government turned its attention to Cape York, where six major parks, including the Jardine River National Park, were established in 1977, and where the 528,000-hectare (1,304,160-acre) Lakefield Park was proclaimed in 1978.

In Western Australia the dual system was maintained. A National Parks Board was created from the State Gardens Board in 1956, and in 1976 this became the National Parks Authority. Most of the major parks, such as the Rudall River (1,569,500 hectares, 3,876,665 acres) and Hamersley Range (617,000 hectares, 1,523,990 acres), date from the 1960s and 1970s, and by 1981 the Parks Authority had responsibility for 4,364,000 hectares (10,779,080 acres). In 1967 the Fauna Protection Advisory Committee was replaced by the Western Australian Wildlife Authority, which, with the wildlife section of the Department of Fisheries and Wildlife, controlled 9,883,200 hectares (24,411,504 acres), including major nature reserves in the north and east of the state. In 1985 both the parks and wildlife functions became the responsibility of a new Department of Conservation and Land Management.

Victoria was also slow to consolidate control of parks and wildlife. A National Parks Service set up in 1970 became part of a Ministry of Conservation in 1972 along with a Fisheries and Wildlife Division. From 1958 to 1972 the wildlife reserves had been controlled by the Department of Fisheries and Wildlife under the Land Act. In 1975 an organic Wildlife Act amalgamated various provisions for the wildlife reserve system. In 1983 both functions were incorporated in a new Department of Conservation, Forests and Lands, and the government prepared proposals to legally consolidate the provisions for both parks and wildlife reserves.

Until the 1970s the majority of Victoria's parks were relatively small. This was changed with the proclamation in 1978 of the 86,000-hectare (212,420-acre) Croajingolong National Park, protecting 100 kilometers (62 miles) of the state's eastern coastline, and in 1984 of the 167,000-hectare (412,490-acre) Grampians National Park. Even more significant was the establishment in 1989 of a 690,000-hectare (1,704,300-acre) Victorian Alpine National Park incorporating three existing parks. With Namadgi and Kosciusko national parks this created a contiguous series of parks for virtually the full length of the Australian Alps.

The administration of parks and wildlife in the Northern Territory was amalgamated first with the formation of the National Parks and Wildlife Service (1978) and later the Conservation Commission (1980). However, the extent of the areas controlled by this body was restricted by the handing back of several wildlife sanctuaries, including the 3,752,900-hectare (9,269,663-acre) Tanami Desert Wildlife Sanctuary to the aboriginal owners and by assumption of control of Ayers Rock and Kakadu by the federal parks agency.

1975–1986: Birth of a National Approach

Between 1971 and 1974 an unsuccessful last-ditch effort by conservation groups to save Lake Pedder National Park from inundation provided the impetus for the new government of Gough Whitlam to assert a federal role in nature conservation, notably through the Environment Protection (Impact of Proposals) Act of 1974, the Great Barrier Reef Marine Park Act of 1975, the Australian National Parks and Wildlife Conservation Act of 1975, and the Australian Heritage Commission Act of 1975.[4] The federal government also used its powers to ban the export of mineral sands from Fraser Island in 1976.

The Australian National Parks and Wildlife Conservation Act met a perceived need for the protection of major national parks in the Northern Territory and important wildlife reserves in the External Territories. In the Northern Territory parks and reserves had been managed since 1955 by the Northern Territory Reserves Board, whose responsibilities included the Ayers Rock–Mount Olga National Park created in 1958. Under authority of the new law, the commonwealth government took responsibility for developing Kakadu National Park on a site proposed by the Reserves Board in 1965. A park of 1,755,200 hectares (4,335,440 acres) was established in three stages between 1978 and 1987.

A decade after the Whitlam government moved to give the commonwealth powers to protect the national heritage against anticonservation activities of state governments, the federal government faced a stiff test in the South-West where further development of the hydroelectric power scheme that had destroyed Lake Pedder now threatened the Lower Gordon and Franklin River gorges. The area had been nominated for the World Heritage list at the suggestion of Tasmanian Premier Doug Lowe, and Prime Minister Malcolm Fraser ignored requests to withdraw the nomination when a new state government announced it would press ahead with plans to construct the power scheme. When three western Tasmanian wilderness national parks were inscribed on the list in December 1982, the dam became a federal election issue. Eventually, a new commonwealth government enacted the World Heritage Properties Conservation Act to prohibit the dam. This decision was upheld by the High Court in July 1983.

Other Australian areas inscribed on the World Heritage list in 1981 and 1982 included Lord Howe Island, where a permanent park preserve was established; the Great Barrier Reef; and Stage 1 of Kakadu National Park. In the case of Kakadu, by identifying the international importance of the area, the listing assisted with the proclamation of Stage 2 and helped the resistance to mining in Stages 1 and 2 of the park. Realizing the electoral advantage of this approach, the government of New South Wales actively promoted the inscription of fifteen national parks and nature reserves containing rain forest. These were listed in 1986 with the title "Sub-tropical and Temperate Rainforest Parks of Eastern Australia."

On the other hand, in 1984–1986 the commonwealth resisted strong public pressure to nominate the Wet Tropics area of North Queensland[5] and to prevent destructive road building and logging in the area. In late 1986 the commonwealth government nominated Uluru National Park but was temporarily blocked by court action from nominating Stage 2 of Kakadu. Both Uluru and Kakadu Stage 2 were inscribed in 1987. In the July 1987 federal election the government promised that, if it were re-elected, it would nominate the Wet Tropics in spite of opposition from the prodevelopment government of Queensland. A 920,000-hectare (2,270,000-acre) area was nominated in December 1987 and inscribed a year later. In 1988 additions to the western Tasmanian site were nominated.

Agents Influencing the Pattern of Parks

Reference has already been made to the influence of land surveyors, citizens, and conservation groups in the expansion of the park and reserve systems. Until after World War II, with the notable exception of Myles Dunphy, most worked for the preservation of individual areas rather than networks of parks. The formation of the National Parks Association of Queensland in 1930 marked the beginning of a statewide approach, but the most influential of these associations, those of Victoria and New South Wales, were not formed until the 1950s.[6] Even then most effort was directed to individual parks. The Australian Capital Territory National Parks Association, for instance, devoted most of its efforts to the successful establishment by stages of Namadgi National Park, 94,000 hectares (232,180 acres) covering 40 percent of the territory.

The effect of these agencies was the creation of a considerable bias toward the establishment of parks and reserves on the coastal periphery of the continent where over 80 percent of the population live. The emphasis in this zone was on the protection of the most dramatic natural scenery and the habitat of the most conspicuous native plants and animals.

The earliest suggestions on making the park and reserve systems representative of all the natural environments of the states and territories were made between 1958 and 1968 by the Australian Academy of Science.[7] The Academy's Committee on National Parks and Reserves established state subcommittees, a number of which produced comprehensive sets of proposals. Several states then set up their own committees, which continued the work of the academy,[8] and as the new parks and wildlife services were established, these committees became active in investigating new areas to add to the park systems.

In Victoria since 1970 the process of establishing parks and reserves has been facilitated by the work of the Land Conservation Council, which was given the task of evaluating all Crown lands and, after consultation with the public, making recommendations on their allocation. Efforts to extend the representativeness of the park systems were assisted by the report of the Australian Subcommittee for Section CT of the Australian National Committee for the International Biological Program (IBP) on the results of a survey organized by Professor Ray Specht and completed in 1971, and by the suggestion for a network of major reserves sampling ecosystems made in 1974 by a group of Australian ecologists at the end of the IBP.[9] Professor Specht's survey indicated the extent to which each of the major vegetation communities was represented in existing parks and reserves. New parks were selected to fill the gaps. Between 1971 and 1976 the Man and the Biosphere Bureau in Paris approved twelve Australian biosphere reserves, but unlike the listing of World Heritage sites, these have not had much influence on decision making.

The overall effect of the efforts discussed above was the extension of the parks and reserves into the interior and the more remote corners of the continent.

Although enormous strides were made toward securing new parks and reserves, interest in management was relatively slight. No doubt this reflected the general view on priorities. The main exception was again Myles Dunphy, who made important suggestions about the classification of parks and reserves. Dunphy's wilderness conservation efforts were taken up in the early seventies by the Australian Conservation Foundation, which instituted a regular series of national wilderness conferences, and by the Wilderness Society, formed in 1976. Wilderness inventories were completed for all of the states of southeastern Australia, and in 1984 a nongovernment National Wilderness Coordinating Committee was formed to promote all aspects of wilderness conservation. In 1987 New South Wales passed a Wilderness Act, the first in Australia.

Marine Parks

Reservation of the marine environment around Australia's 36,800-kilometer (22,852-mile) coastline was relatively slow to develop, but some protection was given to marine organisms, in coral reef environments around Green Island in 1938, and through marine national parks legislation in Queensland in 1974. In New South Wales marine areas adjacent to national parks were gazetted under national parks legislation beginning in 1967.

After a nationwide campaign for the protection of the Great Barrier Reef, which was threatened by oil-drilling proposals, the Great Barrier Reef Marine Park Act was passed in 1975. It provided a means for conservation of the 2,000-kilometer (1,242-mile) reef region. Between 1979 and 1983 the marine park was extended until it covered 98.5 percent of the region. Strong government resistance to the rapid extension of the park was reduced by continuing public pressure and by the inscription of the whole region on the World Heritage list in 1981.

Although still comparatively neglected, by 1984 a diverse range of marine ecosystems had been protected in twenty-two categories of reserves, and there was a growing movement for the establishment of marine parks and reserves.[10]

PARKS AND RESERVES

By June 1988 there were 2,156 nature conservation reserves in Australia covering 4.38 percent of the country. The system protects some part of each of the sixteen major terrestrial biogeographical provinces of the Australian realm as defined by Miklos D. F. Udvardy in his revised classification of 1982. A statistical summary is presented in Table 2.1.

Unfortunately, the last assessment of the adequacy of these reserves in protecting samples of the major plant formations was made in 1981.[11] Since then the system of parks has been greatly expanded, but the major deficiencies appear still to be in its failure to adequately represent samples of temperate tussock grasslands and tropical/subtropical tussock grasslands. The Australian National Index of Ecosystems program is now underway, and this will provide information on the conservation status of the vegetation communities.

An evaluation of the representation of Australia's marine regions in parks and reserves indicated that half had no protected areas, and others, such as the Great Australian Bight and the New South Wales Coast, were very poorly represented.[12]

Not surprisingly, in view of the size of the continent, Australia exhibits a wide range of functional reserve types, including all of the IUCN categories. In spite of the considerable number of terms used—twenty-eight for terrestrial and twenty-two for marine reserves—there has been some convergence as in the development of a dual national park and a nature reserve system in most states.

The variety, splendor, and essential character of the natural environments

Table 2.1
Australia's Terrestrial Nature Conservation Reserves[a]

DESIGNATION	NUMBER	AREA IN HECTARES (acres)	% OF STATE OR TERRITORY	OTHER CONSERVATION RESERVE CATEGORIES
Queensland -- 1,727,200 km^2				
National Park	315	3,512,867 (8,676,814)		Environmental Park Fauna Refuge
TOTAL		3,512,867 (8,676,814)	2.03	Scientific Purposes Reserve Dept'l. & Official Purposes Reserve
New South Wales -- 801,600 km^2				
National Park	68	3,101,742 (7,661,303)		Historic Site Aboriginal Area
Nature Reserve	185	521,651 (1,288,478)		State Recreation Area Flora Reserve
TOTAL		3,623,393 (8,949,781)	4.52	
Victoria -- 227,600 km^2				
National Park	30	1,073,567 (2,651,710)		Other Park (3): Historic Park
Other Park (Schedule 3): State Park Coastal Park Wilderness Flora and Fauna Reserve	48	459,684 (1,135,419)		Other Park (Schedule 4) Forest Reserve (including Forest Park)
State Wildlife Reserve: Nature Reserve	89	70,709 (174,651)		
TOTAL		1,603,960 (3,961,780)	7.05	
Tasmania -- 67,928 km^2				
State Reserve: National Park	13	851,046 (2,102,084)		State Reserve: Historic Site Aboriginal Site.
State Reserve	55	19,999 (49,398)		Conservation Area: Wildlife Sanctuary
Nature Reserve	38	29,427 (72,685)		Mutton Bird Sanctuary Protected Area
TOTAL		900,472 (2,224,167)	13.26	State Recreation Area. Forest Reserve
South Australia -- 984,000 km^2				
National Park	12	2,648,453 (6,541,679)		Recreation Park Native Forest Reserve
Conservation Park	193	4,072,526 (10,059,139)		
TOTAL		6,720,979 (16,600,818)	6.83	
Western Australia -- 2,525,500 km^2				
National Park	53	4,649,732 (11,484,838)		Conservation and Recreation Management Priority Area
Conservation of Flora and Fauna Reserve	1,041	9,994,972 (24,687,580)		
TOTAL		14,644,704 (36,172,418)	5.80	

Table 2.1 (continued)

DESIGNATION	NUMBER	AREA IN HECTARES (acres)	% OF STATE OR TERRITORY	OTHER CONSERVATION RESERVE CATEGORIES
		Northern Territory -- 1,346,200 km²		
Territorial Legislation				
National Park (including Aboriginal National Park)	6	508,713 (1,265,211)		Nature Park Historical Reserve Other lands under Conservation Commission Management
Conservation Reserve	12	33,776 (834,267)		
Commonwealth Legislation				
National Park	2	1,979,900 (4,890,353)		
TOTAL		2,522,389 (6,989,831)	1.87	
		Australian Capital Territory -- 2,400 km²		
National Park	1	94,000 (232,180)		
Nature Reserve	2	10,020 (24,749)		
TOTAL		104,020 (256,929)	43.34	
		External Territories		
Australian Antarctic Terr.: Specially Protected Area	3	unknown		
Christmas Island: National Park	1	1,600 (3,952)	11.85	
Norfolk Island: National Park	1	460 (1,136)	13.26	Reserve
Terr. of Ashmore & Cartier Islands: National Nature Reserve	2	215 (531)		
Coral Sea Island Territory: National Nature Reserve	1	112 (277)		
TOTAL		2,387 (5,896)		
		AUSTRALIA -- 7,682,300 km²		
TOTAL	2,156	33,635,164 (83,078,855)	4.38	

Note:
[a] Data current to June 30, 1988 except Northern Territory and Tasmania, where data current to June 30, 1987. In 1987 there were also 162 marine and estuarine reserves in 22 categories protecting 2,351,629 hectares (5,808,524 acres) in addition to the Great Barrier Reef Marine Park.

Figure 2.1
Australia: Major National Park Groupings

protected in Australia's national parks and nature preserves can best be indicated by looking briefly at ten major representative parks. Please refer to Figure 2.1.

The Great Barrier Reef Marine Park

Embracing 34,480,851 hectares (85,166,960 acres) on the continental shelf off the coast of Queensland, this is the world's largest marine reserve and one of the largest parks of any kind.

The park does not extend above the low water mark and does not include the hundreds of high and low islands. The islands are, however, a part of the World Heritage site, and most are national parks under Queensland legislation.

The park's main feature is a broken maze of 2,500 coral reefs and 71 coral cays, the most extensive in the world. These were formed from the accumulated remains of plant and animal calcium carbonate skeletal material between 15,000 and 6,000 B.C. during which the sea rose 45 meters (148 feet) to its present level.

The whole reef ecosystem is extremely diverse. There are some 400 species of coral in 60 genera, over 4,000 species of mollusks, 1,500 species of fish, and 242 species of birds. The park provides major feeding grounds for endangered dugongs (*Dugong dugon*) and green (*Chelonia mydas*) and loggerhead turtles (*Caretta caretta*). Investigations into the destruction of areas of hard coral by what appear to be large numbers of crown of thorns starfish (*Acanthaster planci*) have not yet reached any certain conclusions.

The park is being developed along multiple-use lines by means of a zoning system, but mining and drilling are banned throughout. Of six zones in general use, two are "marine national park" categories, one of which prohibits recreational fishing. There is also a "preservation" zone.

Parks of the Wet Tropics of North Queensland

The forests of the Wet Tropics between Cooktown and Ingham are the most extensive parts of a chain of rain-forest "islands" extending down the east coast of Australia. Fifteen million years ago closed forest covered most of Australia; today it covers about 0.29 percent.

From an evolutionary standpoint the area is exceptionally important because it contains the greatest concentration of primitive gymnosperms and angiosperms (flowering plants) in the world. The forests are relics of the Tertiary and Cretaceous flora and fauna of Gondwanaland before Australia separated from Antarctica and before the development of the sclerophyllous woodlands that now dominate the Australian landscape. In northeastern Queensland, conditions remained moist and hospitable enough for a large number of primitive plants to survive the cool dry periods of the Pleistocene glaciation. One of these, *Austrobaileya Scanders*, has pollen that closely resembles that of the oldest known fossil flowering plant. There are 1,160 species of plants, 435 of which are endemic to the region, and the area is also an excellent locale in which to study the mixing of Australian and Asian plants.

This plant richness is matched by the great diversity of animal life. Included are a third of Australia's species of marsupials and frogs, a quarter of the species of reptiles, two-thirds of the species of butterflies and bats, and a fifth of the birds. Fifty-four species of vertebrates are unique to the area. Australia's two species of tree kangaroo (Genus *Dendrolagus*) are restricted to the Wet Tropics.

There are 214,300 hectares (529,310 acres) of land in national parks in the region, but major areas of virgin or selectively logged rain forest were threatened by timber interests before the area was nominated for World Heritage listing in 1988 and restrictions placed on logging. The major national parks in the region are Daintree River, Hinchinbrook, Bellenden Kerr, and Cape Tribulation. Cape Tribulation National Park is the most accessible, the most scientifically important, and the most spectacularly beautiful with rain forests that extend from the 1,375-meter (4,510-foot) Thornton Peak to the beaches and fringing coral reefs of the

Great Barrier Reef Marine Park. The park is the home of an aboriginal rain-forest community with a continuous history of occupation of at least 10,000 years.

The Sand Mass National Parks

The coastal sand masses of southeastern Queensland—the highest in the world—are represented in a number of major national parks, including Great Sandy (52,000 hectares, 128,440 acres) and Cooloola (39,400 hectares, 97,318 acres). The sand masses, which reach a maximum height of 282 meters (925 feet), exhibit a large number of distinct dune systems formed over 140,000 years on a hard rock foundation that is generally below sea level.

The surface of the sand masses is diversified by sixty freshwater and nutrient-poor lakes, most perched on organically bonded sand rock. The rain forest of the region is the only rain forest in the world growing on dunes of over 200 meters (656 feet). Wet and dry heath, known locally as "Wallum," is a major plant formation in the parks. Mangroves line the shores of the Great Sandy Strait, which provides significant habitat for dugongs. The sand masses constitute one of the two areas of greatest species diversity for birds in Australia. Politically powerful commercial and timber interests have prevented the two national parks from incorporating major sections of the rain forest, but public pressure for protection is likely to continue from conservation groups and visitors who now number over half a million a year.

Australian Alpine National Parks

The 500-kilometer (311-mile) long Australian Alps are of modest height among the world's mountain ranges, but their environments provide internationally important evidence of the effect of the Pleistocene glaciation and periglacial action on the Southern Hemisphere. The alpine biota contains representation of elements derived from many areas and is rich in old endemic species. Internationally, the parks in the region are most significant for the display of a wide range of sclerophyll open forest communities dominated by eucalypts. Unlike the other areas around the world characterized by sclerophyll vegetation, the forests are extensive and relatively undisturbed. Kosciusko, Namadgi, and the Victorian Alpine national parks collectively cover 1,430,893 hectares (3,535,737 acres).

The area has all of Australia's highest peaks, including Mount Kosciusko (2,228 meters, 7,308 feet), and about 100,000 hectares (247,000 acres) of land above the tree line. Glaciation during the last Ice Age was restricted and mild so that there are few lakes but much evidence, particularly in the form of deep soils, of the severe and extensive periglaciation. The large altitudinal range of 2,100 meters (6,888 feet) is reflected in a wide range of plant formations from the dry scrub and native pines of the lower Snowy Valley to the alpine and subalpine communities above the tree line. Frost hollows in upland plains have created striking inversions of the normal sequence of vegetation formation.

There is a variety of unusual flora and fauna. The snow gum varieties (*Eucalyptus pauciflora*) are an interesting example of the adaptability of the eucalyptus species, in this instance to intense cold and damage by heavy snow. The mountain pygmy possum (*Burramys parvus*), a short furred marsupial, long thought to be extinct, lives in subalpine rock screes and herb fields.

Summer grazing was completely eliminated from Kosciusko National Park nearly twenty years ago, but in Victoria the Alpine National Park Act of 1989 entrenched the position of summer grazing as a traditional use. The decision, which runs counter to the agreed national definition for a national park, could well jeopardize a planned World Heritage nomination. Timber interests are being phased out of the alpine parks in Victoria.

A long-distance walking track has been developed in the Victorian section of the Alps, but it has yet to be linked with the New South Wales and ACT sections.

Western Tasmanian Wilderness National Parks

The contiguous South-West, Franklin–Lower Gordon Wild River, and Cradle Mount Lake St. Clair national parks (769,355 hectares, 1,900,307 acres) together protect a part of one of the most extensive wilderness areas left in the temperate zones of the world.

A series of north to south trending mountain ranges face the prevailing westerlies, giving the area the highest rainfall in Australia after the Wet Tropics. There are deep gorges where rivers such as the Gordon have cut through the ranges, and the 400-kilometer (248-mile) coastline comprises cliffs, beaches, and the drowned valley of Port Davey.

Since the end of the Ice Age some 15,000–12,000 years ago, the natural vegetation of the area has been closed temperate rain forest with many Gondwanaland elements in both the flora and fauna. The extensive area of sedge and grass and the small pockets of eucalypts are largely the result of widespread burning by aborigines over several thousand years. The intricate mosaic of vegetation in the area also results from several other factors including soil, aspect, and hydrology.

The dominant species in the rain forest is the *Nothofagus*, the southern beech. Also of interest are the *Podocarps*, particularly the Huon pine (*Lagarostrobus franklini*), which lives up to 2,000 years. The rare orange-bellied parrot (*Neophema chrysostoma*) breeds in the sedge lands around Port Davey.

In 1981 conclusive evidence was found in limestone caves in the Lower Franklin of 5,000 years of human occupation between 20,000 and 15,000 years ago. In 1989 another cave extended the date to 30,000 years ago. During the Ice Age, these were the southernmost settlements in the world.

This immense system of parks is accessible by road at a number of points, and there are cruise launches on the Gordon River and an 84-kilometer (52-mile) walking track with huts in the Central Highlands. The distinctive activity is wilderness travel on foot and by river.

The heavily timbered eastern sections of the wilderness remain ouside the national parks and the World Heritage site. These are severely threatened as road making and logging extend westward into the region. The swamp gum (*Eucalyptus regnans*) reaches over 90 meters (300 feet) in this area—the world's tallest flowering plant. In early 1987 the federal government intervened to halt logging during a one-year inquiry into the competing heritage and timber interests in the area and, at the conclusion, nominated an additional 312,645 hectares (772,546 acres).

Parks of the Eastern Mallee Heath

Wyperfeld National Park, the Big Desert Wilderness in Victoria, and three conservation parks in the Ninety Mile Desert of South Australia together form a 359,000-hectare (886,730-acre) suite of protected areas representative of the eucalyptus scrubs, shrub lands, and open heaths of the semi-arid parts of Australia.

The eucalyptus species of the parks growing on jumbled sand ridges characteristically have a multistemmed form known as "Mallee." The trees typically have large lignotubers developed as a survival mechanism against wildfires.

Wyperfeld has over 300 plant species and 180 species of birds, of which the Mallee fowl (*Leipoa ocellata*), which incubates its eggs in large mounds, is the best known. No vehicles are allowed into the Big Desert Wilderness.

Most of the land in this region has been cleared for agriculture, but a rural industry slump in the 1970s resulted in the South Australian government establishing the Ngarkat Conservation Park. Together the parks of the eastern mallee heath constitute the largest area of uncleared native vegetation in the agricultural regions of western Victoria and eastern South Australia.

Forest and Wildflower Parks of the South-West

Isolated for millions of years by a broad desert barrier, nearly a quarter of the genera and 70 percent of the species of the moister South-West of Western Australia are endemic.

This rich endemism achieves its most dramatic form in the wet sclerophyll karri forests. Karri (*E. diversicolor*), which grows to heights of over 80 meters (262 feet) and creates a magnificent spectacle as one of the world's largest living trees, is poorly protected. Only a small percentage is in national parks—mainly in the Shannon and Walpole-Nornalup parks—and most of the remainder could be eliminated in its mature form by proposed logging.

Three hundred kilometers (186 miles) to the east, the 242,739-hectare (599,565-acre) Fitzgerald River National Park, an international biosphere reserve, has 1,232 recorded plant species, 58 of them believed to be restricted to the area. Wildflowers, such as the Royal Hakea (*Hakea Victoriae*), attract attention for their unusual forms, and there are several rare vertebrates.

Roughly halfway between Walpole and Fitzgerald the 115,671-hectare (285,707-acre) Stirling Range National Park also exhibits a flora of great diversity with a substantial degree of endemism.

Prince Regent River Nature Reserve (Kimberleys)

This reserve of 634,952 hectares (1,568,331 acres) in the Kimberleys is one of the most remote and inaccessible in Australia. An international biosphere reserve, its main physical feature is the gash of the straight-running Prince Regent River gorge. The area has the highest rainfall in tropical Western Australia. There are monsoon vine thickets with both evergreen and deciduous species. Saltwater crocodiles occur in the estuary, and there is a rare scaly-tailed possum (*Wyulda squamicauda*). The first biological survey was not made until 1974, so the environment is not fully investigated.

Kakadu National Park (Arnhem Land)

Kakadu National Park has an area of 1,755,200 hectares (4,335,440 acres) and is one of the most important national parks in the world. Such preeminence is based as much on the quality of its natural scenery and its cultural features as its great size.

The park contains parts of all of the major landforms of Arnhem Land, including the sandstone plateau and the flood plains. A 400-meter (1,300-foot) high sandstone escarpment runs over 500 kilometers (310 miles) through the park. During the heavy rains of the monsoon, the South and Alligator rivers and their tributaries inundate much of the lower-lying areas. Large lagoons and marshes remain in winter to provide dry season refuges for vast flocks of waterfowl. There are barramundi (*Lates calcifer*) and two species of crocodile (*Crocodylus johnsoni* and *Crocodylus porosus*) in the river systems.

The full richness of the flora and fauna is still being discovered, but there are over 1,000 plant species, 270 species of birds, and 50 native mammal species.

Overhangs and caves at the foot of the escarpment feature one of the world's greatest collection of cave paintings. The aborigines appear to have been in the area for 30,000 years, and there are over 1,000 painting sites with the oldest estimated to be 18,000 years old. The several styles relating to different periods include the so-called x-ray art, in which the shape of the internal organs and bones is shown.

The national park is commonwealth territory, and the greater part is owned by traditional aborigines who in 1978 leased it for the purpose of a national park for a period of ninety-nine years. The management plan provides for the interests of both the national park and the traditional owners, who live in the park.

Unfortunately, large-scale mining is taking place on an enclave within the park, and the supposedly temporary mining town of Jabiru has been established in the park. In June 1987 a 447,900-hectare (1,106,313-acre) section in Stage 3 was added to the park, and mining was banned in Stages 1 and 2. However, a 225,200-hectare (556,244-acre) area of the proposed Stage 3 was gazetted as a conservation zone to allow mining exploration to continue for another five years.

Uluru National Park (Western Arid Region)

The 123,538-hectare (327,368-acre) Uluru National Park is representative of the dune fields, Spinifex grasslands, and Mulga scrub of the Central Australia desert but also includes famous rock formations. Visitors' attention focuses on the giant sandstone monolith Uluru (Ayers Rock) and on Katatjuka (the Olgas), an astonishing group of twenty-four rock domes—the hard tips of buried folded strata—covering 35 square kilometers (13.5 square miles).

The park was part of an aboriginal reserve until 1958. In 1985 it was handed back to its aboriginal owners, who immediately leased it to the commonwealth director of national parks, creating a further experiment with this new reserve concept. Many of the rock features of the monoliths are of spiritual significance to the aborigines.

ADMINISTRATION

The natural environments in Australia's national parks and nature reserves enjoy a relatively high level of protection similar to that in the United States, Canada, and New Zealand, and the staff and resources available for their management, although not lavish, would be the envy of most developing nations. Unlike most other developed nations, however, the park systems of Australia are still far from complete. The emphasis still devoted to securing new parks results in less energy being devoted to management of the existing estate. There are two main threats to the future of the parks. First, mining, timber, and grazing interests pose serious obstacles to the expansion of the parks to their logical boundaries. Second, an aggressive mining sector continues its attempt to gain access to lands already within the park estate.

Allocation of Responsibilities

The major role in the administration and management of the protected areas in the states is still played by the state governments. With the exception of Western Australia, each state has a combined national parks and wildlife agency. In Western Australia, although the control of wildlife and national parks is still administratively separated within the Department of Conservation and Land Management, national parks, nature reserves, and marine reserves are all vested in a National Parks and Nature Conservation Authority, which has the responsibility to produce management plans and advise on overall policy.

The role of the Australian National Parks and Wildlife Service in direct land management has not extended beyond the internal and external territories. In the case of the Great Barrier Reef Marine Park, although the park is established under federal legislation that vests overall control in the Marine Park Authority, day-to-day management is by the state parks and wildlife agency. The Great Barrier Reef Ministerial Council coordinates policy between the two governments at the ministerial level.

A similar cooperative device—the Tasmanian World Heritage Council—forms part of the management arrangement for the wilderness national parks. Co-ordination of national policy overall is attempted through the regular meetings of the Council of Nature Conservation Ministers (CONCOM). Although this body has no statutory powers, it has encouraged the development of a basically similar approach to philosophy, classification, and management. Except in the case of marine reserves, however, it has rejected the introduction of a uniform terminology.

Protection and Use Policy

In 1970 the Conference of National Parks Ministers adopted the following definition of a national park based on the 1969 definition of the Tenth General Assembly of IUCN:

a relatively large area set aside for its features of predominantly unspoiled natural landscape, flora and fauna, permanently dedicated for public enjoyment, education and inspiration and protected from all interference other than essential management practices, so that its natural attributes are preserved.[13]

The priority given to nature conservation in legislation and government policy statements suggests that there should be almost complete exclusion of incompatible uses from the parks and reserves. In general this is true, but there are a few worrying exceptions. In Victoria, for instance, areas scheduled to be included in parks have been made available for logging and mineral exploration for a restricted period, and grazing has been allowed to continue in the Alpine National Park. In Queensland grazing is allowed in remote parks where it would be difficult to control and as a management tool at Lakefield National Park.

Legislation for both the commonwealth and Tasmania makes it possible for mining activity to be permitted by means of a park plan of management, but it is recognized that such would be inconsistent with the principal aim, and no use has been made of these provisions. Instead, as at Kakadu, the commonwealth has excluded three major mining areas from the park. The South Australian and Western Australian governments allow mineral exploration in their parks.

Hunting and fishing for native fauna is generally banned from Australian parks and reserves. Fishing for introduced species, such as trout, which are usually not under the control of the park authority, and hunting of feral animals, such as pigs and goats, and game animals such as deer, is allowed in most instances. Australia does not have a problem of illegal use comparable with that of developing nations.

Throughout Australia the main difference between the objective of a nature reserve and a national park is that in parks the aim is to cater to recreational and educational uses consistent with conservation. Otherwise, the nature conservation objective is paramount in both. Pedestrian recreation and camping are generally the favored forms of visitor activity and, with the exception of the snow fields, accommodation units are either excluded or of an inexpensive nature. In 1989, however, South Australia began to plan high-cost hotels within its national parks. Scientific research is limited to permit holders.

Even though state park and reserve legislation is quite distinct, the differences in park use policy are mainly ones of emphasis and style. Queensland's park system, for instance, emphasizes the exclusion of motor roads and intensive recreation. This approach can have its drawbacks. In Queensland land can be excised from a national park for the purpose of a tourist resort, and although this keeps the park concept pure, it has facilitated the loss of several valuable island areas.

South Australia's conservation parks give a higher priority to nature conservation than do most of the other state park systems. In contrast, some of Western Australia's national parks, such as the Stirling Ranges and the Fitzgerald River national parks, have extensive internal road systems.

The eastern states and the commonwealth all recognize the need for special management to protect wilderness. Provisions exist for this in most park acts, but only New South Wales has implemented a policy of wilderness dedication with any degree of thoroughness.

Management

The states vary greatly as to the extent to which they have developed management plans. The New South Wales Parks and Wildlife Service, with a work force of 753 and an annual budget of $45 million, has prepared plans for the majority of its parks. In Queensland and Tasmania, on the other hand, most have no plans.

Management planning involves the development of a number of functional zones. The 1982 plan for Kosciusko National Park establishes the following zones, which are probably typical of the approach used in Australia: "outstanding natural resources," "special scientific value," "historic resources," "natural values," and "wilderness." In addition, the plan shows areas available for horse riding and indicates which roads are open to public vehicular use.

Not a great deal of attention has been paid in Australia to defining the biological objectives of park and reserve management. The aim is mainly to limit human influence and mitigate earlier damage so that the natural environments can evolve naturally. Such a policy is varied for a few reserves, chiefly nature reserves, where artificial burning is carried out to maintain the grassy vegetation required to maintain macropod populations.

Fire control is a major facet of park management, especially in the southern half of Australia, where rain-forest species are vulnerable and where there is a need to prevent the spread of fires into or out of the parks. In most cases, though, management is complicated by the fact that the main responsibility for fire control rests with a body other than the park authority.

Threats

The existence of scores of government and conservation group proposals for new or extended parks in the extensive areas of Crown land is evidence of the fact that the park systems are far from complete. Further expansion is likely to meet continuing opposition from mining and timber interests. Overcutting by the timber industry has so depleted timber resources that there is strong resistance to new parks in heavily forested areas such as Tasmania and southwestern Western Australia.

Because dedication of an area as a park effectively closes land to mining activity, mining companies and industry associations are waging a campaign both to block the dedication of new parks and to gain acceptance of the concept of mining within national parks. Conservative governments in the Northern Territory and Western Australia have also shown interest in easing mining restrictions in national parks, and parks legislation in the Northern Territory was amended in 1984 to make it easier for mining to occur.

The Future

Public support for the park systems remains high, and a 1986 government proposal to revoke Queensland's Lindeman Island National Park for a resort had to be withdrawn as a result of vigorous public protest. However, if the history of the last two decades is anything to go by, the future is still uncertain. The personal interest of leading ministers has been a more important factor in park policy than political party platforms.

This is reflected in the differing attitude of the states to the nomination of World Heritage sites. As a result of the support for conservation given by former Premier Neville Wran (1976–1986), three out of Australia's eight World Heritage sites are in New South Wales. The Queensland government, on the other hand, objects to further areas being nominated. In 1987 this persistent opposition to proposed World Heritage sites caused the federal government to abandon a policy (agreed to by CONCOM) of seeking the agreement of the state and Northern Territory governments before making nominations of World Heritage areas under their control.

The fact that such matters are regarded as involving important policy decisions indicates that public interest is high and gives cause for some optimism about the future of the parks.

NOTES

The author would like to acknowledge his appreciation of the assistance given by Neille Radcliffe and Louise Russell in the completion of this chapter.

1. *New South Wales Gazette*, April 26, 1879.

2. *New South Wales Parliamentary Debates* (1880–1881): 899–900.

3. Among other major parks declared in the 1901–1955 period were Bellenden Kerr (1921), Hinchbrook Island (1932), Whitsunday (1936), Carnarvon (1938), and Eungella (1941) in Queensland; New England (1931) in New South Wales; Wilson's Promontory (1908), Mount Buffalo (1908), Wyperfeld (1921), and Kinglake (1928) in Victoria; Cradle Mount–Lake St. Clair (1922), Gordon River (1939), Frenchman's Cap (1941), Ben Lomond (1947), and Lake Pedder (1955) in Tasmania; Flinders Chase (1919), Billiatt (1940), Hambidge (1941), and Hicks (1941) in South Australia; Barrow Island (1908) and Fitzgerald River (1954) in Western Australia; and Palm Valley (1923) in Northern Territory.

4. See Lake Pedder Committee of Inquiry, *Final Report, The Flooding of Lake Pedder, April 1974* (Canberra: Australian Government Publishing Service, 1974); and Committee of Inquiry into the National Estate, *Report of the National Estate* (Canberra: Australian Government Publishing Service, 1974).

5. This was in spite of a recommendation from the Australian Heritage Commission that the area merited inscription. See Rainforest Conservation Society of Queensland, *Tropical Rainforests of North Queensland, Their Conservation Significance*, Report to Australian Heritage Commission (Canberra: Australian Government Publishing Service, 1986).

6. The dates for formation of park associations are Queensland, 1930; Victoria, 1952; New South Wales, 1957; Australian Capital Territory, 1958; Western Australia, 1977; Northern Territory, 1985. Similar roles were played by the Nature Conservation Society of South Australia, formed in 1962, and the Tasmanian Conservation Trust, formed in 1968. A National Parks Council was formed in 1975. The Australian Conservation Foundation has been active in this field since 1965.

7. See Australian Academy of Science (AAS), *National Parks and Reserves in Australia* (Canberra: AAS, 1968).

8. In New South Wales through the Scientific Committee on Parks and Reserves (1967–1973) and in Western Australia through a Reserves Advisory Council (1969), becoming the Conservation Through Reserves Committee (1971–1984).

9. See R. L. Specht, Ethel M. Roe, and Valerie H. Boughton, eds., "Conservation of Major Plant Communities in Australia and Papua New Guinea," *Australian Journal of Botany*, Supplement no. 7 (CSIRO: Melbourne, 1974); and Australian Academy of Science, *A National System of Ecological Reserves in Australia* (Canberra: Australian Academy of Science, 1975).

10. See, for instance, Australian Committee for IUCN (ACIUCN), *Australia's Marine and Estuarine Areas—A Policy for Protection* (Canberra: ACIUCN, 1986).

11. R. L. Specht, "Conservation of Vegetation Types," in *Australian Vegetation*, ed. R. H. Groves (Cambridge: Cambridge University Press, 1981), pp. 393–410.

12. Council of Nature Conservation Ministers, *Summary Report of the Second Technical Workshop on Selection and Management of Marine and Estuarine Protected Areas, February 1985* (Canberra: Council of Nature Conservation Ministers, 1985).

13. Committee of Inquiry into the National Estate, *Report of the National Estate* (Canberra: Australian Government Publishing Service, 1974), p. 75.

BIBLIOGRAPHY

Australian Heritage Commission. *The National Estate in 1981*. Canberra: Australian Government Publishing Service, 1982.

Australian National Parks and Wildlife Service. *Nomination of Kakadu National Park for Inclusion in the World Heritage List*. Canberra: May 1980.

Dunphy, Myles. *Selected Writings*. Compiled and annotated by Patrick Thompson. Sydney: Ballagirin, 1986.

Figgis, P., and G. Mosley. *Australia's Wilderness Heritage*, vol. 1: *World Heritage Areas*. Sydney: Weldon, 1988.

Goldstein, W., ed. "Australia's 100 Years of National Parks." *Parks and Wildlife* 2, no. 3–4 (1979).

Great Barrier Reef Marine Park Authority. *Nomination of the Great Barrier Reef for Inclusion in the World Heritage List*. Townsville, Qsld.: GBRMPA, January 1981.

Hutton, G. *Australia's Natural Heritage*. Melbourne: Collins/Australian Conservation Foundation, 1983.

Ivanovici, Angela M., ed. *Inventory of Declared Marine and Estuarine Protected Areas in Australian Waters*. 2 vols. Canberra: Australian National Parks and Wildlife Service, 1984.

Le Gay Brereton, J., J. C. Webb, and D. Whitlock. *The Last of Lands*. Melbourne: Jacaranda Press, 1969.

Mobbs, C. J., ed. *Nature Conservation Reserves in Australia (1986)*. Canberra: Australian National Parks and Wildlife Service, 1987.

Mosley, J. G. "A History of the Wilderness Reserve Idea in Australia." *Australia's Wilderness: Conservation Progress and Plans*. Melbourne: Australian Conservation Foundation, 1978.

Tasmanian Government and Australian Heritage Commission. *Nomination of the Western Tasmania Wilderness National Park for Inclusion in the World Heritage List*. Canberra, November 1981.

CANADA 3

Harold K. Eidsvik and
William D. Henwood

The national parks system of Canada is one of the oldest and most established in the world. Occupying the northern half of the North American continent, Canada is the only country capable of protecting representative examples of several northern biomes of the Nearctic Realm. As a federal state, Canada provides an excellent example of cooperative and complementary efforts among national, provincial, and territorial governments in the establishment of nationally significant protected areas.

HISTORY

The origin of Canada's national park system is inextricably linked to the construction of the transcontinental railway and, ironically, to expansionist national economic policies that encouraged the development of Canada's natural resources. Completing the railway, and securing its financial success, were fundamental to the implementation of this policy, particularly as it related to the "opening up" of the western Canadian frontier.

As construction proceeded on the final crossing of the Rocky Mountain cordillera in November 1883, members of the railway construction crew discovered two natural hot springs, one emanating from the depths of a cave and the other feeding a natural basin. Consequently, they came to be known as the Cave and Basin Hot Springs. Following two years of legal battles to establish their ownership, the government of Canada unexpectedly passed an order-in-council declaring an area of approximateely 26 square kilometers (10 square miles) around the springs to be protected from sale, settlement, or exploitation, thereby creating the nucleus of what was to become Banff National Park. The date was November

25, 1885, a date commemorated one hundred years later in 1985 when Canada celebrated the centennial of its national park system.

This original reserve was given legislative sanction in November 1887 under the Rocky Mountains Park Act. It was expanded to an area of 670 square kilometers (260 square miles) and officially established as Canada's first national park. In the words of Sir John A. Macdonald, then prime minister of Canada, this legislation reflected his government's policy that "it was of great importance that all this section of country should be brought at once into usefulness. . . . The intention is to frame such regulations as will make the springs a respectable resort, as well as an attractive one in all respects."[1]

The establishment of a national park was consistent with the government's thrust of utilizing the newfound resource wealth of the west for the benefit of the nation. The purpose of this new national park was clearly oriented toward tourism and recreation, although a protectionist element was also evident in that the act provided that no leases, licenses, or permits would be issued that could "impair the usefulness of the park for the purposes of public enjoyment and recreation."[2] In apparent contradiction, however, it was also possible under the act for the minister of the interior, by order-in-council, to permit grazing, lumbering, and mining within the park area. In the words of park historian Robert Craig Brown,

It seems that there was an evident choice of priorities in the policy: the preservationist sections were there to enhance the function of the Park as a playground for the Canadian people—to restore the depleted wildlife, for example—but these sections were not to conflict with the exploitation of other resources within the park reserve.[3]

The Banff Hot Springs Hotel development began an era of railway tourism that was to continue to have an impact on the future growth of the park system. Railway construction played a major role in the establishment of Glacier and Yoho national parks in 1886 and Jasper National Park in 1907. In a similar manner, the construction of the Trans-Canada Highway led to the establishment of Kootenay National Park in 1920.

The protection of scenic beauty and natural attractions also played a major role in park establishment, especially when those values became threatened by resource development. Local enthusiasts and mountaineering clubs can be given much of the credit for the establishment of Waterton Lakes National Park in 1895 and Mount Revelstoke National Park in 1914. Similarly, local politicians recognized the value of national parks in providing recreational opportunities for their constituents as well as a base for a regional tourism economy, and often lobbied successfully for the establishment of national parks such as Georgian Bay Islands National Park in 1929 and Cape Breton Highlands National Park in 1936.

The establishment of national parks for the expressed purpose of wildlife protection and for the preservation of specific landscape types appeared relatively early in the evolution of the national park system. Elk Island National Park and Wood Buffalo National Park were created in 1913 and 1922 respectively for wildlife protection. Prince Albert National Park was established in 1927 "for the purpose of preserving in perpetuity a portion of the primitive forest and lake country of Northern Saskatchewan and to provide for the people of Saskatchewan as well as other parts of the Dominion, a great recreational area."[4]

The establishment of Riding Mountain National Park in 1929, created from a former federal forestry reserve, marked the end of an era as it was the last park to have been created from unalienated federal public lands within the provinces (this is still the case in the two northern territories). By virtue of the Canadian constitution, as defined by the British North America Act of 1867, the ownership and administrative control of the natural resources of the Railway Belt of British Columbia, and the provinces of Alberta, Saskatchewan, and Manitoba were vested with the federal government until 1930. It was, therefore, a relatively simple matter for the federal government to establish national parks on these lands.

Between 1887 and 1930, fourteen national parks were created in Canada, eleven of which were located in the four western provinces (Table 3.1). Of the total area of 76,040 square kilometers (29,359 square miles) encompassed within these parks, almost 90 percent was contributed by the western provinces. This is in direct contrast to the population distribution of the day, as only about 25 percent of the population lived in the west.

The year 1930 also saw the enactment of the National Parks Act, a very significant event in the evolution of the national park system in Canada. For the first time in their history, the national parks were responsive to their own legislation. The so-called dedication clause of the act has provided the basic mandate for resource conservation in the national parks, and still applies to this day:

The parks are hereby dedicated to the people of Canada for their benefit, education and enjoyment, subject to the provisions of this act and the regulations, and such parks shall be maintained and made use of so as to leave them unimpaired for the enjoyment of future generations.[5]

In direct contrast to the priorities that pervaded resource-management decisions in the early years of Banff National Park, the priorities clearly expressed in the act are the reverse, where resource protection in perpetuity became the dominant objective. While the act gave new purpose and direction to national parks, a clear interpretation of its provisions in the form of detailed management policies had to wait until 1964.

Between 1930 and 1968 the pace of growth of the national park system slowed considerably. The depression years of the early thirties placed severe limitations on further expansion, and by 1932 the economic situation was such that the federal government had to temporarily suspend any action on proposals to establish new national parks. In spite of this, two new national parks were added

Table 3.1
Canada's National Parks and National Park Reserves

NAME AND LOCATION	YEAR ESTABLISHED	PARK AREA (sq. km.)	(sq. mi.)
1) Banff, Alberta	1885	6,640.8	2,564.0
2) Glacier, B.C.	1886	1,349.6	521.0
3) Yoho, B.C.	1886	1,313.1	507.0
4) Waterton Lakes, Alberta	1895	525.8	203.0
5) Jasper, Alberta	1907	10,878.0	4,200.0
6) Elk Island, Alberta	1913	194.3	75.0
7) Mount Revelstoke, B.C.	1914	262.6	101.4
8) St. Lawrence Islands, Ont.	1914	0.8	0.3
9) Point Pelee, Ontario	1918	15.5	6.0
10) Kootenay, B.C.	1920	1,406.4	543.0
11) Wood Buffalo, Alberta/N.W.T.	1922	44,807.0	17,300.0
12) Prince Albert, Saskatchewan	1927	3,874.6	1,496.0
13) Riding Mountain, Manitoba	1929	2,975.9	1,149.0
14) Georgian Bay Islands, Ont.	1929	14.2	5.5
15) Cape Breton Highlands, N.S.	1936	950.5	367.0
16) Prince Edward Island, P.E.I.	1937	25.9	10.0
17) Fundy, New Brunswick	1948	205.9	79.5
18) Terra Nova, Newfoundland	1957	396.5	153.0
19) Pacific Rim, B.C.	1970	388.5[a]	150.0[a]
20) Gros Morne, Newfoundland	1973	1,942.5[a]	750.0[a]
21) Kejimkujik, Nova Scotia	1974	381.5	147.3
22) Forillon, Quebec	1974	240.4	92.8
23) Kluane, Yukon[b]	1976	22,015.0	8,500.0
24) Nahanni, N.W.T.[b]	1976	4,765.6	1,840.0
25) Auyuittuq, N.W.T.[b]	1976	21,471.1	8,290.0
26) La Mauricie, Quebec	1977	543.0	210.0
27) Pukaskwa, Ontario	1978	1,877.8[a]	725.0[a]
28) Kouchibouguac, N.B.	1979	238.8	92.0
29) Grasslands, Saskatchewan	1981	906.5[a]	350.0[a]
30) Mingan Archipelago, Quebec[b]	1984	150.7	58.2
31) Northern Yukon, Yukon	1984	10,168.4	3,926.0
32) Ellesmere Island, N.W.T.[b]	1986	37,775.0[a]	14,584.9[a]
33) Bruce Peninsula, Ontario	1987	270.0[a]	104.2[a]
34) South Moresby, B.C.[b]	1988	1,470.0[a]	567.6[a]
TOTALS		185,198.1	71,504.8

Notes:
[a] Lands not yet scheduled under the National Parks Act.
[b] Officially a National Park Reserve, meaning that final proclamation of the park awaits resolution of native land claims.

in the mid–1930s. The dedication to the war effort in the 1940s also stalled further growth of the system. In this thirty-eight-year period, a total of six new national parks were established, bringing the total to 20 national parks representing every province with the exception of Quebec. While this period of growth was slow, it served well to improve the balance of park establishment across the country.

Also in 1930, the ownership of natural resources in the four western provinces was transferred from the federal to the provincial governments. This transfer had a profound effect on the rate at which new national parks could be established in the provinces. The establishment of new parks now required the full cooperation of provincial governments in transferring to the federal government administration and control of the resources. Because regional objectives were not always coincident with national objectives, achievement of the agreement necessary for the formation of new national parks was a slow process.

In 1968, Canada held its first national conference on national parks. In recognition of the slow pace of growth, the conference called for the establishment of more national parks and for the development of a more integrated system of national parks representing the biological and geographic diversity of Canada.

The 1970s witnessed what has been called a revolution in the approach to national park establishment and was the most turbulent decade in the history of the national park system. This decade was also a period of unprecedented growth in the system. The period between 1968 and 1974 was particularly fruitful, with ten new national parks being created. There was a strong federal initiative to achieve a better balance in the national park system across the country, and finally all ten provinces and the two northern territories in Canada had national parks. This expansion effectively doubled the total area protected in the national park system. The federal government had also put into effect a policy innovation that enabled the federal and provincial governments to share the costs of land acquisition, greatly increasing the level of cooperation between the two levels of government.

A new initiative also began in northern Canada where most lands are still owned by the federal government and where new development interests were competing for the use of northern resources. In the 1970s, arrangements were made for the creation of four new national park reserves, and six more were identified for further study and negotiation.

Perhaps one of the most significant achievements of this period was the development and implementation of a systematic approach to planning the national park system. This systems approach divided Canada into thirty-nine terrestrial natural regions and formalized the goal of establishing a system of national parks representing each of these regions (Figure 3.1). Within each region, areas are identified that best represent the biogeographic features of the region and are given the status of Natural Areas of Canadian Significance (NACS). From among these NACS, potential national parks are chosen on the basis of natural heritage values and socioeconomic and political criteria. This system also recognizes that national parks are not the only way to protect nationally significant natural areas and encourages other levels of government and private conservation agencies to take appropriate actions within their mandates to protect areas not within the national park system.

In total, the protected area system in Canada is an amalgam of national parks, migratory bird sanctuaries, and national wildlife areas, all created by the federal government, and the many provincial parks and other protected areas established by the ten provincial governments of Canada. The two territorial governments in Canada's north are also developing their own systems of protected areas.

As the national park system began to take shape in the late 1880s, the provinces

Figure 3.1
The National Parks of Canada and the Natural Regions Systems Planning Framework

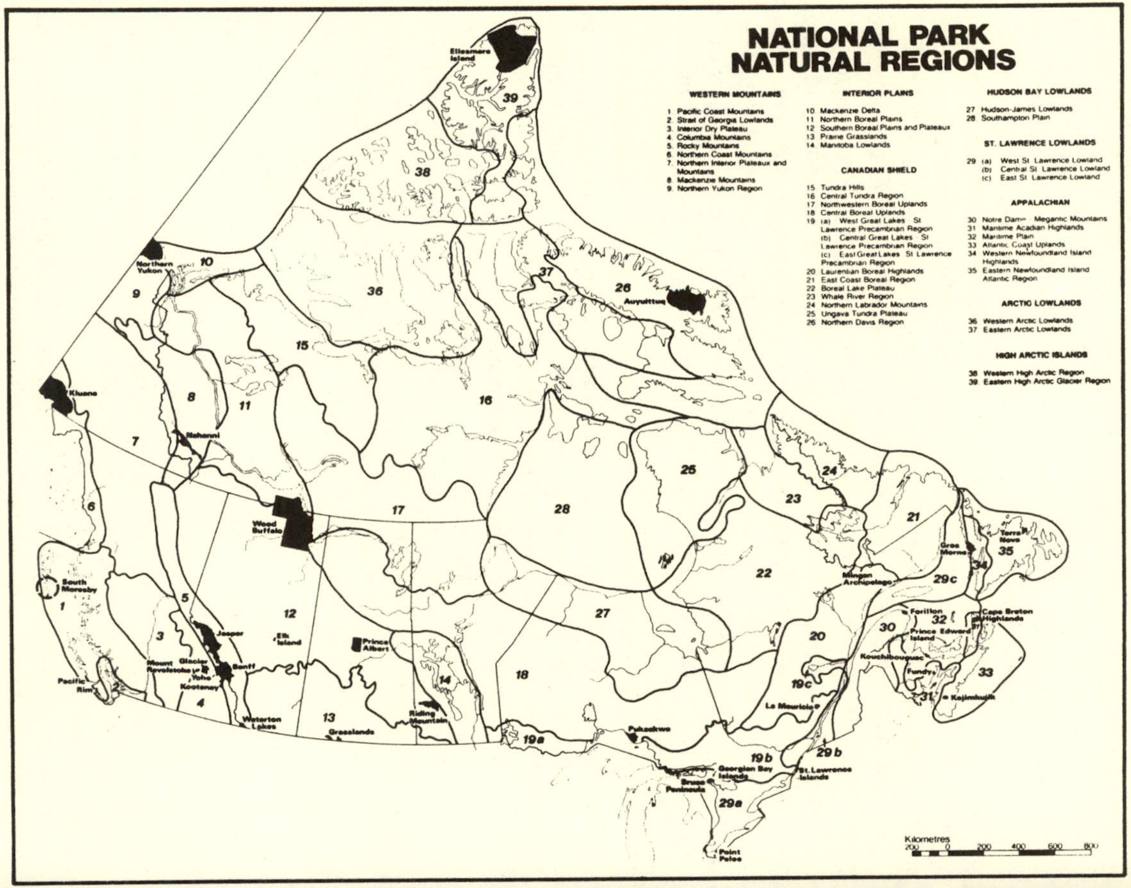

of Ontario and British Columbia had begun to establish their own provincial park systems. Beginning in the 1930s, following the transfer of natural resources to provincial ownership, the three western provinces of Alberta, Saskatchewan, and Manitoba also embarked on the development of their own protected areas. Today, every province in Canada has a provincial park system, and several also have programs to establish natural areas, ecological reserves, wilderness areas, and special wildlife management areas. In total, the cumulative area of these provincially protected areas far exceeds, and is an invaluable complement to, the federal protected area system.

The provincial park system in Ontario is the oldest in Canada, having begun with the establishment of Algonquin Provincial Park in 1893. Quebec followed with Laurentide Provincial Park in 1895. Encompassing an area of 7,540 square kilometers (2,900 square miles), Algonquin was one of the largest protected areas in the country at that time. Established on the recommendation of the Royal Commission on Forest Reservation and National Parks, Algonquin was created for the "maintenance of water supply in a half dozen major water systems, preservation of a primeval forest, protection of birds and animals, a field for experiments in forestry, a place of health resort, and beneficial effects on climate."[6]

It was typical in these early and formative years for provincial governments to establish either small recreation parks or large wilderness parks such as Algonquin. In 1894, Ontario established Rondeau Provincial Park on the shores of Lake Erie, a park of 46 square kilometers (18 square miles) that, while also providing for resource protection, was primarily intended to provide recreation opportunities for the local public. In 1913, Ontario established its second large wilderness area in Quetico Provincial Park, with an area of 4,655 square kilometers (1,800 square miles). Like Algonquin, Quetico protected a large expanse of rugged Canadian Shield country, but the concept of wilderness protection at that time did not exclude the continuation of logging, mining, and trapping activities. Often a source of controversy for the Ontario government, extractive activities in Quetico were terminated in 1973, but logging still continues in Algonquin.

On the Pacific coast, the province of British Columbia established its first provincial park in 1911 at Strathcona, a mountainous area in the interior of Vancouver Island. By 1930, there were thirteen provincial parks in British Columbia covering over 7,000 square kilometers (2,700 square miles). By 1944, this figure had increased to 30,000 square kilometers (11,580 square miles) with the addition of several large wilderness parks such as Tweedsmuir, Wells Gray, and Manning Provincial Parks. These parks were managed under a multiple-use concept, where resource extraction, particularly logging and mining, was as important as tourism and recreation. Logging and mining are no longer permitted in these parks.

The provinces of Alberta, Saskatchewan, and Manitoba started to build their provincial park systems after 1930, and several of the Atlantic provinces waited

Table 3.2
Provincial and Territorial Protected Areas

PROVINCE/ TERRITORY	NUMBER OF AREAS	TOTAL AREA (sq. km.)	PERCENT OF PROVINCE/ TERRITORY
British Columbia	415	51,900	5.5
Alberta	172	7,908	1.2
Saskatchewan	31	5,050	0.8
Manitoba	76	43,088	6.6
Ontario	490	56,980	5.3
Quebec	22	4,866	0.3
New Brunswick	29	3,402	4.1
Nova Scotia	35	1,331	2.4
Prince Edward Island	6	29	0.5
Newfoundland	17	1,287	0.3
N.W. Territories	14	173,090	5.1
Yukon Territory	2	5,918	1.1
TOTAL	1,237	354,849	

Adapted from: Lands Directorate. Natural Heritage Areas Study--Draft. Ottawa: Environment Canada, 1986.

much longer. Nova Scotia, for example, passed its first Provincial Parks Act in 1959. For the most part, these provincial parks systems have been comprised of small recreation parks, and only in relatively recent years have these systems been expanded to incorporate larger wilderness areas.

The many provincially protected areas in Canada make a significant contribution to the development of a comprehensive system of protected areas in Canada (Table 3.2). The provincial park system of British Columbia, for example, now includes 367 parks totaling in area over 46,400 square kilometers (17,900 square miles), almost 5 percent of the provincial land base. In addition, the Ecological Reserves system of British Columbia has established 115 reserves totaling 1,545 square kilometers (600 square miles). Ontario's system now includes 219 provincial parks covering 56,660 square kilometers (21,875 square miles). Collectively, the federal, provincial, and territorial protected areas cover an area of approximately 553,000 square kilometers (213,530 square miles) or about 5.5 percent of Canada's landmass.

While provincially administered, several provincial protected areas are recognized as being nationally and internationally significant. Dinosaur Provincial Park in Alberta, for example, has been declared a World Heritage Site. Several others such as Mount Edziza Provincial Park and the Spatsizi Plateau Wilderness Park in British Columbia, Polar Bear Provincial Park in Ontario and the Avalon Wilderness Area in Newfoundland are recognized as being protected areas of national significance.

Protected areas established by the federal government include not only national parks, but also migratory bird sanctuaries created under the Migratory Birds Convention Act, and national wildlife areas created under the Canada Wildlife

Act. Both of these types of protected areas are administered by the Canadian Wildlife Service of Environment Canada. Today, there are ninety-nine migratory bird sanctuaries covering approximately 11,620 square kilometers (4,485 square miles), and forty-five national wildlife areas covering approximately 2,870 square kilometers (1,108 square miles). Canada established its first migratory bird sanctuary at Last Mountain Lake in Saskatchewan in 1887.

The Federal-Provincial Parks Conference is an organization of federal, provincial, and territorial park agencies with the purpose of coordinating federal, provincial, and territorial efforts and exchanging information and experience in the establishment and management of protected area systems. Through its annual meetings, the conference aims at cooperation among all levels of government in the development of a comprehensive and integrated system of protected areas in Canada.

PARKS AND RESERVES

Canada is the second largest country in the world, spanning 85° longitude and 48° latitude, with a total area of 9,970,610 square kilometers (3,849,650 square miles). Within such a large landmass, there is a very high diversity of ecosystems and habitats. As mentioned previously, in the context of national parks system planning, it is the ultimate objective of the national park system in Canada to protect representative examples of the major biophysical land types in the country. For this purpose, Canada has been subdivided into thirty-nine terrestrial natural regions, each of which will be represented by a national park upon completion of the system. The terrestrial natural regions are identified on the basis of physiographic characteristics coupled with ecological, geographical, and geological considerations.

As of the end of 1987, there were thirty-four national parks in Canada protecting a total of approximately 185,200 square kilometers (71,500 square miles). See Table 3.1. In terms of natural region representation, of the total of thirty-nine terrestrial natural regions, twenty-one are now considered to be adequately represented in the system of national parks. There are nineteen natural regions that are not represented by national parks, and there are currently several proposals under active consideration. Figure 3.1 illustrates the terrestrial natural regions of Canada, upon which have been superimposed the existing national parks. In that sense, Canada has only just passed the halfway mark toward achieving a completed system of national parks.

In September of 1986, Environment Canada approved a new National Marine Parks Policy for Canada, enabling Parks Canada to commence a new initiative of establishing national marine parks in the Canadian territorial waters of the Arctic, Atlantic, and Pacific oceans and the Great Lakes. A systems planning procedure, similar to that used for planning the terrestrial national park system, has been put in place where twenty-nine distinct marine natural regions have been identified for Canada. As with the terrestrial national park system, it is the long-term objective to have each marine natural region represented by a national marine park.

Canada established its first national marine park in 1987 at Fathom Five in the fresh waters of Georgian Bay in Ontario. Created in conjunction with the new Bruce Peninsula National Park, Fathom Five protects one of the best assemblages of historic shipwrecks in the Great Lakes and, with its cold, clear waters, provides some of the best wreck diving in the world. Four additional national marine parks have been proposed, one each in the Atlantic and Pacific oceans, one in the Bay of Fundy on the Atlantic coast, and one at the confluence of the Saguenay and St. Lawrence rivers in Quebec.

Geology

The history of national park establishment in Canada clearly illustrates the importance of geology in influencing park-establishment decisions. The grandeur of high mountains and the fascination with hot springs, and the subsequent perceived need for scenic protection, led to the creation of the first national park in Canada. The basic geology of Canada forms the foundation of the natural region system, whether it be coastal mountains, the central plains, or the massive Canadian Shield.

The four western mountain parks of Banff, Jasper, Kootenay, and Yoho, which collectively constitute a World Heritage Site, protect a very large and representative example of the four geological subprovinces of the Rocky Mountain cordillera. As a result of continental tectonic forces, the sedimentary layers of shale, dolomite, sandstone, limestone, quartzite, and slate, spanning time from the Precambrian forward, have been uplifted, faulted, and folded to produce the spine of the North American continent. The Burgess Shale fossils, considered one of the most significant fossil sites in the world, and a World Heritage Site in their own right prior to the Rocky Mountain designation, are found in these mountains within Yoho National Park. These ranges are also particularly illustrative of the role of glacial and climatic forces in shaping the landscape.

In eastern Canada, on the island province of Newfoundland, Gros Morne National Park contains exceptional geological features that illustrate key concepts of earth science, and particularly the theory of plate tectonics. The result of a series of complex tectonic forces spanning over 600 million years, the rocks of Gros Morne are vestiges of the ancient Iapetus Ocean floor, its underlying crust and mantle, and the previous continental shelf and slope.

By the very nature of the natural regions systems planning framework, the various geological formations found in Canada will be well represented in the national park system.

History and Archaeology

Environment Canada, Parks also administers a system of National Historic Parks and Sites intended to "protect for all time historic resources at places associated with persons, places and events of national historic significance."[7] For example, another World Heritage Site, L'Anse aux Meadows National Historic Park, both protects and re-creates an eleventh-century Viking settlement, one of the earliest known European settlements in North America.

The national parks of Canada also house many nationally significant historic and archaeological resources that are protected and managed with the same vigilance as are National Historic Parks and Sites. Many national parks such as Pukaskwa in Ontario, La Mauricie in Quebec, and Kejimkujik in Nova Scotia contain petroglyphs, pictographs, and other rich archaeological evidence of previous habitation by Canada's indigenous peoples. Where necessary, efforts are made to retard the natural processes of erosion to preserve such sites for as long as possible.

Pacific Rim National Park is located in an area still occupied by the Nootka Indians, and several Indian reserves are located within park boundaries. Shell middens, village sites, petroglyphs, and burial caves are among the most important archaeological resources of the park and take on special meaning when directly associated with living descendants. Further, the more recent human history associated with maritime shipping is also well represented in the park area by a large number of shipwrecks, reflecting the area's reputation as the "Graveyard of the Pacific." The historic West Coast life-saving trail in the park was constructed to assist shipwrecked people to walk to safety after reaching the shore.

Archaeological digs in Forillon National Park, as well as written historical accounts, have documented human habitation there for nearly seven thousand years. Where strict protection is afforded the prehistoric sites of Forillon, the relatively recent evidence of agricultural use of some lands within the park is also retained and interpreted to the public in the context of historical land-use change.

Biology and Ecology

The National Parks Act requires that "the National Parks shall be maintained and made use of so as to leave them unimpaired for the enjoyment of future generations." This clause has been interpreted into policy as follows: "Natural resources within national parks will be given the highest degree of protection to ensure the perpetuation of a natural environment essentially unaltered by human activity," and "natural resources within national parks will be protected and managed with minimal interference to natural processes to ensure the perpetuation of naturally evolving land and water environments and their associated species."[8]

There is a strong correlation in Canada between geological patterns and vegetation distribution patterns and, consequently, wildlife distribution, a pattern further influenced by the extreme variations in altitude, latitude, and longitude. The concept of biophysical representation that underlies the systems-planning approach to national park establishment in Canada should ensure comprehensive protection of the biotic diversity of the country.

The terrestrial natural regions of Canada, while based primarily on physiographic parameters, have also been designed to reflect the gross vegetation patterns across the country characterized by forest type, including Arctic tundra, boreal forest, subalpine forest, montane forest, coast forest, Columbia forest, deciduous forest, Great Lakes–St. Lawrence forest, Acadian forest, and grasslands. Within these biophysical regions are found myriad ecosystems defined by distinct plant and animal associations or communities.

Pacific Rim National Park on the west coast of Vancouver Island, for example, protects a representative example of the Pacific Coast Mountains natural region. This park is characterized by extensive sand beaches and dunes, rugged rocky shorelines, island environments, coastal lowlands, west coast temperate rain forest, and abundant marine life. The park protects a variety of plant communities, ranging from coastal Sitka spruce (*Picea sitchensis*) forest to mature rain forest of western hemlock (*Tsuga heterophylla*) and western red cedar (*Thuja plicata*) with a diverse assemblage of understory species. Marine mammal and seabird habitat is also well represented in the park, in particular for northern (*Eumetopias jubata*) and California (*Zalophus californianus*) sea lions, harbor seals (*Phoca vitulina*), gray whales (*Eschrichtius robustus*), killer whales (*Orcinus orca*), pelagic (*Phalacrocorax pelagicus*) and Brandt's (*Phalacrocorax penicillatus*) cormorants, glaucous-winged gulls (*Larus glaucescens*), tufted puffins (*Fratercula cirrhata*), pigeon guillemots (*Cepphas columba*), and rhinoceros auklets (*Cerorhinca monocerata*).

In contrast, Auyuittuq National Park on Baffin Island of the Northwest Territories represents an environment that few Canadians have experienced or ever will experience. The name "Auyuittuq" is an Inuit word meaning "the land that never melts" and aptly describes the environment of this relatively new park. A large park, encompassing approximately 21,470 square kilometers (8,290 square miles), it is dominated by the Penny Ice Cap, a vast expanse of ice and snow mantling 6,000 square kilometers (2,320 square miles) of the park on the Cumberland Peninsula. Emanating from the ice cap are several outlet glaciers, some up to 25 kilometers long. Much of the park is dominated by rock, but much of the ground that has been exposed by retreating glaciers has been colonized by plant and animal communities.

The rock desert community is characterized by open vegetation with crustaceous and foliose lichens growing on the rocks and between them other lichens, mosses, and cushion plants such as moss campion (*Silene acaulis*) and various saxifrages. The yellow arctic poppy (*Papaver radicatum*) is one of the hardiest and initial colonizers of recently glaciated terrain. The tundra community, a more continuous vegetation cover, consists of a drawf shrub-heath cover of creeping willows, drawf birch, and members of the heath family. The grassland tundra, shore communities of salt-tolerant grasses and sedges, and the snow patch communities of saxifrages complete the scene.

The park is inhabited by a variety of mammals including the arctic hare (*Lepus arcticus*), arctic fox (*Alopex lagopus*), polar bear (*Ursus maritimus*), caribou (*Rangifer tarandus*), wolf (*Canis lupus*), and the wolverine (*Gulo gulo*). The brown lemming (*Lemmus sibiricus*) and the collared lemming (*Dicrostonyx torquatus*) are preyed upon by a number of predatory birds and mammals and are thus a key element in the food chain. Extreme fluctuations in their numbers have a dramatic effect on the entire ecosystem.

Recreation and Wilderness

National parks in Canada have a dual mandate to perform: to provide for resource protection and also to provide for the "appreciation, understanding and enjoyment of the public." Since the inception of the national park system, the various park administrations have embarked on recreation and interpretation programs to encourage Canadians to utilize the parks for the purposes for which they were intended. Camping, picnicking, and hiking have traditionally been the most popular activities in national parks, and virtually every park has the facilities to accommodate them. Even the new parks in the Far North will be equipped to a certain extent to provide for those activities, although the park visitor to Auyuittuq or Ellesmere Island will have to be considerably more self-sufficient than would be necessary in the southern parks.

In recent years such endurance sports as cross-country skiing, mountain climbing, long-distance hiking and white-water canoeing have become very popular. While national parks are ideal for these activities, park staff have had to respond by increasing their own levels of training in these outdoor skills and in the techniques of search and rescue. Public safety has now become a major concern in park management.

Downhill skiing has long been a popular sport in the mountain parks of Banff and Jasper, where four major downhill skiing resorts have developed along with two town sites. The presence of these activities and the development that goes along with them have caused considerable controversy over the years. Recently announced amendments to the National Parks Act have banned any further expansion of downhill skiing areas and placed strict limitations on the expansion of park town sites.

The provision of a wilderness experience has long been associated with national park management in Canada. A national park experience, particularly in the mountain parks, was often synonymous with wilderness and the opportunity to travel in solitude for days on foot, on horseback, or by canoe. As the pursuit of outdoor recreation increased in popularity in the 1960s and 1970s, maintaining a wilderness character in many national parks became a serious management challenge. In some cases it became necessary to institute trail and campsite quotas and reservation systems to control the number of wilderness users and to enforce regulations regarding camping and trail-riding practices. These efforts were directed both to maintaining the wilderness experience for the user and to protecting the wilderness environment from the effects of overuse.

The zoning system utilized by the Canadian Parks Service to guide park planning and management incorporates a wilderness zone. This zone is used to define extensive areas that well represent the natural history themes of the park and to restrict visitor activities and facilities to those compatible with the wilderness experience, including primitive and dispersed design standards for facilities and nonmotorized access.

To stem the trend of diminishing wilderness values in national parks, recent planning efforts have stressed wilderness protection, such as the recently completed planning process for the four mountain parks of Banff, Jasper, Kootenay, and Yoho, together comprising the Rocky Mountain World Heritage Site. There, the wilderness zone has been applied to almost 90 percent of the total area of these four parks.

Amendments to the National Parks Act establish the authority legally to define wilderness areas in national parks by regulation under order-in-council. Through this procedure, the boundaries of wilderness areas would be legally defined and could be changed only by amending the regulation through the governor-in-council.

ADMINISTRATION

Administratively, Canada has one federal, ten provincial, and two territorial governments. In addition, there are regional and municipal governments that in law are subunits of the provincial or territorial governments. Thus, there are thirteen major agencies involved in park and protected area administration. To add to the complexity, there are several "commissions" or "authorities" managing protected areas. These include the National Capital Commission, the Conservation Authorities of Ontario, the St. Lawrence Parks Commission, the Niagara Parks Commission, and the Roosevelt-Campobello Park Authority. There are also two "Peace Gardens" that straddle the border between Canada and the United States, one in British Columbia, and one in Manitoba. This chapter focuses on national parks with secondary references to select provinces.

Unlike the United States, where each national park is created by a specific act of Congress, all of Canada's national parks are established under one piece of legislation, the National Parks Act, 1930. The schedule of the National Parks Act provides a legal description of all lands subject to the legislation.

The act itself leaves considerable scope for interpretation and the development of policies and regulations. Thus the national parks have been shaped by constitutional factors, economics, politics, and by practice and precedent.

The national parks are administered through a central office in Ottawa and five regional offices located in Halifax, Quebec, Cornwall, Winnipeg, and Calgary.

As noted in Table 3.2, provincial park systems in several provinces are large in area, in staff, and in their sophistication of policy, planning, and administrative mechanisms. In some provincial protected areas there is a commitment of parklands to multiple-use resource extraction. Policies during the 1980s are in the process of clarifying the "missions" of many Canadian park agencies.

Ontario has a parks' classification system defining specific roles for parks as wilderness areas, nature reserves, natural environment parks, recreation parks, provincial waterways, and historic parks. Such a classification system improves public understanding and leads to clear management policies. In the early 1980s a "Strategic Land Use Planning" exercise was carried out defining future land use in northern Ontario, including parks. The administration of these parks is highly decentralized with overall direction provided through the provincial headquarters in Toronto.

In summary, each province has parks legislation and an appropriate administrative agency. Large wilderness parks are found in every province except Prince Edward Island, which is primarily agricultural.

The Federal Park Mission

The national parks have evolved over one hundred years and consequently reflect changing social and economic circumstances. As set out in the National Parks Act, the basic mission is to protect the natural resources without impairment for future generations. Paralleling this primary mission is the need to provide for the benefit, enjoyment, and education of park visitors. Balancing these two responsibilities has been a challenge for park administrators since Canada created the world's first national park administration in 1916.

With a few exceptions, hunting, logging, mining, hydroelectric development, grazing, and any form of resource extraction are prohibited in national parks. Regulated sports fishing is permitted, and tourism, research, and education are encouraged.

In recently established parks in northern Canada, special regulations have been designed to permit the continued use of resources by indigenous peoples as a means of accommodating traditional life styles.

Excessive tourism development in parks is a major concern of most nongovernmental conservation organizations in Canada. This controversy reaches its zenith in Banff National Park.

Banff was established in 1885 when the transcontinental railway was built. The town has a year-round population of approximately 4,500. Located in the Rocky Mountains some 80 miles west of Calgary, the park has for years been a recreational destination. In addition to the town site, there are three major ski areas located in the park: Sunshine, Lake Louise, and Mount Norquay. Compounding the management problems is the Trans-Canada Highway, the major east-west route in Canada.

Other similar developments are related to the town site of Jasper in Jasper National Park, and smaller seasonal communities are found in Waterton, Prince

Albert, Yoho, and Riding Mountain national parks. All lands in the town sites are owned by the federal government and are managed under a complex leasehold system. Municipal regulations and zoning controls are also enforced.

Park Management

Park management is directed by legislation and regulations and guided by policy. The *Parks Canada Policy Manual* was first published in 1964. It was revised and updated through a major public participation program during 1977–1978 and was published in 1979.[9]

The manual sets out "corporate" policy for all national parks, national historic parks, and canal systems.

The National Parks Policy provides guidance for the identification, establishment, and management of national parks. Specific sections of the policy deal with

The National Parks System

The National Parks Zoning System

Protecting National Park Resources

Public Understanding, Appreciation and Enjoyment of National Parks

Research

Management Plans

The National Parks System

National parks are intended to protect representative examples of the diversity of Canada's landscape and marine areas for the benefit of present and future generations. As discussed previously, the Canadian Parks Service has divided the nation into thirty-nine terrestrial natural regions and twenty-nine marine natural regions. Each of these natural regions should be represented in the system of national parks and national marine parks. In order to achieve this goal, certain natural areas are identified within each natural region, which include the greatest diversity of natural themes (biologic, geologic, physiographic, geographic, and oceanographic) and which are therefore representative of the natural region. These areas are referred to as "Natural Areas of Canadian Significance" (NACS). Potential national parks and national marine parks are selected from among the Natural Areas of Canadian Significance.

National Parks Zoning System

Zoning is one of the most important tools for the planning, development, and management of national parks. The national parks zoning system is a resource-based approach by which land and water areas of a national park are classified according to their need for protection and their capability to accommodate visitors. It provides a guide for the activities of both visitors and managers within a national park and assists in managing the tension between use and preservation. The zoning system will reflect parks' policies and facilitate their application in individual national parks.

The zoning system provides a means to ensure that the majority of national park lands and their living resources are protected in a wilderness state with a minimum of man-made facilities. Zones permitting a concentration of visitor activities and supporting facilities and services will occupy no more than a small proportion of lands in a national park. Moreover, in certain national parks in remote areas no provision will be made for such zones. In national parks where traditional uses are permitted, the park zoning plan will accommodate such activities.

A zoning plan will be an integral part of each national park management plan. The zoning system is briefly outlined below.

Zone 1—Special Preservation. Specific areas or features that deserve special preservation because they contain or support unique, rare, or endangered features or the best examples of natural features. Access and use will be strictly controlled or may be prohibited altogether. No motorized access or man-made facilities will be permitted.

Zone 2—Wilderness. Extensive areas that are good representations of each of the natural history themes of the park and that will be maintained in a wilderness state. Only certain activities requiring limited primitive visitor facilities appropriate to a wilderness experience will be allowed. Limits will be placed on numbers of users. No motorized access will be permitted. Management actions will ensure that visitors are dispersed.

Zone 3—Natural Environment. Areas that are maintained as natural environments and that can sustain, with a minimum of impairment, a selected range of low-density outdoor activities with a minimum of related facilities. Nonmotorized access will be preferred. Access by public transit will be permitted. Controlled access by private vehicles will be permitted only where it has traditionally been allowed in the past.

Zone 4—Outdoor Recreation. Limited areas that can accommodate a broad range of education, outdoor recreation opportunities, and related facilities in ways that respect the natural landscape and that are safe and convenient. Motorized access will be permitted and may be separated from nonmotorized access.

Zone 5—Park Services. Towns and visitor centers in certain existing national parks that contain a concentration of visitor services and support facilities as well as park administration functions. Motorized access will be permitted.

Protecting National Park Resources

Within national parks, effort is directed toward protecting our natural heritage by maintaining the physical environment in as natural a state as possible. This fact has far-reaching implications for the resource management of national parks in that many concepts or ideas that are relevant or essential to the successful management of other lands have limited relevance to the management of national parks. Therefore, caution is exercised before any active manipulation of park resources is undertaken, with preference given to allowing natural processes to function unless they have been clearly altered or made inoperative by man-induced changes.

Public Understanding, Appreciation, and Enjoyment of National Parks

National parks offer rare and outstanding opportunities to experience and learn about the natural environment in a wilderness setting. They cannot, however, provide for every kind of use requested by the public. Because national parks are dedicated to future as well as present generations, impairment by overuse, improper use and inappropriate development must be avoided. As a general guideline, simplicity in facilities and self-reliance on the part of visitors will be encouraged.

The Canadian Parks Service also has a responsibility to inform the Canadian public about their national parks and to provide programs that encourage a better understanding of these Natural Areas of Canadian Significance. Cooperative action with the many agencies, groups, and citizens concerned about national parks can supplement the Canadian Parks Service's own efforts to increase public awareness of national parks objectives and issues. In these ways, public support and wise use, which are necessary for continuing protection of national parks, may be achieved.

Research

The Canadian Parks Service strives to learn about the natural environment so that national parks can be identified, protected, and accurately interpreted to the public. In addition, research is important to assess public needs and the impact of visitor use and facilities.

National parks also offer opportunities for basic scientific research. While such research may not be essential for park management, it may expand man's fund of knowledge and enable parks to serve as benchmarks for ecological research and for studies of the effects of modern technology on lands outside park boundaries.

Management Plans

The park management plan contains a statement of management objectives and the means and strategies for achieving them, stated in a broad but comprehensive manner. The level of detail is confined to the definition of the type, character, locale of developments, and the provision of guidelines for more detailed plans concerning resource management, interpretation, and visitor use. The management plan is not an end in itself; rather it constitutes a framework within which subsequent management, implementation, and detailed planning will take place. Zoning is a vital component of the management plan. Therefore, proposed changes to a zoning plan require public participation and ministerial approval.

The management of protected areas in Canada, as earlier noted, is a responsibility of thirteen governments through a large number of specific agencies. The agencies are guided by legislation, regulations, and policies that are aimed at maintaining conservation values.

From a broad perspective, Canadians are well served by these agencies. The agencies in turn are subject to the scrutiny of a well-established network of private voluntary organizations such as the Canadian Parks and Wilderness Society, the Canadian Wildlife Federation, and the Canadian Nature Federation. In addition to the national organizations, there are regional groups such as the Federation of Ontario Naturalists and the Alberta Wilderness Association.

Public consultation processes are generally well established, and through these forums, the media and the public are alerted to threats to conservation values.

Threats to Protected Areas

As economic development progresses, protected areas become increasingly isolated as "islands in a sea of development." As yet, we have little scientific data on the impact of isolation on animal species in the parks. We do know, however, that many of the parks are too small to ensure protection through the full life cycle of many species. Thus, incremental development outside the parks will put increasing pressure on the species protected in the parks.

Poaching as an organized international venture places increasing threats on trophy species such as dall sheep, polar bears, and peregrine and gyr falcons. Acid rain in central and eastern Canada has had devastating impacts on species such as the Atlantic salmon and on the full range of freshwater species in lakes such as those in Kejimkujik National Park in Nova Scotia. Tourism is seen by many to be a major threat to the values of large national parks such as Banff and Jasper. Logging, road construction, and hydroelectric development continue to pose real threats to existing and proposed protected areas.

It is clear that many threats to protected areas arise outside of the protected areas themselves. In the same manner, remedies must be found to control deleterious impacts both inside and outside the parks. Acid rain controls must be enacted, and these are the subject of ongoing negotiations in Canada and between Canada and the United States.

Environmental impact assessments are carried out on all development projects, and where necessary, mitigative measures are incorporated. Much remains to be done to ensure the effectiveness of these processes. Enhanced deterrents to poaching have been incorporated in new amendments to the National Parks Act.

These amendments will increase fines related to threatened species from $500 to $150,000 and impose jail terms of up to six months.

An aware and concerned public remains the most effective protective device for national parks. Supporting the nongovernmental movements can be an effective public means of enhancing protected areas and reducing threats to them.

THE FUTURE OUTLOOK

Protected areas represent only a small part (5 percent) of the national landscape. Sound management of the other 95 percent of the landscape will be essential to ensure their viability into the twenty-first century. From this perspective, there is little doubt that the quality of the existing protected area system will deteriorate over the next fifteen years.

In early 1987 economic circumstances were leading to reduced budgets and staff levels in almost all park agencies. Realignment of capital development projects and increasing efficiency are the basic guidelines.

There remain extensive potential park areas in the country, and it is anticipated that a slow and measured growth of the park system will continue.

NOTES

1. Robert Craig Brown, "The Doctrine of Usefulness: Natural Resources and National Parks Policy in Canada, 1887–1914," in *Canadian Perspective*, ed. J. G. Nelson (Montreal: Harvest House, 1970), p. 49.

2. J. I. Nicol, "The National Park Movement in Canada," in J. G. Nelson, p. 22.

3. Robert Craig Brown, pp. 58–59.

4. Fergus Lothian, *A History of Canada's National Parks* (Ottawa: Environment Canada), p. 66.

5. Parks Canada, *Parks Canada Policy* (Ottawa: Environment Canada, 1979), p. 7.

6. Ontario Ministry of Natural Resources, *Algonquin Provincial Park Master Plan* (Toronto: Government of Ontario, 1974), p. 5.

7. Parks Canada, p. 28.

8. Parks Canada, p. 41.

9. Parks Canada, p. 69.

BIBLIOGRAPHY

British Columbia Ministry of Lands, Parks and Housing. *The Provincial Park and Ecological Reserve Systems of British Columbia*. Victoria, British Columbia, 1985.

Davidson, A. T. *Canada's National Parks: Past and Future*. Ottawa: Environment Canada, 1978.

Dooling, Peter, ed. *Parks in British Columbia: Emerging Realities*. Vancouver: University of British Columbia, 1985.

Environment Canada, Parks. *The National Parks of Canada: Date of Establishment and Size.* Ottawa: Environment Canada, 1986.

Environment Canada. *National Marine Parks Policy.* Ottawa: Environment Canada, 1986.

Falkner, A. C., and J. A. Carruthers. *National Parks of Canada.* Ottawa: Environment Canada, 1978.

Hummel, Monte. *Arctic Wildlife.* Toronto: Key Porter Books, 1984.

Lands Directorate. *Natural Heritage Areas Study—Draft.* Ottawa: Environment Canada, 1986.

Lawrence, R. D. *Canada's National Parks.* Toronto: Collins Publishers, 1983.

Murphy, Peter, ed. *Tourism in Canada: Selected Issues and Options.* Western Geographical Series, vol. 21. Victoria: University of Victoria, 1983.

National Geographic Society. *Canada's Wilderness Lands.* Washington, D.C., 1982.

Nelson, J. G., ed. *Canadian Parks in Perspective.* Montreal: Harvest House, 1970.

Nelson, J. G., and D. W. Hoffman, eds. *Sharing Heritage Management.* Vol. 17, No. 3 Management, Waterloo, University of Waterloo, 1985.

Nelson, J. G., and R. C. Scace, eds. *The Canadian National Parks: Today and Tomorrow.* Conference Proceedings. 2 vols. Calgary: University of Calgary, 1968.

———. *The Canadian National Parks: Today and Tomorrow.* Conference II. 2 vols. Waterloo: University of Waterloo, 1979.

———. *Heritage for Tomorrow.* Proceedings, Canadian Assembly on National Parks and Protected Areas. Ottawa: Environment Canada, 1986.

Russel, Andy. *The Rockies.* Edmonton: Hurtig Publishers, 1975.

Théberge, John. *Kluane: Pinnacle of the Yukon.* Toronto: Doubleday Canada, 1980.

Wilson, Roger. *The Land That Never Melts: Auyuittuq National Park.* Ottawa: Supply and Services Canada, 1976.

CHILE

4

Carlos A. Weber

Chile's highly unusual shape makes it stand out as a unique country not only in South America, but perhaps in the whole world as well. It covers some 750,000 square kilometers (290,000 square miles), exclusive of an Antarctic claim of 1,250,000 square kilometers (480,000 square miles), and stretches over 4,200 kilometers, from 17°30′ south latitude at the intertropical zone to 56° south near the Antarctic Circle. If Chile were to be superimposed at an equivalent location in the Northern Hemisphere, it would stretch from Jamaica to the Belcher Islands in Hudson Bay.

In contrast to her considerable length, Chile's width averages no more than 180 kilometers (110 miles), with a maximum of 350 kilometers and a minimum of 15 kilometers. The long north-to-south extension, the altitude variations, and the mountainous topography have important ecological consequences, which bear upon the natural and cultural heritage, as well as on the characteristics of the existing protected areas.

Chile's climate, in general terms, features great aridity in the north, increasing precipitation toward the south, and copious rainfall in the country's deep south. Arica, a coastal city at Chile's northern tip, averages less than 1 millimeter (0.04 inches) of rainfall a year, while on the southern coast annual figures of 5,000 millimeters (200 inches) are not uncommon. Temperatures show an inverse gradient with higher values in the north and lower in the south, although extreme differences are dampened by the cold Humboldt Current that flows northward along the coast. Central Chile has a Mediterranean climate characterized by precipitation concentrated in the winter months and intense drought in the summer. The distribution of rainfall throughout the year is particularly negative for plant life, for water is available when the low temperatures limit biologic activity and is scant during the vegetatively active period.

The ecologic and physiographic conditions obtaining in Chile show a number of similarities with those of North America's west coast, from a warm desert drier than Baja California in the north, through a semi-arid section with climate resembling southern California's, then a temperate rain-forest climate similar to Oregon's and Washington's, to end up in a fjord and island system akin to that of southern Alaska. Despite these similarities, which may help the reader more familiar with the Northern Hemisphere visualize the prevailing conditions in this part of the world, it must be reiterated that biologic similarities (i.e., plant and animal species) are scant, owing to the dissimilar evolutionary history of North and South America.

While Chile is one of the two Latin American countries without tropical rain forests—Uruguay is the other—her flora and fauna make up for this lesser diversity with a very high degree of endemism, i.e., with species found exclusively within her territory and nowhere else in the world. This exclusivity results from the fact that Chile is an ecologic island, surrounded by the Pacific Ocean, the Atacama Desert, the Andes Mountains, and the Patagonian deserts. Thus, 57 percent of her 5,000 fern and flowering native plant species are endemic, a proportion normally reached only at comparably sized oceanic islands.

Another relevant natural feature in so elongated a country is the sea surrounding it and the coastline acting as an interface between land and water. The coastline is very long, hugging the country's western and southern flanks. Along its southern third, spanning over a thousand kilometers, the land breaks into a labyrinth of hundreds of fjords and thousands of islands, with no reliable statistics available regarding either the total number of islands and islets, or regarding an accurate coastline length.

The oceanic islands, terrestrial environments closely related to the marine environment, include Easter Island, Sala y Gómez, the Juan Fernández Archipelago, and the Desventuradas group (San Félix and San Ambrosio). Despite their small area, these islands are extraordinarily important in terms of both natural and cultural heritage, a fact reflected in over half of their area having been placed under national park status.

Chile lies at the edge of a continental plate that originates frequent earthquakes. The geologic instability and variability, added to the existence of a great diversity of altitude, slope, exposure, temperature, and precipitation, give rise to numerous heterogeneous ecologic conditions, with a patchy distribution that produces a large number of different and interspersed plant communities, even within small-sized areas. Thus, although biologic diversity is more limited than in the rest of the Neotropical Realm, the ecological diversity is high, with a great number of unique ecosystems.

HISTORY

The idea of setting aside areas to protect native vegetation started taking shape as early as the nineteenth century, when concern was aroused among some people by the rapid destruction of central and southern forests brought about by the homesteading drive.

By 1850, and to a greater extent after agreements in 1880 between the Chilean administration and the Indian chieftains, the temporate rain forest zone, known as the lake district, began to be homesteaded by European settlers arriving from Germany, Italy, France, and Switzerland, as well as by residents of the Chilean Mediterranean zone. The drive to occupy an increasing amount of land by the equally increasing rural population, with the resulting sequel of fires and devastation, gave rise to a concern about the preservation of the forests. This, in turn, prompted the passing of legal norms that, among other effects, produced the first nature reserves in Chile, some of the oldest in Latin America.

Environmental awareness in Chile was very low at the turn of the century, when the first protected areas were established. Nevertheless, there was concern among certain private individuals regarding the depletion of natural resources and the deterioration of landscapes. This concern was taken up by a small number of government professionals, among whom Federico Albert, a German-born scientist who carried out his entire professional career in Chile, was one of the most noteworthy. The combination of scientific activity and practical work he advocated was frowned upon by the local scientific community, but he did receive a degree of support from the government, which assigned him to head a Forests and Waters Bureau, predecessor to the present-day Forest Service. From that post Albert waged an unceasing campaign aimed at the conservation of renewable natural resources, a campaign that resulted in establishment of the first fish-farming operations, stabilization of shifting sand dunes, planting of forests. and the creation of national parks and forest reserves.

Albert and other concerned individuals succeeded in seeing Malleco Forest Reserve established in 1907. This is considered to be the first protected area in Chile, as it benefited from protection in law, defined borders, and an agency charged with its management with personnel qualified for the task. Until 1935, all protected areas in the country were located in the lake district, and until recently the popular image of any nature reserve invoked snow-capped volcanoes, lakes, and dense forests. The establishment of protected areas in desert locations in the north or in scrublands above timberline, as in the fjord area, was regarded with a certain degree of puzzlement by many people.

As in the establishment of forest reserves, the lake district also figured prominently in the creation of early national parks. Vicente Pérez Rosales National Park (est. 1926), the oldest in Chile, is located here. Almost all the protected areas in this zone were created from public domain lands, which have always belonged to the community as a whole. Because these lands were forested, the Forest Service always had a marked presence and a clearly defined profile of activities that favored the establishment and maintenance of the protected areas.

The first protected areas outside the lake district were established in 1935, when the Juan Fernández Archipelago and the Easter Island—now Rapa Nui—national parks were created. Both are located in oceanic islands removed from the South American continent. A few years later, in 1941, Fray Jorge National Park was created, becoming the first such area established within the Mediterranean arid zone. This area was at the core of the Spanish colonization efforts, and land was transferred into private hands as early as the colonial period. The absence of public domain lands in this part of the country has hindered the establishment of protected areas: acquisition costs are high, and years of human activity have left very few sites in natural or seminatural condition. As a result, the process of establishing protected areas in the Mediterranean zone has been slow and spotty. This history is reflected in the small size of the existing protected areas and in the predominance of national reserves, with flexible requirements and management standards. National parks, by contrast, are subject to more stringent rules and are found more frequently both to the north and to the south of this zone.

Chile's fjord district is characterized by fragile soils unsuitable for farming, grazing, or forestry. In 1945, Cabo de Hornos (Cape Horn) National Park was the first to be created here. During the 1960s many large national parks and forest reserves were established in this part of the country.

The oldest protected area in the northern Andean highlands is Lauca National Park, established initially as a reserve in 1965. It was followed by the Isluga Volcano National Park, the Surire Salt Flat Nature Monument, and the Las Vicuñas National Reserve, with a combined area of 533,056 hectares (1,317,181 acres). The task of securing representation of the high plateau's natural and cultural heritage is not yet complete, with a number of units in a planning stage, particularly in the more arid ecosystems of the southern puna highlands.

In the Atacama Coastal Desert, a vast region stretching for over a thousand kilometers between the Andes and the sea, the process of establishing protected areas has just begun. To date, three areas have been designated, and a number of additional units are under consideration. Scientific and technical data are being gathered to help identify areas of interest for subsequent inclusion in the system. For this reason, the description here is not strictly limited to the areas already established, but also includes areas that could soon be granted national park, nature monument, or national reserve status.

As of January 1, 1989, the entire system of protected areas covers 13,671,249 hectares (33,781,656 acres) in seventy-five units: thirty national parks (8,383,941 hectares, 20,716,718 acres), thirty-six national reserves (5,272,902 hectares, 13,029,341 acres), and nine nature monuments (14,436 hectares, 35,671 acres).

PARKS AND RESERVES

Due to Chile's great length, descriptions are traditionally ordered after a north-to-south pattern, which I shall also employ here. As a result of the large number of protected areas—seventy-five, sixty of which have resident park rangers—this chapter will describe only those that are most representative of the ecologic characteristics of the country, those that possess unique and highly relevant features, and those that serve as examples of management problems and their

Figure 4.1
Chile, National Parks, and Nature Reserves

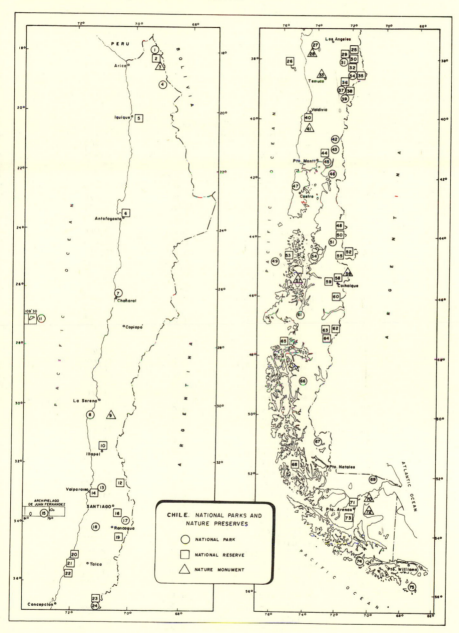

Table 4.1
National Parks and Nature Reserves of Chile

MAP NUMBER	NAME	CATEGORY[a]	AREA (hectares)
	Andean High Plateau		
1	Lauca	N.P.	137,883
2	Las Vicuñas	N.R.	209,131
3	Salar de Surire	N.M.	11,298
4	Volcan Isluga	N.P.	174,744
	Atacama Coastal Desert		
5	Pampa del Tamarugal	N.R.	100,650
6	La Chimba	N.R.	2,583
7	Pan de Azúcar	N.P.	43,754
	Mediterranean Climate Zone		
8	Fray Jorge	N.P.	9,959
9	Pichasca	N.M.	128
10	Las Chinchillas	N.R.	4,229
12	Río Blanco	N.R.	10,175
13	La Campana	N.P.	8,000
14	Peñuelas	N.R.	9,094
16	Río Clarillo	N.R.	10,185
17	El Morado	N.P.	3,000
18	Palmas de Cocalán	N.P.	n/d[b]
19	Río de los Cipreses	N.R.	38,582
20	Laguna de Torca	N.R.	604
21	Federico Albert	N.R.	145
22	Los Ruiles	N.R.	45
	Lake District		
23	Ñuble	N.R.	55,948
24	Laguna del Laja	N.P.	11,600
25	Ralco	N.R.	12,421
26	Isla Mocha	N.R.	2,368
27	Nahuelbuta	N.P.	6,832
28	Contulmo	N.M.	82
29	Malleco	N.R.	17,371
30	Nalcas	N.R.	13,775
31	Tolhuaca	N.P.	6,374
32	Malalcahuello	N.R.	28,910
33	Cerro Ñielol	N.M.	89
34	Conguillío	N.P.	60,832
35	Alto Biobío	N.R.	35,000
36	China Muerta	N.R.	11,168
37	Huerquehue	N.P.	12,500
38	Villarrica	N.R.	43,263
39	Villarrica	N.P.	61,000
40	Valdivia	N.R.	9,727
41	Alerce Costero	N.M.	2,308
42	Puyehue	N.P.	107,000
43	Vicente Pérez Rosales	N.P.	251,000
44	Llanquihue	N.R.	33,972
45	Alerce Andino	N.P.	39,255
46	Hornopiren	N.P.	48,232
47	Chiloé	N.P.	43,057
48	Lago Palena	N.R.	41,380

Table 4.1 (continued)

MAP NUMBER	NAME	CATEGORY[a]	AREA (hectares)
	Fjord Area & Western Patagonia		
49	Isla Guamblin	N.P.	15,915
50	Lago Rosselot	N.R.	12,725
51	Queulat	N.P.	154,093
52	Lago Carlota	N.R.	27,110
53	Las Guaitecas	N.R.	1,097,975
54	Isla Magdalena	N.P.	157,640
55	Lago las Torres	N.R.	16,516
56	Dos Lagunas	N.M.	181
57	Cinco Hermanas	N.M.	228
58	Coihaique	N.R.	2,150
59	Río Simpson	N.P.	41,160
60	Cerro Castillo	N.R.	179,550
61	Laguna San Rafael	N.P.	1,742,000
62	Lago Jeinemeni	N.R.	38,700
63	Lago General Carrera	N.R.	178,400
64	Lago Cochrane	N.R.	8,361
65	Katalalixar	N.R.	674,500
66	Bernardo O'Higgins	N.P.	3,524,648
67	Torres del Paine	N.P.	181,414
68	Alacalufes	N.R.	2,313,875
69	Pali-Aike	N.P.	3,000
70	Los Pingüinos	N.M.	97
71	Magallanes	N.R.	13,500
72	Laguna de los Cisnes	N.M.	25
73	Laguna Parrillar	N.R.	18,814
74	Alberto de Agostini	N.P.	1,460,000
75	Cabo de Hornos	N.P.	63,093
	Oceanic Islands		
11	Rapa Nui	N.P.	6,666
15	Arch. de J. Fernández	N.P.	9,290

Notes:
[a] N.P. = National Park
N.R. = National Reserve
N.M. = Nature Monument
[b] Boundaries still undefined.

correspondinFcompanying map (Figure 4.1). Corresponding summary data is provided in Table 4.1.

The country has a considerable array of ecologic communities and formations. For the purposes of this discussion, the continental area is divided into five large ecologic-geographic units. The oceanic islands are treated as a sixth group.

Andean High Plateau

As is most of the country, Chile's north is made up by the western shelf of the great Andes Mountain Range. Stretching over 1,000 kilometers, the Andes do not constitute a single range, but branch out into several ranges, with vast plateaus between them known locally as "punas." The average altitude of the punas exceeds 4,000 meters (13,400 feet) and constitutes a prime ecological factor that conditions the existence of flora and fauna and the activities of human residents.

The puna highlands feature dramatic temperature variations between day and night—usually some 25° Celsius (60° Fahrenheit)—with frost almost every night and sunshine and high temperatures during the day. All life forms have had to adapt to a daily cycle with winter each night and summer each day. Temperature fluctuations throughout the year are less marked. Annual precipitation is scant, between 300 millimeters (12 inches) in the north and 100 millimeters (4 inches) further south. There is a high proportion of cloudless days.

For twenty years Lauca National Park has been the focus of preservation and education efforts, with a visitors center at the town of Parinacota and a network of ranger/game warden outposts at key locations. The remaining units have only one ranger outpost each but are run jointly and coordinately with Lauca. Some 3,000 visitors arrive at Lauca every year despite the long distance separating it from the population centers, the lack of accommodations and tourist services, and the severe constraints imposed on physical exertion by the high altitude where oxygen pressure amounts to only half that normal at sea level.

Prevailing plant cover at the four units, and throughout the high plateau, is the Andean steppe, dominated by Gramineae and a brush formation known locally as "tolar." There are numerous cacti species, and on rocky wind-sheltered sites thrives the only arboreal species of the high plateau, a Rosaceae called queñoa (*Polylepis* spp.). The llareta also grows in this area. This Umbelliferae species, which takes the shape of large ground-hugging, pillow-shaped woody formations, may take centuries to reach a one-meter diameter.

The biologically most productive vegetation grows along the streams. However, this is not an entirely natural formation but the product of human intervention. Many centuries before the arrival of the Spanish conquerors, the Indian population tamed two species of indigenous camelids and increased the grazing capacity of these cold arid lands by expanding the vegetation that grew along stream banks with simple irrigation methods.

There is a high diversity of fauna, with over a hundred bird species, from the lofty condor to others as improbable in these environments as a parrot species and a woodpecker that, lacking trees, has learned to seek its nourishment in the ground and among rock cracks. The highland salt flats are home to three of the six flamingo species in the world. Among the mammals stand out four species of camelids: two tamed by the Indians, llama and alpaca, and two still wild, vicuña and guanaco.

The vicuña has an interesting history in South America. Numbered in the millions prior to the European conquest, its population had been reduced to barely a few thousands in the 1960s. The high value of its wool—the finest fiber in the world, worth over $100 per kilo in the black market—made poaching an extremely lucrative business. Unfortunately, there is no easy way to capture and shear a wild animal adapted to vast open expanses, so poachers routinely killed the animals to acquire their wool.

In view of the situation, the governments of Chile and Peru started vicuña protection and management programs in their respective countries and, combining surveillance and education, have produced a dramatic increase of vicuña populations in both countries, with a total of some 125,000 individuals at present. These efforts are a model for the successful preservation of endangered species. In Chile, the protective measures were centered at Lauca National Park, spreading from there to Las Vicuñas National Reserve, to the Surire Salt Flat Nature Monument, and to adjacent lands not included within any protected area. The success achieved has prompted the planning of a rational utilization program, focused at the Las Vicuñas National Reserve. This type of program is much more complex than mere protection, as a considerable prior investment in research is necessary, as well as legal and operational measures to prevent the program-related trade in wool from tempting poachers to engage once more in their activities.

The four protected areas under discussion contain an Indian population practicing a culture and tradition that predates the arrival of the Spaniards. The Aymara Etnia counts among its more outstanding accomplishments the creation of the Tiawanaku culture. It withstood relatively successfully the Inca conquest, for although it was incorporated into the empire, it relinquished neither its language nor its cultural identity. Throughout the centuries its members evolved a stable productive relationship with the natural environment surrounding them.

The management philosophy for both national parks includes maintaining the local Indian cattle-raising and farming activities, provided they do not stray from the traditional usages. However, it is not possible to turn a blind eye to the imbalances that may already be observed, resulting from pressures and customs foreign to the traditional Indian culture. Such pressures include the raising of crops for the export markets, large-scale mining operations, water tapping for coastal city consumption or for irrigation of piedmont oases, and destruction of flora and fauna for legal and illegal short-term commercial purposes. These realities should be dealt with in the coming years with a view to reaching, through an adequate combination of protection and management measures, a new balance that takes into account the identity of the Indian population, ensures its evolution, and preserves the area's natural heritage, the equilibrium and continuity of its life support processes, and the relics of the cultural past found integrated into the natural environment. These range from work sites and living quarters of hunting-gathering groups dating back at least 10,000 years, documented evidence of which exists at the Lauca National Park, through the colonial-time churches and villages, to the contour terraces and the pre-Hispanic trade and communication routes.

Atacama Coastal Desert

The Atacama Desert stretches in Chile from the Pacific Ocean in the west to the Andes Mountains in the east; from the boundary with Peru in the north to approximately 1,000 kilometers (600 miles) southward, where a gradual transition to a semiarid zone occurs. The Atacama Desert being the driest in the world, one could assume that the only natural sites of interest would be geological. However, this is a desert that, despite its relentless aridity, harbors a rich diversity of plant, animal, and human life, illustrating the extraordinary capacity for adaptation to extreme situations boasted by all life forms.

Desert vegetation is scant in quantity but rich in floristic diversity; it occurs in any place with some water supply, regardless of how meager this supply may be. For instance, coastal fogs provide the greatest part of the moisture to sustain Cactaceae and lichen formations as well as for a number of associated species, such as *Tillandsia spp.*, which dot the coast. Each one of these communities has a unique structure and species assemblage, a fact that makes every one of them important.

Strictly terrestrial fauna is not abundant, owing to the fact that animals, particularly vertebrates, cannot wait years until favorable conditions occur, as some plants do. Nevertheless, the Pacific Ocean, which borders the entire western edge of the Atacama Desert, is rich in nutrients that support a great marine biomass that, in turn, provides sustenance to millions of sea birds of varied species, as well as to sea lions and sea otters.

From the cultural standpoint, groups of hunter-gatherers inhabited the coastal area thousands of years back, while farming tribes settled the desert oases. There was active trade between coastal dwellers and those in the Andean areas. One of the earliest coastal groups, known as the Chinchorro culture, developed an elaborate technique of funeral preparation ten thousand years ago, producing the oldest mummies found in the world and predating their better-known Egyptian counterparts by several millennia.

In historical times, the desert's mineral riches attracted other groups that settled down in the area, moving from site to site as work sources opened or closed. Their ephemeral settings remain to this day in the form of ghost towns and processing plants that constitute a valuable historical-cultural heritage.

Each of the three protected areas existing in the Atacama Coastal Desert, besides representing flora, fauna, and cultural aspects, offers an opportunity for recreation, education, and appreciation of Chile's natural and cultural heritage to both Chilean and foreign visitors.

In 1986 Pan de Azúcar National Park, with 43,754 hectares (108,116 acres), was established on the coast in the environs of parallel 26 south in order to protect several plant communities. There is also a population of guanaco, a wild camelid, and the largest native herbivore in Chile. Pan de Azúcar is also home to 40 percent of the world's Humboldt penguins and their most important rookery. Cultural resources include numerous seashell deposits and rock ledges evidencing the activity of ancient hunter-gatherers, as well as the remains of one of the earliest copper smelters erected on the Pacific coast.

The educational and recreational needs of Antofagasta, the most important city in Chile's north, were determinants in the establishment of La Chimba National Reserve, an area of 2,583 hectares (6,383 acres) located in the coastal mountains a few kilometers from the city limits. At this site, flora and fauna protection will combine with both formal and informal education, a task facilitated by excellent accessibility, permitting the local inhabitants to become familiar with and learn to appreciate the region's natural environment.

At the southern portion of the Atacama Coastal Mountain Range an interesting biologic phenomenon takes place: thousands of square kilometers support plant communities dominated by annual plants that survive for years as seeds in a dormant state or as bulbs buried in the ground. In those infrequent years (perhaps one out of ten) when brief but torrential downpours occur, these communities sprout back to life and bloom in the space of a few weeks, coloring the desert with their bright red, yellow, or blue flowers. This phenomenon is known as "the flowering desert" and strikes the visitor with seemingly endless expanses of brightly colored ephemerals that are forced to complete their life cycle in a short time before the relentless dryness of the desert sets in once more. There is no protected area yet to represent this interesting phenomenon, but one is planned.

Another unusual biologic phenomenon in so arid a desert is the presence of natural forests of Leguminoseae of the genus *Prosopis* (same genus as mesquite from the U.S. Southwest) at places where the water table is relatively close to the surface, as in certain salt flats. The Pampa del Tamarugal National Reserve (100,650 hectares, 248,706 acres) was established in 1988 precisely to ensure the survival of the genetic diversity of *Prosopis tamarugo* and the adequate management of the plantations of this species established in areas adjacent to the natural forests. Other interesting elements include the existence of an endemic bird, tamarugal conebill (*Conirostrum tamarugensis*), and the numerous relics of past human settlement, among which monumental geoglyphs stand out, large-sized stone patterns on hill slopes. Their precise meaning for the pre-Hispanic inhabitants is unknown, but they tend to be concentrated at locations close to the old trails connecting coast and mountains. Hundreds of these figures decorate many kilometers of hill slopes adjacent to a salt flat called, precisely, "Pintados," the name given by the present inhabitants to the geoglyphs. There is a considerable number of other historical and cultural remains dating back to the last century and the turn of this century, related to the Saltpeter or Pacific War between Chile and a Peru-Bolivia coalition in 1879–1883, and to the saltpeter mining activity, an industry that brought great wealth to the country while Chile enjoyed a world monopoly of this commodity. The windfall ended with the development of synthetic saltpeter by the Germans during World War I.

The establishment of a number of further units is also envisioned at likely locations along the coast, with the purpose of affording the maximum protection to the biologic diversity of the coastal mountain and, particularly, to their cacti, which range from mostly subterranean dwarf species to giant column cacti, many of them endangered by excessive collection, habitat destruction from mining operations, and overgrazing by goats.

Mediterranean Climate Zone

This part of the country holds the largest share of the nation's 12 million inhabitants. Here, therefore, the natural heritage has suffered most from human intervention, which has taken the form of extensive deforestation to meet the needs for fuel or construction materials, overgrazing, land clearing for farming, and forest fires. The latter are particularly damaging. Unlike many plant communities in the Northern Hemisphere where natural fire was common, the vegetation here has not evolved to withstand fire or to effectively recover from its effects.

The Mediterranean zone has a large number of endemic flora species, because the coastal areas served as refuge against the glacial onslaught during the Pleistocene. In the north, this zone borders on the Atacama Desert; toward the south, it adjoins the temperate forests of the lake district. The establishment of borders is, in both cases, arbitrary, as in reality there is a continuous gradual transition from one type to the next.

The typical plant cover is a sclerophyll forest with generally small-sized trees and hard coriaceous leaves adapted to checking water loss by transpiration. Here occur the first southern beech forests (*Nothofagus* spp.), found also in the lake district and fjord zone. *Nothofagus* fulfill many ecologic roles that in the Northern Hemisphere fall on the species of the genus *Pinus*, which do not occur naturally in South America.

The oldest unit existing in this zone is the Fray Jorge National Park, established in 1941. This park illustrates some of the notions that guided creation of parks during the pioneering years and that today might seem questionable. Fray Jorge ("Friar George") was established to protect a small forest-like community sustained by the heavy fogs that almost constantly shroud the Coastal Mountain Range peaks. Regarding this forest island in a sea of aridity, legend has it that it was discovered by a friar of that name who needed timber for the construction of churches in La Serena, a town 100 kilometers to the north. Although the addition of more land has made it include a sizable stretch of scrubby vegetation typical of arid Mediterranean sites, at the beginning interest was focused only in the forestlike vegetation that, while biologically interesting, was not representative of the area. It is rather a curiosity, a leftover from the time when climate changes pushed back the forests that covered a large portion of this area.

Las Chinchillas National Reserve was established to protect the only known wild population of *Chinchilla lanigera*, a species that provided the genetic pool for the chinchillas raised in confinement in many parts of the world. Additionally, the wild chinchilla habitat studies have shown that the reserve provides a haven for many threatened plant species.

La Campana National Park has many plant communities typical of the Mediterranean area, and includes significant Chilean palm forests, the only palm native to continental Chile (another species grows in the Juan Fernández Archipelago). This unit, covering less than 10,000 hectares (25,000 acres), demonstrates many problems associated with protected areas in heavily populated zones and subject to competition for natural resources. The park was itself established in 1967 through a complex process of land and rights exchange. Several mining operations are active within its boundaries, predating the national park and subject to different legal norms than the park. The five million inhabitants living within a 100-kilometer radius from the park demand services that cannot be satisfied with the scant area suitable for educational and recreational activities; although the size of the park might sound large enough, the predominance of steep slopes and the lack of water restrict public use.

Peñuelas National Reserve has the basic purpose of producing drinking water for the city of Valparaíso. Additionally, it has established itself as an excellent haven for fauna, where more than 100 of the 430 bird species known to Chile may be found. This is a good example of multiple-use management. Although primarily a water-producing basin, a certain amount of public visitation, grazing, wildlife management, and tree felling is permitted.

The Río Clarillo National Reserve, established in 1981, is a mere 45 kilometers from downtown Santiago, Chile's capital and a sprawling city of over four million. The reserve consists mainly of high mountains, but on its lower reaches it has a small area of sclerophyllous forests, a type of forest that is little represented in the Protected Wildlands System. The proximity to the most heavily populated area in the country offers great opportunity for educational programs; however, massive public access must be restricted due to the small size and limited number of areas with moderate slopes and free of flood or landslide hazards, which are appropriate for public use. The small proportion of areas suitable for public use is easily explained. As in many other countries, the protected areas of Chile result less from a conscious process of land-use allocation than from their being unwanted by anyone else or being unsuitable for the traditional uses. Nature protection is, to a considerable extent, an afterthought.

The Federico Albert National Reserve, while of recent establishment, covers land that has been public property since the turn of the century. It was named after the man who pioneered dune control, as well as many other conservation activities. It consists of dunes stabilized by planting a large number of tree species, most of them exotic. This unit is a good example of the difference between the management afforded national parks and nature monuments on the one hand, and that afforded national reserves on the other. In the reserves the environment is not necessarily natural or untouched, and its management may include drastic manipulation, provided there is a management purpose behind the effort.

The Los Ruiles National Reserve covers only 45 hectares (111 acres) and was established to ensure the survival of the most endangered of the southern beeches, *Nothofagus alessandri*, whose common name in Spanish is "ruil." In this case, the fundamental objective is to preserve the genetic diversity, and the small size of the reserve makes it possible to carry out only educational activities, precluding multiple use in a traditional sense.

There are six other protected areas in the Mediterranean zone: the Pichasca Nature Monument, a paleontological site; the El Morado National Park, the Río Blanco, and the Río de los Cipreses national reserves, all three high-mountain sites; the Palmas de Cocalán National Park, with Chilean palm forests; and the Laguna Torca National Reserve, consisting of a small lake with numerous bird fauna and dunes stabilized through planting.

Lake District

The lake district stretches 500 kilometers north-to-south, from the lands bordering on the Mediterranean zone to the Reloncaví Sound, where the fjords and archipelagoes spread toward the south. The area receives abundant rainfall, giving rise to broad-leaved temperate rain forests less diverse floristically but physiognomically similar to tropical forests, with numerous lianas and epiphytic plants. This type of cool, moist forest with few conifers is extremely scarce throughout the world.

The southern beeches tend to occupy pioneer ecologic niches; among the few conifers, there are two species of great interest, which tend to form pure or nearly pure stands: Araucaria and Alerce.

As already mentioned, Malleco National Reserve is the oldest unit in the state's Protected Wildlands System. It is located in the front range of the Andes and has mixed temperate rain forests and southern beech forests, with some Araucaria stands. Numerous research projects have been and continued to be carried out here, as well as field-training programs for forestry students. Recreational attractiveness is somewhat less than at other units in the same area, and there are fewer visitors. Throughout Malleco's first fifty years as a reserve, peripheral areas were settled by farmers, whose situation was legalized later by reducing the reserve's size. This trend to settling the land has disappeared over the past few decades, at least in this area of the country.

Nahuelbuta National Park includes the highest peaks in the Coastal Mountain Range, with altitudes up to 1,500 meters (5,000 feet) above sea level. The establishment of this park in 1939 aimed mainly at the preservation of *Araucaria araucana* forests, an ancient umbrella-shaped conifer whose seeds were once important food for the native Indian population. The flora and fauna dependent on this ecologic community, particularly invertebrates, are unique, and their conservation depends totally on the continued existence of vast forests of this species. This shows that ensuring the preservation of a few individuals of a species is not enough, but that to conserve a community it is necessary to maintain one or more functional samples sufficient to ensure the survival of the entire assemblage of dependent species.

Although nearly encircled by settlers who have destroyed vegetation and soils in their efforts to live off little parcels of poor lands, a small number of efficient administrators and rangers have been able to maintain the integrity of Nahuelbuta National Park. In spite of its limited size, the flora and fauna of this part of the country are well represented here, including the top carnivore, the puma.

Conguillío National Park was established on volcanic lands surrounding the 3,000-meter Llaima volcano, one of the highest Andean peaks in an area where the mountains are markedly lower than further north. Volcanism and its consequences, such as lava flows and lakes formed by dikes of molten rock that cut off river flow, are the dominant features of the landscape. Here it is possible to see a succession of biological communities associated with the time elapsed since this active volcano erupted. Lichen communities with some accompanying Gramineae predominate at sites affected by the most recent eruptions, and small pockets of climax rain-forest species survive at those few sites long sheltered from eruption effects. Forests cover less than half of the park's area. Species of pioneer character or those resistant to extreme conditions predominate: southern beeches (genus *Nothofagus*), four species of which may be found here, and the hardy long-lived *Araucaria araucana*, growing here in soils very different from those of the Coastal Mountain Range, although always under difficult conditions that preclude competition from faster-growing species.

The Alerce Andino National Park is both a new and an old protected area. While the decree that established it as a national park dates from 1982, all its land had been included within the Llanquihue Forest Reserve, created in 1912, and thus has been part of the protected area system for three-fourths of a century. This unit consists of a granite massif some 500 square kilometers (200 square miles) in area, dotted with lakes and ponds, and cut by short, swift streams. The dominant species is a conifer called Alerce, the name given in Spanish to larch, as it reminded the Spanish conquerors of some European species. Commercially known as Chilean false larch and scientifically as *Fitzroya cupressoides*, Alerce is a paradox in the plant realm. Its wood is so resistant to rot that it may remain decades or even centuries felled or fallen on the ground, being none the worse for it. On the other hand, its slow growth rate and its particular regeneration cycle, which may take centuries between successive generations, make it in practice unsuitable to be considered a renewable natural resource. The oldest are between 2,000 and 4,000 years old. Like the Araucaria, the Alerce is a conifer with a restricted geographic range, possessing extraordinary biologic and ecologic interest on account of its adaptation to extremely demanding soil and climatic conditions, as well as for being the key species in a community that includes a significant number of dependent species.

The Cerro Ñielol Nature Monument was established fifty years ago under the national park category. This small area of 80 hectares (197 acres) nestled on a hill overlooking Temuco—the most populated city in the lake district—illustrates the confusion in classification concepts existing in the past, as well as the nearly intuitive capacity of those working in this field half a century ago without the experience and access to information common nowadays. Today an area too small to be a self-sustained ecosystem would not be classified as a national park, but the concept of establishing areas of floral, faunal, and ecological interest at locations near population centers, so as to provide education and nature appreciation opportunities, is incredibly "modern." For many, Cerro Ñielol provides the only chance to see Chile's national flower—the copihue—in the wild.

In recent years, a protected area reclassification program was undertaken. As a result, this unit changed from national park to nature monument. The general conclusion arrived at through this process is similar to that taught by Cerro Ñielol: while many units were classified under the wrong category, most of the area included in the system clearly deserved to be a part of it. Thus, while many classifications were changed and the national park category was increased at the expense of lands formerly classified as reserves, the total area in the system remained almost unchanged.

Created in 1982, the 43,057-hectare (106,394-acre) Chiloé National Park is a recent addition to the system in an area characterized by the old age of its protected areas. Located on the Pacific Coast of Chiloé Island, an old Spanish enclave within an area generally dominated by the Indians, this national park has some unusual features. There is considerable seashore, including an island that serves as a rookery for sea lions and where elephant seals, whose males can reach a weight of 4,000 kilograms (9,000 pounds), are regularly seen. With the exception of those in the fjord district, most of the old areas in the system have a terrestrial orientation. The inclusion of a marine dimension, as in this case, is rather recent. Another distinctive feature is the absence of roads. Although they would be easy enough to build, there is a plan to keep this national park free of them and require visitors to use foot trails. Doing so will maximize appreciation of temperate rain forests, which here offer great diversity of tree species, and of forest fauna, which is varied but difficult to spot. Among the latter are pudú, the world's smallest deer with a maximum weight of 7 kilograms (15 pounds); Chiloé fox, a restricted-range species first collected by Charles

Darwin during his visit to the island, and the chucao, a noisy restless bird inhabiting the more impenetrable forests.

The Vicente Pérez Rosales National Park, the last unit to be described in the lake district, was established in 1926. It is the oldest in the country, having some of the most extraordinary landscapes in an area known for scenic beauty. Theodore Roosevelt, one of the earliest visitors, when the area was still a forest reserve, expressed his admiration at the views. Presided over by the snow-covered cone of the Osorno Volcano, its area, more than 200,000 hectares (500,000 acres), corresponds mainly to the basin of the Todos Los Santos Lake, also known as Emerald Lake for the intense green waters. With forests, lakes and snow-covered volcanoes, this unit symbolizes perfectly the image long associated with the national park concept. It attracts 75,000 visitors annually, in spite of its distance from important urban centers. Although this is a small figure by Northern Hemisphere standards, it accounts for fully 12 percent of visitors to the system nationwide.

Fjord Area and Western Patagonia

Low summer temperatures severely limit biological productivity in Chile's deep south, an area aptly called the southernmost part of the world. There is almost no agriculture, and the areas suitable for traditional land uses, such as forestry or grazing, are concentrated in the east, away from the fjords and mountains. The location of the protected areas sharply reflects this fact, for almost every one of them is along the Andes or among the Pacific coastal archipelagoes. Many large parks and reserves adjoin each other, contributing to the survival of one of the few extensive wildernesses of the Southern Hemisphere outside Antarctica.

Among the existing units, Cape Horn is the world's southernmost park, protecting the place where America's landmass ends. The seas surrounding the park were feared by navigators until the opening of the Panama Canal shifted commercial traffic to safer waters. Bernardo O'Higgins National Park, at 3,524,648 hectares (8,709,405 acres) the largest protected area in Chile, extends from the international boundary to the outer seashores, with islands, lakes, bogs, and a 350-kilometer (200-mile) long ice field. Torres del Paine, a park with spectacular scenery, is depicted in every travel guide referring to Patagonia; being at the contact point of western forests and eastern grasslands, it has an important biological diversity for such latitudes. Pali-Aike, near the place where the Strait of Magellan joins the Atlantic Ocean, is a small but important park. Temperate grasslands are poorly represented everywhere in the world including the United States and Canada, and Pali-Aike protects a remnant of the original Patagonian prairies as well as remains of human occupation 10,000 years ago.

Oceanic Islands

There are two national parks in the Chilean oceanic islands. Juan Fernández Archipelago National Park is located 670 kilometers (360 nautical miles) from the South American coast at latitude 33° south; 98 percent of the archipelago's land area is within the park. This small group of islands, under 100 square kilometers (40 square miles) in area, has a very high proportion of endemic species of plants and invertebrate fauna. More than 70 percent of the 140 native flowering plants are endemics. There is also a sea lion species found only here.

Different plants and animals are related to Andean Patagonic, tropical American, and Asia-Pacific groups, providing scientists with a natural experiment in evolution. Over 500 papers about the park's flora and fauna have been published in scientific journals.

The other oceanic island park is Rapa Nui National Park, covering 40 percent of Easter Island, 4,000 kilometers (2,500 miles) west of the continent, and about the same distance east of Tahiti. The unit's boundaries have been drawn with the purpose of including the majority of the island's archaeological monuments. The local cultural heritage is much more than the stone "heads" pictured by popular books and magazines, which actually represent the upper part of unfinished statues never carried out of the quarry, and half buried by the rubble. Hundreds of stone statues, called "moai" in Polynesian, were transported with great effort to ceremonial altars scattered all along the coast; many got red scoriae topknots quarried at the other extreme of the island. Pictographs, petroglyphs, and structures, both ceremonial and utilitarian, have also survived to the present.

A number of plant species and a variety of marine life are endemic to the island. Natural heritage, albeit important in its own right, tends to be obscured by the magnificent cultural heritage sharing this tiny spot lost in the middle of the earth's largest ocean.

ADMINISTRATION

National parks, national reserves (some of them still called forest reserves), and nature monuments fall under the authority of the Forest Service. The service, known in Spanish as Corporación Nacional Forestal and better recognized by Chileans by the acronym of CONAF, is a public autonomous agency within the Ministry of Agriculture. It has four technical programs: forest law enforcement, forest management, fire control, and protected wildlands. The protected wildlands program carries out its activities through four sections: national parks, national reserves, wild fauna, and native flora. The Forest Service has thirteen regional offices, one in each of the administrative regions of the country. The parks and other protected areas are managed by the regional offices.

The program is staffed by approximately 30 university graduates; 300 rangers, many with technical degrees; and 200 support staff including drivers, maintenance personnel, and so forth. Personnel for legal and logistical support and brigades for fire suppression are provided by CONAF through other programs.

The legislative mandate for national parks and other protected areas is broad and general. Different laws refer to different issues, creating problems of compatibility and interpretation. The main sources of the legal mandate are the Forest Law; the Government Property Administration Law, which makes specific reference to parks and reserves; and the Convention of Nature Protection and Wildlife Preservation in the Western Hemisphere. A Protected Wildlands Law has been published but has not yet come into effect. The parks, reserves, and monuments can be created and decommissioned by a supreme decree, a kind of presidential order that does not require legislative approval. This eases the task of establishing new areas, but at the same time gives less stability to the system if pressures arise to make commercial use of resources or to carry out activities that do not conform with the standards of each category.

A strong and coherent body of policies, developed over the last two decades, make up to a certain degree for the deficiencies of the legislative mandate. Master plans have been applied regularly as a management tool for over a decade, and are now well established, both as a guide for those in charge of managing the areas and as a deterrent for those that want to carry out activities that conflict with the rules and purposes of each management category.

The first management priority, systemwide, is the protection of natural and cultural resources. Most manpower and operating expenditures are devoted to this end because the Forest Service recognizes that a lost cultural feature or an extinguished species cannot be recovered regardless of the expenditure.

There are three categories of protected natural areas: national parks; nature monuments, which are essentially small-scale parks; and reserves. They share basic philosophy and goals: to conserve biological diversity, to minimize human impacts upon fragile ecosystems, to provide certain services to the public, and to protect cultural resources set within natural environments.

The real difference lies in the way these objectives are achieved, because each category has its own set of rules. While parks and monuments are committed to strict preservation, with no extraction or modification of natural resources allowed, the reserves may be subject to more active management including any kind of manipulation needed to achieve the objectives established in each unit's management plan. There are few commercial forests within the reserves and therefore no opportunity for a management style similar to the national forests in the United States. In some reserves where there are small quantities of timber it may be sold for profit through public auction. Grazing permits are allotted to the highest bidders as well. No commercial extraction of any kind is admitted in the parks.

Fishing and hunting are forbidden in parks and usually also in reserves. As an exception, sport fishing of introduced species may be allowed in a park or reserve, provided there is no possibility of incidental catch of native species.

Agricultural lands do not exist within protected wildlands, and there are no urban centers within them, except the Andean highland Indian villages, which are classified as compatible uses.

Public use for recreation is allowed in all three categories, in places zoned for that purpose and under the appropriate regulations set in each master plan. The number of visitors has increased from 250,000 in 1978 to 600,000 in 1988. The rate of growth was higher in the late 1970s and early 1980s; it has moderated since then. Individual areas show different patterns: some are still sharply increasing while others have leveled off. The Forest Service does not actively promote tourism because available facilities are being used to capacity, but visitors are welcome. Lodging and food services are operated through concessionaires. Concession arrangements for the ski slopes found in some units of the lake district are handled differently. During the last few years, local governments have realized how important these may be as a source of local income and tax revenues, and CONAF has entered into long-term concession agreements with them because the level of investment required for ski development is much higher than for campgrounds or cabins.

A major concern for administrators of the parks and reserves is the interpretation of protected area values to the public. This is a difficult task in a country where few published materials exist regarding native flora, fauna, or ecological features. Besides the work done in the field at each unit, strong technical and logistic support has been granted to the national television networks, resulting in five to ten one-hour programs each year. These programs have been very popular and have done a lot to increase public awareness about natural heritage and protected area values and philosophy.

Research in protected areas is also supported by the Forest Service, and many national and overseas specialists carry out investigations in them. As part of this effort, eleven parks, reserves, and monuments constitute the seven biosphere reserves so far established in Chile.

The work of individuals or small groups alarmed by the rate of destruction of certain environments was instrumental in the establishment of the early parks and reserves. Today, environmental awareness is much more developed, but there are relatively few nongovernmental organizations (NGOs) in Chile waging campaigns to such ends. In general, NGOs are small and have a limited influence in the development of public policies. The establishment of new protected areas is a decision made within the agency charged with managing such areas; this makes it possible to select the places to be protected in accordance with well-defined priorities if the agency's upper echelons support the proposals. The lack of organized support from the community at large becomes a liability when it is necessary to acquire privately held lands of ecological interest.

Park managers all over the world face similar problems, the predominance of some particular subset of them depending on each country's economic development, level of urbanization, rate of population increase, and specific cultural traits. In the Chilean case, during the first fifty years of the system the main problems were the "traditional" ones, usually associated with developing countries, namely homesteading by land-hungry peasants, poaching, illegal felling of timber, and cattle grazing. Although some of these problems still exist in certain areas, they are not the most important or widespread. "New" problems have taken their place, requiring new strategies and responses by managers. Paramount among them are water rights, mineral and oil exploration, poorly planned tourism development, off-road vehicles, hydropower development, and archaeological resource destruction.

The protected area establishment process still goes on. Four new units were created in 1988, and additional ones are in the planning stage. Unlike during the 1960s, when stress was laid on the creation of large-sized units aimed at preserving the ecological balance of fragile ecosystems, the focus now and during the coming decade is on improving representation of biological diversity and of cultural resources linked to natural environments and on fulfilling other objectives of interest to the national community, such as making areas available for undertaking long-term environmental research. New areas are likely to be small because a country where 18 percent of the territory has already been alloted to protected areas does not have much room available for further expansion of the protected system.

Looking at the overall picture, it is possible to finish with a cautiously optimistic view. Chile has a rural population that has remained stable at two million people for the last thirty years, and total population increase is moderate. The country has a team of well-qualified protected area personnel, and public awareness is consistently increasing. Although many problems and limitations exist and the going will be rough at times, the country's natural heritage has a good probability of emerging almost intact into the twenty-first century.

BIBLIOGRAPHY

Note: There are few formal publications about Chilean nature preserves either in Spanish or English. Most information belongs to the so-called gray literature category: unpublished reports, personal notes, internal agency reports, and so forth. Interested researchers could gain access to the archives that hold these materials, but they are seldom available for the general public. The following will be of interest to the nonspecialist and are available in many countries.

Gajardo, R. *Chile, sus parques nacionales y otras áreas naturales*. Madrid: Instituto de la Caza Fotográfica y Ciencias de la Naturaleza 1982.
Miller, K. *Planificacion de parques nacionales para el ecodesarrollo en Latinoamerica*. Madrid: Fepma, 1980. (Includes a number of examples about the Chilean park system; there is an English version in typescript.)
Oltremari, J., and E. Fahrenkrog. "Institutionalization of National Parks in Chile." *Parks* 3, no. 4 (January-March 1979): 1–4.
Rockefeller, M., et al. "Parks, Plans and People." *National Geographic* 131 (January 1967): 74–119.

Weber, C. "Conservacion y uso racional de la naturaleza en areas protegidas." *Ambiente y Desarrollo* 2, no. 1 (1986): 165–81.

Weber, C., and A. Gutierrez. "Areas silvestres protegidas." *Medio Ambiente en Chile*. Santiago: Ediciones de la Universidad Catolica de Chile, 1985.

REPUBLIC OF CHINA   5

Lung-Sheng Chang
and Shin Wang

Taiwan, a continental island with an area of 36,000 square kilometers (13,900 square miles), is located in the marginal area between the Asian continental shelf and the oceanic crust of the Pacific. Situated between the latitudes of 20°53' and 25°18' north (the Tropic of Cancer crosses the island at 23°30'), Taiwan is endowed with a variety of topography featuring vertical distances as great as 4,000 meters (13,123 feet). Approximately 30 percent of the land area is plains with the remainder occupied by hills and mountains, which parallel the long north-south axis of the island. More than two hundred of the mountains are higher than 3,000 meters (9,842 feet) above sea level. Average annual temperatures are generally above 22° Celsius (72° Fahrenheit), and the average annual rainfall measures more than 2,500 millimeters (100 inches).

Corresponding to the varied topography is a range of climatic zones, including the tropical, subtropical, warm temperate, and cold temperate. Atop the higher mountains the climate is comparable to that of the arctic frozen plains. Within these different zones may be found coniferous and broadleaf forests, grassland, savanna, and alpine vegetation. In all, 55 percent of the land is covered with forests rich in floral and faunal resources. Aquatic plants grow in localized areas.

HISTORY

Just four hundred years ago, Taiwan was but a wild island with a small indigenous population. These native people, now numbering over 300,000, come from nine tribes, constituting less than 2 percent of Taiwan's population. Since 1650, the Portuguese, the Dutch, and the Japanese have successively occupied the island. Population figures available for the 1680s suggest that the aboriginal peoples already numbered about 300,000 by this early date. Beginning in the seventeenth century (Ch'ing Dynasty), Han people from the Chinese mainland immigrated to Taiwan in significant numbers, swelling its population to more than 3.2 million by 1900. The rapid economic development of the past forty years has accounted for an even more dramatic increase in Taiwan's population. In the 1950s there were 8.6 million inhabitants, and by 1987 there were over 19 million, giving Taiwan one of the highest population densities in the world.

Taiwan's natural resources are seriously threatened by the quickening pace of agricultural and industrial developments. Hence, the government is now actively engaged in nature preservation and other measures to improve the quality of the environment. The creation and operation of four national parks by teams of specialists trained in park management signified a major step taken by the government in this direction.

In 1972 the government of the Republic of China promulgated the National Park Law as the legislative basis for managing and controlling Taiwan's national parks. However, with the government giving full priority to economic development projects, it was not until 1979 that the Ministry of the Interior joined with concerned agencies and specialists to form the National Park Planning Committee, and the first national park—Kenting—was proposed. In 1981, the Ministry of the Interior formed the Construction and Planning Administration (CPA) to be responsible for land-use planning.

Altogether, there are six departments under the CPA, the National Parks Department being one of them. The National Parks Department is responsible for creating and managing national parks, as well as investigating their resources of natural and cultural importance. In the formulation of its plans, the department has solicited cooperation from domestic universities and from specialists in landscape architecture and natural resources management from the United States, Japan, and Europe.

By the end of 1986, the government had designated four national parks. These four parks are listed below in the order they were proposed and their headquarters established.

1. Kenting National Park
   Designated—September 1, 1982
   Headquarters established—January 1, 1984

2. Yushan National Park
   Designated—April 6, 1985
   Headquarters established—April 10, 1985

3. Yangmingshan National Park
   Designated—September 1, 1985
   Headquarters established—September 6, 1985

4. Taroko National Park
   Designated—November 12, 1986
   Headquarters established—November 18, 1986

In April 1982, the government ordered the Ministry of Interior to survey the coastal region and draw up a management plan. Since the length of Taiwan's coastline is 1,140 kilometers (708 miles), a plan for the entire coast would take a long time. The ministry set priorities according to the relative importance of the coastal regions. First, the ministry joined with other pertinent agencies to select coastal areas that have unique natural values. The ministry then surveyed these areas and drafted a management plan including a program of conservation.

A report was submitted within six months. The first recommendation of the ministry's plan was to designate seven coastal reserves. These are the Northeastern Coast, the Su-Hua Coast, the Hua-Tung Coast, the Ken-Ting Area, the Lan-Yang Coastal Area, the Chang-Yun-Chia Coastal Region, and the estuary of the Tamsui River. The ministry drew up a "Taiwan Coast Environmental Protection Plan" to protect the natural resources of the above areas, and it became effective in February 1984.

Following the establishment of these seven reserves, the ministry drew up a new plan for establishing an additional five reserves. The new plan includes Pei-Men, Hao-Mei-Li, Chin-Shan, Chiu-P'eng, and the Northern Coast. In 1986, the ministry cooperated with the provincial and city governments in investigating and planning for the coastal reserves. They will be established as coastal protected areas on the basis of regulations for nonurban land use control. The authorities will manage these lands in accordance with the planned zoning regulations, with the ecological protection zone receiving the strictest level of protection in the plan.

PARKS AND RESERVES

Kenting National Park

Kenting National Park is located on the southern tip of Hengchun Peninsula, which forms the southern end of the island of Taiwan. The park is bordered by the Pacific Ocean to the east, the Taiwan Strait to the west, the Nanjen Mountains to the north, and the Bashi Strait to the south. The park environment may be divided into two parts—a terrestrial zone of 17,731 hectares (43,813 acres), and an aquatic zone (referring to the marine environment within one kilometer of the coastline) of 14,900 hectares (36,800 acres). Kenting lies within the tropical latitudes.

Topography and Geology. Kenting is characterized by varied terrain, including isolated peaks, shell sand beaches, coral reefs, rocky coasts, limestones, and sea-washed and eroded tablelands. In addition, there are ancient lakes and aeolian topographies (sand hills, sand cascades, sand rivers, and the like).

Ecology. The Nanjenshan area of Kenting is covered by a natural tropical monsoon forest, home for a rich variety of wild flora and fauna. The Hengchun Peninsula itself is a winter resting area for East Asian migratory bird populations including brown shrike, the gray-faced buzzard, other birds of prey, and many species of waterfowl. About 215 different kinds of birds have been identified in this area. In addition, there are some 210 species of butterflies and many of reptiles, amphibians and fresh-water fish.

Floral communities include virgin forests, tropical monsoon rain forests, grassland, bushes, and coastal plants. All together there are 1,300 different species of plants including Taiwan ebony and the reef pemphis found on coral reefs.

Surrounded by the sea on three sides, Kenting features a rich variety of marine life including rare tropical fishes, shells, and bracken. They contribute in no small measure to Kenting's reputation as one of the most beautiful of all national parks in Asia.

Cultural Importance. According to a report detailing the prehistoric remains of Hengchun Peninsula, the earliest inhabitants in the area may date back 3,000 years. Near Kenting Ranch and Oluanpi Lighthouse, several ancient cultural sites have been discovered. In the Nanjenshan area, the remains of stone-slab houses nearly 600 years old are of special importance to the archaeological record of southern Taiwan. A cemetery belonging to the Paiwan tribe, one of the native peoples of the region, is located at Kenting. Han Chinese settlers reached the Hengchun Peninsula by the time of the late Ch'ing Dynasty, and among the important historical remains left by these early settlers is the Oluanpi Lighthouse, built in 1882, in the latter part of the reign of Emperor Kuangsu. These are all important resources reflecting the rich and diverse cultural history of the park.

Yushan National Park

Located in the central mountains of Taiwan, Yushan National Park has an area of 105,490 hectares (260,666 acres) with many special topographical features. Yushan Peak, in the center of the park, is 3,950 meters (12,960 feet) in height and is the highest mountain in East Asia. About 250,000 visitors reach Yushan National Park each year, partaking mainly in long-distance hiking. With snow in the winter and cool weather in the summer, Yushan is a magnificent mountain park belonging to the temperate zone of the subtropical region.

The high-elevation mountains of the Yushan range account for a topography sharply dissected by peaks and valleys. Landscapes include several watersheds, isolated peaks, and a wide variety of mountain ranges, valleys, and passes.

Aside from climatic features such as snowscapes in the winter, the scenery of Yushan is further enhanced by changing cloud formations and the seasonal characteristics of local vegetation. Rivers of eastern, central, and southern Taiwan originate in the mountain reaches of the park.

Plant Ecology. Plant communities of Yushan are diversified according to elevation and life zones. Trees belong to two general forest groups: coniferous and broadleaf. The coniferous trees include six main species: Taiwan fir, Morrison spruce, Taiwan hemlock, Japanese cypress, Taiwan red cypress, and pines.

The virgin forests—mixed with alpine scrub, Yushan rhododendron, and white forests (dead trees in previously burned areas)—are remarkable representatives of Yushan's grace. As for the broadleaf forests, they are scattered along Pa-tungkuan Trail, between Tungpu and Tuikuan, Tafen and Walami. These broad-leaf forests include plant species particularly worthy of study and appreciation, such as Chinese walnut, wild orchids, oads, and laurels.

Animal Ecology. Yushan fauna is nourished by the abundant native plants. Field surveys have identified 123 species of birds, 28 species of mammals, 17 species of reptiles, 12 species of amphibians, and 186 species of butterflies. Among the endemic fauna, serow, sambar, black bear, pangolin, Mikado pheasant, Swinhoe's blue pheasant, and two species of salamander are especially precious and have been designated as endangered species. The salamanders, survivors from the last glacial epoch, are now found only in high-altitude mountains.

Cultural Importance. Historical records and recent investigations suggest that the development of the Yushan area may be best divided into two periods—before and after the construction of Patungkuan Trail.

Before this passage was constructed, the cultural importance of the area was represented by the traditional ways of the mountain natives living amid the forests and valleys. The construction of the trail enabled the plains-dwelling Han Chinese to settle and cultivate the eastern part of Taiwan. Eventually, however, adverse climatic conditions and the difficulties involved in crossing the high central mountains led to the virtual abandonment of the trail as an important route of east-west travel.

The construction of Patungkuan Trail can be dated to the reign of Tungchih (1874), the thirteenth emperor of the Ch'ing Dynasty. Its total length is approximately 110 kilometers (68 miles). During its heyday as the most important east-west corridor in central Taiwan, it took ten days to traverse its length on foot.

At present, the only surviving remains of the Ch'ing barracks, which once stood along this passage, are located at Lele, Nan, and Kuankao. The only surviving remains (stone walls, slates, stone steps, and earthen walls) of the original Ch'ing period construction of the passage itself may be found in the section between Tungpu and Lele.

Today there are native Bunun people living in Tungpu and Meishan villages of Yushan National Park. Their music is one of the treasures of ethnomusicology in the world.

Bunun are skillful mountaineers and farmers. Unfortunately, their precious cultural traditions are not well preserved. They no longer hunt, as it is prohibited in Taiwan, or collect plant materials for their excellent weavings. Their society is patrilineal and democratic. Their brotherly nature is revealed in their music and daily lives. They are an invaluable part of Yushan National Park.

Yangmingshan National Park

Yangmingshan National Park occupies an area of 11,456 hectares (28,308 acres) in the Taipei basin of northern Taiwan. The park is dominated by the peaks of the Tatun and Chi-Shin Shan, with hot springs dotting their slopes. Owing to its unique proximity to the Taipei metropolis, the annual number of tourists exceeds three million.

Topography and Geology. The majority of geological structures in this area are composed of volcanic and sedimentary rocks. The Kanchiao and Gin-Shin cliffs, sulfurous craters, volcanic cone formations, lakes, basins, hot springs, valleys, and cascades are among the most notable geological formations. Chi-Shin Shan, the highest mountain in this area, is 1,120 meters (3,675 feet) in height.

Plant Ecology. The broadleaf forests consist of indigenous species including red nanmu, large-leaved nanmu, incense nanmu, birdlime tree, Japanese cleyera, Chinese hydrangea, narrow-petaled hydrangea, dark-spotted cherry, Formosan sweet gum, Japanese euscaphis, and green maple. Grassland plants include Kunishi and Usawa cane, and a small area covered by the grass *Miscanthus sinensis.* Groves of Tibet Lyonia and wild peony are also found. Six native species of azaleas are found in this area: red-spotted rhododendron, Taiwan rhododendron, *Rhododendron longiperulatum*, Oldham azalea, Maries azalea, and red-haired rhododendron. *Rhododendron longiperulatum* is an endemic species. There are other flora of interest, among them the unusual plant communities associated with the sulfurous hot springs and the rare and precious *Isoetes* found growing at Munhuan Lake on the Chi-Shin Shan.

Animal Ecology. Resident birds and summer migrants number 88 species. Among them, the Formosan blue magpie is an endemic species, and the Chinese bulbul, black bulbul, the grey-eyed nun babbler, and white-belled yuhina are frequently seen. Butterflies of 133 different species can often be seen fluttering along the trails in this area. Lizards and snakes are very common, and more than 30 species of reptiles have been collected in the park. There are 8 species of frogs and toads.

Taroko National Park

Taroko National Park, an area of 92,000 hectares (227,000 acres), is situated in the central region of eastern Taiwan. The Cross-Island Highway, stretching along the course of Liwu River, provides access to the park's beautiful mountain and valley scenery. The marble gorges in this area are considered by many to be among the greatest scenic attractions of the world.

Topography and Geology. The main topographic features of Taroko are mountains and gorges. The marble gorges form an extraordinary phenomenon. At altitudes ranging from 2,000 to 3,700 meters (6,560 to 12,100 feet), there are mountains, gorges, cascades, natural lakes, cliffs, valleys, river terraces, and a wide variety of other striking features.

Plant Ecology. Vegetation varies according to elevation. Four major life zones may be distinguished: tundra, alpine grassland, forest, and limestone vegetation zones. Nearly all of Taiwan's floral species can be found at Taroko, with the exception of those characteristic of the coastal forest. Preliminary research has identified about 1,100 species of vascular plants in this area, and among them, more than 50 species have been designated as rare or worthy of special protection.

Animal Ecology. Many birds have been identified in field surveys throughout the area of Taroko. They may be distinguished according to vertical zonation such as high-, mid-, and low-altitude species. Aquatic birds and amphibians live beside river banks. Butterflies tend to flutter along trails. The Taiwan macaques congregate in the gorges, on the cliffs, or on steep mountain slopes. Other mammals, such as the black bear, Chinese muntjac, serow, and wild boar, reside in the mountains and valleys at elevations around 2,000 meters (6,100 feet) above sea level.

Cultural Importance. Few ancient cultural remains survive in this area, except the former dwellings of mountain aborigines and an ancient passage along Liwu stream cliff. The cultural relics that have been discovered are mainly scattered within a 10-kilometer area along both sides of the East-West Cross-Island Highway.

ADMINISTRATION

The operating agencies for natural environmental protection include the Council for Agricultural Development, Council for Environmental Protection, Council for Economic Planning and Development, Council for Cultural Planning and Development, Ministry of Communication, Ministry of Interior, and, of course, local governments.

Coastal Reserves

Selection standards have been developed for Taiwan's coastal reserves. The proposed reserves should possess at least one of the following four features: they must be representative of Taiwan's coastal ecosystem, be natural, have extraordinarily unique features, or have a combination of these. The definitive or selective standards are as follows:

A. Faunal resources: the area should contain
   1. rare or endangered animals;
   2. animals valuable for research or for nature studies;
   3. animals of value for visual appreciation and enjoyment by people;
   4. animal communities that are still natural and have not been seriously disturbed by people;
   5. animals of great economic value.

B. Floral/vegetative resources: the area should contain
   1. plant communities that still maintain their natural characteristics and that have not been seriously affected by people;

  2. rare or endangered plant species;

  3. plants valuable for research or for nature studies;

  4. the only existing propagation sources (i.e., seed sources).

C. Marine resources: the area should contain

  1. rare marine organisms;

  2. marine communities that still retain their natural characteristics, uninfluenced by human modifications;

  3. marine resources valuable for research or nature studies;

  4. areas that possess unique and natural landscape features that cannot be reconstructed by people;

  5. areas that have special fishery resources or are suitable for special fishery resource cultivation.

D. Topographical and geological resources: the area should contain

  1. rare or unique geological and geomorphological scenic resources that are unmodified by people and that still retain their natural characteristics;

  2. landforms that are valuable for research or for nature studies;

  3. areas that contain high quality scenic resources and can be utilized as recreational areas for the public.

The coastal reserves can be divided into two categories according to their level of protection. In the "preservation" or "core" areas any action that will change the present ecological uniqueness and natural landscape is forbidden. The authorities are charged to actively protect the natural resources of the reserves. In the "conservation" or "buffer" areas authorities can maintain the present level of resource use if there will be no deleterious influence on the uniqueness of the ecosystem or the natural landscape.

The Coastal Environmental Protection Program of Taiwan was promulgated by the Executive Yuan. Supervisory responsibility lies with the Ministry of the Interior, which administers the program under existing law. Unfortunately, operational effectiveness is limited by a shortage of professional staff and by inadequate financial resources. Coastal areas are also threatened by the activities of local governments intent on maximizing economic development; they show little interest in coordinating their programs with policies of protection and preservation. Real effectiveness in preserving the coastal environment awaits passage of a strong coastal protection law.

National Parks

Although the scope of applicability of the National Park Law is broad, the management of Taiwan's national parks is still dependent on the expertise and training of park personnel. Many of the specialists responsible for planning, establishing, and managing the national parks have experience from the American and Japanese park systems. Their management objectives thus reflect the guidelines set forth by the International Union for the Conservation of Nature (IUCN).

Park planning procedure is similar to that adopted in the United States. First, the Ministry of the Interior selects certain regions for study. Once the review reports are accepted by the Planning Committee, they will be evaluated by the premier of the Executive Yuan and subsequently enacted by the Ministry of the Interior if approved. At this stage, the national park can establish its management headquarters. The management agency consists of planning, interpretation, research and conservation, recreation, and engineering units.

Controlling land use is the fundamental objective of national park management. To this end, the land within a national park is classified into five categories with respect to appropriate usage: the ecological protection zone, the special scenic zone, the recreational zone, the historical protection zone, and the general management zone. Moreover, there are detailed specifications concerning the management and use of each of these categories of land.

Over the period from 1985 to 1991 the government of the Republic of China has determined to embark on "Fourteen National Construction Projects." The conservation work of the national parks has been designated as one of these fourteen projects, and the government has allocated a budget of U.S.$350 million to be devoted to park management in these six years. Such funding is needed if Taiwan's national parks are to overcome the major difficulties and problems still facing them. Pressure on recreational areas is increasing rapidly with overall population growth. Economic development remains a potent threat even to protected lands supposedly under the jurisdiction of park management. Adequate funding, however, is not a solution in itself; it must be accompanied by the formulation of a comprehensive and effective plan by the Ministry of Interior and concerned specialists for improving and strengthening national park management in Taiwan.

BIBLIOGRAPHY

Note: This chapter is based upon the following sources as well as more specialized documents not listed here.

Hsu, T. L. "A Study of the Coastal Geomorphology of Taiwan." *Proceedings of the Geological Society of China*, No. 5 (1962), pp. 29–45.
Republic of China, Ministry of Interior, Construction and Planning Administration. 1981. *The Ecological Resources in Kenting National Park*. Taipei.
———. 1984. *Coastal Zone Natural Environment Protection Program of Taiwan*. Taipei.
———. 1984. *The Protection of Ecological Environment and Promotion of Quality of Life*. Taipei.
———. 1984. *Yushan National Park*. Taipei.
———. 1985. *The Development of Natural Reserve and National Parks Construction in R.O.C.* Taipei.

————. 1985. *The National Parks in Taiwan*. Taipei.
————. 1985. *Seminar Papers on the Management of National Parks*. Taipei.
————. 1986. *Yangmingshan National Park*. Taipei.
Wang, Shin. *Landform of Taiwan*. Taipei: Du-Chia Publishing Company, 1980.

COLOMBIA 6

Heliodoro Sánchez Páez

Colombia's national parks and other natural reserves are important for their cultural, scientific, educational, and recreational values. They make a permanent and ongoing contribution to knowledge by allowing for the free evolution of nature within relatively undisturbed ecosystems. The areas of our national park system are open to the world community for investigation, education, and recreation. They are also the only natural patrimony that we all own and the most precious heritage that we will pass on to future generations.

HISTORY

In 1941, in Washington, D.C., Colombia signed the Pan-American Convention on Nature Protection and Wild Life Preservation in the Western Hemisphere. This event encouraged, for the first time, the government of Colombia to create national parks, natural monuments, and virgin land reserves, in accord with the definitions established in that convention.

The Reserva Natural La Macarena, the first wild protected area in Colombia, was created by Law 52 of 1948, but its boundaries were not properly established until 1965. With the promulgation of the second law of 1959 "about the Forest Economy of the Nation and Conservation of Renewable Natural Resources," Colombia created its first legal framework for the establishment of natural national parks. This law designated the snow mountains and surrounding areas to be natural national parks and areas of public use; however, no boundaries were established. The same law created seven large forest reservations, which together covered almost half the total area of the country.

In 1960, Decree 2631 established Cueva de los Guácharos (Oilbird Cave) Natural National Park, the first national park in Colombia to have fixed boundaries. In 1964 the Colombian Institute of the Agrarian Reform created three national parks on the Caribbean Coast: Isla de Salamanca, Sierra Nevada de Santa Marta, and Tayrona. Between 1968 and 1975, seven new national parks were added. In 1977 the national government declared nineteen new protected areas, including national parks and fauna and flora sanctuaries. In 1983 the Gorgona Islands, previously a penal colony off the Pacific Coast, were declared a national park. That same year two new areas were created, and one fauna and flora sanctuary was removed from the national park system.

Although the process of national parks creation has been virtually continuous, Colombia is still very far from having a complete network of national parks that would be fully representative of its distinctive biogeographic units, endemism centers, and ecosystems.

The earliest national parks were established for the perpetual preservation of areas with special significance in fauna, flora, and gea. The parks were to be used for research, education, and recreation and to be properly managed so as to avoid disturbing the resources or altering the ecosystems.

The recognition of severe environmental damage provided the primary motivation for national park creation. Natural ecosystems were under heavy utilitarian pressures. The uncontrolled exploitation of timber endangered many species of fauna and flora, and some were threatened with extinction. The reaction of the government to these threats was stimulated by the outstanding efforts of several Colombian naturalists, including the late Federico Carlos Lehmann Valencia, Enrique Pérez Arbeláez, and Armando Dugand Gnecco, as well as Jorge Hernández Camacho, Simón Max Franky Vásquez, Manuel del Llano, and Julio Carrisoza Umaña.

The legal status of the national park system of Colombia has been secure since the fundamental law of the system was promulgated in 1971, establishing basic rules for the management, administration, and development of the areas. Three years later a comprehensive environmental law, the Código de Recursos Naturales Renovables y de Protección al Medio Ambiente (Law Decree 2811 of 1974), was promulgated. It includes a whole chapter devoted to the national parks system and provides a definitive legal structure. In March 1977, Decree 622 further amended the code in relation to the national park system.

PARKS AND RESERVES

The Republic of Colombia has an area of 1,141,748 square kilometers (440,875 square miles) including its oceanic territories. It is located in the intertropical zone on the northwestern tip of South America, and it is the only South American country with both Caribbean and Pacific coasts. Colombia's complex orographic system is dominated by three main branches, or "cordilleras," of the northern Andes Mountains. The Cordillera Occidental paralleling the Pacific Coast is the lowest and the most recently raised. The Cordillera Central is the highest, rising to elevations of 5,400 meters (17,700 feet). It includes several snowy peaks and is mainly volcanic in origin. The Cordillera Oriental is the broadest of the three and connects with the Sierra de Perijá and the Cordillera de Mérida in Venezuela. It is primarily sedimentary in origin and reaches its maximum altitude of 5,300 meters (17,400 feet) in the Sierra Nevada de Chita, Güicán, and Cocuy.

Adjacent to the Caribbean Coast is the Sierra Nevada de Santa Marta, a large and isolated mountain massif, with the highest peaks in Colombia.

In the Departamento del Chocó near the Pacific Coast is the Sierra de Baudó, and an isolated mountain range, the Serranía del Darién, forms a portion of the boundary between Colombia and Panama. There are other isolated, low mountain ranges on the Caribbean coastal plain and on the Península de la Guajira.

The eastern part of the country is primarily plain, but there are isolated, low table mountains and inselbergs in the basins of the Guaviare, Negro, Vaupés, and Caquetá rivers. East of the Cordillera Oriental there is an isolated mountain range, the Serranía de la Macarena, which stretches approximately 120 kilometers (75 miles) in length and reaches over 2,500 meters (8,200 feet) in elevation.

The mean atmospheric temperatures are isothermal, with the differences between the coldest and hottest months less than 5° Celsius (9° Fahrenheit) for any given locality. In the daily cycle, however, the temperatures may fluctuate 20° Celsius (36° Fahrenheit) or more as on the summits of high mountains. In the dry sector, on the Caribbean Coast, the mean temperature at sea level is between 27° and 31° Celsius (81° and 88° Fahrenheit), and on the Pacific Coast the corresponding range is 25° to 27° Celsius (77° to 81° Fahrenheit). Elsewhere, mean annual temperature is primarily a function of elevation, with a drop of approximately 0.58°–0.66° Celsius (1.04°–1.10° Fahrenheit) associated with each increase of 100 meters (330 feet) in elevation. The climate is characterized by sharply defined alternating dry and wet seasons, and the average annual rainfall ranges from about 120 millimeters (5 inches) in the desert of the northern Guajira Peninsula to more than 12,000 millimeters (500 inches) in the lowlands of the Pacific coast. Indeed, the southeastern part of Chocó Department may be the wettest area in the world.

The Colombian classification of altitudinal zones is as follows:

1. Lowlands, or *tierra caliente*, 0 to 1,000 meters (0 to 3,300 feet) in elevation.

2. Sub-Andean Zone, 1,000 to 2,000 meters (3,300 to 6,600 feet) in elevation, improperly called the Subtropical Zone.

3. Andean Zone, or *tierra fría*, 2,000 to 3,000 meters (6,600 to 9,900 feet) in elevation and near to the timber line, improperly called the Temperate Zone.

4. Paramo Zone, located between the timber line and the snow line, approximately 3,000 to 4,700 meters (9,900 to 15,400 feet) in elevation and generally equivalent to the Alpine Zone of other regions. The vegetation of the Paramo is mainly herbaceous, with sparse shrubs or dwarf trees. Sometimes an additional belt, the Superparamo, is

recognized for the upper Subnival Zone, which is characterized by the absence of woody plants and large patches devoid of any vegetation.

5. The Nival Zone, over 4,700 meters (15,400 feet) in elevation.

Colombia's unusually complex geological, paleogeographical, and ecological history, its diversity of physiographic and climatic conditions, and its geographical position as a portal for the biotic exchanges between North and South America, result in a true mosaic of ecosystems and biogeographic units together with a high percentage of endemisms.

Although inventories of animal and plant species are still far from complete, about 10 percent of the world's living species are believed to exist in Colombia. This enormous diversity appears much more striking considering that Colombia constitutes just 0.8 percent of the earth's land area.

The Colombian national parks are areas of exceptional value, reserved for the benefit of the nation's inhabitants as a result of their outstanding natural, cultural, or historic characteristics. The system includes five categories of reserves: natural parks, natural reserves, unique natural areas, fauna and flora sanctuaries, and parkways.

As of December 1988, the national park system consisted of thirty-seven areas: twenty-nine natural national parks, a natural reserve (La Macarena), six fauna and flora sanctuaries, and one unique natural area. Collectively they cover approximately 5,928,000 hectares (14,648,000 acres) equivalent to 5.6 percent of the total area of the country. To date no parkways have been set aside. (See Figure 6.1)

The code also permits the establishment of reservations outside the national park system for the more effective management of renewable national resources. There are forest reserve areas (either productive, protective, or protective-productive), faunistic territories, private game reserves, integrated management districts, recreation areas, soil conservation districts, etc. Foremost among these are the forty-five forest protection reserves, which have been established mainly to protect the upper basins of important streams and rivers for diverse uses, particularly on a local scale.

In the following paragraphs I will attempt to give an overview of some of the reserves of the national park system, ordered according to biogeographical region.

La Macarena Biogeographical Complex

This unit is characterized by the integration of typical Guianan and Amazonian biota in a comparatively reduced area, and further complicated by the occurrence of definite Andean elements at the upper elevations of the mountains.

La Macarena Natural Reserve. The Sierra de la Macarena is a small cordillera rising 250 to 300 meters (800 to 1000 feet). It is located near the eastern Andean slopes but isolated from them by humid forest lowland. It was established as a

Figure 6.1
The National Parks System of Colombia

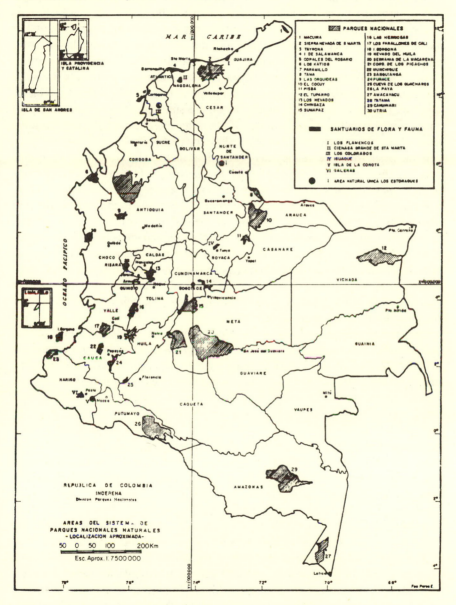

Source: Courtesy of INDERENA-UNIFEM, Bogotá, Colombia.

natural reserve in 1948. At 1,131,350 hectares (2.8 million acres) La Macarena is the largest unit in the national park system and the only natural reserve. According to biogeographic criteria, this mountain is the westernmost of the Tepuis, the large complex of table mountains of the Guianan region, endowed with a particular biota but with a strong Andean influence.

The reserve covers the cordillera, with its bizarre topography including table mountain peaks, spectacular escarpments, and canyons all surrounded by low, rolling country. The basement belongs to the Precambrian Guiana Shield, overlapped by Paleozoic, Cretaceous, Tertiary, and Quaternary sediments. Most of the reserve is covered by semi-evergreen tropical forest that gives way to cloud forest on the slopes and elfin woodlands on the summits. This is particularly so on the southern half, where a complex of litho-chasmo-chersophytic communities results from the scarce development and poverty of soils.

In the basal forest the canopy may exceed 40 meters (130 feet) with enormous trees like the kapok tree, or *ceiba* (*Ceiba pentandra*); wild fig trees, or *chibechas* (*Ficus spp.*); a relative of the Indian almond tree, the *macano amarilla* (*Terminalia amazonica*); and *Sterculia macarenesis*, endemic to the area. In the low hills the tree growth is reduced to 10–15 meters (30–50 feet), and in the microvalleys with peaty undrained soils, there are abundant palms of the genera *Attalea, Bactris, Euterpe, Iriartea, Jessenia, Mauritia, Scheelea,* and *Syagrus.* Toward the summits, the forest becomes mossy, dwarfed, and very thick, with elements like *Weinmannia* that clearly suggest Andean affinities. An outstanding endemic monotypic genus is *Macarenia clavigera*, an aquatic plant devoid of roots but firmly adherent to the rocks.

The fauna, still poorly known, includes at least 420 species of birds, with a subspecies of the Andean sparrow (*Zonotrichia capensis roraimae*). Endangered mammals include giant otter (*Pteronura brasiliensis*), jaguar (*Leo onca onca*), giant armadillo (*Priodontes maximus*), and puma (*Felis concolor discolor*).

The Orinoquia Province

This province covers the lowlands of the Orinoquia drainage with elevations from 100 to 500 meters (330 to 1,640 feet). Most of this province is covered by natural savannas, conditioned climatically (a rainy season alternating with a very dry season) and edaphically (soils with a high water table, with a high water-retention capacity, or with topographic or drainage factors). Fire, both spontaneous and man-made, is also a determining factor changing the floral composition, affecting the surrounding forests, and deteriorating the soil.

El Tuparro National Park. This park is the second largest in the system with an area of 548,000 hectares (1,354,000 acres). It extends westward from the Colombian bank of the Orinóco River. About 75 percent of its area is covered by natural savannas of different types. Open woodland types occur with stunted, gnarled trees of *Byrsonima crassifolia, Curatella americana, Bowdichia virgilioides*, etc., and in the sand soils *Caraipa llanorum* appear. Semi-evergreen gallery forests are well developed and very rich in species diversity. In most of the rivers or close to swamps or shallow lakes, floddely or swampy forests occur, and among its characteristic species one usually finds the *moriche* (*Mauritia flexuosa*). A very particular flora with elements like *Vellozia lithophila* appears on Precambrian and Paleozoic rocks.

Among the mammals in the park are species like the otter (*Lutra longicaudis enudris*), giant anteater (*Myrmecophaga tridactyla*), freshwater dolphin (*Ignia geoffrensis*), and a large population of white-tailed deer (*Odocoileus virginianus gymnotis*).

About 320 bird species have been reported, and the several reptile species include the Orinoquian crocodile (*Crocodylus intermedius*) and terecay turtle (*Podocnemis unifilis*).

In some areas of the park there are important cultural values including archaeological ruins and ritual burial sites.

The Amazonian Province

The physiognomy of the province is reasonably uniform as most of the variation in relief is inconspicuous. The expanse of plateaus, terraces, and alluvial plains is interrupted in some places by ranges of hills and isolated hills. The area has a mean annual rainfall of 2,500 millimeters (100 inches) and a mean annual temperature of more than 24° Celsius (75° Fahrenheit). However, the biota, geology, and soils are heterogeneous. A large number of permanent waterways form a rather complex hydrographic network. The surface of Colombian Amazonia is about 380,000 square kilometers (150,000 square miles), one-third of the country's land area.

In this part of Colombia there are three national parks: Cahuinarí, Amacayacu, and La Paya, but the last is relatively unknown.

El Amacayacu National Park. It is located in southern Colombia in the area called Amazonian Trapeze. It is characterized by a relief of low hills with moderate slopes, alluvial plains, and swamp areas. Regarding geology, there are three formations: the plateau of the Tertiary, a terrace with low hills corresponding to the Quaternary, and the other integrated by the flood beds.

The most spectacular aquatic plant is *Victoria amazonica*, a giant water lily; its petioles and peduncles are invested with spines, and it has circular floating leaves that reach 1.5 meters (5 feet) in diameter. Indigenous trees include *munguba* (*Pseudobombax sp.*), mahogany (*Swietenia macrophylla*), *uipo* (*Genipa americana*), Guianan rubber tree (*Hevea guyanensis*), cannonball tree (*Couroupita guianensis*), and many palms.

There are 150 species of mammals and possibly 450 species of birds. A snake called anaconda or *sucuriyu* (*Eunectes murinus*) reaches 11 meters (36 feet) in length, which makes it the world's largest nonpoisonous species. The group of the fishes has enormous diversity. Among them the *piraíba* or *valentón* (*Brachyplatystoma filamentosum*) is the largest of the South American catfish group, weighing 200 kilograms (440 pounds) or more, and the *pirarucú* or *paiche* (*Arapaima gigas*) reaches 300 kilograms (660 pounds).

Inside the park there are two Indian communities of the Ticuna Tribe.

Caribbean Complex and the Massif of Santa Marta

In this province there are eight areas of the national park system: five national parks and three fauna and flora sanctuaries, which correspond to the Atlantic Coast plains and mountains with a vegetation that ranges from xerophytic and subhygrophytic forests; its also has mangroves and saline communities. The massif of Santa Marta is located in this province and contains each of the country's altitudinal zones. Its biota is related to that of the Andes, especially to that of the Cordillera Oriental of Colombia and the cordilleras of Mérida and of the coast of Venezuela.

Sierra Nevada de Santa Marta National Park. With 383,000 hectares (946,000 acres) this park is a part of the massif of the same name, which is the highest mountain in Colombia. It is an isolated mountain whose foot is located at sea level and whose primary peaks, Simón Bolívar and Colón, reach heights of 5,770 meters (18,900 feet). From base to summit the Sierra Nevada de Santa Marta is probably the highest intertropical mountain in the world.

There is evidence that the region has experienced six periods of glaciation giving rise to glacial circs, U-shaped valleys, and several lakes that are considered to be sacred sites by the Indian people.

The park's vegetation is humid or hygrophytic with forest of the lowlands, sub-Andean, and Andean zones. There are paramo, from 3,400 to 4,200 meters (11,000 to 14,000 feet), superparamo, from 4,200 to 5,100 meters (14,000 to 17,000 feet), and nival zones, the last above 5,100 meters (17,000 feet).

Among the endemic elements of the flora are the aboreus *fraylejon* of the family Asteraceae (*Libanothamnus glossophyllus*), the palms (*Dyctiocaryum schultzei* and *Ceroxylon schultzei*), and *tachuelo* (*Berberis nevadensis*). Seventy species and subspecies of birds are unique to the Sierra Nevada de Santa Marta National Park, including hummingbirds (*Lafresnaya lafresnayi liriope* and *Oxypogon guerinii cyanolaemus*) and the thrush (*Turdus fuscater sanctamartae*).

In 1975 a group of Colombian anthropologists confirmed the discovery of a lost city, La Ciudad Perdida, one of several that had been reported by the Spanish chroniclers of the sixteenth century. It is located in the tropical forest 1,300 meters (4,250 feet) above sea level, inside the Sierra Nevada National Park. The lost city may be one of the biggest pre-Spanish cities in the Americas.

The structures discovered include a remarkable system of ditches and drains, designed to prevent both floods and erosion; terraces, retaining walls, stairways, and abundant home sites. Three types of pottery have been classified: black, red, and beige.

The Tayrona culture was known for its gold work, some of which has been found at the lost city. At present, the Sierra Nevada of Santa Marta is inhabited by the Kogis, Ijka, and Bintukua Indians. The park's unique geography, geology, topography, biota, ecology, and anthropological characteristics are sources of continuing scientific interest.

With special permission the public may visit the lost city, but for now there are no provisions to visit other zones of the park.

El Tayrona National Park. Located in the foothills of the Sierra Nevada de Santa Marta Massif, at altitudes ranging from sea level to 900 meters (3,000 feet), El Tayrona has beautiful beaches and vestiges of another city of the Tayrona culture, called Pueblito. The vegetation includes xerophytic and subxerophytic forest up to humid cloud forest.

The fauna is varied with approximately 100 species of mammals, 300 species of birds, 50 species of corals, and 50 species of reptiles.

The Tayrona National Park offers major visitor facilities including a camping zone, picnic zone, several interpretive trails, visitor center, and places for swimming or bathing in the sea.

Isla de Salamanca National Park. Isla de Salamanca National Park is located near the city of Barranquilla. It is an exceptional formation of marshes, playones, and forest in the ancient estuary of the Magdalena River. In this area the subxerophytic forest with its canopy of only 3 to 6 meters (10 to 20 feet) may well be the climax vegetation.

In places adjacent to the Magdalena River, where the influence of salt is slight, a riparian mixed forest grows. Mangrove, however, is the bioma that occupies most of the park. The mangrove consists mainly of three species: red mangrove (*Rhizophora mangle*), white mangrove (*Laguncularia racemosa*), and yellow or black mangrove (*Avicennia germinans*). Today, hypersalinity, due in part to drainage changes caused by road construction, is rapidly killing the mangroves.

Two hundred species of birds are represented in the park including several migratory species from North America. Among the endemics are the hummingbird (*Lepidopyga liliae*) and the cowbird (*Molothrus armenti*).

The park has an elevated trail, picnic area, and visitor center. Several communities of plants are located on the beaches of the maritime littoral.

The Andean Biogeographic Complex

The Colombian Andes is a complex of biogeographic units characterized by flora and fauna related to the biota of the central and southern Andes, as well as of the sub-Antarctic forests and Patagonia. Many of the biotic elements of the three cordilleras are similar, but there are great differences of endemism between them because each cordillera is a barrier to the distribution of many animals and plants. Within this biogeographic complex there are sixteen national parks, one unique natural area, and three sanctuaries of flora and fauna.

Los Nevados National Park. On the axis of Colombian Central Andes, it includes areas from 2,600 meters to 5,400 meters (8,500 to 17,700 feet) above sea level. The park is of special interest as the source of countless streams, and also because it contains the upper basins of several rivers that supply water to irrigate the country's largest coffee plantations and the northern agricultural zone of Tolima Department. These watersheds are also important for human consumption and production of electricity.

The park's system of protuberant relief is provided by snow-capped volcanic peaks including the Ruiz, Tolima, Santa Isabel Cisne, and Quindío. The Nevado del Ruiz is a complex stratovolcano dissected by radially draining, and glacially modified river valleys. The volcano has been episodically active for at least 1.2 million years.

A small Plinian eruption of the Nevado del Ruiz volcano ejected a mixture of dacite and andesite tephra on November 13, 1985. Small pyroclastic flows and surges generated during the initial stage of the eruption caused surface melting of approximately 10 percent of the volcano's ice cap, which resulted in meltwater floods. The erosive floods incorporated soils and loose sediments from the volcano's flanks and developed into lahars that claimed at least 25,000 lives in nearby Armero City.

The natural vegetation of the area is a mixture of cloud and semi-evergreen forests, which locally reach an altitude of 4,000 meters (13,000 feet) above sea level. Among others there is a defined complex of plant associations dominated by *Clethra ferruginea*, encenillo (*Weinmannia tolimensis*), dulumuco (*Saurauia spp.*), *Hesperomeles sp.*, and *Polylepis sericea*. One of the most outstanding elements is the wax palm (*Ceroxylon guindiuense*), which may form an almost homogeneous forest. This palm is an exclusive Colombian species considered to be the most magnificent in the world. It reaches a height up to 60 meters (200 feet) and is designated by law the national tree of Colombia.

From 3,600 to 4,200 meters (12,000 to 14,000 feet) the vegetation is paramo type dominated by *fraylejon* (*Espeletia hartwegiana*) and bunchgrass (*Calamagrostis spp.*). The landscape is gradually impoverished in diversity and coverage toward a level of 4,200 meters, being replaced by the subparamo, where isolated individuals like *Senecio rufescens* can be found.

The animal biota comprehends a great number of endemic species or subspecies including the hummingbird (*Oxypogon guerinii stuebeli*).

Puracé National Park. This park is also located on the Cordillera Central and represents one of the most spectacular mountain areas in Colombia, the Almaguer or Colombian Massif. Within the park is the Sierra de los Coconucos, which has seven volcanic peaks. The one active peak is Puracé at 4,760 meters (15,600 feet), and the peak that has permanent snow is Pan de Azúcar at 5,000 meters (16,400 feet). Fifty lagoons and the upper basins of the Magdalena, Cauca, Caquetá, and Patiá rivers are other elements of this park.

Among the trees of the Andean forest, some of the most interesting are nasua (*Vallea stipularis*), pino colombiano (*Podocarpus oleifolius*), motilón (*Hieronyma colombiana*), and quina (*Cinchona pubescens*). In the paramo grow the *fraylejon* (*Espeletia hartwegiana*), the bamboo (*Swallenochloa tessellata*), *chite* or *guardarrocío* (*Hypericum spp.*) and bunchgrasses with *Calamagrostis spp.* predominating.

The fauna include some endangered species like spectacled bear (*Tremarctos ornatus*), northern Pudu deer (*Pudu mephistophiles*), and the Andean tapir (*Tapirus pinchaque*). There are more than 250 species of birds, such as the Andean condor (*Vultur gryphus*), the Andean crest eagle (*Oroaetus isidori*), the Andean cock of the rock (*Rupicola peruviana aequatorialis*), and the Andean guan (*Penelope montagnii montagnii*).

A visitor center, several trails, and a recreational area with camping and picnic zones have been established for the use of the public.

El Cocuy National Park. This 306,000-hectare (756,000-acre) park is located on the Cordillera Oriental, and it includes the Sierra Nevada del Cocuy, Chita, and Güicán with the highest crests of the cordillera (5,400 meters; 17,700 feet). The park has 22 snow peaks and is the largest mass of ice and snow north of the equator in South America. The great influence of glacial activity is evident in different parts of the park.

In the paramo and subparamo there are a large number of regionally endemic plants, such as *Senecio cocuyanus, Senecio cleefii, Espeletia lopezii,* and *Espeletia congestiflora.*

The park contains all the wildcats reported in Colombia. The birds are varied, and among them the Andean condor, the tanager (*Anisognathus igniventris*), and the ant-pitta (*Grallaria quitensis alticola*) are important.

Chocó Biogeographic Complex

This province is characterized by saturated rain forest, except in the south and Urabá, where there is a short period of annual drought. Some of the animals and plants are similar to those of the Amazonian zone.

It is believed that many plant and animal species originated in the Chocó Province and later extended their range toward the rain forest of Panama and Costa Rica. Conversely, the formation of the Panamanian isthmus contributed to the fact that many biotic elements of Central and North America were introduced to South America through the Chocó Province.

There are four national parks in this biogeographic complex: Katíos, Utría, Sanquianga, and Gorgona Island.

Los Katíos National Park. It is within the drainage of the Caribbean Sea, but its ecosystems are more representative of the geography of Chocó. Located at the frontier with Panama, Los Katíos embraces a mountain sector, the Sierra del Darién, and a flood or swampy plateau.

Among the hygrophytic vegetation there are *arracacho* (*Montrichardia arborescens*), *pangana* (*Raphia taedigera*), *cativo* (*Prioria copaifera*), *salero* (*Pachira acuatica*), and the palm *naidí* (*Euterpe precatoria*). In the hills there are several associations of plants, one of them, almost homogeneous, of *guipo, bonga*, or *ceiba bonga* (*Cavanillesia platanifolia*), and another dominated by the *palma mil pesos* (*Jessenia bataua*).

This is the habitat of several endangered mammals, among them the Central American tapir (*Tapirus bairdii*), the otter (*Lutra longicaudis*), giant anteater (*Myrmecophaga trydactila*), and manatee (*Trichechus manatus*). The spectacled bear (*Tremarctos ornatus*) has recently been recorded in the area. There are more than 400 species of birds, among which the eagles (*Spizaetus ornatus vicarius* and *Spizaetus tryannus serus*) and the green macaw (*Ara ambigua*) are endangered.

Gorgona National Park. The park embraces Gorgona and the Goronilla Islands as well as a marine sector that has coral reefs. It is located 56 kilometers (35 miles) from the continent.

Park topography is mountainous, with its highest point, Trinidad Peak, 330 meters (1,080 feet) above sea level. The islands are compounded of fundamental volcanic rocks covered by sedimentary deposits from the Quaternary and perhaps a vestige of a primitive cordillera. Twenty-five rivulets originate from the summit of Gorgona Island and flow outward to a shoreline notable for its beaches.

The vegetation includes a rain forest very rich in species, some of them endemic.

Endemic mammals include the sloth (*Bradypus variegatus gorgonae*), spiny rat (*Proechymis gorgonae*), aguit (*Dasyprocta punctata pandora*), and capucine monkey (*Cebus capucinus curtus*). There are mountain, marine, aquatic, and shore birds. The reptiles include three species of the genus *Anolis*, several species of snakes, one variety of spectacled caiman (*Caiman crocodilus chiapasius*), and five species of turtles, three of them marine. Among the marine mammals the most important is the humpback whale (*Megaptera novaeangliae*).

ADMINISTRATION

Since 1968, the National Institute for Renewable National Resources and the Environment (Instituto Nacional de los Recursos Naturales Renovables y del Ambiente or INDERENA) has had the duty of establishing and administering the reserves of the national park system. INDERENA is an independent institute belonging to the Agriculture Ministry. Within INDERENA the Division of National Parks is part of the Department of Forests, Water, and Soils and is responsible for the administration, planning, and supervision of the areas belonging to the national park system.

The aim of INDERENA with regards to the national park system is to achieve perpetual conservation of each area that has been set aside, permitting public use but avoiding any significant alterations of resources and ecosystems.

The Division of National Parks has a director and 6 other professionals. In the field there is a staff of 258 people, including 21 professional and 237 auxiliaries, park rangers, and workers. This staff is insufficient to effectively manage all the areas. For this reason seven areas have no staff people, and a park of 383,000 hectares (946,000 acres) has a staff of only 8 persons.

As a strategy for conserving the country's natural heritage with the concomitant objectives, the areas of the Colombian national park system have been a positive force, and despite the problems and defects that exist, they are the epitome of a suitable management project on the part of the national government. Consistent with the basic principles of the national park system, the economic development of park resources is prohibited. This prohibition extends to agricultural and livestock activities, industrial and commercial developments such as hotels, mining, and petroleum exploitation, and to timber harvest, hunting, and commercial fishing. Activities permitted in the national park system of Colombia are those required for conservation, recuperation, and control. Research, education, and recreation are also permitted.

Aside from inadequate funds, there are several important management problems:

1. In order to preserve self-regulating ecosystems, it was necessary to declare boundaries that included some private lands and legal settlements.
2. The public lacks sufficient awareness of and support for the national parks.
3. There is a lack of qualified personnel and virtually no opportunity for training of staff.
4. The parks lack management plans and a long-term planning process.
5. The Division of National Parks lacks sufficient status within the government.
6. The illegal removal of plants or animals continues.

I believe two changes are required for the national parks of Colombia to survive and flourish. First, a National Park Service or National Park Institute that reports directly to the Presidency of the Republic or the Agriculture Ministry must be created. Second, the programs of the reserves must be included within the National Development Plan.

BIBLIOGRAPHY

Cuatrecasas, José. *Observaciones geobotánicas en Colombia*. Serie botánica 27. Madrid: Museo Nacional de Ciencias Naturales, 1934.

De Schauensee, Rodolphe Meyer. *The Birds of Colombia*. Narberth, Pennsylvania: Livingston Publishing Co., 1964.

Franky, Simón, and Pedro I. Rodríguez. *Parque Nacional Isla de Salamanca*. Bogotá: INDERENA, 1976.

Hernández, C. Jorge, Heliodoro Sánchez, and others. *Plan de Manejo del Parque Nacional Los Nevados*. 4 vols. Bogotá: INDERENA, Carder, Cortolima, Cramsa and CRQ, 1985.

INDERENA. *Colombia Parques Nacionales*. Bogotá: Financiera Eléctrica Nacional 1984.

Meganck, Richard A. "Colombia National Parks: An Analysis of Management Problems and Perceived Values." Ph.D. dissertation, Oregon State University Corvalis, 1975.

Prahl Von, Henry, Felipe Guhl, and Max Grögl. *Gorgona*. Bogotá: Universidad de los Andes, Comité de Publicaciones, 1979.

Proyecto Radargramétrico del Amazonas. *La Amazonia Colombiana y sus Recursos*. Bogotá: Talleres gráficos Italgraf, 1979.

Rodríguez, José Vicente. *Aves del Parque Nacional Los Katios Chocó Colombia*. Bogotá: Proyecto Instituto Colombiano Agropecuario-INDERENA-U.S. Department of Agriculture, 1982.

Sánchez, Heliodoro. *Los Parques Nacionales de Alta Montaña. Un estudio de caso El Plan de Manejo del Parque Nacional Natural Los Nevados*. Caracas, Venezuela: INDERENA 1987.

Sánchez, Heliodoro, Victor Vasquez, and Luis E. Valderrama. *Diagnostico de las areas del Sistema de Parques Nacionales de Colombia*. Bogotá: INDERENA, Oficina de Planeación del Sector Agropecuario, 1983.

Van der Hammen, Thomas, Alfonso Pérez Preciado, and Polidoro Pinto, eds. *La Cordillera Central Colombiana Transecto Parque Los Nevados. Introducción y datos iniciales. Studies on Tropical Andean Ecosystems*. Vaduz: J. Cramer, n.d.

FEDERAL REPUBLIC OF GERMANY

7

Hans Bibelriether

The national parks of Germany demonstrate the importance and the difficulty of nature preservation in a densely populated nation where almost every area has been radically modified by economic utilization for a period of centuries.

HISTORY

National parks in the Federal Republic of Germany do not have a long tradition. The first national park, Bayerischer Wald, was opened only in 1970. Since then, three more national parks have been created, and the first goals and objectives of national parks have been laid down in the Bavarian Nature Conservation Law of 1973.

Actual parks may be recent, but the idea of creating national parks in Germany dates back more than seventy years. In 1911 a suggestion for the establishment of a national park came before the Prussian *Landtag,* the territorial parliament. World War I and postwar events prevented its realization. Similarly, in 1938 a large Böhmerwald National Park was proposed, but World War II prevented its realization.

Finally, in 1966 private nature conservation organizations promoted the establishment of a national park in the Bavarian Forest. The idea was supported by local politicians who hoped that a national park would contribute to the development of tourism in the region. After a discussion lasting for three years the Bavarian parliament passed a unanimous resolution to establish Germany's first national park, Bayerischer Wald. In 1972 a second national park, Berchtesgaden, was established, also in Bavaria. Bayerischer Wald is managed by a State Forest Administration, which reports to the Bavarian Ministry of State for Food,

Agriculture, and Forestry. Berchtesgaden is managed by the Bavarian Ministry of State for Environment.

In 1985 and 1986 two more national parks were established in the north of Germany. These are Schleswig-Holstein's Wattenmeer National Park, created by the state parliament, and Lower Saxony's Wattenmeer National Park, created by the state Ministry of Agriculture (Figure 7.1). At present plans are being discussed that aim at creating a fifth national park to be located in Hesse and protect a large area of deciduous forest.

There is a different situation with regard to nature reserves. The first of these areas was established more than 100 years ago. According to 1980 statistics, there were 1,262 nature reserves covering 203,176 hectares, 0.82 percent of the total area of the Federal Republic of Germany. In addition, there are eleven nature reserves located along coastlines and primarily protecting waters. German nature reserves are limited with regard to the quality of their protective function. Normally they are relatively small and therefore exposed to stress factors resulting from their environment. Effective management is frequently absent, and the larger nature reserves often suffer from common agricultural and forest use, hunting, fishing, and mass tourism. There are only a very few nature reserves in the Federal Republic of Germany where entry is forbidden. So it is only natural that they often fail to fulfill their goals in the field of nature conservation.

PARKS AND RESERVES

Bayerischer Wald (Bavarian Forest) National Park

The largest continuous forest area in central Europe stretches along the mountain ridge between Bavaria and Bohemia, the present frontier between the Federal Republic of Germany and Czechoslovakia. The core area, with its two highest parks, Rachel (1,453 meters) and Lusen (1,373 meters), is a landscape of great beauty, composed of seminatural forests, moors, rivers, and lakes and is home to a wide variety of rare species of flora and fauna.

On June 11, 1969, 13,000 hectares in the heart of this extensive area of forested mountains was established as Germany's first national park by unanimous decision of the Bavarian parliament. On October 7, 1970, the National Park Bayerischer Wald was officially opened to the public by Dr. Hans Eisenmann, the Bavarian minister of state for food, agriculture and forestry, as Bavaria's contribution to the European Nature Conservation Year.

The objectives laid down in the parliamentary decision were consistently pursued by the Bavarian Ministry of Food, Agriculture and Forestry, which manages the area in accordance with the 1969 recommendations of the International Union for the Conservation of Nature (IUCN) and of the Bavarian Nature Conservation Law of 1973. The biocenoses are allowed to develop according to their own natural laws. Gradually, commercial exploitation of timber and other forest products is being eliminated and human intervention discontinued.

Figure 7.1
National Parks of the Federal Republic of Germany

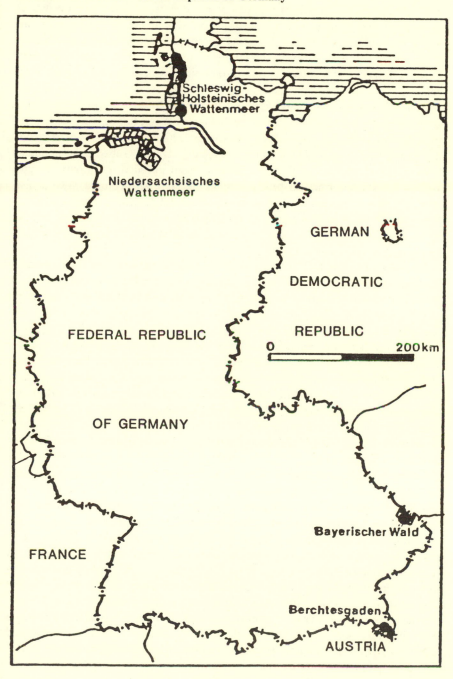

Today Bayerischer Wald National Park is firmly anchored in the public consciousness. The consistency with which the planned nature conservation program has been carried out (nearly two-thirds of the area has already been designated as strict reserves), the complex scientific work that has made the national park one of the best researched wooded areas in central Europe, and the wide variety of amenities and facilities for visitors have won international acclaim and gained for it the respect and recognition of a number of bodies as a national park in the genuine sense of the term.

General Geology. The Bavarian and Bohemian forest occupy the area of a complex mountain range. During the early Paleozoic era, this region was covered by a shallow sea. Erosional debris, chiefly sand, mud, and marl, was carried to the marine basin from surrounding mountains. During subsequent mountain building (orogeny), these marine sediments were intruded by granitic magma and complexly deformed to produce rocks like the dark-colored mica schists now exposed at Rachel Peak and in the Rachel Lake wall. During the late Paleozoic Variscan orogeny, molten granitic magma again penetrated the earlier rocks and cooled to form granite porphyry containing large feldspar phenocrysts. These rocks comprise the Lusen massif.

Weather and Climate. The climate of the national park region is continental, marked by comparatively low temperatures, averaging 3° Celsius at the highest elevations and 6° Celsius in the valleys. The difference in elevation between the 1,453-meter Rachel Peak and valleys of the national park lying about 700 meters lower is the cause of substantial climatic differences corresponding to those between southern Bavaria and northern Sweden. In the high altitudes snow remains on the ground for an average of seven months and in the other areas five to six months.

Biocenoses. For a long time the raw climate prevented man from settling on the frontier ridge and cultivating it. Here he actually exploited the wealth of the forests later than anywhere else in central Europe.

Around 1850 about half of the mountain frontier was still covered with primary forests. In the following 120 years, commercial exploitation often produced a fundamental structural change in the forest cover. In spite of all the pressures on forest resources resulting from two world wars and the subsequent redevelopment, German foresters succeeded in conserving for posterity the actual substance of the forests. Extensive areas have retained a seminatural character. An ecological evaluation by the University of Munich reported that 45 percent of the surface of the national park was planted with ecologically high-quality forests and vegetation units; only 5 percent of the surface was occupied by ecologically low-quality biotopes (e.g., timber stands alien to the site). This analysis supports the appropriateness of designating this site as a national park.

The forest is the formative element and the determinative habitat of the national park; it covers more than 98 percent of the park's surface. The forest is composed essentially of three natural woodland communities: mountain spruce forest, meadow spruce forest, and mountain mixed forest.

Mountain spruce forest is the natural form of vegetation under the extreme climatic conditions associated with altitudes above approximately 1,150 meters. In the summer growth periods, spruce, with their narrow canopies and dense branching, often reaching the ground, mature slowly. The individual trees are widely separated and can withstand the exceptional loads of snow and ice.

The natural regeneration of the mountain spruce forest follows an unusual course. The young spruce grow in small clearings on the leaf mold of fallen trees or decayed tree stumps. Here they find a nutritious and uniformly moist germinating and root bed. They are favorably situated compared with the soil flora and avoid the extreme climatic conditions obtaining directly on the ground.

The natural meadow spruce forest in the wet valleys provides a contrast to the mountain spruce forest. The cold air descending from the slopes collects here.

The trees of the meadow spruce forest are branched to the ground; the more boggy the soil, the more loosely they stand. Here, to a greater extent than at the high attitudes, the regeneration of the forest is brought about by wind throw, for on the wet soils the spruce strike only very shallow roots.

A plant community rich in peat mosses, cranberries, and black alder shrubs merges into the often extensive sphagnum bogs of the valleys. The Grosse Filz and the Klosterfilz on the periphery of the national park are examples of this type of particularly extensive and primeval bog.

The natural site of the mountain mixed forest is the warm slope zone of the national park. Its principal tree species—spruce, fir, and beech—complement one another in their characteristic features and build up mighty forests in terraced form, strong in growth and very diverse in type. In primary mountain mixed forests, mighty old trees tower over the canopy and protect the forest from storm. The trees reach an age of 400 to 500 years and a maximum height of over 50 meters.

The remnants of primary forest around Rachel Lake give us an idea of its wild and primeval character. In the jungle of Rachel Lake trees are born, live, and die in complete accord with the laws of nature.

Up to 25 percent of all wood in the primary forests consists of dying and fallen trees. The dead wood is not only of great importance for the regeneration of the forest but also provides the basis for a rich animal and plant life.

The seminatural, mountain mixed forest of the national park provides critical habitat for many species of rare or endangered fauna. The white-backed woodpecker needs dried up, decayed, and soft broad-leaved wood. Rotten spruce with brittle crowns are absolutely vital for the three-toed woodpecker. The black woodpecker needs rotten but huge old broad-leaved trees for drilling its nest holes and bolt holes.

Goals and Objectives. According to the Bavarian Nature Conservation Law of 1973, the national park serves the interests of nature conservation, research, education in biology, and recreation insofar as it does not clash with conservation.

Nature Conservation. Nature conservation enjoys unconditional priority in the

Bayerischer Wald National Park. The natural environmental forces in this area are allowed to develop as far as possible without human intervention. The objective is to preserve natural and seminatural ecosystems rich with indigenous flora and fauna.

In strict compliance with the nature conservation policy, the 8,000 hectares of forest that are most valuable and worthy of protection have been declared reserved zones in which no more human intervention of any sort can take place. This means that the national park is now one of the largest continuous forest protection areas in central Europe. In other areas, the forests that have suffered structural changes through commercial exploitation in the last 120 years are being returned to a seminatural state by carefully planned measures. An essential requirement for this was the restoration of a reasonable balance between the stocks of red and roe deer and the vegetation upon which they feed. As a result of this restoration, natural forest rejuvenation is again feasible. These and other interventions have been carried out to restore forests and inland waters that suffered structural changes in the last century.

Commercial use of the forests in the past has reduced the wide variety of fauna; particularly affected were the big predators, birds of prey, owls, and the black stork. The return of the forest vegetation now provides an opportunity for restoring the number of fauna species to its original level. A number of rare species, e.g., eagle owl and common raven, have been established. The capercaillie, threatened with extinction in our country, finds one of its last refuges in the national park. Capercaillie are bred in the national park and released to improve the natural stocks.

Research. Successful nature conservation entails research of the habitats of endangered species of flora and fauna and their reciprocal relationships. This is why large-scale basic and applied research is carried out in the national park. A complete assessment of the diverse interrelations and laws governing comparatively undisturbed biocenoses can provide valuable aids for nature conservation as well as for the safeguarding in general of our basic natural resources.

Education in Ecology. The education of our fellow citizens in nature conservation and environmental protection is today a central sociopolitical task. Bayerischer Wald National Park provides unusually good possibilities for this purpose. It is visited by about 1.5 million interested persons annually, and its research supplies comprehensive information. Here the workings of nature can be observed and learned under the guidance of experts.

Successful nature conservation is possible only with the support of the general public, so the existence of the national park must be used to foster a better understanding of these matters. Opportunities afforded by the sometimes unconscious readiness to learn of most national park visitors are being exploited, and several educational facilities have been set up. The ''Nationalparkhaus,'' a generously designed information center, offers a wide range of information and opportunities for education. It was recently renamed to honor the memory of

Dr. Hans Eisenmann, the minister of state for food, agriculture and forest and the "father" of the first German national park, who died in 1987. A botanical and geological terrain near the visitors center contains specimens of all fauna species and rocks to be found in the national park. A large open-air game enclosure allows visitors to observe numerous indigenous species of fauna and also species that formerly occurred here. A youth forest center enables school classes to stay for longer periods so that they can make a more intensive study of the national park.

Recreation and Tourism. With the establishment of the national park the Bavarian parliament intended to strengthen the economic power of the frontier zone by the promotion of tourism. The Bavarian Nature Conservation Law envisages the development of national parks for recreational purposes insofar as conservation permits.

Expectations that the establishment of the national park would lead to a boom in tourism have been fulfilled. Tourism is one of the pillars supporting the economic development of the region surrounding the national park. Through the provision of attractive recreational and visitor facilities and the use of selective control measures, it has been possible to accommodate tourism without prejudicing the national park's main objective of conservation.

Organization. The whole national park area of about 13,300 hectares is the property of the Free State of Bavaria. The Nationalparkverwaltung (National Park Administration) Bayerischer Wald with offices in Grafenau is responsible for the management and upkeep of the national park and subordinate to the Bavarian State Ministry for Food, Agriculture and Forestry.

Berchtesgaden National Park

The history of this reserve dates back long before it became Germany's second national park in 1978. As early as 1910, in an effort to prevent further changes due to the human exploitation that has shaped this landscape for centuries, Königssee, a scenic lake situated in the Bavarian Alps, was declared a "flora reserve." Eleven years later an area of 21,000 hectares became a nature reserve. Still, the area continued to be exploited for hunting, forestry, fishing, and increasingly modern forms of agriculture in spite of the fact that the land was owned by the Bavarian state.

During the postwar era, demands for improved protection became audible, increasingly so since 1970, the European Year of Nature Protection. On August 1, 1978, regulations concerning Berchtesgaden National Park came into effect. The 21,000 hectares of the original nature reserve were declared a national park, and an additional 25,000 hectares adjacent to the northern border were designated as a buffer zone.

The national park area is determined by the Reiteralm, Hochkalter, and Watzmann mountain ranges, by Steinernes Meer, and by three deep valleys, Königssee, Klausbach, and Wimbach. The important ecosystems being protected include high mountain regions with alpine meadows, fields of dwarf pines, and rocky areas; mountain forests including mountain spruce forests, larch and cembra pine forests, and the mixed forest of spruce, white fir, and beech at lower elevations; the mountain lakes of Königssee and Obersee; and the alpine pastures resulting from traditional use.

Many species of endangered fauna and flora are found here. Among them are the golden eagle, owl, wood grouse, black grouse, and snow grouse. A great number of interesting mammals are here as well: the chamois, the ibex, the red deer, and the marmot. Preparations have been made to reintroduce the lynx and the vulture, which were extirpated in this area more than 100 years ago.

For more than a century nature enthusiasts and tourists have visited this area because of its outstanding scenic variety. As a consequence, certain localities like St. Bartholomä and the area near the Obersee have suffered significant environmental degradation.

Here, as in other German nature reserves, the legal regulations are insufficient to direct the visitors, who do damage by trampling the vegetation. There are many marked trails, and protective huts are available. A small information center is located in Königssee, and a large one with various museums and exhibits was opened, in 1988, in the ancient monastery of Berchtesgaden.

The forest has suffered major changes brought about by its exploitation in past centuries. Appropriate measures will be taken to restore its natural structures. A problem that must still be solved is that of pasturage in forest areas. Based on long-established rights, a number of private persons are allowed to drive cattle and sheep into national park forests for the purpose of grazing. Another problem to be solved is that of an excessive population of red deer, which have been preserved in the past few decades for hunting reasons. In some places they inhibit the natural regeneration of the forest. Interference from military maneuvers is also a threat to the park. Negotiations with competent authorities are required to halt this practice.

Wattenmeer (Wadden Sea) National Park in Schleswig-Holstein

Federal Germany's latest national park extends along the North Sea coastline between the Elbe estuary and the Danish border. It covers an area of 285,000 hectares encompassing wadden mud flats, small man-made islands called "Halligen," sand cliffs, and some offshore islands. The larger Halligen and islands are excluded from the national park because of their intensive use.

The park is split into three zones. Zone 1, covering 30 percent of the park, prohibits all farming and other economic uses except for traditional fishing and restricted grazing that aids coastal protection. There is no significant public access. This zone provides an important resting, nesting, and molting site for marine birds. Seals bask on the traditional sandbanks, and there are various important sites of geomorphological interest. Zone 2 acts as a protective buffer for zone 1. Farming is permitted here as long as it is compatible with wildlife interests. The public is excluded from certain sensitive sites. Zone 3 consists of the remaining areas. Certain types of economic activity such as sand extraction, harbor developments, and recreation are allowed by permit in zone 3. The Wattenmeer National Park of Schleswig-Holstein complies only partly with the international criteria for a national park. Because different patterns of use and coastal protection measures are accepted over a majority of the area, it probably will not qualify for the IUCN list of national parks, category II.

This area provides several natural habitats. The underwater sections, the mud flats, and the wadden themselves are subjected to much tidal movement. The rich wadden are of outstanding importance for the propagation of fish, for wadden and marine birds, and as a food resource for seals. The so-called salt meadows are only flooded by tidal waves. They support specific plant communities and are very rich in invertebrates. They are also important as breeding sites of threatened marine bird species and as high-water resting sites. The primary dunes and sands, as well as offshore islands without vegetation, provide breeding sites, especially for marine swallows, and serve as resting sites for wadden birds.

The size of the national park and the inclusion of traditional areas of use led to great conflicts with the native population. These conflicts were reduced by giving higher priority to coastal protection, cleansing of island pollution, and control over fishing than to nature conservation. Today it is unclear whether the long-term conservation objectives of a national park will be compatible with this development. Another important problem is the damage caused by visitors. The Wadden Sea is very attractive to tourists. It will be necessary to provide greater protection to sensitive areas and to channel visitor movement to the least sensitive areas of the park. In this context public relations and education are very important.

Zone 3, the outermost zone of the national park, is radically altered by military flying and artillery practice, merchant marine traffic, and even exploratory oil drilling, which is carried on as a result of permits granted several decades ago. Additional concerns include the dwindling numbers of living creatures in the North Sea and the increasing pollution discharged from the estuaries of the Elbe and the Weser. Also increasing are discharges into the North Sea, burning of industrial waste, oil slicks, and solid waste disposal at sea. Indeed, ever-increasing water pollution poses the greatest threat to the park. In 1988 approximately 4,000 seals—half the existing population—died as a result of this sea pollution. The battle against these considerable threats will have to be fought in interregional and international arenas. For the present, there is no victory in sight.

Wattenmeer (Wadden Sea) National Park in Lower Saxony

It was not until 1986 that the fourth German national park was founded. In comparison with Wattenmeer National Park in Schleswig-Holstein, the situation for nature conservation in Lower Saxony is even worse. This national park covers 280,000 hectares and generally serves the same purposes as the Wattenmeer National Park in Schleswig-Holstein. Its zoning is also similar. Zone 1 contains the most important breeding sites for birds and critical habitat for seals. Here human intrusion is forbidden. Zone 2 embraces 54 percent of the park's area. Here, as in German landscape reserves, regulations are relatively permissive and generally ineffective with regard to nature conservation. The only actions forbidden are those that transform the character of the Wadden Sea including the islands, the natural features of the landscape, or the enjoyment of nature. There are no significant regulations limiting use for hunting, fishing, exploitation of mineral resources, etc. Zone 3 has the weakest regulations for conservation and protection and serves primarily as a recreational area. It may be used as a beach or an area where people can take a cure.

Like Wattenmeer National Park in Schleswig-Holstein, this national park fails to meet IUCN standards. It remains to be seen whether it will be possible in the course of time to actually achieve conservation objectives or whether these areas will only have the character of landscape reserves.

ADMINISTRATION

In the Federal Republic of Germany nature conservation is a responsibility of the various regional or state governments, called *Bundesländer*. The national parks and most of the larger nature reserves are owned by the *Länder*. Land in some of the smaller nature reserves is owned by local communities or private persons. Because the *Bund* (federal government) itself owns no land, its role is limited to establishing a legal framework for conservation. Therefore, in Germany, as in Australia, national parks are established not by the federal government but by the governments of the different *Länder*. They are the highest competent nature conservation authority in Germany.

As there are no uniform laws, each of the four presently existing national parks is founded on a different legal basis. Without uniform regulations the ability of each park to fulfill the most urgent tasks of nature conservation also varies.

From the description of the different parks it is evident that each park has a different set of objectives and a different degree of importance for nature conservation. While the Bayerischer Wald, the first and smallest of the German national parks, is fulfilling tasks of nature conservation in a relatively consequential way, the national parks along the North Sea coast do this only to a small extent. Berchtesgaden National Park lies between the two extremes with respect to the quality of its protective function.

The strictest regulations concerning national parks are laid down in the Bavarian Nature Conservation Law of 1973, which defines national parks as follows:

- landscapes that are of outstanding importance because of their balanced nature potential, their topographical features, their scenic variety; that cover an area of at least 10,000 hectares; and that have the necessary qualifications for nature reserves.

- areas devoted to the conservation and scientific observation of natural and seminatural biocenoses with indigenous flora and fauna, as rich in species as possible, and free from economic exploitation.

- areas open to the public for purposes of education and recreation insofar as these do not clash with conservation.

In Bayerischer Wald National Park all human exploitation and intervention have been discontinued in forests covering over 8,000 hectares. Control of the deer population has also been stopped, and visitors may enter the park only on designated trails. Caring for visitors and catering to their recreational and educational interests also play an important role. Every year at least 30,000 visitors are guided through the park. Instructional trails and other means of education are available, and a large visitor center provides information about the original forest.

A high standard of research supplies important information for management decisions and visitor education. Bayerischer Wald National Park is subordinate to an autonomous administration that is exclusively responsible for all measures taken in this region. It has far-reaching authority and reports to the director of the Bavarian State Forest Administration.

In Berchtesgaden National Park nature conservation objectives are defined in a similar way, but there are few restrictions on tourist traffic. Nearly all areas can be entered without restriction, insofar as the terrain permits. Management of the area for nature conservation has been uncertain. The administration is part of a subordinate local authority dependent on elected politicians. As a result, Berchtesgaden National Park was denied award of the European Diploma category A by the European Council at Strasbourg while Bayerischer Wald National Park received this honor in 1987.

The national parks along the North Sea coast suffer from their vastness. Too many areas, which will always be used and exploited in a way harmful or contrary to the objectives of nature conservation, have become parts of the national parks. This must lead to conflicts between exploitation and protection that cannot be settled. It is too soon to know whether these national parks will really contribute to better protection of a unique ecosystem in the Wattenmeer along the German coast. It will be several years before one can say whether the establishment of these two national parks has been a contribution to nature conservation of international importance.

BIBLIOGRAPHY

Bibelriether, H. *Nationalpark Bavarian Forest*. Grafenau: Morsak-Verlag, 1987.
―――. *Nationalpark Bayerischer Wald*. Greven: KILDA-Verlag, 1979.
Bibelriether, H., and H. Burger. *Nationalpark Bayerischer Wald*. Grafenau: Morsak-Verlag and München: Süddeutscher Verlag, 1984.
Bibelriether, H., and H. Strunz. *Nationalparkführer Bayerischer Wald*. München: BLV-Verlagsgesellschaft, 1980.
Bibelriether, H., and R. L. Schreiber. *Die Nationalparke Europas*. Müchen: Süddeutscher Verlag, 1989.

Flessner, Günter, ed. *Nationalpark Schleswig-Holsteinisches Wattenmeer*. Kiel: Ministerium für Ernährung, Landwirtschaft und Forsten, 1985.

Haug, M., and R. Strobl. *Eine Landschaft wird Nationalpark*. Grafenau: Nationalparkverwaltung, 1985.

Katalog der naturschutzgebiete in der Bundesrepublik Deutschland. Greven: KILDA-Verlag, 1979.

Meister, G. *Nationalpark Berchtesgaden*. München: Kindler-Verlag, 1976.

Zierl, H. *Nationalpark Berchtesgaden—Geschichte eines Schutzgebietes*. Berchtesgaden: Anton Plenk KG Verlag, 1980.

Zierl, H., et al. *Nationalpark Berchtesgaden - Der Watzmann*. Berchtesgaden: Anton Plenk KG Verlag, 1982.

GREAT BRITAIN 8

Brynmor Hugh Green

In Great Britain conservation of wildlife and landscape and the provision of access into the countryside for people to enjoy these things have developed rather differently from other parts of the world. Millennia of human exploitation has left very little representation of natural ecosystems and brought most of the land into fragmented, private ownership. It has, therefore, not been possible to establish large national parks following the international pattern with extensive areas of state-owned, wild, undeveloped country. But farming, which accounts for some 80 percent of the land area (the remainder being divided almost equally between urban development and forestry), has created a wide variety of habitats and landscapes rich in wildlife, scenic beauty, and recreational opportunity. According to its intensity, these vary from cultivated field and hedgerow landscapes to seminatural rough grazings, such as heaths and moors, closely analogous to natural ecosystems in other parts of the world. State conservation has protected a representative selection of these landscapes and ecosystems with a dual system of large national parks, principally to protect cultural landscapes and provide access, and smaller, more numerous, and more strictly protected national nature reserves to safeguard ecosystems and wildlife.

As the traditional farming practices, which created and maintained this countryside, have been replaced by modern, more intensive and environmentally damaging agricultural technologies, national parks and national nature reserves have become areas where effort has focused on developing land uses where man and nature interact in a more harmonious, sustainable way to maintain Britain's heritage of wildlife and landscape. With burgeoning world population and ever-increasing pressures on land, integrated multipurpose management of this kind must inevitably become an important part of conservation policy everywhere. Indeed, this conclusion is recognized in the World Conservation Strategy. Thus, the British approach may offer a model of increasing relevance for the rest of the world. Conservation in Britain is also unusual for the major role played by private, voluntary organizations. They were instrumental in the development of state conservation and now work in close partnership with it.

HISTORY

The beginnings of conservation in Britain go back over a thousand years to the hunting chases, or forests, set aside by the Norman kings. Some of these, such as the New Forest, still survive today as de facto, if not de jure, national parks. Wildlife and landscape conservation, as distinct from game conservation, is, however, much more recent. The origins of the movement can be traced back to sweeping land-use changes that took place mainly between 1750 and 1850. During the period large open fields and extensive wild heaths and other rough grazing land, previously farmed in common by peasant landowners, were statutorily enclosed into fenced or hedged field systems and the land improved and reorganized into a capitalist agricultural system. Poetry at the time reflected the widespread regret at the loss of the old landscape and its wildlife as heaths were plowed, marshes drained, and trees felled.

It was a poet, William Wordsworth, who in 1810 seems to have been the first to propound the idea of a national park when he suggested that

persons of pure taste throughout the whole island, who by their visits (often repeated) to the Lakes in the North of England, testify that they deem the district a sort of national property, in which every man has a right and interest who has an eye to perceive and a heart to enjoy.[1]

But state conservation was still a long way off in the future. It was nearly 150 years until the Lake District was designated a national park.

Positive moves to protect what was left of unenclosed, wild countryside began in 1865 with the formation of the Commons, Open Spaces and Footpaths Preservation Society. This first British conservation organization, of which the philosopher John Stuart Mill was a founding member, used litigation and parliamentary action to stem the loss of common lands, particularly those near towns that could be readily enjoyed by the now largely urban population. Its secretary, Robert Hunter, saw that this was not going to be enough. If the country's landscape heritage was to be preserved for the long-term benefit of the nation, what was required was an organization that could hold and manage land. With Octavia Hill and Hardwicke Rawnsley, he established such an organization in 1895. It was called the National Trust for Places of Historic Interest or Natural Beauty. In 1907 it was reconstituted under its own act of Parliament and given powers to hold land inalienable. The trust's power to hold land in perpetuity can only be overridden by an act of Parliament. It has become the most important voluntary conservation body in Britain. Leading figures in the

Romantic movement, including John Ruskin, Holman Hunt, and William Morris, played a part in its early activities, and the biologist Thomas Huxley, Charles Darwin's champion in the great debate on evolution, was at the trust's first meeting.

Huxley represented another main force in the developing conservation movement, the increasingly influential natural scientists. Their demonstration of the intrinsic interest and sensibilities of animals was accompanied by a growing concern for animal welfare. This led to the formation of a Society for the Prevention of Cruelty to Animals in 1824 and a Society for the Protection of Birds in 1889. Early in its history the National Trust became more concerned with protecting landscape, ancient monuments, and buildings than wildlife, and in 1912 influential naturalists were stimulated to form the Society for the Promotion of Nature Reserves to encourage the trust to establish more nature reserves. In 1915 the society published a list of potential nature reserves in response to the renewed threat to the countryside presented by the wartime plow-up campaign.

Between the wars these voluntary conservation organizations came to play an important role in promoting government action for conservation, lobbying for a state organization to protect the countryside and establish a system of national parks like those that were already established in the United States and several other countries. The campaign was spearheaded by councils for the preservation of rural England, Scotland, and Wales founded respectively in 1926, 1927, and 1928 to fight urban sprawl and other threats to the countryside. In 1929 a government committee, chaired by Christopher Addison, parliamentary secretary to the minister of agriculture, was established to explore the need for national parks. Although the committee saw potential conflicts between access and conservation, it reported positively in 1931. This was the time of the Great Depression, and the government decided that the economic situation precluded action. This and previous failures to gain access to open country denied by landowners occasioned a famous protest on Easter Day 1932 when ramblers made a mass trespass onto a grouse shooting moor in the Peak District. This outdoors movement, led by bodies such as the Ramblers Association, Youth Hostels Association, and Cyclists Touring Club, was the third great force pressing for national parks. The voluntary conservation organizations continued to lobby the government, their activities focused by a Standing Committee on National Parks established in 1936.

It was not until the early part of World War II that all the years of lobbying at last began to succeed. The government decided to prepare a national plan for postwar reconstruction, and it set up a number of committees whose reports and recommendations still form the basis of land-use planning in Britain. A Committee on Land Utilisation in Rural Areas was established under Lord Justice Scott. In 1942 it recommended the establishment of national and regional parks and nature reserves, and a central authority to control them. The government appointed John Dower, an eminent planner, architect, senior civil servant, and leading advocate of national parks to develop these proposals, which he did in a report published in 1945.[2]

Dower's proposals, which included specific recommendations for ten national parks, met with strong support in some quarters and suspicion in others. The Ministry of Agriculture, the Forestry Commission, and those concerned with developing new planning powers for local government saw them impinging on their areas of responsibility. A government National Parks Committee, under Sir Arthur Hobhouse, was therefore appointed to develop the proposals and prepare the foundations for legislation. At this time those concerned primarily with the protection of wildlife began to see their interests diverging from those more interested in landscape and access. The British Ecological Society, the Royal Society, and the Society for the Promotion of Nature Reserves had all published memoranda to the government making recommendations for a state system of nature reserves, and a "Biological Service" to run them, with the emphasis on their use for scientific research and education. A Wildlife Conservation Special Committee was set up under Sir Julian Huxley to explore these aspects. Hobhouse and Huxley published their reports in 1947. Their recommendations endorsed and elaborated those of the earlier committees and were embodied in the National Parks and Access to the Countryside Act of 1949.

This act established a National Parks Commission for England and Wales with duties to preserve and enhance natural beauty, designate national parks, encourage facilities for the enjoyment of national parks, designate areas of outstanding natural beauty, and give advice and assistance to local authorities. Contrary to the recommendations of the Dower and Hobhouse reports, the new National Parks Commission was given no powers to own and manage land in the national parks. Indeed, it was given no real share in running the parks. This was to be the function of local authorities, who were also given powers to acquire access land by agreement or compulsory purchase. The reason for this was that immense new powers had already been given to local governments as a result of another part of the planning for postwar reconstruction. A Town and Country Planning Act of 1947 gave local authorities far-reaching planning powers, particularly to control development, and this was seen as the main requirement in the national parks. The National Parks Authority was left as a small advisory, rather than executive, body.

In contrast, the recommendations of the Huxley committee were much more fully effected. A separate government agency, the Nature Conservancy, was established independently under Royal Charter with duties to establish and manage national nature reserves; give scientific advice, especially to local authorities; and carry out ecological research relevant to nature conservation. It was given powers under the 1949 act to hold and manage land as national nature reserves, and to acquire it by compulsory process if necessary.

Three further categories of protective designation were made under the 1949 act. Both the Hobhouse and the Huxley committees had recommended that there should be "Conservation Areas" intermediate in size and in the intensity of their management for conservation between national parks and national nature re-serves. This proposal was realized as "Areas of Outstanding Natural Beauty," to be designated by the National Parks Commission and protected by a tightening of the planning control by local authorities. In practice, very large areas have been designated to protect landscape beauty. With no provision for access, however, the effectiveness of this category of protected land has been questioned. To supplement the series of national nature reserves, local authorities were also given powers to establish local nature reserves. No government grants were made available for this purpose, but some important areas have been thus protected, especially where the local authority already owned the land. More significant, the Nature Conservancy has notified local planning authorities of sites of special scientific interest. Thereby the conservancy's views must be taken into account before any development affecting these sites is permitted. These sites form a national network of protected areas. The notification procedure was originally intended to help protect them until such time as they could be made nature reserves. Many have been so protected, and subsequent legislation has also made it possible to give them additional protection in their own right, through man-agement agreements with landowners.

By 1957 ten national parks, covering 1.36 million hectares (5,250 square miles), had been designated in England and Wales, amounting to 9 percent of the total land area. (See Figure 8.1 and Table 8.1.) Ironically no national parks have been designated in Scotland, arguably the only part of Britain with sufficient wild country to justify national parks in the sense of the international definition. A committee under Sir Douglas Ramsay had recommended the establishment of five parks in Scotland at the time of the Hobhouse report. But its proposals were not implemented as pressures on land were felt to be much less in Scotland and landowners were not sympathetic. Nevertheless, planning control has been strengthened over the areas—now designated as national scenic areas—that had been proposed as parks, and additional areas in Scotland have been protected as forest and regional parks. The Nature Conservancy's authority covers Scotland as well as England and Wales, and some of its large Scottish national nature reserves, notably the Cairngorms (25,948 hectares, 64,120 acres), Inverpolly (10,861 hectares, 26,840 acres), and Beinn Eighe (4,755 hectares, 11,750 acres), are Britain's closest approximations to national parks in other parts of the world. In England only two of the twelve areas identified in the Hobhouse report as potential national parks have not been so designated. These are the Norfolk Broads and South Downs. In 1988 a form of national park status and many aspects of national park protection were conferred on the Broads by means of a Broads Authority. The South Downs has been designated as an area of outstand-ing natural beauty. Parts have been protected as national nature reserves, and additional protection is anticipated for much of the area.

Because land use has intensified far more than was envisaged, national nature reserve designation has proceeded much further than was proposed in the Huxley report. By 1985 there were 197 national nature reserves in Britain covering an

Figure 8.1
National Parks and National Nature Reserves in the U.K.[a]

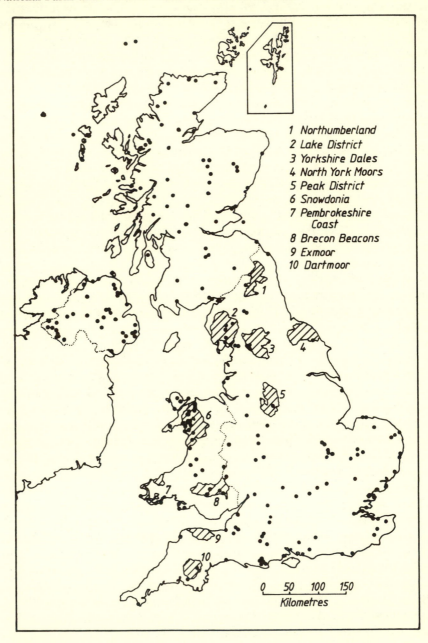

1 Northumberland
2 Lake District
3 Yorkshire Dales
4 North York Moors
5 Peak District
6 Snowdonia
7 Pembrokeshire
  Coast
8 Brecon Beacons
9 Exmoor
10 Dartmoor

0   50   100   150
Kilometres

Note:
[a] National parks are represented by shaded areas and
identified by number. National nature reserves are represented
by dots.

area of 150,470 hectares (371,800 acres). Of this, some 26 percent was owned by the Nature Conservancy, the remainder held under lease or management agreement. In addition, 1.43 million hectares (3.53 million acres) were designated as 4,497 sites of special scientific interest.

Since 1949 two important statutes have conferred additional protection to wildlife and landscapes. In 1968, reflecting growing public recreation pressures on the countryside, particularly in the southeast where there were no national parks, a Countryside Act was passed with measures to accommodate it. Foremost among these was the establishment of a new category of protected land, the "country park." These were to be relatively small areas of open countryside near towns for picnicking, rambling, and other kinds of informal recreation. By 1983 there were 164, covering 21,296 hectares (52,600 acres). Some contain important wildlife habitats and are also designated in whole or part as sites of special scientific interest or even local nature reserves. Similarly, some parts of national parks are designated as sites of special scientific interest or as national nature reserves. Country parks are mostly held and managed by local authorities who are given government grants for doing so. The National Parks Commission was reconstituted as the Countryside Commission in the 1968 act, reflecting wider duties thereby given to it, particularly the selection of country parks and channeling of state funds to them. The Nature Conservancy was also reconstituted soon after. In 1973 its research arm was separated as the Institute of Terrestrial Ecology, and the new Nature Conservancy Council was left to concentrate on practical conservation.

Further powers were given to the Nature Conservancy Council and National Park Authorities in the 1981 Wildlife and Countryside Act. In response to a growing threat to the environment from modern intensive farming, they were given powers to enter into management agreements to control environmentally damaging practices and compensate landowners for income forgone. This act, and those of 1968 and 1949, included conservation measures beyond those concerned with protecting land. All, for example, included provisions for securing public access to the wider countryside, and the 1949 and 1981 acts also included provisions to protect individual species.

New national nature reserves continue to be established under a program established in 1977. The goal is 0.91 million hectares (2.25 million acres) in the nature reserve system. Since the present system falls substantially short of the goal, designations are likely to continue for some time. A nature conservation strategy published by the Nature Conservancy Council in 1984 calls for 10 percent of the land area of Britain to be specially safeguarded for nature. Although there are no plans to establish more national parks, additional areas of outstanding natural beauty may be designated. In the future, state conservation activity seems likely to be increasingly redirected toward financing voluntary conservation bodies and landowners to protect reserves and the wider countryside. An important recent development is the designation of environmentally sensitive areas where some state support for agriculture will be modified to encourage farmers to manage their land in ways more beneficial to the environment.

PARKS AND RESERVES

Although the international concept of a national park as a very large, publicly owned area of outstanding natural scenery, devoid of human settlement, underlaid much of the early thinking of those pressing for national parks in Britain, it was clear that it could not be directly applied to such a densely populated, largely farmed, and privately owned country. In his influential 1945 report John Dower set out a definition of a British national park as

An extensive area of beautiful and relatively wild country in which, for the nation's benefit and by appropriate national decision and action:
  a. the characteristic landscape beauty is strictly preserved;
  b. access and facilities for public open-air enjoyment are amply provided;
  c. wildlife and buildings and places of architectural and historical interest are suitably protected, while
  d. established farming use is effectively maintained.[3]

There were, therefore, to be three main functions of national parks. First, they were to preserve the best examples of the nation's heritage of landscape, including its geological, physiographic, wildlife, and architectural and archaeological components. Second, they were to provide access for people to enjoy these things, and third, they were to sustain the livelihoods of those living in them. Such purposes obviously create the potential for clashes of interest, particularly between those who are primarily concerned with the conservation of the landscape resources and those who are concerned with its use, be that recreation, industrial development, or farming. In 1945 recreational use and industrial development were perceived to be the principal threats. Indeed, the earlier Addison committee of 1931 had taken the view that there was no alternative but to create two kinds of parks, "regional reserves" devoted to outdoor recreation to be located near population centers and "national reserves" devoted to landscape and wildlife preservation.

When it came to selecting potential national parks, both the Dower and the Hobhouse committee made landscape beauty the most important criterion. With the exceptions of the spectacular cliff scenery of the Pembrokeshire and Cornish coasts, all of Dower's ten choices were fairly remote upland areas in the north and west of the country. For the most part Hobhouse endorsed this selection, but he made some concessions to recreation by adding three new areas to the list. One was the North Yorkshire Moors, another upland area, but one very close to the urban and industrial centers of the northeast. It was established as a national park. The Norfolk Broads and the South Downs are in the lowlands. The Broads is a wetland area of rivers and lakes much used for fishing, sailing,

Table 8.1
National Parks in Britain

NAME	DESIGNATION DATE	AREA (sq. km.)	POPULATION (thousand)	ESTIMATED ANNUAL VISITOR DAYS (million)	PUBLIC OWNER-SHIP (%)	MOOR AND OPEN LAND (%)
Peak District	1951	1,404	37	20	28	39
Lake District	1951	2,243	40	20	39	50
Snowdonia	1951	2,171	24	9	31	60
Dartmoor	1951	945	30	8	56	53
Pembrokeshire Coast	1952	583	22	1.5	13	11
North York Moors	1952	1,432	25	11	19	33
Yorkshire Dales	1954	1,760	17	7.5	2	55
Exmoor	1954	686	10	2.5	19	28
Northumberland	1956	1,031	2	1	46	71
Brecon Beacons	1957	1,344	32	7	20	42

Source: compiled primarily from J. Allan Patmore. "Change for National Parks." In Changing Perspectives on National Parks. Cheltenham: Countryside Commission, 1986.

and bird-watching. The South Downs is a long ridge of low rolling hills then covered with an almost unbroken short, springy, thyme-scented sward of prairielike, sheep-grazed grassland. Although neither was established as a national park, both have been given some protection, as outlined earlier. The South Downs was extensively plowed for crop production during the wartime "dig for victory" campaign. Although the national parks attract many visitors (Table 8.1), the main concentration of population in London remains nearly 200 kilometers (125 miles) from the nearest park, and its surrounding countryside receives as many visitor day trips as the national parks. The Cornwall Coast, which had been on the Dower list, was dropped by the Hobhouse committee as it was not considered to be a discrete block of country.

The ten national parks that were finally established (Table 8.1) are rather similar in their general character, containing mostly open wild mountains and moorland with intervening valleys that are settled and farmed. The Pembrokeshire Coast is the one exception, but even this contains the Preseli Mountains. Very different geology, landforms, farming traditions, and other land uses, however, make the parks distinctive. More than 70 percent of the Northumberland National Park, for example, consists of wild, open moorland, with most of the remainder being under commercial conifer forestry. At the other extreme, the main landscape and recreational resource of Pembrokeshire Coast National Park is confined to the cliffs and bays of a narrow coastal strip, so that open country occupies only 11 percent of the park's area with most of the rest being cultivated land, included as the immediate hinterland to the coastline and its clifftop heaths and grasslands. On average in the ten national parks, just less than half their area is open country. Farmland makes up most of the remainder, though most parks contain significant areas of commercial forestry and small areas of more natural deciduous woodlands.

The national parks contain such large proportions of settled and farmed land because considerable emphasis was placed on designating large and contiguous areas but also because much of their wildlife, archaeological interest, and landscape beauty was seen as being the direct result of millennia of harmonious interaction between man and environment. The moorlands, for example, which cloak the hills in a haze of purple in late summer when the heathers flower and are an important wildlife habitat, especially for breeding birds of prey and waders, are not truly natural. They are the result of unenclosed grazing by sheep at low stocking densities and burning to provide the best conditions for grouse shooting. Left unmanaged, they would eventually revert to scrub and woodland.

In the Yorkshire Dales it is the white limestone field walls and barns and villages, which seem to spring naturally out of the surrounding Karstic limestone cliffs and pavements from which they are made, that give the unique character to the landscape. Ruined abbeys, castles, and even tin and lead mines are likewise a testament to the history of human exploitation that has built these national park landscapes, layer upon layer, and now weaves an air of mystery and adventure into the experience of the visitor. Agricultural and forestry developments were therefore not thought to be threats to the landscape; indeed the inclusion of rural populations based on them was felt to be essential to maintain the characteristics of the parks. It was foreseen that the scale and pervasiveness of modern developments, such as dams, reservoirs, quarries, and trunk roads, made them much less likely to be so readily blended or accommodated into park landscapes. Control of such major development was seen as a priority.

Although national parks were selected to fulfill essentially aesthetic and amenity functions, national nature reserves were to be for scientific purposes. In the 1949 act

"nature reserves" means land managed for the purpose—
    a. of providing, under suitable conditions and control, special opportunities for the study of, and research into, matters relating to the fauna and flora of Great Britain and the physical conditions in which they live, and for the study of geological and physiographical features of special interest in the area, or
    b. of preserving flora, fauna or geological or physiographical features of special interest in the area, or for both those purposes.[4]

These statutory objectives came to be known respectively as the "outdoor laboratory" and "living museum" functions of national nature reserves. Unlike in national parks, access, other than that for research or educational purposes, is not an intended purpose of national nature reserves. In practice, however, many reserves do provide access to the general public, sometimes as an unavoidable result of public footpaths or other rights of access having been acquired with the land, more often as a deliberate policy to provide facilities for bird-watchers and other naturalists or to interpret the wildlife and ecosystems of the area as part of the educational function. Many reserves thus have camouflaged areas from which to view wildlife, information centers and nature trails, but the protective function remains primary, and these facilities are often used as a means of channeling people away from the more sensitive parts of the reserve. Being much smaller than national parks, national nature reserves do not normally contain any development, or cultivation, or land uses other than traditional forms of agriculture or forestry necessary to maintain particular kinds of ecosystems. Restricted hunting is sometimes permitted where it is necessary to control pest species or maintain good relations with landowners. Local bylaws can be imposed on national nature reserves to control undesirable activities.

In the Huxley report there was a list of proposed national nature reserves that represented the collective knowledge and experience of naturalists and academics as to which sites were most worthy of protection. It was based on the list originally drawn up by the Society for the Promotion of Nature Reserves in 1915. The intention was that the reserve series should

preserve and maintain as part of the nation's heritage places which can be regarded as reservoirs for the main types of community and kinds of wild plants and animals represented in this country. . . . Considered as a single system, the reserves should comprise as large a sample as possible of all the many different groups of living organisms, indigenous or established in this country as part of its natural flora and fauna.[5]

This decision to aim for a representative sample of species, ecosystems, and physical features has guided the acquisition of national nature reserves ever since, but it has been distorted by a number of factors. In particular, threats to and the availability of different areas of ecosystems have greatly influenced the acquisition program. Upland areas, for example, accounted in 1977 for more than half the total area of national nature reserves, perhaps largely because the land is least useful for other purposes.

In 1977 the Nature Conservancy Council completed a review of its reserve acquisition program. The exercise involved a survey and classification of British ecosystems and a comparative assessment of sites using a number of newly defined criteria. It identified and described 702 sites covering 0.91 million hectares worthy of protection as national nature reserves. Features of geological or physiographic interest were not included in this review but are the subject of a separate review yet to be published.

ADMINISTRATION

Three main kinds of measures were seen as being necessary to achieve the objectives of national parks: planning control of major developments; sympathetic land management by private landowners; and the acquisition of land by national park authorities, local authorities, and other agencies to protect particularly important areas and secure access. Following earlier, less satisfactory arrangements, since 1974 each park has been administered by a single executive committee or board, of which two-thirds of the members are appointed by the local authorities and one-third by the government. The committees appoint their own national park officer and his staff. The costs of park administration are shared between the government and the local authorities, with the government contributing 75 percent of the support. Without the direct operational powers recommended in the Hobhouse report, the National Parks Commission and, subsequently, the Countryside Commission have guided the program of park development by advising the government on the development of policies relating to national parks, including the allocation of the government funds between the parks, and also by financing park activities such as land acquisition, interpretation, and ranger services.

By such means visitor facilities have been greatly improved and some key features of the parks' landscape heritage brought into public ownership. Quite large proportions of land in the parks are publicly owned (Table 8.1). Some is held by conservation bodies specifically to promote park purposes; much of the remainder is held by public agencies such as water authorities whose use of it does not conflict with the national park. There are large military training areas in three parks, constituting 22 percent of the park area in Northumberland and 5 percent in Dartmoor and Pembrokeshire Coast. These are greatly resented by amenity interests denied access, but naturalists have few objections to them since this use prevents most others, and the training areas are in consequence rich in wildlife.

Control of major developments has been less successful. Absent an overriding national interest, it is government policy to prohibit major developments in the parks. This has not prevented some major road and mineral schemes and even the construction of a nuclear power station. Surprisingly, however, the main threat to the parks has come from the quarter least expected when they were designated. At that time the maintenance of farming was one of the main aims of park policy. Farming was seen as the main agency maintaining the landscape, and no threat was seen to the amenities of the countryside from it. Consequently, no measures to control farming or forestry were built into the planning legislation. Postwar agricultural expansion and intensification, however, rapidly began to change park landscapes. In Exmoor and the North York Moors, for example, over a fifth and a quarter respectively of the moorland—the parks' most characteristic landscape—have been lost to agricultural enclosure and reclamation. The traditional pattern of rural society has also changed as farm holdings have amalgamated into larger, more efficient units at the expense of farmers, farm laborers, and employment in industries ancillary to agriculture. In the North York Moors farmers fell in number by 39 percent between 1951 and 1974, full-time male employees by 65 percent. Although this out-migration has now slowed, and even reversed in some areas, the maintenance of rural communities and their infrastructure remains a formidable and fundamental problem with considerable potential for clashes of interest between national park purposes and local interests, who may naturally consider the jobs offered by a new quarry or factory far more important than its effects on the scenery.

These growing pressures on national parks led the government in 1971 to appoint a National Parks Policies Review Committee under Lord Sandford. Reporting in 1974, it affirmed that the overriding purpose of national parks should be the conservation of the heritage with all other functions, including access and recreation, subordinate to this. It recommended planning control over forestry in the parks and much more coordination of agricultural and environmental policies. Because of the large area of national parks, amounting to some 9 percent of England and Wales, the committee felt it would be unrealistic to regard the parks as inviolate, particularly with regard to their use as water catchments. Nevertheless, it concluded that the presumption should always be against development. Some members of the committee, however, were of the view that the intrinsic conflicts built into the parks would be best resolved by giving special protection to "national heritage areas" that would remain as unspoiled heartlands preserving the best wild country, surrounded and buffered by the rest of the parks. A similar "two tier" zoning system, comparable with those used in national parks in other countries, was later proposed by a Countryside Review Committee set up by the government. The idea was rejected by both the majority of the Sandford committee and, later, the government, on the grounds that it would inevitably lead to diminished status for the remaining parts of national parks and increased difficulty in protecting them. Some concession toward this proposal has, however, been made in the 1981 Wildlife and Countryside Act, which requires national park authorities to map areas of moor and heath—the presumption being that they will receive extra protection. These maps become part of the National Park Plan, the main instrument by which ends and means are chosen and reconciled.

Detailed management plans also form the basis of the Nature Conservancy Council's administration of national nature reserves. They are more preoccupied with resource manipulation than with the socioeconomic issues that inevitably determine the nature of national park plans. In Britain there are very few climax ecosystems that would remain unchanged if left to themselves in a nature reserve. Even peat bogs and forests may require some control of water regimes, or of species, because of ecosystem fragmentation or isolation, or because the full natural complement of species is not present, and the ecosystem balance is, therefore, not maintained. Many predatory animals once present in Britain, such as wolves and some birds of prey, are long extinct, so that the herbivore populations on which they would have preyed are more abundant than they would otherwise have been. These prey species must sometimes be culled if damage to the vegetation is to be avoided. The creation of habitats and reintroduction of species may also be desirable if more complete ecosystems are to be restored. The sea eagle (*Haliaeetus albicilla*), which became extinct in Britain around the turn of the century, has recently been successfully reintroduced to the Isle of

Rhum National Nature Reserve in Scotland. Lost species of butterflies have also been restored to nature reserves.

Most British ecosystems have been modified by human exploitation. Some are subnatural, such as coppice woodland that has been structurally modified from the natural climax. Others are seminatural, such as heaths and moors, which have been qualitatively changed from the climax to another spontaneous, unsown ecosystem, usually by stock grazing. These modifications have simulated natural patch catastrophes—such as fire and windthrow, or the grazing of wild herbivores—which diversify climax ecosystems and create species-rich ecosystems analogous to more natural steppe and prairie ecosystems in other parts of the world. If such ecosystems are to be maintained, traditional forms of coppice woodland management or unintensive grazing with domestic stock must continue. On many reserves wardens and estate workers now manage domestic stock as substitutes for wild herbivores. They use complex grazing regimes, with seasonal rotations in stocking patterns and densities, to generate conditions suitable for wild plants and animals. Traditional farming once created such ecosystems as an incidental by-product. Since traditional farming practices are no longer an economic means of food production, they must be subsidized in reserves and national parks in order to maintain the desired ecosystems and landscapes. This is accomplished by payments to farmers under management agreements. Much of the work being done on reserves is experimental to establish the best means of achieving this.

In all these activities the work of the national park authorities, the Countryside Commission, and the Nature Conservancy Council is greatly extended and supplemented by the work of private voluntary conservation organizations who work in close collaboration with them. Their membership, political influence, and their own land acquisition programs have all grown dramatically since the war. The National Trust is the largest, with more than 1.7 million members. It owns 1 percent of England and Wales, including 7.5 percent of national park land and 25 percent of the Lake District National Park. The Royal Society for the Protection of Birds has nearly half a million members and manages 107 reserves covering over 54,000 hectares (133,000 acres). Locally based county trusts for nature conservation also own large numbers of nature reserves, and organizations such as the Commons, Open Spaces and Footpaths Preservation Society still exist and campaign effectively for improvements in access and conservation. Their pressure led to the establishment of state conservation, and their great strength today is an essential buttress to national parks and nature reserves that seems destined to become even more important in the future.

Agricultural overproduction seems likely to transform the socioeconomic context in which conservation must operate in Britain. Whether less food is produced by a return to less intensive forms of production, or by withdrawing land from agriculture, pressures on the environment from the land use that has most profoundly affected it since the war seem bound to ease. Opportunities for positive countryside management through subsidizing appropriate kinds of farming are already being exploited. It may also be possible to return some of the countryside to genuine wilderness—a prospect to delight both the conservationist and ardent devotee of outdoor recreation.

NOTES

1. William Wordsworth, *Guide to the Lakes* (Oxford: Oxford University Press, 1977), p. 92.

2. John Dower, *National Parks in England and Wales*. Cmd 6628 (London: HMSO, 1945).

3. Ibid., p. 6.

4. *National Parks and Access to the Countryside Act* (London: HMSO, 1949), section 15, pp. 13–14.

5. J. S. Huxley, *Conservation of Nature in England and Wales: Report of the Wildlife Conservation Special Committee*. Cmd 7122 (London: HMSO, 1947), p. 17.

BIBLIOGRAPHY

Bell, M., ed. *Britain's National Parks*. Newton Abbot: David and Charles, 1975.

Cherry, G. E. *Environmental Planning 1939–69. II: National Parks and Recreation in the Countryside*. London: HMSO, 1975.

Countryside Review Committee. *Conservation and the Countryside Heritage*. London: HMSO, 1979.

Green, B. *Countryside Conservation: The Protection and Management of Amenity Ecosystems*. 2nd ed. London: George Allen and Unwin, 1985.

Hobhouse, Sir Arthur. *Report of the National Park Committee (England and Wales)*. Cmd 7121. London: HMSO, 1947.

Mabey, R. *The Common Ground. A Place for Nature in Britain's Future?* London: Hutchinson, 1980.

MacEwen, Ann, and Malcolm MacEwen. *National Parks: Conservation or Cosmetics?* London: George Allen and Unwin, 1982.

Patmore, J. Allan. "Change for National Parks." In *Changing Perspectives on National Parks*. Cheltenham: Countryside Commission, 1986.

Ramsey, Sir J. D. *National Parks and the Conservation of Nature in Scotland*. Cmd 7235. Edinburgh: HMSO, 1947.

Ratcliffe, D., ed. *A Nature Conservation Review*. 2 vols. Cambridge: Cambridge University Press, 1977.

————. *Nature Conservation in Great Britain*. Peterborough: Nature Conservancy Council, 1984.

Rogers, Alan, John Blunden, and Nigel Curry. *The Countryside Handbook*. London: Croom Helm, 1985.

Sandford, Lord. *Report of the National Parks Policies Review Committee*. London: HMSO, 1974.

Scott, Lord Justice. *Report of the Committee on Land Utilisation in Rural Areas*. Cmd 6378. London: HMSO, 1942.

Sheail, J. *Nature in Trust*. Glasgow: Blackie, 1976.
Shoard, Marion. *The Theft of the Countryside*. London: Temple Smith, 1980.
Tansley, A. G. *Our Heritage of Wild Nature: A Plea for Organized Nature Conservation*.
          Cambridge: Cambridge University Press, 1945.

GREECE   9

Kostas Kassioumis

Apart from its important historical and archaeological interest, Greece is also endowed with splendid scenery and a diversity of flora and fauna including many rare species of worldwide significance.[1] In an area of only 131,957 square kilometers (50,954 square miles) there is dramatic variation of climatic conditions and geomorphological characteristics, which—combined with the geographical position of Greece, between the three continents of Europe, Asia, and Africa—creates an impressive variety of vegetation types and interesting habitats.

Important colonies of aquatic birds, endangered birds of prey, rare animal species such as sea turtles, the monk seal, and the Cretan wild goat, are found in wide estuaries and lakes, on remote islands, in almost untouched sand dunes and beaches, and in mountains and forests that remain natural and unexploited to the present day. Greece also possesses perhaps the most diverse flora of any country in Europe and a floristic abundance that is unrivaled by other Mediterranean countries of its size.[2] With nearly 6,000 species, more than 700 of them endemic, it represents an immense range of genetic resources, ecosystems, and natural beauty.

Both fauna and flora have benefited from the relatively low levels of economic development and agricultural intensity. The existence of undisturbed isolated areas has assisted the survival of important mammals such as the bear, the wolf, and probably the lynx, which has been extirpated from most other European countries. A wide variety of marvelous landscapes, possessing aesthetic and cultural significance, complements Greece's biological richness and creates additional incentives for the protection of particular areas in their natural state.

HISTORY

Greece was early among European countries in recognizing the need for special protection of forest areas. The first forest code (Law 4173/1929), issued in 1929, provided for special measures to be taken in the management of certain areas characterized as "protected forests" in order not only to protect their soils and other natural or man-made features and works, but also to preserve wildlife and amenity values for the benefit of people.

Another early law that established a protected status for certain areas in Greece was the archaeological law (Law 5351/1932), enacted in 1932 to protect antiquities and the areas within a radius of 500 meters (1,640 feet) around them. This law, which is still valid, is very strict and prohibits not only damage or alterations to the ancient monuments themselves but also any kind of activities in the surrounding areas that might endanger the archaeological structures either directly or indirectly.

The archaeological law protected not only sites with monuments remaining from ancient times but also certain areas with special historical interest, called "historical places." In 1950 it was extended (Law 1465/1950) to monuments of modern times including "landscapes of natural beauty" and thus has become a useful tool for nature conservation. About 300 landscapes of natural beauty and historical places have been designated throughout Greece although very few of them have been protected effectively. These problems are discussed more fully in the section on administration.

The idea of setting aside certain areas to safeguard their natural characteristics was initiated in 1937 by the Greek Forest Service in cooperation with the Greek Alpine Club. A law (856/1937) was enacted that recommended the establishment of five national parks, the first of which was created in 1938 at Mount Olympos, the sacred residence of the twelve gods of Greek mythology.

Preservation of national parks has been accomplished by special orders and regulations issued and applied by local Forest Service authorities to protect the natural environment (flora, fauna, natural features), and also by the construction of the necessary infrastructure (fencing, roads, paths, forest rangers, huts, etc.) for better management and protection.

In 1971 (Law 996/1971) an amendment to the 1937 law abandoned the limitation of five national parks and recognized two more categories of protected areas: "aesthetic forests" and "protected natural monuments." In principle, the Forest Service preserves these areas in the same way that national parks are preserved, but in practice less effort and fewer resources are expended for their management.

Law 996/1971, which is still in use today, is part of a forestry code that also addresses faunal, floral, and habitat protection. It regulates hunting and provides for the establishment of "game refuges," "game breeding stations," and "controlled hunting areas," the first of which was established in 1939. Although these territories are set aside primarily to conserve birds and mammals for hunting, the Forest Service provides significant protection of flora, fauna, and the natural environment generally. Thus, these areas have also contributed importantly to nature conservation.

The archaeological law, the national parks law, and the hunting law provide the legal foundation that has been used to designate protected areas, and authorize governmental bodies to administer, protect, and manage special areas for nature conservation.

In addition to these laws, governmental decisions to protect natural areas have also been based on planning laws, international conventions ratified by Greece, and relevant directives of the European Economic Community (EEC).

The regional and environmental planning law (360/1976) issued in 1976, provided institutional procedures for national and regional plans as well as specialized plans covering particular sectors or activities. It established the National Council for Planning and the Environment and its Secretariat, which has been very useful in resolving conflicts between development and environmental protection. In three decisions taken in 1980 and 1981, the council identified more than twenty natural sites to be protected and instructed the appropriate authorities to take the necessary steps for their conservation.

The ratification by Greece in 1974 of the Convention on Wetlands of International Importance especially as Waterfowl Habitat, known as the Ramsar Convention, and the inclusion of some valuable Greek wetlands under its provisions, has forced relevant governmental bodies to take certain protective measures (e.g., prohibition of hunting and restriction of certain forms of development in some areas), even though this type of reserve is not yet covered by special nature protective legislation.

Greece is also party to the World Cultural and Natural Heritage Convention. It is a signatory of the Berne Convention on the Conservation of European Wildlife and Natural Habitats and the Protocol on Mediterranean Specially Protected Areas, and it is in the process of including specific areas in the relevant lists. Many sites have also been identified as important areas for bird preservation as required under the EEC Birds Directive (79/409/EEC).

Application of the various laws and relevant decisions has revealed many areas that contain important natural values. Not all of them, however, are effectively protected or managed at the present time. There are always political difficulties associated with placing specific areas under special protective control. In recent years deficiencies in institutional procedures were widely recognized. There were no marine parks. There was a lack of public involvement. There were administrative difficulties including insufficient authority.

In recognition of these deficiencies new legislation about "the protection of nature and the landscapes" has been incorporated, as a special chapter, in a fundamental law "on the protection of the environment" (Law 1650/1986), ratified by the Greek Parliament in October 1986.

This new law, which is designed to complement existing legislation, introduces certain changes in the establishment and administration of protected areas. Five new categories of reserves are recommended: (1) Absolutely Protected Natural Areas (Nature Reserves), (2) Protected Natural Areas, (3) National Parks, (4) Protected Natural Formations, Protected Landscapes and Elements of Landscapes, and (5) Areas for Ecodevelopment. Three ministries—Agriculture; Environment, Physical Planning and Public Works; and Manufacture, Energy and Technology—are responsible for initiating the establishment of new reserves in these categories. Individual areas will be designated by special presidential decrees that will also specify which authorities are to be responsible for administration of each area and the necessary means and measures for their protection. Greek authorities have already begun to apply the new law to areas recognized as important for conservation but not yet covered by special protective legislation, such as wetlands, marine parks, and so forth.

PARKS AND RESERVES

Greece is fortunate in the variety, quality, and quantity of natural and semi-natural environments that it contains.[3] To date, many areas have been identified as important to nature conservation. Not all of them, however, have been designated as protected under the relevant legislation. Other areas have been designated, but no specific measures have been undertaken for their preservation and management. Still others have widely recognized values and are treated in practice as protected areas despite their lack of full legal protection.

The descriptions that follow refer to areas or sites that, independent of their legal status, combine important natural values and practical measure from competent authorities to preserve these values. Please refer to Figure 9.1, the System of Reserves in Greece. The total area of parks and other reserves (land area) included in this section amounts to about 360,000 hectares (890,000 acres). It represents 2.72 percent of the national landmass and an area of about 37 hectares (91 acres) per thousand people. The statistical characteristics of the system are summarized in Table 9.1.

National Parks

Nature conservation efforts find their best expression in national parks, the most important type of reserve in Greece. According to the relevant law (996/ 1971), national parks are defined as "mainly forested areas of special conservation interest on account of flora and fauna, geomorphology, subsoil, atmosphere, waters and generally their natural environment, the protection of which seems necessary; also on account of the need for the conservation and improvement of their constitution, form and natural beauty, to permit aesthetic, psychic and healthy enjoyment and, moreover, for carrying on special research of any kind."

Ten national parks were designated between 1938 and 1974 containing some of the loveliest and most important landscapes in Greece and covering a wide

Figure 9.1
The System of Reserves in Greece

⭕ National Parks

△ Selected Aesthetic Forests

▢ Selected Natural Monuments

x Internationally Important Wetlands

⬤ Selected Other Protected Areas

⊢─── 100 Km ───⊣

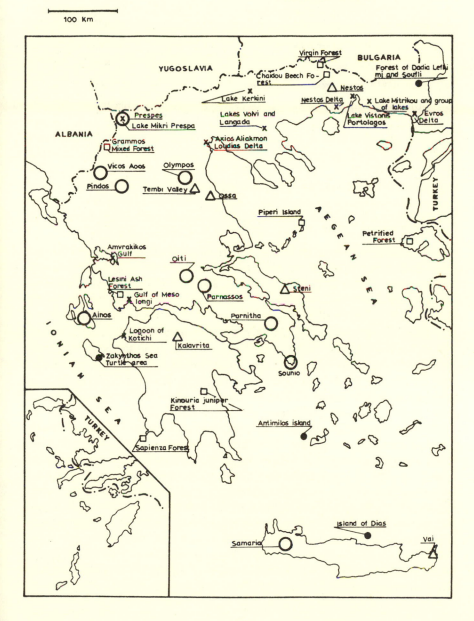

Table 9.1
Synopsis of Parks and Protected Areas in Greece

CATEGORY OF PROTECTED AREA	NUMBER OF AREAS	AGGREGATE AREA (hectares)
National Parks	10	95,000
Aesthetic Forests	19	33,000
Protected Natural Monuments	51	16,500
Hunting Reserves	7	10,500
Internationally Important Wetlands[a]	10	100,000
Other Areas	2	105,000
TOTALS	99	360,000

Note: [a] excluding Lake Mikri Prespa, which is part of Prespes National Park.

range of ecosystems from the most northerly point south to the Libyan Sea and the Greek islands. One of the most important wetlands—Lake Mikri Prespa, with its surrounding land area—is also included in this category of protected areas.

The total area of Greek national parks is 95,000 hectares (235,000 acres). Of this total, 34,488 hectares (85,220 acres) are in fully protected core zones. Of the remaining area, 34,254 hectares (84,642 acres) are in the peripheral zones of Oiti, Pindos, Vicos-Aoos, Prespes, and Sounio national parks. Peripheral zones exist also for the rest of the national parks, but they have not yet been formalized. An additional 26,000 hectares (64,000 acres) are estimated to be protected in these yet-to-be-defined peripheral zones.

The main characteristics and the most important values of the ten Greek national parks are described in the following paragraphs.

Olympos. Situated near Litochoro in the Pieria district, Olympos was established in 1938 as the first Greek national park. It has also been declared a biosphere reserve. The park comprises a core area of 3,996 hectares (9,874 acres) on the eastern slope of Greece's highest mountain, the mythical residence of the Olympian gods. There is a variety of topographic features and altitudes extending from 600 meters (1,970 feet) above sea level to 2,917 meters (9,570 feet) at the Myticas or Pantheon summit. There are more than 1,700 plant species, many of which are rare and endemic to Greece. Aesthetic and alpine resources are also of interest.

Parnassos. Designated in 1938, this mountainous park includes a fully protected core area of 3,513 hectares (8,681 acres) in central Greece, covered mainly with Greek fir (*Abies cephalonica*) and also including some rare plant species, noteworthy fauna, and interesting geological formations. Great cultural and tourist interest centers on archaeological sites (Delphi) and ski areas in the vicinity of the park.

Parnitha. Situated 40 kilometers (25 miles) north of Athens and easily accessible by asphalt roads, Parnitha contains a variety of topographic features and scenic beauty in a core area of 3,812 hectares (9,419 acres). With vegetation consisting mainly of fir forest, interesting fauna, and many open fields at high altitude, this park provokes great recreation interest. It was established in 1961.

Ainos. Situated on the island of Cephalonia in the Ionian Sea, this park covers a core area of 2,862 hectares (7,072 acres) and contains important forest stands of pure Greek fir, a spectacular mountainous landscape near the sea, and special floristic interest.

Samaria. This park is also a biosphere reserve and has been awarded the European Diploma, Category A from the Council of Europe. It extends over the White Mountains in western Crete and protects impressive and dramatic geomorphological features including one of the longest and most beautiful gorges in Europe. Altitude ranges from sea level to 2,116 meters (6,942 feet). In and around the fully protected core zone of 4,850 hectares (11,984 acres) there are rich and diverse isolated biotopes, including rare and endemic plant and animal species of worldwide significance such as the famous Cretan wild goat (*Capra aegagrus Cretica*).

Oiti. One of the loveliest mountainous landscapes, this park encloses a total area of 7,210 hectares (17,816 acres), providing full protection to a core area of 3,010 hectares (7,438 acres). It is located in the Giona Mountain Range of central Greece, Phthiotis prefecture. It includes forests of *Abies cephalonica,* various mixed woods, and also bushes and grasslands, and it is an important biotope for many plant and animal species.

Pindos. This national park protects the exemplary features of the Pindos Mountain Range in northwestern Greece. The total area is 6,927 hectares (17,117 acres) with a core of 3,393 hectares (8,384 acres). It is an isolated area covered with thick forests of pine, beech, and fir, rising to bare and rocky peaks. The landscape is dramatic in the extreme, with vast precipices plunging into narrow valleys, and fast-flowing rivers coursing along wide, boulder-scattered gorges. Pindos provides habitat for interesting fauna, especially large mammals.

Vicos-Aoos. Vicos-Aoos is one of the most outstanding geological formations in Greece. It boasts an impressive landscape characterized by the Aoos and Voidomatis rivers, rich vegetation, alpine areas, and gorges. The flora, fauna, and geomorphological formations, which include caves and lakes, are scientifically important. There are important cultural elements and monuments of traditional architecture in the peripheral zone. The park is located in the Epirus region of northwestern Greece and comprises a total area of 12,600 hectares

(31,100 acres), of which 3,400 hectares (8,400 acres) are within the fully protected core.

Prespes. An inland lake and lakeshore on the Greek-Albanian-Yugoslavian border provides excellent habitat for waterfowl and a genetic reservoir for endangered water birds. The park's core area is the lake proper, an area of 4,900 hectares (12,100 acres). The total area of 19,470 hectares (48,110 acres) contains a large variety of biotopes and geomorphology with many species of plants and animals, especially birds, a marvelous landscape, and unique ecosystems.

Sounio. The park is located about 60 kilometers (37 miles) southeast of Athens near Lavrio. Its 3,500 hectares (8,650 acres) are covered with forests and scattered trees of *Pinus halepensis,* bush, and grass. The area possesses great recreation interest and significant historical, geological, mineralogical, and paleontological values.

Aesthetic Forests

Important protected areas are also included among the nineteen aesthetic forests declared between 1973 and 1980 and covering a total area of 33,106 hectares (81,805 acres). This type of reserve, also established according to Law 996/1971, contains "forests or natural landscapes which possess particular aesthetic, hygienic and touristic significance and which have also characteristics that demand the protection of their fauna, flora and natural beauty."

A full list of all Greek aesthetic forests with relevant information about their important characteristics is given below.

Vai is a 20-hectare (50-acre) valley in the northeastern part of Crete with a natural stand of the Cretan palm tree (*Phoenix theophrasti*), one of only two palms in Europe. An impressive landscape and a marvelous sandy beach make Vai a major tourist attraction.

Kaisariani is an area of 640 hectares (1,580 acres) near Athens covered mainly by forests composed of *Pinus halepensis* and other species that, for the most part, have been introduced and cultivated by man. It includes an important Byzantine monastery and other monuments and has great recreational value.

Tempi Valley, 1,762 hectares (4,354 acres) along the Pinios River spanning the national road between Larissa and Thessaloniki in the prefecture of Larissa, contains impressive geomorphology and vegetation and is famous for its spectacular beauty.

Karaiskaki is a beautiful area of 252 hectares (623 acres) near Mouzaki, in the prefecture of Karditsa. It boasts a varied topography, forests composed mainly of broadleaf trees, and interesting caves that have special historical interest.

Pefkias is a seashore pine forest of 27.5 hectares (68 acres) adjacent to the town of Xylocastro in Peloponissos. It is a popular recreation area with a beautiful beach that is crowded during the summer.

Patras comprises 1,850 hectares (4,570 acres) of mostly forested watershed above the campus of the University of Patras.

Ioannina is a pine plantation with scattered other species. Its 86 hectares (213 acres) above the town of Ioannina have great recreational value.

Farsala is a 34.5-hectare (85-acre), artificially forested area near the town of Farsala, prefecture of Larissa, comprising mainly pines with certain other species. It also includes areas where vegetation is allowed to grow naturally and provides many recreation opportunities.

Steni is a beautiful and ecologically significant mix of fir and chestnut forests. Its 674 hectares (1,665 acres) are located at Mount Dirfi on the island of Evia.

Ossa comprises forests, pastures, and agricultural land with great aesthetic and ecological value in an area of 16,900 hectares (41,760 acres) extending over Mount Ossa in central Greece. Its varied topography includes many streams and 4.4 kilometers (2.7 miles) of coast.

Mogostos is a beautiful oak forest with a scattering of other species, varied topography, and impressive view points. It occupies an area of 520 hectares (1,285 acres) in the prefecture of Korinthos.

Mytikas-Nicopolis is a 66-hectare (163-acre) man-made forest of pinus-eucalyptus and other scattered species. Adjacent to the sea, near the ruins of the ancient town of Nicopolis in the district of Preveza, it has special aesthetic and recreational values.

The Skiathos Island Reserve comprises all the forested areas on the island of Skiathos. It covers an area of 3,000 hectares (7,400 acres) with great aesthetic interest and includes a magnificent forest of *Pinus pinea*.

Nestos is an area of 2,380 hectares (5,080 acres) including the narrowest part of the Nestos River valley in the prefecture of Xanthi. It possesses impressive landscape features including lush vegetation, steep slopes, rock formations, streams, and unique species of flora and fauna.

Kalavrita, an area of 1,750 hectares (4,320 acres) with varied topography, mixed forests, and other vegetation, has great aesthetic, historic, and cultural interest.

Tithorea, a beautiful forested area of 200 hectares (494 acres) above the town of Tithorea in the prefecture of Magnisia, exhibits interesting geomorphological characteristics, cultural monuments, and sites with historic interest.

Kavala is composed of artificial pine forests with a scattering of other species and also includes some open and agricultural land. It is situated above the town of Kavala and covers an area of 2,816 hectares (6,958 acres).

Trikala comprises areas of pine plantation intermixed with scattered other species and naturally grown vegetation. Its 28 hectares (69 acres), with fine scenery and old castles, lie within the town of Trikala.

Kouri-Almyros protects the remnant of an eliminated plain oak forest with important ecological, aesthetic, and recreational values. It covers an area of 100 hectares (247 acres) and is situated near the town of Almyros, prefecture of Magnisia.

Protected Natural Monuments

Areas or sites that possess important values for nature conservation but do not have the size or diversity to be designated as national parks or aesthetic forests are classified as "protected natural monuments." These include areas that present a special paleontological, geomorphological, or historical significance; and trees, clumps of trees, or rare species of plants presenting special botanical, phytogeographical, aesthetic, or historical significance.

There were fifty-one protected natural monuments designated between 1975 and 1985, fifteen of which comprise specific surface areas, amounting to a total of 1,676 hectares (4,141 acres). Some of these fifteen contain natural features of international importance. Each is described briefly:

Kinouria Juniper Forest is an area of 74 hectares (183 acres) in the prefecture of Arcadia. This pure forest of rare *Juniperus drupacea* is important for its botanical and ecological interest.

Mouries Oak and Ash Forest is a very attractive natural mixed forest (9.2 hectares, 23 acres) composed mainly of oak (*Quercus pedunculata*) and ash (*Fraxinus oxycedrus*) and important also for its ecological and recreational significance.

The Virgin Forest of Central Rodopi is an area (550 hectares, 1,350 acres) of unique ecological value, near the Greek-Bulgarian border in the Rodopi Mountains of the Paranesti district. Here the original forest ecosystem, fauna as well as flora, has remained completely intact until present times. It has an exceptionally high percentage of old trees, mainly spruce (*Picea excelsa*), beech (*Fagus silvatica*), pines (*Pinus silvestris*), and fir (*Abies alba*), and is widely known for its very important scientific value.

Tsichla-Chaidou Beech Forest comprises 18 hectares (44 acres) of ecologically valuable virgin forest in the Rodopi Mountains, prefecture of Xanthi. The forest is composed mainly of beech (*Fagus silvatica*) but also includes open grass lands and wetlands.

Pefkoto Beech Forest, part of a natural forest of *Fagus silvatica* with important ecological characteristics, has been protected primarily for scientific reasons. The monument includes 3.3 hectares (8 acres) within a large forest complex in the prefecture of Pella.

Piperi Island is an isolated island of 438 hectares (1,082 acres) in northern Sporades with important ecological and scientific value. It is covered by pines (*Pinus halepensis*) and bushes and surrounded by a rugged coast, the home of some important birds of prey. The steep rocky coasts, which are full of many holes and caves, together with the deep waters around the island, are part of an important biotope for the rare and endangered monk seal (*Monachus monachus*). It is scheduled to be designated as a marine park.

The Petrified Forest of Lesvos Island is a unique area of immense scientific interest, where there are many petrified trunks, branches, and so forth, created 15–20 million years ago, from various species of trees, some of them now extinct on the island. The 52-hectare (128-acre) strictly protected area includes concentrated specimens at particular places, but there are also samples dispersed throughout an area of 15,000 hectares (37,000 acres) that is also protected for its unique and rare paleontological and geomorphological interest.

Endangered Cretan Cephalanthera is a tiny (0.2 hectares, 0.5 acres) protected area that provides habitat for the rare and endangered orchid *Cephalanthera cuculata Boiss et Heldr*. This is one of the five species of genus Cephalanthera that grow in Greece. It is endemic to Crete and found in the Ida Mountains in Iraclio prefecture.

Lesini Ash Forest is a 45.9-hectare (113-acre) remnant of a large natural swamp forest in a plain area, near the village of Lesini, district of Messolongi. It is composed mainly of ash (*Fraxinus angustifolia*) and constitutes a biotope of great ecological significance and special aesthetic value.

Lailias Sphagnum Area is a 3.9-hectare (10-acre) peat bog within a large forest complex in Serres prefecture. It is important for scientific and educational reasons and has special floristic interest due to the occurrence of species rare among the Greek flora.

The Istiea Remnant is a 0.8-hectare (2-acre) area near the town of Istiea on the island of Evia. It comprises clumps of old trees, mainly elm (*Ulmus campestris*), in an area that also includes wetlands and agriculturally used areas. These clumps have special botanical and ecological value as remnants of a swamp forest that was once extensive.

Sapienza Forest of Evergreen Broadleaves is a 24-hectare (59-acre) relict of a typical Mediterranean forest of sclerophyllus evergreen broadleaves, which appear in a treelike form and reach heights of 8–10 meters (26–33 feet). It is part of the uninhabited island of Sapienza at the southwest end of Peloponissos. The entire 850-hectare (2,100-acre) island has important conservation value and has been designated as a controlled hunting area.

Almopia Natural Mixed Forest comprises 192 hectares (474 acres) in the prefecture of Pella. The monument is a valuable mixed forest with special aesthetic and ecological importance. The latter due primarily to the presence of significant numbers of *Pinus peuce*, a tree species rare in Greece.

Embonas Natural Cypress Forest protects important stands of pure Mediterranean cypress (*Cupressus sempervirens* var. *horizontalis*) in the northeast part of the island of Rodos. The forest of 135 hectares (334 acres) consists mainly of old trees. It has special scientific value as a biogenetic reserve, and a high aesthetic value.

Grammos Mixed Forest is a tract of 130 hectares (321 acres) within a large forest complex at Mount Grammos in Kastoria prefecture. It is composed of unexploited stands of beech (*Fagus silvatica*), fir (*Abies borisiiregis*), and black pine (*Pinus nigra*), which have great ecological and scientific value.

Apart from the above important areas, there are also thirty-six protected natural monuments, single trees or small clumps of trees that nevertheless possess significant botanical, aesthetic, or historical value. Among these is the Plane Tree of Hippocrates in the island of Kos. This is a massive and ancient plane tree (*Platanus orientalis*) connected in popular imagination with Hippocrates, the father of modern medicine, who was born in Kos in 460 B.C. According to legend, this tree marks the spot where he taught. Other important trees designated as natural monuments include the Evergreen Plane Trees of Crete, a variety of *Platanus orientalis* having green leaves throughout the year, and the Pafsanias Plane Tree in the town of Egio, one of the oldest and largest plane trees in Greece, with a hollow trunk and great botanical and historical value.

Hunting Reserves

Numerous areas have been also specially designated according to the hunting legislation. Thus there are more than 500 sites declared as game refuges, where hunting is prohibited. These cover about 800,000 hectares (1.98 million acres) of mainly natural areas. Twenty-one game-breeding stations with a total area of about 13,000 hectares (32,000 acres) and eight controlled hunting areas extending to about 120,000 hectares (297,000 acres) complete the system. Very few of these areas, however, are really important to nature conservation because few specific measures are taken to preserve their natural values. Moreover, some of them are also included in the lists of other types of protected areas, including Ramsar sites and national parks, and receive their primary protection from those designations.

In a few areas, however, the application of hunting legislation does play a fundamental role in the protection of the important natural values. Preeminent among these are the Dadia-Lefkimi and Soufli forests, where 7,200 hectares (17,000 acres) are designated as a game refuge. It is a hilly area covered with various species of trees as well as open and grazing lands. The area has a special scientific and conservation value because it provides crucial habitat for seriously endangered tree-nesting raptors, such as the black vulture (*Aegypius monachus*) and valuable eagle species.

Important natural areas protected as game-breeding stations include Antimilos Island (795 hectares, 1,964 acres) in the central Aegean Sea and the Island of Thodorou (60 hectares, 148 acres) in the Gulf of Hania-Crete. Both are uninhabited places where typical Mediterranean ecosystems with representative species of fauna and flora are able to survive in natural conditions. Two uninhabited islands designated as controlled hunting areas are the Island of Dias (1,250 hectares, 3,090 acres) north of the town of Iraclio, in Crete, and Sapienza Island (850 hectares, 2,100 acres), part of which has been also declared a protected monument. In both cases, valuable undisturbed ecosystems are effectively protected under the hunting legislation.

Internationally Important Wetlands

Several of the Greek wetlands are among the most important in the whole Mediterranean basin, mainly for the support of aquatic species. With the accession of Greece to the Ramsar Convention, eleven areas have been designated as "wetlands of international importance." Although not yet administered as protected, these areas are included in this chapter because they are eminently important for nature conservation in Greece and because assessment studies have already been conducted for all areas, and formal protective measures will soon be applied under the authority of Law 1650/1986, discussed below.

Great habitat diversity is characteristic of the Greek Ramsar wetlands, which include sand dunes, lagoons, riverine forests, delta, and halophytic coasts. These areas serve not only as wintering or intermediate stations for migratory birds but also as breeding and feeding sites of rare and endangered species of birds, mammals, reptiles, and amphibians. These wetlands have not yet been delimited either on the map or on the ground. At the time of their nomination, however, provisional areas were identified totaling about 100,000 hectares (247,000 acres), the smallest 2,400 hectares (5,930 acres) and the largest 25,000 hectares (62,000 acres). The eleven designated wetlands are (1) Evros Delta; (2) Lakes Vistonis-Portolagos; (3) Lake Mitrikou, together with surrounding lakes; (4) Nestos Delta; (5) Lakes Volvi and Langada (Koronia); (6) Lake Kerkini; (7) Axios, Aliakmon, Loudias Delta; (8) Lake Mikri Prespa; (9) Amvrakikos Gulf; (10) Gulf of Messolongi; and (11) Lagoon of Kotichi.

Other Protected Natural Areas

To complete the list of national parks and nature reserves included in this description, we also add two additional biotopes, which, although not yet formally declared, contain valuable features of international importance.

One is the Sea Turtle Nesting Area in Zakynthos, an area with sandy beaches, dunes, reefs, and the most important breeding sites for loggerhead turtle (*Caretta caretta*) in the Mediterranean. The area is subject to heavy touristic pressure during the nesting season, and there are special regulations and guards to inform the people and control the use of lights and other activities on the beaches. The biotope comprises a strictly protected zone of about 400 hectares (990 acres). Some restrictions on development also apply to about 4,200 hectares (10,400 acres) of the surrounding sea and land area.

The other important area is the Marine Park of the Northern Sporades Islands, where measures for protection have already been applied and formal designation is imminent. The proposed park covers a sea and land area of more than 100,000 hectares (247,000 acres). It lies off central Greece and includes a strictly preserved zone around the islands of Kyra Panagia, Piperi (also a designated protected natural monument), Gioura (also a controlled hunting area), Skantzoura, and Psathoura. It is one of the last strongholds of the endangered monk seal (*Monachus monachus*). It includes a unique population of wild goats on Gioura and important biotopes for endangered birds of prey.

ADMINISTRATION

The efforts of the government to protect and manage parks and preserves in Greece have not been completely satisfactory to date. This is the result of organizational and institutional difficulties, a lack of informational and educational programs to raise public awareness, and a rather limited political commitment to conservation.[4]

A special conservation agency does not exist in Greece, and the main authority charged with the responsibility for nature conservation and with the administration of the reserves has been the Forest Service, which is a part of the Ministry of Agriculture.

Other agencies, however, have also played a role. The Ministry of Culture, which is responsible for the preservation of antiquities and cultural heritage, also had the responsibility for administration of landscapes of natural beauty until 1984. This responsibility was then transferred to the Ministry of Physical Planning, Housing and the Environment, itself created in 1980 and later renamed the Ministry of Environment, Physical Planning and Public Works. Although actual measures for the administration of landscapes of natural beauty have not yet been implemented, in some cases the mere existence of a ''protected status'' has helped to preserve amenity values by discouraging certain forms of development and exploitation.

For some time the Ministry of Coordination, later renamed the Ministry of National Economy, had the responsibility to coordinate conservation policy through its National Council for Planning and the Environment. This council and its secretariat were transferred to the Ministry of Environment, Physical Planning and Public Works in 1985.

According to the organizational structure existing today and the applicable laws and practices, two ministries now have the responsibility for nature conservation and for the administration of parks and reserves described here.

The Ministry of Agriculture with its Forest Service, an institution with more than a century of history in the protection of wild flora and fauna, is formally responsible for national parks, aesthetic forests, and protected natural monuments, established according to Law 996/1971, as well as for game refuges, game-breeding stations, and controlled hunting areas established under the hunting law. Individual areas are protected and managed by the Forest District Offices or Directorates in their respective localities and supervised nationally by the Section for the Forest Environment, National Parks, Forest Recreation, and the Game Management Section respectively.

The Ministry of Environment, Physical Planning and Public Works, with its Directorate for the Environment, has overall responsibility for conservation, but it has no real presence on the ground. Nevertheless, in recent years it has taken the initiative to protect the Ramsar wetlands, the proposed Marine Park of Northern Sporades, and the important sea turtle nesting in Zakynthos.

The national parks, which are designated according to a presidential decree published in the official gazette, consist of a nucleus or core area of at least 1,500 hectares (3,700 acres), which is strictly protected, and a peripheral zone of a size at least equivalent to the core area. According to the relevant legislation, the core is owned by the state, which has the power to buy all private rights, and there are strict prohibitions against any kind of development or exploitation. The activities prohibited include the excavation and exploitation of minerals, digging, placement of advertising billboards, industrial activities, housing and other construction, as well as agricultural and forestry activities, pasturing, hunting, and fishing. In the peripheral zone all activities are controlled by the competent authority, so as not to create any negative effects to the core. The organization, function, and management of each national park is governed by a regulation issued by the minister of agriculture.

The prohibitions appropriate to the core areas of national parks also apply to protected natural monuments. Aesthetic forests have functions and regulations similar to those in the peripheral zones of the national parks. These areas are also designated by a presidential decree or relevant decisions published in the official gazette.

Designated hunting reserves are also backed by special legislation (Law 177/1975, article 254, and Presidential Decree 453/1977) giving power to the Forest Service to take all appropriate measures, not only to protect and multiply game for hunting purposes, but also to preserve the natural environment of these areas.

The status of the "internationally important wetlands" and "other protected natural areas" described above is less secure. These areas contain important natural values, but there is no specific legislation that guarantees their protection. There are many difficulties confronting the national parks and other reserves on the ground. Most of the national parks, and other protected areas administrated by the Forest Service, not only face the serious danger of fire and other natural hazards but are also threatened by uncontrolled hunting and grazing. Pressures for mining, forest exploitation, road construction, hydroelectrical projects, and industrial and tourist development also pose serious threats to some of these areas. Wetlands are threatened mainly by draining and land reclamation but also by extension of saltworks, construction of river dams, illegal hunting and fishing, and pollution from agricultural, urban, and industrial sources. Tourist, agricultural, and industrial development projects including land irrigation schemes, waste disposal, and other activities sometimes occur without full consideration being given to the ecological consequences. To date, governmental response to these threats has not been very successful. Policy coordination is difficult to achieve, and as a result, environmental considerations often take second place to short-term economic and social aims.

Administration of parks and reserves faces many other obstacles. National parks, the most important category of reserves, are poorly understood and infrequently visited by large numbers of people, and very little has been done to provide recreational, educational, and research facilities. The estimated number of Greek and foreign visitors to all national parks does not reach 500,000 a year.

Visitors congregate primarily at Samaria, where annual visitation exceeds 200,000; Vicos-Aoos; Olympos; Prespa; and Parnitha, where people are concentrated in specific recreation sites established within the park.

Staff functions are carried out on a part-time basis by forestry employees under the supervision of the director of forest district offices, and the budget for national parks is quite insufficient. Management plans are the exception rather than the rule, and the concept of park manager is largely absent. There is no national park career structure, and although some permanent park wardens have been employed since 1983, none of them has been trained in protected area management.

Very few of the other reserves under the authority of the Forest Service—aesthetic forests, protected natural monuments, and those hunting reserves important to nature conservation—have established management goals and effective organization on the ground. This is also true for wetlands and other important biotopes recently recognized as worthy of protection. A series of assessment studies have been conducted, however, resulting in some provisional regulations and restrictions and the employment of special guards to oversee certain of these areas.

Nevertheless, the system of parks and other reserves in Greece and its administration are slowly but steadily improving. Measures already taken and those projected for the future are cause for optimism.

The application of a new legal framework "on the protection of the environment" (Law 1650/1986) will undoubtedly be very helpful in terms of policy coordination. It has already resulted in establishment of procedures for official designation of some important biotopes: the Northern Sporades Marine Park, the sea turtle nesting area in Zakynthos, and also certain of the Ramsar wetlands. It also provides for the assignment of the competent authorities, or the establishment of special ones, to be responsible for administration and management of these areas at the local level. The new law also provides for public participation in management decision making, for economic measures to compensate owners for damages, restrictions of their rights, and so on, and for special resources to be allocated for protection and management. Funding from the Economic Commission of Europe and other international organizations will assist investigations, research, and measures to preserve rare or endangered species in protected areas.

Steps that have already been taken or are underway also demonstrate a commitment on the part of the government to better administration of parks and other reserves in Greece. Management plans are being developed for all national parks and already have been completed for three of them. The budget for national parks has increased at a higher rate than for other activities of the Forest Service. Facilities for the reception of the public are also expanding each year, and three information centers with natural history museums are already under construction. Another encouraging development is imminent. Separate sections are to be set up within the forest district offices to deal with all matters of protection and management for all national parks and for some other important reserves.

Finally, it must be emphasized that there is an increasing public awareness about conservation matters, as evidenced by growing press and television coverage of issues related to protected areas. Interested groups are increasing the pressure on governmental bodies for better protection and management of parks and other reserves, and for educational programs for these areas. This environmental awareness, which is the necessary foundation of political commitment, is clear evidence that the exceptional natural heritage of Greece, as expressed in its national parks and nature reserves, will be more effectively protected and managed in the years to come.

NOTES

1. OECD, *Environmental Policies in Greece* (Paris: OECD, 1983), p. 105.
2. IUCN Threatened Plants Committee Secretariat, "The Rare, Threatened and Endemic Plants of Greece," *Annales Musei Goulandris* 5 (1982): 69.
3. Phillips Adrian, *Report on a Visit to Greece 8–14 February 1987* (Cheltenham, England: Countryside Commission, 1987), p. 2.
4. Ibid.

BIBLIOGRAPHY

Brousalis, Peter. *The Prespa National Park*. Athens: Hellenic Society for the Protection of Nature, 1974 (in English).
Diapoulis, X. A. "The Flora of Mount Parnitha." *To Vouno—Bulletin of the Hellenic Alpine Club* (November–December 1958): 163–88.
Duffey, E. *National Parks and Reserves of Western Europe*. London: MacDonald and Co., 1982.
Ganiatsas, K. "Botanical Research on the Vicos Gorge." *Ipirotiki Estia* 228–30 (Ioannina 1971): 1–28.
Hallman, Ben. "Notes on Bird Nesting and Conservation in Some Greek Wetlands." *Nature-Bulletin of the Hellenic Society for the Protection of Nature* 25 (1981): 44–48.
Hellenic Society for the Protection of Nature. *Proceedings, Conference on the Protection of the Flora, Fauna and Biotopes in Greece*. Athens, 1979.
Joensen, A. H., and J. Madsen. "Waterfowl and Raptors Wintering in Wetlands of W. Greece." *Nature Jutlandica* 21, no. 11 (1985): 169–200.
Kassioumis, Kostas. "The Vicos-Aoos National Park." *Motion,* the magazine of Olympic Airways (July 1987): 64–73 (in Greek and English).
Larsen, J. *National Park System Plan for Greece*. U.S. Department of the Interior, National Parks Service, 1974.
Malakou, M., et al. "Pindos (Valia Calda) National Park." *Nature-Bulletin of Hellenic Society for the Protection of Nature* 31 (December 1985): 3–17 (in Greek).
Mavromatis, George. "The Ecology of the Vai Palm-Forest of Criti." *To Dassos* 59–60 (1973): 21–24 (in Greek).
———. "Research on the Samaria's National Park Ecosystem." *Announcements of the Forest Research Institute of Athens* 4 (1976): 77–106 (in Greek with English summary).

Ministry of Agriculture, National Parks Section. *Proceedings, Conference on Management of National Parks and Other Protected Areas*. Athens, 1984 (papers in Greek and some in English).

Pavlidis, G. *Geobotanical Study of Lake Prespa National Park*. Thessaloniki: Aristotelian University, 1985 (in Greek with English summary).

Phitos, D., and J. Dambold. "The Flora of the Island of Kefalonia." *Botanika Chronika* 5 (1–2) University of Patras, 1985.

Schultze-Vestrum, G. *The White Mountains National Park of Greece. A Report on Its Conservation Status*. Assehhausen, Germany, 1969.

Scott, D. A. *Preliminary Inventory of Wetlands of International Importance for Waterfowl in West Europe and North-west Africa*. Slimbridge, England: International Waterfowl and Wetlands Research Bureau Special Publication No. 2, 1980.

Sevastos, C. G. "Greece." In *Proceedings, International Conference on Conservation of Wetlands and Waterfowl. Heleigenhafen 2–6, Dec 1974*, edited by E. M. Smart. Slimbridge, England: IWRB, 1976.

Stein, J. "The Kentriki Primary Forest in the Rodopi Mountains (North Greece)." *Nature and National Parks* 19 (1981): 10–12.

Strid, Arne. "The Endemic Plant Species of Mount Olympos." *Nature-Bulletin of the Hellenic Society for the Protection of Nature* 5, nos. 19–20, (1979): 42–54 (in English).

————. *The Flora of Mount Olympos*. Athens: Goulandris Natural History Museum, 1980 (in Greek).

Waycott, Angus. *National Parks of Western Europe*. Southampton: Inklon Publications, 1983.

Zaaijer, J. N. *National Park and Environmental Forestry in Greece*. Rome: FAO, 1971.

HONDURAS   10

Jaime Bustillo-Pon

The history and management of Honduran national parks and nature reserves exemplify the common tension between preservation and economic development. Honduras has a vast genetic pool of subtropical and tropical plants and animals, many rare or endangered, deserving of protection. Such protection, however, might curtail the production of wood, the export of which is important to the Honduran economy as well as that of a number of more economically developed countries that provide the export market.

HISTORY

Through our history as a nation, there have been men of wisdom who desired to declare certain areas of the country as national parks or forest reserves, but it took many years for a government to take those ideas and convert them into laws. The basic development needs of Honduras—housing, road construction, education, etc.—were given higher priority. Furthermore, there was no scarcity of nature. As recently as fifty years ago Honduras was largely undeveloped, with surpluses of forest, water, and soil suitable for agriculture.

A few nature reserves had been declared prior to 1980. Among them were the Lake Yojoa Watershed Protected Area and the Cusuco, San Juancito, Mangroves, Guanaja Island, and Olancho protected forest zones. The Protected Forest Zone of Olancho set aside pine reserves to be used by the pulp and paper industries. Most of the other nature reserves were declared primarily to protect the watersheds of important rivers or catchments that provide water to important cities, like Tegucigalpa, the capital, and San Pedro Sula, the second largest city in the country.

In a few cases, nature reserves were established to protect important ecosystems. This is the case for the Mangroves Reserve adjoining the Gulf of Fonseca on the Pacific coast of Honduras. Most of the reserves prior to 1980 were created by the government in the absence of significant public support.

By 1980 conditions had changed. In June 1976 the Honduran government and the national university jointly convened the First National Seminar on Renewable Natural Resources and the Environment. As a result of discussions held here, it was proposed to establish a Honduran Ecological Association (HEA), a private, nonprofit organization dedicated to environmental education and to the creation and defense of national parks and reserves in partnership with the Honduran government and the international conservation community. The HEA was formally chartered in April 1979 when its bylaws were approved by the government.

The most significant decisions to date concerning Honduran nature reserves have occurred in the last ten years, as a direct result of the combined efforts of the government and the HEA. In 1980 the government created two reserves, each with a clear management status. A cloud forest called La Tigra became the first national park, and the Río Platano watershed was designated a biosphere reserve. In 1987 the government promulgated Decree 87–87, establishing eleven new national parks, nine wildlife refuges, and eighteen biological reserves. This decree represents the most important development in the history of Honduran conservation and in the development of a genuine system of national parks and nature reserves.

These reserves have solid legal protection; however, social and political problems of national scope prevent either the government or the private sector from effectively enforcing the forestry law or the nature reserve decrees. The Honduran system of land tenure forces landless peasants to cultivate their corn in the forest and on the hillsides. These peasant farmers migrate from one area to another, practicing the slash-and-burn method of agriculture. This process is destroying more than 100,000 hectares (247,000 acres) a year, most of it broadleaf forest. A second problem arises from the Honduran dependence on the export of wood. From the government's viewpoint, that export remains a high priority, for it creates jobs and generates dollars of foreign exchange.

PARKS AND RESERVES

Honduran nature reserves exist primarily to protect watersheds by conserving the forest. Preserving the diversity of plants and animals within the watershed is a by-product of forest conservation. Although the development of recreation and tourism has been declared to be a national priority, it has not had much influence on the creation of reserves. This is evident in the descriptions of important parks and reserves that follow. Please refer to Figure 10.1 for the locations of areas discussed below.

Figure 10.1
National Parks and Protected Areas of Honduras

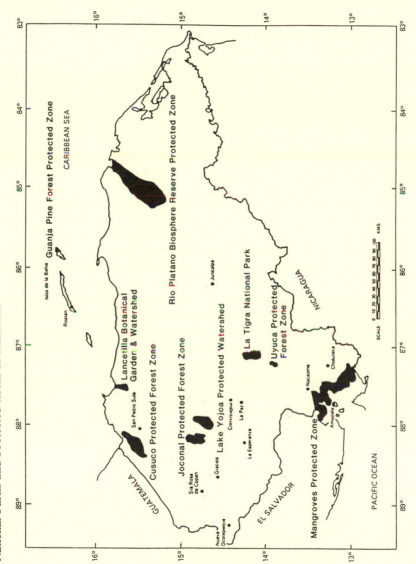

La Tigra National Park

La Tigra National Park was created on July 14, 1980, by Decree 976. The park is almost 8,000 hectares (19,800 acres) in size and has a maximum elevation of nearly 2,300 meters (7,550 feet) above sea level. La Tigra is one of the main sources of water for the capital city of Tegucigalpa. Moreover, La Tigra is the only protected area in the national park category for which special management policies have been established.

This cloud forest has a high potential for tourism and recreation because it is located only one hour from Tegucigalpa, a city of 750,000 population. Here you can find the legendary quetzal (*Pharamacus mocino mocino*) and a host of other birds and animals.

The Río Platano Biosphere Reserve

The second important nature reserve is the Río Platano Biosphere Reserve, which is part of the Man and the Biosphere Program sponsored by the United Nations Educational, Scientific, and Cultural Organization (Unesco). This reserve was declared on July 14, 1980, by Decree 975. It was intended to protect most of the 100-kilometer (62-mile) long watershed of the Platano River and parts of other important rivers including the Paulaya, Guampu, and Sicre. It extends over more than 500,000 hectares (1.24 million acres) of diverse landforms providing habitat for an incredible diversity of plants and animals. Here there is a fantastic genetic pool almost certain to contain unknown plants and animals waiting to be discovered and named.

This reserve is the Honduran forest's last frontier, but its future is not bright. Nearly 50 percent of the forest has been cut. Cattle have been introduced, and slash-and-burn agriculture is being practiced with very low yield in commodities but great and irreversible damage to the watershed. If present trends continue, the reserve will be gone in a decade.

Mangrove Nature Reserve

Another very important nature reserve was created many years ago. It protects the mangroves located on the Gulf of Fonseca, a part of the Pacific Ocean on the southern coast of Honduras.

The reserve's primary value is in the preservation of five different species of mangrove, which together sustain the reproduction of shrimp and provide for a commercially viable shrimp industry. Although legal protection exists in theory, management is totally absent. The mangroves are allowed to be cut for domestic as well as for industrial purposes, e.g., salt and tannins.

Lake Yojoa Watershed Multiple-Use Nature Reserve

There is only one multiple-use nature reserve in Honduras, the Lake Yojoa Watershed Nature Reserve, declared on October 27, 1971, by Decree 71. Lake Yojoa is the major natural lake in Honduras and the primary resource of this nature reserve. The lake provides hydroelectric power and has a very high potential for recreation and tourism. The lake itself covers an area of 79 square kilometers (49 square miles) at an altitude of 632 meters (2,073 feet) and drains a watershed of almost 337 square kilometers (209 square miles). Nearby Santa Barbara Mountain rises to 2,744 meters (9,000 feet) in height.

Although the Lake Yojoa Reserve is protected by decree, management is lacking, and the forests are being converted to agriculture. On hillsides coffee and corn are cultivated, and cattle are grazed. Soil erosion is accelerating and reducing the watershed's capacity to hold the water that feeds Lake Yojoa. The lake is slowly being killed.

Cusuco Nature Reserve

Cusuco reserves the northernmost part of the Meredon Mountain chain in the northwestern part of Honduras, an area known as Sierra Omoa. A cloud forest with a diversity of little-known animals and plants, it was once home to the tallest trees in Central America. It is located near San Pedro Sula, the second largest city in Honduras with a population of half a million.

This reserve was declared on March 10, 1959, by Decree 53. The decree stated that this reserve should eventually be converted into a national park, but thirty years later the conversion has not been accomplished.

Lancetilla Botanical Garden and Nature Reserve

This botanical garden was established in 1926 by the United Fruit Company, a multinational corporation with headquarters in the United States. It is located next to the Caribbean Sea on the eastern coast of Honduras. Its collection of more than 600 species of tropical plants spreads over 400 hectares (1,000 acres). This extensive collection results primarily from the efforts of Wilson Popenoe, a botanist for United Fruit whose studies carried him far beyond the plants of potential commercial value for which he was presumably being paid. The surrounding nature reserve, nearly 1,000 hectares (2,500 acres) of humid forest, includes a portion of the Lancetilla River and its watershed. The watershed provides water to the nearby town of Tela. The town and its harbor are frequented by tourists all year round, but during summer the beautiful beaches are a particular attraction.

Other Nature Reserves

The other nature reserves in Honduras are smaller. The Uyuca Botanical Nature Reserve protects nearly 350 hectares (865 acres) of cloud forest. It provides water and research possibilities to one of the main agricultural schools in Latin America, the Pan-American Agricultural School in El Zamorano Valley.

The Joconal Nature Reserve was recently declared. This area of humid rain forest has suffered extensive deforestation. Its restoration would be very significant because it is part of the watershed of Yojoa Lake.

Least known is the protected pine forest of Guanaja Island, named Island of the Pines by Christopher Columbus because of the abundance of these trees. Guanaja is one of the three *Islas de la Bahía* in the Caribbean Sea off the northern coast of Honduras.

Unfortunately, most of the national parks, wildlife refuges, and biological reserves created by Decree 87–87 exist only on paper. They lack management plans and protection.

ADMINISTRATION

Governmental efforts to protect and manage our national parks and nature reserves are minimal, limited both by budget and by lack of political will.

More people are being trained, both within the country and abroad, and more governmental representatives are attending international meetings on natural resources management. More areas are being designated as national parks or nature reserves. However, few improvements are observed in terms of better management of the areas already extant.

In 1974, the government created the Honduran Forestry Development Corporation (*Corporación Hondurena de Desarrollo Forestal,* COHDEFOR) to commercialize the forests and provide proper multiple-use forest management. This was to be accomplished under a series of decrees that create a kind of partnership between COHDEFOR and private forestry interests. Unfortunately, the combination of agriculture and forestry—designed to assimilate and stabilize the population of peasants already planting within the forests—has had a tremendous deleterious impact on watersheds, and the emphasis on exploitation of resources was not balanced with proportional efforts to create and manage nature reserves.

By contrast, the responsibility for creating nature reserves and especially national parks, was placed in the Directorate of Renewable Natural Resources (*Dirección General de Recursos Naturales Renovables,* RENARE), also created in 1974. Unfortunately, neither RENARE nor COHDEFOR had the budget or the political power effectively to create, protect, and manage national parks and nature reserves, so their efforts have been very limited. Neither COHDEFOR nor RENARE has enough trained personnel and vehicles to patrol the few areas that have been set aside as nature reserves.

The primary impetus for nature conservation has come from a private, nonprofit environmentaLturn has been dependent on international resources. Between 1983 and 1986 funding for the HEA's environmental education and field projects came initially from the United States Agency for International Development and later from the World Wildlife Fund of the United States and the International Union for the Conservation of Nature. The HEA, the biology department of National University, and the Peace Corps contingent in Honduras have also supported conservation activities.

The HEA promotes the slogan, "a green Honduras for the year 2000." A green Honduras is a Honduras with healthy forest and soil, clean air, pure water, and vibrant fauna, all contributing to an improved quality of life. This is a goal toward which we should all strive—in Honduras and around the world.

NOTE

The author wishes to acknowledge the assistance of Ms. Jennifer Barker, United States Peace Corps, with the English version of this manuscript.

BIBLIOGRAPHY

Betancourt, J., and P. Dulin. *Yojoa Lake Multiple Use Plan*. Tegucigalpa: Consejo Superior de Planificación Economica, 1978.
Consejo Superior de Planificación Economica (CONSUPLANE). *National Plan for Development, Environmental Sector*. Tegucigalpa: CONSUPLANE, 1979–1980.
Corporación Hondurena de Desarrollo Forestal (COHDEFOR). *Gerencia de Comercializacion*. Tegucigalpa: COHDEFOR, 1974–1985.
Dirección General de Recursos Naturales Renovables (RENARE). *La Tigra Management Plan*. Tegucigalpa: RENARE, 1981.
———. *Plan de Manejo de la Biosfera de Río Platano*. Tegucigalpa: RENARE, 1979.
———. *Plan Maestro del Parque Nacional la Tigra*. Tegucigalpa: RENARE, 1979.
———. *Río Platano Management Plan*. Tegucigalpa: RENARE, 1984.
United States Agency for International Development. *Environmental Profile of Honduras*. Washington, D.C.: Government Printing Office, 1982.

INDIA

11

Samar Singh and
W. A. Rodgers

Why should an international audience be concerned with the wildlife protected areas system in India? There are several reasons, of which the most important are the enormous value of India's natural resources and the enormous pressures to which those resources are subjected. India has arguably the world's greatest diversity of biological communities as well as the most acute set of pressures on land and natural resources from a huge and still-growing human population. If conservation can be made to work in India, then it can work anywhere.

The biological diversity of India is a consequence of physical and climatic factors plus its geographical position. Altitudes range from sea level to 8,000 meters (26,000 feet) in the Himalayas; rainfall varies from the wettest place on earth with 12,000 millimeters per annum to absolute desert. Deserts themselves vary from hot arid sands with summer temperatures of 50° Celsius (120° Fahrenheit) to high-altitude cold deserts with virtual permafrost. India forms a meeting place of three great zoogeographical regions of the earth: the western African, the northern Eurasian, and the eastern Oriental. All three regions contribute species to India's faunal and floral diversity.

Currently, India has a network of some 460 wildlife protected areas—national parks, and sanctuaries—covering about 3.5 percent of the country's land surface. The network continues to grow, increasingly according to a scientific plan designed to assure adequate coverage of India's biogeographical and biological diversity. Such national networks are seen as a cornerstone of conservation policies. The network planned for India envisages some 600 protected areas to cover about 5.0 percent of the land surface of the country.

The history of conservation in India goes back thousands of years. Scientific management of the forests themselves dates from the late 1800s. More recently there have been significant contributions to integrated resource use and management involving total protection of core areas and regulated use of buffer areas. India, therefore, has much to demonstrate to other tropical nations in the field of wildlife management.

Practical wildlife management derived from rational land-use planning will become increasingly necessary as human population pressure grows. India today has 800 million people, which will grow to 1.3 billion by the year 2030. There will continue to be great pressure on forest lands for fuel, fodder, and other products. The forests, and especially the network of protected areas, will be of even greater importance for maintaining watershed capacities.

The great majority of people, however, do not consider issues of management, biogeography, and watersheds when they think of wildlife protected areas. They think of species, the animal values themselves. India has a wealth of species instilling a variety of emotions. The tiger is the focus of most attention, revered in religion and mythology, a symbol of power, majesty, and fear in the forest. India has more tigers than all other countries. Elephant, rhinoceros, lion, snow leopard, three crocodilians, a variety of bears, lesser cats, Himalayan sheep and goats, and pheasants are all of great conservation importance.

HISTORY

India has a long tradition of wildlife and wildland conservation. The ancient Hindu scriptures or Vedas directed people to protect their environment and wildlife. In the fourth century B.C., a manual of statecraft, the *Arthashastra,* advocated the establishment of "Abhayaranyas," or forest sanctuaries. Sacred groves of forest may go back several thousand years, before agrarian societies. Later in history ruling kings and princes set aside areas as their hunting reserves. Many of these reserves remained intact until after independence in 1947, when they were constituted as national parks and sanctuaries.

After a century of uncontrolled exploitation the British developed policies to conserve resources of economic value: timber and, to a lesser extent, water. The forest reservations often led to great rural hardships. The reserved forests allowed the British to regulate hunting and also to introduce conservation concepts.

The growth of communications, large-scale cultivation, forest clearing, and population pressure, as well as hunting, led to the rapid decline of many species. This prompted the declaration of protected areas for animal populations. The great Indian one-horned rhinoceros in Kaziranga in Assam was reduced to a population of twelve animals early this century. As a result, a rhinoceros sanctuary was set up in 1911. Elephants were similarly protected in Periyar in Kerala.

The need to conserve species of importance for hunting resulted in a plethora of hunting rules and regulations: bag limits, closed seasons, firearm types, closed areas, scales of fees, etc.

In the 1930s wildlife conservation developed an international image, following the creation of national parks in the United States and in South Africa. The Empire Faunal Conference in London in 1933 urged all British territories to develop parks for conservation. India's oldest park, now Corbett National Park in Uttar Pradesh, was created in 1935 following this conference.

Conservation efforts follow from the National Forest Policy statements in 1894, 1952, and a revised policy adopted in December 1988. The Indian Forest Acts of 1865 and 1927 and their amendments provided considerable protection to wildlife by means of the systems of reserved and protected forests. The constitution of India exhorts government and citizens to protect wildlife:

The State shall endeavor to protect and improve the environment and to safeguard the forests and wildlife of the country. (Article 48)

It shall be the duty of every citizen to protect and improve the natural environment including forests, lakes, rivers and wildlife, and to have compassion for living creatures. (Article 51A)

In 1972 the Wildlife (Protection) Act was introduced and has since been adopted by all the state governments. In 1976 forestry and wildlife protection were placed on the concurrent list of subjects under the constitution, giving the central government a decisive role in these matters.

The Wildlife (Protection) Act provides for the creation of national parks and wildlife sanctuaries. National parks are not to have any form of exploitation or habitation, and boundary changes require resolutions of state legislatures. Wildlife sanctuaries may have limited forms of regulated use.

Today the reasons given for the creation and development of protected areas are far more complex than in earlier days when valued resources such as timber or sporting trophies were the major objectives. Modern conservation movements see value in naturalness, diversity, maintenance of genetic resources, aesthetics, science, education, etc. An interesting aspect of wildlife conservation in India is the relatively low importance given in protected areas to tourism. To the average man in the street the most important aspect of protected areas is his ability to go there and watch animals; this is given no emphasis by management agencies or government.

Many organizations have been involved in the development of protected areas. Ultimately, the state governments make the decision to notify and declare the sanctuaries and parks. State governments are often influenced by the central government. Both state and central governments may be lobbied by nongovernmental conservation organizations and by individuals. The creation of the Silent Valley National Park in the evergreen forests of Kerala was a major conservation victory for the NGOs in the face of strong opposition by vested interests.

PARKS AND RESERVES

National parks and wildlife sanctuaries in most cases have been created to conserve the "total natural ecosystem," and the physical substrate, vegetation, and animal components are all of importance. Current philosophy does not see

Table 11.1

Representative Protected Areas in the Biogeographic Zones of India

BIOGEOGRAPHIC ZONE: PROVINCE	MAJOR REPRESENTATIVE PROTECTED AREAS[a]			
	NAME	STATUS	STATE(S)	km²	IMPORTANT FAUNA
1A. Trans Himalayan: Ladakh	Hemis	NP	Jammu & Kashmir	600 (3,000)	Snow leopard, sheep & goats.
2A. Himalaya: North West	Dachigam	NP	Jammu & Kashmir	141	Hangul (red deer), black bear.
	Great Himalayan	NP	Himachal Pradesh	1,716	Snow leopard, brown bear, ibex.
2B. Himalaya: West	Nanda Devi	NP	Uttar Pradesh	630	Snow leopard, blue sheep.
	Kedarnath	NP	Uttar Pradesh	930	Musk dear, tahr, blue sheep.
2C. Himalaya: Central	Khangchendzonga	NP	Sikkim	849	Snow leopard, bear, blue sheep, etc.
	Neora Valley	NP	West Bengal	98	Wide range of plant formations.
2D. Himalaya: East	Namdapha	NP	Arunachal Pradesh	1,807 (2,050)	Plant formations, primates, cats.
3A. Desert: Kutch	Wild Ass	WLS (NP)	Gujarat	5,000 (1,000)	Wild ass, gazelle.
3B. Desert: Thar	Desert	NP	Rajasthan	(500)	Gazelle, bustards.
4A. Semi-Arid: Punjab	Keoladeo Chana	NP	Rajasthan	28	Water fowl.
4B. Semi-Arid: Rajwar-Gujarat	Ranthambor	NP	Rajasthan	397	Tiger, sambar, etc.
	Gir	WLS+NP	Gujarat	1,412	Asiatic lion, sambar, etc.
5A. Western Ghats: Plains	Sanjay Gandhi	NP	Maharashtra	86	Leopard
5B. Western Ghats: Hills	Nagarhole	NP	Karnataka	572	Elephant, bison, sambar, etc.
	Silent Valley	NP	Kerala	89	Forest species.
	Periyar	WLS+NP	Kerala	900	Elephant, bison, forests.
	Anamalai	WLS	Tamil Nadu	960	Nilgiri tahr, elephant, primates

Region	Protected Area	Status	State	Area	Species
6A. Deccan: South Plateau	Nagarjunasagar	WLS	Andhra Pradesh	3,300	Tiger, sambar, etc.
6B. Deccan: Central Plateau	Tadoba	NP	Maharashtra	117	Bison, sambar.
6C. Deccan: Eastern Plateau	Kanger Valley	NP	Madhya Pradesh	200	Plant formations.
6D. Deccan: Chota Nagpur	Simlipal	WLS+NP	Orissa	2,200	Tiger, elephant, plants.
	Palamau	WLS+NP	Bihar	967	Tiger, sambar, etc.
6E. Deccan: Central Highlands	Kanha	NP	Madhya Pradesh	940	Tiger, swamp deer, bison, etc.
	Melghat	WLS (NP)	Maharashtra	1,300	Tiger, bison, sambar, etc.
7A. Gangetic Plains: Upper	Corbett	NP	Uttar Pradesh	521	Tiger, sambar, crocodile.
7B. Gangetic Plains: Lower	Buxa	WLS	West Bengal	360	Elephant, forest species.
8A. North-east: Brahmaputra	Manas	WLS	Assam	390 (1,097)	Elephant, rhino, wild buffalo, primates.
	Kaziranga	NP	Assam	696	Elephant, rhino, wild buffalo, birds.
8B. North-east: Hills	Balphakram	NP	Meghalaya	220,330	Elephant, primates, forest spp.
	Keibul Lamjao	NP	Manipur	40	Brow-antlered deer.
9A. Andaman Islands	Wandour Marine	NP	Andamans	282	Salt water crocodile, mangroves.
	Mount Harriet	NP	Andamans	47	Forest communities.
9B. Nicobar Islands	Several protected areas are proposed.				
9C. Lakshadweep	A marine protected area is being established at present.				
10A. West Coasts	Marine	NP	Gujarat	163	Mangroves, birds.
10B. East Coasts	Sunderbands	NP	West Bengal	1,330	Mangroves, tiger, crocodiles.

Note: a A status or an acreage enclosed in parentheses denotes a proposal.

Source: W. A. Rodgers and H. S. Panwar. Planning a Wildlife Protected Area Network in India. New Delhi: Wildlife Institute of India, 1988.

187

a role for permanent human settlement, including forest-living tribal people, in this natural system, even though some groups still maintain a hunter-gatherer culture and others have high forest resource dependency. This holistic ecosystem approach contrasts with the many fewer protected areas created for individual species, often those of critical population status, for example, the Asiatic lion in Gir National Park, the *hangul* or red deer in Dachigam National Park, the brow-antlered deer of Keibul Lamjao National Park, etc. Protected areas are not created for recreation, although in a few cases seminatural areas near large cities have been made into national parks for education purposes, e.g., Van Vihar National Park at Bhopal, Borivli National Park at Bombay, and Guindy National Park at Madras.

Biogeographic Region and Biological Communities

The fact that India has laid stress on the holistic or community approach to conservation necessitates discussion of conservation efforts at these broad levels, before describing species values themselves. Ten biogeographic zones are recognized in the country, split into twenty-six biotic provinces. The zones separate the major areas of biological diversity, for example, the Himalayas from the Gangetic Plains and from the Deccan Peninsula. The provinces recognize secondary differences. Within the Himalayas, for example, the eastern biota are distinct from those of the western areas.

Conservation plans are to ensure that each state has a major national park covering each biome (i.e., in the Himalayas, the broadleaf forests, the coniferous forests, the subalpine forests, and the alpine communities) in each province or subsidiary region of a large province. Secondary values would be covered by additional protected areas. The 1988 protected area planning report by W. A. Rodgers and H. S. Panwar recognizes that several provinces are still poorly protected and proposes new areas to fill the gaps. Provinces 1A in Ladakh, 6A in the far south of the Deccan, 8B in the North Eastern hills, and 9B in the Nicobar Islands are immediate examples.

Table 11.1 gives examples of major protected areas and their typical faunal values within each zone. Table 11.2 indicates both the existing and the proposed protected area network status for each biogeographic zone.

Geology

Existing and proposed protected areas will cover the broad range of geological formations and landforms in the country. India's highest peaks, Khangchend-zonga and Nanda Devi, are both within national parks. This coverage will include three parks for fossil plants near Jaisalmer, Jabalpur, and Chandrapur. The Shivalik vertebrate fossil beds are partially included in Rajaji National Park. The wide range of coastal formations, however, are still poorly represented.

Table 11.2
Protected Area Status in Each Biogeographic Zone in India

BIOGEOGRAPHIC ZONE	EXISTING STATUS			PLANNED STATUS		
	No.of PAs	Area	% of Zone	No.of PAs	Area (km²)	% of Zone
1. Trans Himalayan[a]	2	800	–	18	12,000	–
2. Himalayas	56	12,908	6.0	92	23,529	9.2
3. Desert	5	8,897	4.0	20	8,553[b]	3.8
4. Semi–Arid	53	11,723	2.3	75	17,876	2.5
5. Western Ghats	44	15,935	10.0	69	15,528[b]	9.7
6. Deccan	115	48,110	3.4	190	56,013	3.9
7. Gangetic Plain	25	4,524	1.3	49	6,221	1.7
8. North–East India	17	1,882	1.1	67	9,381	5.5
9. Islands	100[c]	710	8.3	40	2,323	27.5
10. Coasts	17	4,433	–[d]	37	4,948	–[d]
Total	426[e]	109,652	3.3	651[e]	151,342	4.6

NOTES:

[a] Part of this zone is occupied by Pakistan and China and so percentage data are misleading.

[b] New "planned area" totals are after some very large protected areas have been degazetted.

[c] Figure includes 90 tiny islands as separate sanctuaries.

[d] It is not possible to give a meaningful figure for "percent area" of linear coastline.

[e] Totals do not add up, as some protected areas stretch over two zones. This is the figure for 1987. There have many new protected areas implemented since the report was published.

Source: W. A. Rodgers and H. S. Panwar. *Planning a Wildlife Protected Area Network in India*. New Delhi: Wildlife Institute of India, 1988.

History and Archaeology

Historical monuments do not come under the protected area legislation but are administered by the Archaeological Survey of India (ASI). However, the widespread nature of India's rich archaeological heritage means that many protected areas do have significant religious and historical monuments. Examples include the ancient hilltop fortified city of Ranthambore in Ranthambore National Park, Kankwarhi Mughal fort in Sariska National Park, Ramgarh tribal fort in Palamau National Park, and Nagdwari and Mahadeo temples in Pachmarhi Wildlife Sanctuary. The U.S. National Park Service is starting a cooperative venture with ASI to improve conservation and interpretation activities.

Biological Values

Flora. India has over 16,000 higher plant species, of which some 4,800 are considered endemic. Endemism is especially high in five centers of diversity: the Western Ghats, the North East, the Himalayas, the Andaman and Nicobar islands, and, to a lesser extent, the western desert. Of the total flora several hundred species are of conservation significance.

The protected areas network was initially constituted for larger animals; plants and lesser animal species were neglected. This picture is slowly changing, and several protected areas are being developed for plant values: Valley of Flowers National Park in the high Himalayas and Silent Valley National Park in the Western Ghats evergreen forests of Kerala are two immediate examples. Many smaller protected areas have been suggested for rhododendrons, orchids, sacred groves, riverine vegetation, Himalayan forests, the red sanders forests, and mangroves in different parts of the country. The community approach to conservation management and the wide distribution of protected areas have ensured that the great majority of species are within the protected areas system.

Fauna. India has 341 mammal species, 1,400 bird species, 400 reptile species, and 181 amphibian species. Protected areas, however, have traditionally been concerned only with the larger mammals and birds. Of the larger mammals, most have populations in the protected areas system. However, according to the criteria of the International Union for the Conservation of Nature (IUCN), many species are not yet adequately conserved. For example, out of 34 ungulate species and significant subspecies, only 10 have 2 or more populations of over 1,000 animals in the protected areas system.

Northeast India is still poorly protected; an analysis of the distribution of pheasant taxa shows over half of the pheasant species in northeast India (the highest center of diversity) are not in national parks. New protected area proposals will ensure adequate coverage.

India has achieved considerable success in the conservation of the moist and dry deciduous forest animal communities. The population of tigers, for example, has more than doubled in the past fifteen years. Much of the credit must go to ambitious conservation schemes such as Project Tiger. Planned schemes for similar Project Elephant and Project Snow Leopard should greatly strengthen conservation efforts in the protected areas of the more fragile evergreen forest and Himalayan environments.

Table 11.3 lists mammal species still not represented within a national park. Many are from the Himalayas or the evergreen forests. For several species there is inadequate survey information on which to base conservation efforts. There is still a need for much greater levels of research and species status survey.

Table 11.3
Threatened Mammal Species with No Viable Population in a National Park in India

SPECIES	NOTES
Crabeating Macaque	New proposals in Nicobar Islands
Pigtailed Macaque	Survey needed in Assam
Stumptailed Macaque	Survey needed in Assam
Golden Langur	Upgrade Manas Wildlife Sanctuary
Pygmy Hog	Upgrade Manas Wildlife Sanctuary
Hispid Hare	Upgrade Manas Wildlife Sanctuary
Indian Wild Ass	Upgrade Wild Ass Wildlife Sanctuary
Malabar Civet	Survey in southern Western Ghats
Malay Sun Bear	Possibly extinct in India; Survey
Markhor	Create Wildlife Sanctuary/National Park in Pir Panjal Mountain Range
Argali Sheep	Survey Ladakh and North Sikkim
Tibetan Antelope	Survey Ladakh
Tibetan Gazelle	Survey Ladakh
Grizzled Giant Squirrel	Wildlife Sanctuary is planned for sole relict population
Rusty Spotted Cat	Survey in northern part of Western Ghats

NOTE: Threatened is defined here as inclusion in Schedule 1 of the Wildlife (Protection) Act.

ADMINISTRATION

Administrative Agencies

The protected areas are administered by the wildlife agencies of the state governments. Forests (and hence wildlife) were originally classified as a state function under the constitution, but in 1976 they were placed on the concurrent list, giving the central government legislative powers. The central government maintains a national wildlife directorate within the Ministry of Environment and Forests.

Several sets of legislation control the practice of wildlife conservation. As most wildlife areas were originally forest lands, the provisions of the Indian Forest Act and the more recent Forest (Conservation) Act of 1980 apply. The Wildlife (Protection) Act of 1972 is the principal legislation.

Conservation Philosophies

Two schools of management philosophy are discussed in wildlife forums. These are the "let nature take its course" or laissez-faire policy, typical of eastern Africa, and the more manipulative-interventionist policy of the intensive management school typical of southern Africa. The very small size of most of India's wildlife protected areas, and the level of past and present human interference, necessitate considerable management input. Management has sought to reduce adverse impacts and restore some degree of naturalness to the ecosystem.

Increasingly, however, India will have to face problems of local overabundance as conservation efforts raise population levels to situations where excess animals disperse to adjacent settlements, causing loss of life, livestock, and crops. Solutions to such problems will not be easy within a society that has reverence for all forms of life.

Yet another crucial management aspect is the interface between people and wildlife. It is increasingly realized that when planning conservation efforts wildlife administration must also consider the views of local rural populations having a high material dependence on forest resources. This realization has led to the development of the core and buffer zone concepts, the need to seek public cooperation, and the need to provide ecologically sustainable life styles to human populations within and adjacent to the protected areas.

Levels of Protection

India maintains several categories of conservation estates. Wildlife populations still exist on private and revenue (public) lands, particularly the arid zone communities of black buck, nilgai, and gazelle, all of which, together with the wild boar, can cause considerable crop damage. Religious sentiment, especially by the Bishnoi community of western India, gives great protection to the bovids. The reserve forest system still has low density but widespread wildlife populations especially where forest block size is large and human interference is low. Reserve forests have multiple functions including catchment, timber, and provision of fuel, fodder, and minor produce to local communities, as well as protection of wildlife. Reserve forests vary from intact natural forest to degraded forest to plantation; they obviously vary in their ability to maintain wildlife populations.

The Wildlife (Protection) Act lays down two levels of protection: the wildlife sanctuary, where some resource exploitation may be allowed by the chief wildlife warden provided it does not affect conservation interests, and the national park, where no exploitation may be allowed at all.

At an administrative level, wildlife areas may also be designated as "tiger reserves"—India has seventeen—and, beginning in 1990 when they become eligible for increased funding, also as "snow leopard reserves" and "elephant reserves." Some fourteen areas of wildlife estate and adjacent settlements are also to be designated as "biosphere reserves" with enhanced planning and research provisions as suggested by Unesco's Man and the Biosphere Program.

Establishment Procedure

The legislation setting up protected areas recognized that the legal procedures could not be carried out immediately. Implementation involves a two-stage approach. The initial notification is followed by a period when existing exploitation and settlement rights and privileges are revoked and compensated. This is followed, in the case of parks, by final declaration.

Often, this settlement phase has taken much longer than planned. Many parks have not achieved final declaration and still suffer exploitation.

Recreation, Education and Research

Recreation itself is not thought of as a primary purpose of protected area development. However, the wildlife tourist industry is growing, and most parks and sanctuaries have limited facilities for tourist board and lodging. Although tourism is not openly encouraged and, in some cases, may even be thought of as a major problem for management, there is growing support for the provision of educational and interpretive programs in the protected areas. These programs are still largely for the educated urban elite, but attention is turning to the development of programs for the poorer rural people adjacent to, and often antagonistic toward, the protected area.

Educational programs in wildlife management are undertaken at the central government level for managers and range officers at the Wildlife Institute of India in Dehra Dun. The institute is also actively engaged in research into wildlife conservation and management, a subject that was slow to develop in the regular university system.

Level of Resource Management

Resource management in the Indian context is very much more than anti-poaching. With the exception of rhino in the northeast, musk in the Himalayas, and ivory in the south, poaching is not a major problem as it is in many other countries. Major problems include stoppage of illegal livestock grazing and fodder collection and the stoppage of illegal minor produce collection, such as fuelwood, gum, and leaves. Adopting a system of core and buffer zones allows the protected area administration to permit resource exploitation in the buffer while rigidly preventing use of the core zone. It has become increasingly obvious that much greater attention has to be given to mechanisms by which buffer-zone resource use can be regulated. Demand for produce is much higher than annual production.

Exploitation is not only by the local people. The past history of protected areas as regular working forests has involved a variety of activities: legal timber operations (often involving plantations of exotics), mining, communication access (roads, railways), access of pilgrims to religious shrines, village settlements, and so forth. These adverse factors cannot be stopped overnight, and they constitute a major management problem.

Frequently there are villages located within what is needed as core zone area. Management plans call for their relocation to peripheral areas, preferably near forests where they can maintain natural life styles. Such relocation, however, involves many political and administrative problems, of which finding suitable and acceptable land is only the first. Still, there have been success stories; the relocation of villages from western Kanha National Park is a major example.

The variety of resource exploitation, access, village presence, and so on, affects the protected areas adversely. Naturalness is reduced. Domestic livestock compete with wildlife populations and have been responsible for the introduction of diseases such as rinderpest, which infected bison in the 1970s. Scarce water holes are occupied by human settlement, and the regeneration of natural plant species is greatly reduced. In some areas livestock may form three-quarters of the ungulate biomass; weeds—especially aggressive woody shrubs such as *Lantana* and *Eupatorium*—may dominate over much of the reserve.

These are the major threats to successful long-term conservation of wildlife and wilderness values. They cannot be stopped by aggressive policing, using more and better armed protection staff, checkposts, barriers, fences, and so forth. Long-term solutions will have to come through a combination of sociopolitical processes. People have a high dependency on forest produce; alternative supplies must be developed by ecodevelopment and rational use of buffer zones.

It is too early to say if conservation is meeting this challenge successfully. Only in the past few years have managers realized the enormity of the people problem facing them and the need to meet it through cooperation, not conflict.

What are the prospects for the future? Planning has to contend not only with today's population pressures but with a population of 1.3 billion by the year 2030. India has the ecological potential to produce the essential components of water, food, and fuelwood for such a population and allow the development of an enlarged protected area network. But—and this is a major constraint—the potential will only be realized with very much greater investment into ecological concerns, social equality (including the problem of the unemployed landless), and environmental education. All aspects of environmental concern must be integrated into India's planning and political processes if the protected areas system is to continue.

BIBLIOGRAPHY

Agarwal, A. "Human-Nature Interactions in a Third World Country." (Fifth Annual World Conservation Lecture.) *Ecologist* 15 (1985): 1–12.
Ahmedullah, M., and M. P. Nayar. *Endemic Plants of the Indian Region*. Howrah, India: Botanical Survey of India, 1987.
Ali, Salim, and S. D. Ripley. *The Handbook of the Birds of India and Pakistan*. London: Oxford University Press, 1984.
Anderson, R., and W. Huber. *The Hour of the Fox*. New Delhi: Sage Publications, 1988.
Bedi, R., and R. Bedi. *Indian Wildlife*. New Delhi: Brijbasi Printers, 1984.
Center for Science and Environment. *The State of India's Environment*. The First and Second Citizens Reports. New Delhi: Center for Science and Environment, 1982 and 1984.
Cubitt, G., and G. Mountfort. *Wild India*. London: Collins, 1985.

Daniel, J. C. *The Book of Indian Reptiles*. Bombay: Bombay Natural History Society, 1983.

Directory of Wildlife Protected Areas in India (4 vols. to date). New Delhi: Indian Institute of Public Administration, 1989.

East, R., ed. *Antelopes, Global Survey and Regional Action Plans: Part I. East and Northeast Africa*. Gland, Switzerland: IUCN, 1988.

Ghorpade, M. Y. *Sunlight and Shadows*. London: Victor Gollancz, 1983.

Guha, R., and M. Gadgil. *State Forestry and Social Conflict in British India: A Study in the Ecological Bases of Agrarian Protest*. Technical Report no. 51. Bangalore, India: Indian Institute of Science, 1988.

Harrison, J., K. Miller, and J. McNeely. "The World Coverage of Protected Areas: Development Goals and Environment Needs." *Ambio* 10 (1982): 238–45.

Indian Board for Wildlife. *Eliciting Public Support for Wildlife Conservation*. New Delhi: Task Force, Indian Board for Wildlife, Department of Environment, Government of India, 1983.

Insight Guide. *Indian Wildlife*. Hong Kong: APA Productions, n.d.

Jain, S. K., and R. R. Rao. *An Assessment of Threatened Plants of India*. Howrah, India: Botanical Survey of India, 1983.

Lal, J. B. *India's Forests: Myth and Reality*. Dehra Dun, India: Natraj Publishers, 1989.

Kothari, A., P. Pandey, Shekhar Singh, and D. Variava. *Management of National Parks and Sanctuaries in India: A Status Report*. New Delhi: Indian Institute of Public Administration, 1989.

McNeely, J. A., and K. R. Miller, eds. *National Parks, Conservation and Development*. Washington, D.C.: Smithsonian Institution Press, 1984.

Mani, M. S., ed. *Ecology and Biogeography in India*. The Hague: W. Junk, 1974.

Panwar, H. S. "What to Do When You've Succeeded: Project Tiger, Ten Years Later." In *National Parks, Conservation and Development,* edited by J. A. McNeely and K. R. Miller. Washington, D.C.: Smithsonian Institution Press, 1984, pp. 183–89.

Polunin, O., and A. Stainton. *Flowers of the Himalaya*. New Delhi: Oxford University Press, 1984.

Prater, S. H. *The Book of Indian Animals*. 3rd ed. with corrections. Bombay: Bombay Natural History Society, 1980.

Puri, G. S., V. M. Meher-Homji, R. K. Gupta, and S. Puri. *Forest Ecology*. 2nd ed. 2 vols. New Delhi: Oxford and IBH Publishing Co., 1983.

Rao, K. "Legislative and Organizational Support for Protected Areas in India." In *Conserving Asia's Natural Heritage,* edited by J. W. Thorsell. Gland, Switzerland: IUCN, 1985.

Rao, K. "Management Problems within India's Wildlife Protected Area Network." In *Wildlife and People,* edited by W. A. Rodgers, H. S. Panwar, and K. Rao. Dehra Dun, India: Wildlife Institute of India, forthcoming.

Rathore, F. S., T. Singh, and V. Thapar. *With Tigers in the Wild*. New Delhi: Vikas Publishing House, 1983.

Rodgers, W. A. "A Rational Wildlife Protected Area Network." In *Wildlife and People,* edited by W. A. Rodgers, H. S. Panwar, and K. Rao. Dehra Dun, India: Wildlife Institute of India, forthcoming.

Rodgers, W. A., and H. S. Panwar. *Planning a Wildlife Protected Area Network in India* New Delhi: Wildlife Institute of India, 1988.

Rodgers, W. A., H. S. Panwar, and K. Rao, eds. *Wildlife and People*. Proceedings of a workshop held at Dehra Dun, April 1989. Dehra Dun, India: Wildlife Institute of India, forthcoming.

Roonwal, M. L., and M. S. Mohnot. *Primates of South Asia*. Cambridge, Mass.: Harvard University Press, 1977.

Saharia, V. B. *Wildlife in India*. Dehra Dun, India: Natraj Publishers, 1982.

———. "The Human Dimension in Wildlife Management: The Indian Experience." In *National Parks, Conservation and Development*, edited by J. A. McNeely and K. R. Miller. Washington, D.C.: Smithsonian Institution Press, 1984.

Sahgal, B., ed. *Sanctuary Asia Magazine*. Bombay: n.d.

Sankhala, K. *Tiger! The Story of the Indian Tiger*. London: Collins, 1978.

Schaller, G. B. *The Deer and the Tiger*. Chicago: University of Chicago Press, 1967.

———. *Mountain Monarchs, Wild Sheep and Goats of the Himalaya*. Chicago: University of Chicago Press, 1977.

Singh, Samar. "Protected Areas in India." In *Conserving Asia's Natural Heritage*, edited by J. W. Thorsell. Gland, Switzerland: IUCN, 1985.

———. *Conserving India's Natural Heritage*. Dehra Dun, India: Natraj Publishers, 1986.

Stracy, P. D. *Wildlife in India, Its Conservation and Control*. New Delhi: Department of Agriculture, Government of India, 1963.

Thorsell, J. W., ed. *Conserving Asia's Natural Heritage*. Gland, Switzerland: IUCN, 1985.

Thapar, V. *Tiger: Portrait of a Predator*. London: Collins, 1986.

Tikader, B. K. *Endangered Animals of India*. Calcutta: Zoological Survey of India, 1983.

World Conservation Monitoring Centre. *India: the Conservation of Biological Diversity*. Cambridge, England: IUCN, 1988.

INDONESIA 12

Alan H. Robinson and Effendy A. Sumardja

Indonesia is a tropical land whose tremendous natural resource richness and diversity are challenged by varied and powerful pressures. An expanding population, growing demands of an increasingly educated citizenry, a colonial history, and varying expectations of diverse ethnic groups are common to many developing nations of the world. Even against this background, nature conservation and national park development have made important progress in Indonesia and may provide some useful examples to other nations.

HISTORY

"Indonesia" as a nation is still young, having been created in 1945 out of the diverse 13,000-island Dutch East Indian Archipelago that stretches eastward for 5,000 kilometers (3,000 miles) off the southeast corner of Asia. See Figure 12.1.

Within the Moslem, Hindu, and other cultures now joined together here are many examples of a deeply rooted ethical respect for man's dependence on the earth for food, water, fuel, and sacred places. Nature reserves in the more modern Western sense are also a long-established concept in Indonesia, dating from the late 1800s, not unlike early park movements in the United States and Europe.

The first true nature reserve in Indonesia was established by decree of the Dutch colonial government in 1889 in an undisturbed montane rain forest in West Java known as Cibodas. The reserve was actually an extension of the older, highly respected Cibodas and Bogor botanical gardens. It was intended to facilitate research as well as to provide protection to the natural forest. Though its management was delegated to the garden's director, the impetus to establish the reserve really came from a private group, the Society for Nature Protection

Figure 12.1
National Parks Development Plan in Indonesia

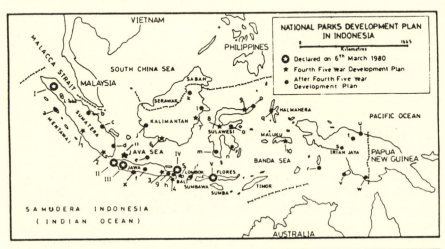

MAP REFERENCE	NAME	AREA (hectares)
	Declared March 6, 1980	
I	Gunung Leuser	1,094,868
II	Ujung Kulon	136,656
III	Gunung Gede-Pangrango	17,000
IV	Baluran	27,868
V	Komodo	75,000
	Fourth Five-Year Development Plan, 1984-1988	
1	Kerinci-Seblat	1,484,650
2	Barisan Selatan	356,800
3	Bromo Tengger-Semeru	58,000
4	Meru Betiri	50,000
5	Bali Barat	77,723
6	Tanjung Puting	355,000
7	Kutai	200,000
8	Lore Lindu	231,000
9	Dumoga Bone	300,000
10	Manusela	189,000
11	Kepulauan Seribu Marine	108,000

	After Fourth Five-Year Development Plan	
a	Siberut	56,000
b	Siak Dua	100,000
c	Berbak	100,000
d	Way Kambas	123,500
e	Karimun Jawa	111,625
f	Merapi-Merbabu	10,000
g	Yang Plateau	14,145
h	Ijen	unknown
i	Rinjani	40,000
j	Gunung Palung	100,000
k	Khayan River	150,000
l	Sangkulirang	100,000
m	Bantimurung Goa Leang	100,000
n	Rawa Opa	100,000
o	Morowali	200,000
p	Tangkoko Batuangus	8,867
q	Halmahera	458,000
r	Aru	183,000
s	Lorenz	2,150,000
t	Poja/Memberamo	835,000
u	Cyclops	22,520
v	Wasur	350,000
w	Dolok	690,000
x	Nusa Kambangan	11,000

of the Dutch East Indies. This society continued to encourage creation of dozens of reserves over the next fifty years and was largely responsible for passage of specific ordinances dealing with wildlife and nature protection, whale conservation, and hunting control.

The location, type, and small size of early selections suggest that scientific research and the protection of unique habitats, rare plants, and animals were the society's principal goals. Management of the reserves continued to be the responsibility of the research-oriented botanical gardens, but in reality little was accomplished in areas away from the centers of colonial power. From early colonial times watershed protection and large-scale forest management have been functions of an extensive system of forestry areas, classified for either protection or production.

The chronology of the Cibodas nature reserve illustrates the increasing national awareness of nature conservation and eventual recognition of national parks.

The first step, in 1889, was creation of a 240-hectare natural forest reserve merely as an extension of the botanical gardens. Over the next eighty-five years the reserve was expanded by small amounts on three different occasions until in 1975 the 17,000-hectare (42,000-acre) Gunung Gede–Pangrango National Park was created, encompassing the earlier reserves and large expanses of protected forest that had continued undisturbed.

The expanding, changing status of Cibodas highlights complexities and deficiencies in Indonesia's legal basis for reserve establishment. Because of difficulty in reconciling early Dutch colonial law with postindependence philosophy, there still exist a variety of nature conservation decrees, ordinances, and laws that are often contradictory or ambiguous. In 1988 there was still no comprehensive nature conservation law under which all categories of reserves could be established. Such legislation has been in draft for over ten years, but declaration of national parks in Indonesia continues to be accomplished only by decree of the minister of agriculture.

Despite these administrative and legal frustrations, the process of national park and reserve identification, declaration, and development continues. Initial establishment of five national parks in 1980 was followed by eleven more in 1982, and a dozen or more are planned in the nation's next five-year planning cycle ending in 1992. In 1988 there were 5.5 million hectares (13.6 million acres) of national parks in Indonesia, and total area protected in some form of reserve approached 14 million hectares (30.1 million acres). Though this latter figure exceeds 10 percent of the 120 million hectares of Indonesia's lands nominally considered forested—a respectable proportion—it is clear that many of the older reserves are either very much degraded or were not the most representative areas. Therefore, along with additional national park development, much reclassification is anticipated in the next decade.

Several recent international aid projects and an important conference have focused on nature conservation and national park development in Indonesia.

• The World Wildlife Fund (WWF), and particularly its Dutch Appeal, has sponsored dozens of individual projects dealing with the endangered Javan rhino, endangered subspecies of tiger, unique primates, and the saltwater crocodile, as well as reserve evaluations and management plans for nearly twenty years.

• The Food and Agriculture Organization (FAO) with funding by the United Nations Development Program completed several phases of a National Parks Development Project from 1974 to 1982. Early emphasis was on strengthening existing institutional structures, drafting comprehensive legislation, training high-level staff and, with WWF, identifying the first candidate reserves to become national parks. Work continued on a systematic survey to assure that the most threatened and valuable reserves were being chosen, on nationwide marine conservation initiatives, and on an eight-volume, long-range conservation plan.

• A Netherlands-Indonesia bilateral aid project developed the School for Environmental Conservation and Management near Bogor in West Java. Parallel to successful training centers in Africa, the school is the first institution in Asia to concentrate on training park managers and planners. Beginning with existing reserve staff whose backgrounds are in forestry, the school has been successful in providing a theoretical background in park philosophy as well as practical operations and management skills to several hundred mid- and upper-level park staff. These men and women are already having very positive effects as managers of the newly designated parks. Training is now being extended to lower-ranking park guards and interpreters through regional training centers in selected parks.

• The World Bank has provided loan assistance to the Indonesian government to support development of Dumoga-Bone National Park in North Sulawesi, which provides watershed conservation for an adjacent Bank-funded irrigation scheme.

• The World Congress on National Parks selected Bali, Indonesia, as the site of its third meeting following 1962 and 1972 conferences in the United States. For the first such meeting to be held in the developing world, the International Union for the Conservation of Nature (IUCN) and other sponsors of the congress felt Indonesia was an especially appropriate location to highlight not only substantial progress but also a spectrum of continuing problems and opportunities facing parks in many different parts of the globe.

Though considerable foreign technical assistance has been provided to Indonesia in its park development history, there has also been a very substantial response by government. In terms of construction and maintenance of facilities, establishment of staff positions, implementation of conservation programs, and expansion of institutional responsibilities, this response is a long-term commitment of manpower and funds that will ultimately far exceed the initial foreign aid contribution.

PARKS AND PRESERVES

Overview

Preservation of Indonesia's cultural resources (historic and archaeological sites) is the responsibility of the Ministry of Education and Culture, not the nature conservation agency that manages national parks and reserves. However, cultural sites incidentally located within nature reserves are dealt with in each area's management plan.

The nation's natural resources and landscapes—and its reserves—include a very broad spectrum from coral reefs to permanently snow-capped peaks at nearly 5,000 meters (16,400 feet) elevation. Indonesia's vast extent, complex shoreline, wide range of climates, and location spanning the zoogeographic gap between Asia and Australia have resulted in an area of incomparable faunal and floral richness. The archipelago is host to more than 1,500 species of birds, 500 species of mammals, 3,000 species of fishes, 10,000 species of trees, and a correspondingly large number of other life forms, many of which have yet to be described.

The terrestrial ecosystems show considerable difference across the breadth of the island chain. They are especially complex because they include both an Indomalayan (Asian) component in Sumatra, Java, Bali, and Kalimantan and an Australian element in Irian Jaya. Between the two is a fascinating and much-studied transition zone known as Wallacea, which includes the Lesser Sundas east of Bali, Sulawesi, and Maluku. The evolutionary explanation for these distinctions involves the deep ocean trenches that prevented dry land connections between various islands even in times of worldwide lower sea levels during which Sumatra and Java were joined to mainland Asia on the west and New Guinea to Australia on the east. The populations of certain ground-dwelling birds, most mammal species unable to swim long distances, and many plants were effectively divided by these water barriers, leading to genetic isolation and the development of remarkably complex affinities between modern species found on either side of "Wallace's Line." The distributions continue to puzzle modern zoogeographers and make the area an important source of information on the evolution of species.

Marine resources are an essential element in the life style and economy of this island nation where 80 percent of the population lives within easy reach of the sea and derives perhaps 70 percent of its protein from ocean products. The resources range from productive nearshore shrimp fisheries to coral reefs with their food fishes, edible invertebrates, algae, and colorful aquarium fishes, to mangrove swamps and estuaries.

Lacking geographical barriers, and lying essentially within the same tropical latitude, the marine resources are more uniform from east to west than are the terrestrial systems. What makes many marine areas candidates for protected status is not uniqueness but representativeness and the importance of providing shelter, spawning, and nesting sites so surrounding areas can be sustainably harvested. Since marine resources can be very sensitive to human-caused stresses like overfishing, pollution, and siltation, it is essential to have a selection of marine areas identified and routinely monitored.

The following description provides examples of major resource values within the protected areas system. They are grouped under (a) marine ecosystems and resources, (b) lowland and montane forests, (c) endangered species habitat, (d) geological phenomena, (e) scenic and esthetic places, and (f) wilderness values. Of course many of Indonesia's reserves contain several or even all of these categories.

Marine Ecosystems and Resources

Eight major categories are included: mangroves, coral reefs, invertebrates and bony fishes, dugongs, cetaceans, sea turtles, seabirds, and algae.

Concern for marine conservation has lagged behind the terrestrial, but a major effort is now being directed toward identification of critical habitats and representative areas. Emphasis is on finding habitat conservation areas, such as large undisturbed reef tracts and complete island-reef complexes, and on identifying protection areas that meet particular species needs, like nesting beaches for sea turtles and sea-grass feeding beds for dugongs. Areas directly or indirectly maintaining subsistence or commercial fisheries, such as mangrove swamps and estuaries, are also being selected for reserve status.

The first marine national park, Kepulauan Seribu (Thousand Islands), immediately off the West Java coast near Jakarta has been selected for several reasons. Properly managed, a buffer zone around its large reef tracts can sustain a fishery harvest essential to Jakarta; appropriately zoned, its many coral islands can accommodate a variety of uses from tourist development to marine conservation training centers to bird and turtle sanctuaries. Close to the nation's capital, it can serve as a showcase of the value of a marine protected area and help generate support for reserve management in the far less visible reaches of the Indonesian seas.

Over eighty of the other existing reserves and national parks including Baluran, Komodo, Bali Barat, and Ujung Kulon contain substantial marine components. In some fortunate cases the marine areas are already formally within reserve boundaries. In others, steps are being taken to establish the parks' control over these marine resources.

Several huge marine areas in Irian Jaya are either already in reserve status or approved in principle. At 450,000 hectares (1.1 million acres), the Bintuni Bay proposed mangrove reserve would be the largest protected area of mangroves in the world.

The 10 million hectares (25 million acres) of marine reserves now protected or projected constitute only a small proportion of the vast Indonesian territorial sea that extends outward 322 kilometers (200 miles) from all its islands' coastlines. It will be essential for marine reserve managers not only to protect the reserves but also to conduct extensive external programs of marine conservation education. These programs must help to create an appreciation of the basic role and value of marine resources, as well as educate local fishermen on specific issues like how destructive it is to fish with explosives or poisons, the need for controlling mining of coral rock, and the importance of leaving spawning areas and nesting beaches intact even if they are not in identified reserves. It will also be important to reach other departments of government and foreign aid donors to ensure that planning for coastal development for human transmigration, aquaculture, and agricultural improvement adequately assesses potential impacts on mangroves, coastal wetlands, and nearshore reefs and fisheries.

Lowland and Montane Forests

The dipterocarp forests of Indonesia, particularly those remaining relatively undisturbed in Kalimantan, Sulawesi, and Irian Jaya, are arguably the richest terrestrial ecosystems in the world. In species mix there are differences between lowland and montane forests, but the two types are roughly equivalent in overall diversity and value as habitat for associated fauna. The more significant difference is that the gentle topography of lowland forests makes them far easier to exploit commercially. In fact, a large proportion of the original lowland forest on the densely populated islands of Sumatra, Java, and Bali has already been permanently converted to other uses. It is not surprising that on these islands the existing rain forest reserves and "protection" forests are located on extremely rugged, steep ground where the capital cost of logging, and incidentally the environmental cost, would be very high.

Given the extremely high commercial export value of dipterocarp forests, and the legitimate need of capital to fund social development programs including nature conservation, proposals for additional reserves within these forest ecosystems must be accompanied by the highest possible justification. It is simply unrealistic to argue that all Indonesia's forests must be saved; in practice, only the most significant, the most representative, and the truly unique can be singled out. Hopefully, in combination with effective management of surrounding buffer zones, these will provide enough genetic diversity and habitat expanse to save the bulk of the rain forest's animal and plant species from local extinction.

A priority of the protected area system in Indonesia is to secure reserve or park status for several large rain forest areas on each of the major islands, with emphasis on lowland forest where it still exists. There are theoretical advantages to having large reserves, but smaller forest reserves should also be identified in order to include a particular forest habitat or a variant of a habitat not included in a large reserve. Having several reserves as reservoirs also decreases the likelihood that rare species will become extinct and may provide for interchange of genetic material between reserves. Additional reserves would be retained or added to preserve unique forest species, e.g., *Rafflesia*, the world's largest flowering plant, or to provide necessary educational, research, and recreational needs.

Several million hectares of existing rain forest reserves have already been awarded national park status. Most extensive are Gunung Leuser and Gunung Kerinci-Seblat in Sumatra, Ujung Kulon and Meru Betiri in Java, and Bali Barat in Bali. Huge national parks including Dumoga-Bone in North Sulawesi and Kutai and Tanjung Puting in Kalimantan also preserve the rain forest type.

Virtually none of these reserves can be said to be free of serious and continuous threats. These include constant encroachment from settlements of illegal migrants, slash-and-burn agriculture by indigenous ethnic groups, and even misguided efforts of externally funded development projects.

Endangered Species Habitat

Though they protect ecosystems valuable in their own right, a number of Indonesian parks and reserves are best known for and probably owe their existence to highly publicized or unique endangered species. In West Java the Ujung Kulon National Park is known worldwide as home to the last 50-60 specimens of the Javan rhinoceros, and in Bali the existence of the last remaining 200 pairs of wild Bali starlings was a major argument for expanding and converting an existing small game reserve to national park status. For its protection of most of the remaining populations of *Varanus komodoensis*, the world's largest lizard, Komodo National Park has received similar improvement in recognition and status, including identification as a Unesco Biosphere Reserve.

Even if official listing as endangered is not applied, other unusual or scarce wildlife species have been major factors and beneficiaries of reserve declaration: Sumatran tigers, the piglike babirusa of Sulewesi, endemic primates of Siberut Island, banteng (wild ox) of Java, and orangutans of Sumatra and Kalimantan are all examples.

Geological Phenomena

Indonesia's location at the rim of the Pacific tectonic plate explains the extraordinary number of active or recently active volcanic features, particularly in Java, Bali, Lombok, and Sumbawa. Many of these spectacular sites have been designated as reserves or included within larger reserves for many years. They range from the jagged smoking remains of Krakatoa in Ujung Kulon National Park, West Java, to the 3,000-meter (9,800-foot) active summit of Mount Semeru in Bromo Tengger National Park, East Java. They include huge calderas, multicolored steaming lakes, and puzzling cold mud pots. One reserve in Sumbawa contains Mount Tambora, site of the 1825 explosive eruption considered to be the largest in recorded human history.

Indonesia's most spectacular mountain range is also substantially covered by two major reserves in Irian Jaya: Gunung Lorentz and Jayawijaya. At 4,884 meters (16,024 feet), Mount Jaya is the highest peak in Southeast Asia and supports equatorial glaciers such as can be found in only two other locations on earth.

Scenic and Aesthetic Places

A number of smaller, long-established reserves probably received initial support because of special scenic characteristics as perceived by influential colonial scientists and administrators. Penanjung-Pangandaran on Java's south coast is an area of attractive beaches, natural caves, and accessible coral reefs, but its small size (530 hectares, 1,310 acres) and generally disturbed character give it limited conservation value. However, since this is a popular recreational destination, it is well worth retaining in the system because it provides an important and accessible showcase for visitors who will probably never have the opportunity to see the large remote reserves.

Perhaps Java's most dramatic and scenic mountain landscape is the huge Bromo Caldera in the highlands of East Java. It measures 10 kilometers (6 miles) in diameter and is 300 meters (1,000 feet) deep. The caldera's reputation for beautiful sunrises, misty moonscape feeling, and traditional ceremonial calendar—and its tourist potential—were major factors in generating political support for expansion of the small Bromo reserve to the 67,000-hectare (166,000-acre) Bromo-Tengger National Park in 1982. The park now protects thousands of hectares of adjacent undisturbed montane rain forest that previously faced an uncertain future because they were classified only as a "protection" forest. Without its association with the caldera, it is unlikely the forest would have generated enough conservation interest to have permanently avoided logging or piecemeal encroachment by migrants.

Wilderness Values

One internal national park zone chosen by Indonesia's park planners carries the English translation "wilderness," but there has been little of the traditional North American debate over limiting human recreational impact. Appreciation of wild nature in solitude is not a priority value for recreational visitors in this crowded, intensely social country. There are, however, huge areas of de facto wilderness in many of the remote reserves, particularly in Kalimantan and Irian Jaya. As a practical matter, wilderness values are threatened far more by slash-and-burn agriculture, poaching, and illegal settlement than potential developments for visitors.

ADMINISTRATION

Structure

Second only to oil resources as a hard currency generator, Indonesia's forests understandably figure prominently in long-range government planning. It is not surprising that a very powerful and influential government forestry ministry has developed. Important components of the ministry are the quasi-commercial divisions called Perum Perhutani and Inhutani, whose task it is either to log suitable forests or to award and manage the tremendously valuable private foreign or domestic logging concessions.

As in many nations, tropical or temperate, the forestry ministry has traditionally been reluctant to grant substantial responsibility and authority to a parks and nature conservation branch. Yet having such authority and stature is crucial to real progress. In fact, a rather small nature conservation branch was created within forestry in 1971; prior to that time, responsibility for reserves had remained essentially with the botanical gardens and research-oriented institutes like the Bogor Herbarium. The branch gradually expanded until an important milestone was achieved. In 1984 the Directorate General of Forest Protection and Nature Conservation (Direktorat Jenderal Perlindugan Hutan dan Pelestarian Alam, PHPA) was created in the forestry ministry at roughly the same administrative level as timber production and reforestation.

The creation of an autonomous state minister for environmental development and control, whose mandate is to see that sound ecological principles are applied in all major government programs, also had an impact in increasing the status and influence of PHPA. Though not granted formal powers of oversight, this cabinet-level position has quite effectively begun to exert the intended coordinating function on ministries such as Forestry, Agriculture, and Planning, including giving support to increased autonomy for PHPA.

Management Philosophy

PHPA's basic management philosophy realistically accepts the need for integrating nature conservation into the nation's overall social and economic development. The philosophy also recognizes that good management of national parks has the potential to enhance the government's domestic and international prestige. To receive political and social support, in addition to being qualified as significant in the traditional resource protection sense, Indonesia's national parks must (a) contribute to the perception of the state as being ecologically sensitive and responsible, (b) have at least some foreign exchange benefits, and (c) have relevance to local and regional development strategies.

Domestic and International Image. Indonesia's fortunate position as owner-manager of much of the richest rain forest in Southeast Asia brings not only potential capital wealth but also an obligation to responsibly manage this resource in the eyes of its citizens and neighbors. There are, sadly, a number of examples where this management has not been responsible, where both logging operations and programs for economic development have caused grave ecological damage. Perhaps the most frustrating problems have occurred where poor oversight of logging operations has failed to enforce conservative logging techniques even when such requirements are clearly written into the concession contracts. Though these circumstances have not been completely reversed, in the past ten to fifteen years there have been significant improvements, improvements that Indonesian authorities are anxious to publicize both at home and overseas.

Foreign Exchange Benefits. In addition to reinforcing the national image as responsible managers, international nature tourism focusing on the national parks generates modest foreign exchange income (see *Recreation and Tourism*, below).

Relevance to Local and Regional Development. Surpassing image and foreign exchange values is the need for a park or reserve to contribute to local social and economic development. So important is this criterion that PHPA's goal is to consider a new national park as simply one element in an overall socioeconomic development package. Other central government departments would contribute to tie park establishment to improved education, increased health benefits, irrigation and agricultural projects, and better communication facilities. Such integration is ambitious and expensive, but past experience has shown that failure to provide clear compensation for local residents for loss of traditional resources drastically reduces chances for a park's long-term survival.

Employment within the national park and indirect economic stimulation by increased tourism are elements in the package of compensation. However, the Indonesian experience has been that these economic elements alone cannot offset losses to the large numbers of local people affected by parks established in densely populated areas.

Zoning and Permitted Activities

PHPA has adopted zoning as the primary mechanism by which to rationalize permitted recreational, managerial, and consumptive uses of parkland. Until the proposed legislation is passed, this zoning will continue to be based on definitions in existing forestry law. National park zones generally consist of

sanctuary zones, where the strictest protection is required, meaning virtually no management activities other than guard protection and scientific research, and where regular visitors cannot enter;

wilderness zones, where nature protection is also required but where recreational visitors are permitted and minimum developments such as hiking trails, signs, and primitive campsites or shelters are provided, and limited habitat management is permissible;

intensive use zones, where heaviest recreation and visitor use occurs, including roads, car parks, visitor and administration buildings, developed overnight camping grounds, and picnic areas are allowed, and considerable landscaping is permitted to support these activities; and

rehabilitation zones, where disturbed or damaged habitat is intended for natural or accelerated recolonization by native vegetation, and eventual reclassification.

Conservation *buffer zones*, usually located outside park boundaries, are considered an integral element in overall national park management. In Indonesia, these areas may consist of commercially managed plantations of teak or other hardwoods, tea or coffee, or agroforestry developments. Buffer zones may be managed by PHPA's sister division Perum Perhutani, by provincial forestry departments, or by private entities. The most successful buffers have been those that emphasize the rapid production of alternatives for forest products that local people are denied by creation of the park in their traditional area of exploitation:

poles for house building, fuelwood, rattan and bamboo, animal fodder, and berries or fruits. The fact that some buffer zones are controlled by forestry interests that favor export-earning products over local-value items is still a serious problem.

The following sections discuss specific activities permitted or prohibited in the national parks.

Human Habitation. Permanent human habitation is not allowed within any of the national park zones, nor within buffer zones. Nonetheless, there are illegal human settlements in a number of the existing or candidate national parks and older reserves. In some cases the extent of residential clearing, settled agriculture, or slash-and-burn is simply irreversible, and the area should be dropped from reserve status completely. Though sometimes painful, accepting this reality can free scarce resources of PHPA to concentrate on less disturbed or more critical or representative reserves.

Where lesser extents of human habitation occur, two basic strategies have been adopted: complete removal of the inhabitants for resettlement or continued acceptance with consolidation into a manageable unit.

The resettlement approach has been tried in a number of old reserves and new parks, including Gunung Leuser and Bali Barat, with varying success. Where migration into the park has been fairly recent and the illegal residents have no long-standing local cultural identity, it is tempting to remove them entirely either to just outside the area (translocation) or to a considerable distance (transmigration). Translocation has been most successful when a properly functioning buffer zone has been established that effectively provides resources no longer available in the reserve. For transmigration to be successful it is essential that government agencies outside PHPA actually provide the services promised in the new area. Where these services are not provided, migrants may simply return to the reserve or even refuse to leave in the first place. Where this has occurred, it is unlikely that forcible removal will be employed, and the second strategy is adopted, where widespread illegal settlements are consolidated and zoned as enclaves that usually require their own surrounding buffer zones to provide fuelwood and animal fodder.

The consolidation and control approach has been adopted in Komodo National Park. There, two villages of 500-800 inhabitants each have been incorporated within this island park of about 75,000 hectares (185,000 acres). Each village has a several-hundred-year history of occupancy in the area, its own language, and a distinctive culture. Their principal economic activity is fishing for small nearshore schooling fishes and squid. There is virtually no agriculture, and animal husbandry consists of keeping a few free-ranging goats.

After some indecision, the park's management plan concluded it was best to leave these villages intact within the park so long as their traditional nondestructive fishing life style did not alter. However, their demands on terrestrial resources would not be allowed to increase. Uncontrolled increase in village size, development of satellite villages, and destructive activities like poaching native deer, setting wildfires to encourage grass growth, and using explosives to harvest coral reef fishes would not be permitted. The "compensation package" offered—which has proved successful for the first few years—has included providing a clean domestic water source, more regular health clinic service, hiring some villagers in construction and operation, developing a fish-marketing cooperative, and prohibiting villagers outside the area from fishing inside the park. Housing for several dozen permanent park staff was constructed within the village, and a limited area for goat grazing was designated. The grazing restrictions are self-enforcing: goats grazing very far from the village are generally stalked and killed by Komodo dragon lizards!

Agriculture, Domestic Livestock, and Timber Harvest. None of these activities are permitted within a national park, nor within the buffer zone. In the buffer zone, however, animal fodder may be cut and removed to be fed to domestic livestock. Also in the buffer it would be common to permit taking of small trees or poles, bamboo or rattan for noncommercial use, harvest of berries and fruits, and fuelwood for personal consumption. Commercial timber harvest, either selective cutting or clear-felling, is prohibited in the buffer zone. It is also prohibited in "protection" forests outside the buffer, but it is quite possible these forests will be reclassified for commercial production.

Hunting and Fishing. Hunting is strictly prohibited in parks, buffer zones, and all forest and reserve types except the hunting reserve, where only such species as deer, wild pig, and wild water buffalo are considered game. Despite being prohibited, however, poaching remains a very serious problem, particularly in remote, understaffed reserves. Since firearms in Indonesia are strictly limited to military and police personnel, relatively few villagers have legal arms with which to hunt. However, hunting deer with dogs and snaring for smaller animals are still commonly practiced by residents near or within parks. In some instances, large groups of organized deer poachers with dogs and firearms will operate in a park to provide middlemen with meat to sell on the black market, but more often the problem is a matter of individual family subsistence. Although seldom sought for food in this predominantly Muslim country, wild pigs are still often killed around villages to reduce destruction of agricultural crops and home gardens.

Illegal trade in protected wildlife is also a serious problem, and some animals are obviously still being taken from the parks and reserves. Indonesia's early record on controlling this traffic is not good, but recently there seems to have been some genuine commitment to improve. For example, Indonesia has been a signatory of the Convention on International Trade in Endangered Species (CITES) since 1978 and has taken steps to stem export of listed species on this basis. Internal trade in wildlife is a domestic regulatory problem, and to deal with it there have been established lists of nationally protected species that cannot be traded or transported inside the country. However, the magnitude of the problem is vast: 13,000 islands stretching across 5,000 kilometers (3,000 miles) provide limitless points of departure, often to another Southeast Asian nation that may neither have signed CITES nor particularly care about being a transfer point to affluent nations providing an almost irresistible market.

Realizing that there may be a problem of illegal sport hunting by the few people having legal access to firearms, PHPA has recently been putting more emphasis into hunting reserves. It is hoped that sport hunters can be directed to these areas, where regulations permit habitat management like controlled burning to enhance wildlife numbers, thus relieving the temptation to illegally hunt in parks.

Fishing is prohibited in sanctuary and wilderness zones of national parks and also in the strict nature and games reserves outside parks, but not necessarily in buffer zones. In marine parks, terrestrial parks, and reserves with marine components, the pressure for subsistence and even commercial fishing can be very great. This is being resolved on a case-by-case basis, in most situations by establishing the largest possible buffer zone. As research identifies critical fish spawning and shelter areas and other sensitive habitats in these zones, they must be given sanctuary status. Areas are already fairly well known for marine turtles, but they are not as easily identified for reef and pelagic fishes, shrimp, or dugong.

Recreation and Tourism. As elsewhere in the developing world, the past few decades in Indonesia have seen a substantial increase in recreational interest in natural areas. An increasing proportion of the national population has become better educated and has the financial resources for leisure-time recreation. This is especially true around the national capital of Jakarta and around provincial capitals in densely populated areas of Java and Bali. Youth "nature lover" organizations in these areas have shown phenomenal growth and are especially active in group-oriented hiking, camping, and exploring. In the sparsely populated provinces of Kalimantan and Sulawesi, and especially Irian Jaya, there is very little domestic demand for recreation in parks and reserves, although it can certainly be anticipated around growing provincial centers.

To meet recreational demand in Java the approach has generally been to direct development to forest recreation parks outside national parks. In many cases these parks (Wana Wisata) are managed by Perum Perhutani in areas being reforested or where selective logging does not interfere with recreational use. Perhutani's commercial orientation has given it considerable experience in facility construction, road building, and multiple-use management. Providing recreational facilities also returns a public relations benefit. In some cases, however, the national park's own intensive use zone may be developed for fairly heavy recreation. This is true in several showcase parks, including Gunung Gede-Pangrango, a mountain park, and Palau Seribu, a marine park, both close to Jakarta.

Currently few Indonesians travel considerable distances from their home areas to visit parks. Providing facilities for domestic tourists remains a long-range goal in national park management plans, since it is anticipated that ultimately this market will increase. Some planners believe that, over the long term, domestic tourism may be the most effective means of developing broad-based social awareness and support for nature conservation and parks. It might eventually be a critical factor in the success or failure of the system.

National park tourism for an overseas market is also little developed, but there is a recognized potential for international tourism as both a foreign exchange earner and image communicator. Tourist facility development has already taken place at parks like Komodo and Bali Barat, which are logistically within reach of current cultural tourism in Bali and East Java. There is a consistent history of low-level international visitation to these areas and to Ujung Kulon/Krakatoa and Bromo Tengger in Java and Gunung Leuser in Sumatra. As of 1988, however, there are still relatively few foreign tourists reaching these parks.

Little information about the wildlife, rain forests, and scenic resources of Indonesian parks has yet been circulated in appropriate foreign markets. This has been coupled with lack of physical facilities for overnight accommodation, unreliability of public transportation, and the perception that park staffs were unprepared to deal with foreign visitors. Airfares to reach Indonesia from Europe or North America remain high, but internal transportation, food, and accommodation, at low but acceptable standards, are extremely inexpensive.

Official government interest in park-oriented international tourism is cautiously positive. The policy is not to promote mass tourism with its capital-intensive, potentially foreign-dominated hotel development at high cost and comfort standards. More appropriate are simple, low-fee facilities in local architectural styles that would (a) make the park attractive as an additional destination for tourists already visiting Bali or Java, (b) be an adequate "draw" to a small number of adventure- or nature-oriented individuals or groups having special interest in parks and who would make this their primary reason for visiting Indonesia, and (c) be of a design and standard to also serve domestic tourists.

It is recognized that not all the parks are appropriate for development as accessible tourist destinations. Some reserves in West Irian, Sulawesi, and Kalimantan, regardless of whether they receive designation as national parks will—and should—remain inaccessible for decades to come. These areas, if adequately protected, will continue to be sanctuary zones serving as research laboratories, storehouses of genetic diversity, and undisturbed habitat for thousands of unnamed plant and animal species of little interest and appeal to visitors. Carefully planned, the foreign currency and international or domestic publicity gained by a few accessible, developed parks can help support maintenance and management of a larger number of undeveloped reserves whose collective conservation value is probably much higher.

Education and Research. Indonesia has very obviously recognized the importance of environmental education and interpretation in parks and reserves as a mechanism for raising public awareness of environmental and developmental issues. Lack of facilities to deal with more than a few visitors in most parks has hampered educational contact "on-site." However, there is a rapidly expanding body of literature in the Indonesian language produced by private conservation organizations such as the Green Indonesia Foundation and by PHPA and the environmental minister. This literature, which often takes as its themes endangered species and habitat preservation, is now being effectively used outside parks through local print and television media and in "extension" work with the "nature lovers" groups.

On-site programs with exhibits and visitor centers are being emphasized only in parks that have high potential to reach visitors. Interpretation is given low priority in remote parks, where emphasis shifts to conservation education in adult populations resident around or even inside the parks. Communication skills are absolutely essential for park managers in this situation, where a different language may be required to reach older villagers, and modern concepts of park value must be radically simplified and made relevant to local life styles and values.

Basic scientific research, as well as that specifically directed toward management, is continuing in many parks and reserves. For many years this research was predominantly stimulated and supported by foreign academic or aid sources. Increasingly PHPA is insisting on stronger roles for indigenous research institutes of the central government and provincial universities.

In many cases the most urgent research is still on a very broad scale, not on individual animal species but on identifying and evaluating the most rare, most representative, most threatened remaining natural areas to be added to the reserve system. Much work on area identification has been done, but much remains to be done.

In terms of geographic areas, there is still underrepresentation from Irian Jaya, Kalimantan, the Lesser Sundas, and Maluku, though a number of sites in these areas have been recommended for consideration. Ecosystems still poorly represented include most importantly the tropical lowland dipterocarp forest so economically important in Indonesia, as well as major marine ecosystems representing vital domestic food products and export items.

Management Problems

In addition to problems described in examples cited above, there are some specific management and staffing problems common to the protected areas system.

- Boundaries of many parks and reserves are still not clearly marked or obvious in the field.
- Park guards are inadequately directed and supervised.
- At all levels there is a lack of staff discipline and little accountability.
- Staff receive low rewards in both salary and status, and consequently may be poorly motivated.
- Field staff lack adequate personal equipment and physical support facilities like vehicles, housing, and guardposts.
- Training for the lower field staff is inadequate.

• Institutional support to prosecute a violation or otherwise encourage enforcement of regulations is lacking.

The Future

Indonesia is a complex society and an island nation where challenges and barriers to conservation and park development equal or perhaps surpass those in North America or Europe. Nevertheless, a great deal of progress has been made in recent decades in building legal and institutional frameworks, training and supporting staff, identifying and establishing parks, and in gaining domestic and international understanding of Indonesian conservation priorities.

The long-term viability of parks and reserves in this nation, as in other developing countries, is very much dependent on successful implementation of development programs in other sectors of society. Human population stability is essential; improved agricultural productivity is necessary; alternative energy sources are needed to relieve pressure on fuelwood resources; industry to provide manufactured goods for export is needed to replace pressures for export of raw natural resources.

The full burden in all these sectors can hardly be placed on the nature conservation and parks administration alone. But Indonesia is fortunate to have far more diverse and valuable natural resources than many countries. It also has a population that is intelligent, increasingly educated, and capable of making its own choices. Ultimately, as it should, success or failure will rest with them.

BIBLIOGRAPHY

Duryat, H. M., and L. P. van Lavieren. "Indonesia's Experience in Training Protected Area Personnel." In *National Parks, Conservation and Development: The Role of Protected Areas in Sustaining Society*, edited by Jeffrey A. McNeely and Kenton R. Miller. Washington, D.C.: Smithsonian Institution Press, 1984, pp. 228–32.

FAO. "Nature Conservation and Wildlife Management in Indonesia." FO/INS/73.013. Terminal Report, UNDP/FAO, 1979.

———. "National Parks Development and General Topics." In *National Conservation Plan for Indonesia, Vol. 8*. FO/INS/78.061. Field Report 19, UNDP/FAO, 1982.

———. "Introduction, Evaluation Methods and Overview of National Nature Richness." *National Conservation Plan for Indonesia, Vol. 1*. FAO/INS/78.061. Field Report 34, UNDP/FAO, 1982.

Petocz, Ronald. "Irian Jaya: Nature Reserve Design in a Pristine Environment." *Parks* 9, no. 3/4 (October-December, 1984): 8–12.

Salm, Rodney V. *Marine and Coastal Protected Areas: A Guide for Planners and Managers*. Gland, Switzerland: IUCN, 1984.

Sumardja, Effendy A. "First Five National Parks in Indonesia." *Parks* 6, no. 2 (April-June 1981): 1–4.

Sumardja, Effendy A., Tarmudji, and Jan Wind. "Nature Conservation and Rice Production in the Dumoga Area, North Sulewesi, Indonesia." In *National Parks, Conservation and Development: The Role of Protected Areas in Sustaining Society*, edited by Jeffrey A. McNeely and Kenton R. Miller. Washington, D.C.: Smithsonian Institution Press, 1984, pp. 224–27.

Sumardja, Effendy A., Harsono, and John MacKinnon. "Indonesia's Network of Protected Areas." In *National Parks, Conservation and Development: The Role of Protected Areas in Sustaining Society*, edited by Jeffrey A. McNeely and Kenton R. Miller. Washington, D.C.: Smithsonian Institution Press, 1984, pp. 214–23.

JAPAN 13

Noriyuki Ito

The national parks of Japan are set apart to preserve areas of superb natural scenery and thereby to contribute to the health, recreation, and culture of the Japanese people. These parks also offer visitors from around the world an opportunity to experience the beauties and wonders of nature. In these aims, there is no difference whatever between the national parks of Japan and those of other countries.

The system of national parks in Japan, however, differs essentially from those in the United States and Canada. The differences are a consequence of Japan's large population, small land area, and long history of land occupation and development. Two such differences deserve emphasis. First, Japanese national parks are designated without regard to landownership; second, even if they include government-owned lands, designated park areas are not necessarily used exclusively for park purposes.

For the present, a national park is established when it seems necessary and proper to add an area to the park system. Since park areas are chosen for their aesthetic and environmental characteristics, there is no assurance that the areas designated will be publicly owned. It follows that the management of these areas becomes a matter of zoning. When parks are established, certain restrictions are applied in order to control the activities or industries that might destroy the area's natural beauty. In its emphasis on zoning and land-use regulation, the Japanese park system seems to be similar to those of Great Britain and West Germany.

Management action strives to achieve a degree of mutual cooperation with other users of the parks. Through this system of cooperative management, Japan comes to achieve, as far as circumstances will permit, the long-term preservation of outstanding natural landscapes and the multifarious and abundant blessings and inspirations that only such landscapes can provide.

HISTORY

Enforcement of the National Parks Law

The establishment of Yellowstone National Park in the United States in 1872 created a precedent that was widely emulated. Japan was no exception. The first movement for creation of national parks appeared in Nikko, about 120 kilometers east of Tokyo. "A Petition for Designation of Nikko National Park" was introduced in the Imperial Diet and adopted in 1912.

In 1930, the National Park Commission was established in the Ministry of the Interior, and a year later the National Parks Law was enacted. Under this law, the National Park Commission undertook a nationwide survey of scenic spots with the result that three national parks, Setonaikai, Unzen, and Kirishima, were established on March 16, 1934. Akan, Daisetsuzan, Nikko, Chubusangaku, and Aso national parks were designated in December of the same year, and four more national parks, Towada, Fuji-Hakone, Yoshino-Kumano, and Daisen, were added in 1936.

These twelve national parks just began to sample the rich variety of mountains and coasts in a country that extends in a long chain from north to south, and many scenic spots worthy of preservation remained outside the park system. There was unabating demand from the nation for additional parks, and the authorities responsible for national park administration continued to investigate the possibility of additional designations.

In the 1940s the demands of Japanese foreign policy and military activity took priority over cultural and social welfare programs including national park preservation. With the outbreak of the Pacific War, park administration was practically suspended, and by the time of Japan's surrender in August 1945, the Japanese national parks existed in name only.

Development of the Natural Parks System

The war created poverty and chaos in Japan. In its aftermath, however, the national parks took on new importance as Japan attempted to stimulate the development of a tourist industry. Ise-Shima National Park was designated in 1946, and several others were established from 1949 to 1950.

In 1949 the National Parks Law was amended to allow for the designation of quasi-national parks, which are second only to national parks in natural scenic beauty and scale, and "special protection areas" within the parks in which there is a higher standard of scenic preservation than in the parks generally. These two amendments contributed greatly to the advancement of national parks administration following the war. The first three quasi-national parks, Sado-Yahiko, Biwako, and Yaba-Hita-Hikosan, were designated in 1950.

The National Parks Law was superseded by the Natural Parks Law in 1957. This law aims to protect areas of scenic beauty while promoting utilization of the parks for their contribution to the health, recreation, and culture of the people. With the enactment of the 1957 Natural Parks Law, the concept of natural parks was clarified, and a Natural Parks System was created. It consists of three kinds of natural parks: national parks, quasi-national parks, and prefectural natural parks.

National parks are areas of extraordinary scenic, scientific, and recreational value. Quasi-national parks are beautiful areas, close to large cities, which fall somewhat short of meeting the criteria for national parks. They are set aside primarily as outdoor recreation areas. Prefectural natural parks, designated locally, complete the system.

Throughout the 1960s the Japanese economy grew dramatically. This economic growth challenged the natural parks on two fronts. First, parks were threatened by mining, timber harvest, electrical generation, and other power developments that were difficult to harmonize with nature conservation. Second, economic growth resulted in overcrowding of urban areas, a rise in income level, and an increase of free time. These trends led to a rapid expansion of outdoor recreation in natural areas, and the increasing demand for outdoor recreation brought about the problems of overuse in natural parks. Securing new opportunities for outdoor recreation in the suburbs of big cities became an urgent task.

In order to meet the demand for outdoor recreation, cheap and clean accommodations and recreational facilities have been required in the national and quasi-national parks. A National Vacation Village System was created in 1961 to meet the needs of family recreation. In addition, a Peoples' Outdoor Recreation Areas System was established in 1970 to provide a variety of outdoor recreation facilities within the prefectural natural parks near urban areas and to propagate the concepts of nature conservation among urban citizens.

The construction of Tokai long-distance nature trail, extending over 1,343 kilometers (835 miles) in total length from Tokyo to Osaka, was begun in 1969 and completed in 1973. This trail was the first full-scale, long-distance nature trail in Japan and was designed to ensure opportunities for outdoor recreation for the urban citizens living within the Tokaido megalopolis by protecting natural environments on the urban fringe.

A year later, the Natural Parks Law was amended to provide for the establishment of marine park areas protecting tropical fish, coral reefs, and seaweeds in coastal waters. These measures are intended to provide for the needs of the near future when stricter regulations and more opportunities for many types of outdoor recreation will be required.

Establishment of the Nature Conservation Law

The economic growth of the 1960s also produced severe environmental pollution, and the combination of economic growth and environmental deterioration in turn caused serious political and social problems. In July 1971, the Environment Agency was established and given the responsibility to promote comprehensive administration of environmental conservation nationwide. Administration of the natural parks and hot springs, which had been conducted by the National Park Department of the Ministry of Health and Welfare, and the administration of wildlife protection and hunting, which had been conducted by the Forestry Agency, were transferred to the new Environment Agency. With the help of the Nature Conservation Law enacted in June 1972, the Environment Agency has brought a uniform and integrated management to Japan's environmental affairs.

The Basic Policy on Conservation of the Natural Environment was decided by the Cabinet in November 1973, in accordance with the Nature Conservation Law. For the first time, the basic principles and general direction were established for governmental regulation of the natural environment.

The Nature Conservation Law includes two new systems of protected areas. Any region that retains its virgin state without being influenced by human activities is designated a wilderness area, and any region of natural environment that it is socially desirable to conserve is designated a nature conservation area. In a wilderness area, all human activity is prohibited except academic research.

In the process of rapid economic growth, many kinds of developments were accelerated all over the country. Even in the natural parks, road construction for tourism, land development for second houses, construction of golf courses, and development of large-scale industrial parks invaded the central parts of these areas and resulted in serious environmental problems. Since the enactment of the Nature Conservation Law, a variety of policies have been implemented to improve the quality of the natural parks and address their environmental problems.

A review of park planning was initiated in 1973. Prior to that time most of the conservation and utilization plans for national and quasi-national parks were seriously outmoded. Many had not been changed since the parks were established and were, as a result, unable to cope with the changing social conditions around the parks. New park conservation and utilization plans are to be reviewed and updated at five-year intervals.

Another change is a policy that allows for the purchase of private lands important for nature preservation. Historically, the Japanese government has created natural parks where there was a recognized need for preservation and without regard to landownership. The aim was to preserve natural beauty through mutual cooperation with landowners. However, trouble has arisen concerning private rights, and this has made protection more difficult. When it is desirable to purchase private lands in special protection areas or class 1 special areas, the prefectural government may issue bonds for that purpose. Since 1972, the national government has subsidized the prefectural governments for principal and interest expenses associated with these bonds. So far, approximately 4,000 hectares (10,000 acres) of private land have been purchased by the national government. This system of purchase is a new tool for adjusting private rights in the natural parks, but zoning remains the primary mechanism.

PARKS AND RESERVES

The Nature Conservation Law and the Natural Parks Law hold an important position in the systems of nature conservation in Japan with the object of preserving valuable and large-scale natural environments.

Wilderness Areas and Nature Conservation Areas

Three kinds of areas designated in accordance with the Nature Conservation Law are wilderness areas, nature conservation areas, and prefectural nature conservation areas. Brief descriptions of each type follow:

Wilderness Area: An area that retains its original natural features without any influence of human activities.

Nature Conservation Area: An area that preserves a unique natural environment such as valuable forest, swamp, sea coast, etc.

Prefectural Nature Conservation Area: An area that preserves a natural environment almost equivalent to Nature Conservation Area.

The areas designated as of March 31, 1988, are depicted in Figure 13.1. Five wilderness areas total 5,631 hectares (14,000 acres); they are detailed in Table 13.1. There are nine nature conservation areas (Table 13.2) protecting a total of 7,550 hectares (18,700 acres). There are 496 prefectural nature conservation areas embracing 71,887 hectares (177,632 acres).

Natural Parks

The Natural Parks Law provides the legal basis for three types of natural parks:

National Parks: Nationally significant areas of outstanding natural beauty.

Quasi-National Parks: Areas of great natural beauty approaching that of the national parks.

Prefectural Natural Parks: Areas of scenic beauty designated by the prefectures (regional governments).

The parks designated as of March 31, 1988, are portrayed in Figure 13.2. The 28 national parks comprise an area of 2,050,106 hectares (5,065,812 acres), 5.43 percent of the land area of Japan, and 54 quasi-national parks an area of 1,288,774 hectare (3,184,561 acres), 3.41 percent of Japan's land area. Brief descriptions of national and quasi-national parks are provided in tables 13.3 and 13.4 respectively. Another 5.27 percent of Japan is devoted to 299 prefectural natural parks covering 1,990,583 hectares (4,918,731 acres).

Figure 13.1
Map of Wilderness Areas and Nature Conservation Areas in Japan

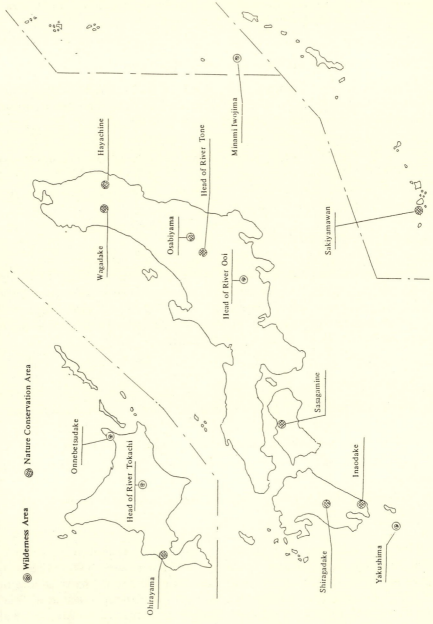

◉ Wilderness Area   ◍ Nature Conservation Area

Onnebetsudake

Head of River Tokachi

Ohirayama

Wagadake

Hayachine

Osabiyama

Head of River Tone

Head of River Ooi

Minami Iwojima

Sasagamine

Shiragadake

Inaodake

Yakushima

Sakiyamawan

Table 13.1
Outline of Wilderness Areas in Japan as of March 31, 1988

DISTRICT	LOCATION (prefecture)	AREA (ha)	LAND OWNERSHIP	DATE	NATURAL FEATURES
Onnebetsudake	Hokkaido	1,895	National Forest	1980	Alpine vegetation mainly composed of Pinus pumila
Head of River Tokachi	Hokkaido	1,035	National Forest	1977	Subarctic evergreen coniferous forest of Picea jezoensis and Abies sachalinensis
Head of River Ooi	Shizouka	1,115	National Forest	1976	Cool-temperate broad-leaved deciduous forest mainly composed of Tsuga Sieboldii and subarctic evergreen coniferous forest
Minami Iwojima	Tokyo	367	National Forest	1975	Tropical and subtropical broad-leaved evergreen forest, including tree ferns and mist forest, geographical features eroded by the sea, and seabirds
Yakushima	Kagoshima	1,219	National Forest	1975	Warm-temperate coniferous forest mainly composed of Cryptomeria japonica and laurel forest of Distylium racemosum and Quercus stenophylla
TOTAL		5,631			

Table 13.2
Outline of Nature Conservation Areas as of March 31, 1988

DISTRICT	LOCATION (prefecture)	AREA (ha)	LAND OWNERSHIP	DATE	NATURAL FEATURES
Ohirayama	Hokkaido	674	National Forest	1977	Natural forest of Fagus crenata located near its northern limit, and limestone vegetation
Hayachine	Iwate	1,370	National Forest	1975	Alpine vegetation, subalpine evergreen coniferous forest, serpentine vegetation, and natural forest of Picea Glehni
Wagadake	Iwate	1,451	National Forest	1981	Natural forest of Fagus crenata and Quercus mongolica var. grosseserrata, Pinus pumila community and snow-bed grassland
Osabiyama	Tochigi	545	National Forest	1981	Natural forest of Fagus crenata and Abies Mariesii
Head of River Tone	Gunma	2,318	National Forest	1977	Natural forest of Fagus crenata and Quercus mongolica Tone var. grosseserrata, dwarf-shrub heath and snow-bed grassland
Sasagamine	Ehime Kochi	537	National Forest Private Forest	1982	Natural forest of Fagus crenata and Abies shikokiana
Shiragadake	Kumamoto	150	National Forest	1980	Natural forest of Fagus crenata located near its southern limit
Inaodake	Kagoshima	377	National Forest	1975	Laurel forest mainly composed of Distylium racemosum and Quercus stenophylla
Sakiyamawan	Okinawa	128	Sea Surface	1983	Giant coral colony of Galaxea faciularis and coral reef
TOTAL		7,550			

Figure 13.2
Map of National Parks and Quasi-National Parks in Japan

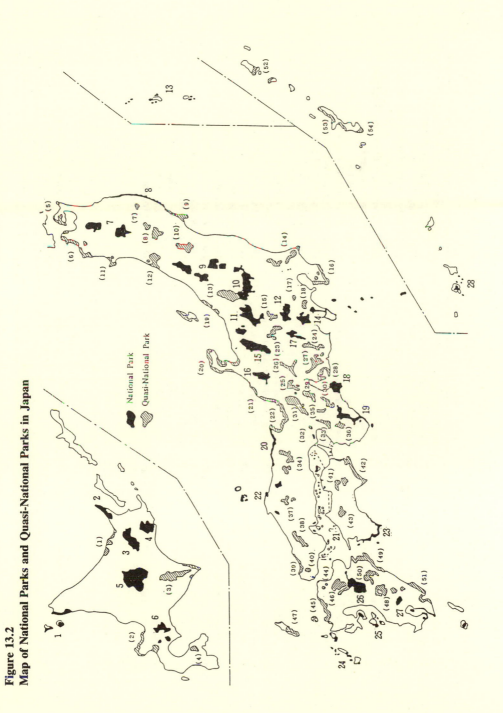

National Park
Quasi-National Park

Figure 13.2 (continued)

1	Rishiri/Rebun/Sarobetsu	(1)	Abashiri	(29)	Suzuka
2	Shiretoko	(2)	Niseko/Shakotan/Otaru-kaigan	(30)	Muroo/Akame/Aoyama
3	Akan	(3)	Hidaka-sanmyaku/Erimo	(31)	Biwako
4	Kushiro-shitsugen	(4)	Onuma	(32)	Meiji-Memorial-Forest Minoo
5	Daisetsuzan	(5)	Shimokita-hanto	(33)	Kongo/Ikoma
6	Shikotsu/Toya	(6)	Tsugaru	(34)	Hyonosen/Ushiroyama-Nagisan
7	Towada/Hachimantai	(7)	Hayachine	(35)	Yamato/Aogaki
8	Rikuchu-kaigan	(8)	Kurikoma	(36)	Koya/Ryujin
9	Bandai/Asahi	(9)	Minamisanriku/Kinkazan	(37)	Hiba/Dogo/Taishaku
10	Nikko	(10)	Zao	(38)	Nishichugoku-sanchi
11	Joshinetsu-kogen	(11)	Oga	(39)	Kitanagato-kaigan
12	Chichibu/Tama	(12)	Chokai	(40)	Akiyoshidai
13	Ogasawara	(13)	Echigosanzan/Tadami	(41)	Tsurugisan
14	Fuji/Hakone/Izu	(14)	Suigo/Tsukuba	(42)	Muroto/Anan-kaigan
15	Chubu-sangaku	(15)	Myogi/Arahune/Saku-kogen	(43)	Ishizuchi
16	Hakusan	(16)	Minamiboso	(44)	Kitakyushu
17	Minami-arupusu	(17)	Meiji-Memorial-Forest Takao	(45)	Genkai
18	Ise/Shima	(18)	Tanzawa/Oyama	(46)	Yaba/Ilita/Hikosan
19	Yoshino/Kumano	(19)	Sado/Yahiko/Yoneyama	(47)	Iki/Tshushima
20	Sanin-kaigan	(20)	Noto-hanto	(48)	Kyushuchuo-sanchi
21	Setonaikai	(21)	Echizen/Kaga-kaigan	(49)	Nippo-kaigan
22	Daisen/Oki	(22)	Wakasawan	(50)	Sobo/Katamuki
23	Ashizuri/Uwakai	(23)	Yatsugatake/Chushin-kogen	(51)	Nichinan-kaigan
24	Saikai	(24)	Tenryu/Okumikawa	(52)	Amami-gunto
25	Unzen/Amakusa	(25)	Ibi/Sekigahara/Yoro	(53)	Okinawa-kaigan
26	Aso/Kujyu	(26)	Hida/Kosogawa	(54)	Okinawa-senseki
27	Kirishima/Yaku	(27)	Aichi-kogen		
28	Iriomote	(28)	Mikawawan		

GLOSSARY			
arupusu: alps	kaigan: coast	sanchi: mountain land	shitsugen: wetland
gunto: islands	ko: lake	sangaku: mountains	wan: bay
hanto: peninsula	kogen: plateau, heights	sanmyaku: mountain range	yama: mountain
	san: mountain	senseki: battlefield	zan: mountain

Table 13.3
Outline of National Parks (March 31, 1988)

MAP	NAME	LOCATION	DATE	AREA (ha)	DESCRIPTION
• 1	Rishiri Rebun Sarobetsu	northern Hokkaido	1974	21,222	Rishiri & Rebun islands, coast of Bakkai and Sarobetsu plain: volcanic islands, sea cliffs, sand dunes.
• 2	Shiretoko	eastern Hokkaido	1964	38,633	65-km peninsula covered with primeval forests protruding into the Sea of Okhotsk; nation's last area of virgin land where many wild animals and sea fowls live.
• 3	Akan	eastern Hokkaido	1934	90,481	Surrounded by the three calderas of world scale--Akan, Kussharo, and Mashu--with volcanoes of Mount Oakandake and Mount Meakandake: primeval forests and caldera lakes.
• 4	Kushiro-shitsugen	eastern Hokkaido	1987	26,86l	Kushiro, a Ramsar Convention wetland 7 the largest in Japan, Lake Toro, Shiraruto marsh, & the surrounding hills.
• 5	Daisetsuzan	Hokkaido	1934	230,894	Largest national park: virgin forests, beautiful valleys, & the volcanic range of Mount Tokachidake and Mount Idhikaridake; many ski areas & hot springs.
• 6	Shikotsu Toya	near Sapporo, Hokkaido	1949	98,332	Well-developed sightseeing spot consisting of three main landscape districts--Mount Yotei, Lake Toya, & Lake Shikotsu--including various types of volcanic landforms, hot springs, etc.
• 7	Towada Hachimantai	northern Honshu	1936	85,409	Mount Hakkoda & Lake Towada district; Hachimantai Plateau district covered with natural forests and alpine flora.
• 8	Rikuchu-kaigan	Iwate Miyagi	1955	12,348	180 km of Pacific Ocean seashore: precipitous cliffs in the north & much-indented coastline and many beautiful inlets in the south.
• 9	Bandai Asahi	Yamagata Hukushima Niigata	1950	189,582	2nd largest park: volcanic range of Mt. Bandai, scared mountains of Dewa-sanzan, virgin forests, & many beautiful lakes.
•10	Nikko	Hukushima Tochigi Gunma Niigata	1934	140,164	Historic shrines and temples harmonize with the excellent scenery, including volcanoes, plateaus, rivers, cascades, waterfalls, lakes, & deep forests.
•11	Joshinetsu-kogen	Gunma Niigata Nagano	1949	189,028	Many volcanoes, plateaus, lakes, forests, & alpine plants; valued for outdoor recreation; steep mountains including Tanigawa, Asama, & Shirane.
•12	Chichibu Tama	Saitama Tokyo Yamanashi Nagano	1950	121,600	One of the few parks in a sedimentary rock area; three main landscape districts--Chichibu & Tama mountain ranges & Shosenkyo gorge.

Table 13.3 (continued)

MAP	NAME	LOCATION	DATE	AREA (ha)	DESCRIPTION
•13	Ogasawara	1,000 km south of Tokyo	1972	6,099	Volcanic archipelago of Ogasawara islands, between subtropical and tropical zones, including a rich variety of fauna & flora and beautiful seascapes designated as "marine park areas."
•14	Fuji Hakone Izu	Tokyo Kanagawa Yamanashi Shizuoka	1936	122,686	Mt. Fuji, highest in Japan, is a graceful and solitary conic-shaped volcano; Hakone is a large double volcano; Izu Peninsula has beautiful seacoast and many springs.
•15	Chubu-sangaku	Niigata Toyoma Nagano Gihu	1934	174,323	"Japan Alps National Park": a series of mountains - including Yari, Hodaka, & Tateyama over 3,000 m high - with sharply cut cliffs & snowy valleys, a mecca for mountaineers.
•16	Hakusan	Toyama Ishikawa Hukui Gihu	1962	47,700	Hakusan Mountain--the object of religious worship--forms the backbone of Hokuriku district noted for heavy snowfall, virgin forest, beautiful alpine flowers, & many wild animals.
•17	Minami-arupusu	Yamanashi Nagano Shizuoka	1964	35,752	"Southern Alps of Japan" includes Japan's second highest mountain, Mount Kita, & other high peaks.
•18	Ise Shima	Mie	1946	55,549	Ise is noted for Ise Shrine, the most sacred site of Shintoism, & virgin forest; Shima has typical rias seacoast with many small inlets & nurseries of cultured pearls in Ago Bay.
•19	Yoshino Kumano	Mie Nara Wakayama	1936	58,546	Yoshino is a mountainous region with Mount Yoshino, which is famous for its cherry blossoms; Kumano is rich in rivers, gorges, & seashores
•20	Sanin-kaigan	Kyoto Hyogo Tottori	1963	8,996	75-km shoreline on Sea of Japan: topographically & geologically complex & rich in bays, capes, inlets, cliffs, & sea-eroded rock holes. To the west, Tottori dune, the largest in Japan, reveals a beautiful seacoast.
•21	Setonaikai	Hyogo Wakayama/Okayama Hiroshima/Yamaguchi Tokushima/Kagawa Ehime/Hukuoka Ooita	1934	62,839	Inland sea surrounded by four straits, full of manifold beauties, extending for about 400 km from east to west, embracing the beauty of the sea, its small islands, its coastal points and beaches.
•22	Daisen Oki	Tottori Shimane Okayama	1936	31,927	With Mount Daisen as its center, the park embraces a cluster of surrounding mountains including Hiruzen & Sanbe, the Shimane Peninsula, & the Oki archipelago.

Table 13.3 (continued)

MAP	NAME	LOCATION	DATE	AREA (ha)	DESCRIPTION
•23	Ashizuri Uwakai	Ehime Kochi	1972	10,967	Magnificent seacoast of southern Shikoku Island with many tall & steep granite cliffs, sea-eroded rocks, & other marine scenery, given the illusion of subtropics by many beautiful groves of camellia & other plants.
•24	Saikai	Nagasaki	1955	24,653	More than 400 islands extended over northwestern Kyushu including Hira-dojima, the Kujukushima islands, & the Goto archipelago, with beauti-ful seas & zigzag shoreline.
•25	Unzen Amakusa	Nagasaki Kumamoto Kagoshima	1934	25,496	Unzen area is a famous sightseeing spot, with extinct volcanoes of Mount Unzen & many hot springs; Amakusa Islands are more than 70 islands with sea-eroded coasts.
•26	Aso Kujyu	Kumamoto Ooita	1934	72,680	Two mountain groups in the center of Kyushu Island: Mt. Aso, which has the world's greatest caldera basin & vast grassland sprawling at the skirt; Mt. Kuju, which is the highest peak on Kyushu.
•27	Kirishima Yaku	Miyazaki Kagoshima	1934	54,833	Located in southern Kyushu, this park embraces the Kirishima range, Kinko Bay overlooking Sakurajima Island, & Yakushima Island, which is noted for its giant Yaku-sugi (cedar) forests.
•28	Iriomote	Okinawa	1972	12,506	1,200 km south of Kagoshima in the East Sea, Iriomote Island has been called the last virgin area; it contains subtropical evergreen forests & rare fauna.
	Total			2,050,106	

ADMINISTRATION

Wilderness and Nature Conservation Areas

Process of Designation. Wilderness and nature conservation areas are designated by the director general of the Environmental Agency after consultation with related governmental agencies and the Nature Conservation Council. Prefectural nature conservation areas are designated by the prefecture by ordinance.

Conservation Policies. Wilderness areas are managed according to one central principle: ensuring natural conditions in the areas concerned.

1. Within wilderness area boundaries, management attempts to maintain primeval conditions, and any artificially induced change is forbidden. Unnatural intrusions arising outside wilderness area boundaries are limited as much as possible.

Table 13.4
Outline of Quasi-National Parks (March 31, 1988)

MAP	NAME	PREFECTURE	DATE	AREA (ha)	MAP	NAME	PREFECTURE	DATE	AREA (ha)
1	Abashiri	Hokkaido	1958	37,412	30	Muroo/Akame/Aoyama	Mie	1970	26,308
2	Niseko/Shakotan/	Hokkaido	1963	19,009			Nara		
	Otaru-kaigan				31	Biwako	Shiga	1950	98,144
3	Hidaka-sanmyaku/	Hokkaido	1981	103,447			Kyoto		
	Erimo				32	Meiji-Memorial-	Osaka	1967	963
4	Onuma	Hokkaido	1958	8,853		Forest Minoo			
5	Shimokita-hanto	Aomori	1968	18,728	33	Kongo/Ikoma	Osaka	1958	15,564
6	Tsugaru	Aomori	1975	25,966			Nara		
7	Hayachine	Iwate	1982	5,463	34	Hyonosen/	Hyogo	1969	48,803
8	Kurikoma	Iwate	1968	77,137		Ushiroyama/Nagisan	Tottori		
		Miyagi					Okayama		
		Akita			35	Yamato/Aogaki	Nara	1970	5,742
		Yamagata			36	Koya/Ryujin	Nara	1967	19,213
9	Minamisanriku/	Miyagi	1979	13,902			Wakayama		
	Kinkazan				37	Hiba/Dogo/Taishaku	Tottori	1963	7,808
10	Zao	Miyagi	1963	40,089			Shimane		
		Yamagata					Hiroshima		
11	Oga	Akita	1973	8,156	38	Nishichugogu-sanchi	Shimane	1969	28,553
12	Chokai	Akita	1963	28,373			Hiroshima		
		Yamagata					Yamaguchi		
13	Echigosanzan/Tadami	Hukushima	1973	86,129	39	Kitanagato-kaigan	Yamaguchi	1955	8,021
		Niigata			40	Akiyoshidai	Yamaguchi	1955	4,502
14	Suigo/Tukuba	Ibaraki	1959	32,237	41	Tsurugisan	Tokushima	1964	20,870
		Chiba					Kochi		
15	Myogi/Arahune/	Gunma	1969	13,123	42	Muroto/Anan-kaigan	Tokushima	1964	7,216
	Saku-kogen	Nagano					Kochi		
16	Minamiboso	Chiba	1958	5,677	43	Ishizuchi	Ehime	1955	10,683
17	Meiji-Memorial-	Tokyo	1967	770			Kochi		
	Forest Takao				44	Kitakyushu	Hukuoka	1972	8,249
18	Tanzawa/Oyama	Kanagawa	1965	27,572	45	Genkai	Hukuoka	1956	10,974
19	Sado/Yahiko/	Niigata	1950	29,464			Saga		
	Yoneyama						Nagasaki		
20	Noto-hanto	Toyama	1968	9,672	46	Yaba/Hita/Hikosan	Hukuoka	1950	85,023
		Ishikawa					Kumamoto		
21	Echizen/Kaga-kaigan	Ishikawa	1968	8,992			Ooita		
		Hukui			47	Iki/Tsushima	Nagasaki	1968	12,625
22	Wakasawan	Hukui	1955	21,870	48	Kyushuchuo-sanchi	Kumamoto	1982	27,096
		Kyoto					Miyazaki		
23	Yatsugatake/	Yamanashi	1964	39,857	49	Nippo-kaigan	Ooita	1974	8,506
	Chushin-kogen	Nagano					Miyazaki		
24	Tenryu/Okumikawa	Nagano	1969	25,756	50	Sobo/Katamuki	Ooita	1965	22,000
		Shizuoka					Miyazaki		
		Aichi			51	Nichinan-kaigan	Miyazaki	1955	4,643
25	Ibi/Sekigahara/Yoro	Gihu	1970	18,920			Kagoshima		
26	Hida/Kisogawa	Gihu	1964	18,193	52	Amami-gunto	Kagoshima	1974	7,861
		Aichi			53	Okinawa-kaigan	Okinawa	1972	10,208
27	Aichi-kogen	Aichi	1970	21,721	54	Okinawa-senseki	Okinawa	1972	3,127
28	Mikawawan	Aichi	1958	9,763					
29	Suzuka	Mie	1968	29,821		TOTAL			1,288,774
		Shiga							

2. When necessary to conserve species of flora or fauna that are rare or unique to the area concerned and that are easily influenced by human activities, "restricted entry districts" are established.

3. When the areas concerned are damaged by natural disasters, official policy allows for their restoration only by the process of natural transition, and not through artificial methods.

4. Wilderness areas are to be observed, surveyed and studied, and the necessary conservation work is to be executed so as to have the minimum impact on the natural environment.

Proper conservation measures also serve to protect specific features of the natural environment in designated nature conservation areas.

1. To the extent it is deemed necessary, zones that are important structural components of their respective ecosystems and require aggressive management measures, or that are particularly necessary for the conservation of a certain natural environment, or that are essential parts of a larger conservation goal, are protected through designation as "special areas" or "special marine areas."

2. Within these special areas, localities harboring populations of rare or endangered fauna and flora are designated "wild animal and plant protection areas."

3. "Ordinary areas" are to be conserved in a manner permitting them to function as buffer zones.

4. When damage is incurred through natural disasters and the like, disaster control and restoration work may be undertaken using artificial means so long as the important ecological characteristics of the area are respected.

5. Within nature conservation areas, necessary conservation work is executed under a proper administration.

6. Efforts are made to harmonize land conservation and other public interests including the welfare of local residents who use these lands and waters for agriculture, forestry, fishery, and the like.

The regulation of activities in wilderness and nature conservation areas is summarized in Figure 13.3.

Natural Parks

Process of Designation. National parks are designated by the director general of the Environment Agency after conferring with related governmental agencies and consulting with the Nature Conservation Council. Quasi-national parks are designated by the director general of the Environment Agency upon the recommendation of the governor of the prefecture concerned and after conferring with related governmental agencies and consulting with the Nature Conservation Council. Prefectural natural parks are designated by prefectural ordinance.

Natural Parks Plan. The basic principles of conservation, management, and

Figure 13.3
Regulation of Activities in Wilderness Areas and Nature Conservation Areas

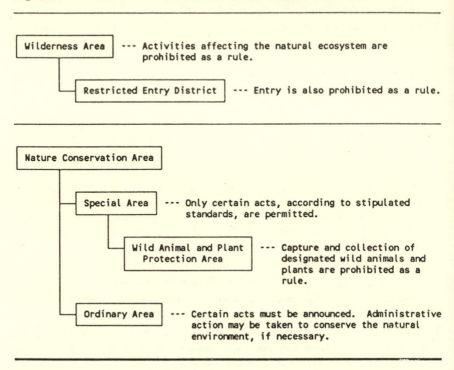

utilization of parks are set forth by the Natural Parks Plan. The Natural Parks Plan, which is established by the director general of the Environment Agency, is divided into the Conservation Plan and the Utilization Plan.

1. Conservation Plan. Within the boundaries of natural parks there are national lands (mostly national forest), lands belonging to prefectures, and private lands. About 24 percent of the total national park area is privately owned, and land utilization varies widely. Forests, fields, farms, and pastures are included, and there may be settlements as well. Under these circumstances a coordinated conservation plan is vital.

In order to protect the outstanding scenic beauty of national parks, "special areas" (Class 1, Class 2, and Class 3), "special protection areas," and "marine park areas" are designated within the various parks by each park's Conservation Plan. Within these designated conservation zones activities inconsistent with nature conservation—such as building, mining, logging, clearing land, harvesting protected plants, or polluting lakes or rivers—may not be undertaken without a permit from the director general of the Environment Agency. In ordinary national park areas, outside these designated conservation zones, anyone planning such activities must notify the director general of the Environment Agency. Upon notification the director general may enter into negotiations to mitigate the environmental damage and conserve scenic beauty. A more detailed synopsis of regulations by type of area is presented in Figure 13.4.

Acts that might damage the scenery of a national park must not be carried out without the permission of the director general of the Environment Agency. The prefectural governors exercise equivalent powers with respect to quasi-national parks. The approval or denial of requests involving the construction or modification of structures or the gathering of soils and stones has been determined on a case-by-case basis relying on precedent. In October 1974 these precedents were compiled into one publication, the *Judgment Guideline for Various Acts in National Parks*. The publication of this document has created a more objective and detailed standard for decision making in these cases.

2. Utilization Plan. Just as the Conservation Plan serves to preserve natural conditions by regulating use, the Utilization Plan serves to organize and regulate the development of suitable park facilities. These plans include the arrangement of "developed areas" and the development of facilities for traffic, lodging, nature observation, and various outdoor activities.

Facilities central to the operation of the national parks, such as nature trails, visitor centers, mountain lodges, and camping sites are provided directly by the national government or by prefectural governments with financial assistance from the national government. Other park facilities, such as overnight accommodations, are provided by private investment in accordance with the Utilization Plan.

Natural Parks Work. It is stipulated by law that the national government shall, as a principle, have the responsibility of providing and improving the facilities for utilization and conservation in the natural parks. However, the irregular patterns of landownership and the system of zoning, both discussed above, suggest that it is often more reasonable that the responsibility for national park facilities not be undertaken at national expense alone but also by the respective local governments or private persons.

As a consequence, the Natural Parks Law provides that the national park work, if it fits in well with the Natural Parks Plan, may be undertaken by local governments or private persons with the approval or permission of the director general of the Environment Agency. The usual result is that government is responsible for the construction of such basic facilities as roads, nature trails, picnic grounds, parking lots, camping grounds, and toilets, while accommodation and transportation facilities offering various services for pay are owned and operated by private enterprises.

The fact that large investments in national parks are made by the nongovernment circles well illustrates that business enterprises connected with the parks can be a success because of the great number of their visitors. Here lies the very reason why the administration of natural parks is making constant exertions to confine the damage on natural environment to the minimum under the present system and to revise the system itself.

Figure 13.4
Regulation of Activities in National Parks

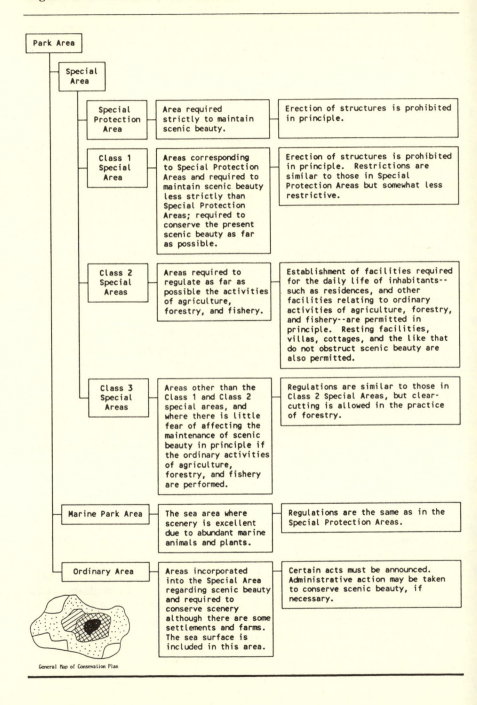

Park Area			

Special Area

Special Protection Area | Area required strictly to maintain scenic beauty. | Erection of structures is prohibited in principle.

Class 1 Special Area | Areas corresponding to Special Protection Areas and required to maintain scenic beauty less strictly than Special Protection Areas; required to conserve the present scenic beauty as far as possible. | Erection of structures is prohibited in principle. Restrictions are similar to those in Special Protection Areas but somewhat less restrictive.

Class 2 Special Areas | Areas required to regulate as far as possible the activities of agriculture, forestry, and fishery. | Establishment of facilities required for the daily life of inhabitants--such as residences, and other facilities relating to ordinary activities of agriculture, forestry, and fishery--are permitted in principle. Resting facilities, villas, cottages, and the like that do not obstruct scenic beauty are also permitted.

Class 3 Special Areas | Areas other than the Class 1 and Class 2 special areas, and where there is little fear of affecting the maintenance of scenic beauty in principle if the ordinary activities of agriculture, forestry, and fishery are performed. | Regulations are similar to those in Class 2 Special Areas, but clear-cutting is allowed in the practice of forestry.

Marine Park Area | The sea area where scenery is excellent due to abundant marine animals and plants. | Regulations are the same as in the Special Protection Areas.

Ordinary Area | Areas incorporated into the Special Area regarding scenic beauty and required to conserve scenery although there are some settlements and farms. The sea surface is included in this area. | Certain acts must be announced. Administrative action may be taken to conserve scenic beauty, if necessary.

General Map of Conservation Plan

Conclusion

In areas with outstanding examples of nature, such as national parks, it is possible for people to come into contact with scenery, animals, and plants that they would not experience in the course of their daily lives and to have refreshing and satisfying experiences. Therefore, provision of facilities that are necessary for contact with nature should be promoted. The demand for areas with outstanding natural environment is expected to increase, both for outdoor recreation and regional development. The large number of park visitors ensures the success of business enterprises connected with the parks and attracts large investments from the private sector.

When viewed from the standpoint of conservation, however, this may not be a desirable social phenomenon. Critics of present park policy fear the possible destruction of the nature in the parks by the encroachment of commercialism, an encroachment that is attributed to the weakness of the zoning system. Although these encroachments are individually insignificant, when aggregated the dangers associated with these commercial developments are far greater than those that might be associated with a more obvious intrusion like the construction of a dam for hydroelectric power.

If the natural parks are to fulfill their twin purposes of nature conservation and proper utilization, the trends related to patterns of utilization must be carefully investigated. Studies must include types of developmental activities, techniques for maintaining and recovering natural functions, etc. Finally, these studies must be the foundation upon which effective administration of the nature conservation system is built.

BIBLIOGRAPHY

Environment Agency. *Environmental Laws and Regulations in Japan (Nature)*. Tokyo: Environment Agency, 1983.

Ikenouye, Osamy. "National Parks and Tourism." *World National Parks: Progress and Opportunities*, compiled under direction of Jean-Paul Harroy. Brussels: Hayes, 1972.

Oi, Michio. "The Role of National Parks in Social and Economic Development Progress." *Second World Conference on National Parks*, ed. Sir Hugh Elliott. Morges, Switzerland: IUCN, 1974.

Shimada, N., O. Shakudo, N. Ito, and H. Onodera. "Nature Conservation of National Land." *Journal of the Japanese Institute of Landscape Architecture* 48, no. 4 (1985): 227–33.

Simmons, Ian G. "The Balance of Environmental Protection and Development in Hokkaido, Japan." *Environmental Conservation* 8, no. 3 (1981): 191–98.

Sutherland, M., and D. Britton. *National Parks of Japan '81*. Tokyo: Kodansha International, 1981.

Nature Conservation Bureau. *Natural Parks System of Japan*. Tokyo: Environment Agency, 1975.

————. *Outline of Nature Conservation Policy in Japan*. Tokyo: Environment Agency, 1977.

————. *Nature Conservation Administration in Japan*. Tokyo: Environment Agency, 1985.

KENYA

14

G. Wesley Burnett

When Kenya obtained its independence on December 12, 1963, the new nation inherited from the former British Kenya Colony and Protectorate several national parks and parklike reserves and a long tradition of the safari and the big-game hunt. With independence, elements of the world press and some international conservationists predicted the decline, if not outright pillage, of these reserves. But these doomsayers seriously underestimated the sagacity of the new nation and its leaders. Rather than having been pillaged, reserves have been increased to include more than 10 percent of Kenya. Conserving a wide variety of natural and cultural landscapes, these reserves are the basis of a tourist industry that, after export of tea and coffee, is the nation's largest source of foreign trade. However, the parks and reserves remain isolated—foreign ground visited by foreigners—and separate from the Kenyan people and their world. Reconciling Kenyan national parks to most Kenyans and integrating the areas into a pattern of Kenyan nationalism remain the salient problems facing conservationists in Kenya.

HISTORY

Among the most important historical figures in East Africa is the soldier-administrator-naturalist Hermann von Wissmann, the German high commissioner to East Africa in the final decades of the nineteenth century.[1] Recognizing that much of East Africa's land is exceedingly unproductive and that wildlife is likely in many places to be the only acceptable product, he suggested the creation of game reserves that would contribute to scientific research and protect the interests of African pastoralists. His ideas influenced the 1900 London Conference on African Wildlife, to which he was Germany's delegate, and the 1933 London

Convention on African Wildlife, which provided the legal model for subsequent park formation in much of Africa. Although his visionary concepts attracted little attention in East Africa at the time, many of his ideas have been implemented or are being experimented with by modern Kenya.

In the early years of the twentieth century huge reserves were established in northern and southern Kenya, but these reserves were little more than controlled hunting blocks giving Europeans a monopoly over big-game and trophy hunting while neglecting other aspects of management. The arrangement did little to endear the colonial government to Africans. Following the 1933 London Convention, smaller reserves, subject to more careful definition and, in theory anyway, to more intense management, began to emerge. The process of creating these equivalents to national parks was interrupted by World War II but began again in the latter half of the 1940s. In 1946, the Nairobi commons, a former grazing and army training area, became Kenya's first national park in the full modern sense.

David Sheldrick, as chief warden of Tsavo National Park after World War II and into the first decade after independence, applied skills and techniques gained as a British guerrilla in Burma to control poaching, particularly of elephants and rhinoceroses, in Tsavo. To do so he gave the guards a military organization including uniforms and martial discipline, and he instilled in them the deep sense of pride, duty, sacrifice, and *esprit de corps* that continues to characterize Kenya's park guards. Veterans of the antipoaching units, many reformed poachers themselves, are justly proud of their records and accomplishments.

No clear administrative structure for national parks emerged during the colonial period. While national Kenya quickly demonstrated its serious intention with respect to its parks, considerable organizational experimentation has ensued. By 1976 what had emerged, apparently as stable and certain as any government organization, is a ministerial level department, the Kenya Ministry of Tourism and Wildlife, to manage directly the reserved lands, and a policy body/oversight committee, the Park Trustees. Both work broadly, of course, under Parliament and the president. Another organization, the National Museums, is responsible for several parklike areas of historical importance, while a number of private citizens' organizations such as the East African Wildlife Society provide popular, though unofficial, review of park policies and management decisions.

Kenya's national parks are based, however, in pragmatism as well as ideals. By the 1960s, there was general scientific and administrative acceptance of what von Wissmann had long ago realized: much of East Africa, and much of Kenya particularly, is of exceedingly low productive potential with wildlife, in many areas, the best product that can be hoped for. Rangeland evaluations and classifications conducted in the 1950s and 1960s, the basis of Kenya's modern land-use policies, continually stressed the low agricultural potential, the importance of wildlife, and the need to protect watersheds.[2] Fortunately, politicians have listened, if not always closely. Fortunately, too, visionary business concerns, organizing the East African Tourist Travel Association in 1948, defined a market for wildlife—the tourist. Although, the most important tourist resource for Kenya is its Indian Ocean coast, parks and the wildlife also play an important role.[3] For most European tourists, Kenya is beach and wildlife in a unity that Kenya will do well to leave undisturbed.

THE PARKS AND RESERVES

The image of Kenya's wildlife is that of the bush and savanna, and it is here that Kenya's parks are their most classic and dramatic—some might add monotonous. At first glance, parks in the savanna and bush seem remarkably similar in both landscape and faunal composition, and the subtle differences in ecological organization escape the casual tourist's appreciation. Indeed, too fast a trip through too many parks that look too much alike by tourists already suffering from jetlag and some degree of cultural disorientation may prove a disappointing experience.

Parks of the Savanna and Bush

Among most popular areas, Masai Mara National Reserve probably offers the greatest opportunity and widest variety for wildlife viewing, while Amboseli, with the backdrop of Kilimanjaro, provides the most consistently dramatic views (see Table 14.1 and Figure 14.1). Masai Mara, an extension of the Serengeti Plain, has a large population of resident animals, which are supplemented by hundreds of thousands of wildebeest and zebra from the Serengeti, generally between August and October of each year. The prey species support the largest population of lions in Kenya, and other predators, particularly cheetah, hunting dogs, hyena, and jackals, are common. The bird life is immense. The mammalian life at Amboseli is both less rich and less abundant, focusing on swamps and seasonal lakes. Views are everywhere dominated by Kilimanjaro. The combination is the quintessential Africa, a photographer's paradise.

Tsavo National Park, an area of 20,800 square kilometers (8,034 square miles), defies generalization by sheer immensity. Really two parks divided by the Nairobi-Mombasa highway and railway, the area has a bitter history. A major and ancient source of East African ivory, Tsavo has been the scene of near warfare between poachers and park guards since World War II. Large herds of elephants in Tsavo led to a management debate over the wisdom of culling, and this to a scientist-conservationist-manager controversy, often as acrid as it was productive of scientific research. In Tsavo East, tourists are generally confined to the area south of the Athi-Galana rivers and in Tsavo West they seldom venture beyond the area surrounding Mzima Springs and the Tsavo River. The country is striking, which is fortunate, since the quality of wildlife is unpredictable, glorious when present, but not always present. Lake Tipe, in the extreme

Table 14.1
National Parks and Reserves of Kenya's Semi-Arid Areas

NAME	AREA (km^2)	CLASS[a]
Rift Valley		
1. Sibiloi[b]	1,673	NP
2. Central Island	5	NP
3. South Island	39	NP
4. South Turkana	1,091	NR
5. Kerio Valley - Kamnarok	---	NR
6. Nasalot	925	NR
7. Losai[b]	1,088	NR
8. Lake Bogoria[b]	107	NR
9. Lake Nakuru[b]	58	NP
10. Hell's Gate (Njorowa Gorge)	68	NR
11. Karianquos - Longonot	52	NP
Tana-Ewaso Nyiro River Area		
1. Meru[b]	877	NP
2. Mwea[b]	68	NR
3. N. Kitui	745	NR
4. Kora[b]	1,788	NR
5. Bisanadi	606	NR
6. Rahole[b]	1,280	NR
7. Arawala[b]	533	NR
8. Tana River Primate[b]	168	NR
9. Samburu[b]	225	NR
10. Buffalo Springs[b]	339	NR
11. Shaba[b]	239	NR
Southern Kenya		
1. Amboseli[b]	392	NP
2. Masai Mara[b]	1,673	NR
3. Ruma[b]	308	NP
4. Nairobi[b]	117	NP
5. Tsavo (East and West)[b]	20,821	NP
6. South Kitui	1,833	NR
7. Ngai Ndethya	212	NR
8. Chyulu Hills	375	NR

Notes: [a] NP = Park Status; NR = Reserve Status.
[b] Areas listed in Secretariat of IUCN. _World Directory of National Parks and Other Protected Areas_ (Morges, Switzerland; IUCN, 1977).

southwest, has a fantastic bird population though the area is infrequently visited by tourists.

Nairobi Park, though small and often criticized as being little more than an extended city zoo, remains rightly among the most studied and visited parks in Africa. With the Nairobi skyline often the backdrop, the apparent tameness is deceptive, and the drama is real. The west side of the park is highland woodland. The northeast is a portion of the Embakasi Plain, an open grassland with scattered acacia bush, and to the south is the Athi River basin with its mature yellow-barked fever trees (_Acacia xanthophloea_). Such variety of habitat in such a small area results in exceptional richness and diversity, and the area is commended to

Figure 14.1
Selected Kenya National Parks and National Reserves

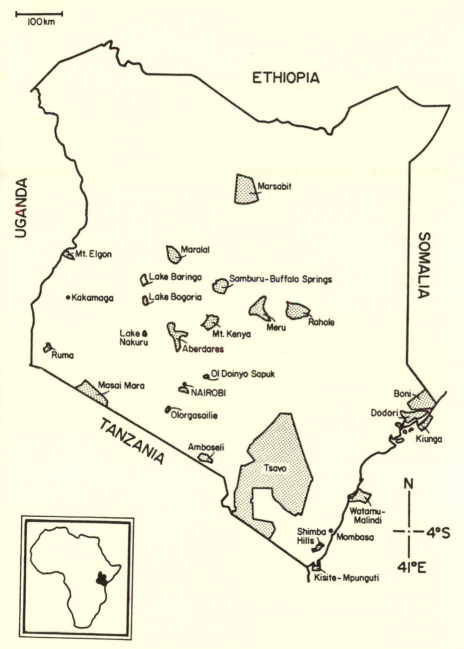

tourists as a good introduction to more extended safaris. A cement plant at Athi River, just beyond the eastern park boundary, often casts its plume in the park and is shamefully too visible in many areas. The number of tourists, which at times exceeds that of the wildlife, is presenting environmental problems.

Several of Kenya's newer areas in the north, such as the contiguous Samburu and Buffalo Springs reserves, north of Mount Kenya, are proving exceptionally popular with visitors, and their use and development have profited much from road paving and improvement north from Nairobi. Here the thorn bush is sparse, and the environment and people suggest a wild frontier district. Indeed, while one might argue the location of Kenya's frontier zone, Samburu is undoubtedly on, if not beyond, it. Certain of the resident species—notably the Grevy's zebra, the reticulated giraffe, the Beisa oryx, and the blue-necked Somali ostrich—are decidedly semi-arid and northern. Distant mountains and the Ewaso Nyiro River with its dramatic riparian vegetation provide a varied, formidable background.

Many of the areas added to Kenya's list of national parks and reserves since independence are isolated, little known, and seldom visited. Such an area is Rahole National Reserve, described in one tourist brochure as "Somewhere out there, somewhere between nowhere and Kora and the [Northern Frontier District] is this elusive 1,270 square kilometer reserve about which so many know so little."[4] These remote areas exemplify Kenya's commitment to the future and to conservation in theory as well as practice. Not long ago, Samburu National Reserve and Meru National Park were isolated and nearly impossible to visit while the Lambwe Valley Reserve, a similarly remote, tsetse-infested bush in the chronically impoverished area south of Homa Bay on Lake Victoria, has recently become Ruma National Park and is currently undergoing improvement. Most wildlife was long ago eliminated in the Lambwe Valley, resulting in bush encroachment. The infamous Ruma bush and adjacent unsuccessful forest plantation provided shade and shelter for the tsetse, the vector of sleeping sickness, and the surrounding region became associated with endemic sleeping sickness as settlement and herds increased under colonialism. The conversion of the Lambwe Valley Game Reserve, which harbors a rare and remarkably tenacious herd of roan antelope, into Ruma National Park is being accompanied by application of fire to the bush with periodic and predictable vengeance. As grasslands have succeeded bush in the wake of the fires, work has begun on wildlife translocations, and it is hoped that Ruma, as a restored landscape, will soon enter the tourist circuit and help stimulate the local economy.

Mountains and Lakes

Mount Kenya and Aberdare national parks, and a more recent acquisition, Mount Elgon National Park, conserve examples of the tropical montane forest and high alpine environments (see Table 14.2). Although the wildlife abundance is less spectacular, and the individuals more illusive, the vegetation is varied, attractive, and unique, and there is a myriad of birds. Tourists and recreationists

Table 14.2
Kenya's Other Parks and Reserves

NAME	AREA (km^2)	CLASS[a]
Mountain Areas		
1. Mt. Kenya[b]	716	NP
2. Aberdare[b]	766	NP
3. Ol Doinyo Sapuk[b]	18	NP
4. Mt. Elgon[b]	169	NP
5. Maralal		NR
6. Marsabit[b]	2,088	NR
Coastal Areas		
1. Malindi-Watamu[b]	235	NP-NR
2. Kiunga	250	NR
3. Kisite/Mpunguti[b]	23	NP-NR
4. Shimba Hills[b]	193	NP
5. Dodori[b]	877	NR
6. Boni[b]	1,340	NR
Historical-Cultural Complex		
1. Gedi	3	NP
2. Olorgasailie	.21	NP
3. Ft. Jesus	.02	NP
4. Hyrax Hill		
Special Natural Reserves		
1. Saiwa Swamp[b]	2	NP
2. Kakamaga Forest	96	NP

Notes: [a] NP = Park Status; NR = Reserve Status.
[b] Areas listed in Secretariat of IUCN. <u>World Directory of National Parks and Other Protected Areas</u> (Morges, Switzerland; IUCN, 1977).

also have greater freedom to camp and roam, particularly on Mount Kenya, an internationally prestigious climb. Unfortunately, the lions of Aberdare are wise to man's wandering instinct and have now severely restricted activities in that park. Mount Elgon, a newer area in far western Kenya, is distant from the main tourist circuits and is less visited though it is popular with Kenya residents.

The many lakes that dot the floor of Kenya's Rift Valley are a paradise for bird-watchers. Two of these lakes have been reserved: Lake Nakuru National Park and Lake Bogoria National Reserve (formally Lake Hannington). Both lakes are alkaline and useless for agriculture. Both are world renowned for their greater and lesser flamingo, but particularly so for Lake Nakuru, established in 1960 as a bird sanctuary. Urban and agricultural pollutants entering Lake Nakuru from Nakuru town and the surrounding exceptionally rich agricultural lands have apparently damaged the lake's environment and somewhat reduced bird populations in recent years. Proximity to Nakuru town and readily controlled access to the reasonably sized area (58 square kilometers, 22 square miles) make Nakuru National Park a potentially attractive rhinoceros sanctuary, which it is destined to become. In recent years, it has also become an important focus for research, particularly in aquatic ecology. At Lake Bogoria geysers and hot springs supplement birds, and the eastern shore shelters a population of greater kudu, which are widespread but uncommon in Kenya. The east side road is generally accessible only by four-wheel-drive vehicles and not at all when the bridge across the river that feeds the lake from the north is out (which is most of the time).

Marine Parks

The Kenya coast is paralleled by fine fringing and barrier reefs that Kenya has undertaken seriously, if not always successfully, to conserve. The oldest and best known of Kenya's marine reserves is the Malindi-Watamu Marine Reserve. The reserve extends from about Malindi south to include the Mida Creek estuary and includes within its boundaries two national parks, appropriately Malindi and Watamu. The conserved birding areas, particularly in the Mida Creek estuary, are almost as spectacular and valuable as the beach and reef areas. At opposite ends of the coast are the offshore Kisite National Park/Mpunguti Reserve at the southern extreme and the Kiunga Marine National Reserve in the extreme northeast. The former may be visited by boat through the Pemba Channel Fishing Club and Shimoni Reef Fishing Lodge. Kiunga Reserve remains more a proposal than a reality though lodge facilities do exist. Together with the adjacent Dodori and Boni national reserves, on the mainland extending southwest from the Somalian frontier, the areas are a rich biological preserve of immense, though little realized, value. Kiunga Reserve is approachable by sea, and it is possible to drive there in the dry season though the journey requires a self-contained vehicle and considerable planning and caution. Journeys to Boni and Dodori reserves are more serious still. The country is thinly populated, the forests ancient and dense, and the wildlife reputedly profuse, if sometimes obscured by the forest.

Beyond the formal reserves, Kenya has taken steps to conserve its entire reef and offshore fishery by regulating fishing, shelling, and the trade in shells in addition to the harvesting of mangrove and estuarian products. The cynic may rightly assume some difference between expressed purpose and actual accomplishment, but the purpose is nonetheless clear and clearly not intended to be hypocritical. Kenya intends to conserve its coastal resources.

Historical and Cultural Areas

Generally in conjunction with the Kenya National Museum, a number of archaeological and historical resources have been stabilized and made available to the public. Southwest of Nairobi is Olorgasailie National Park, a middle paleolithic site originally excavated by L.S.B. and Mary Leakey in the 1940s and completed by G. L. Isaacs in 1962 and 1963. Near Watamu National Park north of Mombasa is Gedi National Park, an Arab city occupied beginning in the late thirteenth or early fourteenth century and ending in the early seventeenth century. Gedi was apparently founded by a splinter group from Malindi, though why a maritime people would have chosen this unusually inland site is unknown. Nonetheless, from the size of its remains its citizens seem to have been prosperous. The site was abandoned, precipitously, for reasons yet to be discovered. Hypotheses abound: Portuguese punitive expeditions, Galla Somali pressures, a fear among the residents that the mosques were incorrectly oriented, or befouled water. Extensive excavations have shed little useful light on Gedi's origin and decline.

The most famous and frequently visited of the conserved archaeological-historical sites is undoubtedly Fort Jesus, a dramatic example of sixteenth-century Portuguese military architecture, its walls and bastions towering impressively over access to Mombasa Harbor. Here visitors cannot help but marvel at the rich, if often violent and shameful, history of Africa's Indian Ocean coast. The grounds include an impressive collection of artillery pieces and the museum a collection of pottery and ceramics arranged chronologically. On the northwestern bastion is a restored Omani Arab house with a fine collection of material objects from that culture.

Gedi became a national park in 1948, and Fort Jesus became a national park in 1958 following a generous grant for restoration from the Gulbenkian Foundation. Both areas were transferred from the National Park Trustees to the Museum Trustees in 1969.

ADMINISTRATION

The Ministry of Tourism and Wildlife is charged with administration of all park areas, though the National Museums of Kenya do administer a number of areas such as Fort Jesus and Gedi in addition to a number of regional museums of cultural and natural history. Several of the regional museums, designed to preserve elements of regional material culture and natural history, are sometimes included on tourist circuits. Tourist visits to these regional museums, and particularly to the National Museum in Nairobi, can hardly be sufficiently encouraged. Kenya is critically short of domestically produced wood and wood products so that national forests are largely serious working plantations of low direct tourist or recreational value, domestic or foreign. Generally, recreation is not encouraged, and neither is it advisable among those unfamiliar with or unprepared to contend with African wildland conditions. Areas of remnant natural vegetation with watershed protection values generally have values of recreational and touristic interests. There has been a concerted effort to place these areas under the administration of the Ministry of Tourism and Wildlife. Biological inventories of Kenya are incomplete and there remain many small areas, until recently little intruded upon, in desperate need of conservation as agricultural populations increase and exploit increasingly marginal niches. The future of these areas is indeed bleak.

Further Park Creation

Further park and reserve designations of large areas in the densely settled highlands of central and western Kenya and in the coastal margins is unlikely though there is ample opportunity to preserve very small areas of critical habitat such as the Kakamaga Forest. There may be some need to develop some unorthodox approaches to nature conservation in highly settled areas. An example is the Lake Baringo area, a highly eroded, impoverished area, where domestic and foreign tourism has become important without the help of the Ministry of Tourism and Wildlife. Leadership in these types of areas will undoubtedly combine local interests supplemented by the National Museums and private organizations.

It is not inconceivable that large areas of northern Kenya could yet be designated as parks and reserves; however, this eventuality depends on many factors that yet remain to be clarified. Too, Kenya has reserved huge areas of little-known land, particularly in the north. As these lands become better known, it may become obvious that portions of the reserve are not needed to meet conservation objectives. Deregulation has happened in the past and can be expected in the future. This is neither unreasonable nor a reversal of national policy, the too frequent external criticism notwithstanding.

Given the situation throughout most of Africa, a surprising number of private organizations provide both support for and review of park activities. The most obvious of these organizations is the East African Wildlife Society. With offices in the Nairobi Hilton and an international membership, this organization publishes *Swara*, a glossy wildlife tabloid of exceptional standards and quality.

Reserves versus Parks

A source of confusion in discussion of Kenya's parks and equivalent reserves is a nomenclature and classification system that is presently unclear and that has been historically unstable. In theory, national parks are supposed to be the most important resources, and therefore totally nationalized. National reserves are in theory a little less important and are created by declaration of the minister of tourism with the permission of a competent authority, generally a land-management agency. Nonconservation uses may be permitted in reserves if they are stated at the time of declaration. If the competent authority is a county council, a management committee appointed by the county council may alter allowable uses as the situation warrants. In parks, no human use is permitted in theory. In practice, one may, with proper contacts, obtain concessions and permits, and build hotels and swimming pools, though livestock may not be driven through park areas. The obvious contradiction does not escape local residents.

Reserves, particularly county council reserves, are more flexible in the uses permitted. For example, a core portion of Masai Mara National Reserve is treated as a national park with grazing by Masai pastoralists permitted at least periodically on the periphery. A similar arrangement existed on the now-deregulated Masai Amboseli Reserve, which surrounds and buffers Amboseli National Park. Both areas have a rich and confusing administrative history. In the buffering reserve of Watamu-Malindi, however, no use is permitted.

National parks are indeed fully nationalized areas with the cost and benefits of development and operation falling on the central government. In reserves, local government often maintains policy and administrative prerogatives and generally gains some of the revenues from the development and operation of the area. Not surprisingly, if an area seems to have a profit-making potential, local government would be interested in maintaining reserve status and often takes the initiative in designation, but areas with little or no development prospects might as well become national parks. Hence, there is the apparent anomaly of the 20-square kilometer (7.7-square-mile), rarely visited Ol Doinyo Sapuk National Park, Sir Northrup McMillan's former estate just east of Thika, but the 1,812-square-kilometer (700-square-mile) Masai Mara National Reserve. Students of the subject are also warned not to confuse these reserves with other types of "reserves" that may exist, or may have existed, in Kenya—for example, game reserves and forest reserves. Further confusing the issue, at least two reserves are nationally administered (Marsabit and Maralal), and at least three national parks are administered by the National Museums and sometimes referred to as national monuments.

The reserve status, particularly county council reserves, can encourage local support beyond what can be mustered for parks. Gate and concession fees from reserves that remain with the county councils encourage local cooperation in development and management, and the council is permitted to shape policies, some of which may bring additional money to local peoples. For example, at Samburu and Buffalo Springs reserves, all game drives must be accompanied by a park guard, though no payment is required. It is unlikely that the guard contributes to the tourist's safety, but an important service may be provided. The park guard is likely to convey information to drivers that will improve wildlife viewing, and in exchange, drivers are likely to encourage larger tips to successful guards. These tips remain in the local economy.

Hotels

In theory, hotels are excluded from the parks and less so from reserves. In practice, however, hotels have sometimes been placed within park boundaries, and they will probably continue to be built in the larger parks and reserves. Since nationally and locally powerful political interests tend to be in the hotel business, it is unlikely that the practice can be stopped. Hotel building is doubtlessly self-limiting. With business dependent upon wildlife viewing, there is only so much local competition a well-established bush hotel can be expected to tolerate or accept graciously. Hotels probably do help control poaching simply by the concentration of people and rapid communication that accompany them.

Unfortunately, hotels in and adjacent to national parks tend to make the industry overcommitted to the area. Package tourists are simply going to be taken to parks with hotels whether they should be taken there or not. Several areas are probably in need of rest, and tourists will continue to be taken to areas where wildlife populations are temporarily depleted. Conversely, many beautiful parks without hotels, such as Shimba Hills National Reserve, are avoided just because there is no hotel. Whether this situation is good or bad is largely a matter of viewpoint; however, unvisited parks tend to be undermanned, unmanaged, and wide open to poaching rather than benignly neglected wilderness areas.

Both the safari companies and tourist-class hotels in and out of the parks are increasingly Kenyan-owned, and many, such as African Tours and Hotels, are wholly Kenyan and/or parastatial. Kenyan, and often local, produce is used, and where it is not, as is the case with most wines and spirits, the tourist pays dearly for the luxury through the high duties that are passed on. Foreign employees, including managers, are increasingly rare, and standards of service are exceptionally high. The Utalii College, the nationally operated training school for most hotel-tourism industry employees, is supported through a training levy appended to the accommodations bills of tourist-class hotels and restaurants. Given the difficulties imposed by isolation, service is generally excellent and always gracious.

Law Enforcement

Unlike its forest reserves, Kenya's parks are little subject to intrusion by squatters. Undoubtedly some illicit or accidental pastoral use is made of parks, particularly in the more isolated, undeveloped parks where boundaries are poorly marked and locally misunderstood. Most Kenyan groups are uninclined to savor bush meat, so subsistence poaching is less a problem than in some other areas of Africa. Nonetheless, poaching has been and remains the single major conservation law-enforcement problem. The war against commercial-scale poaching, victimizing principally elephants and rhinoceroses, is reflected in the military organization and discipline of the park guards and wardens, and confrontations have more than once produced death and serious injury on both sides. Certainly Kenya's 1977 decision to ban sports hunting and its curtailment, in 1978, of trade in or export of animal parts and curios involving animal parts is intended, at least in part, to assist in poacher control. Commercial-scale poaching, however, must involve powerful officials and politicians if export operations are to be successful and profits made. Game officials can find it difficult and even dangerous to implicate such people.

Poaching threatens Kenya's coastal parks, reserves, and marine areas. Within the national parks and reserves, removing shells and disturbing sea life are unlawful, and fishing and shelling are severely restricted throughout the reef. In practice, shell removal and harvesting is difficult to control. Most commercial poachers intend resale to tourists, and since tourists are selective about the shells they purchase, the trade radically affects the population balances, particularly the predator-prey relationships and the grazing food chain, ultimately altering, if not destroying, the entire reef and lagoon ecology. Removal of mangrove poles and posts for local use and for export, largely to the Arabian peninsula, damages the delicate mangrove swamps and increases erosion along the entire coastal margin.

A further law-enforcement problem is the banditry within parks or on routes between parks. Bandits, supposedly from Tanzania, have attacked tourists in Masai Mara and Amboseli while Shifta "rebels," with their weak claim to the status of an "independence movement," have harassed tourists in northern Kenya. Incidents are fortunately rare but profoundly embarrassing to the Kenyan government when they do occur. The topic is seldom publicly discussed in Kenya, and in fact tourists are much more likely to be robbed in Nairobi or to be injured or killed in a traffic accident. But a confrontation with bandits in the bush sounds far worse and is a constant threat to the stability of the tourist industry.

Education and Science

At least in theory, the parks and reserves serve the public educational interests of Kenya. In practice these educational interests are pursued through the schools and youth wildlife clubs and are generally limited to infrequent field trips by those schools with the resources to enjoy such luxuries. Although hostels for educational use are available or are being developed at, for example, Masai Mara, Tsavo, and other areas, they are too small to be of any use to most African schools. The National Museums of Kenya, fortunately, has taken its educational responsibility far more seriously than the Ministry of Tourism and Wildlife.

The interested tourist is likely to find the educational programs within the parks frustratingly inadequate. The signboards and interpretive plaques now expected in American parks are generally impractical in Africa and consequently conspicuously (and gratefully) absent. The Utalii College has added programs for drivers and tour guides that emphasize environmental education, ecology, and wildlife. A variety of published natural history guides are commercially available, and good guides exist for Fort Jesus and Gedi.[5] Reasonably available tourist quality maps, except for Mount Kenya, are out of date and only marginally adequate.[6] The popularized ecological analysis for Amboseli by David Western is singular and of exceptionally high quality, the type of summary that should exist for other areas.[7] Achieving some degree of enlightenment for the serious tourist/amateur naturalist, whether domestic or foreign, will probably always require considerable effort and serious study.

If the park contribution to domestic education remains marginal and an opportunity yet to be exploited, scientific research has been pursued with a vengeance in many of the areas.[8] Von Wissmann argued for a strong research component in East Africa's reserves, and his ideas are reflected in the legal structure of Kenya's parks. However, throughout much of the twentieth century, research beyond gathering and describing museum specimens was restricted by a lack of well-defined problems and the paradigms necessary to their analysis. The gradual maturing of ecology and the respectability gained by the new field of ethology, the study of animal character and behavior, have reinvigorated field observation in the natural sciences. By the late 1950s investigators were scurrying to the field, and many of them chose as their laboratory East Africa's national parks.

Research began, supposedly, in Kenya's national parks in 1956, and an almost immediate schism developed between administrative managerial research and theoretical research.[9] The split is seldom as neat as its proponents would suggest. A large amount of worthy applied research is undoubtedly lost to the scholarly world in Nairobi file cabinets, but a substantial body of applied as well as theoretical research from Kenya's parks and reserves has entered the scientific literature.

The oldest established national parks and reserves have been the most frequently utilized research laboratories. This is probably a reflection of the extreme ecological importance of the areas reserved in the final years of colonialism and the greater accessibility of these areas to the scientific community. Any review of the literature would probably underestimate the importance of Masai Mara, which is generally included in the research conducted in Tanzania's Serengeti National Park. Nairobi National Park has served as a laboratory for two decades of faculty and students at the University of Nairobi. Initial studies of population dynamics and feeding behavior provided a firm basis for the study of individual species, some of which, such as J. A. Rudnai's study of the lion, have become classics in their own right.[10] The prospect of culling Tsavo's elephants resulted in international funding and a massive and highly productive research project under the direction of Walter Leuthold. Studies went far beyond elephants to include many aspects of the area's ecology from dung beetles to water holes.

Amboseli is probably further along in developing a permanent research focus and facility than any other park in Kenya. Initially, T. T. Struthaker and S. A. Altmann developed a focus on primates, the vervet monkeys and baboons specifically, which endures to this day. This research, deeply theoretical, has influenced contemporary developments in the study of behavior generally, but recently has taken a startling turn toward applied research—the study of primates as pests in tourist areas.[11] Studies of large mammals and general ecological studies have been conducted and will probably become more important in the future. The ecologist David Western has observed tourists as ecological subjects and, more significantly, has studied the relationship of Amboseli to surrounding pastoral peoples, a study that contributed significantly to solving many of the park's managerial problems. Managerial research of this quality needs to be initiated in other areas, particularly Masai Mara and potentially in areas of northern Kenya.

By the late colonial period, because of its botanical wealth, Mount Kenya had developed a tradition of vegetative study that has changed in emphasis from taxonomic concerns to ecology. Species identification on Mount Kenya, however, is by no means complete. Studies of small mammals began in the immediate postcolonial period by M. J. Coe, whose book remains the best general description of the mountain's ecology.[12] Recently, studies have increasingly been concerned with comparison of tropical alpine environments and ecologies.

Recent trends in research in the parks include increases in the amount of material being published and a diversification of areas where studies are being conducted. Lake Nakuru, in particular, has had its birds, water quality, geology, and general ecology scrutinized. Despite the importance of Kenya's parks and reserves to science, the future of research in the parks is not particularly bright. Funding has never been easy to obtain, and inflation results in less being accomplished at more expense. For foreign researchers, required research permits are increasingly difficult to obtain particularly in the absence of Kenyan colleagues, and Kenyan scientists with interests in the type of scientific work that has been conducted in parks are rare. Nonbiological studies, such as economic evaluations and surveys of visitor behavior and satisfactions, are troublesome if not dangerous topics because of the political and economic importance of parks, while ecological studies of a park's relationship to neighboring people are generally beyond the ethnological and linguistic skills of foreign scientists. Tourist facilities have undoubtedly encouraged research by easing problems of access and providing some margin of comfort and convenience, but there are obvious limits to scientist-tourist cordiality. The baboons of Nairobi had become so habituated to humans by Kenya's independence that they had become useless to science, and there are increasing indications of scientist-tourist conflicts at Amboseli.

Prospects

It is possible to produce a long list of problems, from trivial to substantial, confronting Kenya's national parks. It is also possible for foreign conservationists to wring their hands too much over these issues. Blessed with uncommon political stability since 1963, Kenyans have demonstrated their will to face and solve their problems. The greatest problem before Kenya is, of course, a calamitous population growth rate that could damage a lot more than just the parks. A closely allied issue, however, is precisely the place of the parks in society. Kenyans as a group are simply not very much interested in their parks.

There are a number of interdependent hypotheses that can be offered to explain this lack of involvement. A most simple and direct explanation is that while resident fees for entering the parks are almost nonexistent, the cost of getting to a park, or of staying there any length of time, is simply beyond the financial ability of most Kenyans, even the middle class and even at off season and special resident rates. Steps are being taken to encourage and to reduce the cost of domestic tourism; however, evidence indicates that the coast, rather than the national parks, is both the preferred and the least expensive destination for the Kenyan vacationer.

It appears that Kenyans will simply not seek out their parks as a matter of preference. For the majority of rural farm Kenyans, wilderness and wildlife are anything but a refreshing, renewing experience, and the urban middle class is still decidedly close to its rural farm experience. The bush is a place to be respected, feared, and avoided. Men and women who spent years of their youth herding and guarding livestock in the bush or driving baboons and birds out of the family fields can hardly be expected to regard a Sunday drive in a national park with the same romantic enthusiasm as does a German tourist.

There also remains the taint of the colonial experience. For many Kenyans, wildlife and the luxury of enjoying landscape are the privilege and priority of Europeans. Indeed Kenyans' reaction to tourists seems to vary between bewilderment and insult. The tourist is perceived as only wanting to photograph lions and possibly "natives" as "natives" doing "native" things but not seeing, much less experiencing, a people struggling to build a new nation. Behind such cultural and racial conflicts may simply be generations of implied inferiority and diseducation. As a Kenyatta University geography student stated in discussing his reaction to a field exercise, "Professor, we don't look out the bus windows because we have not been taught that it is a beautiful land." And in fairness to tourists, Kenya markets wildlife, beaches, and often "natives"—not development, a topic hardly likely to captivate the foreign tourist.

Less subjective, but still hard to get objective data on, is who benefits and how much from national park-tourism related activities. Kenya is a capitalist country and respects investment and the risks and profits that go with it. That park investments create private wealth is not surprising and certainly hotels at, for example, Masai Mara do pay local government for the privilege of doing business. That the tourist industry will help support local government is well established, but the proper amount of that help is subject to debate. It is also well established that the tourist who wants first-class accommodations in isolation from the day-to-day Africa surrounding him and who wants foreign food and drink will pay for the service and dearly so. The jobs provided by tourism in and around the parks certainly do benefit Kenyans of all classes, from Masai ladies stringing together plastic beads to aspiring hotel managers. However, that a landless farmer looking at land devoted to wild animals might fail to appreciate the need for conservation and for foreign exchange is also understandable.

The social problem before Kenya's national parks undoubtedly centers on and will increasingly center on this "non-productive" use of conserved fields. So far, the conflict has largely been between the pastoralists and the parks. The problem was anticipated by von Wissmann, and practical solutions, at least in part, were developed by Western at Amboseli while the flexibility of the reserve concept presents the opportunity for Kenya to experiment with new mechanisms of local-park conflict resolution. In fact, the national policy of decentralization of planning and administration processes adopted in July 1983 suggests that local governments must eventually take more responsibility for national parks and reserves, and the further denationalization of national reserves is not beyond speculation.

Continued high population growth, particularly in a population that is 85 percent agricultural, can only result in intensifying land shortages and intensifying conflicts between the people and their parks. A landless farmer can hardly be expected to accept graciously that a marginal piece of land is more productive nationally when devoted to antelope and tours than to a crop of pigeon peas. There is little to suggest that the average rural Kenyan is ready to accept the scientist's dismal assessments of Kenyans' marginal lands, and much of the rhetoric of development, of necessity expansive and optimistic, may in fact reinforce the rural Kenyans' hopes that surely hard work will convert the wilderness into a garden. The hope is optimistic and characteristic of frontiersmen, but as naive, nonetheless, as the belief that rainfall will follow the plow.

NOTES

1. The classical study of Kenya's wildlife management and conservation programs in the colonial period is Noel Simon, *Between the Sunlight and the Thunder* (London: Collins, 1962). For a more critical and unorthodox view, see A. D. Graham, *The Gardeners of Eden* (London: George Allen and Unwin, 1973).

2. D. J. Pratt and M. D. Gwynne, *Rangeland Management and Ecology in East Africa* (London: Hoddler, 1977).

3. S. E. Migot-Adolla, K.G.C.M. Kangi, and J. Mbindyo, *Study of Tourism in Kenya* (Nairobi: University of Nairobi, Institute for Development Studies, 1982), p. 20.

4. Nation Newspapers Ltd., *What's On*, no. 54 (May 1986): 16.

5. J. Kirkman, *Gedi* (Nairobi: National Museum of Kenya, 1975); and J. Kirkman, *Fort Jesus* (Nairobi: Museum Trustees of Kenya, 1981).

6. A new series of maps of high cartographic standards is available for the Aberdares and Mount Kenya. The trend is a hopeful sign. The maps are published by the Survey of Kenya and are available from the Public Map Office, City Square, P.O. Box 30089, Nairobi.

7. D. Western, *A Wildlife Guide and a Natural History of Amboseli* (Nairobi: General Printers, 1983). M. J. Coe's classic study of Mount Kenya (see note 12) and his recent *Islands in the Bush, a Natural History of Kora Reserve, Kenya* (London: G. Philip, 1985) are too extensive to be considered park guides but they are highly readable and would be interesting to serious students.

8. For a general and readable review of wildlife research in East Africa and the national parks particularly, see C. Moss, *Portraits in the Wild: Behavior Studies of East African Mammals* (Boston: Houghton Mifflin, 1975).

9. J. K. Mutinda, "How Far Has Wildlife Management Benefited from Research?" in *Wildlife Research Priorities in Kenya* (Nairobi: Kenya Ministry of Environment and Natural Resources, 1977), pp. 5–11.

10. J. A. Rudnai, *The Social Lion* (Lancaster, England: MTP, 1973).

11. E. J. Brenman et al. "Ecology and Behavior of a Pest Primate." *African Journal of Ecology*, 23 (1985): 35–44.

12. M. J. Coe, *The Ecology of the Alpine Zone of Mount Kenya*, Vol. 17 (The Hague: Junk, Monographiae Biologicae, 1967).

BIBLIOGRAPHY

Altmann, S. A. *Baboon Ecology*. Chicago: University of Chicago Press, 1970.
Yeager, Rodger, and Norman N. Miller. *Wildlife, Wild Death; Land Use and Survival in Eastern Africa*. Albany: State University of New York, 1986.

MALAYSIA 15

Susan Kay Jacobson

Concomitant with its rapid economic development, Malaysia has pursued a successful conservation strategy by preserving samples of its unique natural heritage in an extensive system of parks and reserves. These protected areas preserve a variety of ecosystems from spectacular coral reefs beneath the sea to the peaks of Southeast Asia's tallest mountain. Malaysia's forests are among the richest in the world. They are home to three of the rarest mammals, the Malaysian gaur, Sumatran rhinoceros, and tiger. In East Malaysia, on the island of Borneo, orangutans, proboscis monkeys, and rare species of insectivorous plants and orchids add to the astonishing diversity protected by the parks. The success of this park system has been shaped by Malaysia's political and biophysical history.

HISTORY

The Federation of Malaysia is composed of eleven states of Peninsular Malaysia that gained their independence from Britain in 1957 and the two Bornean states of Sabah and Sarawak. These latter two states joined the federation in 1963 and are separated from the Peninsula by a 1,000-kilometer (600-mile) stretch of the South China Sea. The history of natural area preservation in Peninsular Malaysia, Sarawak, and Sabah all began under British occupation. However, their subsequent administration and future development differ because of the terms under which the Bornean states joined the federation. Therefore, these three areas will be discussed separately.

Peninsular Malaysia

In Peninsular Malaysia the need for some kind of environmental protection was first recognized in the late 1800s by the British colonialists. The decimation of several bird species hunted for their exotic plumage triggered the passage of the first protective laws for birds in 1884. At this time, wildlife was protected mainly by gazette notification, which would impose a temporary moratorium on the slaughter of an affected species. Game species like rhinoceros (*Dicerorhinus sumatrensis*), gaur (*Bos gaurus*), and deer (*Cervus unicolor*) could be temporarily protected in this manner.

In 1902 protection was extended to include habitats as well as populations of animals. The first game reserve was established at Chior, Perak, to protect a herd of gaur. In the following years, more reserves were created under the influence of the colonial planters and hunters. Between 1922 and 1928, ten game reserves were created, but most of these were oriented only toward preserving game species. Minimal management was carried out by voluntary game wardens as the state governments refused to pay any salaries. Meanwhile, wildlife populations continued to decline. This was caused by habitat modification for rubber plantations and other agricultural uses, severe hunting pressures, and wanton destruction of "pest" species, such as elephants.

In 1930, the government appointed a Wildlife Commission to ascertain the status and need for the protection of wildlife in Peninsular Malaysia. The commission produced a three-volume report with recommendations for the administration of wildlife conservation in the country. The commission recommended establishment of a national park around Gunung Tahan, the Peninsula's tallest mountain. This area had already been set aside as a wildlife reserve in 1924. In 1938 it was incorporated with land from parts of the states of Kelantan and Trengganu to become the first Malaysian national park. At this time, the first state game warden took office, and the chief game warden post received a salary.

During World War II, the Japanese occupation, and the subsequent communist emergency, which lasted until 1960, the government gave little attention to the cause of wildlife conservation. Upon independence, the Wild Animals and Birds Protection Ordinance of 1955 was continued under the new constitution. The law requires states to meet federal standards for wildlife protection, but allows them to enact additional protective legislation.

Under the constitution of Malaysia, the states retain power over their land and collect revenues from its exploitation. It is an arduous task for the federal national parks department to convince a state government to relinquish jurisdiction and set aside land for a new protected area. In order to establish parks and reserves in Peninsular Malaysia, the Department of Wildlife and National Parks makes an application for the land through the Ministry of Science, Technology and the Environment to the federal commissioner of lands and mines. The application is then forwarded to the appropriate state government. Because the areas are usually large, the State Executive Committee will meet with the Ministry to evaluate the application and suggest any modifications. The state may take years to decide on the application. For example, the Endau Rompin National Park, which was proposed in 1972, remains ungazetted. In large part this is because of the slowness of one of the states involved to ratify the proposal.

Once the proposed areas are accepted, they are established as reserves or parks under current laws by the Department of Wildlife and National Parks. Wildlife reserves or sanctuaries are established under the 1972 Protection of Wildlife Act. In Malaysia these are defined as follows:

- A wildlife reserve is "an area under government control established for the conservation of natural resources. This protection will be given to wildlife consistent with other uses of the reserve such as forest protection, water catchment, research, education, recreation, etc. The establishment of this reserve will recognize wildlife and its habitat in the context of total land use planning."

- A wildlife sanctuary is "an area where indigenous wildlife exists in good number and where it may be given full protection. Such an area may be established for one or a few species, but generally they will be intended to protect all species. The area is restricted to authorized persons undertaking activities compatible with the purpose of the area, e.g., research, etc."[1]

National parks can be established under the 1980 National Parks Act. This act defines the purpose of national parks as the "preservation and protection of wildlife, plant life and objects of geological, archaeological, historical and ethnological and other scientific and scenic interest and through their conservation and utilization to promote the education, health, aesthetic values and recreation of the people."[2] Under this act the reservation of an area cannot be revoked by the state authority except with the written concurrence of the federal minister. This act has yet to be used. States remain reluctant to give up any land to the federal domain.

Most of the existing protected areas in Peninsular Malaysia were established under the old Federated Malay States Ordinance, Wildlife Ordinance, or Land Code. Because they were set up by legislative order or gazette notice, they can be altered or eliminated in the same way.

Since independence, three new reserves have been established in Peninsular Malaysia. Along with the older reserves, the tenure of these areas remains insecure. Some of the older reserves have been substantially modified by timber extraction or agricultural and residential developments. For example, W. E. Stevens reported that Chior, the first game reserve, "long ago died from neglect but was never interred."[3] Other reserves no longer serve their original function. The smallest reserve, the Port Dickson Islands, was established in 1926 to protect Imperial pigeons (*Ducula sp.*). These birds no longer inhabit the island. Currently the Department of Wildlife and National Parks is reviewing the existing protected areas to strengthen their security by reestablishing them under the more secure legislative enactments of the National Park Act of 1980 and the Wildlife Protection Act of 1972.

No new preserves have been created under these enactments, although proposals for the establishment of additional protected areas have been made. In the federal government's development plans for 1976 through 1980 (the Third

Malaysia Plan), twenty-three new reserves and parks were recommended with an approximate area totaling 897,806 hectares (2,218,480 acres). Because of jurisdictional conflicts between state and federal governments and a shortage of personnel and staff in the Department of Wildlife and National Parks, these areas remain unconstituted.

East Malaysia

In contrast to Peninsular Malaysia, in the East Malaysian states of Sarawak and Sabah, the establishment of protected natural areas is a relatively new phenomenon. Most of the parks and sanctuaries in these states have been gazetted during the last two decades. The recent establishment of protected areas in these two states reflects their greater land areas, lower population densities, relatively less developed conditions, and the growing awareness of the need for preservation spurred by the severe depletion of natural areas in recent years. For example, in Sabah, 61 percent of the land area was in natural forest in 1971. By 1980, primarily because of timber extraction, only 27 percent of the natural forest remained.[4]

In Sarawak, the first National Parks Ordinance was enacted in 1955. This delineated the procedure for constituting a national park that would be managed by a board of trustees. After a preliminary inquiry into objections and claims for prior land rights, the state granted development funds to establish the park. Selection of the park site was based on the following criteria: (1) situated near the capital city, Kuching; (2) contained unspoiled and beautiful country with considerable scientific interest; (3) not encumbered by native customary rights that would render its protection difficult, and (4) "provided natural facilities for quiet holidays."[5] After considering several possibilities, the board decided on a coastal area that was constituted as Bako National Park in 1958. The 2,728-hectare (6,741-acre) area had been reduced from the original proposal in order to provide the local population with a continued source of forest products.

The board of trustees managed the park until 1973. At that time the National Parks Ordinance was amended to abolish the board and give responsibility to the conservator of forests for the establishment, administration, and management of national parks. As a result, a national parks section was created in the Forest Department in 1975.

In Sarawak, the legal constitution of a national park can be a lengthy process and involves the following steps: (1) initial proposal, (2) initial Supreme Council approval, (3) publication of gazette notification stating the intent of the government to constitute a park, (4) hearing of local peoples' claims against the land in question by the district officer and resident concerned, after which the admitted claims are forwarded to the clerk of councils, (5) final approval by the Supreme Council, (6) federal government concurrence, and (7) publication of final gazette notification. However, in 1973, when Gunung Mulu was established, the sixth step was skipped.

Since the National Parks Ordinance was amended, five new national parks have been established and six new ones have been proposed. As in Peninsular Malaysia, legal constitution of the parks often takes a long time. In Sarawak this is mainly because years may pass while local people make claims on the land or forest involved. For instance, the Gunung Gading National Park proposal was first approved in principle in 1965. The park was not established until 1983.

In the state of Sabah on the northern tip of Borneo, the establishment of protected areas lagged behind the movement in Sarawak. Again, it traces its roots to British rule. The legal protection of Mount Kinabalu, Southeast Asia's tallest mountain, as Sabah's first national park owes its conception to the Japanese occupation of Sabah during World War II when it was still a British Crown Colony. The Japanese marched 2,400 Australian and British prisoners of war for eleven months from the east coast to the foothills of Mount Kinabalu, 386 kilometers (240 miles) west. Only six men survived. In a desire to honor the Allied men lost, a Kinabalu Memorial Committee was formed to construct a monument to the war dead. The memorial was the nucleus of the concept to preserve Mount Kinabalu itself as an entity. Later, a British botanist led two expeditions for the Royal Society of London to explore the little-known flora of the mountain. In 1961, he sent a report, entitled "The Proposed National Park of Kinabalu," to His Excellency the Governor of the Crown Colony of North Borneo.

This resulted in the 1962 National Park Ordinance, which paved the way for the creation of the first park. Under the ordinance, His Excellency was empowered to constitute any state land as a national park. He could appoint a board of trustees to manage and maintain the parks with the right to appoint officers, make regulations, and provide for penalties. Following this, Kinabalu National Park was established in 1964.

In 1963, Sabah, along with Sarawak, joined the Federation of Malaysia. Under the terms of this agreement, all land matters reside with the state government. Since then, state interest in the protection of natural areas has grown. Six more parks have been gazetted in Sabah, although one was later degazetted.

In 1984, the State Legislative Assembly passed a new Parks Enactment. Under this enactment the boundaries of each park were re-delineated, and a land title for each park for 999 years free of all liabilities and encumbrances was vested in the name of the Board of Trustees of the Sabah Parks. The names of the five existing parks were changed to reflect their new status as state, rather than national, parks. For example, Kinabalu National Park became Kinabalu Park. This would ensure that the parks would remain under the jurisdiction of the state in the event that the federal National Parks Act was extended to Sabah. The enactment also established a new national park, the Crocker Range National Park, which would fall under the administration of the federal government.

PARKS AND RESERVES

Malaysia lies a few degrees north of the equator. Its warm climate, high annual rainfall, and relative lack of disturbance have led to one of the richest floras and faunas in the world. This diversity is reflected in the tremendous range of biophysical features protected in Malaysia's parks and reserves. Malaysia's natural vegetation belongs to the Malesian floristic region of archipelagic Southeast Asia. Over twenty-four major forest types have been classified in Malaysia, including such diverse ecosystems as lowland and montane rain forests, mangrove and peat swamps, and cloud forests and alpine meadows. In Peninsular Malaysia alone there are over 8,500 species of flowering plants, 200 mammal species, 675 bird species, 350 species of reptiles and amphibians, and over 150,000 species of insects.

In Malaysia, there are currently thirteen national parks and 20 major wildlife sanctuaries and reserves (Table 15.1 and Figure 15.1). They range in size from 0.5 hectares to 434,351 hectares (1 to 1 million acres). In order to describe the rich biophysical features protected by these areas, several representative areas from Peninsular Malaysia, Sarawak, and Sabah are examined below. These parks and reserves indicate the major ecosystems found in Malaysia and illustrate their diversity.

Peninsular Malaysia

Of the nineteen protected areas in Peninsular Malaysia, the Department of Wildlife and National Parks actively manages four main preserves. Taman Negara, the premier park of Malaysia, is the largest and oldest of these. Taman Negara National Park, 434,351 hectares (1,073,280 acres) in area, stretches across the boundaries of three states. Much of the park lies on sedimentary rocks, although the eastern section is mostly granitic. Limestone hills, sandstone outcrops, and the tallest mountain in Peninsular Malaysia (2,156 meters, 7,073 feet) create a varied landscape. Much of the park supports a profusion of life in its undisturbed lowland dipterocarp forest. The vegetation is characterized by huge trees dominated by the family Dipterocarpaceae, and a complex, multilayered forest structure. Lianas and other epiphytic plants are abundant. The diversity of plant life is legion. In a 1.6-hectare (4-acre) plot, 136 different tree species have been recorded.[6] This lowland forest harbors one of the richest mammal faunas in the world. This includes Sumatran rhinoceros (*Dicerorhinus sumatrensis*), Malayan gaur (*Bos gaurus*), tiger (*Panthera tigris*), gibbons (*Hylobates spp.*), slow loris (*Nycticebus courang*), civets (Viverridae), barking deer (*Muntiacus muntjak*), sambar deer (*Cervus unicolor*), elephant (*Elephas maximus*), tapir (*Tapirus indicus*), panther (*Panthera pardus*), sunbear (*Helarctos malayanus*), serow (*Capricornis sumatrensis*), and Malayan wild dog (*Cuon alpinus*). Two hundred and fifty bird species have been recorded in the park,

Table 15.1
Parks and Reserves in Malaysia

MAP REFERENCE	NAME	LOCATION BY STATE	AREA (hectares)	DATE ESTABLISHED
		Peninsular Malaysia		
1.	Sungkai	Perak	2,428	1928
2.	Batu Gajah	Perak	4.5	1952
3.	Krau	Pahang	53,095	1923
4.	Cameron Highlands	Pahang	64,953	1962
5.	Pahang Tua	Pahang	1,336	1954
6.	Pulau Tioman	Pahang	7,160	1972
7.	Endau-Rompin	Johor	101,174	1933
8.	Endau-Kota Tinggi (East and West)	Johor	69,372	1933
9.	Four Bird Islands	Johor	2	1954
10.	Port Dickson Islands	Negeri Sembilan	0.5	1926
11.	Fraser's Hill	Selangor	2,979	1922
12.	Kuala Selangor	Selangor	44	1922
13.	Bukit Kutu	Selangor	1,943	1922
14.	Klang Gates	Selangor	130	1936
15.	Bt. Nanas	Selangor	9	1906
16.	Templer Park	Selangor	1,011	1956
17.	Sungei Dusun	Selangor	4,330	1964
18.	Sungei Puteh	Selangor	40	1932
19.	Taman Negara	Pahang Kelantan Trengganu	434,351	1939
		East Malaysia		
20.	Bako	Sarawak	2,728	1957
21.	Gunung Mulu	Sarawak	52,887	1974
22.	Niah	Sarawak	3,140	1974
23.	Lambir Hills	Sarawak	6,952	1975
24.	Similajau	Sarawak	7,067	1979
25.	Gunung Gading	Sarawak	5,430	1983
26.	Samunsam	Sarawak	6,092	1979
27.	Lanjak-Entimau	Sarawak	168,755	1983
28.	Kinabalu	Sabah	75,370	1964
29.	Tunku Abdul Rahman	Sabah	4,929	1974
30.	Turtle Islands	Sabah	1,740	1977
31.	Pulau Tiga	Sabah	15,864	1978
32.	Tawau Hills	Sabah	27,972	1979
33.	Crocker Range	Sabah	139,919	1984

including endangered hornbills (*Bucerotidae*) and the great argus pheasant (*Argusianus argus*).

The lowland forest gives way to hill dipterocarp forest above 300 meters (1,000 feet). Although structurally similar, different tree species are common such as *Shorea curtsii* and *S. platycladus*. Above 1,000 meters (3,300 feet) the montane forest begins. Trees in the families Fagaceae and Lauraceae grow. On the Tahan Mountain this changes to ericaceous vegetation at higher elevations.

The park is located a full day's drive from the capital city, Kuala Lumpur. The headquarters can be reached only by boat, a 59-kilometer (37-mile) journey up the Tembeling River. Accommodation includes a 16-room resthouse, 12 chalets, and a 64-bed hostel. Six platform hides are equipped for nighttime

Figure 15.1
Major Parks and Reserves in Malaysia

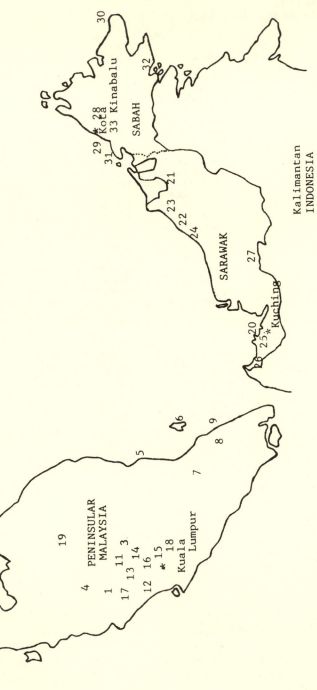

Note: Areas are not shown to scale.

wildlife viewing. In 1984, the park received 8,117 visitors; 56 percent of these were local Malaysians.

Recreational facilities at the park are oriented toward exploring the rich environment. Wildlife viewing is a popular activity. Wild animals are abundant around the headquarters. Deer and wild pigs have become habituated to people and often graze or grovel near the accommodations. A number of fruiting trees (*Ficus spp.*) were strategically planted in the area and attract flocks of beautiful frugivorous birds. Many pristine rivers flow from the mountain chain that runs across the center of the park. River cruises and fishing are two popular visitor sports. Mountain climbing expeditions are possible, but problematic, as they require preparation and about a week's time to reach the tallest peak.

Not far from Taman Negara, in the state of Pahang, lies the 55,080-hectare (136,000-acre) Krau Game Reserve. Established in 1923, it is one of Malaysia's oldest game reserves. It is a valuable tract of pristine lowland rain forest, hill dipterocarp forest, and montane oak forest. The topography is varied. The largest hill, the Benom Massif, rises 2,073 meters (6,800 feet). The Krau River drains a valley that supports the lowland rain forest.

The faunal diversity at Krau is similar to the wildlife at Taman Negara. The reserve was established to protect a large population of gaur. The Department of Wildlife and National Parks estimates that about forty head of gaur still inhabit the reserve.

Of the remaining reserves in Peninsular Malaysia, two others are actively managed by the Department of Wildlife and National Parks. Like the Krau Reserve, the Sungkai Game Reserve was established in 1928 primarily to protect a population of gaur. Further south, the Sungei Dusun Game Reserve encompassed 4,330 hectares (10,700 acres) of lowland dipterocarp forest and marine alluvial swamp forest. The reserve was established in 1964 to protect rhinoceroses, which are currently under study by the department. Three rhinoceroses continue to utilize the reserve, and an extension to enlarge the reserve by 3,000 hectares (7,400 acres) is being considered by the Selangor government.

East Malaysia

In contrast to Peninsular Malaysia, the East Malaysian states of Sarawak and Sabah have constituted most of their protected areas as national or state parks. In spite of land bridges that formed several times between East and Peninsular Malaysia during the Pleistocene, some of Sabah and Sarawak's wildlife remains unique. This includes orangutans (*Pongo pygmaeus*), tarsier (*Tarsius bancanus*), and endemic proboscis monkeys (*Nasalis larvatus*), as well as many species of orchids (Orchidaceae) and pitcher plants (Nepentheaceae).

Sarawak's protected areas preserve 253,051 hectares (625,289 acres) of land, about 2 percent of Sarawak's total area. This includes unusual heath forests, bogs, swamps, enormous limestone caves and mountains, and significant anthropological sites.

Sarawak's first and smallest park is Bako National Park situated 60 kilometers (37 miles) from the capital city, Kuching, on a sandstone peninsula on the southwest coast of Sarawak. Within the 2,728-hectare (6,741-acre) park, twenty-five different vegetation types have been identified. Mangrove forests, characterized by tree genera like *Rhizophora*, *Bruquiera*, *Avicennia*, and *Sonneratia*, grow where the rivers meet the sea. These are fast growing trees with unique adaptations for surviving life in brackish water and thick mud. Beach forest lines the coast. On the tops of plateaus the soil consists of white podzolized sand, which is acidic and lacks organic material. Heath forest is predominant here, called "kerangas" forest after the Iban word meaning "sites with soils unsuitable for rice cultivation." Common species of trees include conifers in the genera *Casuarina* and *Dacrydium*, as well as *Callophyllum* and *Tristania* species. The kerangas forest is succeeded by more impoverished vegetation on the exposed, horizontal sandstone plateaus. Plant life is stunted and confined to shallow depressions where organic matter can accumulate. An interesting array of plants grows here, including insect-eating pitcher plants (*Nepenthes*) and sundews (*Drosera*), which are able to obtain supplementary nutrients from a carnivorous life style. Myrmecophytic plants like *Myrmecodia* and *Dischidia* host ant colonies that can supply additional nutrients.

In more fertile areas mixed dipterocarp forest grows. It is small in stature because of the shallow, sandy clay soil that supports it. Common genera are *Dryobalanops*, *Hopea*, *Shorea*, and *Vatica*.

The forests bordering the sea are home to Borneo's proboscis monkey. In other areas, deer, leaf monkeys (*Presbytis cristata*), otters (*Lutra sumatrana*), monitor lizards (*Varanus spp.*), and bearded pigs (*Sus barbatus*) are common. The great floral variation provides habitats for a myriad of birds; Palearctic migrants and waders are abundant.

Bako's beautiful beaches, interesting plant life, and proximity to Kuching attracted over 50,000 visitors in 1985, more than any other Sarawak park. Visitor facilities include two rest houses, six hostels, and camping areas. An exhibit center and nature trails through a variety of habitats are well maintained.

Sarawak's largest park, Gunung Mulu National Park, has an area of 52,866 hectares (130,630 acres). It features a sandstone-based mountain towering 2,376 meters (7,800 feet) high and limestone cliffs up to 1,750 meters (5,740 feet). Enormous caves have formed in the limestone, including the largest indoor chamber in the world: 600 meters (1,970 feet) long, 450 meters (1,480 feet) wide, and 100 meters (330 feet) high. So far 150 kilometers (93 miles) of cave passages have been surveyed, and perhaps another 350 kilometers (200 miles) remain to be explored.

The park contains all the major inland vegetation formations found in Borneo. As the elevation increases, the mixed dipterocarp forest and peat swamps are replaced by heath forests and limestone forests, and finally by montane and moss forests at the highest altitudes. In 1977–1978 the Royal Geographic Society of

London sponsored an expedition to Gunung Mulu. It described the park as having the richest, most extraordinary and beautiful tropical rain forest in the world.

The park's fauna is abundant. It includes the endangered clouded leopard (*Neofelis nebulosa*) and all eight species of hornbills found on Borneo. The hornbills are among the 272 species of birds recorded in the park. The park is also home to anteaters (*Manis javanica*), porcupines (Hystericidae), pigs, deer, civets, squirrels, 74 species of frogs, 48 species of fish, 458 species of ants, and a myriad of other organisms. The cave-dwelling wildlife includes 12 species of bats, 3 species of swiftlets, and 25 troglobite invertebrate species including a rare scorpion and white crab.

Although the park was constituted in 1974, it was not until a detailed management plan had been completed in 1985 that it was opened to the public. It is located at least a one-day boat trip from Miri, the nearest town. There are two bungalows for accommodation and 50 kilometers (30 miles) of walking trails.

The other parks and preserves in Sarawak protect a broad array of wildlife. The Samunsam Wildlife Sanctuary, located on the western end of Sarawak, was established specifically to protect proboscis monkeys, which mainly inhabit the mangrove swamps. There is now a population of about 100 of these leaf-eating monkeys. The 6,478-hectare (16,000-acre) sanctuary protects a variety of other animals, from gibbons in the tree canopy to marine turtles (*Chelonia mydas*) nesting on the beach.

Further inland, the Lanjak-Entimau Wildlife Sanctuary provides protection for a population of orangutans as well as protecting the upper water catchment areas of seven rivers. One of the most famous national parks in Malaysia is Niah. It was established in 1974 to protect the flora and fauna surrounding limestone caves where archaeologists found human remains dating back 40,000 years. Millions of swiftlets (*Collocalia spp.*) and bats live in the caves. Their guano and swiftlets' saliva-plastered nests are regularly collected for sale by the local people. The Sarawak Museum has retained jurisdiction over the caves, which were declared a National Historic Monument in 1958. The surrounding 3,140 hectares (7,760 acres) of heath and dipterocarp forest is managed by the National Park and Wildlife Office.

In the East Malaysian state of Sabah, six parks have been established since 1964. The two most spectacular ones protect the tallest mountain in Southeast Asia and the rich underwater life of a coral reef. The others protect important water catchment areas, turtle nesting beaches, and pristine coastal islands. In total, the parks preserve an area of 265,794 hectares (657,000 acres), 3.6 percent of Sabah's land.

Sabah's most famous park, Kinabalu, features Mount Kinabalu, a granite pluton that was forced upward through the earth's crust only a million years ago. It is still adding a few millimeters annually to its 4,101-meter (13,455-foot) height. The 75,400-hectare (186,000-acre) park includes terrain stretching from lowland rain forest to montane forest, cloud forest, and alpine meadow, before finally reaching a crown of bare granite, the tallest point between the Himalayas and New Guinea. The vegetation of the lowland and montane forests is similar to those described previously. Above 2,600 meters (8,500 feet), stunted forms of *Leptospermum*, *Dacrydium*, and *Schima* tree species grow. The soil disappears above 3,300 meters (10,800 feet), and only a few sedges, grasses, and herbs survive.

The broad altitude range results in a remarkable diversity of plant life. This includes over 450 species of ferns, 1,500 species of orchids, 70 species of figs, 26 species of rhododendrons, and 9 species of insectivorous pitcher plants. Also noteworthy is the presence of the world's largest flower (*Rafflesia*) and tallest moss (*Dawsonia*).

The animal life on Kinabalu is equally diverse. It includes over 100 mammals, the more distinctive being orangutan, gibbons, slow loris, tarsier, and clouded leopards. About 300 species of birds have been seen in the park, representing over 60 percent of the birds ever recorded in Borneo. More than 40 species of frogs and 100 species of reptiles have been collected from Mount Kinabalu.

The park is also important for preserving the cultural heritage of the local Kadazans, Sabah's largest indigenous group. They have long esteemed the mountain as the homeland of their spirit world. The mountain's name is derived from the Kadazan "aki nabalu," meaning "the revered place of the dead." When the first European explorer ascended the mountain in 1851, his local guides performed special rituals to appease the spirit of the mountain. An annual ceremony is still conducted by Kadazan guides on the summit of the mountain.

Because of its spectacular scenery and the cool climate around park headquarters at 1,550 meters (5,100 feet), it is a major attraction for both international and local tourists. In 1985, 163,337 people visited the park. About 70 percent of these were Sabahans, and only 7 percent attempted the climb to the summit.

The park is located 90 kilometers (56 miles) from the capital city, Kota Kinabalu. When the road was paved completely in 1981, visitation numbers tripled the following year. The park has accommodation for several hundred people, ranging from luxury cabins to student hostels and mountain huts. There are 11 kilometers (7 miles) of graded trails at park headquarters, an interpretive center, and mountain garden collection. Natural sulfur baths and additional accommodations have been developed in the southeastern corner of the park.

The second most popular park in Sabah is a fifteen-minute boat ride from the capital city across the South China Sea. The Tunku Abdul Rahman Park, named for Malaysia's first prime minister, encompasses 4,929 hectares (12,180 acres), including five small islands and the surrounding coral reefs.

The land area, formed from shale and sandstone covering more ancient, harder rocks, probably became islands near the end of the Pleistocene. Their rain forest vegetation is depauperate compared to the diversity found on the mainland. On several of the islands, mangrove forests grow into the ocean. The fauna is also limited, although some interesting species, like megapode birds (*Megapodius freycinet*), inhabit a few of the islands. These chickenlike birds scratch up huge mounds of sand and vegetation. The females then lay their eggs in this giant incubator and abandon them to hatch and crawl out of the mound on their own. Long-tailed macaques (*Macaca fascicularis*) and bearded pigs (*Sus barbatus*) inhabit some of the islands, as well as a variety of bird, reptile, and insect life. The endangered estuarine crocodile (*Crocodilus porosus*) has been seen on the largest island.

It is the marine life that makes this park special. Located at the center of the diversity of the Indo-Pacific region, Sabah's reefs probably support one of the richest faunas in the marine world. There are sixty-one genera and several hundred coral species in Sabah's tropical waters. An equally rich fish fauna inhabits it.

The islands are a major recreational area for the nearby urban dwellers. They provide picnic facilities, sandy beaches, and good snorkeling for its many visitors. A resthouse is available for hire on one of the islands, and a glass-bottom boat tour is offered for exploring the coral reefs.

ADMINISTRATION

The management of protected areas in Peninsular Malaysia by the Department of Wildlife and National Parks comes under the direction of the Ministry of Science, Technology and the Environment. In contrast, in East Malaysia, Sarawak's parks and wildlife are managed by the Forest Department. Sabah's parks are administered by state-appointed trustees, and wildlife falls under the direction of the game branch in the Forest Department.

Concomitant with this array of jurisdictions in Malaysia, the Peninsula, Sabah, and Sarawak have differing laws governing the administration of protected zones and wildlife. The federal National Parks Act has yet to be extended to East Malaysia. In addition, Taman Negara National Park is exempt from its jurisdiction because the states in which it lies have their own National Park Enactments.

Peninsular Malaysia

The federal government's official conservation strategy covering protected areas has been outlined in its five-year development plans. The Third Malaysia Plan (1976–1980) proposed twenty-three new areas in Peninsular Malaysia, totaling 897,806 hectares (2.2 million acres). However, few of these plans have been realized. The difficulty lies with the states' reluctance to surrender any power over their land to the federal government. In the Fourth Malaysian Plan (1981–1985), two national parks, Endau Rompin and Kuala Koh, were proposed.

The existing parks and reserves in Peninsular Malaysia are administered by the Department of Wildlife and National Parks. In 1984, the department was allocated a budget of about U.S.$3 million, and employed 731 people. Staff positions were associated with an assortment of duties, ranging from law enforcement to rhinoceros research (Figure 15.2). Only 3 percent of the posts are A-level jobs requiring university degrees. Most (83 percent) are untrained D-level positions. About a sixth of all these posts are associated with the national parks and reserves.

Taman Negara National Park constitutes almost half of Peninsular Malaysia's wildlife reserve land. Here, the department's administrative activities include both wildlife and visitor management. No exploitation is permitted within the park, except for licensed fishing, as outlined in the 1939 Taman Negara (Pahang) Act. Border patrols are conducted regularly. In 1984 twelve offenses of this act were detected. These included transporting fish nets, and taking rattan, fish, rocks, and plants.

An exception to this enforcement is made for the "orang asli," indigenous people of Negrito stock. They are traditionally nomadic, with a hunting and gathering economy. They are permitted to continue their traditional practices within the park. Although most live in outside settlements, about 1,000 orang asli still use the park. Others occasionally work as expedition guides, where they are in demand for their keen knowledge of the forest.

The department has considered the ramifications of the increasing influx of visitors to the park. Recommendations were made to set a limit on visitor numbers. A carrying capacity of under 200 people was suggested for overnight accommodation at park headquarters. This figure was intended to maintain the "wilderness-experience" quality of a visit to Taman Negara, rather than in consideration of human impact on the flora and fauna. Recently the government has been considering privatizing the transportation and lodging facilities and making the mountain range more accessible with a road. This will lead to greater human impact in the park and may call for more stringent regulations as expansion occurs in the future.

Taman Negara is an important area for research and education. The Department of Wildlife and National Parks has been conducting ecological studies on the resident populations of gaur, elephant, tapir, rhinoceros, and tigers. Small areas have been experimentally cleared to provide forage to attract and increase populations of gaur and deer. In other areas, such as at Krau Wildlife Reserve, the department has been carrying out deer- and pheasant-breeding projects. The collection of data for baseline studies, such as bird banding projects, are being conducted in Krau and six other reserves. In the 1970s, a nature study center was built at Taman Negara to accommodate student groups for an intensive natural history course. In 1984, 557 students and 75 teachers participated in this program.

Taman Negara National Park has remained inviolate for the past forty-seven years. Perhaps the gravest threats to its pristine nature have come recently in the form of government proposals for hydroelectric and timber extraction schemes. In 1971 the National Electricity Board first proposed a multipurpose dam on the Tembeling River, which would have flooded a critical area of Taman

Figure 15.2
Organization of the Department of Wildlife and National Parks

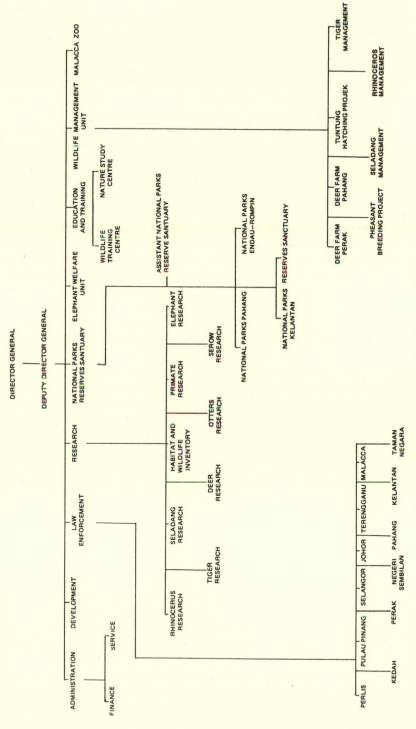

Source: Department of Wildlife and National Parks. 1984 Annual Report. Kuala Lumpur, Malaysia.

Negara. As a government department, the Wildlife and National Parks staff must support government development plans. Opposition to the hydroelectric project came from the public, spearheaded by a variety of nongovernmental nature and environmental organizations. By early 1983, the campaign to save the national park had gained the support of about 100,000 Malaysians, and the government discarded its plans.

Other reserves in Peninsular Malaysia are threatened by state government plans for exploitation. There is stiff competition for land, particularly in the species-rich lowlands where human activities are concentrated. Forest clearance for agriculture and selective logging has accelerated in the past few decades. In 1976 only 14 percent of the entire area of Peninsular Malaysia was considered virgin forest. Even in the protected areas, only about a third of the existing reserves remain in a pristine condition. The value of the other reserves has been diminished by having substantial areas excised for logging, mining, agriculture, or housing. The states' primary interest in immediate profits, although under-standable, also affects the likelihood of new areas being protected.

Take the case of Endau Rompin, an area proposed as a national park in 1972. This area would represent the last remaining tract of undisturbed lowland rain forest in the southern part of the peninsula. An agreement was reached between the federal and state governments to allow sustained-yield logging in a buffer zone of 110,480 hectares (274,000 acres), while constituting a core area of 91,865 hectares (227,000 acres) as an inviolate reserve. However, in 1977 logging concessions were granted in the core area by the Pahang state government. Protests by the federal government, nongovernmental organizations, and the public helped persuade the authorities concerned not to issue any new logging licenses starting in 1978. The publicity of this ''Save Endau Rompin'' campaign generated national pride in a protected area. Later, this enthusiasm helped launch the first all-Malaysian scientific expedition to explore the ecology of Endau Rompin.

East Malaysia

In East Malaysia, the human population is only about an eighth as dense as in the more industrialized peninsula. Yet there is still competition for land. Only 23 percent of Sarawak is classified as suitable for agriculture, and much of the rest of the state is covered by infertile soils. Native groups, like the Ibans, Dayaks, Kenyahs, Penans, and others, have the right to practice shifting culti-vation on more than half the area of Sarawak. This involves burning a plot in the forest, planting crops, then moving on in a few years because of leached soils and heavy weed infestation. The Forest Department estimates about 10,120 hectares (25,000 acres) of forest are slashed and burned annually. Native cus-tomary rights include not only the right to farm, but also the right to hunt, fish, and collect forest produce like rattan, fruit, and timber for personal use. When a park or sanctuary is constituted, native customary rights may be recognized and specified in the constitution. Alternatively, they can be abrogated and compensated, which is often expensive.

The position of Sarawak's National Parks and Wildlife Office within the Forest Department has allowed the park staff to recommend conversion of other Forest Department land to protected area status before the land is logged. This has helped reduce or avoid completely the conflicts with other claims on the land. By 1983, 2 percent of the state land had been converted to protected areas because of this action.

The administration of the parks and reserves in Sarawak is overseen by the assistant conservator of forests, who is responsible to the director of forests. Detailed management plans have been drawn up for Lanjak Entimau Wildlife Sanctuary and Gunung Mulu National Park. These plans include the regulation and management of both people and wildlife. In Gunung Mulu the settled people living around the Tutuh and Medalam rivers exercise their limited hunting, fishing, and gathering privileges over parts of the park. The nomadic Penan have similar privileges as long as they maintain a nomadic existence. About twenty families make full use of the park.

Illegal activities within Sarawak's parks and reserves are monitored by the Forest Department. In 1978, eight persons were fined U.S.$40 for felling trees in Gunung Mulu National Park. In Bako National Park in 1982, seven people were arrested for illegal felling of trees and another fined for carrying a shotgun into the park. Regulations are sometimes difficult to enforce because of a shortage of Forest Department personnel, or occasionally because of political problems in prosecuting the cases. In Samunsam Wildlife Sanctuary patrols were conducted to check the high incidence of poaching, but "as the culprit(s) may involve security personnel operating in the vicinity, arrests have proved not only difficult but risky as well."[7]

Until recently, the management of visitors in the parks has been minimal because the numbers did not warrant it. However, increasing visitor pressure is necessitating some future planning. In the case of Bako National Park, the completion of a road connection from the capital city to the park resulted in a tenfold increase in the number of visitors. As a result, the parks are becoming increasingly important facilities for conservation education. Bako and several other parks in Sarawak have interpretation centers and audiovisual programs that introduce visitors to the human and natural history of the parks. Over 3,000 people viewed the interpretation center at Niah National Park in 1982, many of whom stayed overnight at the park hostel. A variety of pamphlets and brochures are available in several languages about the wildlife at many of the parks.

The Forest Department maintains an active research program studying wildlife ecology and management. Bako National Park has been the site of extensive botanical research on heath vegetation and mangrove forests. A number of animal species have been studied here as well. In Samunsam Wildlife Sanctuary, studies have been made of habitat use by rare proboscis monkeys, the effects of logging on other wildlife, and the breeding biology of nesting marine turtles. When the

Lanjak-Entimau Wildlife Sanctuary was proposed, a study of the hunters in the area was conducted to ascertain their harvesting methods and the wildlife populations involved. The Forest Department oversees the Semengoh Rehabilitation Center, which was set up to reintroduce confiscated animals back into the wild. These animals, protected under the Wildlife Protection Ordinance, were trapped or were being kept illegally before confiscation. In 1985, two orangutans, four gibbons, and a hornbill were rehabilitated.

The Sabah park system, a quasi-governmental institution, is under the administration of the Sabah Parks Trustees. In the 1970s, a need for an official national park policy was recognized. The 1962 National Parks Ordinance had not provided any guidance in the regulation of the parks. This had led to "conflicts in administration, planning and development."[8] In 1974, the Board of Trustees accepted a proposal outlining a national parks policy based on the Canadian national park system. This was submitted to the State Cabinet for ratification and publication. Chapter 2, Section 5 pertains to human activities inside a park. It prohibits grazing livestock; harvesting plants or animals; mining; polluting the air, soil, or water; or altering rivers.

However, these prohibitions are followed by the caveat that "Sabah is a developing country, and exploitation of these resources of land and water may be necessary for the well being of the State. Where no alternative resources are available, then impairment may be accepted if these resources are of such national importance that the sacrifice of park values can be justified."[9] Consistent with this policy, in 1981, only three years after it was established, Klias Peninsula National Park was degazetted for use in a paper and pulp mill project. Land has been excised from Kinabalu Park on several occasions. In the 1970s, 2,512 hectares (6,200 acres) were leased for a joint Japanese-Sabahan copper mining project. In 1982, 1,882 hectares (4,650 acres) were excised for a golf course, cattle farm, agricultural station, and farming schemes. And again in 1984, a further 1,620 hectares (4,000 acres) were taken out. Subsequent to this, the excision of park land was made more difficult with the passage of the new Sabah Parks Ordinance in 1984. This decreed that the degazettement of any park land must be approved by the state assembly.

Illegal threats to the park in Sabah vary depending on the location. Illegal collection of rare orchids and pitcher plants growing in Kinabalu Park has been a problem in the past. These plants fetch as much as $1,000 per plant in international markets. Closer park surveillance and cooperation with other government departments has helped lessen this threat. A current threat is the unmarked boundaries left by the recent land excisions. These have been the site of increased illegal logging and crop cultivation.

In Tunku Abdul Rahman Marine Park, illegal fish bombing and sand excavation have destroyed some areas of the coral reefs. A well publicized arrest of a construction worker excavating sand in 1985 helped to advertise both the illegality and the ecological damage committed. This episode is expected to deter potential offenders.

In Sabah, the level of resource and human management varies among the six parks. The Turtle Islands Park, encompassing three islands off Sabah's west coast, is intensively managed for the two species of sea turtles (*Chelonia mydas* and *Eretmochelys imbricata*) that lay eggs on its beaches. Park rangers survey the beaches nightly for nesting females. Since the program started, they have measured and tagged over 17,000 turtles. The eggs are transplanted to a fenced hatchery to help improve the reproductive success of the turtles. In 1984, 104,288 eggs were transplanted, and 80 percent of these hatched.

At Kinabalu Park, the Ecology Section staff has had success transplanting rare plants to protected areas in the park. Propagation of some plants, like the pitcher plants and orchids, may be tried in the future. A deer-farming project is being considered for the lowland area of the park.

Education programs for casual visitors, school groups, local villagers, and other populations have been developed by the park's Ecology Section. A mountain garden, exhibit center, and guided walks make up a sophisticated program of park interpretation. A number of books and pamphlets are available about the park's wildlife.

Conclusion

The development of parks in Sabah, as well as in the other Malaysian states, has been limited by a chronic lack of funds and trained staff. Administration and planning problems have been exacerbated by the political history of land issues in this nation of federated states. Yet in spite of these shortcomings, the country's parks and reserves serve as a model in Southeast Asia for the skill of their management and research activities, and their utilization for recreation and education. The prospect for protected areas in Malaysia is promising. The government is currently reviewing the potential of these areas for tourist development as a source of foreign exchange. Under careful management, the positive effects from this could be an increased budget and staff, and the constitution of some of the newly proposed parks and reserves. As Malaysians' income levels and leisure time continue to increase, the parks will become even more important for recreation. The interpretive programs and school courses at some of the parks should help increase the public's interest in and support of the protected areas that preserve Malaysia's rich natural heritage.

NOTES

Many people in the Malaysian park system provided valuable information and assistance. I am especially grateful to Director General Mohd. Khan of the Department of Wildlife and National Parks, Director Lamri Ali and Deputy Director F. Liew of Sabah Parks, and Planning Director D. Cotter of Sarawak's National Park Office. D. Yong and F. Lambert, as well as Sabah park wardens G. deSilva, S. Janardhanan, E. Wong, and Park Ecologist A. Phillipps, were also most helpful. I thank L. Maguire, M. Meade, and C. Richardson for reviewing this manuscript. The Shell Foundation and Duke University's Asian/Pacific Studies Institute funded my research in Sabah, Malaysia.

1. W. E. Stevens, *The Conservation of Wildlife in West Malaysia* (Kuala Lumpur, Malaysia: Game Dept., 1968), p. 108.

2. S. Robert Aiken and Colin H. Leigh, "A Second National Park for Peninsular Malaysia? The Endau-Rompin Controversy," *Biological Conservation*, 29 (1984): 253–76.

3. Stevens, p. 29.

4. I. H. Sario and T. C. Liew, "Basis for Future Forest Management in Sabah" (1980), in *A Faunal Survey of Sabah*, ed. Glyn Davies and John Payne, (Kuala Lumpur: IUCN/WWF-Malaysia, n.d.), p. 2.

5. *Annual Report of the Board of Trustees, Sarawak Parks* (Sarawak, Malaysia: Government Printing, 1956), p. 2.

6. P. W. Richards, *The Tropical Rain Forest* (London: Cambridge University Press, 1952), p. 249.

7. *Annual Report of the Forest Department* (Sarawak, Malaysia: Government Printing, 1982), p. 30.

8. D. V. Jenkins, F. Liew, and P. Hecht, *A National Parks Policy for Sabah* (Kota Kinabalu, Malaysia: Government Printing, 1976), p. 1.

9. Ibid, p. 4.

BIBLIOGRAPHY

Chai, Paul P. K. "Bako National Park." *Nature Malaysiana* 4 (September 1978): 4–11.
Gunung Mulu National Park. Sarawak, Malaysia: Forest Department Publication, 1984.
Heang, Kiew Bong, and Ruth Kiew. "Samunsam Wildlife Sanctuary." *Nature Malaysiana* 7 (January 1981): 5–10.
Jacobson, Susan Kay. *Kinabalu Park.* Sabah, Malaysia: Sabah Parks Publication, 1985.
Kavanagh, Michael. "Planning Considerations for a System of National Parks and Wildlife Sanctuaries in Sarawak." *Sarawak Gazette* (March 1985): 15–29.
Luping, Margaret, Wen Chin, and E. Richard Dingley, eds. *Kinabalu Summit of Borneo.* Sabah, Malaysia: Sabah Society Monograph, 1978.
Nordin, Musa. "Management of Wildlife Preserves in Peninsular Malaysia." *Journal of Wildlife and Parks* 2 (October 1983): 103–14.

NEW ZEALAND 16

Patrick J. Devlin, Paul R. Dingwall, and P. H. C. Lucas

New Zealand's national parks and reserves are part of a protected natural area system that includes more than 2,000 areas and covers about 5 million hectares (12.4 million acres). See Table 16.1 and Figure 16.1.

These areas represent approximately 18 percent of New Zealand's total land area and include national, maritime, and forest parks as well as a number of different classes of reserves. This system of parks and reserves has a major responsibility for the conservation of a flora and fauna noted internationally for its large endemic component, as well as preserving areas of distinctive beauty and diverse recreational opportunities.

HISTORY

New Zealand's main islands lie between latitudes 34° and 46° south and are some 1,900 kilometers (1,200 miles) southeast of Australia, its nearest neighbor. Occupying the country are 3.3 million people, of which 350,000 are Maori. Their ancestors were the original Polynesian people of New Zealand who settled these lands over 1,000 years ago. Subsequent settlement by Europeans began only 150 years ago and was accompanied by rapid landscape changes as land was cleared for agriculture and habitation.

Prior to European impact, some modification of forests and other vegetation occurred—principally through fire. Whether such fires were lit deliberately by the Maori or by accident has been long debated and will never be resolved. What is certain, however, is that within the value system of the Maori, nothing stands out more clearly than their veneration of the land, forests, and waters. Conservation values were inherent within their social structures, and *rahui*, or

Table 16.1
Number and Area of New Zealand Protected Natural Areas by Protective Status Class (January 1988)[a]

PROTECTED NATURAL AREA CLASS	NUMBER OF UNITS	AREA (HECTARES)	PERCENT OF N.Z. LAND AREA[b]
National Park	12	2,203,644	8.20
National Park Specially Protected Area	5	190,234	0.71
Nature Reserve	50	185,577	0.69
Scientific Reserve	46	8,537	0.03
Scenic Reserve	1,219	354,439	1.32
State Forest Park	21	1,775,384	6.61
State Forest Sanctuary	14	16,288	0.06
State Forest Ecological Area	92	219,283	0.82
Wildlife Sanctuary	16	424	----
Wildlife Refuge	131	74,000	0.28
Government Purpose (Wildlife Management) Reserve	146	12,484	0.05
Marine Reserve	2	2,687	0.01
Open Space Covenant	178	5,000	0.02
Protected Private Land	64	3,209	0.01
Conservation Covenant	19	589	----
TOTAL	2,015	5,051,779	18.80

Notes:
[a] Compiled from information provided by various governmental agencies. Not all data is equally current.
[b] Based on a total land area of 26,868,400 hectares, excluding island territories.

prohibitions, were conservation practices used to ensure the maintenance of balance and continuity of habitats and species.

There are other aspects of Maori tradition that are of great importance in examining the history of New Zealand's developing parks system. For the Maori, the relationship with land holds a deep spiritual significance. In their cosmology, the sky (*Te Rangi*) and earth (*Papatuanuku*) are the primeval parents and all natural phenomena their children. The progeny of the earth mother includes all plants and animals as well as the rivers, lakes, sea, mountains, and other land-forms. All aspects of nature and natural phenomena are capable of explanation within their concept of creation. For the Maori to harvest (exploit) the earth mother's children (fish, forest products), strict attention to ritual detail was required, and transgression would be unthinkable. Even inanimate objects such as rocks and mountains shared a life force (*Mauri*) lending a spiritual dimension to non-living as well as living components of nature. The Maori were thus enabled to understand and explain their relationships with the world in which they lived.

Although the Maori view of the world is described above in a brief and oversimplified way, its significance as a belief system is considerable. It provides New Zealand with an enriched base from which to approach its management of protected areas. The spiritual dimension offered through Maori philosophy can

Figure 16.1
New Zealand National Parks, Maritime Parks, and State Forest Parks

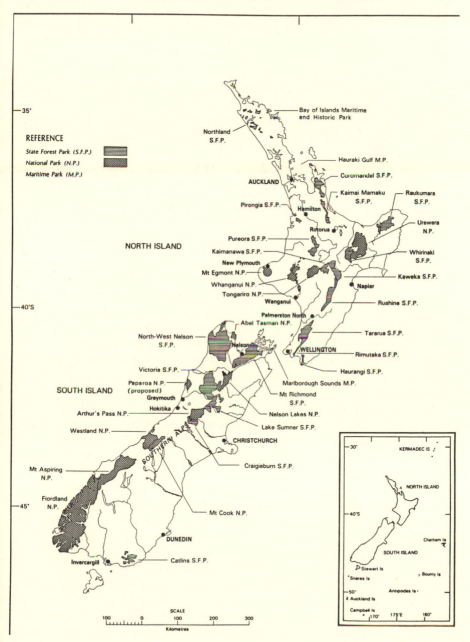

REFERENCE

State Forest Park (S.F.P.)
National Park (N.P.)
Maritime Park (M.P.)

—35°

Bay of Islands Maritime
and Historic Park

Northland
S.F.P.

Hauraki Gulf M.P.

Coromandel S.F.P.

AUCKLAND

Kaimai Mamaku
S.F.P.

Raukumara
S.F.P.

Pirongia S.F.P.

Hamilton

Urewera
N.P.

Rotorua

NORTH ISLAND

Pureora S.F.P.

Whirinaki
S.F.P.

Kaimanawa S.F.P.

New Plymouth

Mt Egmont N.P.

Kaweka S.F.P.

Whanganui N.P.

Napier

Tongariro N.P.

Wanganui

—40°S

Ruahine S.F.P.

Palmerston North

Abel Tasman N.P.

Tararua S.F.P.

North-West Nelson
S.F.P.

Nelson

WELLINGTON

Rimutaka S.F.P.

Victoria S.F.P.

Haurangi S.F.P.

Paparoa N.P.
(proposed)

Marlborough Sounds M.P.

SOUTH ISLAND

Greymouth

Mt Richmond
S.F.P.

Hokitika

Arthur's Pass N.P.

Nelson Lakes N.P.

Westland N.P.

Lake Sumner S.F.P.

CHRISTCHURCH

SOUTHERN ALPS

Craigieburn S.F.P.

Mt Aspiring
N.P.

Fiordland
N.P.

—45°

Mt Cook N.P.

DUNEDIN

Invercargill

Catlins S.F.P.

SCALE

100   0   100   200   300
Kilometres

—30°

KERMADEC IS

NORTH ISLAND

—40°S

Chatham Is

SOUTH ISLAND

Stewart Is

Snares Is

Bounty Is

—50°

Antipodes Is

Auckland Is

Campbell Is

170°   175°E   180°

stand alongside the intellectual dimension of ecological representativeness and other biological and physical imperatives. In association, they combine the concept of stewardship with that of management.

The first reserves in New Zealand were set aside under Royal Instructions from the British Crown in 1840. Many of these were for quite pragmatic reasons in that they facilitated government purposes such as acquiring sites for harbors, docks, and buildings. In 1877, an act of Parliament (the Land Act) enabled the reservation of areas for the growth and preservation of timber, thus providing for production, or protection for subsequent use, rather than for ecological purposes.

It was in 1887 that New Zealand received its first National Park when Te Heuheu Tukino of Ngati Tuwharetoa,[1] on behalf of his and associated people, bequeathed the mountain peaks of Tongariro, Ngauruhoe, and Ruapehu to Queen Victoria and the people of New Zealand. This nucleus of volcanic peaks in the central North Island was a highly sacred (*tapu*) area to the local Maori people. The fires of the still-active volcanoes were lit by their ancestors through the intercession of gods. It was unthinkable that these sacred lands could be subdivided or alienated, and the option of placing them under permanent protection as a national park was a means through which their ancestral lands would remain intact. A Maori belief in the life of the mountains with which they identified as a people joined with a Western concept of formally protecting a great natural area as a park for the nation to found the national park system of New Zealand. A Maori proverb sums up the preciousness of land: "Whakangarongaro he tangata; Toitu he Whenua" (People pass but land endures).

It was 1894 before Tongariro National Park was formally constituted by act of Parliament, but prior legislation (the Land Act of 1892) allowed for scenery reserves and flora and fauna reserves. Indeed, the significance for protected areas of this decade and the first two of the twentieth century must be emphasized. This period has been described by M. M. Roche as a "phase of acquisition, during which large areas of land were gazetted providing protection in a cadastral sense."[2] A special act of Parliament established Egmont National Park in 1900. Arthur's Pass National Park was established by a further act in 1929, but nearly 61,000 hectares (151,000 acres) of what was to become Arthur's Pass National Park had been set aside in 1901 as a national park reserve. In 1905, 900,000 hectares (2.2 million acres) were reserved in Fiordland to eventually become New Zealand's biggest national park (1.2 million hectares; 3 million acres) in 1952. Between 1892 and 1920, 44 percent of the 1980 area of scenic reserves had been gazetted largely under the Scenery Preservation Act (1903), whose architect was the great conservationist politician Harry Ell.

In terms of quantity, quality, and location of parks and reserves, these early years can be viewed as a somewhat ambivalent period with regard to the significance of these lands to our present-day protected area system. In a biological sense all areas reserved have some value, but these values are diminished if reserves are too small, badly shaped, isolated, or ecologically overrepresented.

The "acquisition phase" was not consciously guided by such criteria and cannot fairly be criticized retrospectively.

The motivations that prompted the acquisition of lands and eventual establishment of parks and reserves must, however, be examined within the wider social and economic context of the years in which they occurred. A second aspect to consider—but one not fully developed in this essay—is the influence of significant individuals and groups who played major catalyst roles in the promotion of a reserves system, as well as the role of central government.[3]

At least initially, much of what historically took place must be seen as the product of special circumstances in random, localized areas. The availability of the volcanoes of Tongariro was a response by the Maori to ensure that their sacred peaks and their inherent spiritual values were not lost or diluted by subdivision or improper use. Thirteen years later, the establishment of Egmont National Park stemmed largely from concern for the lowland consequences if the forests on the mountain (Taranaki) were removed. Flooding from the numerous streams that radiated from the massive watersheds of the volcanic mountain was rightly seen as potentially damaging to the farming industry concentrated on the surrounding ring plain. This curious mixture of self-interest and vision at the turn of the century was reflected by public policy. Agriculture was a primary land use, and the government worked to create small holdings that could support family units. Consequently, much of the land reserved was land considered unsuitable for settlement or development.

At the same time, the eminent botanist Dr. Leonard Cockayne was secretary of the Christchurch Beautifying Society. He used this position to apply increasing pressure for reservation of land in the Arthur's Pass region. He had traveled widely as a botanist, including visits to Tongariro National Park, and saw in the Southern Alps a fine example of trans-alpine flora transition. In the case of Arthur's Pass, this transition occurred on what was, as yet, unalienated Crown land. Cockayne had noted the impact already wrought by grazing, fire, and railroad construction and knew that the seemingly indestructible mountain lands of the Southern Alps would be just as susceptible. He used his influence to gain the support of politicians, and while the area was many years away from being called a national park, the substantial reservations, described above, ensured its future status.

In 1942, Abel Tasman National Park was established. This park included spectacular rocky coastlines, golden sand beaches, and remnant coastal vegetation of botanical interest. It also commemorates Abel Janszoon Tasman, the Dutch navigator, who in 1642 became the first European to visit New Zealand.

By the late 1940s New Zealand had reached the end of a major period in its overall parks and reserves development. Four national parks and over 1,300 reserves had been established for scenic or nature conservation reasons. But to give the impression that this had been easily achieved would be mischievous. The entire seventy-year period from 1880 to 1950 was notable for its economic and political unease. A series of economic depressions, which also affected the rest of the world, had equal or greater impact here. Two world wars likewise involved New Zealand, and politicians were preoccupied with weightier matters. The primary source of motivation for national parks was therefore from private individuals such as already described; from groups such as Federated Mountain Clubs; or, in some cases, from public servants in land-management agencies. Overall, it is unlikely that parks were at all dominant in the thinking and philosophy of average New Zealanders. The recreation boom was still a number of years away, and the impact of the Great Depression of the 1930s and World War II of the 1940s were periods that promoted basic survival and self-interest. This was not a time of outward-looking, future-oriented vision necessary for a philosophy that supported setting aside lands for conservation purposes. It was thus a relatively small group of people who over these first seventy years exerted the influence on government policy necessary for the significant achievements that had been made by the end of this period.

Roche has divided the development of our parks system into three phases. The first he called the "period of acquisition" (already described), which dominated from the 1890s to the 1920s. The second phase, occupying the 1930s and 1940s, he called a "maintenance, or caretaking" phase, in which parks were administered on a day-to-day basis. Staff were few or nonexistent, but external pressures on these places were likewise few. The third phase, which he called "management," was a development toward planned land use and the evolution of the scientific perspectives that currently guide the development of parks and protected areas.

Another useful analysis of the evolution of New Zealand's parks system has been provided by G. Rennison, who also characterized three periods. The first period, 1887 to 1941, he called the years of "trial and error." From the advent of Tongariro three further parks had been added, but "the legislation, thinking and management were chaotic, and centralized control minimal." His second period, 1942 to 1960, was the era of "park ascendancy."[4] Five new parks had been added and the legislation overhauled to reflect new philosophies and practices. Of the new National Parks Act of 1952, Jane Thomson writes,

before 1952 legislation governing the administration of national parks was, to say the least, untidy. It was a matter of conjecture whether some reserves really were, and whether others ought to be, national parks; and although certain clear principles for the administration of the parks had evolved, they were nowhere plainly stated in the legislation.[5]

The new act clearly enunciated the twin responsibilities of parks: to serve first of all a nature conservation role, and second, to fulfill the recreational and inspirational needs of people.

Thomson saw logic in the timing of New Zealand's National Parks Act. The lean and difficult years of the Great Depression and World War II had given way to a postwar boom of relative affluence and optimism. While public opinion had previously been apathetic and money hard to come by, in 1952 prosperity and public opinion made reform both possible and politically advantageous. The enthusiasm that greeted the proposed legislation both inside and outside Parliament was testimony to the new interest and concern of the public for the environment.

Thomson concludes, "It had taken half a century to engender enough concern for the environment to produce such an Act; in the second half century environmental issues have become a general concern."[6] The passage of the 1952 act smoothed the way for a rapid rationalization in several places where large areas of land were already being managed along national park lines. Fiordland and Mount Cook were constituted as national parks in 1953, Urewera in 1954, Nelson Lakes in 1956, Westland in 1960, and Mount Aspiring in 1964. Hauraki Gulf Maritime Park was constituted in 1967 and, subsequently, Marlborough Sounds Maritime Park and Bay of Islands Maritime and Historic Park. Leaving aside the maritime parks, it was twenty-three years (1987) before a further national park was added. During this time, New Zealanders have undergone a comprehensive evolution in their relationships with their environment. Pressures from recreationists, from tourists, from developers, and from environmentalists and conservationists have all played a part.

It is, therefore, hardly surprising that Rennison called his third period (1961–1971) the "years of testing, with nearly all parks subject to sometimes irresistible pressures from alien interests."[7] New Zealand, perhaps in common with other nations throughout the world, was unprepared for the burgeoning interest in parks. Use pressures on parks intensified, and millions of dollars worth of buildings and facilities were constructed in response to this demand. Pressures came not simply from the recreation-oriented visitor. As Rennison has written,

a park system has grown from nothing to one which is perhaps the finest in the world . . . [yet] at the pinnacle of its success it suddenly stands strangely vulnerable and uncertain, attacked over the length and breadth of the country by its natural enemies, the human modifiers, and it is unable to defend itself by falling back on the law, as the Manapouri issue [a hydro-development project in Fiordland National Park] has proved.[8]

The political viewpoint of the 1970s did little to assuage these concerns and uncertainties. A prominent politician, noted for his support of the environmental lobby, responded to a question on the relationship between the inviolate nature of parks as inferred by the 1952 act and parks as areas for potential mineral resources as follows:

Governments and Ministers of Land and Environment come and go; Acts of Parliament can be changed; but the people remain. If a majority of the people demand that we place the wealth from minerals above the longer-lasting wealth of natural beauty, no doubt eventually they will get their way.[9]

The kinds of pressures and concerns described above reached a political and social climax in the middle and late 1970s. The exuberant postwar period and subsequent "years of testing" had in fact become a period of post-exuberance! While the reasons for this are complex, events in the Middle East that threatened our fuel supplies brought dramatic changes to the attitudes of many New Zealanders. For some it was a first-time recognition of the precarious dependence that we have on mineral sources from other countries. It led to renewed interest in prospecting and in the possible discovery of oil and other precious mineral resources somewhere in New Zealand. A second manifestation was the fear that these resources may be locked up by giving new areas national park status, or for that matter, that they may already be locked up in national parks and should be released.

Fears of this nature were compounded by other socioeconomic factors such as increasing unemployment and inflation. All of these may be viewed as threats to basic human needs, and a public that sees basic needs to be under threat does not engender a political climate that enables either the acquisition of new parks or the extension of existing parks to include new and ecologically desirable lands. These lands just may hold resources that can be exploited to improve lifestyles and well-being!

Whether or not this post-exuberant period has really ended is an interesting hypothetical question. The answer is probably not, but what is now clear is that the entire approach to preservation and utilization has undergone dramatic changes within a decade. This has been due to a number of factors, but important among them are the increased professionalization of the principal land-management agencies, the Department of Lands and Survey and the New Zealand Forest Service, and a similar process within those voluntary groups and organizations that constitute the conservation-environmental lobby, New Zealand Royal Forest and Bird Protection Society and the Native Forest Action Council.

Whereas the Lands and Survey Department managed the national parks and reserves primarily for preservation and secondarily for recreation, the Forest Service established a system of forest parks, many of national park size and quality, under a multiple-use mandate. The parallel pathways, and the pros and cons of these two styles of park, are beyond the scope of this chapter, but it is noted here that the range of management and policy options previously available had considerable merit. Historically, forest parks did not satisfy the strict requirements of protected natural areas, but subsequent structural changes in conservation administration have brought many forest parks into the same administrative fold as national parks and reserves. The scope and nature of their management vis-à-vis national parks policy have yet to be detailed. However, any forcing of a common approach to management of national and forest parks would be of concern. The opportunity for a measure of heterogeneity in management options seems a more healthy approach and enables a harder line to be taken where conservation needs are paramount.

The 1980s may well be regarded as a period of coming of age. The last ten to fifteen years have seen conservation groups become increasingly aggressive and well-organized political lobbyists. Their efforts have done much to focus public attention on the inadequacies of ecological representativeness in the existing system. At the same time, their efforts have polarized people in those regions of New Zealand where further setting aside of lands for protection is seen as necessary. As so often has happened, the areas in which such lands have been identified are places in which land has escaped development because of distance from main centers of population. Consequently, these are frequently regions where the economic base is relatively narrow and fragile. The West Coast of the South Island is a notable example in that the mining for gold and coal, and timber milling, all extractive industries, have been the major source of jobs and incomes for West Coasters. Putting further forested lands aside for parks and conservation is met with hostility and resentment. This type of controversy has caused politicians to tread a wary path, and until 1987 numerous proposals to extend parks, or create new ones, foundered at central government level.

The exception to this is the establishment in 1987 of the Wanganui National Park. The major focus of the park is the Wanganui River, which is an important area for recreational canoeing, is historically rich, and is scenically and scientifically of high value. As most of the land involved was already in Crown ownership and involved few competing resources issues, the establishment of the park was not associated with any marked controversy or alienation of interest groups.

The same cannot be said of a proposed national park on the West Coast of the South Island. The new park—the Paparoa National Park—was officially opened in December 1987 and is notable for the acrimony and compromise that have been associated with its stormy pathway. Important mining and milling areas remain outside the boundaries, and the Paparoa National Park will, therefore, symbolize this new era of livable compromise and cooperation. Such an era will require that what remains of our precious natural environments will be worked through similar processes of public and political participation, with due regard to long-term objectives for both protection and development of resources rather than short-term expediency.

The existing parks and reserves system, though comprehensive, is heavily biased toward upland and forested landscapes, thereby inadequately reflecting the true ecological diversity of New Zealand's natural environment. A new protected natural areas (PNA) program, developed on a scientific basis over the past few years, is aimed at extending the geographical and ecological scope of the existing network and protecting a representative sample of all major landscapes and their associated biota. A systematic program to survey and rank the conservation potential of all remaining natural areas of the country has made good progress, and it is hoped that this national survey can be completed in five to ten years. Emphasis will go toward protecting those formerly widespread habitats that are rapidly diminishing and in danger of being lost or irredeemably modified. Among the most important of these are lowland forests, the richest and most complex natural ecosystems nationally and containing most of the rare and endangered biota; mangrove (*Avicennia resinifera*) forest, which are among the southernmost of their type in the world but are much reduced due to reclamation of the estuarine or harbor habitats for farmland, urban and industrial development, refuse sites, and marinas; wetlands, which have suffered widespread loss through drainage, burning, and conversion to exotic pastures; and native tussock grasslands grossly modified by burning, grazing, topdressing with fertilizers, and oversowing with introduced pasture species.

Currently, a boom in international tourism has illustrated that our national parks and reserves are prime visitor destinations. This adds yet another chapter to the chronology of events that have acted, and will continue to act, as threats to parks and reserves. Yet it is the human participant and observer that ultimately translates the intrinsic values of these places into terms we all understand. The challenge is how to achieve a balance between the intrinsic values of ecological complexity and species diversity while still enabling a level of human activity that caters to human needs. New Zealand's parks and reserves have a special international responsibility in terms of nature conservation, and it is toward an understanding of the scope and nature of this role that this chapter is now directed.

PARKS AND RESERVES

New Zealand is a sparsely populated, mountainous archipelago set in the temperate latitudes of the southwest Pacific region, with scenery of world renown and a fascinating assemblage of ancient and unique plants and animals. Ancestors of the indigenous conifer forests, including rimu (*Dacrydium cupressinum*) and kauri (*Agathis australis*), extend back over 250 million years to when New Zealand was part of the Gondwanaland supercontinent, while the tuatara (*Sphenodon punctatus*) is the world's only survivor of an ancient group of reptiles that flourished in the age of the dinosaurs, and the flightless moa (*Dinornithiformes*), kiwi (*Apertyx* spp.), and ancestors of the beech forests (*Nothofagus* spp.) were present 80 million years ago when New Zealand began to drift away from Australia and Antarctica.

The enormous period of biological isolation means that more than half of the species of all major classes of native plants and animals are endemic, i.e., belong exclusively to New Zealand, including all species of amphibians, reptiles, and mammals (2 bat species only); more than 90 percent of the approximately 20,000 species of arthropods (insects, etc.); 80 percent of the approximately 2,000 species of higher plants; and about 60 percent of the terrestrial birds.[10]

Human occupation over the past millennium, particularly the period of planned European settlement beginning 150 years ago, has produced massive and widespread environmental change. Some 60 percent of the original vegetation cover has been destroyed, especially the forests that were once ubiquitous but are now reduced to only 23 percent of the total land area, mainly in the mountains. The introduction of plants and animals has been likened to a biological invasion, and the number of introduced plant species (ca. 2,000) now rivals that of the higher native plants, while among the successfully introduced animals are at least 30 species of birds and 20 species of mammals.[11]

The impacts on the indigenous biota, through predation, disease, competition, and habitat reduction, have been disastrous. In the period prior to or just after arrival of the Europeans, 45 species of birds became extinct. Moreover, of the 41 species of rare and endangered endemic terrestrial vertebrates listed in the *New Zealand Red Data Book*, 17 of the 21 species of birds and 7 of the 14 species of lizards and amphibians have been devastated through predation by introduced rats, cats, or mustelids. Considerable areas of New Zealand are now essentially devoid of native plant communities, and only the mountains remain largely unmodified. Some 10–15 percent of the native flowering plants and ferns are currently regarded as being at risk.

National parks and allied protected areas are bastions against further loss of native wildlife and their habitat. Although New Zealand's parks and reserves were not established with the intention of protecting a representative sample of the nation's biota, the extent to which they achieve this, for the plants at least, is quite remarkable. For example, Mount Cook National Park includes 450 species of native plants in 167 communities. Westland National Park has 650 species in 118 communities, and Mount Aspiring National Park has 550 species in 19 vegetation types. Of the 26 major botanical districts in New Zealand, 14 are well represented in national parks. Fifty-one of the 66 rare or endangered plant species listed in the *New Zealand Red Data Book* are located in parks or reserves. Several reserves were established specifically to protect habitats of rare plants, including Lake Waiparaheka Scientific Reserve protecting *Baumea complanata* and Castle Hill Nature Reserve containing *Ranunculus paucifolius*.

All of New Zealand's major forest classes are represented in national parks and reserves, though in somewhat uneven proportions. The kauri forests, which now have a very restricted distribution north of 38° south, are protected notably in Waipoua State Forest Sanctuary of approximately 9,000 hectares (22,000 acres) and in the 600-hectare (1,500-acre) Trounson Kauri Park Scenic Reserve, which has dense virgin stands of kauri. Lowland podocarp forests (the Southern Hemisphere's conifer forests), now nationally important because of their much-diminished distribution, and characterized by rimu, totara (*Podocarpus totara*), matai (*P. spicatus*), and kahikatea (*P. dacrydioides*), are exemplified on the North Island in Pureora State Forest Park, also famous as the home of the rare kokako (blue wattled crow, *Callaeas cinerea*), and on the South Island in coastal lowlands of Westland National Park. Forests of podocarp/beech/hardwoods at lower altitudes, the typical mixed rain forest of New Zealand, dominate the vegetation of Urewera, Egmont, and Tongariro national parks, and in the more than 100 scenic reserves of the Wanganui River—amalgamated in 1987 to constitute New Zealand's eleventh national park. Beech forests (*Nothofagus* spp.) of the montane and subalpine realms are the most widely represented forests in protected areas, and are especially characteristic of Nelson Lakes, Arthur's Pass, and Mount Aspiring national parks, Craigieburn State Forest Park, and several other major parks and reserves that form an almost continuous belt along the South Island's Southern Alps.

Westland National Park, which extends from mountain crest to sea over an altitudinal range of 3,500 meters (11,500 feet) in a distance of only 27 kilometers (17 miles), has perhaps the widest range of plant habitats in New Zealand parks. This includes, with increasing altitude, podocarp forest of almost subtropical luxuriance, rich in epiphytes and lianes; montane forest of mixed podocarps and broad-leaved hardwoods, with ferns as an almost continuous understory; dense scrub and low forest of the subalpine zone, dominated by species of *Olearia*, *Senecio*, and *Dracophyllum*; tall grasslands of snow tussock (*Chionochloa* spp.) and associated herbs; short tussock (*Poa* spp.) meadows; and mossy or lichen-encrusted fellfield.

Mountains dominate the New Zealand landscape, and about 60 percent of the country is more than 300 meters (1,000 feet) above sea level. The alpine story is well told in national parks—mountains being predominant in all but two parks. They have their greatest expression in the adjoining Mount Cook and Westland national parks, which contain all but one of the twenty-nine mountain peaks in New Zealand above 3,000 meters (10,000 feet). Glacial history is also well represented here, with more than 300 glaciers present, including the 28-kilometer (17-mile) long Tasman Glacier, which is New Zealand's longest and the world's largest midlatitude glacier. The Franz Josef and Fox glaciers, which descend into a temperate rain forest realm only 300 meters (1,000 feet) above sea level, are among the fastest moving in the world.

Fiordland National Park comprises one of the world's most spectacular fiord landscapes. Carved from bold crystalline rocks, the fourteen major fiords here are as much as 44 kilometers (27 miles) long and 500 meters (1,600 feet) deep, with summits rising abruptly to more than 2,000 meters (6,600 feet) above sea level. Their steep slopes are clothed in lush rain forest, reflecting an annual rainfall of more than 6,200 millimeters (244 inches), and have some of the highest waterfalls in the world, such as the 580-meter (1,900-foot) high Sutherland Falls.

New Zealand straddles the hot rim of the Pacific Basin and has a long volcanic history, spectacularly expressed both in Egmont National Park, centered on the almost perfect cone of Mount Egmont/Taranaki, and in Tongariro National Park, which contains the highly active Ruapehu and Ngauruhoe volcanoes that are the most spectacular andesitic mountains in the southwest Pacific region. Mount Ruapehu, 2,979 meters (9,774 feet) high and the highest North Island mountain, is less than 500,000 years old and has erupted more than forty-five times in the last 125 years. One of the few volcanoes in the world with a hot crater lake surrounded by glaciers, it is flanked by an extensive lahar (volcanic mudflow) plain, and on its southern slopes the Rangataua lava flow is one of the world's largest, 14 kilometers (9 miles) long and 150 meters (500 feet) thick.

Extending north from Tongariro National Park to White Island (a large active volcano, which is a privately owned scenic reserve), centered on Rotorua, is one of only five major hydrothermal regions existing anywhere in the world. The region is the focus of the New Zealand tourist industry. Some twenty-five reserves here protect a wide range of features such as geysers, boiling springs, mud pools, and siliceous sinter terraces mantled in brightly colored algae. These are most impressively displayed at Whakarewarewa, which has eleven active geysers, and ranks with Yellowstone National Park as one of the world's few outstanding geyser fields, and at Waimangu, the world's only large hydrothermal system where surface activity has begun in historic times—as a result of the massive Tarawera eruption in 1886. Abnormally warm and mineralized soils on geothermal sites proved special habitats for plants, many of which differ morphologically from plants of the same species on nonthermal sites (e.g., *Leptospermum* and *Dracophyllum* spp.) or are of restricted distribution or unique to a site, such as the swamp fern (*Cyclosorus interruptus*) at Waimangu Scenic Reserve, and the sedge (*Baumea complanata*) at Lake Waiparaheka Scientific Reserve.

Karst and cave landforms, which in New Zealand range from lowland polygonal karst to subalpine marble massifs, are also extensively protected. Approximately 100 parks and reserves contain limestone substrate and/or karst, and 37 such areas have cave systems. Among the best known, and most popular for tourist visits, is Waitomo Cave Scenic Reserve with its spectacular subterranean stream system and well-developed stalactites and stalagmites. Abel Tasman National Park has some of the deepest caves in New Zealand, including Harwoods Hole, which is 357 meters (1,171 feet) deep.

Surrounding the main islands of New Zealand are some 600 offshore islands, of which about half are protected, mostly either as nature reserves or wildlife sanctuaries. This strict protection reflects the vital role that islands play as refuges for species of plants and animals that have become endangered or extinct on the mainland. Examples include the tuatara, now confined to twenty-two offshore islands, and the takahe (flightless rail, *Notornis mantelli*) and kakapo (flightless parrot, *Strigops habroptilus*), which have been introduced to Maud Island Scientific Reserve and Little Barrier Island Nature Reserve, respectively, as part of a desperate strategy to rescue them from extinction. Of particular significance are those islands free of predatory rodents, especially the Norway rat (*Rattus norvegicus*) and ship rat (*R. rattus*), which devastate populations of invertebrates, lizards, burrowing seabirds, and some forest birds. Of the more than 200 islands and islets in northern New Zealand, only 49 are reliably known to be rodent-free, and considerable management effort is devoted to preventing new introductions.

New Zealand territory also includes five subantarctic island groups: Snares, Auckland, Campbell, Antipodes, and Bounties. All are nature reserves and have been declared national reserves. These islands are of outstanding scientific value in the preservation of genetic resources peculiar to the world's southern regions.

They provide habitat for thousands of marine mammals and millions of seabirds of the Southern Ocean and are internationally important as some of the last remaining areas of the world where vegetation is unmodified by man.

All major elements of New Zealand's historical and cultural heritage are prominently recorded in the protected area system. For example, at least 15 percent of the 38,000 recorded prehistoric archaeological sites in New Zealand are in parks and reserves. Tongariro and Egmont national parks are sacred ancestral lands of the Maori people, and Abel Tasman National Park was established in 1942 to mark the 300th anniversary of the first European discovery of New Zealand, by the Dutchman Abel Janszoon Tasman.

The Bay of Islands Maritime and Historic Park, with eleven historic reserves among a total of more than fifty reserves of various types, has been described as the cradle of New Zealand history. Included here are many nationally important sites of early Maori occupation, such as pa (fortified village) sites, garden cultivation areas, and midden (refuse of cooking areas). Notable among these are Kororipo Pa, the home of the famous chief Hongi Hika, and Ruapekapeka Pa, the scene of a famous battle of the War of the North between Maori and European forces.

The emergence of the dual Maori and European cultures in New Zealand is symbolized by the Waitangi Treaty House at the Bay of Islands, where in February 1840 the Treaty of Waitangi was signed between the Crown and the Maori people, thereby establishing British title to sovereignty over the colony of New Zealand.

In the far north, Te Paki Farm Park, which is an amalgamation of many historic, nature, and recreation reserves, along with farming operations, contains many areas sacred to the Maori and more than 700 archaeological sites. The park also has links with early European exploration by the Englishman James Cook and Frenchmen Jean de Surville and Marion du Fresne. Farming here continues a landworking tradition extending back more than 100 years, and the park also protects sites where hoards of gumdiggers settled in the late nineteenth century to hunt for fossilized resin of the kauri tree, highly prized for varnish manufacturing, jewelry, and ornaments.

The mining theme is central to the Otago Goldfields Park, one of the first significant efforts at preserving part of the country's industrial heritage. Containing at present more than twenty sites, the park displays all aspects of life during the region's brief gold-mining bonanza of the 1860s. The town of St. Bathans, for example, which once boasted 2,000 residents, 14 hotels, and 30 stores, but now has only 5 residents, 1 hotel, and some holiday cottages, is being faithfully restored, in part as a major focus for the park.

Other historic sites and relics in protected areas are as diverse as whaling stations, shipwreck sites, and castaway depots on the subantarctic islands; disused timber mills in Westland; original mountain huts and lodges at Mount Cook; and European wartime forts and gun emplacements in Hauraki Gulf within the city of Auckland.

An estimated one-third of New Zealand's land area is regarded as having high value for scenic viewing and wilderness recreation, with most of it in national parks, forest parks, and approximately 1,500 recreation reserves.

Indeed, the national and forest parks, which collectively attract at least 8 million visits annually, are at the heart of New Zealand's burgeoning tourism and commercial recreation industries. The major national parks have demonstrated considerable economic benefit, not only for the regional economy but also for the national economy.

Tourists and recreationalists find New Zealand attractive because of its healthy, unpolluted, safe, and uncrowded outdoor environment, of great scenic beauty and with many diverse landscapes offering a wide range of recreational experience. Fiordland National Park and the combined Westland/Mount Cook national parks are designated as World Heritage (Natural Property) Sites under Unesco's World Heritage Convention, thus ranking among the world's most exceptional sites of rare natural beauty.

Of the five most popular tourist destinations in New Zealand (outside the main cities), four are in national parks and reserves: Rotorua geothermal area, Te Anau–Milford Sound in Fiordland National Park, Franz Josef and Fox glaciers in Westland National Park, and Mount Cook. The country's major walking tracks are also in protected areas, including Milford, Routeburn, Hollyford, and Heaphy tracks.

Mountains have always held great fascination and were among the earliest regions exploited for tourism. Thus, the Hermitage at Mount Cook first opened in 1884, and the Milford Track, often described as the finest walk in the world, was first opened in 1890. The alpine realm shared by Mount Cook and Westland national parks has been a mecca for mountaineering for more than a century and attracts climbers from all over the world. Of the twenty-four skifields in New Zealand, ten are in national or forest parks or in reserves, including many major commercial skifields of international standard. Whakapapa Skifield in Tongariro National Park, the country's busiest, attracts as many as 8,000 skiers in a day.

The 1970s marked the beginning of a boom in outdoor recreation in New Zealand, and there has been a remarkable growth in commercial activities since then, with the trend predicted to continue well into the next century. Protected areas are the major nodes of commercial recreation activities: particularly fishing, hunting, and white-water rafting in the central North Island; yachting in the waters of the Hauraki Gulf and Bay of Islands; and alpine climbing, tramping (trekking), safari hunting, and heli- and downhill skiing in the alps of the South Island.

While the majority of visitors frequent resort areas where facilities are available, increasing numbers are penetrating remote areas seeking solitude, freedom, and the challenge of self-reliance. This has prompted the designation of extensive wilderness areas, many of which are in national and forest parks, where facilities development is absolutely prohibited and where management aims at minimizing human impact. In a world of diminishing wild places, the opportunities for wilderness recreation in New Zealand have assumed international significance.

ADMINISTRATION

Establishment, protection, and management of national parks in New Zealand are provided for in the National Parks Act 1980 which, while it repealed a 1952 act, retained almost word for word the purposes of national parks in New Zealand and the criteria for their management.

The act is "for the purpose of preserving in perpetuity as national parks, for their intrinsic worth and for the benefit, use, and enjoyment of the public, areas of New Zealand that contain scenery of such distinctive quality, ecological systems, or natural features so beautiful, unique, or scientifically important that their preservation is in the national interest."

Land in national parks is almost all in state ownership, the primary exception being land in Urewera National Park leased by the government from its Maori owners for national park purposes.

The act lays down criteria for the management of national parks:

- They shall be preserved as far as possible in their natural state.
- Native plants and animals of the park shall as far as possible be preserved, and the introduced plants and animals shall as far as possible be exterminated.
- Sites and objects of archaeological and historical interest shall as far as possible be preserved.
- Their value as soil, water, and forest conservation areas shall be maintained.
- The public shall have freedom of entry and access to the parks "so that they may receive in full measure the inspiration, enjoyment, recreation and other benefits that may be derived from mountains, forests, sounds, seacoasts, lakes, rivers and other natural features." (This provision is subject to "conditions necessary for preservation of native flora and fauna and for the welfare in general of the parks.")

The act provides for the establishment within national parks of "specially protected areas" with entry by permit, "wilderness areas" with only foot access permitted, and "amenities areas" for appropriate recreational and public amenities. The act lists permissible developments including camping grounds, huts, hostels, accommodation houses, and other buildings or facilities, always subject to the overall aim of the act, and in accordance with the general policy for national parks and the relevant park-management plan.

The only human habitation permitted in parks is that authorized for park management and for public use and enjoyment of the parks. In older established parks—Tongariro, Egmont, Fiordland, and Mount Cook—there are visitor accommodations, but in other cases the parks are serviced by towns outside their boundaries.

Fishing is permitted for species introduced in the past for sport fisheries. Policy is not to introduce sport fish into virgin waters. Hunting, both commercial and recreational, is encouraged for introduced species of animals as a means of reducing the adverse impact of browsing mammals that were brought to New Zealand, generally in the latter part of the nineteenth century, for recreational hunting. Hunting for these species is permitted with permits for both ground and helicopter hunting during periods and in locations that will not restrict or endanger public use.

Timber harvesting is expressly forbidden, and grazing by domestic livestock is permitted only where it is for park management or was an existing use prior to park establishment and then generally on a phasing-out basis.

Mineral prospecting and mining can be authorized only on the joint consent of the ministers of conservation and mines after a procedure that requires extensive public consultation for projects of any significance. No significant mining operations exist or have been authorized.

Recreation and tourism are fostered where compatible with the purposes of national parks. The emphasis is on nature walks and walking tracks with overnight huts for park users, generally operated by the park administration but in some cases by private operators under license. Other huts are provided as bases for mountaineers and skiers.

Tongariro National Park has commercial skifields operated under license, and there are smaller-scale skifields in other parks. Glacier skiing in Mount Cook National Park is facilitated by use of ski-equipped aircraft. Air access and sightseeing are also permitted in the 1.2-million-hectare (3-million-acre) Fiordland National Park, often with float planes, and in Mount Cook and Westland national parks using ski-equipped aircraft.

All the parks have visitor centers with interpretive displays and audiovisual programs. During holiday periods there are nature programs both in the visitor centers and on nature walks and longer-distance tramps.

Educational lodges exist in some parks, but their establishment is now encouraged close to but outside the parks. Research in parks is encouraged where it is management-oriented or cannot be undertaken as well outside the parks.

The National Parks Act sets up a management approach for national parks under which implementation of the act is carried out in partnership between the National Parks and Reserves Authority at the policy-overview level and the Department of Conservation carrying out the policy and undertaking day-to-day management.

The authority, made up of informed private citizens, has advised the minister, adopted general policy for parks, and adopted management plans for each park after reviewing public submissions on the advice of regional national parks and reserves boards. Both the authority and the boards are responsible for reviewing management effectiveness.

The National Parks and Reserves Authority has ten members appointed by the minister of conservation on the following basis:

- one appointed on the recommendation of the Royal Society of New Zealand,
- one appointed on the recommendation of the Royal Forest and Bird Protection Society of New Zealand Incorporated,
- one appointed on the recommendation of the Federated Mountain Clubs of New Zealand Incorporated,
- three appointed after consultation with the ministers of tourism and local government, and
- four appointed on public nomination, "having special knowledge of or interest in matters connected with the policy for and management of national parks and reserves or having special knowledge of or interest in matters connected with wildlife."

National parks and reserves boards are appointed by the minister to operate over various regions of New Zealand decided on a geographic basis.

Both the authority and the boards have responsibility for national parks and for reserves set aside for the nature preservation under the Reserves Act 1977. A key aim of this act is to ensure the preservation of representative examples of all natural ecosystems and landscapes that originally gave New Zealand its unique character.

Under present law, classes of reserves where nature preservation is predominant are nature, scientific, and scenic reserves, and there are also wildlife management reserves.

Nature reserves are "for the purpose of protecting and preserving in perpetuity indigenous flora and fauna or natural features that are of such rarity, scientific interest or importance, or so unique that their protection and preservation are in the public interest." Emphasis is on habitat for rare or endangered species, and entry to nature reserves is generally by permit.

The scientific reserve classification is closely allied to that for nature reserves, but there is greater emphasis on research values.

Scenic reserves are managed essentially as national parks are but are generally smaller in area and do not contain such diverse features as national parks. However, some have substantial public use for recreation and for sightseeing with cave systems, waterfalls, forest, and other features.

Where, in the minister's opinion, on the advice of the National Parks and Reserves Authority, a reserve protects values of national or international significance, it may be declared a national reserve with added protection.

Other areas are protected as nature preserves under the Wildlife Act 1953 or as wildlife sanctuaries and refuges and under the Conservation Act 1987.

Owners of private land also give protection to natural areas on their properties by voluntary covenants under the Reserves Act 1977 or under the Queen Elizabeth the Second National Trust Act 1977.

April 1, 1987, marked a significant change in environmental administration in New Zealand. National parks and other protected natural areas passed from the responsibility of the ministers of lands, forests, and internal affairs to the minister of conservation. At the same time, the Department of Conservation was established to take over national parks and reserves from the Department of Lands and Survey, wildlife sanctuaries and refuges from the Wildlife Service of the Department of Internal Affairs, historical and archaeological sites from the Historic Places Trust, and other protected areas in state forests from the New Zealand Forest Service.

The Department of Conservation was established with a central office in Wellington and with directorates responsible for

- Land and Fauna
- Protected Ecosystems and Species
- Marine and Coastal Resources
- Recreation, Tourism, and Historic Resources
- Science and Research
- Advocacy and Extension
- Finance
- Executive Support Services

Regional offices have been established in Auckland, Hamilton, Rotorua, Wanganui, Nelson, Hokitika, Christchurch, and Dunedin. District offices operate within the regions, with national park staff responsible to these district offices.

The Department of Conservation administers a variety of legislation including the National Parks Act 1980, the Reserves Act 1977, the Wildlife Act 1953, the Wild Animal Control Act 1977, the Marine Reserves Act 1971 and the Queen Elizabeth the Second Act 1977.

Under the Conservation Act 1987, provision is made for public land not already set aside as national parks or reserves to become conservation areas managed by the department or stewardship areas to be managed so that the inherent character is largely maintained. The act provides that any conservation area may become a national park, reserve, sanctuary, or refuge.

Field management for national parks and other protected areas is in the hands of well-trained and highly motivated career rangers (now termed conservation officers) backed up by capable work staff.

With legislation that sets out clearly a preservation philosophy, with the authority-departmental partnership involving private citizens working with officials, with strong support from the public, the tourist industry, and the articulate conservation lobby, national parks and other protected areas enjoy a high measure of security in New Zealand.

There is a continuing battle for adequate resources to manage the protected areas system, but the greatest threat to the integrity of some areas lies in the continued presence of introduced species, particularly animals ranging from deer species to the Australian possum and rodents. Numbers of the larger introduced mammals have been reduced dramatically with the use of helicopters with a corresponding improvement in the health of vegetation on alpine herb fields.

However, the reduction in animal numbers and the establishment of a deer-farming industry has made commercial hunting in the wild less attractive commercially, leaving a potential for future problems of vegetation modification if introduced animal numbers increase.

New Zealand's systems for protected area administration are currently being modified. In May 1988 Fran Wilde, the associate minister of conservation, announced a new structure that would transfer the functions of the National Parks and Reserves Authority and boards to a New Zealand Conservation Authority and nineteen local conservation boards. The new authority and boards would have extended functions covering all the protected lands that are the responsibility of the Department of Conservation as well as general nature conservation responsibilities. Appointments to the authority and boards would be made by the minister of conservation from a range of interests, written into the new statute, with special emphasis on the role of the Maori people.

At the same time, Helen Clark, the minister of conservation, was directing a review of New Zealand's protected areas legislation with the objective of rationalizing the legislation and developing a clear and consistent classification system for protected areas. These changes in management may result in easier or less expensive administration. Whether they will also result in enhanced nature conservation and cultural preservation remains to be seen.

NOTES

1. Te Heuheu Tukino was paramount chief of the Ngati Tuwharetoa tribe, which was centered on the area around Lake Taupo in the central North Island.

2. M. M. Roche, "Some Historical Influences on the Establishment of Protected Natural Areas," in *People and Parks*, ed. Paul Dingwall (Wellington: Department of Lands and Survey, 1984), p. 9.

3. "Significant individuals" and their impacts are not fully developed in this essay because of the relative lack of meaning this would have for international readers. Cockayne is an exception to this, as his reputation will be known to many of the scientific community.

4. G. Rennison, "New Zealand National Parks: Thoughts on the Evolution and Relevance of the New Zealand National Parks System," *New Zealand Environment* 2, no. 1 (1972): 8–11.

5. Jane Thomson, *Origins of the 1952 National Parks Act* (Wellington: Department of Lands and Survey, 1976), p. 8.

6. Ibid., p. 10.

7. Rennison, p. 8.

8. Ibid. Initial proposals were to raise substantially the level of Lake Manapouri, and while this intent was in part successfully fought, the overall hydrodevelopment nevertheless went ahead.

9. D. McIntyre, "The Future of National Parks," *New Zealand Environment* 2, no. 2 (1972): 21.

10. G. C. Kelly, "Landscape and Nature Conservation," in *Land Alone Endures* (Wellington: Department of Scientific and Industrial Research, 1980), p. 64.

11. Carolyn A. Burns, "Protected Areas and Introduced Species in New Zealand,"

in *National Parks, Conservation, and Development*, ed. J. A. McNeely and K. R. Miller (Washington, D.C.: Smithsonian Institution Press, 1984), p. 404.

BIBLIOGRAPHY

Atkinson, I. A. E. "Rodents on New Zealand's Northern Offshore Islands: Distribution, Effects, and Precautions against Further Spread." In *The Offshore Islands of Northern New Zealand*, edited by A. E. Wright and R. E. Beever. Wellington: Department of Lands and Survey, 1986.

Breese, Josephine, and Lester Clark, eds. *Proceedings of an Historical Workshop for National Parks, Reserves, Walkways and Other Protected Areas*. National Park Series no. 31. Wellington: Department of Lands and Survey, 1984.

Davison, J. "Policy Implication of Trends in Supply and Demand for Natural Areas for Protection and Recreation 1970–2000." 2 vols. M. Appl. Sci. thesis, University of Canterbury, New Zealand, 1986.

Dingwall, Paul. "New Zealand: Saving Some of Everything." *Ambio* 11, no. 5 (1982): 269–301.

Given, David R. *Rare and Endangered Plants in New Zealand*. Wellington: A. H. and A. W. Reed Ltd., 1981.

Kelly, G. C., and G. N. Park, eds. *The New Zealand Protected Natural Areas Programme: A Scientific Focus*. Wellington: Department of Scientific and Industrial Research, 1986.

Kerr, G. N., B. M. H. Sharp, and J. D. Gough. *Economic Benefits of Mount Cook National Park*. Paper no. 12, Center for Resource Management, University of Canterbury and Lincoln College, 1986.

Lucas, P. H. C. *Conserving New Zealand's Heritage*. Wellington: Government Printer, 1970.

Mark, A. F. *Vegetation of Mount Aspiring National Park New Zealand*. Wellington: Department of Lands and Survey, 1977.

Molloy, B. P. J. "The Adequacy and Role of National Parks in Preserving Natural and Cultural Landscapes." In *Proceedings of Silver Jubilee Conference*. Wellington: National Parks Authority of New Zealand, Department of Lands and Survey, 1979.

Register of Protected Natural Areas in New Zealand. Wellington: Department of Lands and Surveys, 1984.

Thom, David. *Heritage: The Parks of the People: A Century of National Parks in New Zealand*. Auckland: Lansdowne Press, 1987.

Wardle, P. *Plants and Landscape in Westland National Park*. National Parks Scientific Series no. 3. Wellington: Department of Lands and Survey, 1984.

Williams, G. R., and D. R. Given. *The Red Data Book of New Zealand*. Wellington: Nature Conservation Council, 1981.

Wilson, Hugh D. *Vegetation of Mount Cook National Park New Zealand*. National Parks Scientific Series no. 1. Wellington: Department of Lands and Survey, 1976.

NORWAY 17

Olav Gjærevoll

Norway, including Svalbard, has some of the most magnificent scenery in Europe. Its diverse environments range from the central European deciduous forest to Arctic tundra and include skerries, fjords, mountains, and forests.

HISTORY

The first suggestions for national parks in Norway came at the beginning of this century. The Norwegian Travel Association was particularly interested in having some of the most famous and attractive mountainous areas in the country protected. The scientific community, too, argued that Norway should follow the example of other civilized countries and establish national parks. The Association for Nature Conservation in Norway was founded in 1914.

These efforts resulted in the establishment of some small reserves and some areas where plants were protected, but the dominant opinion remained that there was no need to preserve particular areas. In a country like Norway with a small population and large expanses of wilderness, nature would protect itself. This attitude was mistaken. During the first fifty years of the century, the Norwegian wilderness was considerably reduced. Extensive development of the country's water-power resources led to major technological encroachments even in the most remote areas of wilderness. After World War II there was an increased demand for recreation in undisturbed natural areas, and attitudes about preservation began to change.

A new Conservation Act was passed in 1954. Section 1 of this law read: "The King shall determine that areas of land or water shall be protected when this is considered desirable for scientific or historical reasons, or because of the beauty or distinctive character of the area." This new law also instituted a new body, the National Council for Nature Conservation, which was to function in both an advisory and initiatory capacity in nature conservancy work. The first major task the council undertook was to prepare a nationwide plan for national parks. When the plan was presented in 1964, it contained proposals for sixteen parks comprising an area of 6,300 square kilometers (1.55 million acres) and involving only state-owned ground. The first two parks, Rondane and Børgefjell, had already been established when the plan was presented.

The national park plan received parliamentary approval in 1967, and although it has taken a long time, the plan has been fulfilled. In Norway the usual procedure with a plan is to send it out to all involved parties for hearing before the government prepares a report to parliament, which adopts the plan in principle. As the government completes the individual projects, they are established by royal decree.

The Conservation Act of 1954 soon became obsolete. In 1970 it was replaced by the Nature Conservation Act, which states the following objective:

Nature is a natural asset which must be protected. Nature conservation means the management of natural resources, taking into account the close relationship between man and nature and the need to preserve the quality of nature for the future.

All persons shall show consideration and due care in their relationship with nature. Encroachments on nature should only be undertaken on the basis of a long-term and comprehensive management of resources, based on the principle that nature in the future must be preserved as the basis for human activity, health and welfare.

This new law allows for three types of nature protection: national parks, protected landscape, and nature reserves. The category "protected landscapes" is used for areas that have already been disturbed in some way, but where important conservation assets remain. On the coast it is particularly difficult to find fair-sized areas that have not suffered technological encroachments associated with road building, hydroelectric power generation, utility corridors, etc. If certain features of Norway's exceptionally varied and magnificent scenery are to be protected, some partially disturbed areas will have to be included. By January 1, 1985, forty-five areas of protected landscape had been established. Figure 17.1 shows only the largest of these. Areas of protected landscape are also used as buffer zones bordering several of the national parks, to separate them from more heavily exploited areas.

The national parks contain many different types of scenery, but they cover by no means all the variations to be found in the country. Norway spans 13° of latitude from approximately 58° north to beyond 71° north; in addition, there is Svalbard, which reaches 81° north. The geology shows large variations ranging from hard, acid rocks to soft, readily weathered shales, and the topography varies greatly over short distances. Even though the Gulf Stream moderates the climate from south to north, significant climatic variations remain. Since southwesterly winds bring most precipitation, the mountain and fjord districts in the west are

Figure 17.1
National Parks and Protected Landscapes of Norway

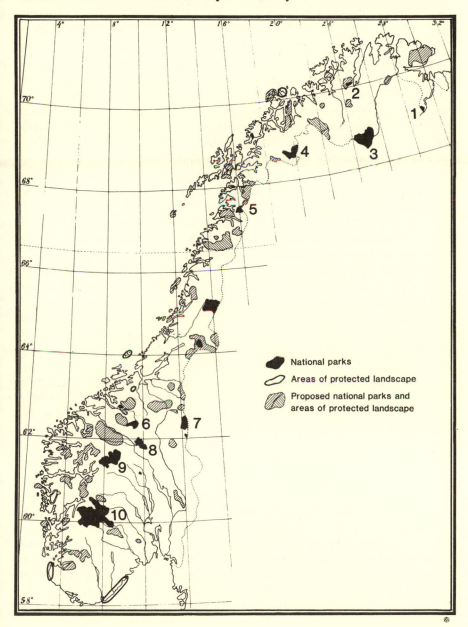

National parks

Areas of protected landscape

Proposed national parks and
areas of protected landscape

characterized by high precipitation, whereas areas east of the mountains, lying in the rain shadow, may have as little as 250 millimeters (10 inches) annually.

These variations result in an infinite number of environments, making Norway into a fantastic patchwork of different types of nature. Many of these fall outside national parks, but they can be given protection as nature reserves. According to Clause 8 of the Nature Conservation Act, "areas of undisturbed or almost undisturbed nature, or which constitute nature types of scientific or educational importance, or have a unique character, may be preserved as nature reserves."

Several national plans have been implemented, with the aim of establishing a network of nature reserves. The Directorate of State Forests has established fifty-four virgin forest reserves, mainly coniferous forests, throughout the country. Another plan deals with temperate deciduous forests. Trees characteristic of the temperate deciduous forests of central Europe play a secondary role in Norway, but since they represent the northernmost outposts of these types of vegetation, areas carrying these trees are of great importance. They are found in eastern and southern Norway and along the coast north to the Arctic Circle, chiefly where soil and climate are favorable. These biotopes are therefore very rich in plants and animals. Many are in vulnerable locations, as a result of building or forestry, and can be easily converted into valuable spruce forest, resulting in a completely different and poor ecosystem.

A similar plan for mires (bogs and fens) is being implemented. Mires are mainly found in the boreal coniferous forest zone. Because of the great variation in soil conditions, precipitation, and evaporation, as well as the altitudinal, longitudinal, and latitudinal spans, mires show extreme diversity in development. They therefore form the most varied type of nature in Norway and are in a class of their own as regards ecological studies. The mire plan is meeting strong opposition from economic interests; rich fens in particular can be easily converted into forest and farmland. A national plan for protecting wetlands, primarily as bird sanctuaries, is closely linked to the mire plan. However, there are many collisions with economic interests here, too. Estuaries, for example, are often found near towns and harbors, and shallow lakes can be drained for agricultural purposes.

The Norwegian coast has numerous bird biotopes—islets, skerries, and nesting cliffs—deserving conservation.

The most recently initiated plan concerns deposits essential to our understanding of the Quaternary geological history of Scandinavia: moraines, drumlins, eskers, raised shorelines, sand dunes, etc.

Each national plan needs lengthy preparation, involving scientific investigations, negotiations with landowners, and public hearings. The plans are now being implemented, and 839 reserves had been established by mid–1989. This number is expected to reach at least 1,300 when the work is complete.

The 1964 national park plan by no means marked the completion of the program for parks and preserves. In 1982 the Ministry asked the National Council for Nature Conservation to prepare a new countrywide plan for national parks and other large protected areas. In view of the decreasing amount of relatively undisturbed ground, everyone was aware that such a plan was a matter of urgency. Whereas the present national parks in Norway mainly consist of ground owned by the state, it was decided that the new plan should not be influenced by questions of ownership but be based on quality and diversity. The plan was presented in June 1986. It proposed twenty-seven new national parks, fourteen new areas of protected landscape, and three large reserves; in some cases a combination was recommended. The plan also recommended extending nine existing parks.

As Norway is a mountainous country, alpine scenery is strongly represented in the new plan, but several protected areas are proposed in coastal and forest districts, too. A biogeographical division of the Nordic countries into sixty regions, presented by the Nordic Ministerial Council in 1977, helps to achieve maximum representativeness when protection plans are being prepared. Norway extends over twenty-seven of these regions, and all except the most densely forested areas of southern and southeastern Norway are represented in the new plan (Figure 17.1).

If, following the usual handling procedure, the plan is adopted in full, there will be forty-three national parks in Norway, exclusive of Svalbard. The national parks, areas of protected landscape, and nature reserves will then cover an area of about 37,000 square kilometers (14,000 square miles), approximately 10 percent of the country.

Some of the largest remaining wilderness areas in this part of the world are to be found astride the borders of Norway and Finland, and Norway and Sweden. These three countries have cooperated closely for many years on questions concerning frontier national parks and guidelines for national park policy.

PARKS AND RESERVES

Out of a total land area of 324,000 square kilometers (125,000 square miles), as much as 47 percent of Norway consists of unproductive or low-productive ground, most of this being above the timberline. Mires, wetlands, and lakes comprise 11.5 percent, 37 percent is forested, 3.5 percent is used for agriculture, and built-up areas make up 1 percent.

The state owns most of the ground above the timberline, and the existing national parks reflect this. However, considerable pressure has also been exerted to preserve some of Norway's most famous mountain areas, especially because they are the most important areas for recreation.

The examples that follow indicate the diversity of reasons for establishing the various national parks. The numbers in brackets correspond to those on the map (Figure 17.1).

Øvre Pasvik National Park [1] lies as far east as longitude 29° and borders the USSR and Finland. It consists mainly of virgin subarctic pine forest and represents a forest landscape transitional between the northeastern and north-western European fauna and flora. It forms a westerly extension of the Eurasian taiga, and many interesting eastern species grow here that are rare or absent elsewhere in Norway, including wolverines and bears.

Stabbursdalen National Park [2] is at present rather small, but the new plan proposes to enlarge it considerably. The main reason for the present park is to preserve the northernmost pine forest in the world at latitude 70°18'. The park is dominated by Stabburselva, a river that has waterfalls and canyons in its upper stretches, whereas its lower portion meanders through flat landscape. The proposed extension of the park will include some vast bogs, some of them palsa bogs where ice beneath the soil pushes both soil and vegetation upward. Some ice-cored palsas reach a height of 7 meters (23 feet).

Anarjokka National Park [3] was established to preserve the special landscape of inner Finnmark, which is very flat and covered by enormous masses of drift deposits. Thousands of small lakes and a mixed forest of pine and birch with a carpet of reindeer moss characterize the landscape. Precipitation is low. The thin snow cover in winter provides excellent grazing conditions for the domesticated reindeer belonging to the Lapps, who are the main inhabitants. The park is adjacent to Lemmenjoki National Park in Finland, and together they cover an area of 4,400 square kilometers (1,700 square miles).

Øvre Dividalen National Park [4] is sufficiently remote to provide a sanctuary for the carnivores: lynx, bear, wolf, and wolverine. The wolf is now extremely rare in Norway, and the wolverine is regarded as a threatened species. The park is very scenic. Plant life is rich, in keeping with the calcareous bedrock.

Rago National Park [5] is the least accessible of Norway's parks. It has extremely varied geology and a wild landscape with large lakes, magnificent waterfalls, canyons, high mountains, glaciers, and virgin forests. It adjoins large national parks in Sweden.

Dovrefjell National Park [6] comprises part of the central mountain area of Norway and is easily accessible from all directions. It has held an international reputation since the middle of the eighteenth century for its unique and rich mountain flora, the richest in northern Europe. A number of species not found elsewhere in Europe outside Scandinavia occur here. Some are endemic, but most are found in Greenland and Arctic North America, thus indicating an ancient biological link between these areas that are now divided by the North Atlantic Ocean. The flora of the Dovrefjell area has been important in helping phyto-geographers to understand the age, origin, and immigration of the Scandinavian mountain biota. The bedrock mainly consists of calcareous schists that easily disintegrate to offer good conditions for a number of basiphilous plant species. The park is the home of wild reindeer. It also contains a thriving herd of musk oxen, which were reintroduced here some forty years ago having become extinct in Norway during the Pleistocene glaciation. The Kongsvoll Mountain Hostel, on the highway between Oslo and Trondheim, forms the main gateway to the park.

Femundsmarka National Park [7] is mainly a flat landscape with pine forests and low mountains. The bedrock is arkose, which produces poor soil, but it is mostly covered by dead-ice moraines. There are numerous rivers and lakes rich in trout and char. Femundsmarka is adjacent to an area in Sweden where a corresponding conservation area is planned.

Rondane National Park [8] was the first national park in Norway, established in 1962. Grand scenery with numerous high and majestic mountains is characteristic of this park. The bedrock is chiefly feldspathic quartzite, and plant life is fairly poor. The park is easily accessible and is one of the most popular mountain areas for walkers, skiers, and tourists in both summer and winter. Just outside the park boundary are many hotels and huts for walkers and skiers, but hotels are not allowed within the park itself.

Jotunheimen National Park [9] comprises some of the grandest mountain scenery Norway has to offer. Galdhøpiggen (2,468 meters, 8,097 feet), the highest mountain in the country, and many other peaks above 2,000 meters (6,500 feet) are found here, along with deeply incised valleys and numerous lakes and glaciers. The bedrock is extremely varied. Carbonate-rich rocks are especially widespread in the north where the flora is in part as rich as in the Dovrefjell National Park.

Hardangervidda National Park [10] represents a unique landscape, not only for Norway but also Europe. The area forms the only large mountain plateau in Europe. Ease of access makes it a very popular recreation area in both summer and winter. Probably no other national park can offer so many and such a variety of rivers and lakes. The geology is extremely varied, reflected by a corresponding variation in plant and animal life. From a zoological viewpoint, Hardangervidda has an arctic character and is the southernmost nesting area and haunt of several arctic bird species. Above all, it is the home of 15–20,000 wild reindeer. Hunting is permitted to maintain the herd at a level compatible with the area's carrying capacity. The park is rich in historic and prehistoric sites, some dated as far back as the Stone Age.

National Parks in the Norwegian Arctic

Svalbard is the group name given to all the islands between latitude 74° and 81° north and longitude 10° and 35° east. The southernmost of these is Bjørnøya (Bear Island) and the easternmost Kvitøya (White Island). The largest island is Spitsbergen (ca. 39,000 square kilometers, or 15,000 square miles), followed by Nordaustlandet (ca. 14,000 square kilometers, or 5,400 squares miles). The islands comprising the Svalbard archipelago cover an area of about 62,000 square kilometers (24,000 square miles), about two-thirds of which is more or less permanently ice-covered.

Svalbard chiefly consists of sedimentary rocks of Precambrian to Tertiary age, many of which are rich in fossils.

A branch of the Gulf Stream flowing along its west coast gives Svalbard the most favorable climate in the Arctic and therefore a flora that, considering the latitude, is both luxuriant and rich in species. The high primary production in the relatively warm sea off the west coast results in some of the largest concentrations of seabirds in the world.

There are three species of land mammals: polar bear, reindeer, and arctic fox. The polar bear is totally protected, and it is estimated that 200–400 cubs are born each year around the coasts of Svalbard. Special interest is attached to the Svalbard reindeer (*Rangifer tarandus platyrhynchos*), a unique race related to the Peary reindeer (*Rangifer tarandus pearyi*) of Greenland and the Canadian Arctic. When Norway became responsible for Svalbard in 1925, the reindeer stock had been decimated, but protection measures introduced immediately have resulted in the number of animals increasing to the present estimate of 10–12,000.

The bioresources of Svalbard were overexploited for centuries, on land but especially offshore. By the time the walrus was totally protected in 1952, a population that once numbered tens of thousands had been almost extinguished. The stock has only recently begun to show signs of recovery.

Norway's responsibility for nature conservation in Svalbard is clearly expressed in the international Svalbard Treaty of 1920. Article 2 states that Norway shall be free to adopt measures to ensure the preservation and, if necessary, reestablishment of the fauna and flora of the archipelago and of its territorial waters. The land areas of the Arctic are among the last surviving intact ecosystems in the world. Economic exploitation of the few remaining areas of undisturbed nature would be a drastic step toward making the world monotonous and far less interesting. Islands and archipelagoes have always played a very important role in biological research. It is sufficient to mention in this connection what Galapagos has meant for the knowledge of the evolution of life on the earth. Svalbard has been described as an "arctic Galapagos."

In 1968 the Norwegian Polar Research Institute started preparing a draft plan for national parks and nature reserves in Svalbard. The matter was urgent because oil exploration was already in progress. Hundreds of claims were located in areas deserving high priority for conservation. The conflict was settled in 1973 when three national parks, two large nature reserves, and fifteen bird sanctuaries were established. The protected areas amount to about 35,000 square kilometers (13,500 square miles), about 56 percent of the total land area. In implementing these conservation measures, the Norwegian government has stressed that the protection of Arctic bioresources is as important as their exploitation for economic purposes.

The protected areas are as follows. (See Figure 17.2.)

South Spitsbergen National Park has an extremely varied landscape. It includes Hornsund, perhaps the most spectacular and scenic fjord in Svalbard. There are many large seabird colonies, inhabited by large numbers of species.

Forlandet National Park is located in waters strongly influenced by the Gulf Stream. These favorable ecological conditions make the island very interesting biologically. It is, for example, the northernmost locality for the harbor seal.

Northwest Spitsbergen National Park is one of the richest biological environ-

Figure 17.2
National Parks and Nature Reserves in the Svalbard Area

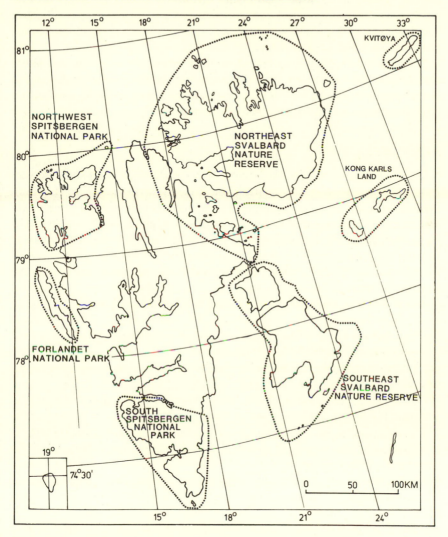

ments in Svalbard and has a large herd of reindeer. The park includes the small island of Moffen, which is a low sandbank strewn with walrus skeletons, a grim monument to former overexploitation of limited natural resources.

Northeast Svalbard Nature Reserve is the largest preserved area in Svalbard, covering about 19,000 square kilometers (7,300 square miles). It represents the Norwegian contribution to the Man and the Biosphere reserve system, and is an almost intact Arctic ecosystem. The northernmost reindeer population in the world is found here. This reserve also includes the isolated, remote group of islands, Kong Karls Land, one of the most important polar bear habitats and denning areas in the Eurasian part of the Arctic.

Southeast Svalbard Nature Reserve comprises the two large islands, Edgeøya and Barentsøya, which have flat or rolling landscape. Polar bears are numerous, and there are about 1,500 reindeer.

The conservation provisions relating to these areas prohibit technological encroachments and installations of all kinds, as well as other activities that would disturb the environment, including the use of cross-country vehicles and landing of aircraft. Flora and fauna are totally protected.

ADMINISTRATION

In 1972 Norway was the first country in the world to get a separate ministry for environmental protection matters, the Ministry of Environment. Environmental protection tasks had become so large and complex that the government considered it necessary to coordinate everything within a single ministry. The philosophy behind the establishment of the new ministry was that it should have superior responsibility for the long-term management of all ecological resources in the same way as the Ministry of Finance has superior responsibility for the economic resources.

The Ministry of Environment is divided into five departments:

1. The coordination and administrative department, dealing with such matters as research and international cooperation.
2. The regional planning department, responsible for the use and management of land and water resources.
3. The department for pollution control, dealing with problems relating to all kinds of pollution, waste disposal, noise, and product control.
4. The department for nature conservation and open-air recreation, responsible for nature conservation, recreation areas, preservation of cultural sites and buildings, and for fish and wildlife management.
5. The department of natural resources, which has budgeting supervision over all the natural resources of the nation.

Each of the eighteen counties has a conservation office dealing with much of the detailed work, including inspection and management of the numerous nature reserves. These offices are also responsible for proposing new conservation areas.

The national parks so far established are largely comprised of state-owned ground. All such ground is administered by the Directorate of State Forests (even though only 8 percent of this area is forested, the remainder being above the timberline). Hence, the directorate controls and administers the national parks, in close cooperation with the local conservation offices.

Norway has very strict legislation governing national parks. No technological encroachments—such as buildings, road construction, mining, quarrying, gravel extraction, river-system regulation, or power-line construction—are allowed. Motorized traffic on land and water is forbidden. Hikers' organizations have permission to discreetly mark routes for walkers. Hunting of small game and fishing is usually allowed. The Lapps are able to use the national parks for reindeer farming as they have from time immemorial. Ordinary grazing is also allowed.

Nature reserves enjoy the strictest type of protection. No interference of any kind is allowed, and access to some bird reserves is forbidden during the nesting season. Some reserves are obvious cultural landscapes, and in these it is necessary to employ management techniques to preserve this particular type of nature. Nature paths are provided in some reserves, for the use of schoolchildren and the general public.

Attempts are made to avoid further technological encroachment in areas of protected landscape, but some commercial activity is allowed, such as timber felling, running of summer pasture farms, and fish farming. Mining, quarrying, and large installations connected with the tourist industry are prohibited. The regulations controlling these areas of protected landscape resemble those relating to national parks in many other countries.

All preserved areas are strongly protected by existing legislation, and likely grounds for dispute have generally been cleared away beforehand. For example, it is not possible to plan hydroelectric or mining schemes in a national park. In a few places, especially nature reserves, wear and tear caused by large numbers of visitors may be a problem, although so far this has been insignificant. International egg collectors, operating commercially, pose a threat to rare bird species. The greatest threat to preserved areas—and to the natural environment of Norway as a whole—is the acid precipitation carried to Norway on southerly and southwesterly winds. Acidic precipitation reduces tree growth, and in the most extreme cases leads to the death of forests. At the present time the most obvious consequences are fish kills in hundreds of lakes and rivers in the southwestern part of the country. This problem is a subject for continuing research and political negotiation.

Conservation in Svalbard is faced with special problems because the Arctic environment is so vulnerable. A modern airport, opened in 1975, has increased the number of tourists. The use of cross-country vehicles represents a threat to the environment, both in winter and summer. Maintaining a watch over the vast unpopulated areas in difficult, and the office of the governor in Svalbard is too understaffed to carry out the supervision necessary during the summer.

Conclusion

In Norway the conservation associated with national parks and reserves enjoys popular support. Most people are proud of their national parks, and their conservation is viewed as a permanent situation.

Public hearings have been completed on the most recent national parks plan.

There was some opposition from landowners and some local officials, who view conservation as an obstacle to economic development. Nevertheless, the plan won general acceptance, and it has great support in the *Storting* (parliament). The National Council for Nature Conservation is very optimistic about the future of national parks and nature reserves in Norway.

BIBLIOGRAPHY

Norderhaug, M. *Svalbard*. Oslo: Universitetsforlaget, 1984.
Ryvarden, L. *Norges Nasjonalparker*. Oslo: Universitetsforlaget, 1983.

PAPUA NEW GUINEA 18

Peter Eaton

Papua New Guinea is a sparsely populated and largely undeveloped country. It is fortunate that much of its natural environment is still unspoiled, and it has extensive areas of wilderness. There are spectacular mountain ranges, offshore islands, coral reefs, and over three-quarters of its land area is still covered by tropical rain forest. The country occupies the eastern part of the island of New Guinea and is at a meeting point of the South East Asian, Australian, and South Pacific regions. As a result, there is a great diversity of flora and fauna. Papua New Guinea has an embryonic national park system and other reserves based on customary systems of land tenure and conservation.

HISTORY

Papua New Guinea became independent in 1975, having previously been administered by Australia. National parks are a relatively new concept although traditional methods of conservation have always been practiced as part of the subsistence economy of the indigenous people. Most of the land, 97 percent of the total area, is still owned under customary systems of tenure with land-use rights being dependent on membership in the kinship group or clan. Farming, hunting, and fishing are controlled by the clan, and outsiders are excluded from exploiting the natural resources of the group's territory.

In the past there have been traditional controls that have helped to protect wildlife. Overhunting and fishing were prevented by seasonal bans; certain species were protected by taboos and could not be killed or eaten. Similarly, certain areas with historical or religious associations were regarded as homes of the spirits and places where the wildlife and natural vegetation should not be disturbed. Gradually these traditional controls and beliefs were weakened, and at the same time new pressures have been imposed on natural resources. These changes have often been associated with population increase, economic development, and technological innovations such as the steel ax and the shotgun. The result is that it has become necessary to search for new ways of protecting the natural environment: conservation legislation has been introduced, and protected areas have been established.

The first area in the country to be given protected status was a forest of hoop and klinki pine (*Auracaria hensteinii* and *Auracaria cunninghamia*) in the Bulolo Valley, a region that had already been very much affected by gold-mining and commercial-logging activities. The Department of Forests wished to preserve the only extensive tract of primary forest that still survived, and in 1962 it established a flora and fauna reserve. It was named the McAdam Park after the forester who had been responsible for the original concept. Later, when a National Parks Board was formed, the park was transferred to its control.

The establishment of the National Parks Board had been initiated by Dirona Abe, one of the Papua New Guinean members of the pre-independence House of Assembly. In 1966 Abe was taken on an official tour of the United States, where he visited several national parks including Yellowstone. These visits made such an impression on Abe that when he returned to Papua New Guinea he successfully introduced a National Parks and Gardens bill into the House of Assembly. This statute gave the government powers to reserve land for national parks, monuments, botanical and zoological gardens, reserves, and sanctuaries. These areas were to be under the care, control, and management of a National Parks Board. A board of five members chaired by Abe took office in 1967, and later a National Parks Service was developed.

In addition to McAdam, another national park was established in 1969 at Varirata, and three smaller reserves were created in 1973 at Nanuk, Talele, and Cape Wom. Earlier the Baiyer River Sanctuary, based on private collections of birds of paradise and other wildlife, had been transferred to the national parks system in 1968. In 1979 an historical reserve was declared at Namenatabu.

A large number of other areas have been proposed as suitable for parks and reserves, several have been investigated and approved, and three are now waiting to be officially declared by notice in the *Government Gazette*. These are Mount Wilhelm, Horseshoe Reef, and Mount Gahavasuka. In addition, the National Parks Service administers and maintains the Kokoda Trail, a proposed national walking track.

Delays in declaring other potential parks have been partly due to financial and administrative problems, but the major constraint has been the land-tenure system. Existing parks have been developed on land owned by the government, but the establishment of any more conservation areas is likely to involve the acquisition or use of customary land. This is often fiercely resisted by the land-owners, and if a purchase is agreed upon, it is likely to be a lengthy and expensive process requiring consensus approval by all right-holders and hindered by the lack of any documented titles and surveyed boundaries. For these reasons, more emphasis is now being placed on encouraging customary landowning groups to establish their own reserves to protect threatened wildlife resources.

These reserves on customary land were given legal status by the Fauna (Protection and Control) Act of 1966, which provided for the establishment of sanctuaries, protected areas, and wildlife management areas. In sanctuaries all fauna is protected unless otherwise specified by the minister for environment and conservation. The reverse applies in protected areas that exist to prevent the hunting of particular species listed in the declaration of the area. In the wildlife management area a committee of representatives of the landowners decides on the boundaries of the area and the rules to conserve its wildlife. These often involve the protection of certain species, prohibitions on the use of firearms, and controls on hunting of outsiders. In addition, there may be provisions for a system of quotas, licenses, charges, and the collection of royalties. The regulations of each wildlife management area vary depending on local problems and needs.

The first wildlife management area was declared at Tonda in 1975. Since then eleven more management areas, three sanctuaries, and one protected area have been created. The relative significance of the wildlife management areas is illustrated by the fact that they occupy 680,184 hectares (1.68 million acres) of land and over 187,810 hectares (464,000 acres) of marine and coastal areas. In contrast, the total area of established national parks is only 4,059 hectares (10,000 acres). There is also considerable interest among landowning groups in forming new areas. They are seen as a means both of formalizing and reinforcing customary land rights and of protecting valuable wildlife resources. Sixty-one management areas have been proposed, and if they are established, they will provide an impressive network of conservation areas across the country.

The history of the development of national parks and reserves is interesting in that it has led to a dual system of conservation. The national park system, established on government land, is largely based on the overseas models provided by countries such as the United States and Australia. The wildlife management areas, established on customary land, are based on traditional forms of resource management that are unique to the South Pacific.

PARKS AND RESERVES

Table 18.1 shows the parks that have already been established and those that are being developed. The classifications used by the Papua New Guinea National Parks Service provide an indication of the values that are being preserved together with the functions of the different parks.

Varirata is classified as a national park, although its area of 1,063 hectares (2,627 acres) is relatively small by international standards. It is located (see Figure 18.1) on the Sogeri Plateau, an upland area of volcanic rock consisting of andesitic agglomerate, deeply weathered tuff, dikes, and lava. The southern

Table 18.1
National Parks in Papua New Guinea

NAME	CLASSIFICATION	AREA IN HECTARES (ACRES)	DATE ESTABLISHED
Baiyer River	Sanctuary	740 (1829)	1968
Cape Wom	International Memorial Park	105 (259)	1973
McAdam	National Park	2080 (5140)	1962
Namenatabu	Historical Reserve	27 (67)	1979
Nanuk	Provincial Park	4 (10)	1973
Talele	Nature Reserve	40 (99)	1973
Varirata	National Park	1063 (2627)	1969

boundary of the park is a steep escarpment, and along its crest are several excellent viewpoints for looking out over the Papuan coast and the Coral Sea.

The natural vegetation is one of hill forest although there are extensive patches of secondary growth and savanna where clearing has taken place in the past. There is a varied fauna with marsupials such as the agile wallaby (*Macropus agilis*), bandicott (*Peroryctes raffrayanus*), and spotted cuscus (*Phalanger maculatus*). Larger animals include wild pig and the rusa deer. Birds of paradise can also be seen in the park, and there are particular display trees where the male birds perform their courtship dances.

The major objectives in establishing the Varirata park have been to protect natural communities of plants and animals, to preserve a scenic landscape, and to provide outdoor recreation.

Traditionally, the park is part of the homeland of the Koiari people, formerly a warlike tribe with a very distinctive culture. Today the information center at the park displays photographs of their tree houses, which were built high above the ground for defensive purposes.

Varirata is 42 kilometers (26 miles) by road from Port Moresby, the national capital, and is popular for day visits by both local residents and overseas tourists. There are picnic areas with barbeque facilities and a number of sign-posted walking tracks. Educational visits to the park are encouraged. A nature trail has been marked out with the main trees identified and a leaflet provided that describes their traditional uses as foods, dyes, and medicines.

The other national park is McAdam, which is rather larger with an area of 2,080 hectares (5,140 acres). It is located in Morobe Province between the small towns of Bulolo and Wau. It is on the southern side of the valley of the Bulolo River, an area of steep and often precipitous relief. The altitude ranges from 670 to 1,980 meters (2,200 to 6,500 feet), and the general geology consists of mesozoic metamorphic rock with intrusions of pliocene porphyr.

The vegetation of the lower slopes is dominated by stands of hoop and klinki pine, which covered most of the region before the advent of commercial logging. Above an altitude of 1,000 meters (3,300 feet) the pines give way to hill forest. Over 180 species of birds have been recorded in the region of the Wau-Bulolo

Figure 18.1
National Parks and Nature Reserves in Papua New Guinea

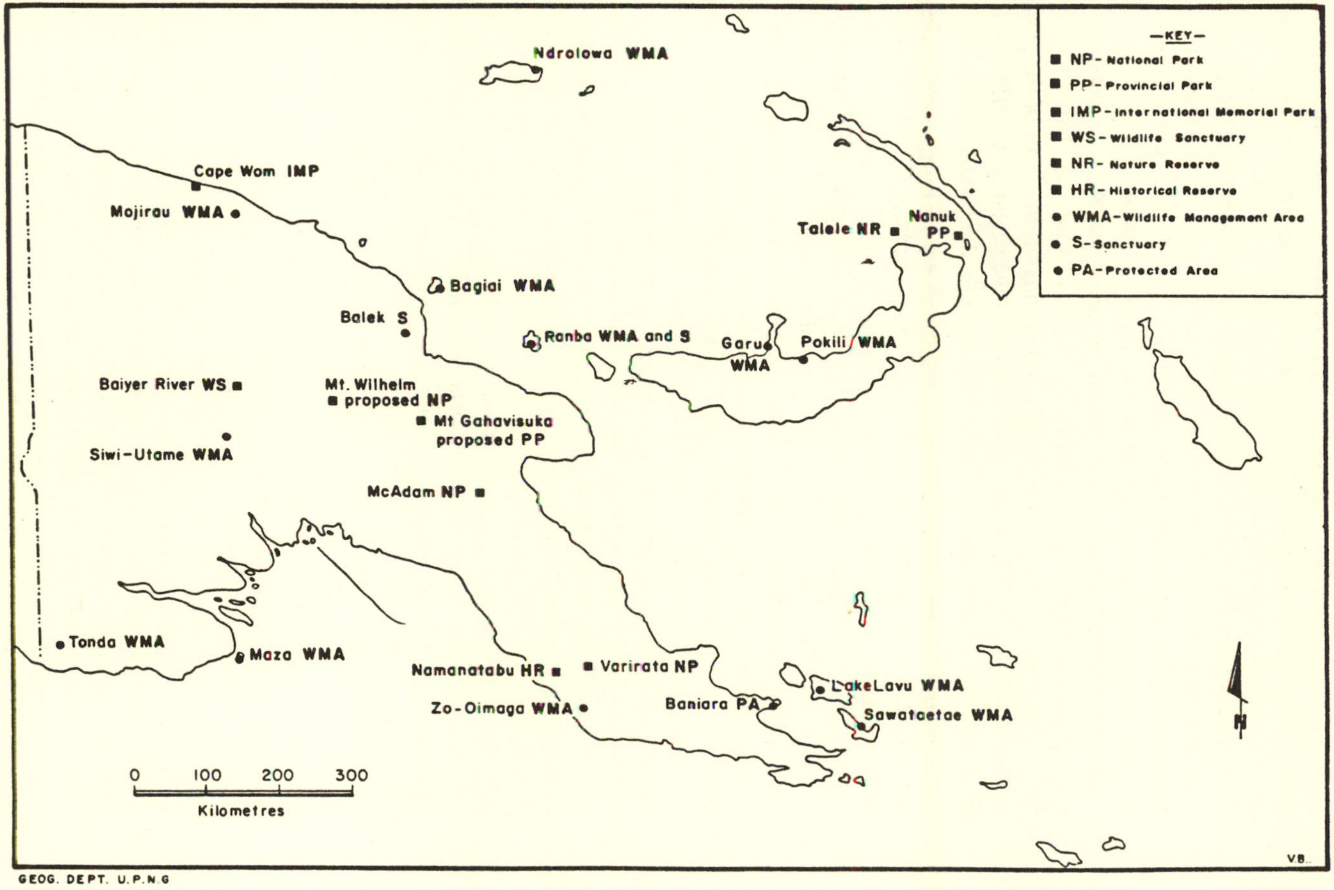

-KEY-

■ NP - National Park
■ PP - Provincial Park
■ IMP - International Memorial Park
■ WS - Wildlife Sanctuary
■ NR - Nature Reserve
■ HR - Historical Reserve
● WMA - Wildlife Management Area
● S - Sanctuary
● PA - Protected Area

Ndrolowa WMA

Cape Wom IMP ●

Mojirau WMA ●

Bagiai WMA

Talele NR ■

Nanuk
PP ■

Ronba WMA and S

Garu ●
WMA

Pokili WMA

Balek S

Mt. Wilhelm ■
proposed NP

Mt Gahavisuka
proposed PP

Baiyer River WS ■

Siwi-Utame WMA ●

McAdam NP ■

Namanatabu HR ■   ■ Varirata NP

Zo-Oimaga WMA ●

Baniara PA ●

● Lake Lavu WMA

Sawataetae WMA

● Tonda WMA

● Maza WMA

0   100   200   300
Kilometres

GEOG. DEPT. U.P.N.G

N

V8

Valley. These include ten types of bird of paradise, the cassowary, New Guinea eagle, the mountain owlet, nightjar, and diverse fruit pigeons. Mammals found in the park include the long-beaked echidna (*Zaglossus bruijni*), an endangered species protected under the Fauna (Protection and Control) Act.

At present there are only a limited number of visitors to the McAdam Park. Development has been restricted to a foot trail that has been constructed along the lower slopes. A road runs along the other side of the valley, but access from it to the park is difficult and involves crossing a fast-flowing river.

The other conservation areas administered under the National Parks Act are much smaller and have been established to fulfill diverse objectives. The Talele Nature Reserve comprises seven small coral islands off the coast of the province of East New Britain. The main aim is to protect the seabirds that nest there and the marine life of the surrounding reefs. Nearby is the Nanuk Provincial Park, a low sandy coralline cay with a vegetation of casuarina pines, coconut palms, and mangroves. In addition to its bird and marine life, it is popular with day visitors for picnicking and swimming.

The Baiyer River Sanctuary is located in the central highlands of New Guinea. It differs from the other conservation areas in that it has aviaries and cages where birds of paradise and other native fauna are kept and bred in captivity. A 1981 census identified sixty-one different species of birds and nineteen types of mammals. The sanctuary has recently acquired more land and now has an area of 740 hectares (1,829 acres), much of it rain forest which is rich in wildlife. The sanctuary has facilities for scientific research and educational visits. There are also walking tracks, a camping site, and picnic places.

The Cape Wom International Memorial Park is located on a small peninsula on the north coast of New Guinea, about 7 kilometers (4 miles) by road from Wewak, the capital of East Sepik Province. It is the site of the Japanese military surrender to the Australian forces at the end of World War II. The main significance of the park is as a war memorial, and it is of limited value for nature conservation. There are attractive beaches on the western side of the peninsula, which are popular with weekend visitors.

Another reserve, which has historical associations with World War II, is Namenatabu, located on the southern side of the country near Port Moresby. It consists of a small lake surrounded by rain forest situated on the steep sides of the Laloki Valley. The area figures in the myths of the Koiari people; an ancient dwelling place is believed to have been submerged by the lake. More recently the area was known as Blamey's Garden, after the Australian general who attempted to develop a botanical garden as a place where his troops could enjoy the diverse plant life of the country. The area is important as a forest reserve in a region of savanna that has been subject to periodic burning.

Four additional areas are being developed as part of the national parks system. All have features of particular interest and should add to the variety of ecosystems represented by the parks. The Mount Wilhelm National Park will have an area of 800 hectares (1,977 acres) and include the 4,510-meter (14,700-foot) peak

Table 18.2
Wildlife Management Areas in Papua New Guinea

NAME	AREA (hectares)	DATE
Tonda	590,000	1975
Pokili	11,000	1975
Garu	8,700	1976
Siwi-Utame	2,540	1977
Ranba	41,922	1977
Bagiai	13,760	1977
Mojirau	5,074	1978
Lake Lavu	5,000	1981
Sawataetae	700	1977
Zo-Oimaga	1,488	1981
Maza	184,230	1979
Ndrolowa	5,850	1985

that is the highest point in Papua New Guinea. Its mountain scenery and vegetation make it important for scientific research as well as outdoor recreation. Another upland area, Mount Gahavasuka, is being established as a provincial park and is of particular interest because of the large variety of orchids found there. A third park is being planned at the Horseshoe Reef, which is a part of the Papuan Barrier Reef off the south coast of the country. The long and varied coastline, with its offshore islands, coral reefs, and sea life, make Papua New Guinea especially suitable for the development of marine parks and reserves. The fourth area is the Kokoda Trail, a walking track across the Owen Stanley Range and the scene of troop movements and bitter fighting during World War II. Its 94-kilometer (58-mile) length provides a challenging walk with steep gradients and fine views.

Details of the twelve wildlife management areas are shown in Table 18.2. Most of these areas have been established on land held under customary tenure. The rules of the areas have been drawn up by management committees of local landowners to solve what they consider to be the problems affecting wildlife resources in their traditional territories.

The wildlife management areas vary considerably. They range in size from Tonda, which is 590,000 hectares (1.5 million acres), to Sawataetae, which is only 700 hectares (1,730 acres). The locations and physical characteristics of these reserves show considerable differences and a consequent diversity in the ecosystems represented.

Wildlife management areas have been established in response to the particular problems experienced by landowners in different situations. In nearly all cases there has been concern about the hunting, collecting, and fishing activities by outsiders, who have no traditional rights in the area. The greater mobility of the population and the weakening of customary controls have increased these problems, and landowners see the establishment of a wildlife management area as a means of protecting their traditional rights. This is especially important as there are few other legal means of defining their land rights and boundaries; establishing a wildlife management area can be a substitute for customary land registration. Most wildlife management rules exclude outsiders from hunting, collecting, or fishing in the area. Other rules allow some hunting by outsiders, but subject to the conditions of obtaining permission of a license and paying royalties or compensation to the landowners or the management committee.

Another major cause of concern in nearly all areas is hunting with shotguns. The indiscriminate use of this weapon is blamed for the decline in wildlife numbers. The management rules deal with firearms in a variety of ways. In some areas they are banned completely; in others they are allowed only under certain conditions. Another constraint on hunting is the exclusion of dogs from certain areas. Sometimes the regulations incorporate limitations on the amount of game that can be killed or specify the periods when hunting is allowed. They may also prohibit killing animals that are breeding or feeding young. In these ways, management rules generally reinforce customary controls that have existed in the past.

Wildlife management rules tend to emphasize the protection of the fauna itself rather than its habitat. However, in both Zo-Oimaga and Sawataetae the rules specifically control the lighting of fires, and in Pokili and Garu tree felling is prohibited. In the larger areas such as Tonda, Ranba, and Bagiai, which generally encompass the whole of a group's land, clearing for subsistence farming is allowed. In smaller areas clearing may be restricted to places where shifting cultivation has taken place before, ensuring that no new patches of primary forest are destroyed.

Tonda is the largest of the wildlife management areas. It is located in a low flat region of savanna grasslands, melaleuca forest, and swamp. The area is rich in wildlife. There are large numbers of rusa deer (*Cervus timorensis*), which have immigrated from the western part of New Guinea. The agile wallaby is also common throughout the region. There are wild pigs, cuscus, bandicoots, forest wallabies, and echidna. Both freshwater and saltwater crocodiles occur; turtles and large monitor lizards abound along the rivers. Fish are plentiful in the rivers and swamps; the main river, the Bensbach, is rich in barramundi, a large species of perch.

However, the most spectacular feature of the area is its bird life. There is a profusion of species. These include a great variety of heron, egrets, cormorants and ibis, large flocks of magpie geese and ducks, and spectacular large birds such as the pelican, cassowary, jabiru, brolga, and bustard. Birds of prey are common, especially the white-breasted sea eagle and the whistling kite. Along the rivers there are large numbers of colorful parrots, lorikeets, and kingfishers; in the evening their place will have been taken by owls, nightjars, and frogmouths.

Hunting plays an important part in the subsistence economy of the villagers who live in the area. Traditional methods are still followed using bows and arrows, snares, spears, and dogs.

Concern over hunting and fishing by outsiders, both foreign tourists and other Papua New Guineans, was one of the major reasons for the establishment of this management area. There was a concern to protect traditional hunting and land rights. The rules of the area now restrict hunting by outsiders to deer and duck; hunters are limited to a maximum of five in each case. Licenses are required for hunting and fishing, and royalties are paid to the landowners.

Two wildlife management areas have been suggested as potential sites for world heritage areas.[1] Both are located on volcanic islands off the northern coast of New Guinea. The Ranba area covers the whole of Long Island. The center of this island is occupied by a large caldera lake formed by an immense volcanic explosion that is thought to have blown out a central peak about three hundred years ago. Since then the island has been recolonized by vegetation, and it has become the home for a variety of wildlife. Sixty-nine species of birds have been recorded, including eleven types of pigeon.[2] Green hawksbill and leatherback turtles breed on the northern and western beaches; wild pig and cuscus are common further inland. The wildlife management committee consists of representatives of the five villages on the island. The rules include a total prohibition of the use of firearms and restrictions on the killing and selling of turtles. Two sanctuaries, where all wildlife is protected, have also been established: one in the interior of the island, the other on nearby Crown Island.

Bagiai Wildlife Management Area is on Karkar Island and derives its name from the crater and volcanic cone in the mountainous center of the island. The coastal regions of the island are relatively densely populated and developed; the establishment of the management area has been a result of local concern over the increased scarcity of wildlife as a result of population pressure and over-hunting. The rules of the area now forbid the use of firearms. Established exceptions allow local residents to shoot kites attacking poultry, flying foxes destroying cocoa pods, and wild pigs in garden areas. Otherwise, traditional methods of hunting must be used, and these are approved only for those with customary rights to the land. Commercially manufactured nets are prohibited to fishermen, as is the use of kerosene lamps for attracting the fish at night.

Three other wildlife management areas are located on offshore islands. The Lake Lavu area occupies a swampy depression in the interior of Ferguson Island. This area was established primarily to conserve the crocodiles living in and around the lake. The collection of their eggs is forbidden, and only customary landowners may hunt them using traditional methods. Other wildlife is also protected by bans on firearms and hunting by outsiders. The Sawataetae Wildlife Management Area is on neighboring Normanby Island. It is based on a plantation but includes coastal mangrove forest, reefs, and, further inland, the surrounding lowland rain forest and secondary growth. No shooting of any birds or animals is allowed except for wild pigs and birds damaging crops. There are also restrictions on the cutting of mangroves and on the burning of vegetation. The Ndrolowa Wildlife Management Area is on Manus Island. It was formed when local villagers became concerned about depletion of both terrestrial and marine wildlife resources. Their rules prohibit the use of firearms, explosives, roots, chemicals, lamps, commercially made nets, and spear guns.

There is one completely marine wildlife management area; this is Maza in the southwest of the country near the mouth of the Fly River. Its main objective is the conservation of the dugong, the marine mammal that now may be hunted only by traditional hand-harpoon methods from canoes.

In the remaining areas the protection of birds of paradise is a major aim. Siwi-Utame is in the highlands region and has rules restricting most forms of hunting and also felling of trees. In the Mojirau and Zo-Oimaga management areas all wildlife is protected in the central core area, but hunting by the landowners using traditional methods is allowed in the surrounding buffer zones. Siwi-Utame and Mojirau both have cassowary farming projects where the villagers are able to gain some cash income from the rearing and selling of birds that are in particular demand for food at wedding feasts and other ceremonies.

There are two other reserves that have been established under the provisions of the Fauna (Protection and Control) Act. One is Baniara Island, a protected area where all hunting of the agile wallaby is prohibited. The other is the sanctuary at Balek near the town of Madang. Balek is the site of steep limestone cliffs with caves that are the homes of large numbers of bats and birds. At the foot of the cliffs a sulfurous stream emerges from underground, and the villagers have made an attractive recreation area to encourage visitors. All wildlife is protected in the sanctuary.

ADMINISTRATION

National parks, wildlife management areas, sanctuaries, and protected areas are now administered through the Papua New Guinea Department of Environment and Conservation. Initially the parks were the responsibility of the National Parks Board, a semiautonomous body that received financial support from the national government. The implementation of board policy and the day-to-day administration were carried out by an executive director.

In 1982 a new National Parks Act clearly designated the director of national parks as the individual responsible for the administration of the act and the management of the parks. The board was abolished, and the National Parks Service became a branch of the Department of the Environment and Conservation.

The constitutional basis for the new National Parks legislation was provided by reference to the fourth National Goal of the country's Independence Constitution, which stated:

We declare our fourth National Goal to be for Papua New Guinea's natural resources and environment to be conserved and used for the collective benefit of us all, and be replenished for the benefit of future generations. We accordingly call for:

1. wise use to be made of our natural resources and the environments in and on the land or seabed, under the land, and in the air, in the interests of our development and in trust for future generations; and
2. the conservation and replenishment, for the benefit of ourselves and posterity, of the environment and its sacred, scenic and historical qualities; and
3. all necessary steps to be taken to give adequate protection to our valued birds, animals, fish, insects, plants and trees.

The objectives of the National Parks Act itself are defined as being

to provide for the preservation of the environment and the natural cultural inheritance by. . . . the conservation of sites and areas having particular biological, topographical, geological, historical, scientific or social importance.

The act contains provisions for the reservation of government land and for leasing and accepting gifts of land. It gives the authority to make regulations to control hunting, fishing, sports, vehicles, and domestic animals. Law-enforcement provisions give staff the authority to remove people breaking the rules and to impose fines.

The National Parks Service in Papua New Guinea presently operates with very limited resources. Staff and funding were reduced in 1982 as a result of budget cuts that led to the important investigative and interpretive sections being abolished. At present there are twenty-five officers in the National Parks Service, twenty of whom are rangers occupied in the management of parks.

Lack of trained specialist staff is a major constraint on the development of parks in Papua New Guinea and in other small countries of the South Pacific region. At present most of Papua New Guinea's rangers receive preservice training in forestry followed by a period of work experience. Further training is provided in New Zealand, where students take the Diploma in Parks and Recreation at Lincoln College, Canterbury, and a practical course at Turangi Ranger Training Center.

Wildlife management areas are controlled by the management committee of customary landowners. However, government wildlife officers play an important role in assisting the establishment and maintenance of the areas.

Wildlife officers are attached to provincial governments, where they should be actively involved in extension activities, and in the instigation and support of the wildlife management areas. Unfortunately, these functions have also suffered. Budget cuts have affected both staffing levels and funds available for travel to the different areas. The result is that in some regions the protected areas are rarely visited by wildlife officers. The local people feel that government has lost interest and that their conservation work needs more support.

The enforcement of rules is one of the major problems of the wildlife management areas. This is partly because of the difficulty of policing some of the larger, sparsely inhabited areas, but also because of uncertainty over procedures.

Landowners are unsure whether they themselves, the police, or government officers are responsible for apprehending offenders. It is also unclear whether prosecutions should be in the local village courts or the more formal district courts.

Papua New Guinea's relatively low level of economic development and sparse population mean that conservation areas do not generally experience the competing land-use pressures that are often found in more industrialized countries. Agriculture and domestic livestock production are not allowed in the national park areas. In the wildlife management areas they may be permitted under certain conditions. The traditional subsistence-farming methods generally involve shifting cultivation, the clearing of forest, and the planting of root crops. In some areas the landowners continue to farm areas to which they have customary rights, but the management rules generally prohibit felling and burning virgin or primary forest. Clearing land for cash crops, such as coconuts, coffee, and cocoa, is generally allowed.

An important factor is the availability of land outside the management area; conservation is likely to be more successful and under less pressure if villagers have sufficient land elsewhere for farming and hunting.

The position is similar in relation to human settlements. There are none in the parks apart from those associated with rangers' residences and park facilities. There are villages in all the larger wildlife management areas. Where management areas are smaller, villages are usually located outside the boundaries.

Mining is not allowed in wildlife management areas or national parks. Unofficial gravel quarrying occurs in the Cape Wom Park, and at McAdam Park the boundary was moved to exclude gold-mining areas along the Bulolo River.

Commercial timber operations represent a threat to tropical rain forest and wildlife habitats in many parts of Papua New Guinea. No logging is allowed in the parks or wildlife management areas. The McAdam National Park was established to protect the indigenous hoop and klinki pine. A major objective of the Pokili and Garu wildlife management areas on the island of New Britain has been to protect the megapode breeding areas from logging. When a Japanese timber company felled twenty-six trees just inside the Pokili area, it was required to pay compensation to the landowners.

Commercial logging is often a threat to conservation on customary land. At present landowners who agree to the felling of timber may receive considerable benefits in the form of royalties, rentals, and timber-right purchase fees. At Ranba on Long Island there has already been some local political pressure to disestablish the management area and allow logging. These pressures have been resisted, but they illustrate the need for integrating programs establishing reserves with those for the management of forest resources, and also for providing alternative means of providing employment and income to those landowners who are conserving their forest and wildlife resources.

One possible source of income for landowners of protected areas is through tourism. Several of the management areas would be attractive to tourists, but at present few have visitors because of their inaccessibility and the relatively high cost of travel and accommodation throughout Papua New Guinea. In Tonda the landowners already receive some income from license fees and royalties paid by visitors for fishing and hunting. In other areas, such as Bagiai and Mojirau, the management committees are discussing the possibility of entrance fees and paid guides, practices already taking place at the Balek Sanctuary.

Several of the national parks are very popular with visitors and are included on the itineraries of organized tours. The most popular are Varirata, Baiyer, and Cape Wom.

The full potential for research and education in the parks and wildlife areas has yet to be realized. Varirata and Baiyer are frequently visited by school and university groups. At Varirata there is a nature trail and a visitors center with display facilities. The Baiyer Sanctuary has a laboratory and library in addition to its collection of Papua New Guinea fauna. There have been research projects in the Tonda Wildlife Management Area, especially in association with deer farming; the area has also been featured in several natural history films.

In Papua New Guinea the concept of protected areas as being places for outdoor recreation is a relatively new one. In the Varirata National Park, for example, the great majority of the visitors are foreigners. However, as people become increasingly aware of the value of parks and other conservation areas, it is hoped that the degree of indigenous participation and support will increase. Future developments, such as the establishment of the Mount Wilhelm National Park and more marine parks, are likely to increase the potential for outdoor activities. Papua New Guineans have always had a close dependence upon and attachment to their immediate natural environment; this can be widened and strengthened by the establishment of a national network of parks and reserves.

NOTES

1. IUCN, *The World's Greatest Natural Areas: An Indicative Inventory of Natural Sites of World Heritage Quality* (Morges, Switzerland: IUCN, 1982).

2. E. Ball, "List of the Island Fauna of Long and Crown Islands, Madang District, Papua New Guinea," Appendix 4 in *Long Island*, by E. Lindgren (Port Moresby: Department of Agriculture Stock and Fisheries, 1974).

BIBLIOGRAPHY

Constitution of the Independent State of Papua New Guinea. *Revised Laws of Papua New Guinea*, Chapter 1.

Eaton, P. *Grassroots Conservation: Wildlife Management Areas in Papua New Guinea.* Land Studies Centre Report 86/1, University of Papua New Guinea, 1986.

———. *Land Tenure and Conservation: Protected Areas in the South Pacific.* South Pacific Regional Environmental Programme Topic Review 17. Noumea: South Pacific Commission, 1985.

Fauna (Protection and Control) Act. *Revised Laws of Papua New Guinea*, Chapter 154.

Morauta, L., J. Pernetta, and W. Heaney, eds. *Traditional Conservation in Papua New Guinea: Implications for Today*. Port Moresby: Institute of Applied Social and Economic Research, 1982.

National Parks Act (1982). *Revised Laws of Papua New Guinea*, Chapter 157.

National Parks Service. *Report of the Baiyer River Sanctuary, 1975 to 1980*. Port Moresby: Office of Information, c. 1981.

Winslow, J. H., ed. *The Melanesian Environment*. Canberra: Australian National University Press, 1977.

PERU 19

Marc J. Dourojeanni

Peru is the best synthesis of South American ecology and the center of South American cultural development for a thousand years. In spite of their being less well studied than those in neighboring countries, the number of identified species and endemisms in Peru is astonishingly high and increasing rapidly. The national territory is an emporium of useful genetic resources for world agriculture, forestry, and animal husbandry. As a consequence, Peruvian protected areas are critical to the conservation of mankind's natural heritage and the preservation of biological diversity on a global scale.

HISTORY

Peru has only recently developed an interest in the problems associated with conserving representative samples of its natural ecosystems and genetic resources. Its first national park, Cutervo, was established in 1961, and there were only two additions to the system prior to 1970: Tingo Maria National Park and Pampa Galeras National Reserve. However, between 1972 and 1987, Peru has recovered lost time, and today there are twenty-three protected areas comprising over 5 million hectares, 4 percent of the nation's land area (see Figure 19.1).

The most fertile period for the establishment of protected areas was between 1972 and 1979, under the regime of the Generals Velasco and Morales-Bermudez. Fifty percent of the existing units, comprising 92 percent of the currently protected area, were established during this period.

Figure 19.1
Conservation Areas in Peru

UNIDADES DE CONSERVACION
EN EL PERU

CDC - PERU
1987

UNIDADES	HAS
1 PN Cutervo	2,500
2 PN Tingo Maria	18,000
3 PN Huascarán	340,000
4 PN Cerros de Amotape	91,300
5 PN Manu	1'532,806
6 PN Rio Abiseo	274,520
7 PN Yanachaga-Chemellén	122,000
8 RN Paracas	335,000
9 RN Pampa Galeras	6,500
10 RN Titicaca	36,180
11 RN Junín	53,000
12 RN Calipuy	64,000
13 RN Lachay	5,070
14 RN Pacaya-Samiria	2'080,000
15 RN Salinas y Aguada blanca	366,936
16 SN Calipuy	4,500
17 SN Huayllay	6,815
18 SN Pampas del Heath	102,109
19 SN Lagunas de Mejía	690.6
20 SH Chacamarca	2,500
21 SH Pampas de Ayacucho	300
22 SH Macchu Picchu	32,592
23 SN Ampay	3,635.5

Table 19.1

Protected Areas in the National Conservation System, 1988

CONSERVATION AREA	AREA (hectares)	LOCATION (department)	YEAR ESTABLISHED
National Parks			
1. Manu	1,532,806	Madre de Dios-Cusco	1973
2. Huascarán	340,000	Ancash	1975
3. Abiseo	274,520	San Martin	1983
4. Yanachaga-Chemillén	122,000	Pasco	1986
5. Cerros de Amotape	91,300	Tumbes-Piura	1975
6. Tingo Maria	18,000	Huanuco	1965
7. Cutervo	2,500	Cajamarca	1961
National Reserves			
1. Pacaya-Samiria	2,080,000	Loreto	1972
2. Salinas-Aguada Blanca	366,936	Arequipa	1979
3. Paracas[a]	335,000	Ica	1975
4. Calipuy	64,000	La Libertad	1981
5. Junin	53,000	Junin	1974
6. Titicaca	36,180	Puno	1978
7. Pampa Galeras[b]	6,500	Ayacucho	1967
8. Lachay	5,070	Lima	1977
National Sanctuaries			
1. Pampas del Heath	102,109	Madre de Dios	1983
2. Huayllay	6,815	Junin	1974
3. Calipuy	4,500	La Libertad	1981
4. Ampay	3,635	Apurimac	1987
5. Lagunas de Mejia	6,691	Arequipa	1984
Historical Sanctuaries			
1. Macchu Picchu	32,592	Cusco	1981
2. Chacamarca[c]	2,500	Junin	1974
3. Pampas de Ayacucho[c]	300	Ayacucho	1980
Total	5,263,360		

Source: General Directorate of Forest and Fauna and Conservation Data Center of Peru.

Notes: [a] Includes 217,594 ha. corresponding to the marine territory not included in the national total.

[b] Really includes some 75,000 ha. not indicated here. Although protected, this area is not legally designated as a National Reserve.

[c] Exclusively historical interest, not developed in text.

PARKS AND RESERVES

Table 19.1 presents the protected areas of Peru, grouped in the categories recognized by the Forest and Fauna Law. Taken as a whole, the conservation system is reasonably representative of Peru's ecological diversity, but it is still far from ideal. The 128 million square kilometers (49 million square miles) of Peru are a true ecological summary of South America, and the diversity is so

Table 19.2
Conservation Areas Proposed to Be Established in Peru to Improve the Ecological Representativeness of the System

CONSERVATION AREA	APPROXIMATE AREA (hectares)	LOCATION (departments)	STATUS OF STUDIES
National Parks			
Loreto	2,000,000	Loreto	Intermediate
Sira	600,000-1,000,000	Ucayali and Junin	Intermediate
Cutibireni	236,000-1,000,000	Junin and Cusco	Preliminary
Tambopata	500,000	Madre de Dios	Intermediate
National Reserves			
Atiquipa	40,000	Arequipa	Intermediate
Loma en el Norte	20,000	La Libertad	Intermediate
National Sanctuaries			
Este del Maranon	98,125	Amazonas	Final studies
Cordillera del Condor	85,000	Amazonas	Preliminary
Valle de los Volcanes	60,000	Arequipa	Preliminary
Namballe	23.690	Cajamarca	Final studies
Manglares	15,000	Tumbes	Preliminary
Huaros	500	Lima	Preliminary
Zarate	600	Lima	Intermediate

great that it will probably be impossible to protect all that should be protected. Still, there are many proposals to augment the system and make it more representative of the ecological diversity of Peru. These proposals are summarized in Table 19.2. If all these proposals were to be adopted, the total area in conservation units could be increased by 3 to 5 million hectares, raising the percentage of protected land at the national level to 6 or 7 percent.

Today, Peru only has one area that protects a marine ecosystem, but legislation is being considered (the Environment Code) that would establish a category of marine parks.

In addition, Peru has three Biosphere Reserves and three World Heritage Sites. See Table 19.3.

Finally, it should be indicated that Peru has other protected areas that are not recognized as components of the conservation system. These include five national forests (5.25 million hectares, 13 million acres), two protected forests, two hunting reserves, and three reserved zones.

Manu National Park

Manu National Park is undoubtedly the highlight of the national conservation system. Its 1.5 million hectares enclose one of the most pristine territories on

Table 19.3
Other Protected Areas in Peru

PROTECTED AREAS AND COMPONENT UNITS	AREA (hectares)	LOCATION (department)	DATE ESTABLISHED
Biosphere Reserves			
Noroeste	231,402		1977
(Cerros de Amotape N. Park	91,300)	Tumbes and Piura	
(de Tumbes National Forest	75,102)	Tumbes	
(El Angolo Hunting Grounds	65,000)	Piura	
Huascarán	399,239		1977
(Huascarán National Park	340,000)	Ancash	
(Agricultural Areas	59,239)	Ancash	
Manu	1,881,200		1977
(Manu National Park	1,532,806)	Madre de Dios and Cusco	
(Manu Reserved Zone	300,200)	Madre de Dios	
(Agricultural Areas	48,194)	Madre de Dios	
World Heritage Sites			
Huascarán	340,000		1985
(Huascarán National Park	340,000)	Ancash	
Machu Picchu	32,592		1985
(Machu Picchu N. Sanctuary	32,592)	Cusco	
Manu	1,532,806	Madre de Dios	1988
(Manu National Park	1,532,806)	and Cusco	

Source: Ministry of Agriculture

earth with one of the highest levels of plant and animal diversity ever recorded. The landscape is incomparable, and there is reasonable evidence that its dense forests protect the ruins of what could well be the mysterious Paititi, with its promises of new revelations concerning the history of Peru.

The park occupies a great part of the Manu Province in Madre de Dios Department as well as a small portion of the Cusco Department. It extends from some 4,500 meters (14,800 feet) above sea level along the eastern range of the Andes to some 500 meters (1,640 feet) in the basin of the Manu River near the Amazon Plains. It includes climates with average annual temperatures of 20° to 24° Celsius (68° to 75° Fahrenheit) in the lower elevations and barely 5° Celsius (40° Fahrenheit) in the higher elevations. There are regions where rains measure 8,000 millimeters (300 inches) per year and other regions where the precipitation is barely 1,500 millimeters (60 inches). Enormous ecological and genetic diversity is the result.

The park's vegetation corresponds to several life zones: wet forest, which is the most extensively represented; rain forest, semisaturated rain forest, and rain paramo in the lower montane; montane and subalpine altitudinal belts of the subtropical latitudinal region; and in very small proportion, the premontane wet forest of the tropical region. Very few botanical studies have been conducted in the area, but its rich flora is known to be unique.

The park's fauna is better known. Some detailed studies have been made concerning birds, primates, caimans, and otters, among other groups. Manu is believed to have the greatest diversity of birds in the world. Almost 600 species have been detected in a few hectares surrounding the Cocha Cashu Biology Station. In all probability 900 or more species exist in the park, more than 10 percent of all the world's known birds. Many animals that face extinction in most of Peru are still common in Manu. Among them are the spectacled bear (*Tremarctos ornatus*), a species of brocket deer (*Mazama chunyi*), the giant armadillo (*Priodontes giganteus*), giant otter (*Pteronura brasiliensis*), the jaguar (*Leo onca*), diverse primates, and the Andean deer (*Hippocamelus antisensis*). In Manu the fauna is easy to see. At the edge of the river one can see hundreds of caimans, river turtles, capyvaras, birds, and frequently a majestic jaguar. From the river one can also observe the famous "colpa de los Guacamayos" where thousands of macaws sometimes gather to obtain salt. In the forest it is possible to easily see monkeys, tapirs, and often the impressive spectacle of a scattering herd of hundreds of peccaries.

Huascarán National Park

Huascarán National Park is most distinguished by its splendid high mountain landscapes. Included within its boundaries is virtually all the Cordillera Blanca that forms the eastern flank of the Huaylas Valley. It is named after Peru's highest mountain, one of seven snowy peaks, each measuring more than 6,000 meters (19,600 feet), which together constitute one of the major international foci of attraction for climbers and mountaineers. Alpamayo Peak is believed by many to be the most beautiful mountain in the world.

Huascarán is important not only for its countryside and for the Andes, but also because it possesses an important treasure of flora and fauna with numerous rare or nearly extinct species. Further, the conservation of its vegetation is of great importance for the prevention of natural disasters like landslides and floods, for the provision of clean water to the Huaylas and Conchucos valleys, and as the source of rivers, especially the Santa.

Huascarán is located in Ancash Department and boasts altitudes that range from 3,200 to 6,768 meters (10,500 to 22,200 feet) above sea level. Its average annual temperature is about 3° Celsius (37° Fahrenheit), but the higher elevations can be much colder. The average annual precipitation is about 880 millimeters (35 inches). The geological materials consist principally of upper Jurassic marine sedimentary rocks, and plutonic rocks of the Cretaceous-Tertiary age that form part of the Andean batholith.

The vegetation is typical of montane moist forest at the lower elevations and subalpine wet paramo and alpine rain tundra at the higher elevations. Beautiful forests of *Polylepis* are found around the Lake of Llanganuco and in many other places. There are smaller forests of *Budleia* (butterfly bush) and an important stand of the rare *Puya raimondii*, probably the best in the country.

Distinctive mammals include vicuna, spectacled bear, gray deer, Andean fox, mountain viscacha, and three species of felines: pampas cat (*Felis colocolo*), mountain cat (*Felis jacobita*), and puma (*Felis concolor*). Numerous birds include the condor and many aquatic species. Among the latter is the endangered torrent duck (*Merganetta armata*).

The countryside of Huascarán National Park exhibits a conjunction of peaks, lakes, canyons, streams, and waterfalls. The area called Llanganuco, after the lake of this name, is the most well known and most frequently visited, but there are other equally beautiful areas including those surrounding Paron and Santa Cruz lakes. The park administration has organized various tourist circuits that permit observation of the countryside during a hike of one or more days' duration. The park is particularly appreciated by mountain climbers, but unfortunately several have sacrificed their lives to its peaks.

Cerro de Amotape National Park

This park protects essential remnants of the dry forests on Peru's northern coast. It begins at the mountain chain known as the Cerros de Amotape, which runs from south to north. Altitudes range from 200 to 1,613 meters (650 to 5,290 feet) above sea level. The geologic materials are principally marine sedimentary facies of Silurian-Devonian age; there are no older Paleozoic rocks. Lithologies include schists, dark-colored quartzite, and black slates.

With an average annual temperature of 24° Celsius (74° Fahrenheit) and an average annual precipitation of 900 millimeters (35 inches), the vegetation is typical of thorn woodland, dry and very dry forest, both tropical and premontane. Common species include *Prosopis* (mesquite), *Loxopterygium*, *Tabebuia*, *Alseis*, *Cesalpinea corymbosa*, *Bombax discolor*, *Capparis angulata*, and *Pithecolobium multiflorum*. *Tillandsin usneoides* (Spanish moss) is common in the trees.

Although wildlife is generally abundant, there is great interest in the many species in danger of extinction. Cerros de Amotape probably contains the last examples of the Tumbes caiman. There are also white-winged guans (*Penelope albipennis*) and jaguars (*Panthera onca*). More than sixty species of birds are endemic to the areas as well as diverse mammals including the white-necked tree squirrel (*Sciurus stramineus*) and a species of leaf-earred mouse (*Phyllotis gerbillus*). In the dry forest of the northeast the fauna of the original Amazon fuse with that of the coast and the sierra. As a consequence, the Andean condor and the jungle condor can both be seen.

Yanachaga-Chemillén National Park

This new national park is located in the central Amazon between the Palcazu and Pozuzo valleys and relatively near Lima. Its topography is very rough, consisting primarily of tropical wet forest and semisaturated rain forest in the

high jungle. It is an important watershed, serving several small towns and adjacent agricultural land.

Many endangered species of plants and animals are present in the park. Among
the animals, the most interesting are the giant armadillo (*Priodontes giganteus*
or *Priodontes maximus*), the naked-tailed armadillo (*Cabassous unicinctus*), the
spectacled bear (*Tremarctos ornatus*), the Pudu deer (*Pudu mephistophiles*), the
jaguar, the giant anteater (*Myrmecophaga tridactyla*), and several species of
primates and birds.

The park's beautiful scenery and its proximity to the nation's capital are
expected to make it a major tourist destination, and it is likely to undergo rapid
development.

Abiseo National Park

This park is important both for its nature—representative of the cloud forest,
high jungle, and jungle summit regions—and for the interesting archaeological
remains known as Great Pajaten. The park is home to a number of endangered
species including the spectacled bear, yellow-tailed woolly monkey (*Lagothrix
flavicauda*), giant armadillo, and possibly the mountain tapir (*Tapirus pinchaque*).

A great part of the Abiseo are well-developed late successional forests. They
correspond to the rain and wet forest appropriate to the montane and lower
montane zones. The general physiography is characterized by steep slopes and
relatively broad valleys typical of the high jungle. In part this area resembles a
Pleistocene wildlife refuge, which enhances its value to scientific research.

Abiseo National Park is today inaccessible to tourism. Plans for protection
and scientific investigation have been initiated, some of them in cooperation
with the University of Colorado and various Peruvian scientific institutions.

Tingo Maria National Park

The main value of this area is the conservation of a large cave of guacharos,
or oilbirds (*Steatornis caripensis*), whose food residues provide the foundation
for a complex food chain composed of more than seventy species of invertebrates.

The cave is found in the high jungle, near the city of Tingo Maria, and
lamentably a large part of the habitat that surrounds the cave has been deforested
and dedicated to the illegal cultivation of coca, destroying the natural palms and
broadleaf trees, whose fruits are a part of the guacharos' diet.

Cutervo National Park

This park is located in Cutervo Province in northern Cajamarca and enclosed
on the eastern part by the Cordillera de Tarros. Cutervo was Peru's first national

park. It is very similar to Tingo Maria, and like Tingo Maria, it was established to protect caves inhabited by owls.

Both Tingo Maria and Cutervo should be reclassified as national sanctuaries.

Pacaya-Samiria National Reserve

This is the largest of the conservation areas in Peru. Despite being classified a national reserve, all of its 2,080,000 hectares (5,140,000 acres) are government-owned thus guaranteeing its protection. Pacaya-Samiria was established with 1,387,500 hectares (3,428,500 acres) and expanded to its present size in 1982. Initially this reserve was managed for fisheries, especially for exploitation of the paiche (*Arapaima gigas*). It has been considered a reserved zone since the 1940s and was administered by the Fisheries Sector for many years, even before its establishment as a national reserve.

The reserve is located in Loreto Department, at the confluence of the Ucayali and Marañón rivers, and encompasses the entire watershed of the Pacaya and Samiria rivers. It is the only protected area in Peru typical of the lower jungle. Its average annual temperature and precipitation are, respectively, 26° Celsius (78° Fahrenheit) and 3,000 millimeters (118 inches).

The vegetation is that of the tropical moist forest with a very complicated structure and enormous diversity. Among the most conspicuous trees are *Chorisia integrifolia*, *Calycophyllum*, *Virola*, *Cedrela odorata* (cedar), and *Calophyllum brasiliensis*. Palm trees are very abundant, among them *Scheelea*, *Phytelephas*, *Socratea*, *Iriartea*, *Astrocaryum*, *Mauritia*, *Euterpe*, and *Jessenia*.

The area is rich in aquatic fauna including a wide variety of fish, tortoises and caimans, manatee, dolphins (*Sotalia* and *Inia*), and a variety of aquatic birds. Almost all species of vertebrates and invertebrates belonging to the lower Amazon of Peru reside here including a variety of interesting primates that have been the subjects of scientific studies.

Salinas-Aguada Blanca National Reserve

This reserve is located in the highest lands of the Arequipa and Moquegua departments. Its habitat is dominated by high plateau, but in addition there are various volcanoes, mountains, and lakes making some of its views extremely beautiful. The average annual temperature varies from less than 3° to 9° Celsius (37°–48° Fahrenheit), and the average annual precipitation is between 200 and 500 millimeters (8 and 20 inches). The vegetation belongs to the formations known as subalpine, montane, and nival desert scrub, and, to a lesser extent, alpine moist and wet tundra, and subalpine moist paramo. The forests of *Polylepis* are noteworthy.

Most notable among the fauna are the vicuna, taruca, gray deer, puma, Andean fox, viscacha, and wild guinea pig. On lakes like Salinas there are three species of flamingos (*Phoenicopterus ruber, jamesi*, and *andinus*) and many other aquatic birds.

The major disturbances to the area, besides the running of livestock by peasants, are the gathering of firewood, poaching, mining, and hydroelectric development.

Paracas National Reserve

Paracas has exceptional value among the national system of protected areas because it is the only reserve that conserves marine ecosystems, which make up 65 percent of its surface area. It is also the only reserve that protects inland desert and a part of the coastal desert. The reserve also contains important remains of the famous culture that bears its name.

The reserve contains 335,000 hectares (827,785 acres), of which 217,594 hectares are marine and 117,406 are terrestrial. Altitudes range from sea level to 786 meters (2,580 feet) where a sparse loma vegetation exists. Located on and south of the Paracas Peninsula, in the Pisco and Ica provinces of the Ica Department, the reserve enjoys a climate where mean temperatures vary between 15.5° Celsius (60° Fahrenheit) in the coldest month and 22° Celsius (71° Fahrenheit) in the warmest. Average annual precipitation is almost nil, measuring barely 2 millimeters (.08 inches). Because the Paracas Peninsula and the San Gallán and Independence islands are part of the so-called Coastal Cordillera, now largely submerged, the sea conditions are very peculiar, giving rise to many endemic species.

The topography is flat or rolling. The highest hills near the sea generally form an abrupt coastline with high cliffs, rocky beaches, or narrow strips of sand. Toward the south the beaches become larger. The wind has randomly eroded the coasts, forming grandiose natural monuments. In the higher hills, *Tillandsia*, *Solanum ferreyrae*, *Cressa*, and other plants grow. The rest of the habitat is absolutely barren of vegetation. Only in the line of the beaches can one see a few halophytes or salt grass species of the genera *Distichlis* and *Sessuvium*. Of course, the sea is rich in phytoplankton and algae.

The fauna is abundant, especially in fish and aquatic fowl. Among the endemic fishes is the *Syngnathus independencis*. Notable among the birds are the condor, guano birds (pelicans, cormorants, and boobies), Humboldt penguin, and flamingo. The dozens of other species include gulls, sea gulls, frigates, avocets, oyster catchers, sandpipers, shear waters, petrels, great grebes, terns, falcons, albatross, cabo dove, golondrinas, dotterel, lapwing, skimmers, and zarcillo. In the sea or along the coastline live the two species of seal that exist in the country: *Otaria flavescens* and *Arctocephalus australis*. *Lutra felina* survives here, and the tortoises *Chelonia mydas* and *Dermochelys coriacea* and different whales can be observed.

Calipuy National Reserve

The essential purpose of Calipuy Reserve is the conservation of a declining population of guanaco (*Lama guanicoe*) in the northernmost extremity of their range. Previously these animals lived primarily on the hills of the coast and in the western spurs of the Andean range. Today 300 to 500 guanaco remain within the reserve.

Within the reserve altitudes range from 800 to 3,600 meters (2,600 to 11,800 feet), with the relief being broken by numerous gorges and canyons. Average annual temperature is estimated to be 11° Celsius (52° Fahrenheit) with precipitation of about 500 millimeters (20 inches), but there are large climatic variations depending upon the elevation.

The vegetation is desert scrub at the levels premontane, lower montane and montane, and montane steppe. Prior to the establishment of Calipuy, this type of flora was not well represented in the national conservation system. The wildlife includes guanacos, spectacled bear, and other species indigenous to the western Andean slope.

Junin National Reserve

The Junin Reserve is unique in Peru because it completely protects the country's second largest lake. It is located on the border of Junin and Pasco departments and encompasses the lake and associated marshes and part of the surrounding plains. Altitudes vary only from 4,000 to 4,125 meters (13,100 to 13,500 feet). The average annual temperature is about 4° Celsius (39° Fahrenheit), and the average annual precipitation is close to 800 millimeters (31 inches).

The vegetation in the lake and its surroundings is typically lacustrine, with diverse species of algae, aquatic and emergent plants like *Scirpus rigida* and *californicus*. At higher altitudes there are highlands with typical pastures and diversified traditional agriculture.

The fauna is particularly rich in birds with almost 100 species identified. Most notable of the species is the Taczanowski grebe, which is endemic to the lake. There are numerous ducks, grebes, herons, ibises, geese, rails, flamingos, etc. The lake is at the center of the range of the Junin frog (*Batrachophynus macrostomus* and *Batrachophynus brachydactylus*). In its waters are two species of fish of the genus *Orestias* (toothed carp) as well as a catfish (*Pygidium oroyae*). Wild guinea pigs (*Cavia tschudii*) live in the marsh surrounding the lake and in the rocks and in the stone walls of the farms.

Titicaca National Reserve

Titicaca is an ecological universe in itself. It is the largest freshwater lake in South America, and at an elevation of 3,814 meters (12,500 feet), it is by far the highest large lake in the world. Titicaca has been given a high priority for protection because of the rapidity with which its most biologically interesting areas were being destroyed.

As a result, in 1978 the reserve was established in two sections, each covering extensive lake vegetation fields and together comprising 36,180 hectares (89,400 acres). The Puno Sector has 29,150 hectares and the Ramis Sector has 7,030 hectares. The primary objective of this and all reserves is the sustained utilization of the wildlife resources, and the need for management to achieve this objective can be fairly urgent in certain cases. In Titicaca, as in Junin and Pampa Galeras, the objective of optimum use has been compromised to avoid conflict with local traditions and customs that, in the case of Titicaca, are ancient.

Centuries ago, an indigenous group called the Uro were exiled to the lake and now live on artificial floating islands. The Uro hunt, fish, and exploit "totora" (*Scirpus*). The initial effort has been to rationalize such use.

The reserve's water temperature varies from 9° to 14° Celsius (48° to 62° Fahrenheit). Its vegetation consists of algae, submerged vegetation of the genera *Elodea* and *Potamogeton*, and "totorales" of *Scirpus*. There are also *Lemma*, *Nostoc*, and other plants typical of this environment. The fowl, like those of Junin, are most abundant and diversified, and there are also various species of fish and amphibians, some of them endemic.

Pampa Galeras National Reserve

Of all the protected areas of Peru the most famous internationally is unquestionably the National Reserve of Pampa Galeras, dedicated to the conservation and rational utilization of the vicuna.

This reserve was established in 1967 based on studies by the National Agrarian University, which had confirmed that the greatest surviving nucleus of vicunas existed in this region. From its beginning in 1965, this project had as its goal to save the vicuna from extinction and to increase the population to the level where its products could be scientifically harvested to benefit the local communities. This goal was accomplished, and at the end of the 1970s it stood as an unprecedented success in Latin America.

Pampa Galeras really includes an area of some 75,000 hectares (185,000 acres) although only 6,500 hectares (16,000 acres) are designated by law. The national reserve should not be confused with the area dedicated to the Ministry of Agriculture's special project for the rational utilization of the vicuna. The latter area includes many hundreds of thousands of hectares, which should grow from year to year, and it is also administered by Pampa Galeras. The reserve is located in the Lucanas Province of the Avacucho Department. Altitudes within the reserve proper vary from 3,950 to 4,500 meters (13,000 to 14,800 feet), but altitudes are higher outside the formally designated boundaries. The average annual temperature is close to 5° Celsius (41° Fahrenheit), and the average annual precipitation is 800 millimeters (31 inches) although prolonged droughts occur frequently.

The area is primarily gramineous steppe, but there are also forests of *Polylepis* and *Buddleia* and a stand of *Puya raimondii*. There are cushions of *Distichia* and extensive areas with *Parastrephia*. There are more than 150 registered species of flora. The vicuna is the most abundant species of wildlife, but there are also tarucas, guanacos, deer, pumas, foxes, skunks, viscachas, wildcats, and a great number of birds, among them the condor.

Lachay National Reserve

Lachay is the only national reserve to protect "lomas," the vegetated hills of the coastal desert. Lachay is classified as a reserve because it belongs to a peasant community and consequently could not legally be designated as a national park. It consists of 5,070 hectares (12,500 acres) in the Chancay Province, 80 kilometers (50 miles) north of Lima and about 100 to 500 meters (330 to 1,640 feet) above sea level. The average annual temperature is 17° Celsius (62° Fahrenheit), and the average annual precipitation is less than 100 millimeters (4 inches).

The vegetation that grows in Lachay is typical of the lomas, where water is obtained exclusively from the condensation of coastal fog. In the higher regions there are forest relicts of *Capparis*, *Caesalpinia*, and *Carica*. Many plants and invertebrates are endemic to the area. A diverse fauna also includes an especially varied population of birds.

Pampas del Heath National Sanctuary

This recently created sanctuary in southeastern Peru conserves the only Peruvian example of the formation known as the wet Chaco province. It is an extensive prairie meadowland interrupted by forest galleries. Among the most renowned species living in the area are the marsh deer (*Blastocerus dichotomus*) and the maned wolf (*Chrysocyon brachyurus*). Both are in danger of extinction.

This area has yet to be opened to tourism, and there has been no development.

Huayllay National Sanctuary

This unit protects a spectacular geological phenomenon consisting of rocks that have eroded to form a gigantic and extensive "stone forest."

Huayllay was established in 1974 and occupies 6,815 hectares (16,800 acres) of the Pasco Department. The terrain varies from 4,100 to 4,543 meters (13,500 to 14,900 feet) above sea level. The geologic material consists of facies of continental and sedimentary volcanic types, which range in age from upper Tertiary to Quaternary. They contain rocks that erode easily, giving rise to shapes that in some places resemble a fossil forest, and in others cyclopean statues, arches, and as many other figures as the imagination can conceive. The rock formations are interspersed with meadows, and there are small streams, caves, and other places of interest.

The average annual temperature is near 5° Celsius (41° Fahrenheit), and the average annual precipitation is some 800 millimeters (31 inches). The vegetation is of the subalpine wet paramo type. The fauna is typical of this altitude, with viscachas, wild guinea pigs, deer, foxes, and skunks, as well as Andean geese (*Chloephaga melanoptera*) and other birds like *Colaptes rupicola*, *Vanellus resplandens*, *Nothoprocta ornata*, and *Tinamotis pentlandi*.

Calipuy National Sanctuary

This sanctuary conserves an important and dense stand of *Puya raimondii*, which also exist in the Huascarán National Park and in the Pampas Galeras National Reserve. Established in 1981, it covers 4,500 hectares (11,100 acres) just to the north of the Calipuy National Reserve in La Libertad Department.

It is between 3,600 and 4,300 meters (11,800 and 14,100 feet) above sea level, characterized by an average annual temperature of 6° Celsius (43° Fahrenheit) and an average annual precipitation of some 750 millimeters (30 inches). The vegetation is typical of the highest regions of the north central Andes, and it appears that the spectacled bear also lives here.

Machu Picchu Historical Sanctuary

Machu Picchu is an Inca fortified city not far from Cusco, the capital of the Inca Empire. It is among the most marvelous of human works, and it has been a worldwide attraction since its discovery in 1911.

In Machu Picchu the most admirable quality is the aesthetic harmony between nature and architecture. To retain this harmony it was important to preserve both the ruins and their natural setting. In 1981, after much delay, a national sanctuary of 32,592 hectares (80,500 acres) was created for this purpose in the Urubamba Province, Cusco Department. The sanctuary encompasses the ruins of Machu Picchu and various others in the proximity.

The sanctuary's altitude varies from 1,452 to 3,600 meters (4,800 to 11,800 feet) above sea level. The average annual temperature is about 16° Celsius (61° Fahrenheit), and the average annual precipitation is 1,500 to 3,000 millimeters (60 to 120 inches). The relief of this region is very rough, and the geology is fairly complex. The vegetation is that of the lower montane moist and wet forest. There are numerous ferns including the tree fern *Cyathea*. There are palms and more than ninety species of orchids. The forests are rich in Lauraceae. Trees include *Cedrela*, *Swietenia*, and *Podocarpus*, all valued for their lumber. Forests of *Polylepis* appear at the higher elevations.

Despite the disturbance to natural ecosystems, the fauna is varied. There are endangered species like the spectacled bear and, probably, the deer *Mazama chunyi*. There are a wide variety of other mammals including sloth bears, otters, wildcats, ocelots, the tayra (*Tayra barbara*) and other weasels, red deer, and various primates. Residents of the heights include gray deer, viscachas, Andean fox, and pumas. The mammals are an amalgamation of the species of the sierra and of the edge of the jungle. This amalgamation is also apparent in the population of birds. The cock of the rocks (*Rupicola peruviana*), Peru's national bird, is very common.

Ampay National Sanctuary

Ampay is the most recently established of Peru's protected areas. Near the city of Abancay in the southeastern part of the Andes, it serves to protect a well-conserved stand of *Podocarpus*, a tropical conifer that was heavily exploited in the past. The area is also rich in endemic birds.

Lagunas de Mejia National Sanctuary

This small sanctuary preserves critical habitat for migratory birds along the South Pacific coast. It consists of coastal ponds and marshes south of Mollendo and provides excellent opportunities for bird-watchers, especially those interested in waders, ducks, and shorebirds.

ADMINISTRATION

Together, the national parks, national reserves, national sanctuaries, and historical sanctuaries of Peru constitute the national system of conservation units. In the parks and sanctuaries the land is legally inviolable and largely untouched. In the national reserves the land is not necessarily government-owned, and other uses are allowed so long as they are compatible with conservation purposes.

Although the national system of conservation units is under the administration of the General Directorate of Forestry and Wildlife of the Ministry of Agriculture, several regional governments do participate in the financing and management of parks and other protected areas under special agreements with the central government.

Generally speaking, the system is underdeveloped. Only Manu and Pampa Galeras are relatively well protected and managed. A second group, including Paracas, Huascarán, Abiseo, Yanachaga-Chemillén, Titicaca, Machu Picchu, Pacaya-Samiria, and Lachay, have little infrastructure and limited staff. The other designated areas are still without permanent protection. The budget for parks and protected areas is very small, probably less than $1 million a year for the entire system. There are only about 160 rangers to protect more than five million hectares of difficult terrain, and most of them are undertrained and ill-equipped. There are fewer than a dozen professional staff (foresters or biologists) in the field. To date, management plans have been developed for Manu, Paracas,

Lachay, Titicaca, Pacaya-Samiria, and Pampa Galeras. Currently, tourism is important only in Machu Picchu, Huascarán, and Paracas.

Almost every protected area in the system is threatened. The most common threats are road construction (Manu, Huascarán, Paracas, Cerros de Amotape), mining (Huascarán, Salinas-Aguada Blanca), oil exploration (Manu, Pacaya-Samiria), coca farming (Tingo Maria, Abiseo), illegal livestock grazing (Huascarán, Manu, Lachay, Abiseo, Cerros de Amotape), poaching and removal of plants and firewood (almost every one), pollution (Paracas, Titicaca, Junin, Pacaya-Samiria), and agricultural, fisheries, or tourism development (Paracas, Cutervo, Huascarán, Machu Picchu) and so on.

The people of Peru are beginning to react to the threats. Leadership is being provided by local private conservation associations. The Peruvian Foundation for Nature Conservancy and the Peruvian Association for Nature Conservancy are two of more than forty relatively new and increasingly active groups devoted to the cause of conservation.

Several universities, but especially the National Agrarian University of La Molina, are offering courses in national parks administration. La Molina is also offering a master's degree in parks and wildlife management, and an increasing number of students are participating every year.

CONCLUSION

Considering that there were no protected areas at all before 1961 and that most of the areas have been established since 1972, the progress Peru has made in only fifteen years is astonishing. The quality of the areas currently under protection is excellent, and thanks to the careful scientific work that went into selecting areas for protection, the system is highly representative of the ecology and of the genetic diversity of the country. When current projects for the improvement of the system are achieved, Peru will have a system of protected areas superior to that of most developed countries. The main problem the system faces today is a lack of public awareness and, therefore, of political support. But the private conservation associations are addressing this lack of awareness, and budgets for conservation work can be expected to increase annually.

BIBLIOGRAPHY

Dourojeanni, Marc J., and Carlos F. Ponce. *Los parques nacionales del Perú*. Madrid: Instituto de la Caza Fotográfica y Ciencias de la Naturaleza, 1977.
Dourojeanni, Marc J., and Manuel A. Rios. ''A Critical Approach to the National System of Conservation Areas of Peru.'' *Revista Forestal del Perú* (Lima) 11, nos. 1–2 (1983): 56–72.

SOUTH AFRICA 20

Leslie M. Reid and
Jacobus N. Steyn

South Africa has rightly been called "the greatest wildlife show on earth."[1] South Africa claims the world's first, second, and third largest land mammals (elephant, white rhino, and hippopotamus, respectively), the tallest (giraffe), the fastest (cheetah), the smallest (pygmy shrew), the world's largest flightless bird (ostrich), and the largest flying bird (Kori bustard), which weighs up to 20 kilograms (45 pounds).[2]

For generations South Africa has been one of the few countries in the world that could boast of apparently limitless herds of free-roaming wild animals. Food, shelter, and climate all seemed to combine to produce huge populations of large game animals.

Visitors come to South Africa from many countries to view and photograph the native wildlife, to collect species unique to South Africa, and also to hunt and capture them. Though only one-seventh the size of the U.S.A., South Africa has 10 percent of the world's known species of birds, more than 22,000 plant species, and over 800 species of butterflies.[3]

The national parks of South Africa contain a bewildering variety of habitats, with rare flora and fauna. Features are included that are found nowhere else on earth. Thus, these parks are an important part of the ecological and environmental diversity that makes of this planet a global ecosystem.

If interdependency of man and natural systems is important, then South Africa offers a variety of examples of man-ecosystem relationships that are unequaled elsewhere in the world.

HISTORY

The nation recognized today as the Republic of South Africa has exhibited a concern for conservation and wise management of natural resources for over

Figure 20.1
Southern Africa Including Republic of South Africa and Neighboring States

300 years. Only four years after settlement at the Cape of Good Hope by Dutch colonists, Commander Jan van Riebeeck drafted hunting regulations when the area still teemed with wild animals. Shortly after, permits were issued for the taking of certain kinds of wild game. In 1672, Governor van der Stel proclaimed certain bok (buck) species as protected game.

But as has been true in other regions of the world, the wild, open, and uncontrolled environment attracted explorers and hunters, some of whom indulged themselves in an orgy of mass destruction, wantonly slaughtering wild game in the belief it was inexhaustible. Successive administrators attempted to curb and control illegal hunting in the late 1600s. In fact, the first game reserve in South Africa was established in Natal in 1697. Nevertheless, just five years later—in 1702—only thirty years after the granting of protected status to certain species, the last surviving elephant near Cape Town was killed.

Widespread publicity about the biological richness of South Africa may have resulted initially from reports of naturalists and scientists who came to the Cape area to study and classify the flora and fauna. But the greatest impetus to settlement of the nation's interior came with the discovery in the 1800s of untold wealth in the form of gold and diamonds. Kimberley, Witwatersrand, Johannesburg—these became the magnets that brought people streaming into the un-developed interior lands and resulted in the creation of what today are major urban centers.

By 1900 the vast animal herds had been thoroughly decimated and the remnants widely scattered. The elephant totally disappeared from large areas of its native habitat. Giraffe, eland, and the unique South African white-tailed gnu (the black wildebeest) all but disappeared. Some species, including the true zebra (*Equus quagga quagga*)—the wild horse of the early colonists—and the Cape lion (*Felis leo melanochaitus*) were driven to total extinction before 1900.[4]

Hunters and sportsmen cannot be blamed entirely for the dramatic collapse and disappearance of the vast migratory game herds. Other people also eradicated wild animals in order to profit from the country's natural outdoor resources. Mines, farms, vineyards, and transport systems all took their toll. Domestic livestock competed with wild animals for scarce forage and water. Farmers modified the characteristics of the natural ecosystems to suit agricultural purposes by cultivating the soil, building fences, eliminating predators, and introducing exotic species—all of which damaged the endemic species.

Why Established

The initial concerns that eventually led to the establishment of national parks in South Africa centered on the protection and preservation of wildlife species. Early actions taken both to protect wild animals and to limit the uncontrolled destruction of wildlife are well documented. The broadening of this narrow view to include the related areas of nature conservation and cultural and historical preservation is a fairly recent development, largely since the beginning of the present century.

How Accomplished

Very early during the white settlement of the Transvaal, attempts were made to conserve wildlife. For example, in 1846 the Ohrigstad Republic prohibited by proclamation the extermination of game. In 1858, the South African Republic (later to become the Transvaal Province) prohibited the unnecessary shooting of game, and the hunting of elephant was drastically curtailed. In 1870 the Volksraad of the Transvaal Republic provided for the appointment of game rangers, out-lawed the use of traps and snares, and proclaimed open and closed seasons.

All sources agree that major credit for wildlife conservation and nature con-servation belongs to Paul Kruger, South Africa's first president of what was then the Transvaal Republic. Paul Kruger was deeply concerned about the continuing destruction of wildlife and natural habitat. He clearly saw that wild animals must lose in any contest with economic development and ''progress.'' As a solution, he envisioned large areas set aside as reserves where wild species could thrive and be protected from outside dangers.[5]

In 1884, barely one year after assuming office as president, Paul Kruger presented his ideas to the Volksraad for protection of various forms of wildlife through the establishment of nature reserves.

Related legislation was introduced in 1891 and 1893. Later proclamations established hunting seasons and shooting licenses. Elephant, hippopotamus, buffalo, eland, giraffe, and rhinoceros were given extensive protection. In 1894, the Pongola Game Reserve was created by government proclamation.

In 1897, four provincial game reserves were established in Natal Province. Three of these first four reserves still exist today—St. Lucia, Umfolozi, and Hluhluwe.

In a landmark action that took place in March 1898, President Paul Kruger succeeded in gaining approval for proclamation of a large land area in the northeastern part of the Transvaal Republic to be known as the Sabie Game Reserve.

The Sabie Game Reserve initially consisted mostly of farmland, part of which was used at that time for sheep pasture. In July 1902, a British army officer, Colonel James Stevenson-Hamilton, was placed in charge of the area. During the ensuing forty-four years he became a legend as he guided this area from its uncertain origins to its status as a world treasure.

The Sabie Reserve was enlarged in 1903 by the addition of Shingwedzi Game Reserve and other related areas. Wildlife species that had previously been exploited again prospered, and elephants began to return from Mozambique.

Major Events

The Transvaal Republic became a province of the Union of South Africa in 1910. By 1926, evidence accumulated over the years demonstrated that wildlife preservation by means of game reserves was a viable concept, but more active programs of conservation and preservation were necessary. In that year, the South African Parliament took action by combining the Sabie Game Reserve and the Shingwedzi Game Reserve into one contiguous area to be known as the Kruger National Park of South Africa. In that same year, Parliament also approved Act 56 of 1926, the National Parks Act.[6]

This law provided for the establishment of other national parks by proclamation of the governor-general. The general purposes of the act were stated to be the propagation, protection, and conservation of wildlife and objects of geological, ethnological, historical, or other scientific interest for the benefit, advantage, and enjoyment of the inhabitants of the Union of South Africa. Provision was also made in the act for a board of trustees, comprising ten members appointed by the governor-general, whose duties were the control and management of the parks.

In 1931, three areas in the Cape Province were proclaimed as national parks under the provisions of the 1926 act. These were the Kalahari Gemsbok, Addo

Table 20.1
Distribution of National Parks by Province

National Park	Date Proclaimed	Purpose	Size (Hectares)
Province			
TRANSVAAL:			
Kruger	1926	Game Herds	2,000,000
CAPE:			
Kalahari	1931	Migrant Game	1,000,000
Addo Elephant	1931	Cape Elephant	7,740
Bontebok	1931	Antelope Herd	2,800
Mt. Zebra	1937	Zebra Herd	6,850
Tsitsikamma	1964	Forest/Coast	3,320
Augrabies Falls	1966	Waterfalls	9,200
Karoo	1979	Ecosystem	18,000
Wilderness			
Lake Area	1983*	Estuarine	10,000
Zuurberg	1985	Wilderness	20,770
Langebaan	1985	Forest/Coastal	
Vaalbos	1985	Prairie	4,575
ORANGE FREE STATE:			6,000 **
Golden Gate			
Highlands	1963	Landscape	6,240

NOTES: * Placed under aegis of National Parks Board for control
      of physical planning and development.
  ** Plus some 59,000 hectares contracted for later
      proclamation.

Elephant, and Bontebok national parks. The Mountain Zebra National Park, also in the Cape Province, followed in 1937.

Act 56 of 1926 was superseded by the National Parks Act of 1962. This act vested comprehensive powers for the maintenance of parks in a National Parks Board of Trustees appointed by the state president.

As recently as 1980, there were a total of ten officially designated, state-owned national parks in South Africa. By 1985, this number had increased to a total of fourteen national parks. See Table 20.1.

NATIONAL PARKS AND RESERVES

Each of the fourteen existing national parks is described below, with special attention given to the outstanding and associated natural features that are found in the designated area.[7] These features can be broadly categorized as biological/ecological, geological, historical/archaeological, aesthetic, recreational, or wilderness. Some added description of the facility infrastructure is included where appropriate, since accommodations are normally provided for visitors, and such developments also have an impact on the perceived character as well as the natural resources of the area itself. Figure 20.2 locates each of the parks.

Kruger National Park (1926)

Considered by many as the premier unit of South Africa's national parks, and doubtless the best known to foreigners, this park is the second oldest national park in Africa. It is located in the extreme northeast part of the country, some 400 kilometers northeast of Johannesburg, abutting South Africa's border with Mozambique.

The primary purpose of this area when it was originally set aside as the Sabie Game Reserve at the urging of President Kruger was to preserve the many species of indigenous wildlife. The park is about 2,000,000 hectares (5,000,000 acres)— approximately the size of the state of Massachusetts.

Kruger National Park is bounded on the north and south by two major rivers: the Crocodile River at the southern border and the Limpopo River at the north. The park averages about 65 kilometers (22 miles) from east to west and extends 320 kilometers (200 miles) from north to south. The topography of the park is fairly flat to gently rolling, generally trending downward from 900 meters (3,000 feet) in elevation in the western sections to 200 meters (650 feet) in the eastern parts. Native vegetation varies from scattered trees to dense brush pockets to open parklike meadows. Indigenous grasses and bush species are critically important sources of forage for browsing and grazing animals.

Kruger National Park boasts more species of wildlife than are found in any other African game sanctuary. Over 120 species of mammals exist, with an additional 55 species of fish, 109 species of reptiles, and over 420 bird species.

Without question the large mammals constitute the greatest attraction of Kruger Park. A game census conducted in 1980 recorded some 7,500 elephants, 30,000 buffalo, 120,000 impalas, and 20,000 zebras. Large numbers of antelope and giraffe also inhabit the park. Major predators include the lion, cheetah, leopard, jackal, and hyena.

Kruger Park is open all year. Times of daily opening and closing of the eight major park entry gates are publicized for various seasons of the year. The park contains about 1,250 kilometers (775 miles) of roads, over one-half of which are hard-surfaced. Visitors are not permitted to leave their vehicles while traveling on roadways within the park. Most animals can be seen at relatively close range from a vehicle in practically all parts of the park; camera-wielding tourists tend to be ignored by wildlife as long as the visitors remain inside. Viewing of large animals is a principal goal of many visitors. Lions, giraffe, or elephants found near a park road quickly result in vehicle congestion as vans, busses, and autos congregate to see or photograph wildlife. Table 20.2 shows the increase in vehicles entering the national parks during a recent six-year period.

Figure 20.2
Location of National Parks in Republic of South Africa

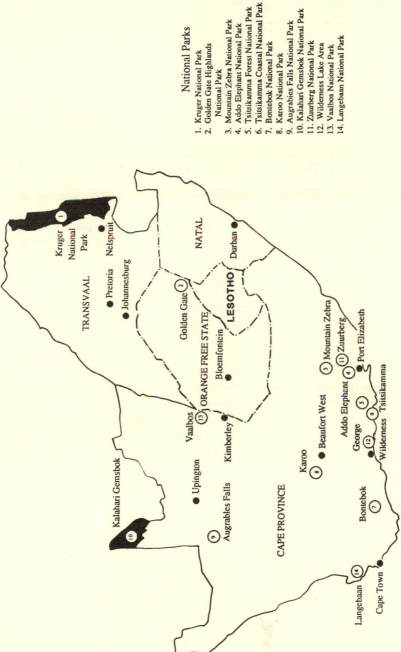

National Parks

1. Kruger National Park
2. Golden Gate Highlands National Park
3. Mountain Zebra National Park
4. Addo Elephant National Park
5. Tsitsikamma Forest National Park
6. Tsitsikamma Coastal National Park
7. Bontebok National Park
8. Karoo National Park
9. Augrabies Falls National Park
10. Kalahari Gemsbok National Park
11. Zuurberg National Park
12. Wilderness Lake Area
13. Vaalbos National Park
14. Langebaan National Park

Table 20.2
Total Vehicles Entering National Parks, 1979–1985

National Park	1979 / 80	1980 / 81	1981 / 82	1982 / 83	1983 / 84	1984 / 85
Kruger	96,541	108,157	120,575	116,535	119,460	134,450
All Others	34,492	45,090	54,547	60,599	63,277	69,415
Total	131,033	153,247	175,122	177,134	182,737	203,865

Within the park, tourist accommodations are provided at seventeen fenced rest camps. The gates at these campgrounds are locked every afternoon. Overnight visitors must remain in camp until the gate is opened the following morning. Thatched huts, bungalows, and camping sites are provided at the major camps, as are souvenir shops and restaurants.

A special attraction of Kruger Park is four popular wilderness foot trails. Located in the north and east-central parts of the park, with the remaining two in the south, they provide an unusual opportunity to observe park features close at hand. These are unlike hiking trails in other national parks where visitors are self-guided, following a designated trail on their own with overnight hut lodging along the route. The Kruger trails are conducted wilderness experiences on foot. Reservations are required in advance. Participants convene at a reception center. Groups are limited to a maximum of eight persons between the ages of twelve and sixty. Groups are led by an experienced guide. No set route is followed on the three-night, two-day hike. The guide is responsible for leading the group safely through the wilderness, arriving each night at bush lodging in the form of wood and thatch hutments. Food is provided as part of the total fee.

Table 20.3 summarizes recent use of the four wilderness trails, revealing how current use is approaching operational capacity of the facilities.

Approximately 500,000 people visit the Kruger National Park in a typical year. Visitation increased each year from 1980 to 1985, the total five-year increase being almost 23 percent.

Kalahari Gemsbok National Park (1931)

The Kalahari Gemsbok National Park was proclaimed in 1931 to protect herds of migrating animals. Major indigenous species include the magnificent gemsbok or oryx, eland, wildebeest, hartebeest, steenbok, and large numbers of springbok. Predators are represented by lions, cheetahs, hyenas, and jackals.

Table 20.3
Visitor Numbers, Hiking Trails in Kruger N.P., 1979–1985

TRAIL	1985 CAPACITY (*Persons*)	1979 / 80	1980 /81	1981 / 82	1982 / 83	1983 / 84	1984 / 85
Wolhuter (1978)	800	612	424	718	716	762	726
Olifants (1979)	800	106	728	729	591	758	779
Nyalaland (1980)	800	——	208	648	768	741	757
Bushman (1983)	800	——	——	——	——	429	724
Total	3200	718	1360	2095	2075	2690	2985

The park covers nearly 1,000,000 hectares (2,500,000 acres), roughly the same size as Yellowstone National Park. The park is situated in the extreme northern part of the Cape Province, extending north into Southwest Africa/ Namibia on the west and bounded by Botswana on the east. This is a land nearly empty of man's intrusions, attractive yet harsh semidesert and drifting sand. Plants and animals struggle for existence. The Kalahari sand dunes glow a dull red in the heat which often exceeds 40° Celsius (over 100° Fahrenheit), while night temperatures in the winter frequently fall below freezing.

Rainfall is minimal, and both plants and animals must adapt to a life of water conservation. Vegetation tends to be concentrated in and along the dry riverbeds, which also serve as roadways. Wells, windmills, dams, and reservoirs provide an adequate supply of drinking water. Visitor accommodations are provided at three rest camps. Bungalows furnish some 120 beds, and there are seventy-five camping sites.

Addo Elephant National Park (1931)

The purpose for which the Addo Elephant National Park was proclaimed in 1931 was to preserve the survivors of the eastern Cape elephant herd. The significance of this herd is that the animals differ from the equatorial elephant. They are smaller and have less tusk ivory, the cows usually having none. These are the descendants of the elephant herds that were decimated by ivory hunters 150 years ago. The herd was now increased to over 100 animals.

This national park is located about 65 kilometers (40 miles) north of Port Elizabeth in the eastern Cape Province. The park consists of approximately

45,000 hectares (111,000 acres). Principal vegetation is a dense forest of inter-twined trees and creepers, mostly evergreen, that reach a mature height of about 3–3.5 meters (10 feet). The warm, temperate climate, coupled with rain most of the year, encourages a dense growth of edible, evergreen plant species that has been termed "a botanist's paradise."[8] This vegetation is said to support three times the number of elephants per unit area than are found in any other nature reserve in Africa.

It is interesting that the entire reserve is fenced as an elephant enclosure. An experimental electric fence failed to keep the elephants in. The eventual solution was to use discarded mine cables strung on posts made of deep-set trolley rails.

Other fauna in this reserve include the black rhino, Cape buffalo, and several varieties of antelope (eland, kudu, hartebeest, bushbok, grysbok, and duiker). The reserve also is rich in smaller mammals, nocturnal species, and a large number of bird species.

Visitor housing is provided in family bungalows and circular thatched-roof cottages called "rondavels." Camping and picnicking sites are also available. Formerly, motor coach tours were the only means of viewing the elephants in the enclosure, but visitors are now permitted to enter the park in their own vehicles.

Bontebok National Park (1931)

The Bontebok antelope is one of the rarest of all mammals. Bontebok National Park was established as a game sanctuary to preserve this almost-extinct species. Early explorers and hunters described vast herds of this handsome mammal. Although several private families struggled to preserve the few remaining animals, by 1930 it was thought that no more than 30 bontebok remained in the area. In 1960, the national park and about 60 bontebok specimens were relocated to an area better suited to the animals' needs. Bontebok in this park now number almost 300 animals.

The national park comprises about 3,000 hectares (7,400 acres) located in the southern part of the Cape Province, less than 200 meters (650 feet) in elevation above sea level, and about 50 kilometers (30 miles) inland from the Indian Ocean. The climate is temperate, and the Breede River, which flows through the park, provides a dependable supply of fresh water.

This part of the Cape Province boasts a great diversity of plant species. Trees are concentrated along the banks of the river and in scattered groves elsewhere. The park becomes a riot of color in winter and early spring (July-September), when many of the plants flower due to the heavier rainfall.

Several varieties of antelope—both indigenous and introduced after the park was created—coexist with the bontebok in the reserve. However, all Cape buffalo were removed in 1975, and evidence of competition between some grazing species and the bontebok resulted in removal of the competitors as well.

Overnight facilities consist of a campground with space for twenty-five caravans (camper vehicles). Picnic facilities are available for day-users. Visitors may also swim in designated areas of the river (at their own risk). A sales shop and an information center are located at the campground, which is open all year.

Mountain Zebra National Park (1937)

As its name implies, this national park was created to ensure the survival of the Bergkwagga, or Cape mountain zebra (*Equus zebra zebra*). Although this reserve is only slightly over 6,500 hectares (16,200 acres), its importance cannot be measured by size alone. It is regarded as one of the most important game sanctuaries in all of Africa since it is the home of the smallest of the three surviving zebra species (the true zebra was driven to extinction before 1900).

The mountain zebra prefers a high-country habitat, and once ranged widely through the mountains of the southern Cape. Nevertheless, by the early 1930s fears of its extinction led, after lengthy controversy, to the purchase in 1937 of a 1,600-hectare (3,950-acre) farm in the mountains north of Port Elizabeth. The controversy and delay stemmed from doubts that this animal was in fact a separate species.

The mountain zebra is a slow breeder. By 1945, numbers had dwindled to the point that serious doubt existed that the species could be saved from extinction. At that time, only two stallions remained, and the last surviving mare died. Fortunately, replacement animals were obtained from nearby private farms. No more than 25 zebra were recorded in the park as recently as 1964. In that year, the size of the reserve was increased, and 30 additional animals were obtained from another farm. Today this park has over 200 mountain zebra. This is considered to be the effective carrying capacity of the reserve but far less than the 500 animals judged to be necessary to assure desirable genetic diversity. Recently, surplus zebra have been transferred to three other game reserves to create additional breeding groups.

The mountain zebra is well-adapted to the mountainous terrain of the park, negotiating rock areas with ease. Mountain meadows provide good grazing. The summer climate is windy, arid, and warm with temperatures reaching 40° Celsius (104° Fahrenheit). Winter days are sunny, but nights are cold, with frost, freezing temperatures, and snow common at the higher elevations. A dependable supply of water is provided by the Willow (Wilge) River, which runs the length of the park.

Creation of the fenced sanctuary has led to increases in the numbers of other species. Some existed in the area prior to its proclamation; others were introduced. Still others wandered in and elected to stay. Removal of major predators is a primary reason for the present problem of overpopulation. Current management practices include the culling of certain species and relocation of surplus animals.

Another important aspect of the park is the large variety of small mammals, insects, and amphibians. Bird life is also abundant, with over 200 species represented.

Overnight visitor accommodations are provided in a rest camp that has twenty two-bedroom chalets plus a campground with twenty campsites. A guest house, souvenir shop, cooking facilities, and other amenities are also available, as is a swimming pool.

A special feature of the park is a 26-kilometer (16-mile) hiking trail that extends for three days and two nights. Two overnight huts are provided on the trail, each capable of sleeping six persons. No more than twelve persons may begin the trail on any given day. Unlike the wilderness trails in Kruger National Park, visitors are permitted on the Mountain Zebra Trail without supervision.

Golden Gate Highlands National Park (1963)

Each of the national parks described to this point was created primarily as a sanctuary for game animals. Proclamation of Golden Gate Highlands as a national park was a landmark departure from the primary purpose for which previous parks had been created.

This area, the first designated after the close of World War II, was established primarily to preserve an example of highveld landscape and scenery. Located in the foothills of the Maluti Mountains in the northern Orange Free State, it is centrally located in relation to the thousands of visitors who come from the nation's northern cities.

The area includes over 6,000 hectares (15,000 acres). The principal attraction is geologic—the scenic grandeur of superb mountain scenery. Colorful rock outcrops, eroded sandstone cliffs, canyons, and meadows dominate the landscape. Elevations within the park range from 2,000 to 3,000 meters (6,500 to 9,800 feet), similar to Denver, Colorado, or Mexico City. The mountain air is cool and clear. Freezing temperatures and snow are common in the winter months. Vegetation is typical of the highveld region—brush and grassland with shrubs in more protected, better-watered situations. Soils tend to be poor. The seven privately owned farms from which this park was created were subjected to overgrazing and erosion.

Early records indicate that this area was a hunter's paradise. One report tells of an early settler shooting more than 300 lions on and near his farm. By 1963 both predators and prey had largely been exterminated. As a result of careful research, many former game animals have been reintroduced into the park. In addition to the large game animals, of which the blesbok is the most typical, the rare lammergeyer (bearded eagle) can be seen here. Sometimes classed as a vulture, this large bird is a noted bone-eater.

No attempt has been made to restock predators, not only because the park is too small to function as a complete ecosystem, but also, as stated by René Gordon in *The National Parks of South Africa*, because this would conflict with the recreational aspect . . . which is part of the rationale for the Park, a rationale which places it outside the generally accepted parameters for a national park. But its role as a means of increasing public awareness of the value of wilderness and its conservation offsets this deviation from the norm.[9]

In keeping with its recreational theme, Golden Gate Highlands National Park is well equipped with visitor facilities. Principal housing is provided in a hotel that has over 200 beds and luxurious appointments including telephone, radio, and television. Banquets and conferences can be accommodated. A grouping of adjoining chalets is similarly equipped. The visitor complex also offers tennis courts, bowling green, golf course, swimming pool, and horseback riding.

A rest camp and caravan park has a capacity of over fifty sites with full camping facilities and a separate area for day visitors. A hiking trail limited to eighteen persons per day extends for two days with a trail-side hut available for one night. A special feature of this park is a permanent youth camp in which up to sixty children can attend classes in environmental education, conservation, and nature study.

Tsitsikamma Forest and Coastal National Park (1964)

This national park is located on the south coast of the Cape Province between Port Elizabeth and Cape Town. It is unique to South Africa in that it was proclaimed as two separate areas, Tsitsikamma Forest National Park and Tsitsikamma Coastal National Park. The two units of this national park were set aside to preserve outstanding examples of important natural features. This was the first coastal or marine sanctuary park to be established on the entire African continent.

Tsitsikamma Forest Park contains slightly less than 480 hectares (1,186 acres) of dense rain forest. It is characterized by huge, ancient trees of several different species, plus shrubs, ferns, and tree ferns. The forest is only a remnant from a colder, wetter climatic period. Thus the gradual drying of the climate plus the destruction of the forest by man for timber products and for agricultural purposes reduced the remaining forest to the point where aggressive actions had to be taken for any of it to be protected from total destruction.

Tourist facilities are provided in a developed area on the outer edge of the forest adjacent to the Garden Route Highway. Included are a restaurant, store, and caravan park with 100 campsites. Special trails and picnic sites are available for visitor use.

The larger unit of the park is the 2,800-hectare (6,900-acre) Tsitsikamma Coastal National Park, which comprises a narrow band of adjacent seacoast. This 1.5-kilometer (1-mile) wide strip, which extends along the coast nearly 80 kilometers (50 miles), consists not only of a narrow coastal plain between the ocean and inland cliffs, but also extends 800 meters (one-half mile) out into the open sea. The magnificent variety of natural features makes this area extremely attractive for nature study, with several rivers plunging down to the sea, intertidal pools, and marine life of many kinds. The Otter Hiking Trail, five days in length, is provided to allow visitors to come into close contact with the natural features of the area.

A central tourist complex at the mouth of the Storms River offers self-contained beach cottages and luxury holiday apartments. A caravan park and camping sites are also available. A restaurant and store provide meals and fishing equipment, and a trained conservationist is available to lead visitors on a snorkel and flipper tour of South Africa's first underwater nature trail.

Augrabies Falls National Park (1966)

Located in the northwestern part of the Cape Province, and south of the Kalahari Gemsbok National Park, the Augrabies Falls National Park was established in 1966 to preserve a magnificent waterfalls, river corridor, and associated landscape features in one of the country's most arid regions. The park contains about 9,000 hectares (22,000 acres). It is located along the Orange River, the largest river in South Africa, which cuts across nearly the entire country from east to west. The Orange River changes at this point from a peaceful stream of intertwined channels to a restricted, roaring monster that cascades and then falls over a granite lip into a ravine and gorge that extends some 18 kilometers (11 miles) downstream.

Whereas the river historically ranged seasonally from low to flood stage, the flow is more even today due to the harnessing of the river above the falls by large dams. The need for these dams as a basis for development was a major reason for delay in proclaiming Augrabies Falls as a national park.

The multiple waterfalls are a major tourist attraction. Both animals and plant life are interesting complements to the geologic attraction and the lure of water in an arid land.

Visitor facilities are developed throughout the park on the south side of the river. Various trails lead to observation points for viewing the river and gorge. A rest camp is provided featuring air-conditioned huts, a store, restaurant, and information center. A campground offers over fifty campsites. Roads extend into various areas of the park. The Klipspringer Hiking Trail follows the ravine downriver, then loops back to the visitor complex. The trail is designed for three days and two nights. Two separate overnight huts are provided that can each accommodate twelve persons.

Karoo National Park (1979)

The Karoo National Park is one of the newer areas to be added to South Africa's emerging system of national parks. This area illustrates the intent expressed in the National Park Act of 1962 to conserve a representative example of each of the major ecosystems in the country. Located near Beaufort West some 480 kilometers (300 miles) northeast of Cape Town, the 18,000-hectare (44,000-acre) park is a sample of the huge inland arid basin known as the Great Karoo. The name is derived from a Hottentot word meaning bare or dry. The Karoo lies between the great mountain escarpment to the north that forms the backbone of South Africa and coastal hills to the south. The Karoo changes from wide level plains in the south to flat-topped buttes or mesas in the north.

The area is subject to severe drought and extremes of temperature. The Karoo is an empty bush- and grass-covered land of widely separated farmsteads, thin soils, erosion, and rock outcrops.

Early records indicate that vast migrations of wild game herds moved periodically through this area. One such report describes a moving mass of springbok covering an area 20 kilometers (12 miles) wide and 200 (120 miles) kilometers long! Naturally, where large concentrations of animals abounded, predators would be close at hand, including leopard, lion, hyena, and the bone-eating lammergeyer. Today, a few species of either prey or predator remain since these animals were hunted, trapped, poisoned, and fenced nearly out of existence. Sheep and goats now populate the Karoo, although several of the larger mammal species have been reintroduced into the park.

Much of the attraction of Karoo National Park relates to the immensity of the open space. Closer examination reveals much of interest in the intricate relationships between flora, fauna, and natural processes. The Karoo is also highly prized for geological and paleontological study of fossils.

This park has no visitor accommodations or camping area, but the three-day, two-night Springbok Hiking Trail provides visitors with the opportunity to experience the charm of the park interior.

The three national parks that follow were all proclaimed in 1985 and thus are so recent that there is little to report other than their establishment. However, they do provide an indication of the vitality of the national parks movement in South Africa.

Zuurberg National Park (1985)

This new national park totaling about 20,000 hectares (50,000 acres) was established in 1985 in three separate units. It is located about 15 kilometers (9 miles) north of the Addo Elephant National Park. The terrain of peaks, hillsides, and valleys is a transition zone of three major vegetation types. Consequently, there is a great variety of plant life ranging from shrubs and bushes to evergreen trees of the coastal forest. The park supports a variety of wild animals, as well as bird, insect, and fish species.

Since the park was so recently proclaimed, the master plan has not yet been completed. However, a primary concern is retention of the natural features to provide visitors with an authentic wilderness experience. Decisions as to what animals are to be reintroduced and what level of visitor accommodations is to be provided have yet to be determined. The hilly character of the park makes it especially suitable for hikers, so it is anticipated that hiking trails will be an integral part of the management scheme.

Vaalbos National Park (1985)

This newly established area consists of 4,575 hectares (11,305 acres) in the northern Cape Province, a short distance west of Kimberley. The principal purpose in the establishment of this park is preservation of the transitional vegetation zone that has some of the characteristics of the Karoo, the Kalahari, and grass plains.

This park is not yet in its final form. Additional parcels of land are expected to be added to the existing core area. Comprehensive surveys of fauna are also necessary prior to the development of a master plan and the construction of appropriate visitor facilities.

West Coast National Park (1985)

West Coast National Park is a 6,000-hectare (15,000-acre) coastal complex of seashore, dunes, saltwater lagoon, and several adjacent islands. Proclaimed by the government as a national park on August 30, 1985, it is undoubtedly the most ambitious attempt at ecosystem management and protection yet undertaken by South Africa. A unique feature is that an additional area of almost 60,000 hectares (150,000 acres) is part of a contractual arrangement for proclamation in the future as an addition to this national park. Figure 20.3 describes the principal features of West Coast National Park.

The Saldanha Bay area, located only about 100 kilometers (62 miles) north of Cape Town, has been known for over 400 years. Even though it offered a protected bay and anchorage, it had limited potential as a watering stop or shipping center because of the lack of fresh water and the extreme aridity of the surrounding country.

Unlike most bay and lagoon systems, which are fed by a major river system, Saldanha Bay is not an estuary; no river empties into it. Instead, it was formed over millions of years by the alternate rise and fall of the world's oceans. These cycles generated a series of sand dunes. Then at some time the ocean broke through the coastal dunes, creating the bay and lagoon behind them. Thus the Saldanha Bay and Langebaan Lagoon are as saline as the ocean, not more or less salty depending on inflows of fresh water from inland.

A second major feature of this unique and fragile marine environment is the presence of numerous islands in the system. These serve as rookeries and nesting sites for colonies of resident and migratory birds—some species coming from as far away as Siberia and Greenland. The 10,000 jackass penguins nesting here comprise the densest colony of that species in the world.

The ultimate development and character of this national park are still imprecise. But the consequences of man-induced activities are already a concern. For ex-

Figure 20.3
Example of "Contractual National Park"

WEST COAST NATIONAL PARK AND SALDANHA BAY AREA

DESCRIPTION:

The policy adopted for the West Coast National Park by the National Parks Board represents a novel initiative intended to afford the highest possible level of lasting protection to an area of extreme ecological importance, but which is also utilized by man at various levels of intensities. The bay/lagoon/island complex includes wild areas, nesting sites for many bird species, an important marine fishery, a military defence installation, an iron-ore terminal and industrial area. In the conservation area, the State-owned features of offshore islands, lagoon, intertidal zone and limited land areas comprise about 16,000 hectares. But natural and cultural activities on at least 60,000 hectares outside this core area impact the ecology of the publicly-owned national park. The State has taken a series of actions to ensure protection of this ecologically-important area.

CONSERVATION BACKGROUND/HISTORY:

1973 - Lagoon proclaimed as marine sanctuary under the Sea Fisheries Act.

1983 - Additional protection provided when placed under administration of National Parks Board

1984 - Adjacent land area proclaimed as a "NATURE AREA" under the Physical Planning Act of 1967.

1985 - State-owned parcels totaling 6,000 hectares proclaimed as "West Coast National Park."

1986 - Decision to administer large areas of private land as a "Contractual Natural Park."

1989 - West Coast National Park covers an area of 18,000 hectares, consisting of State land and contractual park areas, and bordered by natural area.

To ensure the environmental integrity of the total bay complex, the State has defined a "Nature Area" of approximately 60,000 hectares of privately-owned lands. After December 1984, land within the West Coast Nature Area may only be used for the purpose it was legally used immediately prior to reservation. Any change in land use is subject to prior authorization by the Minister of Environmental Affairs and Tourism. Within the Nature Area, the intent is to reach voluntary and mutually-acceptable contractual agreements with private landowners regarding acceptable land management practices. Once agreement is reached between the landowner and the National Parks Board, the land is given the formal status of "Contractual National Park."

Figure 20.3 (continued)

DEFINITIONS

"NATURE AREA:"

The Physical Planning Act 88 (1967) defines a "NATURE AREA" as, "... any which could be utilized in the interest of and for the benefit and enjoyment of the public in general and for the reproductory protection and preservation of wild animal life, wild vegetation or objects of geological, ethnological, historical or other scientific interest.

"CONTRACTUAL NATIONAL PARK:"

The term "contractual national park" has been officially accepted to replace "Schedule 5 National Park" as it is more descriptive and less confusing.

A "CONTRACTUAL NATIONAL PARK" is "any land that is either privately owned or State-owned that is managed by an agreement reached between the owner (State or private) and the National Parks Board and legally specified in a contract will constitute part of a "contractual national park" whose boundaries, identification, ownership and status are established by contract."

SIGNIFICANCE:

The policy of creating a "contractual national park" through voluntary agreements reached with individual private land-owners is an innovative way to gain long-term protection for resources that could otherwise not be acquired by purchase.

From: CUSTOS Vol.14, No.7, June, 1985 and National Parks Board, RSA (1989).

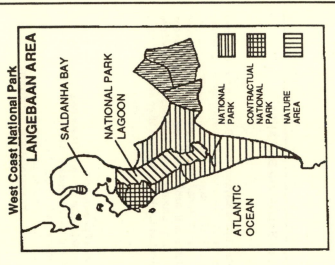

West Coast National Park

LANGEBAAN AREA

SALDANHA BAY

NATIONAL PARK LAGOON

ATLANTIC OCEAN

NATIONAL PARK

CONTRACTUAL NATIONAL PARK

NATURE AREA

ample, the annual harvesting of guano is related to the extent of commercial overfishing. A causeway was built to one of the offshore islands to form a harbor breakwater. This has allowed a number of new predators to invade the island ecosystem. An iron ore terminal on the bay interior at Saldanha is part of a massive industrial complex that has impacted the marine ecology of the area by generating both air and water pollution. Also, the bay entrance was deepened by blasting in order to accommodate large ocean-going ore-carriers.

All of these and other problems must be dealt with by the Advisory Committee of Ecological Studies. Appointed by the government, this body must develop equitable and feasible policies that will ensure the survival of the outstanding ecosystems located at Langebaan Lagoon.

Wilderness Lake Area (1983)

It is necessary before moving on to describe an additional area that, although not officially proclaimed as a national park, is demonstrably of a character to warrant inclusion in any description of nationally significant areas and programs.

The Wilderness Lake Area is located in the extreme south of the Cape Province, east of Cape Town and adjacent to the Garden Route Highway between George and Knysna. The area extends from the Indian Ocean to the foot of the Outeniqua Mountains to the north. Sand dunes, salt marsh, islands, river estuary, and a lagoon are all part of the designated area.

Though not an official national park, this area was placed under the control of the National Parks Board to prevent pollution, ill-advised and uncoordinated development of the lakes, and loss of scenic beauty. The various geologic origins of the lake make the area a complex and unique coastal system, like no other in the country.

Although the lakes area is rich in a variety of life-forms, there are no large mammals in the area. Bird species abound, as well as fresh- and saltwater fish. Nature study is a major activity.

A camp at Wilderness Village is located within walking distance of the sea and bathing beach. Fishing, canoeing, wind surfing, and water skiing are popular activities. Rental pedal boats are available. Hikers can enjoy spectacular scenery on numerous developed trails. Overnight facilities are provided in the form of five fully equipped, two-bedroom chalets. A campground with rental units is also provided.

IMPORTANT RELATED CONSERVATION PROGRAMS

Provincial Game and Nature Reserves

In addition to the areas that have been placed under the aegis of the National Parks Board, the importance of provincially administered nature and game re-

Figure 20.4
Comparison between Number and Total Area in National and Provincial Parks

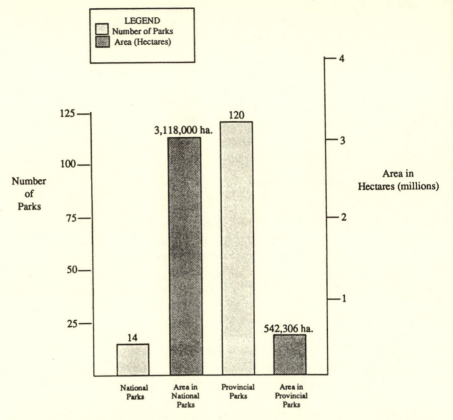

serves must be recognized. Some of the provincial reserves are world-famous, possessing all the attributes of a proclaimed national park.

Figure 20.4 shows that the fourteen national parks include over 3 million hectares (7.4 million acres), more than six times the total area contained in the 120 provincial reserves. Kruger National Park alone, however, accounts for two-thirds of the total national park area.

Each of the four provinces is empowered by the state president to designate and administer areas for nature conservation, including regulation of game and fish. The first such ordinance was recommended by a study commission in the Transvaal Province in 1947. Adoption of this ordinance created the Transvaal Nature Conservation Commission. The action has since been referred to as the Magna Carta for wildlife.

By 1974, each of the other provinces had adopted a similar nature conservation ordinance. These ordinances established procedures for creation of provincial, local, and private nature reserves; provided regulations for hunting, possessing,

Figure 20.5
Number and Total Area of Provincial Parks, by Province

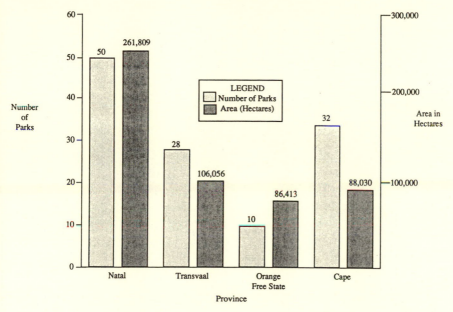

or trading of wild animals; picking or engaging in commerce involving plants; and provided protection for endangered species of both plants and animals.

In the aggregate, provincial game and nature reserves total over 540,000 hectares (1.3 million acres). Figures 20.5 and 20.6 present the growth of provincial reserves in number and total area since the first three areas were proclaimed in Natal in 1897.

Although none of the fourteen national parks are located in Natal Province, Figure 20.5 shows that Natal is the leading province in dedicated provincial parks and reserves.

Nationally, the total number of provincial reserves increased from 11 in 1945 to 120 in 1981. Figure 20.6 shows the relationship over time between the increasing number of provincial reserves and the total area comprising those reserves. Although the number of provincial areas has increased dramatically since 1945, it is readily apparent that the reserves created since that time tend to be much smaller.

It is impossible to adequately describe the bewildering variety of features protected in the reserves established by the four provinces. Some twenty reserves are larger than 10,000 hectares (25,000 acres) in size. But size alone does not adequately describe the value of these reserves. Some smaller areas are mag-

Figure 20.6
Increase in Number and Total Area in Provincial Parks, 1897–1981

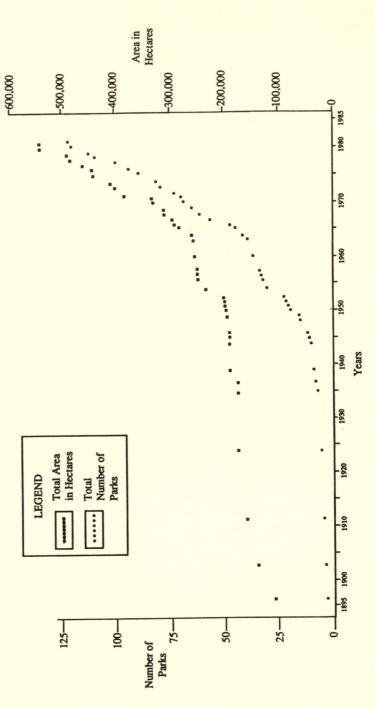

nificent ecological gems; others ensure the survival of an endangered plant or animal.

Though to describe only a few of these provincial areas is an injustice to many others equally deserving of mention, examples from each province illustrate how effective the actions of the provincial governments have been in preserving the natural resources of South Africa.

Blyderivierspoort Nature Reserve, Transvaal Province. The major feature of this reserve, located in the escarpment area of the rugged Drakensberg Mountains, is the Blyde River Canyon, over 1.5 kilometer (1 mile) wide and equally deep. The area, encompassing over 20,000 hectares (50,000 acres), is a showcase of botanical and geological features. Hiking trails extend throughout the reserve. Visitor accommodations are provided at two public resorts within the reserve.

Hans Merensky Nature Reserve, Transvaal Province. This reserve covers over 4,000 hectares (10,000 acres) on the south bank of the Letaba River east of Tzaneen. The chief attraction is lowveld woodland with a variety of resident game animals, especially the rare sable antelope. A special feature is a community of Tsonga craftsmen that maintains traditional activities in a typical village kraal.

Roodeplaat Dam Nature Reserve, Transvaal Province. This 1,600-hectare (4,000-acre) reserve surrounds the Roodeplaat Dam on the Pienaars River about 30 kilometers (19 miles) from Pretoria. Mixed vegetation, bird life, and introduced animal species are the main attractions. Recreation activities are featured, including fishing, wind surfing, sailing, and general boating. Fully equipped camping and caravan facilities are provided for visitors.

Suikerbosrand Nature Reserve, Transvaal Province. Located about 65 kilometers (40 miles) south of Johannesburg, this 13,200-hectare (32,600-acre) reserve offers urbanites a convenient site for outdoor enjoyment and nature study. A wide variety of plant species exists in the area, and antelope and cheetah have been reintroduced. A network of hiking trails extends through the park, and educational bus tours are available. A major visitor center features educational exhibits, an outstanding diorama exhibit, and an auditorium. A public resort within the reserve provides overnight accommodations.

Hluhluwe Game Reserve, Natal Province. The chief attraction of this reserve, which contains over 20,000 hectares (50,000 acres), is a wide variety of large game animals. Black and white rhino, kudu, impala, zebra, and buffalo, to name only a few species, can easily be seen by driving the roads within the reserve. The number of vehicles in the reserve at a given time is strictly controlled. As at other parks, visitor housing is provided in the traditional thatch-roofed rondavels. Hluhluwe and the other reserves of Natal Province are located in Figure 20.7.

Connected to Hluhluwe Game Reserve by a state-owned corridor is the 47,700-hectare (120,000-acre) Umfolozi Game Reserve, dedicated to protection of the rare white rhinoceros.

St. Lucia Game Reserve, Natal Province. The original purpose for the dedication of some 38,000 hectares (94,000 acres) in this coastal wilderness north

Figure 20.7
Map of Natal Province Showing Location of Major Provincial Reserves

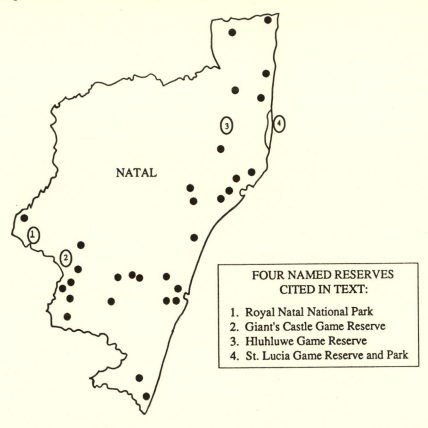

FOUR NAMED RESERVES
CITED IN TEXT:

1. Royal Natal National Park
2. Giant's Castle Game Reserve
3. Hluhluwe Game Reserve
4. St. Lucia Game Reserve and Park

of Durban was protection of bird life. Hippos are numerous, and crocodiles have been introduced. Numerous rest camps are provided for tourists in the park and at the estuary, and launch tours are available.

Giants Castle Game Reserve, Natal Province. This is a high-mountain reserve containing about 34,000 hectares (84,000 acres). It contains the greatest number of eland in South Africa, plus many other species. Hiking and fishing are popular activities in a superb scenic setting.

Royal Natal National Park, Natal Province. The title of this area is misleading because this is *not* a national park. It is a provincial park. The 8,000-hectare (20,000-acre) area features some of the most superb scenery in the Drakensberg Mountains. It has a long-standing reputation based on scenery, plants, animals, and outdoor activities. A modern, fully equipped hotel provides lodging and such related amenities as tennis court, a bowling green, and opportunities for hiking and swimming.

Willem Pretorius Game Reserve, Orange Free State. Located about two hours' drive north of Bloemfontein, this 8,000-hectare (20,000-acre) reserve is built on the banks of the Allemanskraal Dam. The reserve protects a typical sample of mixed-grass prairie plants and animals. Reestablishment of several animal species has been a success, with surplus animals being transferred for reintroduction to other areas. The reserve boasts a wide range of visitor facilities with several kinds of lodging, a restaurant, store, auditorium, swimming pool, tennis courts, bowling green, and golf course.

De Hoop Nature Reserve, Cape Province. Containing 18,000 hectares (45,000 acres), this reserve was created near Bredasdorp to protect a variety of plants and animals indigenous to the region. Rare species such as the bontebok and mountain zebra are found here, and the reserve includes a variety of marine life-forms along three miles of intertidal coastline.

Conservation in Forestry Areas

Mention must be made of the work of the Directorate of Forestry of the Department of Environment Affairs, since this is one of the major conservation agencies of the Republic of South Africa. More than 1,000,000 hectares (2.5 million acres) of nonforested mountain watershed are directly administered by this agency for water production, nature conservation, and outdoor recreation. Over 120,000 additional hectares (300,000 acres) of indigenous forestlands are also controlled by the department. An additional 600,000 hectares (1.5 million acres) of privately owned mountain lands are cooperatively managed for watershed purposes.

Where appropriate, parts of these forest holdings are proclaimed under terms of Forest Act 72 of 1968 (amended by Act 37 of 1971) as nature reserves and wilderness areas. Nature reserves are specially selected for conservation, the study of natural ecosystems, and the protection of indigenous flora and fauna, especially of rare or endangered species.

Undeveloped, uninhabited areas having an intrinsically wild character are selected and proclaimed as wilderness areas to preserve these characteristics. Their primary purpose is to provide areas of a primitive nature isolated from the outside world for those who seek physical and spiritual relaxation. Approximately 300,000 hectares (740,000 acres) of state (national) forests have now been proclaimed as wilderness areas or nature reserves.

Private and Local Conservation Efforts

In addition to the many provincially administered nature reserves, literally hundreds of other game and nature conservation areas have been created by local or private interests. In Natal Province, for example, more conservation-area land is currently protected in private ownership than is administered by the Natal Parks Board. Similarly, although thirty-four nature reserves, sanctuaries, and fish hatcheries are administered by the Cape Province, the province provides subsidies to sixty-five additional nonprovincial reserves.

Under terms of the Environmental Planning Act of 1969, the minister of environmental affairs, in consultation with the appropriate provincial administrator, may proclaim an area a "nature conservation area." This proclaimed use henceforth takes precedence over all other land uses. All subsequent development in the designated area comes under the control of government with the establishment of an advisory management committee to rule on land-use issues in the nature area.

Encouragement of Game Ranching

Act 57 of 1976 provides for the protection of wildlife in the national parks of South Africa. Although wildlife outside the boundaries of a proclaimed national park is the property of the provincial government, the provinces have ceded these rights to individual landowners.

Private owners have been encouraged by each province to protect wildlife and, in some cases, to breed wild animals. Hunting can now take place on a year-round basis on farms that are enclosed by special game fences. The owner receives all financial proceeds. Thus it is in his best interest to protect wild animals. Hunting of wild game animals is also permitted on farms without special game fences, but only in scheduled seasons, and only by permit issued by a local magistrate and signed by the farm owner. The owner thus is obligated to determine what numbers of wild animals can be harvested each season. This policy has resulted in landowners actually stocking their properties with wild animals as an economic inducement to attract hunters—in some cases resulting in a more profitable enterprise than stock farming.

ADMINISTRATION

Administration of proclaimed national parks and major nature reserves in South Africa has gone through three identifiable evolutionary phases over the past 100 years. These phases represent responses to basic changes in the perception of the values inherent in these areas.

Values Underlying Administration of National Parks

A major force in early campaigns (1650–1950) for creation of protected areas always was concern for the preservation of game species, hence the initial designation as "game reserves." From Paul Kruger's continuing struggle in the late 1800s for protected areas to ensure the survival of game animals to the proclamation of Mountain Zebra National Park in 1937—a period of fifty years—the primary concern was herd animal protection.

The major break with this tradition came after World War II. The basic driving social force is not documented. Perhaps it was related to ease of travel—both international and domestic—with consequent overcrowding of existing parks; or perhaps burgeoning populations and the desire to proclaim additional areas while still possible to do so was paramount; or perhaps it was recognition of the massive interest in park development then underway in the U.S.A. under the aegis of the Outdoor Recreation Resources Review Commission (1959–1962). Perhaps it was due to the awakening conscience of a new generation of South African leaders who saw more clearly the necessity to expand the concept of protection of game animals to preservation of representative examples of South Africa's national heritage of outstanding scenic, geological, historical, and biological features.

In any event, the National Parks Act of 1926 was superseded by the National Parks Act of 1962, which granted broad powers for administration of parks to a National Parks Board of Trustees appointed by the state president.

Adoption of the act of 1962 immediately ushered in the second phase of nature conservation with the establishment of three additional national parks having broader purposes:

- Golden Gate Highlands N.P. (1963)—geology; scenery
- Tsitsikamma N.P. (1964)—rain forest; coastal/marine
- Augrabies Falls N.P. (1966)—geology

Establishment of these three national parks can be considered transitional in that the purpose went beyond a narrow concern for preservation of a specific species or habitat. In contrast, the primary concern was protection from a broad range of threats—an ecological posture rather than, at the most restricted, management of a single species.

A major shift in emphasis concerning people also begins to be apparent. Humans had previously been considered intruders into the ecosystem. Visitors were viewed as an externality, separate and distinct from management of the area's habitat and wildlife—as for example, opportunities for game viewing under tightly controlled conditions. Visitors began to be accepted as an integral element in the management of the park. A good example is Augrabies Falls National Park, where hiking trails and visitor facilities are found throughout the area.

This leads to the third or current phase of establishing national parks for the express purpose of preserving outstanding representative examples of the nation's major ecosystems. This policy is evidenced by the proclamation of the following national parks:

- Karoo N.P. (1979)—desert ecosystem
- Wilderness Lake Area (1983)—estuarine ecosystem
- Zuurberg N.P. (1985)—wilderness ecosystem

- Vaalbos N.P. (1985)—prairie ecosystem
- West Coast N.P. (1985)—coastal marine ecosystem

The philosophical maturation from narrow concern for survival of a herd species to emphasis on preservation of viable ecosystems is apparent. However, ecosystem management demands a high order of administration to deal effectively with complex problems. Management policies must be adopted that ensure viable functioning of interrelated system elements. Additional research becomes necessary to obtain needed information on which those management policies can be based.

Along with the broadened focus of recently established areas has come acceptance of the idea that proclaimed areas should be accessible to visitors for enjoyment, education, and recreation. Thus, presence of humans in substantial—and potentially damaging—numbers becomes an integral part of the management scheme, necessitating specific accommodations in administrative decision making.

Finally, a policy of increased public accessibility favors locations closer to urban areas, where the majority of potential visitors reside. But proximity to populated areas exacerbates problems of land acquisition (availability and cost), and also may lead to increased demand for general recreation activities and facilities.

Social values are expressions of the beliefs people hold about their society. As a society changes, values change. National parks and reserves are created because of the belief that they are valuable to society. The value or values ascribed to those parks reflect the benefits the society feels it derives from the existence of those parks. Thus, the evolution of park philosophy described above mirrors a parallel broadening in society's perception of the values inherent in national parks.

Ascribing values and benefits to a park is a risky business. A portion of a society may value parks very highly; another may feel that parks have no value at all. Some people feel very strongly that an ethical and moral obligation exists to preserve all forms of life. Others believe just as strongly in the value of a natural environment that is not degraded by mankind. Attempting to quantify noneconomic benefits of a park is difficult. Yet some seek to bring park values into the marketplace so that benefits can be expressed in terms of potential economic value.

Certainly, South Africa's national parks have economic value in terms of the monetary benefits they yield—through tourism, publicity, product sales, etc. But basing the principal value of national parks on economic considerations alone is both incomplete and short-sighted.

The primary values for which South Africa's national parks have been proclaimed can best be described as an array of ecological values relating to nature conservation. Recognized benefits of nature conservation include the maintenance of genetic diversity—the concept of gene pools or gene banks. Avoidance of species extinction is another benefit. Also, totally protected areas can function as environmental or ecological monitoring stations, providing baseline data by which changes in developed environments can be evaluated. Finally, national parks have value by serving as natural laboratories for environmental education.

Managing a specific area simply for the survival and protection of, for example, a herd of game animals is far different than attempting to stabilize or manipulate an entire ecosystem. This is especially true if external elements (such as visitors) impact the system, or if administrative decisions are imposed on the system (such as policies regarding the disposition of surplus animals, retention of old-growth trees, control of wildfires, etc.).

All of these factors and many others increase the need for management of the parks—another name for interference with or modification of natural processes in order to achieve certain specific and desirable goals.

Research

Research is an important part of the national and provincial nature conservation programs. Not only is exhaustive study made of an area prior to approval of a master plan for a national park, but continuing studies provide both baseline data and longitudinal data on which to base programmatic or policy changes as the park matures.

Currently, there are ten wildlife management scientists assigned to studies in Kruger National Park, with another nine scientists similarly engaged in other national parks.

Level of Protection

Protection of the national parks is a crucial facet of administration. To quote from the introductory chapter written by Prof. Roy Siegfried in *The National Parks of South Africa*:

Within the embrace of the conservation movement at least ten categories of protection are internationally recognized, with national parks at the pinnacle. These parks are specifically conserved areas of special scenic, historical or scientific interest at sea or on land which are actively protected and whose existence is inviolate. Their legal protection is vested in a nation's highest competent authority. Such inviolate protection is not assured in the case of provincial reserves, conservation areas, game parks and a host of other areas designated for some particular conservation objective and which receive some degree of legal protection.[10]

All the national parks are enclosed by game-proof fencing to ensure that animals do not escape into the surrounding countryside where damage could be done to crops or other property. Constant surveillance is provided by park rangers in an attempt to prevent game poaching, especially of such potentially valuable items as elephant ivory or game pelts.

Visitor Regulations and Prohibitions

Thoughtless or illegal actions of visitors can have a significant impact on the wildlife and other resources of a national park. Consequently, the National Parks Board has established a series of regulations and controls in an attempt to prevent or to minimize damage and degradation. No dogs or other pet birds or animals are allowed in any national park. Feeding, harassing, or disturbing indigenous wildlife is not permitted. Plants and other artifacts are not to be damaged or removed. No litter is allowed, nor are unauthorized fires, sales, or public entertainments for a fee. Firearms must be acknowledged at the entry gate and sealed while in the park. Visitor numbers and activities are regulated. Permissible vehicle speeds are posted and enforced. A maximum number of vehicles is permitted in some parks on any given day, based on the calculated carrying capacity of the area. In effect, this means that in some cases latecomers must wait until a vehicle leaves the park before they can enter.

Threats to the National Parks

The national parks in South Africa, as in other countries of the world, are vulnerable to a variety of internal and external factors that threaten their very existence. Unlike natural features such as mountains, glaciers, or waterfalls, national parks are man-made creations—in a sense, artificial contrivances or designations applied to a geographic area, phenomenon, or feature. This very artificiality suggests that, having been created by man, without man's constant reinforcement, attention, and constant intervention to ensure its continuation, the national park would revert to something else—less desirable to those who for one reason or another created it. An appropriate analogy is the suburban lawn painstakingly developed from the original forest by a householder, which if not assiduously tended, will quickly revert to the overgrown, multispecies condition in which it previously existed.

If a national park existed as a complete ecosystem, that is, within itself as an entity there existed all the variable factors capable of modifying it with no external factors impinging upon it, then that national park could be considered as in a state of dynamic equilibrium, with no threats, and consequently no need for "management."

However, most national parks are not complete ecosystems. They are created either deliberately or by chance under very real constraints of limited funds, political exigency, geographical boundary, compass orientation, or other factors totally unrelated to the completeness of the ecosystem. In that sense, the early national park planners in the U.S.A. who said "All I want inside the boundary is everything I can see" may have intuitively expressed an important ecological principle.

Kruger National Park (2 million hectares; 5 million acres) and the Kalahari Gemsbok National Park (1 million hectares; 2.5 million acres) may come the closest in South Africa to being self-contained units. But even in these, and more certainly in the other smaller proclaimed national parks, designated boundaries cut across ecosystems, with the result that only partial ecosystems are included in the protected area. These are not inviolate ecosystems—only less violated.

The above means by definition that the designated park is subject to external threats that have the capability of modifying the protected area. The managing agency is consequently required to respond in an attempt to mitigate the initial failure to establish a complete ecosystem by substituting human interventions for what should have been an automatic response of natural processes. A complete ecosystem shows remarkable long-term stability even while undergoing dramatic changes in the short term. Man's interventions simply accelerate the rates of change, often causing irreversible consequences by the external forces that are brought to bear and with which the ecosystem is unable to cope.

Seen in this light, the best management of a national park may well be the least management. In this scenario, no management intervention would be necessary or permitted. Natural processes would be allowed to proceed without human interference. As a consequence, dramatic swings in wildlife population numbers could be expected based on feast or famine conditions, climatic aberrations, predator numbers, disease, or wildfire, which would maintain the ecosystem in a dynamic, long-cycle state of equilibrium.

The problems with the above scenario are (1) an entire and complete ecosystem is mandatory in order that all relevant controls and actions are included, and (2) human beings, whose desires for outdoor recreation, game viewing, etc., are short-cycle or immediate, would object strenuously to a total "management-by-non-management" policy that permitted natural occurrences (which might take a generation or more to ameliorate) to run unchecked.

Major threats to South Africa's national parks can be categorized under three headings: (1) external threats; (2) internal threats; and (3) official policies, as described below.

External Threats. The environmental consequences of human activities—whether these take place inside or outside the park—constitute a severe threat to the integrity of national parks. Viewed on an individual basis, actions of a park visitor may be entirely appropriate. But in the aggregate, uncontrolled numbers of visitors—all acting properly and responsibly—may over time result in alteration of the park's features and degradation of the intrinsic values for which it was established. A few selected examples illustrate the problem.

1. Visitor Impacts

   a. For years, worldwide publicity has focused on Kruger National Park, making it a prime target for international tourism. The enhanced reputation of the park resulted in increased numbers of tourists, necessitating additional roads, overnight accommodations, sanitary facilities, and service personnel—all the elements of the tourist infrastructure.

b. As national parks increase in popularity with local residents, repeat visitation tends to result in demand for an increased level of services, activities, and facilities, such as the development of resort complexes boasting swimming pools, lodge accommodations, and similar amenities in conjunction with major game reserves. Over time, this tends to favor recreation-related activities over nature-related activities. The primary purpose for which the national park was created becomes secondary.

2. Cultural Impacts

a. Modification of the park's ecosystem can be brought about by man's activities beyond the boundary of the national park. Decreased river flow from upstream irrigation diversions, dam construction with subsequent changes in water tables, flooding, and aquifer characteristics affects the Orange River and impacts Augrabies Falls National Park.

b. Pollutants originating outside national parks can also have serious impacts on the protected ecosystem. For instance, both air and water pollutants generated by the nearby industrial district at Saldanha Bay affect the interior environment of West Coast National Park.

c. Major ecological changes also result from agricultural or industrial developments, such as the mining of economic commodities, livestock grazing, and conversion of wildlands to cropland.

3. Resource Removal

This group of external threats results in the loss of ecosystem components through removal of plants or animals for sale or use. Examples include poaching of animals for sale or food, obtaining materials for handicraft manufacture, and the gathering of firewood and thatch grass.

Internal Threats. The internal element that is an important consideration in protection of a national park is the indigenous wildlife that is itself being protected. Given too great a measure of protection, the population of a protected species can increase to the point where associated values or features of the park are degraded or lost entirely:

1. Inadequate land area can lead to overpopulation of animals per unit area. In specific cases, such as in Kruger National Park, the problem of inadequate space has been compounded by failure to take into account traditional migration patterns.

2. Serious conflicts arise between particular species that have similar environmental needs, such as interspecies competition between elephants and hippos, or between buffalo and bontebok, described earlier.

3. Animals have the capacity to damage, degrade, or destroy the very habitat on which their survival depends. The wide-ranging destruction of trees and other vegetation by elephants and hippos during dry periods is a documented cause of altered landscapes.

Official Policies. This category of threats cannot be classed as internal or external. These are more subtle, yet nevertheless real since they derive from the adopted policies of the managing agency—in this case the National Parks Board of Trustees. Through its selection of adopted policies and procedures, the National Parks Board sets in motion a long-term chain of consequences that result in increased protection or increased vulnerability of the national parks entrusted to its care. Examples include

1. Single species ecosystem management. Manipulating the environment (habitat and life-forms) for the benefit of a single target species (e.g., removing predators to accelerate breeding success of a desired animal).

2. Disposition of surplus animals. Attempting to stabilize an animal population by cropping or culling numbers down to a predetermined acceptable level due to inadequate area for population growth without habitat degradation. Methods variously used include public hunting, hunter disposal, sale, and transfer to private landowners.

3. Loss of Public Support. Though the most indirect, this threat has the potential for destructive impact on the national parks. Parks are vulnerable to deproclamation as a result of economic, social, or political pressures. Only by maintaining a broad base of public support for national parks can existing and future parks continue to be inviolable.

PROSPECTS FOR THE FUTURE

South Africa has made great strides to this point in developing a system of national parks. The avowed objective of preserving a representative sample of each of the nation's major ecosystems is commendable.

However, as a comparatively young country with a low population-land ratio of about 21.3 persons per square kilometer (some 58 persons per square mile), much of the present system of national parks has been designated from extensively used or undeveloped lands where competition from alternative uses has been negligible or absent.

Prospects for the future are altogether different. Most unused lands appropriate to the adopted national park objectives are already included in the system. The necessity remains to incorporate examples of missing ecosystems, or to add to presently proclaimed areas that are incomplete or partial ecosystems. This is especially critical in the case of inadequate size for animal preservation. Examples are Addo Elephant National Park and Mountain Zebra National Park, where existing space is inadequate to permit the threatened populations to increase to a genetically safe level. At Tsitsikamma Forest National Park the existing protected remnant of an ancient rain forest is too small to function as a viable, self-contained ecosystem.

The problems associated with accomplishing the necessary amount of increase are formidable. Adjacent lands are already being impacted by development pressures. Increasing prices make land acquisition expensive and in some cases prohibitive. Conversion to cropland or settlement makes expropriation politically unfeasible. The situation becomes more desperate with each passing year.

The modern approach to national park administration supports an integrated management of biosystems. Mounting evidence clearly shows that decisions to retain animal or plant "collections" as static museum pieces in anything less than a viable complete ecosystem result eventually in costly, time-consuming, and typically unsuccessful attempts to salvage such displays after initial errors in establishment.

South Africa has made major commitments to reduce species extinction in both plants and animals. By signing the Washington Convention on Endangered Species in 1975, the country became an active participant in the movement for protection of threatened wildlife. South Africa also boasts a greater number of plant species than all those found in the U.S.A. or the Soviet Union.[11]

There is recognized worldwide value in ensuring the survival of existing species of both flora and fauna. However, if South Africa's national parks are to survive in the future, they must pay their way. They must be recognized as a truly valued part of the social, historical, and economic framework of the nation. This requires broad-based support of the citizenry.

The population of South Africa is expected to increase from 26 million persons in 1980 to 50 million in 2000. It is dangerous to assume that nearly a doubling of population in less than twenty years will result in a doubling of support for national parks. That might be true. But in fact a doubling of population could also just as easily result in a dramatic loss of popular support. For if the general population perceives the national parks as being elitist, intended primarily for tourists, as an income producer or status symbol for a privileged few, or as the locking up of resources needed for basic food, fiber, commerce, or shelter for the needy, then the consequent loss of popular support could sound the death knell for continuation of South Africa's national parks.

Concerned people representing many political persuasions are working hard to avoid such a calamity. Loss of the rare and unique biological treasures found in South Africa's national parks would constitute an irreparable loss not only to South Africa's patrimony, but to the natural heritage of the entire world as well.

NOTES

1. South Africa, Bureau of Information, *South Africa: 1985/6* (Pretoria, 1986), p. 879.

2. Ibid., p. 880.

3. Ibid.

4. National Parks Board of South Africa, *South Africa's National Parks* (Pretoria, 1985), p. 3.

5. Ibid.

6. South Africa, Bureau of Information, p. 886.

7. No author should attempt the arrogant exercise of describing another country's treasures without expecting to incur substantial criticism from those who know the subject better. I accept the responsibility for errors of fact or interpretation, my primary purpose being to help make the magnificent parks of the Republic of South Africa better known to the people of the world. My sincere appreciation is extended to my colleague and

coauthor, Professor J. N. Steyn, for providing much up-to-date information and for reviews responsible for major improvements in the draft text.

8. South Africa, Bureau of Information, p. 882.

9. René Gordon, *The National Parks of South Africa* (Cape Town: Struik, 1983), p. 138.

10. Ibid., p. 12.

11. South Africa, Bureau of Information, p. 894.

BIBLIOGRAPHY

Cape of Good Hope (Province). Department of Nature Conservation and Environmental Conservation. *Cape Department of Nature Conservation and Museum Services, Report No. 26.* Cape Town, RSA: The Department, 1980.

Levy, Jaynee. *Everyone's Guide to Trailing and Mountaineering in Southern Africa.* Cape Town, RSA: C. Struik Publishers, 1982.

Natal (Province). Natal Parks, Game and Fish Commission. *Resorts, Parks, Game and Nature Reserves in Natal.* Pietermaritzburg, RSA: The Commission, n.d.

————. Natal Town and Regional Planning Commission. *A Planning Guide to Hiking Trails.* Pietermaritzburg, RSA: The Commission, 1977.

Skinner, John. *South African Animals in the Wild.* Pretoria, RSA: Mammal Research Institute, University of Pretoria, 1985.

South Africa (Republic). Bureau of Information. *South African Digest.* Pretoria, RSA: Government Printer (weekly news journal).

————. Department of Environmental Planning and Energy. *National Outdoor Recreation Plan, vol. 3: Terrain Capability Classification.* Pretoria, RSA: Government Printer, 1980.

South Africa (Republic). Department of Foreign Affairs and Information. *South Africa: 1980/1,* and *South Africa: 1984/5.* Official Yearbooks. Pretoria, RSA: The Department, 1981 and 1985.

————. National Tourist Bureau, Department of Tourism. *Guide Map for the Tourist: Republic of South Africa.* Pretoria, RSA: Government Printer, n.d.

————. *The Western Cape—Year Round Tourist Paradise.* Pretoria, RSA: Government Printer, n.d.

South African Tourist Corporation. *The Peace Game.* Pretoria, RSA: The Corporation, 1978.

————. *Travel Digest of South Africa: 1980.* Pretoria, RSA: The Corporation, 1980.

————. *Orchids of the Veld.* Pretoria, RSA: The Corporation, 1977.

Tyack, Maurice. *South Africa: Land of Challenge.* Lausanne, Switzerland: L.A.M. Tyack–France Inter Presse, 1976.

Youngblood, Peter. "Playing God With Nature." *International Wildlife* (Washington, D.C.) (July/August 1986): 4–13.

UGANDA

Frederick I. B. Kayanja

By African standards, Uganda is a small country with an area of 240,000 square kilometers (93,000 square miles) including 44,000 square kilometers (17,000 square miles) of water and swamp. Thirty percent of the dry land is cultivated, 8.7 percent is national parks and game reserves, and 7.6 percent is forest. The balance of 53.7 percent is partly utilized for grazing, partly available for improved mixed crop and animal husbandry activities, and partly available for the development of new parks. Uganda has four parks: Queen Elizabeth National Park, 2,475 square kilometers (956 square miles); Murchison Falls National Park, 3,814 square kilometers (1,473 square miles); Kidepo Valley National Park, 1,344 square kilometers (519 square miles); and Lake Mburo National Park, 380 square kilometers (147 square miles). See Figure 21.1.

HISTORY

During 1951, Sir Andrew Cohen arrived in Uganda as governor. Unlike his predecessors, he enjoyed the wilderness and the wildlife of Uganda. He initiated discussion on wildlife and the possibilities of national parks. In March 1952 the National Parks Act was passed through the Legislative Council, the pre-independence parliament of Uganda.

Ralph Dreschfield, who was attorney general, became the first chairman of the Board of Trustees. The foresight and pioneering spirit of Cohen, and the drive and enthusiasm of Dreschfield for the cause, ensured the smooth take-off of Uganda's national parks.

Kidepo Valley National Park was gazetted in 1962, and during 1982 Lake Mburo National Park was gazetted. In the aftermath of the recent civil war

Figure 21.1
The National Parks of Uganda

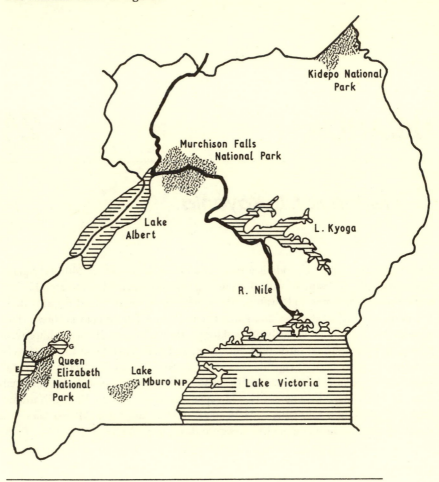

Note: E = Lake Edward; G = Lake George.

(1979–1986) and with the beginning of a new era of peace, the process of park creation is being revived and new forest national parks are being planned.

PARKS AND RESERVES

Queen Elizabeth National Park

In favorable weather, the immense landscape with which one is confronted from Mweya Peninsula is one of the most impressive and beautiful in Africa.

Geology. The park is situated within the southern part of the Western Rift

Valley (Albertine Rift). The valley runs the length of Uganda on the west; it constitutes the Lakes Edward, George, and Albert basins, and the Rwenzori Mountain host block. It is highly asymmetrical in places, faulting being more pronounced on the eastern side.

The park is bounded to the west by Lake Edward and extends northward to enclose Lake George (Figure 21.2). Except for the relief resulting from volcanic piles within the rift and at the northern margin, south of Lake George, the larger part of this park is plain flat land only interrupted by rift margins to the east. The two lakes within the rift are linked by Kazinga Channel, which is the heart of this park. The eastern escarpment is 185 to 250 meters (607 to 820 feet) high in the north, becoming lower and less well defined southward until it disappears. Transversely the rift floor rises gradually from 930 meters (3,050 feet) at Lake George and Kazinga Channel to 1,055 meters (3,460 feet) where it meets the rift escarpment.

The geology in this area is dominated by Plio-Pleistocene rift sediments, the Pleistocene volcanics, and the presently forming swamp and alluvial deposits around the lakeshores. The volcanic regions, each characterized by numerous craters, are exposed. The Katwe-Kikorongo volcanic field is within the rift floor, while the region composed of Kichwamba and Bunyaruguru is at the eastern margin of the rift. Volcanic activity was evidently explosive, as indicated by the numerous craters. The salt (crater) lakes at Katwe and Kasenyi are of economic value and, if treated scientifically, may rank as renewable resources. The highest probability for discovery of commercially exploitable petroleum reserves may be in the rather thick sedimentary section within Lake Albert itself.

History and Archaeology. The Trans-Africa Expedition led by English explorer Henry Morgan Stanley visited the area of Queen Elizabeth National Park in January 1876. In July 1891 Frederick John Dealtry Lugard crossed the channel by canoe and also visited the area known today as Mweya. By 1910 sleeping sickness was a serious problem around Katunguru, and people died in large numbers on the islands in Lake Edward and Lake George. The sleeping sickness areas became "restricted areas," the terms given to depopulated and controlled parts of the country. Queen Elizabeth National Park was eventually created from these "restricted areas."

In 1925, immediately after formation of Uganda Game Department, an area of 689 square kilometers (266 square miles) was established as Lake George Game Reserve. Lake Edward Game Reserve, an area of 559 square kilometers (216 square miles), was declared in 1930. This area, which ultimately formed the Ishasha sector of Queen Elizabeth National Park, was enlarged to include the area south of Kazinga Channel and below Kichwamba escarpment. Queen Elizabeth National Park was declared in 1952.

As president of Uganda, Idi Amin announced that he had renamed the park Rwenzori. The name was used while Amin held power, but it was dropped when he was overthrown because it had never been incorporated in the law.

Throughout the Pleistocene the park's vegetation (where not inundated by

Figure 21.2
Geological Map of Queen Elizabeth National Park

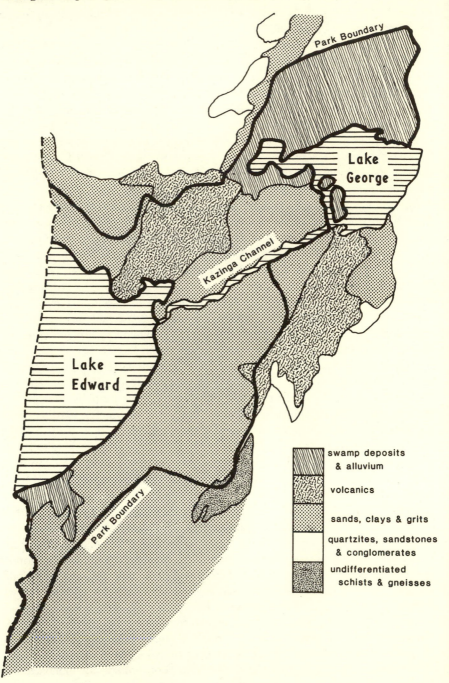

water) was probably much like it is today. The forests were more extensive, and trees were certainly more numerous. Paleolithic hunters and food gatherers of the early Stone Age wandered through these areas. Their way of life was favored by the open savanna type of country, and signs of their presence have been revealed by recent erosion.

The most populous areas were along the lakeshores and the Nile where fishing could supplement hunting and agriculture. Bantu people lived in these areas for many hundreds of years. Successive waves of migration of Hamitic and Nilotic invaders from the north and northeast have left their mark on the populace and are partly responsible for the presence of several different ethnic groups.

The hunter-agriculturalists established a relatively stable ecological equilibrium with the wildlife among which they lived. Man was an integral part of the natural ecosystem, hunting for meat and practicing shifting cultivation. Apparently the wildlife shared man's world as he shared theirs. Wildlife would probably have fared badly had it not been for the African's deep understanding of and respect for animal life.

Birds. Queen Elizabeth National Park is the most interesting park to the enthusiastic bird-watcher. Two species of pelican can be easily distinguished, the white and the pink-backed, and both species breed in Africa. Two species of cormorants are also present: the white-necked and the long-tailed black. The darter, sometimes mistaken for a cormorant, occurs in company with pelicans and cormorants on the beach.

Fish eagles have conspicuous nests on the tops of tall trees along the Kazinga Channel. In the channel one sees the ubiquitous pied kingfisher and the brilliant malachite or crested kingfisher.

The Goliath heron is an imposing bird, sometimes well over four feet in height. The purple heron is similar in appearance but smaller. The black-headed heron is very similar to the gray heron. The rather elegant saddle-bill storks can be seen where there are pools of water in the plains. Four types of egret or lesser heron, all of them pure white, are sometimes seen on the shore, but more often they are to be found in open country following the herds of buffalo and elephant.

Gulls and terns are seen usually in large numbers near the Katunguru Bridge, and a large population of Egyptian geese inhabits the lakes and channel. The ibis family is represented by the sacred and the hadada ibis.

The marabou stork, a repulsive-looking bird, is to be found in large numbers near fish markets and human habitations. The beautiful flamingo is not a permanent resident but comes and goes with changing weather conditions. Flamingos are often present in small numbers on the Katwe Salt Lake.

Bee-eaters are very similar to kingfishers in their bright plumage and nesting habits. Weaver birds build nests on branches and bushes near pools, while hammerheads build huge nests in forks of trees beside the water. Plovers, stilts, ducks, and geese congregate at pools where hippos wallow. Also, a large number of migrant wading birds visit Uganda during the northern winter. Among the migrants are sandpipers, sanderlings, godwits, and the tiny stints. Guinea fowl

Figure 21.3
Geological Map of Murchison Falls National Park

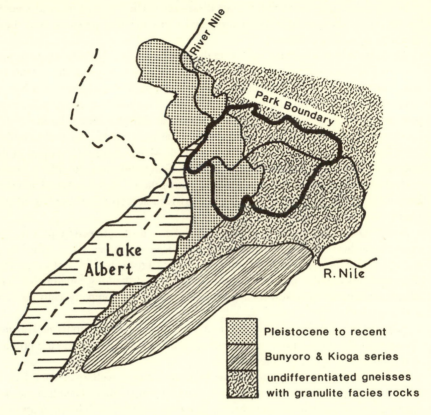

are common. Gray parrots, crowned eagles, and great blue turacos can be seen in the Maramagambo forested area of Queen Elizabeth National Park. Hornbills are also common in the forest.

Eagles, hawks, buzzards, and kites are the most significant birds of prey in Uganda. While the Bataleur eagle is the most impressive of all eagles in flight, the martial eagle is the most magnificent, and Whalberg's eagle is probably the most common. The African kite is found in large numbers. Vultures are also present, with the hooded vulture being most common.

Mammals. The elephants found in Queen Elizabeth National Park have affinities with the forest elephant (*Loxodonta africana cyclotis*). The average number of elephants recorded in this park between 1963 and 1973 was 2,393. In 1974, the population began to decline due to heavy poaching so that by 1976 only 931 elephants were recorded.

The hippopotamus (*Hippopotamus amphibius*) is common in both Murchison Falls and Queen Elizabeth parks (Figure 21.3). The African black buffalo (*Syncerus caffer caffer*) has remained plentiful throughout the parks in spite of uncontrolled poaching. Some buffalo in Queen Elizabeth National Park show signs of integrating with the red forest buffalo (*Syncerus caffer nanus*) of Zaire.

The Uganda kob (*Kobus kob*) is the most widely distributed antelope in Queen Elizabeth and Murchison Falls national parks. Its head is displayed on the crest of the Uganda National Parks. The Bohor reedbuck (*Redunca redunca*) is similar to the kob but is somewhat smaller. The waterbuck (*Kobus defassa*) is perhaps the finest of all antelopes in Ugandan parks. Waterbuck form small herds that almost always remain in the same locality. The topi (*Damaliscus lanatus*) is similar in appearance to the hartebeests but is certainly more handsome. Topi are present in large numbers, forming enormous herds often in association with kob and buffalo, on the grassy plains of the Ishasha sector of Queen Elizabeth National Park.

Side-striped jackals (*Canis adustus*) can be seen as well as the spotted hyena (*Crocuta crocuta*). Little packs of banded mongoose (*Mungos mungo*) scuttle about looking for beetles and other insects. Mongooses are plentiful, and at least four different species occur: slender mongoose (*Herpestes sanguineus*), greater gray mongoose (*Herpestes ichneumon*), marsh mongoose (*Altilax paladinosus*), and white-tailed mongoose (*Ichneumia albicauda*).

The nocturnal African polecat, or zorilla (*Ictonyx striatis*), is rarely seen. The same applies to the African civet (*Civettictis civetta*), which is actually plentiful, as is the bush genet (*Genetta tigrina*).

The ratel, or honey badger (*Mellivora capensis*), is led to the bees' nest by a bird, the honey guide.

The African wildcat (*Felis lybica*) is plentiful although rarely seen. The serval (*Felis serval*) is largely nocturnal and shows a preference for swampy ground near water. The leopard (*Panthera pardus*) is also rarely seen because it seldom moves about during daylight. The lion (*Panthera leo*) is easier to see, being plentiful, especially on the Ishasha Plains, where lions feed on topi and climb *Ficus* or *Acacia* trees to rest in the branches.

The long-haired chimpanzee (*Pan troglodytes*) can be seen in the Maramagambo forest. Baboons (*Papio anubis*) are common. Vervet monkeys (*Cercopithecus aehiops*) are also common. On the other hand, the Uganda blue monkey, a resident of the Maramagambo forest, very rarely seen. The black and white colobus (*Colobus abyssinicus*) is fairly common, but the red colobus (*Colobus badius*) is difficult to see as it occupies the inaccessible region of the Mpanga Dura River.

The African ant-bear, or aardvark (*Orycteropus afer*), is widely distributed but rarely seen because it is completely nocturnal, spending the daylight hours underground. The pangolin, or scaly anteater (*Manis temmincki*), porcupine, and bud hedgehog share this nocturnal behavior.

The East African hare (*Lepus capensis*) is present in large numbers, as are bats and rodents. Squirrels, rates, mice, and shrews are ubiquitous. Warthogs are present in fairly large numbers; and giant forest hogs, squirrels, bushbuck, duikers, and elephants are present in Maramagambo forest.

Fish. Lakes Edward and George, the Kazinga Channel, and the Semliki River on the borders of this park contain many fish. The channel and lakes, especially Lake George, are particularly productive. Organic manure from the many hippos that inhabit these waters sustains a rich microscopic plant life upon which the fish feed.

The most important of the herbivorous fish is *Tilapia nilotica*, known locally as *ngege*. Feeding upon the herbivorous fish are several predatory species. The most interesting of the predators is the lungfish (*Protopterus aethiopicus*), known locally as *mamba*. The mudfish (*Clarias* spp.), known locally as *male*, is another predator. Catfish (*Bagrus docmac*), locally known as *semutundu*, are numerous. Barbel (*Barbus altianalis*), locally known as *kisinja*, abound in the rivers flowing into the lakes from Rwenzori Mountain. The *Mormyrus*, or elephant-snout fish, known to local fishermen as *kasulubana*, lives in the deep water of Lake Edward. A large variety of smaller fish, especially *Haplochromis*, are important especially as a source of food for the larger species.

Reptiles. There are no crocodiles in lakes Edward and George and the Kazinga Channel, but the dull gray-brown monitor (*varanus niloticus*), the gaudy agama and blue-bodied agama (*Agama atricollis*), skinks, and chameleons are common.

Many species of snakes can be found, but only a few will be mentioned. The large python (*Python sebae*) and vipers such as the puff adder (*Bitis arietans*) and the Gaboon viper (*Bitis gabonica*) are easily identified. The rhinoceros-horned viper (*Bitis nasicornis*) is partially aquatic and forest-dwelling. Four species of cobras can be found: the black-lipped cobra (*Naja melanoleuca*), the spitting cobra (*Naja nigricollis*), the Egyptian cobra (*Naja haje*), and the Gold's forest cobra (*Pseudohaje goldii*). The forest mamba (*Dendroaspis jamesoni kiamosae*) is more slender than the cobras. It resembles the back-fanged boomslang (*Dispholodus typhus*), which inhabits woodland and bush country. The sun snake (*Psammophis sibilans*) is found in grassland and bushes. The night adders (*Causus rhombeatus* and *Causus resimus*) are widely distributed.

Wilderness. Queen Elizabeth National Park has areas of open bush country. The plains are studded with Euphobia and thickets among the short grass savanna near the great lakes and the channel. These areas are heavily grazed by the hippopotamus. There are pools on the plains where hippos wallow and other animals drink.

Toward Rwenzori Mountain are hills resulting from past volcanism. Some of the volcanic craters are filled by lakes, while others are covered with forest or grassland. The southern end of the park has the Maramagambo forest. The majority of the trees in this forest are evergreen. Uganda ironwood is the most abundant and conspicuous species. Toward the northern extremity of the main forest are large patches of "swamp forest" dominated by wild date palms (*Phoenix*). The Maramagambo forest is the haunt of chimpanzees, which visit the date palms in season for fruit.

Beyond the Maramagambo forest are the Ishasha Plains, where fig trees and acacias grow in red oat grass. Herds of topi graze this area in company with

Uganda kob. Large herds of buffalo are also present as well as tree-climbing lions. The rapid expansion of the acacias has taken place on the plains at the expense of the grassland, a change that is unfavorable to the topi.

Recreation. Visitors to Queen Elizabeth National Park can be accommodated in Mweya Safari Lodge, which offers luxurious services for up to 100 guests. The lodge is strategically situated on Kazinga Channel so that guests can enjoy launch trips along the channel. The lodge commands a wonderful view over Lake Edward and is right in the heart of abundant game country. Ishasha rest camp has six bandas with twelve beds for guests who wish to see this part of the park.

Murchison Falls National Park

The Victoria Nile of Murchison Falls National Park is a more exciting spectacle than Kazinga Channel. The river enters the eastern end of the park and runs for about 120 kilometers (75 miles), cutting the park almost in half. The Murchison Falls, from which the name of the park is derived, form the most spectacular sight along the course of the Nile from Lake Victoria to the Mediterranean. The bulk of the flowing Nile water plunges through a gap of about 6 meters (20 feet), and drops 40 meters (130 feet) into an incredible cauldron of turbulent water below. This is followed by about 1.5 kilometers (1 mile) of extremely turbulent rapids as the river heads for Lake Albert.

Geology. This national park occupies part of the northern Albertine Rift and is partly outside the rift in the east. The part that is outside the rift is traversed by the Victoria Nile. The geology in this area includes the younger sediments laid down in the rift basin and the much older basement rocks within the eastern park of the park.

Limited original geological work has been done on the basement rocks in the park (Figure 21.3). According to J. V. Hepworth and P. K. Mazimhaka, three rock types based on metamorphic and structural criteria exist. These are the granulites, granite gneisses, and siliceous schists and gneisses.

The Plio-Pleistocene sediments are distributed along the rift floor, with the thickest sediments along the present course of the River Nile. These thin to the west and terminate at a line 16 kilometers (10 miles) from the river.

Some of the sediments along Lake Albert contain mammalian remains of the Miocene age. These Plio-Pleistocene sediments in the park and further north are a continuation of the Lake Albert basin sediments and are a potential source of oil.

The Karuma Falls, to the east of the park, owe their origin to alternation of resistant (quartzitic) horizons with softer (micaceous) rocks. The magnificent Murchison Falls owe their origin to the sudden relief drop from the competent Precambrian basement rocks to the rather incompetent Plio-Pleistocene rift sediments. This geological boundary is marked by a normal fault with a drop to the west. The falls are further modified by the differential hardness of the Pre-cambrian rocks.

History and Archaelogy. In 1862, J. H. Speke and J. A. Grant became the first Europeans to visit Lake Victoria, the headwaters of the Nile. Returning north they crossed the Victoria Nile at Karuma Falls, at the eastern edge of what is now Murchison Falls National Park. On April 3, 1864, Samuel White Baker saw the fabulous Murchison Falls. By 1904, when Sir Albert Cook and Bishop Tucker visited the area, sleeping sickness was rampant. During 1907 Winston Churchill visited the area and was most impressed by the Murchison Falls. Churchill noted the frightful ravages made by the sleeping sickness. A huge area about 13,000 square kilometers (5,000 square miles) was depopulated, and on December 10, 1910, the Bunyoro Game Reserve was established in the depop-ulated area. This game reserve was extended and renamed Bunyoro and Gulu Game Reserve in 1923. In May 1952 the game reserve became Murchison Falls National Park.

Idi Amin renamed this park Kabalega, but again the name did not last beyond the period of his rule.

Fish. The Murchison Falls limit the spread of the Nile fauna. Fish are unable to scale the cataract to reach the waters of Lakes Kioga and Victoria. This explains why the tiger-fish, the Nile *ngege* (*Tilapia esculenta* and *variabilis*), and other typical nilotic species are to be found below the falls and not above, where the waters are populated by the Lake Victoria species. The latter are very similar to those found in Lakes George and Edward of Queen Elizabeth National Park.

The spectacularly large and predatory Nile perch (*Lates albertianus*), locally known as *mputa*, is very common below the falls. In 1955 and 1956 Nile perch were transferred from Lake Albert to the Victoria Nile above the falls and to Lake Kioga. It is becoming clear that this was a tragic mistake as this predator is seriously depleting the waters of other species.

Two species of tiger-fish, the smaller *Hydrocyon forskalli* and the larger *Hydrocyon lineatus*, are also common below the falls. *Alestes baremose* and *Alestes macrolepidotus* superficially resemble the tiger-fish and are plentiful below the falls. The electric catfish (*Malopterurus electricus*) is also common. Moonfish (*Citherinus citherus*), butterfish (*Schilbe mystus*), a large species of upside-down catfish (*Synodontis schall*), and bichirs (*Polypterus senegalus*) are also present.

Mammals. Mammals tend to be concentrated in a few localities, around Chobe, the Buligi circuits, and the Nile below the falls. The park's elephant population was estimated to be as high as 15,000 in the late 1960s and early 1970s, but 90 percent of the park's elephants, most of the rhinos, and large numbers of other species were destroyed through uncontrolled poaching. In the early 1980s, fewer than 1,500 elephants survived. It is reassuring to note that there are now plenty of young elephants in the herds.

The elephants of this park, like those of Kidepo Valley National Park, are typical bush elephants (*Loxodonta africana cyclotis*). Severe damage was caused to the woodlands by elephants stripping bark from trees, especially *Terminalia*, when their population was very high. The trees, deprived of their bark, were very susceptible to fire, which they easily survive if their bark is intact. The present low numbers of elephants are allowing the woodland to regenerate, and the regeneration should increase the diversity of habitats in both Murchison Falls and Queen Elizabeth national parks.

In spite of the efforts made to establish the northern white rhinoceros (*Cerato therium simum*) in Murchison Falls National Park, it is feared that this species is now extinct in the wild. While a very few black rhinos (*Diceros bicormis*) may still exist within the park, it is certain that this species has also suffered from the poachers.

The hippopotamus is abundant here, as it is in Queen Elizabeth National Park. Rothschild's giraffe (*Giraffa camelopardalis rothschildi*) occurs in small numbers in the acacia woodlands near Chobe and along the Nile below the falls. On the other hand, the Cape buffalo (*Syncerus caffer*) occurs in large herds throughout the park.

Jackson's hartebeest (*Alcelaphus buselaphus jacksoni*) is common in Murchison Falls National Park. It is often referred to as the *kongoni*. The bushbuck (*Tragelaphus scriptus*), on the other hand, are relatively commoner in thickets, especially near the Nile. The most numerous species of larger mammal is likely to be the Uganda kob (*Kobus kob*). The waterbuck (*Kobus defassa*) is common near the Nile. The bush duiker and the common (Bohor) reedbuck are also common, the latter at Buligi. Pairs or small family groups of oribi (*Ourebia ourebia*) are common and widespread. Warthogs are numerous in the shorter grass areas of Murchison Falls National Park, while bush pigs are relatively uncommon.

The Cape hare (*Lepus capensis*) is a common species of the grassland areas in all the parks. The Bunyoro rabbit (*Pronolagus majorita*) can usually be seen between Paraa and Buligi. Only a few species of rodents have been recorded in this park, but this reflects lack of study more than lack of rodents.

The aardvark (*Orycteropus afer*) is well distributed in all the parks. The lesser ground pangolin (*Manis temmincki*) is also found in all the parks.

Six species of primates have been recorded for Murchison Falls National Park, including the chimpanzee, which is found in Rabongo forest. Patas monkeys (*Erythrocebus patas*) can be seen in this park. The black and white colobus (*Colobus polykomos abyssinicus*) is common, particularly in the riverside forests. Red-tailed monkeys can also be seen in forested areas, while troops of baboons are commonly seen in open savanna, especially where there are extensive rocky outcrops. Vervet monkeys occur where there are many trees but not dense forest.

Predators are difficult to locate in the long grass areas of Murchison Falls National Park. Leopards, which are quite plentiful, are difficult to see for this reason and also because they are seldom abroad in daylight. Lions are more easily seen, especially along the Buligi Circuit and the rocky kopjes west of Chobe.

Wildnerness. Along the Nile are small patches of evergreen forest, woodland, scrub, rich grassy meadows, and bare eroded ground, where a few tamarind trees and desert dates grow. South of the river the park is almost entirely open grassland. The Chobe section overlooks one of the most turbulent stretches of the Nile. Fine woodlands are a feature of this part of the park. The trees are mainly *Terminalia*, acacia, and albizia. Black rhinos were once numerous around Chobe.

Recreation. Visitors may stay in the Chobe or the Paraa Safari Lodge. Paraa Safari Lodge overlooks the Nile, on which launch trips to the famed Murchison Falls are an unforgettable experience. Both lodges are to be rehabilitated as they were damaged during the civil war. Pakuba Grand Hotel was looted during the war and will take longer to rehabilitate.

Kidepo Valley National Park

The beautiful wilderness of rugged mountains, rocky hills, and open plains of Kidepo Valley National Park supports a range of wildlife that is distinct from other parks. Except for its northwestern border, the national border with the Sudan, the park is an arid plain, albeit reasonably well wooded in places, almost surrounded by wild and rugged mountains. Both Morungole Massif, 2,750 meters (9,000 feet), and the highest point of the Napore Range, 2,286 meters (7,500 feet), are within the park.

Geology. As suggested in its name, the park is centered on Kidepo Valley, which drains northwesterly through the Kidepo River into the Nile. The area is basically a plain dissected by the shallow and broad Kidepo Valley with meandering and braided streams that are seasonally active.

The park is covered by high-grade old basement complex rocks, belonging mainly to the Karamjoa group and partly to the Karasuk group, and much younger spots of the late Tertiary intrusives related to the Zulia complex and some carbonatites (Figure 21.4).

History and Archaeology. Kidepo Valley National Park is part of a harsh, wild country that was in a constant state of unrest because of raids and counter raids by Didinga, Turkana, Karamajong, and the inhabitants of Dodoth. There were no fixed tribal boundaries except on the mountains where most of the more permanent villages were situated. The country was full of game, particularly elephants, which the inhabitants trapped and hunted with their spears. To add to the confusion, Ethiopia laid claim to much of this during Emperor Menelik's reign.

The first military patrol passed through the Kidepo Valley in 1907 in a peacemaking mission, and by 1920 the situation was stable. The Game Department built a permanent camp at the foot of the Napore Hills, and in 1958 a game

Figure 21.4
Geological Map of Kidepo Valley National Park

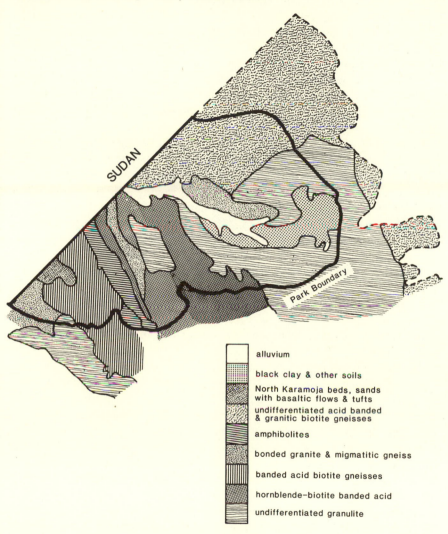

alluvium

black clay & other soils

North Karamoja beds, sands
with basaltic flows & tufts

undifferentiated acid banded
& granitic biotite gneisses

amphibolites

bonded granite & migmatitic gneiss

banded acid biotite gneisses

hornblende–biotite banded acid

undifferentiated granulite

reserve was declared. As part of the preparations for the independence of Uganda, a national park was declared in 1962.

Mammals. It is rather remarkable that the semi-arid Kidepo Valley supports so many different kinds of mammals, and sometimes in large numbers. The park contained a comparatively low population of about 600 elephants in the mid-1970s. However, the population has been less severely reduced by poaching than in other parks. The elephants in this park are of the bush variety and are most frequently seen near the Kidepo and Narus watercourses.

The black rhinoceros is still found in this park, as are the warthog and bushpig.

Rothschild's giraffe (*Giraffa camelopardalis rothschildi*) is often seen in considerable herds throughout Kidepo Valley National Park. The common zebra (*Equus burchelli*) occurs sometimes in large herds in open country and in company with other animals. The buffalo is less common here than in Queen Elizabeth or Murchison Falls.

The greater kudu (*Tragelaphus strepsiceros*), with perhaps the most magnificent horns carried by any antelope anywhere, is found on the Morungole Massif above the park. Lesser kudu (*Strepsiceros imberbis*), elegant miniatures of the greater kudu, inhabit dry country.

The eland (*Taurotragus oryx*) occurs in this park, and large herds can be seen, especially in wet weather, in the short grass country near the Kidepo River. The roan antelope (*Hippotragus equinus bakeri*) is another large antelope that can be seen in Kidepo, usually in small herds or as single bulls. Beisa oryx (*Oryx beisa*) occur in the Kidepo region, but have not been recorded in the park. Where there are husher thickets bushbuck may be seen but in small numbers. The most numerous antelope are Jackson's hartebeest, which are widespread in the park. Defassa waterbuck are less numerous and favor the moister areas.

The oribi, common (Bohor) reedbuck, and Chanler's mountain reedbuck (*Redunca fulvorufula chanleri*) are smaller antelopes that occur in small numbers in this park. The dikdik (*Rhynchotragus kirkii*) is a small animal that occurs only in dry bush country. The only true gazelle in Uganda is Grant's gazelle (*Gazella granti brighti*). Herds as large as thirty animals can be seen in the drier acacia bush country.

The cheetah (*Acinonyx jubatus*) is usually seen in pairs or small family groups. Leopards, although difficult to see, are probably quite common at Kidepo. Lions are easier to see, especially in the Narus valley during the dry season, when the game is concentrated there. The African wildcat (*Felis lybica*) is present in this park, as is the serval (*Felis serval*). In the Kidepo region, servals mostly inhabit thickets along the banks of watercourses. The caracal, or African lynx (*Felis caracal*), occurs in acacia scrub in Karamoja but has seldom been seen in Kidepo Valley National Park. African wild dog (*Lycaon pictus*), or hunting dogs, are relatively common in Kidepo Valley National Park. The side-striped jackal, active during the day as well as at night, is quite often seen, as is its near relative, the black-backed jackal (*Canis mesomelas*). The bat-eared fox (*Otocyon megalotis*) is largely but not entirely nocturnal, and is sometimes seen in the park.

Although rarely observed, the aardvark manifests its presence by characteristic diggings in termite mounds. The aardwolf (*Proteles cristatus*) is a hyena that, unlike its relatives, is both long-legged and long-haired. The common striped hyena can be heard most nights on the plains throughout most of Africa. The striped hyena (*Hyaena hyaena*) is smaller in size, rarer, and inhabits drier habitats, often traveling long distances to drink.

Squirrels, rats, mice, and shrews are ubiquitous. The striped ground squirrel (*Xerus erythropus*) is plentiful in this park, as are the giant rat (*Cricetomys*

gambianus) and the cane rat (*Thryonomys swinderianus*). The nocturnal porcupines and hedgehogs are widely distributed. The East African crested porcupine
(*Hystrix galeata*) is covered with long, sharp quills that effectively protect it
even against lions and leopards. Cape hares are numerous, and the so-called
Bunyoro rabbit is present in this park too. Bats can be seen at dusk.

Five species of primates have been recorded for Kidepo Valley National Park.
The smallest is the lesser galago. The black-faced vervet monkey (*Cercopithecus
aethiops*) can be seen in well-wooded country, but the blue monkey is rarely
seen. Baboons inhabit the park in troops that may number up to 100.

Birds. Although little is yet known about the bird life of this park, the variety
of habitats indicates that there is bound to be an enormous wealth of bird life.
The ostrich (*Struthio camelus rothschildi*) is the most spectacular of them all.
It is seen in the short grass areas of the park, often in flocks of up to ten birds.
The kori bustard (*Ardeotis kori*), the largest of African bustards, is sometimes
seen in the Kidepo plains. Other bustards are common, as are guinea fowl,
francolins, and the colorful yellow-necked spurfowl (*Francolinus leucoscepus*).
Other common bird species include quails, starlings, bee-eaters, and hornbills
(*Bucerotidae*). Kingfishers, herons, storks, and geese have been recorded in
the park.

This park offers ideal conditions for hawks and eagles, with steep rocks and
outcrops serving as vantage points and short grass where the prey is easy to see.
Including vultures, many species of birds of prey have been recorded in this
park. Among them are rare falcons (*Falconidae*), goshawks (*Melie rax* spps.),
the Egyptian vulture (*Neophron percnopterus*), and the swallow-tailed kite (*Chil-
ictinia riocourii*). The rare immaculate Verreaux's eagle (*Aquila verreauxii*) hunts
from rocky crags in the mountains, and a few lammergeyer (*Gypaetus barbatus*)
live high up on Morungole.

Wilderness. Kidepo Valley National Park is traversed by two river systems,
the Narus and the Kidepo. The latter is a sand river for most of the year.
Permanent water is limited to a few waterholes, dams made since the park was
established, and the headwaters of one or two streams flowing into the Narus,
notably the Lorupei. The monotony of the plains is broken by the many tributaries
flowing into the Narus and the Kidepo. These are sand-rivers too, and some
appear to be no more than erosion gullies. Only a few places apart from the
Narus Valley have permanent water. These places are: around the base of Morungole, at Lokudul, and at Kananorok Hot Springs.

The southwestern section of the park is less harsh and has a higher rainfall
than the Kidepo Plains. It provides the main area of concentration for game in
dry weather. Apoka, the park headquarters, Opotipot, and Katurum, are all
located in this southwestern section.

To date, Kidepo Valley National Park is the only Ugandan national park with
any true montane country. The mountains were more heavily forested in the past
than they are today. The tree line has receded up the slope due to recurrent grass
fires on the plains. It supports many of the same animals. The main forest trees

Figure 21.5
Map of Lake Mburo National Park

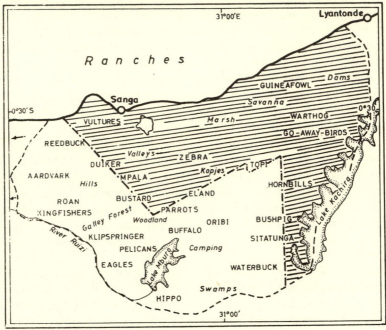

Note: The shaded area will be degazetted for human use.

are *Podocarpus*, a form of yew, and junipers, which carry a good variety of epiphytes and orchids.

The Narus Valley has some fine acacia trees, *Combretum*, and the *Longhocarpus* shrub. Along the Kidepo River are magnificent and extensive groves of Borassus palms. Elsewhere the land is mainly steppe with smaller acacias, a shrubby form of *Albizia*, desert dates, and an occasional tamarind tree. There are great clumps of dry thicket with sword-sharp *Sanseviera* succulents and thorny bushes. The desert rose grows out on the steppe, and colorful herbs burst into flower after the first rains.

Recreation. Kidepo Valley National Park remains the most difficult to visit by road. Visitors to the park can be accommodated in Apoka Rest Camp, which has thirty-two beds. Katurum Lodge, with forty beds, was being constructed when turbulence started in Uganda, and it remains incomplete.

Lake Mburo National Park

Lake Mburo National Park is situated in the scenic Lake District of southeast Ankole in western Uganda. This park, declared in 1982, is the youngest and has been the most problematic (Figure 21.5).

Geology. The topography of this area is lithologically controlled especially in

Figure 21.6
Geological Map of Lake Mburo National Park

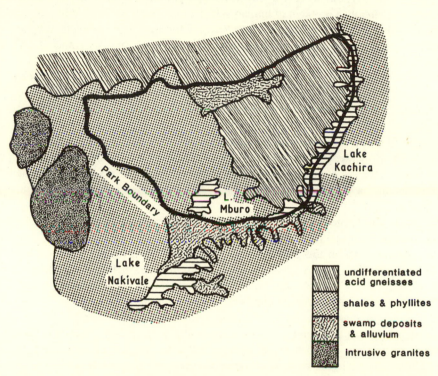

areas occupied by Karagwe-Ankolean rocks. The quartzite outcrops form sharp, high ridges, while the hills covered by phyllites are lower, smooth, and rounded. The lakes occupy the lowest zones, mostly along lithologic boundaries (Figure 21.6).

The lithology covering this park consists of Precambrian undifferentiated acid gneisses, which are part of the basement complex in the east and north, and the Karagwe-Ankolean shales and phyllites with lenses of conglomeratic quartzites in the west and south. Recent alluvial swamp deposits are found within both formations in the valleys adjacent to the lakes. Further west outside the park area, there are two undifferentiated gneissic acid (Arena) granites derived from Buganda-Toro and Karagwe-Ankolean rocks (Masha and Mbarara).

This national park is characterized by hilly landforms typical of central Uganda. The series of lakes and swamps on the eastern and southern sides of the park make it ideal for the purpose.

History and Archaeology. The inhabitants of this area were continuously harassed by wild animals. For this reason, the Enganzi of Ankole (prime minister of the Kingdom of Ankole), Kesi Nganwa, sought help from the colonial government. He made an appeal for game guards to be made available, and this was done in the 1950s. Later the Ankole local government requested that the area be established as a game reserve, which was done.

Unfortunately, the game reserve suffered from serious human encroachment. By December 1982, when the government approved establishing the reserve, there was already a problem of human settlement in the area. In addition, a large part of the area had already been developed through a government ranching scheme. The entire area, including human settlements and the ranches, was unwisely established as a national park on January 7, 1983.

The Obote government was overthrown in July 1985. All park buildings and structures were destroyed as people flocked to resettle the area. Park vehicles were seized by the National Resistance Army, and the park existed in name only.

The Board of Trustees and the international community appealed to the new government, under President Yoweri Museveni, to find a solution to this thorny problem. Interested parties were summoned to discuss the matter, an approach that should have been adopted in 1982. A compromise now has been found (Figure 21.5).

Mammals. Large mammals are absent. Elephants disappeared from the area about fifty years ago, and there are no records of giraffes or rhinoceroses. There are also no lions in the park although some have been reported in the neighborhood. Buffalo were almost eliminated from this park before it was declared, and the surviving few are wary. The habitat, having lush grass and many valleys, is ideal for buffalo, and their numbers should eventually increase.

The hippopotamus is abundant in the various lakes and swamps. Warthogs were not particularly common at the time of the coup in July 1985. It is feared that the hunting that has taken place since then has further depressed their numbers. The African bushpig (*Potamochoerus porcus*) lives in forest or thick bush and has been seen in the park.

The common zebra occurs in open country in many parts of the park. The impala (*Aepyceros melampus*) is by far the most numerous of the larger mammals in this park. This is the only park in Uganda in which impala are found.

Three species of tragelaphine antelope are found in this park: eland, bushbuck, and sitatunga. The area suits the eland, and its numbers have risen since the establishment of the park. The sitatunga (*Tragelaphus spekei*) lives almost permanently in the swamps.

The roan antelope survives in small numbers; so does the topi. Defassa waterbuck are present and graze in the fairly damp longer-grassed areas. In the low hills of the central part of the park, the bush duiker (*Sylvicapra grimia*) is found. The oribi is present in large numbers. The klipspringer (*Oreotragus oreotragus*) is found on rocky outcrops and escarpments. The diminutive dikdik is believed to inhabit some of the drier woodlands.

Baboons (*Papio anubis*) live in troops of up to 100 individuals and are especially common around abandoned banana plantations. Troops of vervet monkeys are spread more widely. Unlike the baboons, they inhabit the wooded areas, avoiding the ground wherever possible. The lesser galago, or bush baby (*Galago senegalensis*), can be seen in the trees at night. The African hare is common, and more than ten species of rodents have been recorded.

Only a few species of predatory mammals are known to occur in Lake Mburo National Park. Leopards have been seen quite often, and it is assumed that they feed largely on the thriving baboon populations. The serval is believed to be present. The spotted hyena can be heard and seen at night.

The dwarf mongoose (*Helogale percivali*) is common, and the marsh mongoose has been recorded near Lake Mburo. The African civet (*Civettictis civetta*) is thought to be common although it is not often seen as it is nocturnal. The bush genet (*Genetta tigrina*) is also nocturnal and is widely distributed in this park.

The spotted-necked otter (*Lutra maculicollis*) has been seen on several occasions in Lake Mburo.

Birds. No record has yet been made of the bird species present. Preliminary observations indicate that over 250 species can be seen in the park.

Wilderness. The small park has outstanding physical scenery with hills intercepted by meandering shallow valleys. There are fourteen lakes in the area, the most prominent of which are Kakyera, Mburo, Kagambirwa, Kajuma, and Misyera. The park contains a variety of vegetation types ranging from gully forests to various types of woodland, shrubs, and grassland. Much of the park is a grassland with scattered trees dominated by *Acacia*. There is also an interesting range of aquatic vegetation in the wetlands.

ADMINISTRATION

Uganda National Parks is a parastatal body established by an act of parliament. Under section 5 of the act a Board of Trustees was set up as an independent body devised to insulate the organization from political pressures and expediency. In practice the wisdom of this action has been proved beyond doubt.

A director and a number of subordinate officers are responsible for the day-to-day running of the organization. See Figure 21.7.

The officers have supporting staff consisting of the rangers, mechanics, coxswains, deckhands, carpenters, nurses, ferry operators, porters, etc. The task of controlling illegal activities falls heavily on the rangers' shoulders.

African wardens first learned their trade on patrol in the field. Later they received professional training in wildlife management. The organization was established as a strong, largely self-sufficient institution, with high standards of management and discipline. The protection afforded to animals was so effective that all national parks in Uganda suffered from overconcentration of elephants. The aim of the organization is to restore this favorable situation.

Threats to the Parks

Among the most significant events of the last decade have been the severe economic problems, the breakdown in political stability, drought, and the proliferation of automatic weapons and their use on wildlife. National parks, by

Figure 21.7
Organization of Uganda National Parks

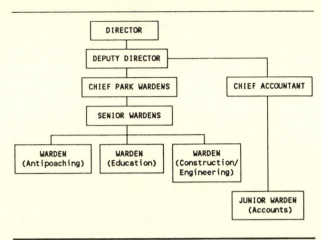

virtue of being vast areas of unpopulated wilderness, are in danger of being overrun by increasing population or by displaced people.

From the very beginning, it has proved difficult to enforce the law on poaching, because hunting is part of African tradition. Fortunately, the traditional hunter, using primitive implements, has not been a serious threat to African wildlife.

In the past twenty years the most serious danger has come from commercial poaching. The commercial poacher uses sophisticated automatic weapons, which have become readily available. Commercial poachers fall into two categories. The first and most recent category is the hunter who trades in game meat on a commercial scale. This poacher is a direct result of economic difficulties and global inflation, which have hit Africa hard. The second category of commercial poacher is the trader in game trophies: ivory, rhino horn, skins, etc. This trophy trade involves complicated international networks with centers in America, Europe, the Middle East and Asia, and with tentacles in Africa.

Totalitarian regimes, such as that of the infamous Idi Amin, have condoned poaching even by senior government officials and the security forces. Political turmoil and war have often been periods of free-for-all. During the war of liberation in Uganda in 1979, hippo, buffalo, topi, and Uganda kob, to name but a few, were shot in large numbers inside the parks by Amin's soldiers and the invading Tanzanian troops.

The Republic of Uganda is looking to hydroelectrical power to meets its growing energy needs. The possibility of harnessing power by building dams inside Murchison Falls National Park is a serious threat to the park's existence.

NOTE

I am deeply indebted to Professor Hassan A. El-Etr and Mr. Steven S. Sinabantu for their help on the geology of the parks. I am also grateful to Mr. P. Ssemwezi for advice and to Mrs. Ben Kawesi for providing secretarial services.

BIBLIOGRAPHY

Beadle, L. C. "The Uganda National Parks in Prehistoric Times: (1) Landscape Changes." In *Uganda National Parks Handbook*. Kampala: Trustees of the Uganda National Parks, 1965.

Bere, R. *The Story of Uganda National Parks*. Unpublished, 1975.

Churchill, W. *My African Journey*. London: Hodder and Stoughton, 1908.

Eltringham, S. K. *Elephants*. Poole, Dorset, England: Blandford Press, 1982.

Eltringham, S. K., and R. C. Malpas. "The Decline in Elephant Numbers in Rwenzori and Kabalega Falls National Parks, Uganda." *African Journal of Ecology* 18 (1980), 73–86.

Grant, J. A. *A Walk Across Africa*. Edinburgh: Blackwood, 1864.

Hepworth, J. V. *Explanation of the Geology of Sheet 19, 20, 28, and 29 (Southern West Nile)*. Geological Survey Report No. 10. Kampala: Uganda Government, n.d.

Kayanja, F.I.B. "Conservation of African Mammals in the Aftermath of Commercial Poaching." *Acta Zoologica Fennica* 172 (1938), 195.

Kayanja, F.I.B., and I. Douglas-Hamilton. "The Impact of the Unexpected on the Uganda National Parks." In *National Parks, Conservation, and Development* edited by J. A. McNeely and K. R. Miller. Washington, D.C.: Smithsonian Institution Press, 1984, pp. 87–92.

Laws, R. M., I.S.C. Parker, and R.C.B. Johnston. "Elephants and Habitats in North Bunyoro, Uganda." *East African Wildlife Journal* 8 (1970), 163–80.

Malpas, R. C. *Wildlife in Uganda, a Survey*. Report sponsored by New York Zoological Society, World Wildlife Fund, IUCN, Frankfurt Zoological Society, African Wildlife Leadership Foundation and Fauna Preservation Society (1980).

Mazimhaka, P. K. *Description and Explanation of the Geology of the North-eastern Part of Map 30/iv, Kabalega National Park, Northern Uganda*. Unpublished geology mapping report. Kampala: Makerere University, 1973.

McGregor, J. P. *Explanation of the Geology of Sheet 10 (Kaabong)*. Geol. Serv. Report No. 9. Kampala: Uganda Government, 1962.

Rhodes, D. H. "Fish and Fishing." In *Uganda National Parks Handbook*. Kampala: Trustees of the Uganda National Parks, 1965.

Speke, J. H. *Journal of the Discovery of the Source of the Nile*. Edinburgh: Blackwood, 1863.

Stanley, H. M. *Through the Dark Continent*. London: Sampson Low, 1878.

Turnbull, C. *The Mountain People*. New York: Simon and Schuster, 1972. Reprint. London: Triad Paladin, 1984.

UNION OF SOVIET SOCIALIST REPUBLICS 22

Yury Yazan

A modern encyclopedic dictionary defines *nature reserves* as "areas of particular scientific and economic value that are specially protected," typically through the prohibition of hunting, fishing, cutting, destruction of vegetation, et cetera.[1] Another defines *nature reserves* as "terrestrial or water area[s] with natural features of great scientific or cultural value (typical or rare landscapes, rare geological formations, animal and plant species, etc.)." It adds, "A nature reserve is also an institution responsible for supervision and management of the territory in question."[2]

This chapter discusses the history of national parks and nature reserves in the USSR, their contributions to the natural and biological sciences, their present organization and management, and their prospects for the future.

HISTORY

Although the meaning of the terms "reserve" and "preserve" as forms of land use began to diverge only in the present century, each type of land use has ancient precedents.

The tradition of protected areas in what is today the USSR began with the various "holy places," "sacred forests," and "sacred groves" set aside from time immemorial by aboriginal peoples who deified the creative forces of nature. These ritual sites, sometimes quite sizable, where not only hunting, fishing, tree cutting, or any other economic activity was prohibited, but where the mere presence of man was forbidden, were the prototypes of the present-day nature reserves that are strictly protected.

Precursors of modern preserves, with their various conservation regimes and regulated use of natural resources, were the communal "forbidden places" that were under the protection of local populations. Here it was forbidden to hunt valuable animal species, but these areas were open for recreation.

Other protected areas are of more recent origin. At the beginning of the twelfth century when the Russian state was just emerging, wildlife reserves were established where native and exotic species of wild animals were kept for hunts of the Great Princes. These "Great Prince's Hunts," "Czar Hunts," and "Royal Hunts" became a custom, and the hunting grounds occupied large virgin areas with abundant and well-guarded big game such as European bison, bear, red deer, roe deer, and wild boar. In one of these forest areas, called "Belovezhskaya Pushcha," a hunting management unit still exists. Another of these areas, "Kubanskaya Okhota," is the site of the present-day Caucasian Biosphere Reserve.

Beginning with the fourteenth century, when falconry became particularly widespread, nesting sites of some daytime birds of prey, mainly gyrfalcons, were "forbidden for entry." Seven islands in the Barents Sea remain protected to this day.

A bit later abatis that stretched for hundreds of kilometers were arranged along the southern border of the Moscow principality. Forest areas within the abatis were painstakingly guarded. During the reigns of Peter the Great and Catherine II, "ship forests" and "reserved groves" were designated for their military and commercial importance. Control over these areas was rigidly maintained, and trespassers were severely punished.

There also existed private nature reserves set up on lands that belonged to landowners and factory-owners. At the close of the nineteenth century F. E. Falts-Fein, a landowner, reserved an area of 500 hectares of sheep's fescue and feather-grass virgin steppe in Askaniya-Nova, in the south of the Ukraine. This reserve has been functioning ever since. Refuges of a kind also existed on lands that belonged to monasteries as, for example, the forests of the Troitse-Sergiev Monastery, forests on the Solovets Islands, the island of Valaam, the Ainov Islands, and Raif Woods.

Prior to the Great October Socialist Revolution of 1917 the decision had been made to set up nature reserves in Moritssala, Barguzin, and Lagodekh, but they were actually organized only with the establishment of Soviet power.

In 1919, in the midst of civil war and economic collapse, V. I. Lenin backed the establishment of Astrakhansky Nature Reserve in the Volga Delta. It was set up by the decision of the Astrakhan regional executive committee. A year later, in 1920, Lenin signed a decree establishing a nature reserve in the Ilmen Mountains in the Urals. The foundation of a formal system of nature reserves in this country was laid by the decree "On Conservation of Natural Monuments, Gardens and Parks," signed by Lenin on September 16, 1921. The decree set forth that

1. Natural areas, animals, plants, rocks, etc., of scientific and historic and cultural value that require conservation, may be declared reserved monuments of nature by the People's Commissariat of Education on agreement, in every case, with the organizations and institutions concerned.

2. More sizable natural areas distinguished by their monuments are declared nature reserves and national parks.

The Presidium of the All-Russian Central Executive Committee issued a decree defining nature reserves as areas set aside for complete conservation and therefore withdrawn from the sphere of economic activities forever. In subsequent years the number of nature reserves rapidly increased. Their development as nature conservation research institutions was, however, far from being smooth.

THE ADMINISTRATION OF RESERVES AND PARKS

The function of state nature reserves answering modern conservation concepts is most fully defined in the joint decision (No. 77/106) of the USSR State Planning Committee and the State Committee for Science and Technology (April 27, 1981), which approved the Standard Regulations for the State Nature Reserves, Monuments of Nature, Botanical and Dendrological Gardens, Zoological Parks, Refuges, National Nature Parks. Here are some important excerpts from this document:

1. State nature reserves are set up in order to preserve areas (natural complexes) typical or unique for a given landscape zone in natural state in the entirety of their components, to study natural processes and phenomena, and to develop scientific principles for nature conservation.

2. Areas on land, entrails of the earth, and water areas with all natural features within their limits are permanently withdrawn from the sphere of economic activities and are handed over, in accordance with established order, to state nature reserves.

3. The responsibilities entrusted to state nature reserves are as follows:

   a. To provide territory conservation of a state nature reserve (including water areas) with all natural features and to maintain the appropriate protective regime;

   b. To conduct research depending on scientific purposes of a reserve, implemented by a reserve scientific staff and research institutions of the country;

   c. To publicize the ideas of protected areas, the problems of nature conservation and rational use of the environment, to promote assistance in training and education of researchers involved in nature conservation.

The USSR has a large and very complex system of protected natural areas. The system comprises natural monuments, preserves of different types and functions, national nature parks, hunting management units, constantly emerging new local refuges, protected stows, natural microreserves, etc. The state nature reserves, national nature parks, refuges, and monuments of nature have won the greatest recognition. The number of monuments of nature runs to over 5,000. There are over 2,500 large refuges, 155 nature reserves, and 19 national nature parks in the country. (See Table 22.1.) The list of specially protected natural

Table 22.1
Strict Nature Reserves, Hunting Reserves, and National Parks of the USSR by Geographic Region[1]

NAME	AREA	DATE
R.S.F.S.R.		
Altaisky NR	881,238	1932
Astrakhansky NR[b]	63,400	1919
Azas NR	337,290	1985
Baikalo-Lensky NR	659,919	1986
Baikal'sky NR[b]	165,724	1969
Barguzinsky NR[b]	263,200	1916
Basegi NR	19,422	1982
Bashkirsky NR	72,140	1930
Bashkirsky NNP	98,134	1986
Bol'shekhekhtsirsky NR	45,044	1963
Bureinsky NR	358,444	1987
Bryansky Les NR	11,778	1987
Dagestansky NR	19,061	1987
Dal'nevostochny Marine Reserve	64,316	1978
Daursky NR	44,752	1987
Darvinsky NR	112,630	1945
Galich'ya Gora NR	231	1925
Il'mensky NR	30,380	1920
Kabardino-Balkarsky NR[c]	74,099	1976
Kandalakshsky NR	58,100	1932
Caucasian NR[b]	263,277	1924
Kedrovaya Pad' NR	17,896	1916
Khingansky NR	97,836	1963
Khopersky NR	16,178	1935
Kivach NR	10,460	1931
Komsomol'sky NR	61,208	1963
Kostomukshsky NR	47,569	1983
Kronotsky NR[b]	1,099,000	1967
Kuril'sky NR	63,365	1984
"Kurshskaya Kosa" NNP	6,621	1987
Laplandsky NR[b]	278,436	1930
Lazovsky NR	116,524	1957
Les na Vorskle NR	1,038	1979
Losinyi Ostrov National Park	10,063	1983
Malaya Sos'va NR	92,921	1976
Marii Chodra NP	36,600	1985
Magadansky NR	883,805	1982
Mordovsky NR	32,148	1935
Nizhne-Svirsky NR	40,972	1980
Oksky NR[b]	22,911	1935
Olyokminsky NR	847,102	1984
Pribaikal'sky NNP	412,750	1986
Priel'brussky NNP	101,000	1986
Vrangel' Island NR	795,650	1976
Pechoro-Ilychsky NR[b]	721,322	1930
Pinezhsky NR	41,244	1974
Prioksko-Terrasnyi NR[b]	4,945	1948
Samarskaya Luka NP	69,000	1984
Sayano-Schushensky NR[b]	390,368	1976
Severo-Osetinsky NR	28,999	1967
"Shul'gan-Tash" NR	22,531	1986

Table 22.1 (continued)

NAME	AREA	DATE
Sikhote-Alinsky NR[b]	347,052	1935
Sochinsky NP	190,000	1983
Sokhondinsky NR[b]	210,007	1973
Stolby NR	47,154	1925
Taimyrsky NR	1,384,316	1979
Teberdinsky NR	84,996	1936
Tsentral'no-Chernozyomnyi NR[b]	4,847	1935
Tsentral'no-Lesnoy NR[b]	21,380	1931
Tsentral'no-Sibirsky NR	972,017	1985
Ussuriysky NR	40,432	1932
Ust'-Lensky NR	1,433,000	1985
Verkhne-Tazovsky NR	631,308	1986
Visimsky NR	13,500	1971
Vitimsky NR	585,021	1982
Volzhsko-Kamsky NR	8,034	1960
Voronezhsky NR[b]	31,053	1927
Yugansky NR	648,636	1982
Yuzhno-Ural'sky NR	254,914	1978
Zabaikal'sky NNP	269,300	1986
Zavidovsky NR	125,400	1929
Zeisky NR	98,899	1963
Zhigulyovsky NR	23,140	1966
Armenian S.S.R.		
Dilizhansky NR	24,232	1958
Erebuninsky NR	89	1981
Khosrovsky NR	29,925	1958
Sevan NP	150,000	1978
Shikaokhsky NR	10,000	1975
Azerbaijan S.S.R.		
Ak-Gel'sky NR	4,400	1978
Basutchaisky NR	107	1974
Gei-Gel'sky NR	7,131	1965
Girkansky NR	2,904	1969
Ilisuinsky NR	9,345	1987
Ismaillinsky NR	5,778	1981
Karayazsky NR	4,855	1978
Kyzyl-Agachsky NR	88,360	1929
Pirkulinsky NR	1,521	1968
Shirvansky NR	17,745	1969
Turianchaisky NR	12,352	1958
Zakatal'sky NR	23,844	1929
Byelorussian S.S.R.		
Belovezhskaya Pushcha HP	98,065	1940
Berezinsky NR[b]	76,201	1925
Pripyatsky NR	63,342	1969

Table 22.1 (continued)

NAME	AREA	DATE
Estonian S.S.R.		
Endlasky NR	8,162	1985
Matsalusky NR	39,697	1957
Lakhemaa NP	64,911	1971
Nigulasky NR	2,771	1957
Vil'sandiysky NR	10,689	1971
Viydumyaesky NR	1,194	1957
Georgian S.S.R.		
Adzhametsky NR	4,848	1957
Akhmetsky NR	16,297	1980
Algetsky NR	6,000	1965
Borzhomsky NR	17,948	1959
Kintrishsky NR	7,166	1959
Kazbegsky NR	4,300	1976
Kolkhidsky NR	500	1959
Lagodekhsky NR	17,818	1912
Liakhvsky NR	6,388	1977
Pitsunda-Myussersky NR	3,761	1966
Pskhu-Gumistinsky NR	40,819	1976
Ritsinsky NR	16,289	1957
Saguramsky NR	5,247	1946
Satapliysky NR	354	1935
Tbilissky NP	19,461	1973
Vashlovansky NR	4,833	1935
Kazakh S.S.R.		
Aksu-Dzhabagly NR	75,094	1927
Alma-Atinsky NR	73,442	1961
Barsakel'messky NR	18,300	1939
Bayanaul'sky NNP	45,502	1985
Kurgal'dzhinsky NR	237,038	1968
Markakol'sky NR	71,367	1976
Naur umsky NR	87,694	1934
Ustyurtsky NR	223,300	1984
Kirghiz S.S.R.		
"Ala-Archa" NP	19,400	1976
Besh-Aral'sky NR	116,700	1979
Issyk-Kul'sky NR	18,994	1948
Narynsky NR	18,250	1983
Sary-Cheleksky NR	23,868	1959
Latvian S.S.R.		
Gauya NP	83,750	1973
Grini NR	1,076	1957
Krustkalny NR	2,903	1977
Moritssala NR	818	1912

Table 22.1 (continued)

NAME	AREA	DATE
Slitere NR	15,054	1921
Teichi NR	18,966	1982

Lithuanian S.S.R.

NAME	AREA	DATE
Chyapkyalyai NR	8,477	1975
Kamanos NR	3,660	1979
Lithuanian NP	30,000	1974
Zhuvintas NR	5,428	1946

Moldavian S.S.R.

NAME	AREA	DATE
Kodry NR	5,174	1971
Redensky Les HP	5,664	1976

Tadzhik S.S.R.

NAME	AREA	DATE
Dashti-Dzhumsky NR	19,700	1983
Ramit NR	16,168	1959
Tigrovaya Balka NR	49,785	1938

Turkmenian S.S.R.

NAME	AREA	DATE
Amudarinsky NR	50,506	1982
Badkhyzsky NR	87,680	1941
Kaplankyrsky NR	570,000	1979
Kopetdagsky NR	49,793	1976
Krasnovodsky NR	262,037	1968
Repeteksky NR	34,600	1928
Syunt-Khasardagsky NR	29,700	1979

Ukrainian S.S.R.

NAME	AREA	DATE
Askaniya Nova NR[b]	11,054	1921
Azovo-Sivashsky HP	57,430	1957
Chernomorsky NR[b]	57,048	1927
Crimea HP	42,962	1923
Dneprovsko-Teterevsky HP	30,544	1967
Dunaiskiye Plavni NR	14,851	1981
Kanevsky NR	1,030	1931
Karadagsky NR	2,885	1979
Karpatsky NR	12,760	1968
Karpatsky NP	50,303	1980
Lugansky NR	1,608	1968
Mys Mart'yan NR	240	1973
Polessky NR	20,104	1968
Rastochie NR	2,080	1984
Shatsky NP	32,515	1983
Ukrainsky Stepnoi NR	1,634	1961
Yaltinsky NR	14,589	1973
Zalessky HP	15,030	1957

Table 22.1 (continued)

NAME	AREA	DATE
Uzbek S.S.R.		
Baday-Tugay NR	5,926	1971
Chatkal'sky NR[b]	35,686	1947
Gissarsky NR	87,538	1983
Kitabsky NR	5,378	1979
Kyzylkumsky NR	5,721	1971
Nuratinsky NR	22,138	1975
People's Park of the Uzbek S.S.R.	31,503	1978
Surkhansky NR	28,014	1986
Zaaminsky NR	15,600	1939
Zeravshansky NR	2,362	1975

Total number:	strict nature reserves	--	155
	hunting preserves	--	6
	national nature parks	--	19

            Total area: 21,307,233 hectares

Notes:
[a] Data of the USSR Central Statistical Board.
[b] Biosphere Reserve
[c] Alpine Reserve

areas grows annually by dozens of natural monuments and refuges and several nature reserves and national parks.

Officially, nature reserves in the USSR are not classified, but they are very different in their functions. Most of them represent a particular pattern of nature undisturbed by human activity. Examples include the Pechoro-Ilychsky, Bashkirsky, Kavkazsky, and Tsentral'no-Lesnoy nature reserves. They are exempt from any economic activity.

Other state reserves, such as the Voronezhsky, Berezinsky, Prioksko-Terrasnyi, Krasnovodsky, and Kyzyl-Agachsky, preserve valuable fauna. These reserves serve in part as patterns of nature, but admit of some economic activities related to their wildlife conservation purpose. In some areas wildlife populations are regulated through capture and subsequent dispersion of valuable animals such as beaver, deer, boars, etc. In other areas some beasts and birds are fed when a sudden deep snow cover, glaze, or lack of feed threaten their well-being. The so-called minor nature reserves are set aside with the aim to conserve unique natural features such as the only naturally occurring grove of relict Pitsunda pine in the Pitsundo-Myussera Nature Reserve or the Eldar pine in the Geigel' Nature Reserve. The biocenoses or natural complexes in such nature reserves are, as a rule, incapable of self-regulation, and compensatory human activity is essential to create favorable conditions for the protection of plant and animal species, their populations and communities. At present some nature reserves are being turned into national nature parks owing to their geographical location and heavy recreational pressure. These are the Teberdinsky, Issyk-Kul'sky nature reserves and, in part, the Stolby and Kronotsky reserves.

National parks are at an early stage of development in the USSR. There are only eighteen national parks. Hunting management units are also nature reserves, but their management allows for tourism and hunting in certain areas. Even national parks and hunting management units, however, have areas where man is admitted under no circumstances, and animals and plants are left undisturbed under strict protection.

Historically, there was no acute need of designated areas for nature recreation. Anyone could freely fish, hunt, wander, or lie on untrampled grass and enjoy the beauty of an unspoiled landscape. In the second half of the twentieth century the situation has changed. The need of the Soviet people for contact with nature and for improved ecological education is growing explosively. Their standard of living has risen; many people have cars, motorcycles, motor- and sail-boats, and they also have more spare time. The drive "back to the lap of nature" has acquired frightening proportions. Nature is no longer threatened by a plunderer who would pull a trigger or wield an ax for profit. It is threatened by an ignoramus who brings harm unintentionally, by picking the occasional flower or crushing some small animal under the wheels of his car.

Accordingly, measures are being taken to meet the growing need of the people, on the one hand, to experience nature, and, on the other hand, to improve their level of ecological awareness and spiritual enrichment. Experts in nature conservation have no doubts that these new functions of the protected natural areas may be best realized in national parks. The need to create an expansive system of this relatively new category of protected areas is self-evident.

In area and diversity of natural conditions as well as in the degree of ecological integrity, the USSR is unparalleled in the world and, therefore, mere copying of national park schemes existing in other countries would hardly suffice. The experience of national parks in this country, though modest in scope, teaches specific forms of organization and management appropriate to the USSR and conforming generally to international definitions and requirements.

A national park is a nature conservation institution. The zoning of a park's territory, with some portions fully protected and others open for tourism and recreation, includes areas developed in accordance with the national patterns of land use and harvesting, local crafts, and specific features of ethnic life styles and culture. These territories also boast monuments of architecture and minor architectural artifacts of local ethnic groups. Lands allotted to a national park are the property of the park, but there may be several land-users. In these cases all economic activities should conform to the goals set by the park. When land-use issues arise, the locally based scientific-technical council serves as arbitrator and coordinator. Its members also perform the functions of trustees.

In fully protected areas, with the regime similar to that in nature reserves, only scientific observations are carried out by the staff and scientists commissioned through scientific cooperation agreements. Areas open for tourism and recreation have no camping sites, which are set up off the grounds. Inside the park, pedestrian traffic is confined to footpath and special transport to bridle ways. Admission is free but regulated. The facilities of national parks should be specially designed and are rather costly. A perfunctory approach to organization of national parks may be the source of a grave negative impact. An unmanageable flow of tourists may simply devastate the park and pilfer the natural attractions, carrying them away in bits and pieces in bottomless rucksacks. Much remains to be done in this field.

State nature reserves are designed to protect complete ecosystems in all their natural diversity; partial reserves protect certain biotic and abiotic features of nature. Therefore, the system of protected areas has been built in accordance with the physical-geographical classification of the country. For the future the system will require an approach that also takes into account industrial development, population density, and the needs for tourism and recreation.

National parks should be established primarily in industrially developed regions in the vicinity of big cities with good access roads where there is still some intact nature with picturesque landscapes. Without these preservation measures, well-intended holiday-hikers will destroy these landscapes. The All-Union Research Institute of Nature Conservation and Reserves has received more than 110 recommendations for new national parks, including 70 in the Russian Federation, 21 in the Ukraine, 6 in Belorussia, and 4 in Kazakhstan. It will be impossible to fully implement each of these projects within the next few years, but long-term priorities have been established through the year 2000. In some areas, development is already underway.

In contrast to national parks, all nature reserves in the USSR are primarily research institutions, laboratories in nature, and centers for education and promotion of the ideas of nature conservation. Most of them have their own staff of scientists and engineers who are ardent devotees of nature. Their effort as chronicles of living and nonliving nature is of great importance for understanding natural processes, for forecasting changes in the biosphere and in particular protected ecosystems, and for development of proposals to prevent negative impacts on natural environment.

A number of statutes and decrees signed by Lenin indicate that nature reserves are the property of the people and that, as such, they are called to solve scientific problems facing the society and the country, and to develop measures for nature protection. The significance of this demand was demonstrated, first, by the specificity of research in nature reserves, and, second, by the prohibition of economic activities. This prohibition helps to reveal the "norm" and a "pattern" of a biota and its vital processes. These include behavior patterns, optimum density of wildlife populations, sex and age ratios, indicators of breeding and mortality, etc.

Nature conservation administrations of the Union republics are responsible for state nature reserves. The control over the activities of nature reserves, the quality of research in particular, is entrusted by the USSR government to the State Committee for Nature Conservation with scientific guidance provided by the USSR Academy of Sciences. Also, there is the All-Union Research Institute of Nature Conservation and Reserves (VNIIPRIRODA) affiliated to the same department. The institute coordinates and provides guidance for the activities of eighteen state nature reserves, including ten biosphere reserves governed directly by the USSR State Agro-Industrial Committee. Scientific recommendations of the institute are also used in state reserves affiliated with other administrations. The original purposes of the VNIIPRIRODA concerning the research conducted in nature reserves included the following:

• the study of phenomena and processes in a natural complex;
• the study of composition and distribution of living and nonliving features of nature;
• the study of biogeocenoses;
• the development of methods to conserve biogeocenoses and the corresponding physical-geographical region (district, province), rational utilization of natural resources in the adjacent areas;
• the development of methods to research features and phenomena of nature (the methodology of research);
• the development of methods for domestication and cultivation of valuable animal and plant species.

In addition, nature reserves were assigned to some other scientific, technical, and cultural measures. They were responsible for compiling an animal census, banding and marking, estimating yield capacity, capturing wild animals for subsequent dispersion in the areas where populations had decreased, keeping breeding records, collecting data and developing a biological data base or "biological" bank, reacclimatizing, preparing scientific publications, maintaining museums and demonstration nurseries for protected common animals, organizing tours, preparing radio and television broadcasts, filming and photographing protected features and landscapes, compiling maps, etc.

Later, in connection with optimization of research, it was found expedient to reduce the number of problems developed in nature reserves to four but to formulate them more broadly:

• the organization of observations of natural processes with elements of the biological and ecological monitoring—Chronicle of Nature;
• the inventory of flora, fauna, and nonliving natural features; mapping and biosurveying of the territory using aerial photography, filming, and satellite imagery;
• the development of ecological baselines for conservation of natural ecosystems in reserves and of methods to manage them;

- the ecological study of common, valuable, or rare animal and plant species as the scientific basis for their preservation, restoration, or economic utilization in the adjacent territories.

What follows are a few examples of the more specific projects that attempt to implement one or more of the four goals articulated above:

- the description of major indicators of the landscapes, components, biomes, and biomic subdivisions for the determination of their stability, extent of degradation, and reproductive potential of animals and plants;
- the development of techniques for integrated assessment of the indirect anthropogenic impact on protected natural ecosystems;
- the development of norms of protection and scientific elements of protective measures, size, configuration, and boundaries of a reserve;
- the identification of hypothetical hazards to a species (population), ecosystem, or entire reserve;
- the assessment of the role of a protected area and its scientific importance in the system of nature reserves, in a region, and in the country.

No other research institutions tackle these problems. The tasks performed by scientists working in nature reserves are of great theoretical and tremendous practical importance. As a result of their work, it is possible to preserve, restore, and control the populations of valuable animals, and the structure of these populations, and to optimize utilization of natural resources in adjacent territories.

The development of the theory of nature conservation would be impossible but for the contribution of scientists working in nature reserves. Concepts such as the carrying capacity of lands and certain biotopes relative to game species of animals; the mechanisms of regulation of populations and population structures; trophic chains; the parameters of environmental control, including indicative species of animals and plants; techniques of quantitative estimates, both absolute and relative; and the place and functional importance of species in biogeocenoses are employed and developed largely through the effort of scientists in nature reserves. It is only in the absence of the direct anthropogenic impact, that is, in nature reserves, that research is free from errors generated, under different circumstances, by the diverse impacts of man. Protected living and nonliving features provide a baseline against which to identify new natural regularities of development, to record and cognize the processes of microevolution, and with which to improve scientific knowledge.

State nature reserves in this country have made an important contribution to the study of wild nature. The total of published papers using materials from nature reserves approaches 3,500 "author's sheets," and recommendations of scientists from nature reserves are used both in this country and abroad. There is no monograph, textbook, or lesson about nature conservation that would not refer to the original research in nature reserves.

State nature reserves in the USSR are, as a rule, specialized according to their geographical position, scientific traditions, and the presence of particular specialists. Thus, the Kyzyl-Agachsky Reserve specializes in study and development of measures aimed at protection of waterfowl species; the Voronezhsky Reserve emphasizes studies of beaver and red deer; the Pechoro-Ilychsky Reserve specializes in the study of elk, beaver, marten, sable, salmon, and cedar; the Tsentral'no-Lesnoy Reserve is engaged in study of firewoods; and the Caucasian Reserve studies mountain ungulates, soils, and so forth.

The populations of such valuable animals as sable, beaver, and elk were restored in the country largely through the work of these reserves, and the European bison was saved from complete extinction. Numerous methods have been developed for the trapping, transportation, and temporary captivation of valuable beasts and birds—particularly those so rare and endangered that they are included in the *USSR Red Data Book*—and for disease prevention, animal marking, age determination, and animal domestication.

The strict protection afforded to reserves admits no human interference into the natural processes. Some relevant problems, however, remain unsolved. One of these concerns the artificial regulation of wildlife populations. The majority of experts both in this country and abroad agree that artificial regulation is appropriate in exceptional situations. What are these exceptional situations? Obviously, these are the situations where there is a danger of destabilization, violation of the established biocenotic relations, and degradation of ecosystems.

Fur-bearing animals and resident birds normally do not develop population densities that exceed an area's natural capacity. If an excess population should accumulate, some members will fail to find their place in the completely occupied habitat and search for new sites. Therefore, there is no reason whatever to regulate populations of fur-bearing animals and bird species. As a rule, these species form stable populations and annually disperse outside the reserve, constantly replenishing the adjacent areas and creating good hunting prospects.

With large carnivores and ungulates the situation is different. These develop excessively dense populations, which affect the numbers of prey species and exhaust feed vegetation, occasionally reducing prey species and pasture productivity to a minimum. In nature reserves that are ecologically incapable of self-regulation, such situations are undesirable and unnatural and should, therefore, be artificially regulated. It appears, however, that the most expedient mechanism by which to reduce numbers of large carnivores (wolves, bears, jackals) and wild ungulates (elk, boars, deer) is to allow for hunting, not in the reserves themselves, but in buffer zones. Wildlife harvest, by shooting or capture, in adjacent hunting management units creates a biological vacuum of sorts and ensures the maximum outflow of animals. Clearly, research of this kind has both theoretical and practical significance.

The recommendations on improvement in the program and techniques for ecological monitoring in biosphere reserves, developed by the workshop of experts from socialist countries which was held in Pushchino (USSR) on October 12–18, 1980, contained the following statements:

Biosphere reserves and stations form the base of the ecological monitoring system and should implement the following tasks:

a. conservation of gene pools of living organisms and standard ecosystems (biogeocenoses) and landscapes; the task of developing standards consists in preservation of ecosystems characterized by the greatest diversity of natural conditions;

b. monitoring of the state of ecosystems and their components in the absence of direct utilization of natural resources, and in the territories subjected to anthropogenic impact;

c. development of techniques for forecasting changes in the environment; policies and strategies of control over natural processes;

d. implementation of functions of ecological education centers.

Monitoring is implemented at three levels: global, regional, and local. Usually it is impossible to demarcate these levels of monitoring as they differ in the scale of negative spatiotemporal impact of human activities and in the extent of unfavorable changes in the biosphere under direct or indirect technological impact.

The monitoring of chemical pollution in the environment is ecological monitoring, and monitoring the effect of this pollution on biota is biological monitoring. In biosphere reserves, as in all other nature reserves in this country, studies involve both the extent of pollution of protected ecosystems and the impact of this pollution on living organisms.

Experts from socialist countries who participated in the workshop already mentioned agreed to differentiate four stages in the organization of ecological monitoring:

1. compilation of the inventory of data on the environment of a reserve and on its history;

2. selection of items for observation and development of certain programs for a biosphere reserve;

3. regular observations carried out in conformity with the approved programs;

4. storage, systematization, and analysis of the information obtained.

It was also suggested that these activities should be carried out by biosphere reserves in collaboration with the USSR State Committee for Hydrometeorology and Environmental Control and a number of research institutes of the USSR Academy of Sciences and other agencies in accordance with programs that could ensure the coordination of information.

Pollution of the environment in biosphere reserves is studied by chromatography and spectrometry. These studies have already been started.

The biological monitoring is a part of the ecological monitoring, though for protected ecosystems, for wild nature, this part is the most essential.

The implementation of biological monitoring with respect to all animal and plant species protected in nature reserves is presently impossible. Such monitoring would be very laborious and expensive. Moreover, techniques have not yet been developed for the majority of biota types. Nonetheless, biological monitoring should be carried out at least at the regional, ecosystem, and component levels. This biological monitoring is new in most nature reserves, including biosphere reserves, and such works have not yet reached full scope.

The program for biological monitoring at the component level has been developed at the All-Union Research Institute of Nature Conservation and Reserves.

The Chronicle of Nature is of great importance in studies of nature reserves. It is the major document where everything that occurs in nature is registered: population density of common animals, intensity of flowering, productivity of fruits and seeds, state of soil and water, weather conditions, relief, adaptational and biotechnical measures, filming, photography, and research records. Though the term Chronicle of Nature was first proposed by A. N. Formosov in 1937, research of this kind started in many reserves as early as 1924. Many prominent naturalists including A. N. Formosov, S. V. Kirikov, S. M. Preobazhensky, O. I. Semenov-Tyan-Shansky, I. V. Zharkov, A. A. Nasimovich, Yu. A. Isakov, A. M. Krasnitsky, K. P. Filonov, and others contributed to the development and improvement of the Chronicle of Nature program.

Records obtained for the Chronicle of Nature are compiled in manuscript form annually and in five-year increments. In view of their particular importance, they are to be kept forever in the reserves and in the bodies providing for their governance. Like other scientific works, these Chronicles require uniform methodology that allows for comparison and provides for continuity of observation, thus ensuring the possibility of using the accumulated material not only in the parent institution but also in other reserves and related scientific institutions.

The effectiveness of research conducted in state nature reserves is enhanced by the collaboration of highly qualified specialists from the USSR Academy of Sciences and the republican academies, universities and other schools of higher education, and by the help of a great number of students and even schoolchildren.

Scientists from reserves participate in research that sometimes goes beyond the scope of a parent institution. This research involves such problems as standardization of terms and concepts, including the standards for the structure of the Chronicle of Nature; nature conservation symbolism; methods of research; the scientific basis for size, configuration, and boundaries of newly established protected areas, i.e., reserves, national parks, preserves, monuments of nature; and the scientific basis for the proposed system of such areas, for protective regimes, for zoning, for regulatory measures, and for staffing and facilities policies.

The scientific staff of the reserves contributes to the development of theory, to national strategies for nature conservation, and to rational utilization of natural resources in various regions and statewide.

The reserves have played a very great role in the conservation and perpetuation of rare plants and valuable game animals, some of which had been near extinction. Among the plant species and biomes saved from extinction or extirpation are yew and box trees, Amur oak tree, Caspian lotus, Pitsunda and Eldar pines, and areas of virgin feather-grass steppes. Among the animal species are bobac marmot, European bison, Asiatic wild ass, sika and Bukhara deer, goral, Caucasian tur, tiger, leopard, panther, and sable. A number of birds, including flamingo, white heron, Asiatic turkey, and pheasant, have been saved from extinction in various regions of this country.

Reserves not only saved rare animals and plants but enriched and continue to enrich adjacent areas through the process of natural dispersion of these species. Furthermore, some reserves played an outstanding role in the reintroduction of some animal species to areas of their former range. The Voronezhsky Reserve, for instance, having restored the population of beaver and red deer, has for many years engaged in capture, temporary captivity, and transportation of these animals in order to distribute them to regions of the country where they had disappeared. Thanks to the effort of the Voronezhsky and Berezinsky reserves, the numbers of beaver have reached a level permitting hunting, and expensive pelts have reappeared on the market.

The work of specialists at state reserves has produced many other successes. What follow are but a few examples. The endemic Russian desman was saved at the Khopersky, Mordovsky, and Oksky reserves. The sable was restored in the Barguzindky, Altaisky, and Kronotsky reserves. The elk was saved in the Pechoro-Ilychsky reserve and the Asiatic wild ass in the Badkhyzsky reserve. The European bison was restored in the Belovezhskaya Pushcha, Prioksko-Terrasnyi, Caucasian, and Oksky reserves and the tiger in the Sikhote-Alinsky and Lazovsky reserves.

Nature reserves in the USSR accumulate data on life patterns, behavior, diurnal activities, and other features of the biology of animals and plants. These data are summarized and published in *Transactions* of reserves, in other periodicals and collections of papers, and are used in special educational television and radio programs.

Nature reserves in the USSR are examples of untouched nature set aside among landscapes transformed by man. They are the majestic monuments that serve to promote understanding of the creative role of nature, harmony, and beauty. Conserved nature helps to disclose the intimate secrets of life on earth and allows man to avoid unnecessary mistakes.

Reserves augment natural wealth and improve hunting prospects in adjacent areas, which results in great economic effect. They promote ideas of nature protection and offer an opportunity to enjoy the beauty of nature and to breathe clean air. At the same time they serve to educate and motivate people.

THE FUTURE OF PARKS AND RESERVES

There are many nature reserves in the USSR. Some of them are vast, but so is the country of which they are a part. The All-Union Research Institute of

Nature Conservation and Reserves and other institutions have developed plans for an expanded system of reserves. The number of nature reserves is to be dramatically increased in such regions as East Siberia, Kazakhstan, and in some other republics.

The projected system will be based upon a scheme of physical-geographical classifications proposed by N. A. Gvozdetsky and others in 1967.[3] It involves eighteen physical-geographical provinces. Proceeding from the necessity of protecting the gene pool of plants and animals most adapted to each classification, at least one nature reserve is proposed for every physical-geographical province. In some cases, as for example in Transcaucasia and the Baltic Republics, where they are already several nature reserves and national parks, the number will be greater.

Following the principle that reserves should be representative of physical-geographical classifications, it follows that the more diverse the natural conditions within a particular physical-geographical province, the stronger the argument for creating additional reserves to represent this diversity.

In this country and elsewhere, nature reserves and national parks may be of various sizes, ranging from several hectares to hundreds of thousands or even tens of millions of hectares. The issue of reserve size is beyond the scope of this chapter. What is undeniable, however, is that the appropriate dimensions of protected areas have not yet been scientifically determined. The time is ripe to consider this issue. The reasons for this are as follows:

- nature conservation implies the technological development of industry and agriculture reasonably combined with conservation of natural wealth, rational utilization of natural resources, and improvement in the quality of life;
- with increasing technological impact entailing deterioration of landscapes and natural complexes and, occasionally, their destruction over considerable areas of land and water, nature conservation signifies the need for balanced strategies of utilization and reproduction of natural wealth and timely restoration of territories in order to prevent irreversible changes.

All territories, however, cannot be reserved, and vast areas cannot be withdrawn from the sphere of economic utilization. Before a reserve is established, three things must be accomplished. First, the need to reserve this or that area of land or water must be convincingly demonstrated. Second, the most appropriate form of the reservation (e.g., a national park, nature reserve, preserve, monument of nature) must be determined. Last but not least, the criteria must be developed to determine the optimum size of the territory to be reserved. The areas should be adequate for preservation of the total adapted genepool of biota and sufficient for maintenance of the conditions necessary for normal development of plants and animals constituting the biota.

It might be claimed a priori that the greater the number of species in the biocenoses under study, the greater the territory necessary for protection of these species and vice versa. Given that the number of species in natural complexes of the Northern Hemisphere generally increases from the north to the south, and in the mountains, from the highest point of microrelief to the lowest, one might falsely conclude that in the north and in the mountains, areas allotted for protection should be substantially smaller than in more southerly areas and in middle- and low-mountain reliefs. Such a conclusion ignores the fact that animals inhabiting the less hospitable northerly and high-altitude areas almost invariably require larger ranges than those in more moderate and southern climatic conditions. The extensive ranges of lemming, snowy owl, willow-ptarmigan, Arctic fox, and reindeer are obvious examples.

In determining the boundaries and the area of a proposed nature reserve it is very important to identify the area that would provide for normal vital functions of particularly valuable animals traveling great distances, such as large carnivores or ungulates. It is not necessary to protect the entire area; it is sufficient to select the area where animals could feed, come to watering places, rest, rut and mate, breed, suckle and bring up progeny, survive in time of deep snow, floods, droughts, etc. In other words, it is necessary to protect the area where animals could exist all year round.

As Professor V. M. Zhitkov aptly noted: "It is better to wait with establishment of a nature reserve than to do it slapdash and then start re-delimiting its boundaries."[4]

Unfortunately, procrastination may be even more dangerous and result in irreversible losses to living nature.

Nature conservation generally and protected areas in particular are nowadays taken very seriously in many countries of the world. The USSR has bilateral and multilateral agreements on cooperation in this field with the countries of the socialist alliance, the United Kingdom, the United States, West Germany, Belgium, France, Sweden, and many others.

The International Union for the Conservation of Nature and National Resources (IUCN), which monitors the state of ecosystems and biological species the world over and develops nature conservation projects based on its *World Conservation Strategy*, has as its symbol a circle representing the biosphere into which are inscribed three interpenetrating arrows that denote

- maintenance of the fundamental ecological processes and life-supporting systems;

- preservation of genetic diversity; and

- sustainable utilization of biological species and ecosystems.

All actions of our country in the field of nature conservation and rational utilization of natural resources are aimed at attainment of these goals.

NOTES

1. *Encyclopedic Dictionary*, vol. 1 (Moscow: Big Encyclopedia Soviet, 1953).
2. *Soviet Encyclopedic Dictionary* (Moscow: Soviet Encyclopedia Publishers, 1980).
3. N. A. Gvoadetsky, Physical and Geographical Province Planning of the USSR (Moscow: 1968).
4. V. M. Zhitkov, "Astrakhansky Nature Reserve" (Moscow: 1940).

BIBLIOGRAPHY

Bannikov, Andreĭ G. *Through the State Nature Reserves of the USSR*. Moscow: Mysl', 1974.
Reymers, Nikolai F., and Felix R. Shtilmark. *Specially Protected Areas of the USSR*. Moscow: Mysl', 1978.
Shalybkov, Anatoly M., and Konstantin V. Storchevoy. *Nature Reserves*. Moscow: Agropromizdat, 1985.
Vasiliev, Nikolai G., et al. *State Nature Reserves of the USSR*. Moscow: Lesnaya Promyshlennost', 1983.

UNITED STATES: NATIONAL PARKS

23

Michael Frome, Roland W. Wauer, and Paul C. Pritchard

Establishment of Yellowstone National Park in 1872 marked the beginning of a systematic effort to preserve natural treasures for public benefit in a democratic society. But U.S. parks, pressed by population growth and technological civilization, approach the twenty-first century increasingly dependent on public understanding and support.

HISTORY

Conflicting Values

Nature reserves are an ancient idea, not even American. From the earliest settlement of the New World, however, open squares, greens, and "commons" were set aside for community purposes. With passing time, new approaches emerged from the old. William Cullen Bryant in 1836 editorialized in the *Evening Post* for a large-scale natural park in New York. With support of two prominent landscape architects Andrew Jackson Downing and Frederick Law Olmsted, Central Park ultimately was established in 1857. Olmsted, destined to become a major advocate and designer of open space and parkland, reasoned that it would humanize the city: that pastoral beauty would bring poetic influence, refinement, and happiness to its inhabitants.

The movement to preserve and protect nature embodies one historic branch of American thought and action, emphasizing nonmaterial, esthetic values. It has long conflicted with another branch, founded on the concept of the American earth as a commodity to be marketed like an agricultural product or manufactured item. George Washington, among others of colonial prominence, was highly regarded for landholdings, promotions, and speculations. Humble pioneers, for their part, sought social justice and dignity through acquiring material goods and by reducing wilderness "to possession."

In the conflict of values, artists, writers, naturalists, and some scientists sought to invoke national and spiritual meaning from the country's wild aspects. Early in the nineteenth century, William Cullen Bryant, poet; Thomas Cole, painter; and James Fenimore Cooper, novelist, stirred Americans to recognize the glory in their surroundings. George Catlin went further. Enthralled by colors, grace, and dignity of native peoples, he painted heroic portraits of red chieftains and ventured the bold proposal of a national park preserving a vast natural area *and* the life cycle of the Indian.

But ambitious entrepreneurs dominated the pages of unfolding history. The Civil War introduced the machine age and the power of money. Affluence, influence, and wealth were confused with virtue. With the opening of the West attention concentrated on the public domain, the vast expanse held in trust by the federal government for all Americans, but many millions of hectares designed to aid settlers passed into the hands of railroads, mining and cattle syndicates, logging companies, and speculators.

Civic and scientific leaders earnestly advanced an alternate course. George Perkins Marsh, congressman and diplomat, in *Man and Nature*, his classic of 1864, urged leaving large and accessible regions as a resource of learning of students, recreation for lovers of nature, and sanctuary for plants, trees and wild animals. John Wesley Powell, Civil War veteran, explorer, geologist, and ethnologist, opposed monopoly control in general, the cattle trusts in particular, and counseled against disposing of the public domain.

The Preservation Surge

As early as 1864 Congress responded to pleas of concerned citizens by withdrawing from the public domain Yosemite Valley and the Mariposa Grove of Big Trees and presenting them to California as a state park, thus safeguarding the choice scenery and cherished groves. Then, barely a few years after the Civil War, when vast areas were being claimed and colonized, came the designation of Yellowstone National Park on the raw Wyoming-Montana frontier. The act to establish Yellowstone has sometimes been treated as an attempt to match the older European culture of castles and cathedrals with nature monuments or has been denigrated as recognition only of spectacular phenomena like the geysers and hot springs. Yet it would have been easier to let the Yellowstone country go into the hands of prospectors, squatters, ranchers, and lumbermen. "The establishment of this first national park, protecting a 2-million-acre [810,000 hectare] wilderness, appears in the context of time as an overt act of idealism— the opening wedge of a conservation era that gradually spread the world over."[1]

The value of Yellowstone and other parks subsequently established is evidenced in the pressures to which they unceasingly have been subjected. During the 1880s legislation authorizing construction of a railroad line through Yellowstone very nearly passed Congress; though it failed, the railroad proponents successfully denied the new park funds for its adequate protection. The preservation ideal from its very earliest has been attacked through such political means, with citizen supporters rallying to its defense, striving to refine and advance the ideal, only to find it attacked anew.

Preservationists persevered through the nineteenth century into the twentieth. John Muir led the fight to protect the forest of giant sequoias above Yosemite Valley from the timberman's ax and the slopes of the Sierra Nevada from devastation by grazing sheep. Congress responded in 1890 by reserving 388,500 hectares (960,000 acres) surrounding the valley as a national park and almost simultaneously established General Grant (now a part of Kings Canyon) and Sequoia national parks south in the Sierra Range. Other parks were designated, including Mesa Verde, protecting the cliff-dwelling ruins of southwest Colorado, following passage of the Antiquities Act of 1906. National parks emerged not simply as scenic spectaculars or natural curiosities, but as reservoirs of wildness and cultural heritage, fragments of an ancient America otherwise certain to be lost to onrushing civilization.

This was the case in the populous East as well as the frontier West. On September 27, 1890, two days following the Sequoia Act and four days before the Yosemite Act, Congress directed the purchase of 710 hectares (1,754 acres) in the heart of Washington, D.C., henceforth officially to be known as Rock Creek Park, vowing thus to protect "its pleasant valleys and deep ravines, its primeval forests and open fields, its running waters, its rocks clothed with rich ferns and mosses, its repose and tranquillity, its light and shade, its ever-varying shrubbery, its beautiful and extensive views."

Legislation and lofty language of this nature reflected wide public feeling. Easterners for years had campaigned to rescue the falls of the Niagara River from private exploitation; their efforts culminated in 1885 with authorization of the New York State Reservation at Niagara, a pioneering state park. In that same year the New York State Legislature established the Adirondack Forest Preserve in the upstate mountains, then nine years later reinforced its intent with a constitutional amendment that lands of the forest preserve must be "forever kept as wild forest lands."

The twofold purpose in setting aside those early reserves was to shield them from private exploitation while making them accessible in natural condition. Frederick Law Olmsted spoke of the individual's right to enjoy public scenery and the government's responsibility to protect that right. Yellowstone was set apart by law "as a public park or pleasuring ground for the benefit and enjoyment of the people." John Muir encouraged Americans to experience wilderness as a beneficial antidote to urbanized living. Muir, however, insisted that wilderness to be wild must be accepted on its own terms. At Yosemite in 1912, when the major question on the agenda of the conference of national park superintendents was "Shall automobiles be allowed to enter Yosemite?" Muir was reduced to despair. To him it seemed that gaseous eloquence was wasted on the question, as though Yosemite's mountains, canyons, glaciers, and rivers had no existence. Good walkers, Muir believed, could go anywhere in hospitable mountains without artificial ways.

Politics of a New Bureau

Muir's greatest battle was the one he lost: damming the Tuolumne River in Hetch Hetchy Valley of Yosemite National Park to provide water to San Francisco, 250 kilometers (155 miles) distant. Muir and others had argued that no part of a national park should be violated, that once allowed it would happen repeatedly until the preservation purpose was meaningless. After years of contest the political issue of Hetch Hetchy was resolved by Congress in 1912: the dam was built, flooding a valley comparable in beauty with Yosemite itself. Nevertheless, out of this defeat came a new determination. Until then the parks had been loosely administered; now their supporters campaigned for a central bureau to coordinate the areas already established and to advance through government the cause of preservation.

Thus in 1916, fully forty-four years following the Yellowstone Act, Congress established the National Park Service as an agency of the Department of the Interior, defining its mission in close accord with the Olmsted principle: "to conserve the scenery and the natural and historic objects and the wild life therein and to provide for the enjoyment of the same in such manner and by such means as will leave them unimpaired for the enjoyment of future generations." The first director of the National Park Service, Stephen T. Mather, a wealthy outdoorsman, and his young assistant, Horace M. Albright (who later succeeded him), formed a vigorous team, aggressively committed to building a loyal, professional staff.

Although insisting on one hand that personnel must be chosen free of political connection or concern, Mather and Albright promoted park visitation and expansion of the park system as a means of building a constituency and support in Congress. They followed the unwritten law of bureaucratic survival: the larger an agency and the more people it serves, the larger its personnel force and appropriations, consequently the greater its influence and security of purpose.

Clearly they (as would their successors) faced continuing challenge from commercial enterprise and from other federal bureaus, even sister agencies in the Department of the Interior, with conflicting congressional mandates—to build roads or dams or to produce commodities such as timber, forage, and minerals. Mather and Albright throughout World War I faced efforts of meat, wool, lumber, and power interests to gain access to park resources, while playing on public emotion as a time "not to worry about the flowers and wild animals." Mather has sometimes been depicted as a slick tourist promoter. It might also be said, however, that the National Park Service became almost his personal vehicle of direct action to save wilderness. This he demonstrated in blocking a proposed cable crossing of the Grand Canyon and an electric steam elevator alongside the

308–foot Great Fall of the Yellowstone. In 1925, while vacationing in Glacier National Park, Mather headed a brigade with thirteen charges of TNT to blow up a sawmill illegally cutting timber.

An Expanding Domain

In 1916, when the National Park Service was born, fifteen national parks covered about 1,919,000 hectares (4,742,000 acres), entirely in the West. Implicit values were little recognized or understood. Nor were the human impacts or means of coping with them understood. Ecology, whether as word or science, was unknown. Wildlife values had been only incidental in the establishment of Yellowstone—the original question had been whether public or private ownership should govern. Nevertheless, after 1885 the last significant herd of bison had found refuge in the park. Yellowstone held the largest elk herds in the country, and beaver and grizzly bear were still common, while outside its boundaries such species had been greatly reduced in number or nearly extirpated. Appreciation of ecosystems and limits of appropriate use were still many years away.

The principal focus was on expanding the National Park System and building the bureau to administer it. In the West, parkland came from the public domain or (almost always grudgingly) from the national forests. In the East, with scant federal estate, new parks were founded on private lands. But Congress, regarding open space acquisition as a budgetary luxury, refused to appropriate any funds for land purchases. In the development of the Appalachian national parks, Shenandoah (Virginia) and Great Smoky Mountains (North Carolina–Tennessee), hundreds of small tracts were painstakingly acquired during the 1920s and 1930s with money appropriated by the states involved and contributed by their citizens.

During the pre–World War II administration of Franklin D. Roosevelt, the park system was significantly enlarged in size and types of areas. These henceforth would include national military parks (commemorating Revolutionary and Civil War battles), historic sites and buildings, memorials like the Statue of Liberty and Washington Monument, and all of the buildings and parks in the nation's capital. As a consequence, some of the parks' strongest proponents became the most critical, insisting that national parks be administered as an elite gallery of nature reserves, that anything less must ultimately dilute their quality. Others, however, including the Park Service leadership, welcomed an expanding budget and constituency. In the same period, the Roosevelt New Deal provided extensive funding for work projects in the out-of-doors. Between 1933 and 1942 thousands of unemployed young people were given jobs in national parks, national forests, and state parks, working under landscape architects, biologists, engineers, archaeologists, and historians. While they did much good work of lasting use and value, they also built roads into areas hitherto wild; in fact, concern during the mid-thirties that scenic roads would overrun unspoiled mountain areas sparked the organization of the wilderness movement in the United States.

All that was forgotten during World War II. National Parks virtually closed their gates, but industries pressed to open them for commercial uses: mining for copper in Grand Canyon and Mount Rainier, manganese in Shenandoah, and tungsten in Yosemite; for timber in Olympic; and forage on rangelands wherever they might be. The National Park Service resisted with courage and surprising success. It did yield to the military for permits for maneuvers, but all of minor, temporary consequence.

Following World War II, the pace of civilization, technology, and population growth quickened, and so too pressures on the parks. Foresters and loggers complained that great trees, 400 to 1,000 years old, were overmature and going to waste in the rain forests of Olympic National Park. The powerful Bureau of Reclamation, a sister agency in the Department of the Interior, in the early 1950s proposed to erect a major dam across the gorge of the Green River in Dinosaur National Monument, Utah. The battle, reminiscent of Hetch Hetchy, was fought for more than five years in Congress until the plan was dropped. Then, in the 1960s, another proposal was advanced to construct two dams across the Colorado River in the Grand Canyon, primarily for water storage and hydropower, but with the Bureau of Reclamation vowing that raising the water level would improve natural beauty and make the canyon accessible to more people. Yet another extensive public effort was required to show the Grand Canyon needed no improvement.

"Progress" did indeed come to the national parks, with varied construction projects, roads, urbanizing tourist developments such as Canyon Village implanted in the heart of Yellowstone's wild country, and opening of Yellowstone to snowmobiles and coastal parks to off-road dune buggies. Passage of the Wilderness Act in 1964 manifested a growing concern over the fate of unspoiled roadless country on federal lands. The National Park Service, however, was slow to respond. In 1966, Great Smoky Mountains became the first national park to be considered for classification under the Wilderness Act, but the Park Service proposal generally was considered weak and inadequate, providing for small blocks of wilderness intersected by roads. That proposal, rejected by the public, years later was refined and much improved.

The National Park System has continued to grow. It includes urban national parks (usually but not always called recreation areas) in New York, Washington, D.C., New Orleans, Atlanta, Cleveland-Akron, San Francisco, and at the edge of Los Angeles. The Wild and Scenic Rivers Act, adopted by Congress in 1968, preserves outstanding sections of free-flowing rivers. The National Trails System Act, approved on the same day, is designed to protect the Appalachian Trail, the longest recreational footpath in the world (which the National Park Service administers), Pacific Crest Trail, and potential other routes. The Alaska National Interest Lands Conservation Act (ANILCA) of 1980 added about 18 million hectares (44 million acres) to the system, creating ten major new national parks, monuments, and preserves.

The National Park Service established in its early years a reputation powered

Table 23.1
Statistical Summary of the National Park System[a]

CLASSIFICATION	NUMBER	HECTARES	ACRES[b]
National Battlefields	11	3,787	9,358
National Battlefield Parks	3	3,015	7,449
National Battlefield Site	1		1
National Capital Parks	1	2,618	6,469
National Historic Sites	64	6,659	16,454
National Historical Parks	26	38,371	94,815
National Lakeshores	4	57,985	143,282
National Mall	1	59	146
National Memorials	25	3,183	7,865
National Military Parks	9	13,395	33,099
National Monuments	78	1,872,378	4,626,647
National Parks	49	18,565,409	45,875,126
National Parkways	4	64,609	159,648
National Preserves	12	8,458,062	20,899,872
National Recreation Areas	17	1,351,213	3,338,848
National Rivers	12	95,968	237,137
National Trails	3	36,869	91,103
National Seashores	10	192,722	476,215
White House	1	7	18
	343	30,779,242	76,055,507

Notes: [a] As of September 30, 1987.
[b] Acres federal government ownership.

Source: United States Department of Commerce. Statistical
Abstract of the United States, 1989. Washington, D.C.:
Government Printing Office, 1989, p. 219.

by professional ethics, largely free of political considerations. Recent times have seen personnel selection, designation of new parks, and management practices in parks more seriously influenced by special-interest politics. In 1979, for example, following detailed studies, the Park Service announced a plan to gradually phase out the use of motors and reduce the number of rubber rafts running the Colorado River through the Grand Canyon. The reason was simple: use had skyrocketed, key camping spots were congested and impacted, and sanitation rules were widely violated. But protests from commercial outfitters to key members of Congress blocked the Park Service plan; the following year visitor numbers *rose* to record high levels.

PARKS AND RESERVES

With establishment of Great Basin National Park, in Nevada, in 1986, there were 49 national parks, plus 289 other units of the National Park System, including national monuments, historic areas, battlefields, seashores, lakeshores, riverways, parkways, and recreation areas. (See Table 23.1.) They extend from Guam, Hawaii, and Alaska across the United States to the Virgin Islands. With their museums, trailside exhibits, guided walks, campfire talks, and audiovisual programs, the national parks have been a major influence in culture, education, science, and tourism, providing to Americans and visitors from abroad a noble view of this country in a world of change.

National parks include grand scenic regions known the world over. (See Table 23.2.) Among them are Yellowstone, largely in northwestern Wyoming but extending also into Montana and Idaho, identified by its geysers, canyons, and abundant wildlife; Yosemite, in the High Sierra of California, identified by its granite domes, plunging waterfalls, and forests of giant sequoias; and Grand Canyon, in Arizona, which President Theodore Roosevelt once called "the one great sight every American should see." But all of the national parks are preeminent in one aspect of nature or another. Among the lesser known, for instance, Petrified Forest, in northeastern Arizona, is part of the Painted Desert, a wide arid land of plateaus, buttes, and low mesas—low in water and plant growth, but lavish in displaying many hues in bands of sandstones, shales, and clays. The national park consists of six separate "forests," with great logs of agate and jasper lying on the ground, petrified relics of the ancient Triassic period, when this region was a low-lying swamp basin, in which ferns, mosses, and trees thrived before volcanic upheavals and climate changes modified land and landscape. Isle Royale National Park, in Michigan, the largest island in Lake Superior, is a roadless sanctuary of forested wilderness, fjordlike harbors, beaver ponds, innumerable lakes, and surrounding islets. Everglades National Park, at the southern tip of Florida, is an expanse of tall, swaying grasses; tropical plants and trees; and dozens of low islands, or keys, rising from the sheltered waters of Florida Bay. The park is a sanctuary for beautiful tropical bird life, including wood ibis, the only stork in the United States, and for rare mammals like the Florida panther.

National parks are established only by act of Congress. National monuments may be established either by Congress or presidential proclamation. Devils Tower National Monument was established in 1906 as the very first national monument, a 264-meter (865-foot) tower of columnar rock in northeast Wyoming, with symmetrical, almost perpendicular sides, the remains of a molten formation born of volcanic activity. By contrast, Dinosaur National Monument, in eastern Utah and western Colorado, contains the world's most concentrated deposit of petrified bones of dinosaurs, crocodiles, and turtles. In addition, the folded and tilted rock layers in the deep canyons of the Green and Yampa rivers show the results of tremendous forces of earth movement.

National preserves represent a new category of national park area, allowing hunting and trapping (in accordance with state law), activities normally prohibited in the national parks. Big Cypress National Preserve, directly north of Everglades National Park in Florida, was established in 1974 to assure the flow of critical water into the park. It also provides habitat for rare and endangered species like the Florida panther, manatee, and brown pelican. Additional preserves of significance were established in Alaska in 1980, when Congress passed the Alaska National Interest Lands Conservation Act. That legislation enlarged existing

Table 23.2
U.S. National Parks over 10,000 Hectares

NAME	LOCATION BY STATE(S)	AREA (hectares)	DATE ESTABLISHED
Acadia	ME	16,069	1919
Arches National Park	UT	29,696	1971
Badlands National	SD	98,463	1978
Big Bend	TX	299,926	1944
Biscayne	FL	70,028	1980
Bryce Canyon	UT	14,502	1924
Canyonlands	UT	136,613	1964
Capitol Reef	UT	97,897	1971
Carlsbad Caverns	NM	18,922	1930
Channel Islands	CA	100,912	1980
Crater Lake	OR	74,151	1902
Denali	AK	1,900,000	1917
Everglades	FL	566,143	1934
Gates of the Arctic	AK	3,000,000	1980
Glacier Bay	AK	1,305,220	1980
Grand Canyon	AZ	493,070	1919
Grand Teton	WY	125,666	1929
Great Basin	NV	31,206	1986
Great Smoky Mountains	TN,NC	210,550	1934
Guadalupe Mountains	TX	30,875	1972
Haleakala	HI	11,597	1960
Hawaii Volcanoes	HI	92,747	1916
Isle Royale	MI	231,400	1931
Katmai	AK	1,504,000	1980
Kenai Fjords	AK	271,145	1980
Kings Canyon	CA	186,822	1940
Kobuk Valley	AK	708,000	1980
Lake Clark	AK	1,067,114	1980
Lassen Volcanic	CA	43,048	1916
Mammoth Cave	KY	21,079	1941
Mesa Verde	CO	21,079	1906
Mount Rainier	WA	95,267	1899
North Cascades	WA	204,282	1968
Olympic	WA	370,124	1938
Petrified Forest	AZ	37,836	1962
Redwood	CA	44,588	1968
Rocky Mountain	CO	107,322	1915
Sequoia	CA	162,885	1890
Shenandoah	VA	78,945	1935
Theodore Roosevelt	ND	28,497	1978
Voyageurs	MN	88,180	1975
Wind Cave	SD	11,449	1903
Wrangell-St. Elias	AK	3,620,000	1980
Yellowstone	WY,MT,ID	898,349	1872
Yosemite	CA	308,041	1890
Zion	UT	59,308	1919

Source: United States Department of the Interior, National Park
        Service. The National Parks: Index 1985. Washington,
        D.C.: Government Printing Office, 1985.

national parks and established new ones; in order to develop a broad base of political support large portions were specified as reserves. Nevertheless, basic protection is assured to outstanding natural areas. These include the Bering Land Bridge National Preserve, containing immense deposits of remains—vestiges of mammoths, horses, giant bison, plus a few human traces—directly relating to the Bering Land Bridge, where prehistoric hunters are believed to have migrated from Asia, and Yukon-Charley Rivers National Preserve, a corridor of the Yukon River, the central artery of a vast Canadian-Alaskan frontier.

ADMINISTRATION

Organizational Structure

The National Park System, with units located all across the continental United States, and in Alaska, Hawaii, Puerto Rico, Virgin Islands, and Guam, is administered under a hierarchical format. It flows from a "headquarters" office in Washington, D.C., to ten regional offices and through them to the diverse park units. A director and deputy director, with assistance from nine associate directors, all at the Washington office, establish policy and guidelines for the entire Park System.

Ten regional directors are responsible for carrying out the mandates. Regional offices are located in Anchorage, Alaska, for all of Alaska; Seattle, Washington, for the northwestern states; San Francisco, California, for California, Nevada, most of Arizona, and the Pacific Islands; Santa Fe, New Mexico, for the southwestern states; Denver, Colorado, for the Rocky Mountain states; Omaha, Nebraska, for the midwestern states; Boston, Massachusetts, for the mid-Atlantic states; and Atlanta, Georgia, for the southeastern states and Atlantic islands.

Although each regional office has planning responsibilities, a larger and more complex planning function is located at the Denver Service Center in Colorado. The center includes an extensive professional staff that addresses all new park area projects and the most significant management plans.

The Park System also includes three training centers: Albright Training Center at the Grand Canyon in Arizona, involved with most "intake" courses (for new park personnel) and those best handled in a western setting; Harpers Ferry Center, West Virginia, involved with most interpretive courses and those best handled in the east; and the Federal Law Enforcement Training Center at Glynco, Georgia, which all park rangers must attend to receive law-enforcement certification. Certification updates are undertaken at various institutions throughout the country.

Management of each park falls under the responsibility of a park superintendent, who in turn reports to the regional director. The park superintendent and his or her staff are responsible for the day-to-day operational activities. The park staff usually consists of four to six divisions, depending upon the size and complexity of the unit. Divisions include park protection, interpretation, maintenance and administration, resource management, and science. Park rangers include representatives from both protection and interpretation, as well as resource management; these personnel usually are readily identified by the typical National Park Service uniform. Maintenance division personnel usually wear a uniform other than the "Class A" ranger wear.

The Challenge of Protection

To critical, preservation-oriented national park watchers, the "innovative" National Park Service thrusts of the 1960s and 1970s did little to enhance protection of natural and cultural resources. The Mission 66 program, launched in 1956, improved visitor comfort and park operations; so did the Parks for People concept that followed, only rendering more difficult the challenge of resource protection. Preservationists felt that perpetuation of natural and cultural treasures had become secondary to legislative and bureaucratic politics. Not until the late 1970s was attention finally focused on what may be considered true park values.

The National Parks and Conservation Association (NPCA) and the Conservation Foundation, both privately funded nonprofit organizations, conducted surveys on threats to park resources derived from the use of adjacent lands. The NPCA report ("NPCA Adjacent Lands Survey: No Park Is an Island") was published in March and April 1979; the Conservation Foundation report ("Federal Resource Lands and Their Neighbors") in December 1979. As a consequence of public attention and congressional concern stirred by these studies, in July 1979 two key members of Congress, Phillip Burton and Keith G. Sebelius, requested a "State of the Parks Report" from National Park Service Director William Whalen.

Many National Park Service employees and members of the conservation community believed that the resultant report, "State of the Parks—1980," provided the first real opportunity for the Park Service to seriously concentrate attention on resource protection. And when the second State of the Parks "Prevention and Mitigation" report followed in 1981, delineating short-term and mid-term strategies necessary to address the critical issues outlined in the 1980 report, the service appeared well directed on its preservation mission. National Park Service budget justifications to Congress utilized these reports to influence the budgetary process. And Congress appropriated an additional $10 million in 1983 to permit the National Park Service to initiate the projects described in its "Prevention and Mitigation" strategy.

An observer might have considered the State of the Parks process a huge success—that natural and cultural resources henceforth would receive the attention they desperately deserved. In actuality, this was only partly true. The bureaucracy of the National Park System itself created limitations. Although great strides were made in some areas, many good intentions were diluted or ignored altogether in others.

On the positive side, the "Prevention/Mitigation Plan" called for an immediate evaluation of all critical resource issues. New National Park Service Director Russell Dickenson summoned all ten regional directors to discuss and rank their "Significant Resource Problems" (SRPs). The SRP exercise created additional visibility of the critical issues and forced the regional directors to give unprecedented attention to park resources.

In addition, the "Prevention/Mitigation Plan" obligated the Park Service to utilize the Resource Management Plan process (already in place but rarely used) for project identification, assessment, prioritization, and resolution. It called for the completion of a Resource Management Plan for every park unit by December 1, 1981. And it also listed four support documents to be prepared to help in resolving or assessing park threats: Information Baseline Standards, Special Protection Zone Guidelines, Boundary Study of Historic/Archaeological Parks, and Biological Monitoring and Environmental Indices.

Six additional support projects were identified, two of which involved personnel training: a Natural Resource/Natural Science Management Development (Trainee) Program, and Natural Resource Management for Superintendents, Mid-level and Beginning Employees. The additional four projects included: Resource Information Tracking System (RITS), Early Warning/Consultation/Response Team, Cooperative Park Study Units Assessment, and Science Program Review by the National Academy of Sciences.

The Unfulfilled Plan

The results of those good intentions? This question occurred in the mid-1980s to Congressman Bruce Vento (D-Minn.), the new chairman of the House Interior Subcommittee (where it all began), and he asked the U.S. General Accounting Office (GAO), a congressionally directed research bureau, to investigate. The resultant GAO report, *Parks and Recreation—Limited Progress Made in Documenting and Mitigating Threats to the Parks*, completed in 1987, found that, despite progress on a few projects, most of the projects were either not started or were prematurely discontinued.[2]

Of those dozen or so thrusts, students of park practice feel that natural resource management training for all levels of the Park Service has been most worthwhile and must continue. Observers are concerned, however, that the shift in the Natural Resource Management trainee program from emphasizing the interface between management and science to that of training scientists may endanger an extremely valuable program. They believe the program must train resource management specialists, not compete with universities in teaching science, nor duplicate university programs.

Although the SRP program provided funds to address key issues at first, the revised program (now called Natural Resource Protection Program [NRPP]) allows regions to allocate funds as desired rather than for the highest-ranked servicewide priorities. Much of the funding originally earmarked for SRPs is now being utilized for non-natural and cultural resource issues.

The Degradation Continues

Progress was made on several of the thrusts identified in the "Prevention/ Mitigation Plan" but were discontinued. Considerable funds were spent on developing Information Baseline Standards, Special Protection Zone Guidelines, and RITS. Each of these programs was stopped after the Washington office was reorganized in 1983, and the responsibility for these efforts was placed under the associate director for natural resources.

What are the results of these inconsistencies? Although "the Field" (park units) generally is primarily concerned with its own responsibilities—of resource, visitor, and facility protection—the mixed signals from the central office cannot help but undermine morale. While the old-timers sit back and wait for the opportunities to come around again, the bright younger employees are oftentimes more affected. They either develop their own agenda, which may be way off the mark, or the best of the lot look for other work with higher salaries and less confusion. The result to this point has been reduced attention to the natural and cultural resources—and their continued degradation.

FUTURE OF THE NATIONAL PARKS

The Difficulty of Keeping Pace

Observers generally predict the number of visitors to U.S. national parks will grow from 250 million in 1987 to 350 million by the year 2000, the turn of the century. Yet no one dares to foresee the number of parks, or the land area they occupy, or the funding to administer them properly increasing by anywhere near the same degree.

The National Parks and Conservation Association (NPCA), a private nonprofit citizen organization (established in 1919 under the auspices of Stephen T. Mather, first director of the National Park Service), has been particularly concerned about such prospects. In 1988 NPCA completed a three-year study, resulting in "a plan for the future of the national parks." Key recommendations of the plan include the following:

• Additional national parks should be established, a number of existing national parks enlarged, and corollary preserves of state, county, and municipal parks likewise expanded.

• Renewed emphasis must be placed on safeguarding both the fundamental national park ecosystems and the quality experience visitors expect.

• As part of the effort to sustain the quality experience, visitor numbers must be limited. Park managers need to overcome their reluctance to set visitation limits.[3]

The National Park System, as conceived and constituted, reflects two elements of the American experience: natural diversity and cultural heritage. Of the former, it may safely be said that significant biological and geological forms are not now represented. The tallgrass prairie of the midcontinent has long been identified as a major gap that needs to be filled, especially considering that very little prairie still remains in the United States. Other gaps that need to be filled include Arctic caribou habitat, tropical rain forest, and underwater ecosystems. Countries elsewhere in the world already have extensive marine national parks, a biota not properly represented in the U.S. system. As for cultural components, these two must be expanded as Americans recognize the values of historic structures and landscapes and their potential contributions to future civilization. Historic preservation in the United States *has* advanced, from safeguarding single buildings to entire neighborhoods and entire communities and industrial sites. But the knowledge of what deserves saving remains far from being fully applied.

Parks Incomplete and Unfulfilled

Studies show clearly that most national parks, even the oldest and most respected, lack the comprehensive resources to assure protection of their plant and animal communities and/or cultural elements—the very values they were established to protect. Following are three examples.

1. Grizzly bears are as vital to Yellowstone National Park as the great thermal features, canyons, rushing streams, and limitless vistas. But grizzly bears are continually on the move; they require space well beyond the boundaries of the national park. With pressures of population growth and advancing civilization, the natural buffers around the park are no longer available to the bears. Grizzly survival plainly depends upon more rigorous protective management in the Yellowstone ecosystem, possibly tripling the size of the management zone, embracing lands administered by the U.S. Forest Service and with certain restraints on private lands as well.

2. Olympic National Park, in Washington State, has long been a threatened and endangered treasure. The park is located on the Olympic Peninsula of the Pacific Northwest, where heavy precipitation and moderate climate create favorable growing conditions for some of the greatest forests of North America. These include luxurious stands of Douglas fir, exceeded only by the redwood and giant sequoia in size of all trees on the continent. The Douglas fir grows to heights of 75 to 90 meters (250 to 300 feet), and some of the largest trees may be 400 to 1,000 years old. Because of the political influence of the timber industry, however, the park boundaries are imperfectly drawn. Only a few choice stands are protected in the rain forests along the Pacific, while many others, in adjoining national forests, state forests, and privately held timberlands, have been subjected to intensive clear-felling, destroying scenic, recreational, and watershed values. To protect the quality of the national park, either its boundaries must be extended or improved practices must be applied to neighboring lands.

3. Everglades National Park, at the southern tip of Florida, has suffered continuing decline even though administered as a national park since 1948. Some

species of wading birds, for which the park is known throughout the world, have declined by as much as 90 percent. The Florida panther has been declared endangered even in this last great stronghold. The American crocodile is virtually extinct. At least a dozen other significant wildlife species are believed facing a dim future. Declining levels of water as a consequence of drainage and urbanization in the south Florida basin and increasing concentrations of toxic chemicals have taken heavy tolls. Confronting the difficult truth, that the national park itself, the most cherished natural symbol of his state, was in serious trouble, Governor Robert Graham in the mid-1980s joined with citizen leaders in setting a goal: to restore the Everglades to their natural condition by the turn of the century. But all concerned recognize that it will not be easy to reclaim the natural quality that once prevailed.

Attaining Quality through Public Desire and Support

In the case of the Everglades 2000 campaign, emphasis has been placed on generating public attention to the goal and public support for the means of achieving it (such as breeding programs to restore decimated species, development of special structures to allow wildlife migration across highways, assembly of baseline scientific data and monitoring facilities). This approach in itself is not new. A review of history shows that virtually all national parks were established through the efforts of concerned citizens and that these same citizens rallied to defend the parks when they were in trouble. One formidable national park personality, the late Benton MacKaye, said that in the 1920s, when he conceived the idea of the Appalachian Trail, the longest recreational footpath in the world, he thought of it first as a physical body, but in due time realized there was also something else involved beyond the physical; it was, he felt, a spiritual quality, a soul, as manifest by the dedication of thousands of individuals who each year would maintain the trail. Involvement of citizens takes diverse forms, some not wholly welcome by those in charge. Nevertheless, the Grand Canyon today might well be flooded by dams were it not for public opposition during a period of controversy during the 1960s. Likewise, Great Smoky Mountains National Park might be cleft by highways actually proposed by the National Park Service had not many citizens expressed to Congress and the media their outraged opposition.

Leaders in preservation foresee public awareness and involvement as critical to the future of U.S. national parks, warning against isolation of park professionals from their public constituency. Professional resource managers must guard against the tendency to presume they know best, but rather be willing to listen to the public and to learn from it. This question relates closely to park accessibility. To play their full and proper role in the future, national parks must be administered as valid, undisrupted ecosystems and yet be accessible to all sectors of society, regardless of age or income. Natural and cultural features must be protected, not so much by rules and regulations but by understanding, a recognition that national parks reflect the common heritage of all people.

Given this approach, the quality of resources within the parks can become the prime indicator of the quality of life of the nation, the barometer of society's health. Manifestly, if air quality is degraded, or if wildlife and plant species are in poor condition inside the parks, so too must it be in the home environment of those who visit the parks.

The collection of scientific data—through baseline inventories and scientific monitoring—has been strongly cited as a weakness and need of coordinated park administration. Yet perhaps the greater need in the United States is a renewal of national commitment to the pioneering spirit of an earlier day, a commitment to an ideal condition coupled with determination to strive consciously and constantly to attain it.

NOTES

1. Michael Frome, *Battle for the Wilderness* (Boulder, Colo.: Westview Press, 1984), p. 110.

2. General Accounting Office, *Parks and Recreation—Limited Progress Made in Documenting and Mitigating Threats to the Parks* (Washington, D.C.: Government Printing Office, 1987), p. 4.

3. National Parks and Conservation Association, *Investing in Park Futures, the National Park System Plan: A Blueprint for Tomorrow* (Washington, D.C.: NPCA, 1988), pp. 5–8.

BIBLIOGRAPHY

Ise, John. *Our National Park Policy*. Baltimore: Johns Hopkins University Press, 1961.

Muir, John. *Our National Parks*. New York: Houghton Mifflin, 1901. Reprint. Madison: University of Wisconsin Press, 1981.

National Park Service Office of Science and Technology. *State of the Parks 1980: A Report to the Congress*. Washington, D.C.: Government Printing Office, 1980.

————. *State of the Parks: A Report to Congress on a Servicewide Strategy for Prevention and Mitigation of Natural and Cultural Resources Management Problems*. (Typescript.) Washington, D.C.: National Park Service, c. 1980.

National Parks and Conservation Association. *National Parks in Crisis*. Washington, D.C.: NPCA,1981.

President's Commission on Americans Outdoors. *Americans Outdoors, The Legacy, The Challenge*. Washington, D.C.: Government Printing Office, 1987.

Runte, Alfred. *National Parks: The American Experience*. Lincoln: University of Nebraska Press, 1979.

UNITED STATES: WILDERNESS AREAS

24

George H. Stankey

The protection of natural values at the national level in the United States has been achieved through a variety of programs. Historically, the National Park Service has been the leader in the creation of a system of parks and reserves designed to ensure that the nation's natural heritage is protected and preserved for future generations. But the extent of the National Park System is limited; much wild, undeveloped land possessing important natural values lies outside it. Development within the national parks to accommodate recreation use has often meant that natural values have been diminished. Finally, the national park designation often has been applied only to those areas with outstanding scenic and natural qualities; other areas possessing less striking qualities yet characterized by a high level of naturalness have not been seen as deserving national park status. Such concerns led to pressures for creation of an additional protective designation for lands possessing a high level of naturalness and ecological integrity. The result of this pressure was the National Wilderness Preservation System, a system of lands managed to protect their natural quality and the processes that created them. In this chapter, we will examine the evolution and institutionalization of wilderness in America and its role in conserving nature and natural values. We will also examine the problems facing the protection and management of such areas and their future.

HISTORY: ORIGINS OF THE WILDERNESS MOVEMENT

Early settlers along America's eastern seaboard faced a vast continent of wilderness, reaching over 5,000 kilometers (3,000 miles) westward. Considered a barrier to settlement and movement, a source of threats to life and property, and the antithesis of the cultured and domesticated landscape that religion and culture favored, the wilderness yielded rapidly to expansion and development. Yet society has always viewed wilderness with ambivalence. Even as westward settlement progressed and wilderness was replaced by civilization, there were early pleas to set aside some areas where the natural qualities of the land and its native people might be protected. George Catlin, an artist and lawyer, proposed in 1832 that, through "some great protecting policy of government . . . a nation's Park, containing man and beast" be created.[1] Two decades later, Henry David Thoreau, the Transcendental theorist, spoke eloquently of the need to preserve segments of wild nature, arguing "in Wildness is the preservation of the World."[2]

In 1872, Yellowstone National Park was established, the first such natural reserve in the world. In 1890, Yosemite National Park was created. These early parks were important steps in governmental involvement in protecting natural values. Nevertheless, the parks clearly were not established to protect wilderness; the enabling legislation for both areas contains no reference to wilderness values or the need to preserve natural quality. Rather, designation as national parks was mainly done to protect unique landscapes (e.g., geysers in Yellowstone) from private purchase and development. The extent to which wilderness and natural values were protected through these designations was only incidental.

But the symbolic importance of these early park reservations cannot be underestimated. They clearly established a governmental role in setting aside land for nondevelopmental purposes. What was next needed were individuals and organizations to catalyze the political process in such a way that this governmental capacity would be fully realized. The first of these was John Muir. Muir's appearance on the scene coincided with growing national recognition that America's natural resource base was under siege from developmental interests. Muir helped dramatize such concerns through his writings, which appeared regularly in national magazines and newspapers. In particular, he helped garner public support for the designation of Yosemite National Park, and despite the lack of explicit legislative recognition of wilderness in the park's enabling legislation, there was little doubt that wilderness was the driving concern for Muir. He declared the area around Yosemite Valley to be "a noble park for the . . . lover of wilderness pure and simple," arguing that his support for the park was to prevent "the destruction of the fineness of wildness."[3]

Following passage of the Yosemite National Park Act in 1890, Muir joined a number of like-minded colleagues in the San Francisco area to form a group whose purpose was to ensure continued protection for the Sierra Nevada. Although formed initially as a regional organization, the Sierra Club quickly became a potent national political force in the effort to preserve the nation's wilderness lands.

The declaration of national parks was a critical phase in governmental efforts to protect natural values. But only a relatively small proportion of the nation possessed those qualities that qualified them for national park protection. Vast acreages that lacked outstanding scenic qualities or spectacular natural phenomena still remained wild and undeveloped. Many of these lands were under administration of the fledgling Forest Service.

In 1891, Congress passed a law giving the president authority to create "forest reserves" by withdrawing land from the public domain. President Benjamin Harrison immediately set aside 5.25 million hectares (13 million acres) under this authority. Because no explicit purpose for these reserves was contained in the legislation, the stage was set for a debate over how these lands should be used. Muir took the position that they were indistinguishable from national parks and should be managed to protect their naturalness. Gifford Pinchot, on the other hand, held an instrumental perspective, favoring the application of scientific forestry principles to these areas to ensure a sustained flow of material goods. Although a brief period ensued during which Muir felt it possible to realize both goals, the inevitable conflict between development and preservation soon brought an end to this. By the end of the century, further congressional action made it clear that the primary purpose of the forest reserves was to "furnish a continuous supply of timber for the use and necessities of citizens of the United States."[4] Mining and grazing also were to be allowed. The forest reserves, forerunners of the national forests, provided little solace to those concerned with the protection of naturalness.

But the history of wilderness protection in the United States is marked by paradox and irony. Despite the fact that the utilitarian perspective of Pinchot and others prevailed in the legislative definition of the forest reserves, there nevertheless was growing public sentiment in support of the concept of wilderness preservation. Roderick Nash has identified three themes underlying this growing swell of public support.[5] First, with the 1890 census, the American frontier had finally passed, with the shift from a rural to an urban society. The shift held major symbolic significance for a country where a frontier that had once seemed endless had influenced the outlook of generations of citizens. With its passage, the wilderness that had both resisted the spread of civilization and shaped the character of the society was lost. Second, the promises of civilization had already been seen to fall short of society's expectations; the squalor of urban slums and the dominance of machine over human spirit were seen to represent the price of an overly materialistic society. From such experiences arose romantic conceptions of the virtues of primitive life and primitive man, products of the wilderness now fast disappearing. Finally, there was a related view that saw the wilderness as the source of values civilization lacked, such as honesty and morality.

In sum, as the twentieth century dawned and America began its metamorphosis from agrarian to industrial society, the conception of wilderness as a powerful symbolic representation of good began to take shape.

This intellectual conceptualization of wilderness in American society was given impetus by the events surrounding proposals to develop the Hetch Hetchy Valley in Yosemite National Park as a reservoir to supply the city of San Francisco with drinking water and hydroelectric power. The intrusion of a dam and reservoir within a national park was bitterly contested by the Sierra Club and many other preservation groups, but to no avail. In late 1913, President Woodrow Wilson approved the proposal opening the way for the development to proceed. Yet in many ways, the loss of Hetch Hetchy proved to be a major factor in awakening public support of nature preservation. It highlighted a fundamental precept in nature conservation: development can lose many times, but preservation can lose only once. Across the country, many people began to concern themselves with the question of how best to protect examples of the primitive landscape.

In 1916, the National Park Service came into being, led by Stephen T. Mather. Together with the Forest Service, established in 1905 to manage the forest reserve program, the two agencies represented a major federal effort to manage the nation's natural resources. But there was sharp conflict between the two organizations. Part of the conflict arose from the differences in their underlying missions: the Forest Service was utilization-oriented, the Park Service preservation-oriented. Virtually all the expansion of the National Park System occurred as a result of the removal of lands from national forest status. As Craig Allin notes, all of this was occurring not because the Forest Service was in disfavor with the Congress, but simply because societal pressures for preservation were so strong and the National Park Service was seen as the most logical agency to administer a system of areas where preservation was the principal management goal.[6]

Although the Forest Service had arisen in a tradition of utilitarian values, recreation was of growing importance on the national forests. Thus, in 1921, the Forest Service had recognized recreation as a legitimate resource use along with the more traditional uses of timber production, grazing, and watershed protection. Yet there remained considerable opposition to any official wilderness preservation.

But pressures to take wilderness preservation values into account in the national forests were building. They arose from the growing number of users seeking recreation in the national forests. They arose from the calls from organizations such as the Ecological Society of America and the American Association for the Advancement of Science. These latter pressures were particularly important in that they called for the protection of wilderness reserves to protect their scientific values. The Ecological Society, for example, recommended setting aside areas of every ecological description.

Pressures also arose from within the agency. In 1919, Arthur Carhart, a landscape architect working on a proposed development at Trapper's Lake on the White River National Forest in Colorado, argued that development of the area was inappropriate. Carhart contended that the area's scenic value outweighed the benefits to be gained by development; he predicted that the "time will come when these scenic spots, where nature has been allowed to remain unmarred, will be some of the most highly prized scenic features of the country."[7] Carhart's training as a landscape architect naturally led him to emphasize the scenic values of retaining land in a preserved condition; nevertheless, his proposal clearly rested on the importance of maintaining the area's natural qualities. His suggestions for Trapper's Lake were accepted; for the first time within the Forest Service, preservation of natural conditions took precedence over development.

Conflict between the Forest Service and National Park Service remained sharp. The growing recreational use of national forest lands had brought the agency in to the recreation-management business irrespective of any official position, and the agency responded by seeking funding to meet this new demand. Mather objected and sought to prevent the Forest Service from receiving such funding, taking the position that the provision of recreation was solely a national park responsibility. At the same time, the National Park Service continued to enjoy significant expansion of the system of park reserves into the 1920s, with the bulk of the expansion drawn from the National Forest System.

Increasingly, Forest Service officials realized that a preservation policy was necessary to prevent further losses of land to the National Park Service and to gain increased support from Congress and the public. In the mid-1920s, the Forest Service took steps to establish such a policy. It took form slowly, initially reflected in decisions to prevent development in certain areas where outstanding scenic values were threatened by roads or structures. In 1922, Aldo Leopold recommended creation of a large wilderness reserve in New Mexico's Gila National Forest; in 1924, his proposal was approved and a 232,400-hectare (574,000-acre) area was set aside.[8] Then, in 1926, the Forest Service took the first step toward creation of a formal system of wilderness reserves. A national inventory of roadless lands on the national forests was initiated to identify all those tracts over ten townships (932 square kilometers, 360 square miles) in size. This inventory revealed 74 tracts totaling 22 million hectares (55 million acres), with the largest area about 2.8 million hectares (7 million acres).

With this inventory information in hand, a new Forest Service wilderness policy was set forth in 1929. The L-20 Regulation called for the establishment of a system of areas "to be known as primitive areas, and within which will be maintained primitive conditions . . . with a view to conserving the values of such areas for purposes of public education and recreation." The L-20 Regulation was in effect for ten years, during which 75 areas and over 5.7 million hectares (14 million acres) were set aside. Both the definition and the administration of these areas were loose. Timber harvesting and road building, for example, continued in many areas, and in only four areas was development completely restricted.

Nevertheless, the L-20 Regulation created the first system of areas managed explicitly and predominantly for nonexploitive purposes. Moreover, it created the core of what would become, three decades later, the National Wilderness Preservation System. But the protection of natural values was only incidental to the L-20 Regulation. It was primarily a response to demands for primitive recreation opportunities on the national forests as well as a strategic response to the pressures for withdrawals for the creation of national parks and for controlling haphazard road building and commercial development in areas of scenic and recreational attraction until such time as management plans could be prepared.

In this latter sense, the L–20 Regulation served as an interim measure rather than a permanent land-use designation.

Although the L–20 Regulation was a major advance in the protection of wilderness values on the national forests, inherent weaknesses in it left those concerned with the permanent protection of such values dissatisfied. In 1937, the Forest Service hired Robert Marshall, then employed with the Office of Indian Affairs in the Department of the Interior. Marshall had already established impressive credentials in the name of wilderness preservation through his writing and work. In 1935, he, along with several like-minded colleagues, had formed the Wilderness Society. Marshall was well aware of the weaknesses of the L–20 Regulation and immediately set about to correct them.

Marshall's efforts led to a new set of administrative regulations to guide the establishment and management of national forest wilderness. They were called the U Regulations and established a more detailed and explicit set of criteria. The U Regulations supplanted the L–20 Regulation and called for the review of each existing primitive area under the new guidelines.

The U Regulations created a three-tiered system of protected areas. Regulation U–1 established wilderness areas—tracts of land not less than 40,469 hectares (100,000 acres). Acting on the recommendation of the chief of the Forest Service, the secretary of agriculture could designate an area as wilderness, and only the secretary could modify or eliminate an area's wilderness designation. Regulation U–2 created wild areas—tracts of land between 2,023 and 40,469 hectares (5,000 and 100,000 acres) that could be established, modified, or eliminated by the chief of the Forest Service. Management of wild areas, however, was the same as for wilderness areas. Finally, Regulation U–3(a) established roadless areas. These areas were to be managed principally for recreational use "substantially in their natural condition." Areas over 40,469 hectares (100,000 acres) were to be established by the secretary of agriculture, those under, by the chief of the Forest Service.

The U Regulations provided much more protection for wilderness than the L–20 Regulation they replaced. For one thing, it was clear they were to be permanent, not just an interim measure to halt haphazard development. They prohibited timber cutting, road development, and special use permits for such things as summer homes and hunting camps. The use of mechanized access, except where well established or in emergencies, was banned. Grazing and water resource development were allowed to continue, as was mining, which was not under the control of the Forest Service; however, the agency could insist that such developments take care to minimize impact on wilderness values.

The first order of business following enactment of the U Regulations was the review of the existing primitive areas to determine their status under the new regulations. Pending completion of review, each area was to be managed under the new, stricter guidelines. Progress, however, was slow. The outbreak of World War II in 1941 effectively halted any progress in the reviews.

Following the end of the war, reviews of the primitive areas began again.

Despite the improvements in the U Regulations over the L–20 Regulation, there remained much concern about the effectiveness of wilderness protection on the national forests. Several factors drove these concerns. First, the rate of progress of the primitive area reviews remained slow; by the late 1940s, only 800,000 hectares (2 million acres) had been reclassified. Moreover, conservationists were concerned about the loss of acreage in the reclassification process. In many areas, they argued, timbered lower-elevation areas within primitive area boundaries had been lost when the area was reclassified. Second, following World War II the United States entered a period of rapid economic growth. Demand for housing, for example, led to increased levels of timber harvest, and with it, increased incursions into much de facto wilderness land. There was also an explosion in the demand for recreational access to the forests. In the mid–1950s, both the Forest Service and the National Park Service responded to this demand with major capital investment programs to create more recreational opportunities on their lands; the bulk of this development was focused on road-accessible recreation. Many conservationists saw such programs as a threat to the continued protection of roadless areas. Finally, despite the improved protection for wilderness values that the U Regulations afforded, they remained administrative edicts; conservationists were concerned that an area's wilderness designation could be overturned by an agency administrator. In other words, wilderness on the national forests lacked the kind of legal protection afforded the national parks. Its future security remained tied to the sympathy and support toward wilderness held by area administrators.

The argument that wilderness required a level of legal protection equivalent to that given national parks was not new. As early as the 1930s, proponents had argued that wilderness should be protected by statute. Periodic reviews of the status of wilderness uniformly concluded that one of the major shortcomings of wilderness protection was the lack of legal protection. A 1949 report by the Legislative Reference Service reinforced this perspective, concluding that without legal status, the future of wilderness was cloudy.[9]

The tenuous status of wilderness, coupled with the various pressures on the nation's wild lands, set the stage for efforts to rewrite the manner in which wilderness was to be protected. The existing situation with regard to wilderness protection had four major shortcomings:

1. Land-administering agencies could put wilderness to other uses.
2. Agencies lacked full jurisdiction over some land uses within wilderness, such as mining.
3. There was a lack of coordinated control over wilderness uses.
4. There was a lack of distinctive management policy.

One of the strongest advocates of a national wilderness system, protected by law, was Howard Zahniser, executive director of the Wilderness Society. Zahniser's major theme was the need for a "persisting program" of wilderness preservation. Beginning in 1949, Zahniser campaigned for a law to ensure adequate wilderness protection within federal land-managing agencies. There was sharp opposition to the idea, both from special interests such as the grazing, mining, and timber industries, and from the Forest Service and National Park Service. Both agencies argued, at least initially, that such legislation was not needed and that it might constrain their execution of other programs.

In 1956, the first bill proposing creation of a national wilderness system was introduced into Congress. The bill was largely drafted by Zahniser, and he played a major role in guiding the bill to eventual passage. Eight years passed, however, before the bill became law. Sixty-five different bills were introduced during this time, numerous public hearings were held across the nation, and thousands of pages of testimony were taken.

After considerable revision and compromise, the Wilderness Act was signed into law in September 1964. The legislation set forth the goals of, and procedures for, establishing a National Wilderness Preservation System (NWPS). Above all else, it provided wilderness with the highest level of permanency and protection possible in the American legal system, thus addressing one of the basic concerns noted by the Legislative Reference Service in 1949. In the next section we will look at the basic features of the act and review the character and extent of the system it has created.

NATURE RESERVES: THE NATIONAL WILDERNESS PRESERVATION SYSTEM

The Wilderness Act includes a statement of objectives for areas classified under its terms and provides a definition for such areas. The statute sets forth its overriding objective as follows:

To assure that an increasing population, accompanied by expanding settlement and growing mechanization, does not occupy and modify all areas within the United States and its possessions, leaving no lands designated for preservation and protection in their natural condition, it is hereby declared to be the policy of the Congress to secure for the American people of present and future generations the benefits of an enduring resource of wilderness.

Wilderness is defined in two complementary ways. First, it is defined in an almost poetic fashion:

A wilderness, in contrast with those areas where man and his own works dominate the landscape, is hereby recognized as an area where the earth and its community of life are untrammeled by man, where man himself is a visitor who does not remain.

The act then goes on to define wilderness in a more pragmatic, objective manner as an area of undeveloped Federal land retaining its primeval character and influence, without permanent improvements or human habitation, . . . and which (1) generally appears to have been affected primarily by the forces of nature, with the imprint of man's work substantially unnoticeable; (2) has outstanding opportunities for solitude or a primitive and unconfined type of recreation; (3) has at least five thousand acres [2,000 hectares] of land or is of sufficient size as to make practicable its preservation . . . ; and (4) may also contain ecological, geological, or other features of scientific, educational, scenic, or historical value.

Wildernesses are defined as areas where natural processes predominate, not where some particular ecological state is maintained. Thus, the specific conditions in an area will evolve in response to natural forces of change such as erosion and succession.

The act establishes a process to create a NWPS. Wildernesses can be designated only by an act of Congress. Upon passage of the act in 1964, all existing Forest Service areas managed as wilderness, wild, or roadless became part of an "instant" wilderness system; approximately 3.7 million hectares (9.1 million acres) formed the core of the NWPS. The act instructed the secretary of agriculture to review the remaining primitive areas—thirty-four areas totaling 2.2 million hectares (5.4 million acres)—within ten years and to make recommendations regarding the suitability of these areas for wilderness classification to the president who, in turn, would advise Congress. A similar review procedure was identified for the secretary of the interior; all areas within the National Park System and Wildlife and Game Refuges Systems were to be studied for their suitability for wilderness within ten years and recommendations made to the president. No Interior Department areas were immediately classified as wilderness.[10]

Growth of the Wilderness System

The NWPS has grown rapidly. As of mid–1989 the system contained 36.73 million hectares (90.76 million acres) distributed over 474 separate units located in 44 states. (See Table 24.1). The National Park Service managed 14.86 million hectares (38.50 million acres); the Forest Service, 13.14 million hectares (32.46 million acres); and the Fish and Wildlife Service, 7.82 million hectares (19.33 million acres). Because the Bureau of Land Management (BLM) has only recently initiated wilderness studies, only about 189,000 hectares (470,000 acres) of its holdings have been classified.

Although the Wilderness Act only referred to the need for the Forest Service to review its existing primitive areas for possible designation as wilderness, the act has become applicable to virtually all national forest lands possessing the basic qualities that define wilderness. A series of legal challenges and court tests have resulted in the review of roadless lands on the national forests for consideration as wilderness. Over 2,900 areas totaling over 25.1 million hectares (62 million acres) were identified. Much of the growth of the NWPS has come from the classification of these national forest areas.

Table 24.1
Statistical Summary of U.S. Wilderness Areas

MANAGING AGENCY OR AGENCIES	NUMBER OF UNITS	AREA (HECTARES)	AREA (ACRES)
U.S. Forest Service	341	11,086,498	27,394,739
National Park Service	41	15,580,322	38,498,978
Fish and Wildlife Service	64	7,822,718	19,329,936
Bureau of Land Management	14	171,979	424,960
U.S.F.S. and B.L.M	10	1,933,565	4,777,838
U.S.F.S. and N.P.S.	2	122,473	302,630
U.S.F.S. and F.W.S	1	12,359	30,540
F.W.S. and B.L.M.	1	196	485
TOTAL	474	36,730,110	90,760,106

Source: Wilderness Society. "National Wilderness Preservation
System, 1964-1989." Supplement to Wilderness 52 (Spring 1989).

A second major source of growth in the NWPS occurred in 1980 when President Jimmy Carter signed legislation setting aside over 22.7 million hectares (56 million acres) of wilderness in the state of Alaska. Lands from the Forest Service, National Park Service, and Fish and Wildlife Service were involved. Included in this total was the largest single wilderness in the NWPS, the 3.5-million-hectare (8.7-million-acre) Wrangell–St. Elias Wilderness, managed by the National Park Service. The largest of the established wilderness areas are listed in Table 24.2.

There remains considerable potential for future growth in the NWPS. Many national parks have large areas still pending consideration for wilderness classification. The addition of BLM holdings to the wilderness review process further increases the potential for growth. The BLM was not included originally in the Wilderness Act because the agency had no authority to manage its holdings; it acted only in a custodial role, and was largely involved in the disposition of the nearly 162 million hectares (400 million acres) of public domain that was its responsibility. In 1976, however, passage of the Federal Land Policy and Management Act provided BLM with authority to undertake wilderness reviews of its holdings and to establish wilderness in accordance with the provisions outlined in the Wilderness Act. The agency has identified 9.3 million hectares (23 million acres) in more than 700 areas for further study for possible wilderness classification.

The process of wilderness classification is likely to continue for many years to come. The eventual size of the NWPS is arguable, but an estimate of 48.6 million hectares (120 million acres), or approximately 5 percent of the land area of the United States, does not seem unreasonable.

The Wilderness Act has many positive effects, but in particular it has brought a high level of protection to the natural values that characterize the landscape. In national parks these values were relatively well protected prior to passage, yet it remained possible that developments to accommodate increasing recrea-

Table 24.2
U.S. Wilderness Areas over 100,000 Hectares

NAME	MANAGING AGENCY[a]	LOCATION BY STATE(S)	AREA (HECTARES)	DATE ESTABLISHED
Absaroka-Beartooth	USFS	MT/WY	382,055	1978[b]
Admiralty Island National Monument	USFS	AK	379,359	1980
Aleutian Islands	FWS	AK	526,000	1980
Alpine Lakes	USFS	WA	123,597	1976
Andreafsky	FWS	AK	526,000	1980
Arctic	FWS	AK	3,200,000	1980
Becharof	FWS	AK	162,000	1980
Bob Marshall	USFS	MT	408,480	1964[b]
Boundary Waters Canoe Area	USFS	MN	323,071	1964[b]
Bridger	USFS	WY	173,278	1964
Denali	NPS	AK	769,000	1980
Eagle Cap	USFS	OR	145,067	1964[b]
Everglades	NPS	FL	523,472	1978
Frank Church - River of No Return	USFS	ID	956,085	1980
Gates of the Arctic	NPS	AK	2,850,000	1980
Gila	USFS	NM	225,746	1964[b]
Glacier Bay	NPS	AK	1,120,000	1980
Glacier Peak	USFS	WA	233,366	1964[b]
Golden Trout	USFS	CA	122,739	1978
Great Bear	USFS	MT	116,000	1978
Gros Ventre	USFS	WY	116,000	1984
High Uintas	USFS	UT	186,000	1984
Innoko	FWS	AK	502,000	1980
Izembek	FWS	AK	120,000	1980
John Muir	USFS	CA	234,996	1964[b]
Joshua Tree	NPS	CA	173,893	1976
Katmai	NPS	AK	1,406,000	1980
Kenai	FWS	AK	546,000	1980
Koyukuk	FWS	AK	160,000	1980
Lake Clark	NPS	AK	1,000,000	1980
Lee Metcalf	USFS/BLM	MT	103,174	1983
Mazatzal	USFS	AZ	101,947	1964
Misty Fjords	USFS	AK	866,954	1980
Noatak	NPS	AK	2,350,000	1980
North Absaroka	USFS	WY	141,861	1964
Nunivak	FWS	AK	240,000	1980
Okefenokee	FWS	GA	143,254	1974
Olympic	NPS	WA	345,783	1988
Organ Pipe Cactus	NPS	AZ	126,500	1978
Pasayten	USFS	WA	214,427	1968[b]
Russell Fjord	USFS	AK	141,117	1980
Selway-Bitterroot	USFS	ID/MT	541,445	1964[b]
Semidi	FWS	AK	100,000	1980
Sequoia-Kings Canyon	NPS	CA	298,252	1984
South Baranof	USFS	AK	129,327	1980
Stephen Mather	NPS	WA	256,825	1988

Table 24.2 (continued)

NAME	MANAGING AGENCY[a]	LOCATION BY STATE(S)	AREA (HECTARES)	DATE ESTABLISHED
Stikine-LeConte	USFS	AK	181,643	1980
Teton	USFS	WY	236,936	1964[b]
Three Sisters	USFS	OR	115,419	1964
Togiak	FWS	AK	919,000	1980
Tracy Arm- Fords Terror	USFS	AK	264,338	1980
Trinity Alps	USFS/BLM	CA	200,000	1984
Unimak	FWS	AK	370,000	1980
Washakie	USFS	WY	284,897	1964[b]
Weminuche	USFS	CO	186,080	1975[b]
West Chichagof- Yakobi	USFS	AK	107,142	1980
Wrangell-St. Elias	NPS	AK	3,500,000	1980
Yosemite	NPS	CA	274,000	1984

Notes: [a] USFS - U.S. Forest Service
NPS - National Park Service
FWS - Fish & Wildlife Service
BLM - Bureau of Land Management
[b] A part of the current area was added by legislation
subsequent to initial establishment.

Source: Wilderness Society. "National Wilderness Preservation
System, 1964-1989." Supplement to Wilderness 52 (Spring 1989).

tional use could compromise natural values. Thus, the Wilderness Act has provided an additional level of protection beyond that afforded by park designation. Outside the national parks, the Wilderness Act has established a process that protects the natural qualities of areas from development, particularly timber harvesting and road building. Without such a process, it is unlikely that the amount of area now classified or likely to be so would, in fact, have been protected.

Although the Wilderness Act covers only federal lands, a number of states have instituted programs of wilderness protection as well. A recent survey of state activity revealed nine states with programs roughly equivalent to that of the federal government, and numerous other states have programs designed to protect natural values.[11]

Wilderness Values

Historically, the debate about wilderness legislation echoes an overriding concern to preserve ecological processes that shape the land. Wilderness is viewed as a dynamic concept, where the ebb and flow of nature are allowed to the maximum extent possible, free to operate outside the control of humans.

Another concern for wilderness focused on the protection of ecological diversity. The Wilderness Act nowhere ensures a diverse, representative sample of ecosystems. Much of the support for specific wilderness arises from their recreational importance or from the presence of outstanding scenic attractions. It is true, in a system as large as the NWPS has grown, that a wide range of ecological representation has been gained, albeit in an unsystematic fashion. Yet serious gaps remain.

For example, George D. Davis has examined the extent to which the nation's various ecosystems are represented adequately within the NWPS.[12] By merging R. G. Bailey's ecoregion concept and A. W. Küchler's potential natural vegetation mapping, Davis divides the United States into 233 distinct ecosystems. Using the criterion that at least two examples of each ecosystem are required within the NWPS to constitute adequate representation, he assesses the present coverage provided by the NWPS. Davis finds only 81 of the 233 ecosystems (35 percent) adequately represented; grasslands, deserts, eastern hardwoods, and coastal lowland ecosystems are particularly poorly represented.

It is estimated that an additional sixty ecosystems could be included within the NWPS through the addition of new areas, particularly those under BLM jurisdiction. But even with these additions, and even if the wilderness management agencies recommended representative examples of each basic ecosystem under their jurisdiction and Congress concurred with these recommendations, fifty ecosystems would still not be represented within the NWPS. Although some of these might be protected under some other designation, typically these are less stringent than what wilderness protection offers.

With the exception of recreation, most other wilderness values have received little attention. No comprehensive assessment, for instance, has been conducted with regard to geological phenomena within the NWPS. Wilderness is typically associated with providing critical wildlife habitat. For example, much of the habitat of the threatened grizzly bear (*Ursus arctos*) is within wilderness. Yet for other species, such as elk (*Cervus canadensis*), wilderness is not necessarily the best land-use designation. Because the focus in wilderness is on allowing natural processes to operate freely, successional changes can lead to habitat conditions not beneficial to wildlife. This poses problems for administrators of wilderness on some Fish and Wildlife Service areas that were established in order to provide habitat for a specific species. Often, without habitat manipulation, these species' habitat requirements cannot be met; however, such manipulation is, on the face of it, contrary to the intent of wilderness.

One natural value not mentioned specifically in the Wilderness Act but given emphasis in subsequent legislation is clean air. The 1977 Clean Air Act and its amendments specify that all wildernesses over 2,023 hectares (5,000 acres) are to be identified as Class 1 areas; air quality in these areas was assumed to be of high quality, and the Class 1 designation provides wilderness managers with the authority to prevent any adverse impacts on the air-quality-related values found within such areas. These air-quality-related values included visibility, but also such things as effects on the growth and productivity of flora and fauna, metals concentration in soils, and changes in pH or alkalinity of water. In effect, any projected measurable change in air quality other than visibility is defined as an adverse impact and therefore subject to control.

Recreation Values in Wilderness

Like the national parks, wilderness is managed according to an apparent paradox in which such areas are for the use and enjoyment of people at the same time their essential natural qualities are to be preserved. The "use and preserve" dilemma poses difficult management challenges. Nevertheless, recreational use remains the predominant direct wilderness use.

The amount of wilderness recreation use is difficult to estimate. The measurements of use by different agencies are reported differently and are not additive. In 1985, however, the Forest Service reported nearly 12 million visitor-days of wilderness recreation use (a visitor-day is defined as a twelve-hour visit by one individual or any combination thereof, such as two people for six hours). In the national parks, about 1.6 million overnight visits were reported in wilderness or undeveloped backcountry (a visit is defined as the entry of any person onto National Park Service lands or waters).[13]

Recreational use of wilderness has grown rapidly. In national forest wilderness areas, use grew 7-fold between 1946 and 1964, over 11 percent per annum. Since 1964, it has increased another 2.5-fold, about 5 percent per annum. In recent years, however, growth rates have slowed. Much of the apparent growth recently is the result of the substantial expansion of the number of wilderness areas. Among the eighty-eight national forest areas designated as wilderness or otherwise protected in 1964, recreational use actually declined by 2 percent between 1980 and 1985. Such declines are even more apparent in national park areas; between 1976 and 1985, recreational use of these areas declined by over one-third.

Most of the recreational use of wilderness occurs on foot, on horseback, or by canoe. Motorized access (e.g., by aircraft or motorboat) is permitted in only a few locations, typically where such use had a long historical precedent. Use densities are relatively light, but high concentrations occur in a few locations. Typically, most travel occurs along trails and often along only a small proportion of them. In many areas, it is not uncommon to find over half of the total use traveling along only 10 percent of the total trail mileage available.[14] Still, the relatively light use levels mean the impacts on natural values are limited to areas along travel routes, at popular campsites, and at attractions such as scenic views. And it is clear from the language of the Wilderness Act that the area's natural qualities underlie the kind of recreational opportunity the area provides. In general, wilderness management agencies give priority to those activities whose enjoyment is dependent on a natural setting where environmental conditions are preserved and only minimal development is permitted.

ADMINISTRATION

The Wilderness Act provided general guidelines for management. Wilderness is protected by federal law; the establishment of wilderness requires congressional approval, as does any addition, deletion, or modification. The overall objective is to protect a system of areas so that natural processes are allowed to continue operating with minimal human influence. Mechanized use is generally prohibited, as are road building and timber harvesting.

However, because the Wilderness Act, like most legislation, was the product of compromise, certain activities generally regarded as inconsistent with wilderness protection are nonetheless allowed. These are often described as "allowable but nonconforming uses." They include such things as livestock grazing and activities conducted in support of grazing, water resources development projects, and mining. Access to private inholdings is allowed. These activities can threaten natural values, yet it is clear that without accommodations to these interests, it would have been difficult if not impossible to secure the necessary political support to pass the Wilderness Act. The managing agencies retain the authority and responsibility to see that these activities are conducted in a manner that minimizes adverse impacts and that steps are taken to mitigate these adverse effects wherever possible.

The educational and scientific values of wilderness are recognized in the legislation. The value of such areas as baselines of ecological conditions and as repositories of genetic material is often cited as a major reason for their protection. However, it is difficult to appraise the extent to which wilderness serves such purposes; it appears to be of more potential than actual value. Moreover, policies on research within the Forest Service and National Park Service strongly advocate that only that research that cannot be conducted in any other setting be permitted in wilderness. Manipulative and experimental research are not permitted. The educational potential of wilderness seems similarly underutilized. Aldo Leopold's conception of wilderness as a "land laboratory"[15] is still with us, but the extent to which areas in the NWPS perform an educational and scientific function is limited.

Although the Wilderness Act created a national system, individual areas remain under the administration of one of the four federal land-managing agencies. Different agency missions, legal directives, and philosophies, however, produce differences in how wilderness is managed. For example, hunting is permitted in national forest and BLM wilderness, in some Fish and Wildlife Service areas, but not in national park wildernesses. Mining is permitted in wildernesses managed by the Forest Service and the BLM, but most national park areas have been withdrawn from mineral entry. Although habitat modification is incompatible with wilderness, it occurs in some Fish and Wildlife Service areas to maintain essential habitat for the species for which the area was established.

The relatively scarce nature of wilderness, coupled with its inherent sensitivity to change, makes such areas particularly susceptible to threats from human activity, including activity outside as well as within the area. Within wilderness, the allowable but nonconforming uses are a principal source of impact on natural values. The potential impact of mining, for example, is extreme, both through the excavation and road-building activities associated with the removal of minerals and through the introduction of air and water pollution. Recent pressures for oil and gas leasing have been a particular source of concern, as many western wildernesses coincide with areas where major oil and gas concentrations occur.

Grazing can also have major impacts on natural values. Compared to mining, grazing is a much more extensive activity, with large areas often involved. Grazing can lead to significant erosion, loss of natural vegetation, and the introduction of exotic plants. Only about 2 percent of total U.S. grazing occurs in wilderness, yet powerful lobbies support its continuance. Recent legislation has reinforced guidelines that support the idea that it will be allowed to continue in wilderness. Only in cases where grazing impacts exceed those judged acceptable by the normal criteria used to evaluate good grazing practices can it be restricted or terminated; simply documenting impacts on the natural values in wilderness is not sufficient reason to halt it.

Fire in wilderness is a controversial issue. The Wilderness Act permits fire control activity. Yet there is an inescapable inconsistency between the control of fire in an area where the predominant objective is to allow natural forces to operate outside human influence. Fire is probably one of the predominant forces shaping the character of many wildernesses in the United States. But the scarcity of wilderness, its recreational and aesthetic importance, the adverse impact of fire on regional air quality, and the presence of important values in areas adjacent to wilderness make the idea of permitting some fires to burn highly controversial.

Nevertheless, management agencies have begun to implement programs designed to allow fire to play a more natural role in wilderness ecosystems. For example, beginning in 1972, the Forest Service has allowed lightning-ignited fires to burn under carefully prescribed conditions in many wildernesses throughout the country. The National Park Service has also undertaken a program of restoring fire in wilderness, including management-ignited fires in addition to those started by lightning. Together, the two agencies have brought over 6.4 million hectares (16 million acres) of wilderness under some form of fire management. The key feature of both agencies' programs is that prescriptions carefully written prior to ignition define how a fire is to be managed.

Fire in wilderness, however, remains a problem. While attempting to rectify the problems associated with long-term fire exclusion, management efforts to restore fire can lead to other problems. For example, smoke from a prescribed fire in Rocky Mountain National Park covered an adjacent community, with the National Park Service eventually being cited for a violation of the federal Clean Air Act. Both fire and associated control efforts can seriously impact archaeological values, values that the wilderness management agency is also required to protect. Perhaps more than any other issue, wilderness fire management illustrates the interdependent nature of the various values that comprise the wilderness resource.[16]

Recreational use is a major source of impact on natural values. In some areas, major disruptions of ecological communities, including loss of vegetation, soil erosion, wildlife disturbance, and water pollution, have occurred. The irony of such areas being "loved to death" has forced managers to consider controls over users and, in some cases, to ration numbers of users and to control where people travel and camp.

Few wildernesses encompass complete ecosystems, and threats from external activities can jeopardize natural values within their boundaries. Air and water pollution are particularly critical. Today aesthetic values are severely threatened in areas such as the Grand Canyon because of increased air pollution. In the wildernesses of northwestern Wyoming, evidence of airborne heavy metal pollution has been documented, with possible sources as far away as Los Angeles or even Mexico City. Pollution associated with coal development in southern British Columbia threatens water quality in the wilderness in northwestern Montana.

Activities on adjacent lands can threaten natural values within wilderness. Although timber harvesting is not permitted within wilderness, the boundaries in many areas are obviously demarcated by harvesting activity. This can lead to impacts within the area, such as shifts in wildlife distribution patterns, thus increasing the stress on wilderness ecosystems and other wildlife species. In areas where grizzly bear or wolves (*Canis lupus*) are found, adjacent grazing interests are likely to poison or shoot these species to prevent real or anticipated losses of cattle or sheep.

Thus, wildernesses, like national parks or other nature reserves, have only a limited capacity to protect the natural values that they contain. Boundaries are often drawn to accommodate local interests or to appease various political demands; they seldom reflect ecological criteria. Yet the NWPS represents a major opportunity to protect natural values and to ensure their continued presence.

Management Response to Threats

To date, much effort has been devoted to wilderness classification, but only limited attention has been given to management. Increasingly, however, there is recognition that without careful planning and management, lands designated as wilderness can quickly be spoiled.

Each of the wilderness management agencies has developed a variety of strategies to protect areas under its jurisdiction. Generally, two levels of activity are involved. First, major efforts are devoted to developing wilderness plans in which specific management objectives are identified, problems identified, and management strategies outlined. A recent survey of wilderness management throughout the NWPS revealed that more than 80 percent of the areas had a plan in effect or in preparation.[17] A major shortcoming in many of these plans, however, is their lack of specificity and detail. Statements of objectives are often so vague or general that it is difficult to define what it was the plans sought to achieve or to measure performance with regard to the objectives. There is an increasing emphasis, however, on establishing management objectives that can be defined in objective and measurable terms. Such objectives provide clear statements as to what conditions are sought within the area as well as a basis for assessing how well management practices achieve those conditions.

For example, the concept of the "limits of acceptable change," or LAC, is now being advocated as an approach to planning that may rectify some of the above problems. The LAC is based on the notion that recreational use inevitably changes resource and social conditions within a wilderness. Thus, the major management task is to define the extent to which such change is acceptable, given an area's management objectives, and to prescribe actions to maintain or restore these desired conditions.[18]

Also important in protecting wilderness are the specific management actions undertaken to achieve the objectives. In general, the predominant focus is on the management of recreational uses rather than the biophysical resource of wilderness. It is generally accepted that where naturalness is threatened by recreational use, the latter must be controlled. Controls take a number of forms, ranging from subtle, light-handed efforts to modify visitor use through education and persuasion (e.g., methods for minimizing impacts on campsites) to direct control of use numbers by rationing and quotas. Other types of controls involve regulations on the number of persons per recreational group, the length of stay in the wilderness, the location of campsites.

THE FUTURE

In a relatively short time, the NWPS has grown tenfold, from about 3.6 million hectares (9 million acres) to 36 million hectares (90 million acres). With this growth have come increased representation of the nation's natural heritage and a strong commitment to protect this heritage for future generations. Further growth is possible, perhaps on the order of another 12 million hectares (30 million acres). Although further expansion of the system would be necessary to protect a broader range of natural environments, future protection of natural values lies more in the area of improved management than it does in the growth of the system.

Impacts on the natural values of wilderness can be expected to increase. Although there is some evidence that recreational use of wilderness is beginning to slow or possibly even decline, it is likely to remain a major source of impact. Policies that promote wider distribution of recreational use, both within as well as between areas, may lead to an increase in the amount of area adversely affected. Other sources of impact will remain serious, particularly those that emanate from outside the wilderness boundary. The many serious effects associated with acid precipitation are of particular concern, given the great difficulty in controlling the sources of such pollution and the very great distances over which it may spread.

The difficulty of managing such impacts on natural values in wilderness must be balanced with the high levels of public interest and support in the maintenance of such areas. Despite shifting social priorities in the country over the past two decades, protection of the environment in general and of wilderness in particular continues to be ranked highly. This public support will be particularly important in achieving additional wilderness designation but needs also to be directed at supporting wilderness management.

The security of the wilderness preserves in the United States is underwritten by the law of the land, yet clearly nothing can be taken as guaranteed or assured in perpetuity. Nevertheless, society apparently sees major benefits in the maintenance of such a system. These benefits occur both directly, as in the use of such areas for recreation and research, and indirectly, through the vicarious pleasures afforded and the values they hold for future generations. These benefits create the public support necessary for the continued survival of the National Wilderness Preservation System.

Like national parks, the American wilderness system serves as a model for other countries to observe and modify to their own particular needs and circumstances. As one component of the overall nature preservation effort in the United States, the NWPS has helped ensure increased representation and protection of the nation's natural heritage.

NOTES

1. George Catlin, *North American Indians*, 2 vols. (Philadelphia: Leary, Stewart, and Co., 1913), 1:ix.

2. Henry David Thoreau, *Excursions* (Boston: Houghton, Mifflin and Company, 1894), p. 275.

3. John Muir, "The Treasures of the Yosemite," *Century* 40 (1890): 483.

4. Act of June 4, 1897, chapter 2; Public Law 55–2; 30 *Stat.* 11.

5. Roderick Nash, *Wilderness and the American Mind*, 3rd ed. (New Haven: Yale University Press, 1983), chapter 9, pp. 141–60.

6. Craig W. Allin, *The Politics of Wilderness Preservation* (Westport, Conn.: Greenwood Press, 1982), chapter 3, pp. 60–101.

7. Memorandum from A. H. Carhart to Aldo Leopold, Dec. 10, 1919, p. 2. Quoted in Donald N. Baldwin, *The Quiet Revolution* (Boulder, Colo.: Pruett Publishing Co., 1972), p. 34.

8. Susan L. Flader, *Thinking like a Mountain: Aldo Leopold and the Evolution of an Ecological Attitude toward Deer, Wolves, and Forests* (Columbia: University of Missouri Press, 1974), pp. 80, 100.

9. John C. Hendee, George H. Stankey, and Robert C. Lucas, *Wilderness Management* (Washington, D.C.: Government Printing Office, 1978), p. 63.

10. Federal natural resource management in the United States is divided among a number of agencies. The principal agencies with which this chapter is concerned are the following: (1) Forest Service, responsible for administration of the 77.3-million-hectare (191-million-acre) National Forest System; (2) National Park Service, responsible for management of the 32-million-hectare (79-million-acre) National Park System; (3) Fish and Wildlife Service, charged with administering the 36-million-hectare (89-million-acre) National Wildlife Refuges and Game Ranges; and (4) Bureau of Land Management, responsible for administering 138-hectares (341 million acres) of National Resource Lands.

11. George H. Stankey, "Wilderness Preservation Activity at the State Level: A National Review," *Natural Areas Journal* 4 (October 1984): 25.

12. George D. Davis, "Natural Diversity for Future Generations: The Role of Wilderness," in *Natural Diversity in Forest Ecosystems: Proceedings of the Workshop*, ed. James L. Cooley and June H. Cooley (Athens: Institute of Ecology, University of Georgia, 1984), p. 143.

13. The use measures of visits and visitor-days are not directly convertible. Moreover, wilderness is not a reporting category for national park areas; a more general "backcountry" category, including formally designated wilderness as well as ones presently undeveloped but lacking wilderness designation, is used. Also, national park use figures do not include day use, a major proportion of total use in many areas. Nevertheless, an extremely rough approximation of the number of visitor-days of national park backcountry use can be calculated by simply multiplying the number of overnight visits by 2; thus, about 3.2 million visitor-days would be a conservative estimate for national park wilderness use.

14. Hendee, Stankey, and Lucas, *Wilderness Management*, pp. 301–4.

15. Aldo Leopold, "Wilderness as a Land Laboratory," *Living Wilderness* 6 (July 1941): 3.

16. Many references exist about wilderness fire management. For a detailed discussion of the topics mentioned here, see *Proceedings—Symposium and Workshop on Wilderness Fire* (Ogden, Utah: Intermountain Forest and Range Experiment Station, 1985).

17. Randel F. Washburne and David N. Cole, *Problems and Practices in Wilderness Management: A Survey of Managers* (Ogden, Utah: Intermountain Forest and Range Experiment Station, 1983), p. 11.

18. George H. Stankey, David N. Cole, Robert C. Lucas, Margaret E. Petersen, and Sidney S. Frissell, *The Limits of Acceptable Change (LAC) System for Wilderness Planning* (Ogden, Utah: Intermountain Forest and Range Experiment Station, 1985).

BIBLIOGRAPHY

Nash, Roderick, ed. *The American Environment: Readings in the History of Conservation.* Reading, Mass.: Addison-Wesley Publishing Co., 1968.

VENEZUELA

25

Jesús M. Delgado

Although its preservation history goes back only about fifty years, Venezuela could be considered relatively successful, compared to other developing nations, in protecting its most representative ecosystems and natural landscapes.

HISTORY

The history of national park preservation dates back to 1937. Henri Pittier, a Swiss scientist, recognized the value of Venezuela's heritage and started a national campaign to protect a very special environment: the tropical cloud forest of Rancho Grande. During several years of intensive work he collected more than 9,000 plants for the National Herbarium and persuaded the politicians of his era to protect a significant part of the cloud forest of the northern coastal range. On March 13, 1937, an area of 90,000 hectares (222,000 acres) became Venezuela's first national park. Today it bears Henri Pittier's name.

Sierra Nevada National Park was the second to be declared. Set aside in 1952, it protects a portion of the Andes of western Venezuela. Here Pico Bolívar (5,700 meters, 18,700 feet) towers over an area of 190,000 hectares (469,000 acres), encompassing several types of forests and climatic regions.

In 1958, after the fall of the military dictatorship, the new government established another national park consisting of 92,640 hectares (228,900 acres) of tropical rain forest in an important network of watersheds draining the interior mountain range. Guatopo National Park subsequently proved that with public concern and government support a natural area can be rescued from man's activities despite enormous difficulties.

El Avila National Park was also established in 1958 in the city of Caracas. Together, Guatopo and El Avila national parks provide the Venezuelan capital

Table 25.1
The Systems of Protected Areas in Venezuela

STATUS	HECTARES	PERCENTAGE
National Parks	7,310,329	7.98
Natural Monuments	20,774	0.02
Protected Zones	9,151,405	8.72
Wildlife Refuges	56,329	0.06
Wildlife Reserves	227,795	0.24
Forest Reserves	11,367,807	12.40
Forest Patches	1,107,590	1.20
Hydraulic Reserves	1,978,583	2.15
Critical Priority Areas	2,727,575	2.97
TOTALS	33,948,187	35.74

both with its water supply and with the scenery that makes Caracas a beautiful city.

In July of that year the first administrative body for national parks and natural monuments was created under the name of Sección de Parques. In 1962 it was elevated to a Division of the Ministry of Agriculture. In 1975 the name was changed again, to Oficina Nacional de Parques Nacionales, and all agencies having to do with renewable natural resources were placed under the new Ministry of the Environment. In 1977 it became the Dirección Sectorial de Parques Nacionales within the National Parks Institute (INPARQUES), an autonomous institute within the Ministry of the Environment. Unfortunately, the various name changes have not been associated with increased influence over national park decision making and management.

Over the last twenty-eight years Venezuela has greatly increased the number of protected areas, but at the same time man's activities have significantly damaged the natural heritage. Prior to 1972 most of the protected environments were forested areas. Thereafter, the government decided to protect fragile and unique marine ecosystems as well.

Between 1974 and 1978 the number of protected areas almost doubled in size. A total of twenty-one areas have been protected since the mid–1970s including two international parks: the Serranía de la Neblina National Park, established in 1979 with 1,600,000 hectares (3,950,000 acres) in Venezuela and 2,200,000 (5,400,000 acres) in Brazil, and Tamá National Park established in 1978 with 141,800 hectares (350,400 acres) in Venezuela and 48,000 hectares (119,000 acres) in Colombia. Venezuela has also declared thirteen natural monuments since 1949.

Before beginning a more detailed discussion of the various national parks and natural monuments, mention should be made of other protected natural areas. All together, more than 35 percent of Venezuela's territory has a legal status that provides some degree of protection. See Table 25.1.

Obviously, Venezuela has done a good job of establishing a system of legally protected areas, but much remains to be done to convert legal documents into genuine protection. The majority of these areas lack management plans, and there are no supervising organizations to prevent their degradation.

National parks, natural monuments, forest reserves, and protected zones were finally recognized by Congress in 1965 under the law governing forests, soils, and waters. In 1970 the Law for the Protection of Wildlife set the guidelines for the creation and management of wildlife sanctuaries, refuges, and reserves. Both laws gave the Ministry of Agriculture the responsibility for administration, protection, supervision, and management of those areas until 1976 when the Administration Law transferred the task to the Ministry of the Environment.

The 1983 Organic Law for Planning the Territory is yet another legal instrument affecting national parks. This law considers all protected areas under the same title: "Areas under Special Administrative Regime." There are serious problems with some features of the law. One example is Article 17, under which the declaration of parks and changes in their status is the responsibility of the president of the country within the Council of Ministers. This is in violation of the Washington Convention of 1940, which established a requirement for congressional approval.

This review of the history of the protection process in Venezuela reveals that the first stage, involving the declaration of protected areas, is nearly complete. Although some areas remain unprotected that ought to be protected, almost 37 percent of Venezuela's area is included under one or another "special administrative regime." The pressing priority at this time is to move beyond the mere declaration of protected areas to effective management, which would include real protection, ecological rehabilitation, land-use zoning, organized research, and public education. Today, the National Park Service of Venezuela has neither the political nor the administrative resources to meet these pressing management needs.

PARKS AND RESERVES

The Venezuelan parks occupy a significant portion of the country's area and include a variety of ecological areas, landscapes, and ecosystems. To present the natural features of some of these areas effectively, we have organized them in physiographic regions: the coastal and marine regions, including insular parks; the mountains; the llanos or savanna; and finally the Guayana Shield area.

Coastal and Marine Region

Seven national parks and four natural monuments have been declared in this region since 1972, three of each being located on islands.

Medanos do Coro National Park was established in 1974 to protect 91,280 hectares (225,550 acres) of desert landscape including an extensive area of dunes, or "medanos," constantly moved by winds from east to west. This park represents one of the special ecosystems of the country and includes patches of

Table 25.2
Venezuelan National Parks System

	NAME	REGION[a]	HECTARES	YEAR
	National Parks			
1.	Henri Pittier	M	107,800	1937
2.	Sierra Nevada	M	276,446	1952
3.	Guatopo	M	122,464	1958
4.	El Avila	M	85,192	1958
5.	Yurubi	M	23,670	1960
6.	Canaima	GS	3,000,000	1962
7.	Yacambu	M	14,580	1962
8.	Cueva Auebrada El Toro	M	8,500	1969
9.	Archipielago Los Roques	I	221,120	1972
10.	Macarao	M	15,000	1973
11.	Mochima	C	94,935	1973
12.	Laguna de la Restinga	I	10,700	1974
13.	Medanos de Coro	C	91,280	1974
14.	Laguna de Tacarigua	C	18,400	1974
15.	Cerro El Copey	I	7,130	1974
16.	Aguaro-Guariquito	S	585,750	1974
17.	Morrocoy	C	32,090	1974
18.	El Guacharo	M	15,500	1975
19.	Terepaima	M	18,650	1976
20.	Jaua-Sarisariñama	GS	330,000	1979
21.	Serrania de la Neblina	GS	1,360,000	1979
22.	Yapacana	GS	320,000	1979
23.	Duida-Marahuaca	GS	210,000	1979
24.	Peninsula de Paria	M	37,500	1979
25.	Perija	M	295,288	1979
26.	El Tamá	M	139,000	1979
	Natural Monuments			
1.	Alejandro de Humboldt	M	181	1949
2.	Aristides Rojas	S	1,630	1949
3.	Maria Lionza	M	11,712	1960
4.	Cerro Santa Ana	C	1,900	1972
5.	Laguna de las Marites	I	3,674	1974
6.	Las Tetas de Ma. Guevara	I	1,670	1974
7.	Cerros Matasiete y Guayamuti	I	1,672	1974
8.	Piedra del Cocuy	GS	15	1979
9.	Cerro Autana	GS	30	1979
10.	Morros de macaira	M	99	1979
11.	Cueva Alfredo Jahn	M	58	1979
12.	Laguna de Urao	M	29	1979
13.	La Chorrera de las Gonzalez	M	126	1980

[a] The physiographic regions are:
C = Coastal and Marine   M = Mountains
I = Insular   S = Llanos or Savanna
GS = Guayana Shield

mangroves along the coastal area. Geologically it belongs to the late Pleistocene, and its soils are the product of aeolian deposits. The vegetation is xerophytic with approximately sixty species from twenty different families. Lizards and iguanas are the most common inhabitants of the park, but wildlife is generally very scarce due to the extreme environmental conditions. Various xerophytic birds are present as well as some mammals such as tamanduas, foxes, and rabbits.

The park is located in Falcón State in western Venezuela and occupies the whole isthmus of the Paraguana Peninsula, where temperatures fluctuate between 27° and 40° Celsius (81°–104° Fahrenheit). Rainfall is only 250 to 500 millimeters (10–20 inches) per year, and the highest elevation is not more than 20 meters (66 feet).

The road connecting the state capital, Coro, with the city of Punto Fijo traverses the park, so access is easy. Still, the park is not heavily used, and there are no facilities or interpretive programs of any type.

Morrocoy National Park is also located in Falcón State, between the towns of Chichiriviche and Tucacas. It was established in 1974 to rescue this high-quality landscape and delicate ecosystem from residents and entrepreneurs who were developing the area without legal title. These "squatters" occupied the islands of Morrocoy, building docks, bridges, and houses; introducing exotic plants; destroying coral reefs; polluting sea water, etc. The change in land status has not solved the area's problems. The park is negatively affected by nearby private development, and it is not well managed. Visitation is uncontrolled, and the environmental impacts are tremendous. Establishment of the park has been associated with real estate speculation, administrative corruption, increases in delinquency and other social problems, and higher cost of living. As a consequence, Morrocoy remains one of Venezuela's most controversial national parks.

Morrocoy covers 32,090 hectares (79,300 acres) of islands, beaches, coral reefs, mangroves, and tropical dry forests. Cerro Chichiriviche, 285 meters (935 feet) above sea level, is the highest point in the park. The geology is similar to that of Los Medanos de Coro National Park, with soils of recent formation and a predominance of limestone in surrounding cliffs. Temperatures vary from 22° to 29° Celsius (72°–84° Fahrenheit), and rainfall from 1,000 to 1,800 millimeters (40–70 inches) a year.

Vegetation is mostly dry tropical forest. Mangroves and Thalassias are found in the marine sector, with dry and evergreen forests further inland. Over 300 species of plants have been recorded in the park. The density of the mangrove forests in some areas of the park and the coral reefs around the islands and channels made Morrocoy a paradise for wildlife before the intervention of man in this area. Mammals may still be found on Cerro Chichiriviche, but the most important zoogeographic groups are birds and fishes. Morrocoy is contiguous with the Cuare Wildlife Refuge, which has managed so far to protect the wildlife of the region despite the absence of any management plan.

Morrocoy receives more than 1,000,000 visitors a year, and the impact on the quality of the experience and on the environment is tremendous. There are no restrictions on camping. There are no sanitary facilities on the islands, and visitors have free access to the park by private boat. There are no visitor centers, no educational or interpretive programs for visitors, nor are recreational activities guided. Studies made in the area have shown that visitors have no concept of correct behavior patterns for a national park. Although Morrocoy is one of the most beautiful places on the Venezuelan coast, with only six rangers to cover sixteen islands, it is also one of the most difficult parks to manage.

Laguna de Tacarigua National Park was established in 1974 to protect a very fragile and significant coastal lagoon in the northern part of the country. It covers a surface area of 18,400 hectares (45,500 acres) of mangroves forest, tropical dry forest, and almost 30 kilometers (19 miles) of beaches.

The lagoon itself is a very dynamic ecosystem, representative of a tropical estuarine environment. It is 30 kilometers long and 6 kilometers wide and receives the drained waters of a 260-square-kilometer (100-square-mile) watershed. Its waters occupy 11,000 hectares (27,000 acres) of the park area and are separated from the Caribbean Sea by two strait barriers with intermittent inlets closing and opening periodically in response to natural processes. As an estuary, it is a very rich and productive ecosystem for fishing operations both within its waters and on the open sea.

The climate is humid and hot with temperatures between 24° and 28° Celsius (75°–82° Fahrenheit). Rainfall is 1,000 to 1,500 millimeters (40–60 inches) per year, and most of the estuary's fresh water comes from the Guapo River and other small streams of its watershed.

The area is rich in wildlife and provides valuable habitat for the feeding, roosting, and nesting of a number of important sea and wading birds as well as the spawning ground of important commercial fishes. The lagoon is of special interest to ornithologists as it is a feeding area for the endangered American flamingo (*Phoenicopterus ruber*) during certain months of the year.

Unfortunately, over the past twenty years human impact has changed the natural processes of the lagoon with regard to the periods of closing and opening of the inlet, the depth of the lagoon, and the variety of fish species. Drainage of the inlet, diversion of waters, indiscriminate fishing operations, and erosion in the watershed have accelerated the degradation of this lagoon.

The three park rangers do not suffice to administer and protect the whole of the park. There is no environmental educational program, and management is rudimentary at best although a management plan does exist. Although the affluence of most park visitors is very low, the housing established within the park caters to the middle class. Most of the local people outside the park depend on the lagoon for their food supply, and commercial fishing is still allowed.

Mochima National Park was established in 1973. Here, too, management has been complicated by significant invasion of people living within the park boundaries.

The park covers 94,935 hectares (234,584 acres) of mountains, beaches, coral reefs and islands, dry forest, gulfs, bays with exotic beaches, mangroves, and coral formations. The boundaries extend from the city of Puerto La Cruz to the city of Cumaná, in the northeast of the country, and the eastern part of the interior mountain range. The climate is semi-arid, with high levels of temperature, insolation, and evapotranspiration. Geologically it corresponds to the Lower Cretaceous period.

Mochima offers a variety of environments: coraline mangroves and thorny, dry, very dry, and humid tropical forests. Each type of ecosystem offers species of vegetation adapted to that particular environment from succulents and cacti to palms and figs. Wildlife is not abundant in the arid areas of the islands and on the continent, but lizards do thrive there.

Mochima has no management plan, and it has been impossible to stop the invasion of the park, which has reached crisis proportions. At the time the area was declared a national park there were approximately 400 families living within its boundaries. It is now estimated that 10,000 families—more than 35,000 people—have invaded the continental areas. Forty percent of the vegetation is being turned into savanna, and 40 of the park's 100 streams have dried up. Erosion is causing damage to the marine environment of the Sante Fe Gulf. It has even been impossible to stop the construction of weekend houses on the islands and along the coast.

In the face of these threats there are only a couple of park rangers and a superintendent, and they lack support. If Mochima is to accomplish the objectives of a national park, these problems and many others will have to be addressed in the very near future. The stakes are very high. Preserving Mochima intact would not only mean saving an unique landscape and natural resource but would also guarantee 60 million cubic meters (16 billion gallons) of fresh water to the inhabitants of the coast of eastern Venezuela.

Laguna de la Restinga National Park was created in 1974 to protect an important estuary with mangroves, beaches, and wildlife on Margarita, Venezuela's largest island. Dense mangrove forests, channels of brackish waters, and green forested islands make its 10,700 hectares (26,400 acres) a perfect habitat for birds.

The island of Margarita has been declared an international free-trade zone, resulting in rapid growth of the tourist industry. The park offers no interpretive or environmental education program, but access is well controlled. Of the five protected areas on Margarita, Laguna de la Restinga is the most significant.

Mountainous Region

There are three mountain chains located between the northern coast and the llanos or savannas of the south. Their forest ecosystems vary with the altitude. Through 1986, thirteen national parks and six natural monuments had been declared in this region. Among the national parks are El Tamá, Perija, Sierra Nevada, Yacambú, Henri Pittier, Macarao, El Avila, Guatopo, and the Paria Peninsula. The natural monuments include the Lagoon of Urao, Chorrera de las Gonzalez, Maria Lionza, Cave of Alfredo Jahn, Morros of Macaira, and Alejandro de Humboldt.

Of the national parks, El Avila, Henri Pittier, and Guatopo are probably the

most significant in that they protect areas of great importance for a large proportion of the population. For example, El Avila, established in 1958, is perhaps
the best known of all parks as it is a recreational, educational, and scenic area
for the capital city of Caracas. It possesses an adequate infrastructure for the
million and a half visitors it receives annually, but it has nevertheless suffered
from the impact of this visitation and from the pressures of land use in the city
below.

Henri Pittier National Park is the oldest and one of the most important parks
in the system. It protects important recreational and hydrologic resources, more
than 500 species of birds, and a variety of ecosystems from xerotropic areas to
cloud forests. Henri Pittier is located in both Aragua and Carabobo states, and
access is easy. For many years it has been a center for numerous biological
studies. Despite the importance and popularity of the park, fifty years after its
establishment it still lacks a coherent management plan, an infrastructure, and
a visitor center.

Guatopo National Park is important as a source of water for human consumption—it serves as a reservoir for the capital city of Caracas—and potentially
for hydroelectric power. Located in the northern mountain chain, Guatopo is
also an important wildlife refuge and boasts an exuberant tropical forest. It has
excellent recreational possibilities, an interpretive center, well-trained park
guards, nature trails, and a high level of protection.

Yacambú National Park is located in the state of Lara and best known for the
variety of its endemic botanical species. This area is also of interest for its
volcanic characteristics. It boasts the only active fumarole in Venezuela. Together
with Terepaima, Quebrada el Toro, Macarao, Yurubi, and Guacharo national
parks, Yacambú was established to protect mountainous areas between 500 and
2,600 meters (1,600–8,500 feet) above sea level.

Terepaima National Park, also in Lara State, not only protects a cloud forest
with many endemic species but also provides true refuge for fauna such as the
jaguar (*Panthera onca*), spectacled bear (*Tremarctos ornatus*), red brocket deer,
tapir, and howler and capuchin monkeys.

Quebrada El Toro National Park protects the largest subterranean river in the
country as it flows through a cave 1,200 meters (4,000 feet) in length. The
national park also protects significant fauna including oilbirds and cave-dwelling
insects.

Macarao National Park, located in the coastal cordillera between the Federal
District and Miranda State, forms part of the green belt of the city of Caracas.
It serves primarily to protect the San Pedro, Macarao, and Lagunetas rivers.
Some areas of the park are noted for the preponderance of epiphytes. At an
elevation of 2,098 meters (6,883 feet) No Leon Peak is the highest point in the
park.

Yurubi National Park is situated in the city of San Felipe, the capital of
Yaracuy State. It was established primarily to protect various rivers that are
important to the region's agriculture. The park covers a variety of vegetation

including a large number of endemic species of plants and is also a refuge for fauna, especially reptiles. Although the park was declared twenty-six years ago, it does not have sufficient program or personnel to educate or even to control the thousands of tourists that visit it annually. Nevertheless, footpaths and re-forestation programs have been carried out to an extent that could well be copied by other parks.

Guacharo National Park was recently created. It includes within its borders the Guacharo Cave, whose name has been changed to Alejandro de Humboldt Natural Monument. Thus one of the most important geological features of Venezuela is guaranteed protection along with the vegetation utilized by the oilbirds that live in the cave. Its geology, fauna, microclimate, and resulting interactions make this cavern a truly spectacular experience for the tourist and a treasure for the scientist.

Sierra Nevada National Park is the only national park with perpetual snow and glaciers covering extensive areas from 500 to 5,000 meters (1,600–16,000 feet) above sea level. Venezuela's highest mountain, the 5,007-meter (16,427-foot) Pico Bolívar, is located here. Other peaks over 4,500 meters (14,750 feet) include Humboldt, Bompland, La Concha, El Toro, El Leon, and El Mucuñuque. The alpine vegetation is well represented by the genus *Speletia*, which is the most colorful of the many plants of the Andes. Among the animals of the area are some that are in danger of extinction, such as the spectacled bear, condor of the Andes (*Vultur gryphus*), puma *(Felis concolor)*, and jaguar.

The park is easily accessible and has an adequate infrastructure and well-trained park guards. There is even a cable car that goes from Mérida to the highest mountains. Although it offers few directed programs, Sierra Nevada is one of the most frequent visited parks in Venezuela and the best known internationally.

El Tamá National Park is located between the states of Táchira and Barinas and borders on Colombia. This park contains alpine or paramo areas crossed by numerous rivers and canyons that provide an excellent refuge for the spectacled bear. The humid forests are rich in plants that are endemic to Ecuador, Colombia, and Venezuela. The elevation averages 3,450 meters (11,300 feet). Unfortunately, the park has neither a management plan nor adequate personnel.

Perija National Park is another area that protects both rain forests and alpine tundra areas. As the access is very difficult and the topography extremely abrupt, it has become an excellent wildlife refuge. This park is located in Zulia State and borders on Colombia in the area known as Sierra de los Motilones. There is no management plan or infrastructure, and the presence of drug smugglers makes it a very dangerous area to visit.

The Llanos or Savanna Region

This enormous area encompasses almost 300,000 square kilometers (116,000 square miles), yet there are only one national park and one natural monument to represent the region.

Aguaro-Guariquito National Park protects an excellent example of the diverse fauna associated with the central llanos. This rich habitat results from the dynamics of area rivers that flood the land during the rainy season from April to October. Far from being monotonous, the diverse scenery is typical of wetlands, with extensive savannas and gallery forests. The park is a refuge for birds, mammals, reptiles, and especially a large number of fish. Recently the park has undergone petroleum exploration, and it is feared that in the future there will be conflict between those trying to conserve the area and the economic interests of the petroleum industry. Access to the park is difficult. There are no facilities, no personnel, and the management plan has still to be implemented.

Aristides Rojas Natural Monument is located within the capital of Guárico State. This natural monument is a scenic jewel characterized by limestone hills raised up in the form of jagged morros with numerous small caves. The vegetation is predominantly grasses although the foothills are covered by deciduous forest. The fauna consists only of bats and red howler monkeys. The maximum altitude within the monument is 1,060 meters (3,480 feet).

The Guayana Shield Region

This region is separated from the rest of Venezuela by the Orinoco River. It has been and continues to be the focus of attention for those attempting to protect examples of tropical rain forest in Venezuela. The Precambrian soils of the region are the oldest on earth, with a typical age of more than 1,700 million years. This region occupies 45 percent of the total national territory. Through 1986, five national parks and two natural monuments had been established here, but only Canaima had received sufficient attention to make it accessible and well known.

Canaima National Park possesses a singular beauty and protects the highest waterfall in the world. Canaima is located in the highlands of the Guayana region, crossed by numerous rivers separating "tepuis," or tabletop mountains of sandstone. The tepuis are biological islands with a large numbers of endemic flora and fauna. The large savannas of the altiplano are one of the scenic attractions of this region. The Gran Sabana is a prominent example.

Canaima is the largest national park in Venezuela with an area of 3 million hectares (7.4 million acres). Its economic importance rivals even its ecological value since the rivers of this region feed the Guri hydroelectric dam, which represents the largest economic investment ever made by the Venezuelan government. These hydroelectric resources have interested the Corporacion Venezolana de Guayana in the management of the park. INPARQUES may be asked to cede control of the park to the corporation, which would surely result in serious controversy.

The vast area of the park, its distance from any settled areas, and its dense vegetation make Canaima a natural refuge for numerous animal species of importance to science. Examples include the giant anteater (*Myrmecophaga tri-*

dactyla), giant otter (*Pteronura brasiliensis*), jaguar, ocelot (*Felis pardalis*), and giant armadillo (*Priodontes giganteus*). The flora of the area is of incalculable richness, and extensive inventories have been undertaken. It is hoped that this will become the national park with the greatest protection in the near future.

Jaua-Sarisariñama, Yapacana, Serranía de la Neblina, and Cerros Duida-Marahuaca national parks represent an intent to protect the region's unique geological formations and its extraordinarily rich flora. The deep collapsed chasms of Jaua-Sarisariñama, the tepuis of Yapacana, the vertical tabletop mountains of Duida-Marahuaca, and the highest elevation east of the Andean mountains in Serranía de la Neblina are some of the outstanding features preserved. These parks are all inaccessible to the majority of visitors. They have no management plans, personnel, or infrastructure.

Cerro Autana Natural Monument is an area of great geological interest since it possesses the only quartzite cave in the world. Autana is a mountainous formation isolated from the surrounding jungle. The monument has only 480 hectares (1,190 acres) and is located in the extreme northwest of the Federal Amazon Territory between the Cuao and Autana rivers.

Piedra del Cocuy Natural Monument is situated between Venezuela, Brazil, and Colombia in the Federal Amazon Territory. The Piedra is a granite formation 400 meters (1,300 feet) in height dating from the Precambrian period. It stands in stark relief to the Amazonian jungle lowlands. The vegetation at the base of the Piedra contains rare and endemic species of the three countries, and the famous cock of the rock (*Rupicola rupicola*) is found among its fauna.

THE FUTURE OF THE PARKS AND RESERVES

Obviously, Venezuela has been able to conserve, at least theoretically, a goodly portion of its natural heritage. What remains is to guarantee effective protection and adequate management for each of these areas. Unfortunately, some grave errors in administration are cropping up that could seriously endanger the original objectives for protecting the regions involved.

First, the National Park Service needs greater autonomy in park management. The service had, and still has, well-trained technicians with real expertise in planning and managing natural areas. Unfortunately, they are subordinate to the National Institute for Parks, which emphasizes management for recreation and is often unduly responsive to private interests.

A second limitation is budgetary. As in many other countries, the Park Service finds itself with a very large job to do and very meager resources with which to do it. The annual budget of about US$1.5 million is far from adequate for the protection and administration of 8 percent of the nation's area, some 8 million hectares (20 million acres). What is protected in theory is often unprotected in practice. Under these severe constraints the National Park Service concentrates its work in just a few of the national parks and in the headquarters in Caracas.

The parks need greater political and popular support as well. The public is conscious of the importance natural areas play and generally supportive of the existing areas. But threats to natural area preservation abound. Plans for economic development are bound to have a degree of popular appeal, and the developers are often very influential in governmental circles. Unless both politicians and public are willing to make park preservation a higher priority, the natural areas of Venezuela will continue to be endangered.

Despite these challenges, Venezuela has the potential to have one of the finest park systems in Latin America. Among its assets are protected areas of beauty, uniqueness, and ecological importance and a well-trained technical staff capable of managing those areas and eager to do so. The future of Venezuela's parks and reserves depends on finding the political will to protect and utilize those assets.

NOTE

The author and editor wish to thank Mario Gabaldón for valuable information and assistance in the preparation of this chapter. Mr. Gabaldón has worked as Chief of the Division of Basic Studies in the Managerial Department of Venezuelan National Parks. He also serves as an Assistant Professor of Environmental Studies in the Faculty of Architecture of the Central University.

BIBLIOGRAPHY

Delgado, Jesús M. *Perspectivas Económicas de los Parques Nacionales de Venezuela.* Bariloche, Argentina: IUCN, 1986.

——. *Impacto Económico del Parque Nacional Morrocoy.* Guanare, Venezuela: Universidad Experimental de los Llanos Ezequiel Zamora, 1986.

Gabaldón, Mario. *Una Characterización del Sistema de Parques Nacionales de Venezuela.* Caracas: Universidad Central de Venezuela, 1985.

Gondelles, Ricardo. *Los Parques Nacionales de Venezuela.* Madrid, Spain: Instituto de la Caza Fotografica y Ciencias de la Naturaleza, 1977.

INPARQUES. *Guía de los Parques Nacionales y Monumentos Naturales.* Caracas: INPARQUES, 1982.

WEST AFRICA   26

Harald H. Roth and
André R. Dupuy

Important differences of natural features, landscape, culture, and history exist
in different parts of the African continent. Most people imagine national parks
with spectacular African wildlife to be found only in eastern and southern Africa.
However, West Africa also contains a wealth of protected areas of great importance. Flora and fauna of these areas vary greatly in accordance with three
major biogeographical zones that extend uniformly from west to east: the arid
Sahel in the north, the humid evergreen forest belt along the Guinean coast in
the south, and the savanna woodlands in between. See Figure 26.1.

Historically, the greater part of West Africa has evolved under French colonial
rule. All French West Africa was governed from Dakar in Senegal until 1960,
and thus political and administrative conditions were very similar across this
vast territory.

Taken together, the differences from the rest of Africa, the uniformity of the
biogeographical zones, and the common historical background warrant dealing
with French-speaking West Africa as one entity for the purpose of this volume.

HISTORY

In 1902 the French government consolidated all its colonial possessions in
West Africa into one federated administrative unit called French West Africa
(Afrique Occidentale Française, AOF). This vast area comprised all the territories
that today are known as Mauritania, Senegal, Mali, Guinea, Ivory Coast, Burkina
Faso, Niger, Bénin and, as of 1918, also Togo. At the head of each of these
territories was a governor, who was responsible to the governor general in Dakar,
who was in turn appointed by and acting on behalf of the French minister of
colonies. Whereas the governor general governed through decrees, the territorial

Figure 26.1
Biogeographical Zones of West Africa

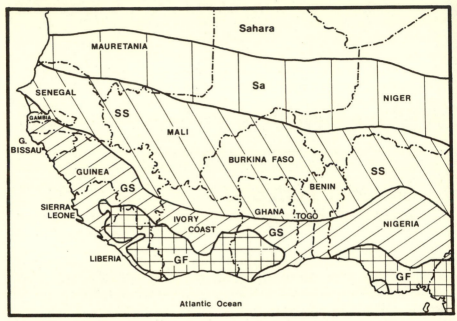

Note: Sa = Sahel
      SS = Sudanian Savanna
      GS = Guinean Savanna
      GF = Guinean Forest

governor could only promulgate ordinances. This political and administrative framework determined the evolution of nature conservation concepts and their implementation in French-speaking West Africa until 1960 and continued to be influential thereafter.

Evolution of Nature Conservation Concepts during the Colonial Era

Nature conservation concepts were essentially metropolitan, emanating from a long French tradition, and unrealistic and ill-adapted to the evolving situation in the AOF. Only more recently was conservation influenced by Anglo-American concepts introduced through Franco-British interregional contacts. In the French tradition game animals constitute "res nullius"—nobody's property—a legal notion leading to continued and disastrous exploitation of wildlife resources. Anything to do with game and hunting was exclusively the responsibility of the Forest Service, the officers of which have had military status since 1824. This responsibility was deeply rooted in specific hunting legislation under which forest officers enjoyed exorbitant legal privileges. Recognizing to some extent that game management constitutes a specialty, the Forest Service introduced a special "Code" establishing inspectors of hunting (*inspecteurs de la chasse*) after World War II. However, as the Code was part of the forestry regulations, these inspectors remained fully dependent upon the forestry administration. This all-embracing responsibility of the Forest Administration for nature and wildlife protection has had many negative but also some positive effects.

The failure to accept wildlife management as a specific biological discipline prevented the development and practical application of this science. Because there was no separate body of specially qualified and responsible game officers, wildlife remained an unimportant aspect of forest administration. Career-conscious foresters had no incentive to fight for wildlife conservation. On the other hand, they were determined to set aside as many protected forest areas (*forêts classées*) as possible. In protecting these forest areas vital habitat for game animals was conserved and thus also wildlife itself.

Nevertheless, for decades hunting in the AOF remained an indiscriminate activity, often becoming a commercially oriented massacre of wild animals in which all sectors of the European society participated. Commercial hunting for ivory was prohibited in only 1936, and in 1943, all hunting in the forest reserves (*domain forestier classé*) was prohibited by decree with very positive results for game conservation. Nevertheless, the extermination of some species, such as crocodiles, continued well into the 1950s. Finally, the application of traditional French hunting laws prevented the serious consideration or desirable legalization of subsistence hunting, which is of tremendous importance to indigenous peoples throughout Africa.

Creation and Management of Protected Areas under the French Colonial Administration

The different categories of protective status that the colonial administration could grant to any particular area comprised *forêt classée* (protected forest area) and *réserve naturelle* (nature reserve). The latter category was subdivided into *réserve naturelle generale* (general nature reserve) and *réserve naturelle à but definie* (nature reserve for specific purposes).

The *forêt classée* status was not very restrictive, but the *réserve naturelle* status would qualify as a conservation area in present terminology. The *réserves naturelles generales* included what would be termed today "strict nature reserves," "managed reserves," and "national parks." The status of *réserves naturelles à but definie* could be used to protect a particular natural feature such as soil, water, flora, fauna, or ethnic groups or to set aside an entire area for forestry, hunting, or fishing activities or as a monument or special landscape.

Responsibility for proposing, establishing, and managing protected areas was entirely vested in the Forest Service. Since its primary concern was to protect areas for forestry purposes, wildlife was of little concern. The procedure for the

Table 26.1
Listing in the London Convention (1933) of Protected Wildlife Areas in AOF

COUNTRY	LOCATION	YEAR ESTABLISHED	AREA IN KM^2	PRESENT STATUS
Mauritania	"Boutilimit"	1926	?	Nonexistent
	"Assaba"	1929	?	El Agher P.F.R.
Senegal	"near Portuguese-Guinean frontier"	1926	3,400	Niokolo Koba N.P.
Soudan[a]	"in Kita District"	1926	?	Boucle de Baoulé N.P.
Guinea	"Boké"	1929	?	Nonexistent
	"Diguirayé"	1926	7,000	"
	"Kankan"	1926	2,550	"
	"Koumbia"	1933	1,300	"
Ivory Coast	"Sassandra"	1926	7,100	Tai N.P.
	"in the north"	1926	2,400	Comoé N.P.
Upper Volta[b]	"in Gaoua district"	1926	5,570	partly forêt classée
	"in Koudougou district" (3 different reserves)	1926	760	partly forêts classées
	"Ouagadougou"	1929	300	Non-existent
	"in Say and Fada districts"	1926	5,720	W du Niger N.P. & adjacent reserves
Dahomey[c]	"on Niger River"	1926	4,800	W du Niger N.P.
	"in Savalou district"	1926	1,400	Nonexistent
Togo	"in Sokodé district"	1927	?	Kéran N.P.

NOTES: [a] Soudan is now Mali.
[b] Upper Volta is now Burkina Faso.
[c] Dahomey is now Bénin.

establishment of a protected area was informal and not particularly authoritative; it included surveying, appointment of a committee, public hearings, and eventually the promulgation of a regulatory ordinance.

The administration's first effort to define and list areas as *réserves naturelles* was undertaken in 1925. Much later, private French organizations like the International Hunting Council, founded in 1930, and the Committee of French Colonial Hunters, created in 1931; research institutions like the Institut Français d'Afrique Noir (IFAN) and the Office pour la Recherche Scientifique et Technique d'Outre-Mer; and statutory authorities like the Federal Committee for Nature Protection, founded in 1951, and the Conseil Scientifique pour Afrique au Sud de Sahara, instituted in 1953, gained some influence on the creation of nature reserves. The London Conference of 1933 had considerable importance for the early recognition of conservation areas. It developed a Convention for the Protection of Flora and Fauna in the African Colonial Territories, which was also adopted by France.

The convention listed the game reserves and national parks in French West Africa (Table 26.1).

It should be noted that almost all reserves were situated in the Sahel and in the Sudanian savanna zone. Only one area was located in the rain forest belt: the Sassandra Reserve, a part of which has become today's Tai National Park.

The management of these and other wildlife reserves was left entirely to the local forestry administration, often located far away from the respective areas. Because reserves have been administered just like other forest areas, management has always and everywhere been inadequate. The key reason for this failure was the absence of the specialized personnel and the technical means required to effectively protect and manage the reserves. As long as the protected areas did not come under settlement pressure, they would persist, but with "civilization" encroaching upon them their existence was in great jeopardy. Nevertheless, as Table 26.1 shows, the majority of the early nature reserves have in fact become the nuclei for the most important national parks in the French-speaking West African countries.

Development of Protected Areas after Independence

In 1960 all territories of the AOF were granted independence. With the exception of Guinea, however, they decided to remain associated with France in a French Commonwealth (*Communauté Française*). Initially, this political change had very negative effects on wildlife conservation. As a demonstration of national sovereignty, the strict hunting laws established by the colonial administration were deliberately modified or relaxed. With the availability of modern firearms, systematic commercial poaching for profit developed with rather serious repercussions on game populations, particularly in the formerly protected game-rich areas. The post-independence era also demonstrated the serious negative consequences of one administrative authority, the Forest Service, having had the sole responsibility for wildlife and conservation:

• Other government services, like animal husbandry, not having been involved previously, remained disassociated from conservation and even became hostile toward rational use of the wildlife resource.

• Without specialized personnel the new nations lacked the capability to administer and develop the protected areas; the remaining French foresters served only two-year contracts with obligatory transfer in case of extension, so neither devotion to any particular conservation area nor administrative continuity could develop.

However, as international influence gained momentum and development proceeded, national awareness and responsibility for the wildlife resource quickly developed. In 1963–1965 IUCN/FAO carried out a Special Africa Project surveying the wildlife resources of all newly independent countries and advising on their great economic and cultural importance. In 1965 FAO set up an Ad Hoc Working Group on Wildlife Management in the framework of its African Forestry Commission, which gave valuable assistance to the developing wildlife authorities. Furthermore, in 1968 it created a regional college at Garoua in

Cameroon for the training of parks and wildlife personnel in French-speaking West Africa.

Although few new conservation areas were created in the two decades that followed independence, many of the existing *forêts classées* were upgraded to national parks and equivalent reserves.

By 1973, Senegal, Ivory Coast, and Upper Volta had started to become seriously concerned about improving the management and conservation of their wildlife resources. In Bénin, Togo, and Niger efforts have been made since 1980. In Mauritania, Guinea, and Mali, however, consciousness of the importance of the resource and the need to conserve it has yet to develop.

PARKS AND RESERVES

West Africa south of the Sahara comprises four quite distinct biogeographical zones, which are shown in Figure 26.1 in relation to present-day political boundaries. Flora and fauna of these zones vary greatly because of the different prevailing climatic and ecological conditions.

In order to present the parks and reserves of West Africa, it is easiest to describe the specific flora and fauna of the different biogeographical zones and to show in which of these zones the forty parks and reserves are located. Such an approach serves to indicate which of the biomes of West Africa are fairly well safeguarded and which ones are endangered. Summary data is presented in Table 26.2, which is keyed to Figure 26.2.

Sahel Zone

The Sahel comprises about 1.3 million square kilometers (500,000 square miles) located between the Sahara Desert and the Sudanian savanna woodland. It represents roughly 31 percent of West Africa south of the Sahara. It is a particularly sensitive, transitional zone consisting of a mosaic of grassland with herbs and thorny acacia scrub. Ecological conditions are governed by the sporadic and very localized rainfall, averaging less than 200 millimeters (8 inches) per annum in the north and as much as 600 millimeters (24 inches) in the south. The rains turn the dry and dusty soil into extensive green pastures during the months of August to October, after which the land gradually dries up again.

Historically, the vegetation in this zone was very much more abundant, providing suitable habitat for a great diversity of game animals. Notable among them were elephant, giraffe, topi, gazelles, the large desert antelopes addax and scimitar oryx, barbary sheep, warthog, ant bear, cheetah, hunting dog, hyenas, jackals, and lynx. The zone also provided habitat for baboons and patas monkeys, as well as a great diversity of bird life including the ostrich. In recent decades, however, severe conflicts with cattle husbandry, the traditional form of nomadic land use in this zone, and significantly increased hunting pressures have severely

Figure 26.2
National Parks and Reserves in the French-Speaking Countries of West Africa

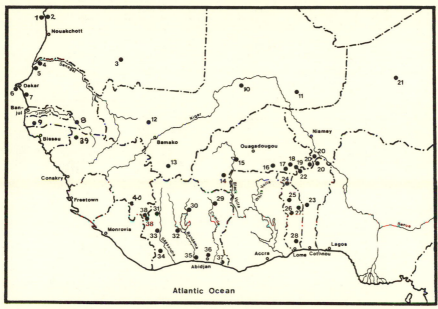

Note: See Figure 26.1 for names of countries and Table 26.2 for
names of protected areas corresponding to the numbers here.

depleted wildlife in the Sahel. In fact, many of the larger species are presently threatened with extinction.

In spite of the particular need for conservation in this zone, efforts at protection of the Sahara-Sahelian wildlife continue to be very inadequate. Only four areas, totaling about 54,000 square kilometers (21,000 square miles) and representing roughly about 4 percent of the Sahel zone, have been granted a partial conservation status.

In Mauritania an area known as the *El Agher Elephant Refuge*, in the Affolé Mountain Range of the Assaba region between the towns of Kiffa and Aioun-el-Atrouss, had been identified as early as 1929. However, it remains only a partial fauna reserve of unknown size and has never even been given full legal protection, much less any physical protection. It has failed its primary objective of ensuring the conservation of the most northerly occurring elephants, which today are very close to extermination. Giraffe, also historically present in the area, have already been extirpated.

In Mali the situation is similar. The *Réserve des Eléphants*, an area of some 12,000 square kilometers (4,600 square miles) was established in 1959 in the *Gourma* area south of the bend of the Niger River, yet it has never attained any status more protective than that of a partial fauna reserve. This reserve is po-

Table 26.2
National Parks and Equivalent Reserves in French-Speaking West Africa

MAP NO.[a]	NAME OF PROTECTED AREA	AREA (km^2)	LEGAL STATUS[b]	DATE ESTABLISHED	ZONE[c]
		Mauritania (1,118,604 km^2)			
1	Baie du Lévrier	3,100	SNR		Co (Sa)
2	Banc d'Arguin	11,743	NP	1976	Co
3	El Agher	2,500	PFR	1926	Sa
	TOTAL	17,343 (1.6% of country)			
		Senegal (197,160 km^2)			
4	Djoudj	160	NP (WH)	1971	Co (Sa)
5	Langue de Barbarie	20	NP	1976	Co (Sa)
6	Iles de la Madeleine	5	NP	1976	Co
7	Delta du Saloum	730	NP (BR,WH)	1976	Co
8	Niokolo Koba	9,130	NP (BR,WH)	1954	SS (GS)
9	Lower Casamance	50	NP	1970	GS (GF,Co)
	TOTAL	10,095 (5.1% of country)			
		Mali (1,204,022 km^2)			
10	Réserve des Elephants	12,000	PFR	1959	Sa
11	Ansongo-Menaka	17,500	PFR		Sa
12	Boucle du Baoulé	3,500	NP (BR)	1953	SS
	(adjacent reserves)	4,210	FR+PFA		SS
13	Sounsan	380	FR		SS
	TOTAL	37,590 (3.1% of country)			
		Burkina Faso (274,200 km^2)			
14	Bontioli	127	FR	1957	SS
	(adjacent reserves)	254	PFA		SS
15	Deux Balés	560	NP[d]	1967	SS
16	Pô	1,550	NP	1976	SS
17	Pama	2,235	PFR	1955	SS
18	Singou	1,928	FR	1955	SS
19	Arli	760	NP[d]	1954	SS
	(adjacent reserves)	3,070	PFR + CHA		SS
20	W du Niger	2,350	NP	1954	SS
	(adjacent reserves)	390			SS
	TOTAL	13,224 (4.8% of country)			
		Niger (1,267,000 km^2)			
20	W du Niger	2,200	NP	1954	SS
	(adjacent reserves)	756	FR	1962	SS
21	Massif de l'Air	(77,360)[e]	FR[e]		Sa
	TOTAL	2,956 (0.23% of country)			
		Bénin (112,622 km^2)			
20	W du Niger	5,680	NP	1954	SS
	(adjacent reserve)	2,250	CHA		SS
22	Pendjari	2,755	NP (BR)	1961	SS
	(adjacent reserves)	3,750	CHA		SS
23	Mts. Kouffé	1,080	PFA		GS
	(and Wari-Maro)	1,076	PFA		GS
	TOTAL	16,591 (14.7% of country)			
		Togo (56,500 km^2)			
24	Fosse aux Lions	30	PFR	1950	SS
25	Kéran	1,700	NP	1985	SS
26	Fazao-Malfakassa	1,920	NP	1975	GS (GF)
27	Abdoulayé	(300)[e]	FR[e]		GS
28	Mandouri	(1,800)[e]	FR[e]		GS
	TOTAL	3,650 (6.5% of country)			

470

Table 26.2 (continued)

MAP NO.[a]	NAME OF PROTECTED AREA	AREA (km^2)	LEGAL STATUS[b]	DATE ESTABLISHED	ZONE[c]
		Ivory Coast (322,462 km^2)			
29	Comoé	11,500	NP (BR,WH)	1968	SS (GS)
30	Haute Bandama	1,230	FR	1973	SS (GS)
31	Monts Sangbé	950	NP	1975	GS (Mo)
32	Marahoué	1,010	NP	1968	GS (GF)
33	Mont Péko	340	NP	1968	GF
34	Tai	3,400	NP (BR,WH)	1972	GF
	(adjacent reserves)	1,390	FR		GF
35	Azagny	190	NP	1981	GF (Co)
	(adjacent reserve)	30	FR	1981	GF (Co)
36	Banco	30	NP	1953	GF
37	Iles des Ehotiles	5	NP		Co
38	Monts Nimba	50	SNR (WH)	1943	Mo (GS)
	TOTAL	**20,125 (6.2% of country)**			
		Guinea (245,855 km^2)			
38	Monts Nimba	130	SNR (WH)	1944	Mo (GS)
39	Vallée de la Kouloutou	---[e]	NP[e]		GS
40	Massif du Ziama	1,162	BR	1980	GF
	TOTAL	**1,292 (0.52% of country)**			

SUMMARY DATA

Total of country areas (including Sahara)   4,798,425 km^2

Number and Area of Protected Areas by Zone:

Zone	Number of Units		Area in km^2	
	Existing	Proposed	Existing	Proposed
Sahel Zone	3	1	32,000	77,360
Sudanian Savanna Zone	15		62,295	
Guinean Savanna Zone	5	3	6,086	2,100
Guinean Forest Zone	5		6,542	
Montane Zone	1		180	
Coastal Zone	7		15,763	
TOTAL	36		122,866	79,460
(percentage)			(2.6%)	(1.7%)

Notes:
[a] Refer to Figure 26.2.
[b] Legal statuses are identified as follows:
   NP = National Park
   FR = Fauna Reserve
   PFR = Partial Fauna Reserve
   SNR = Strict Nature Reserve
   PFA = Protected Forest Area
   CHA = Controlled Hunting Area
   BR = Biosphere Reserve
   WH = World Heritage Site
[c] Biogeographical zones are identified as follows:
   Sa = Sahel Zone
   SS = Sudanian Savanna
   GS = Guinean Savanna
   GF = Guinean Forest
   Mo = Montane Zone
   Co = Coastal Zone
[d] Never legally established as a national park.
[e] Proposal only; excluded from totals.

471

tentially the most important conservation area in the Sahel. It still includes the whole range of the original Sahelian fauna as well as the largest surviving population of Sahelian elephant, some 500 animals. However, conservation can only be achieved by multiple-use management as proposed by Robert Oliver in 1983.[1]

Similarly important is the *Ansongo-Menaka Giraffe Reserve*, an area of 17,500 square kilometers (6,760 square miles) east of the Niger River along the border with Niger. Tourists traveling from Niamey to Gao and traversing this reserve frequently see what are probably the last surviving giraffe herds of West Africa.

More recently efforts were also initiated in Niger to conserve the Sahelian fauna of the Massif de l'Air northeast of the town Agadez. An area of 77,360 square kilometers (29,870 square miles) has been proposed as the *Air and Tenere Nature Reserve*. The area is still sporadically frequented by the rare desert antelopes, addax, and scimitar oryx, and may contain some barbary sheep as well as many other smaller Sahelian species.

Sudanian Savanna Zone

This zone extends all through Africa, from Senegal to Ethiopia. Its West African part comprises about 1.7 million square kilometers (660,000 square miles), which represents 39 percent of West Africa south of the Sahara. Annual rainfall in this zone varies between 600 millimeters (24 inches) per annum in the north and 1,200 millimeters (47 inches) in the south. Most of the zone has been inhabited for centuries, and practically all vegetation has been extensively modified by cultivation, cutting of trees, grass fires, and grazing. Only the southern parts of the zone comprise original woodland, in which *Isoberlinia* trees predominate. This is physiognomically comparable to the East African "miombo" woodland savanna in which tree coverage may be as much as 40 percent.

On heavy soils along the rivers and on seasonally inundated plains dense and tall grass predominates, and these areas sustain a great variety of wildlife quite similar to that of the East African savanna plains. However, a number of the more spectacular species, like zebra and wildebeest, and browsers like impala and kudu have apparently never occurred in West Africa. Giraffe have never inhabited savanna areas south of the Niger River, and today they still occur only in a few localities north of it. Rhinos were exterminated early, and the Derby eland, a greater cousin of the East and South African eland antelope, has survived in only a few areas of Senegal and Mali, and perhaps also in Guinea.

According to surveys by Harald H. Roth and I. Douglas-Hamilton, elephants occur only in isolated localities, but buffalo are still widely present.[2] The most common large antelopes are roan, hartebeest, waterbuck, kob, and bushbuck; smaller species include oribi, grey and red-flanked duiker. Hippopotamuses are still found in most of the larger rivers, and both wild pig species are common. Carnivores are represented by all the species known from East Africa: lion, leopard, hyena, jackal, serval, lynx, and many smaller species. Wherever there is water there is abundant bird life, and in contrast to East Africa there are three different species of crocodiles widely occurring.

Due to its spectacular manifestation of wildlife, the savanna zone, as in East Africa, has attracted the greatest conservation attention. No less than fifteen national parks or equivalent reserves, totaling about 59,000 square kilometers (23,000 square miles), have been established in the French-speaking West African countries. If one adds the conservation areas of English-speaking countries, an area of about 81,000 square kilometers (31,000 square miles) is protected, representing about 5 percent of West Africa's Sudanian savanna.

The Sudanian savanna zone comprises the best developed, largest, and most frequently visited national parks of West Africa.

The *Niokolo Koba National Park* is located in the southeastern part of Senegal on the upper reaches of the Gambia River about 560 kilometers (350 miles) from Dakar. It may be visited by road via Tambacounda entering the park at Simenty, where there is a tourist lodge; or by traversing the northern section of the park to arrive at Niokolo Koba Village, where there are camping facilities. After inclusion of adjacent forest reserves the park now comprises 9,130 square kilometers (3,525 square miles), extending to the border of Guinea. Its landscape is characterized by the various upper tributaries of the Gambia River, all of which spring from the most northern slopes of the Fouta Djalon mountain massif in Guinea. They are accompanied by grass plains that become inundated during the rainy season and provide for good grazing during the dry season. Whereas the greater northern part of the park is typical Sudanian woodland savanna, the southern part has some typical Guinean elements. Some of the Sudanian species, notably giraffe and topi, were exterminated some decades ago, but efforts are being made to reintroduce them. Most others, like hippo, buffalo, kob, water-buck, hartebeest, oribi, red-flanked duiker, and warthog are still plentiful; among the carnivores wild dogs are also common. Bird life comprises about 370 different species, and all three African crocodile species are present.

The park has particular importance as the last refuge of Africa's most westerly elephants, already exterminated in the rest of the country and very rare in the adjacent territories. After an apparent increase in their population in the 1960s, severe poaching has now reduced them to a mere fifty animals despite enormous efforts by the national parks administration. The park is also the last stronghold of West Africa's magnificent Derby eland antelope.

The Guinean fauna is manifest by the occurrence of chimpanzees in the Mount Assarik area, the most northerly outcrop of the Fouta Djalon massif, and by red colobus monkeys inhabiting some of the gallery forests.

The Niokolo Koba National Park is one of the most easily accessible and best developed and protected national parks of West Africa.

The *Comoé National Park* is located in the northeastern part of Ivory Coast, about 530 kilometers (330 miles) from its capital Abidjan. It is accessed via Bouaké to its southern entrance at Kakpin, or via Ferkéssédougou to its northern entrance at Kofolo (Ferké), at which points there are both tourist hotels and camps. The park comprises 11,500 square kilometers (4,440 square miles) and is flanked in the south by several forest reserves totaling another 907 square kilometers (350 square miles). The main feature of the park is the picturesque Comoé Valley with a broad river meandering for more than 160 kilometers (100 miles) from north to south through the center of the park, accompanied by extensive alluvial plains and, in the south, by gallery forest of up to two kilometers wide. The river is the home of many hundreds of hippopotamuses, and the plains abound with kob antelopes, displaying their territorial behavior. Whereas the northern part of the park represents typical Sudanian woodland savanna, the southern part extends into the Guinean zone, featuring numerous patches of moist semideciduous forest and broad bands of dense riverine forest. This habitat contains many typical forest species as the black, blue, and yellow-backed duikers, colobus and mangabey monkeys, and forest pangolins. In the southwestern part of the park toward the mountains, even chimpanzees, bongo, and giant forest hogs have been seen. The buffalo are mostly of the transitional type and favor the moist southern habitat.

The Comoé National Park with its adjacent, sparsely inhabited areas is also the range for one of West Africa's most important elephant populations, estimated at about 1,200 head in 1982.

The changing landscape and the proximity of savanna and forest wildlife of Comoé National Park make a visit during the dry season from November to May very worthwhile despite its distance from the capital.

The *Boucle du Baoulé National Park* is located in the bend of the Baoulé River, a tributary of the Senegal, in the northwestern part of Mali about 110 kilometers (68 miles) northwest of its capital, Bamako. It can be reached either directly via Kolokani and the Missira tourist camp; or via Negala and the Baoulé tourist camp from where one traverses the Fina Game Reserve, which adjoins the park in the southeast. If one includes the adjacent game reserves, the entire Baoulé conservation complex comprises 7,710 square kilometers (2,980 square miles) of typical northern Sudanian savanna. Apart from the typical Sudanian species, the area contains perhaps the last giraffe west of the Niger bend and Derby eland antelope in the southern Fina Reserve. Buffalo are rare and elephants on the verge of extirpation; topi, gazelle, and kob no longer occur in the park.

In the 1950s the Baoulé area was still one of the most remarkable wildlife habitats of the AOF, and tourist development aimed exclusively at promotion of sport hunting. Ever since—and despite the gazetting of the national park and the transformation of the hunting reserves into game reserves—the entire zone has suffered severely and continuously from livestock and agricultural pressures, but mainly from indiscriminate hunting. Wildlife is increasingly depleted, and with the lack of infrastructure tourism is not likely to increase.

The *Pô National Park* is located in the southern part of Burkina Faso (formerly Upper Volta) along the Upper Red Volta River, about 120 kilometers (75 miles) from the capital, Ouagadougou. From there it can be easily visited as the main road south to Ghana traverses the park. With only 1,550 square kilometers (600 square miles) it is a relatively small savanna reserve that has only recently been upgraded to a national park. Nevertheless, it contains a good sample of all Sudanian game species, and it is one of the few reserves in West Africa where one can usually view elephants easily.

The *Pendjari, Arli*, and *W du Niger* national parks are located in Burkina Faso, Niger, and Bénin (formerly Dahomey) and constitute together with a large number of adjacent reserves the largest and most important conservation area in West Africa, totaling some 25,000 square kilometers (9,700 square miles). The area can be visited from Niamey, the capital of Niger, via Tamou, reaching after 120 kilometers (75 miles) the Tapoa tourist lodge in the Nigeran part of W National Park. From here one can continue southward to the Arli and Pendjari national parks. Otherwise, the visitor has to travel from Cotonou or Lome, the capitals of Bénin and Togo, about 550 kilometers (340 miles) northward to Nattitingou, where there is a pleasant tourist hotel. The next day one continues another 120 kilometers (75 miles) to the entrance of the Pendjari Park at Porga or directly to the tourist lodge in the center of the park.

The Pendjari National Park is situated between the Pendjari River, a tributary of the Oti and White Volta, and the Atakora Mountain Range in Bénin. The river constitutes the border between Bénin and Burkina Faso, and the adjacent Arli National Park. It is characterized by extensive grass plains, on which large numbers of kob antelope and most of the other Sudanian species can be easily viewed. There are also numerous large water pans at which hippos and varied bird life can be observed.

The W National Park derives its name from the W-like bend of the River Niger south of which the park is situated. The Mecrou River, a tributary of the Niger with impressive rapids on its upper course, traverses the park and forms the border between Bénin and Niger. It has permanent water pools and thus attracts much wildlife during the dry season from November to May. Whereas the Nigeran part of the park is easily accessible from the south, the Bénin part remains undeveloped.

Next to the Niokolo Koba and Comoé national parks, a visit of the Pendjari, Arli, and W national park complex is probably most rewarding to tourists. It should be undertaken as a circuit between Niamey and Lome/Cotonou or vice versa. Although the vast area is inhabited by several thousand elephants, these migrate far and are very difficult to see.

Guinean Savanna Zone

There is no clear distinction between the Sudanian and the more southerly Guinean savanna; the transition from one to the other is very gradual. The latter is relatively moist and rainfall is nowhere less than 1,200 millimeters (47 inches) per year. Much of the Guinean savanna has historically been derived from moist semideciduous forest, so large parts of this zone still constitute a mosaic of moist forest islands, large bands of riverine forest, grassland, and savanna woodland that is characterized by fire-resistant tree species such as *Daniella olivieri*, *Lophira lanceolata*, *Philostigma thoningii*, and *Borassum aethiopicus*.

As the moist Guinean forest is increasingly converted into agricultural lands, the Guinean savanna is expanding. Presently it covers about 796,000 square kilometers (307,000 square miles), which represents about 18 percent of West Africa south of the Sahara.

Due to its ecological evolution the Guinean savanna contains both the savanna wildlife described above and the typical moist forest fauna associated with the Guinean forest zone.

Elephants and buffalo in this zone are morphologically intermediate between the typical savanna and forest subspecies. Hippos migrate down the rivers and become resident where there is enough pasture. Typical savanna antelope species occur, sometimes in close proximity to typical forest species.

Although the fauna are particularly interesting, only nine conservation areas, comprising less than 8,000 square kilometers (3,100 square miles) have been established in the French-speaking Guinean savanna zone. If one adds the conservation areas of the English-speaking West African countries, about 11,000 square kilometers (4,250 square miles) of the Guinean savanna zone is legally protected, representing only about 1.4 percent of the total.

Among the national parks and reserves in this zone the following are of particular interest.

The *Lower Casamance National Park* is located in the southern part of Senegal, bordering the estuary of the Casamance River, about 480 kilometers (300 miles) from the country's capital, Dakar. It may be reached from Ziguinchor by road or boat. The park comprises 50 square kilometers (19 square miles) of a transitional zone between woodland and semideciduous dense forest but also includes patches of evergreen primary forest, mangroves, secondary forest, and degraded grassland.

Wildlife is correspondingly varied. Apart from savanna species, like hippopotamus, kob, and patas monkeys, the park is inhabited by typical forest species, such as forest buffalo, blue and yellow-backed duiker, Campell's Mona monkey, red colobus, and chimpanzee. Rare species include the sitatunga, clawless otter, and manatee.

The diversity of its natural features make this small park worthy of visitation.

The *Marahoué National Park* is located near Bouaflé in Ivory Coast on the southern bank of the Marahoué River, a tributary of the Bandama, only about 320 kilometers (200 miles) from the capital, Abidjan. About one-third of its 1,010 square kilometers (390 square miles) are dense semideciduous forest; the remainder is either forest-woodland mosaic or open grassland. The park has no tourist facilities and suffers from heavy poaching and invasion by illegal squatters. Nevertheless, a visit of the park is rewarding as one can drive onto some hilltops from where one can observe the forest animals, such as buffalo and elephant, coming out into the grassland.

The *Fazao Malfakassa National Park* is located in the central part of Togo southeast of Sokodé, extending into the Fazao Mountain Range, about 320 kilometers (200 miles) from the country's capital, Lome. It was created recently to supplement the tourist circuit to the northern Pendjari, Arli, and W national parks. Including the two former forest reserves of Koué and Kimassi, it comprises 1,920 square kilometers (740 square miles). It is situated in a transitional zone between Sudanian and Guinean savanna with elements of moist montane forest. A comfortable hotel was built to enhance tourism, but wildlife is rather depleted and difficult to observe. The park is nevertheless an important conservation area and offers refuge to Togo's last southern elephants.

Guinean Forest Zone

This includes both moist-semideciduous forest and lowland evergreen rain forest, often intermingling with each other and forming a closed canopy. The Guinean Forest Zone extends from Sierra Leone through Liberia and Ivory Coast to Ghana, comprising about 395,000 square kilometers (153,000 square miles), which is approximately 9 percent of West Africa south of the Sahara. The only French-speaking countries that have typical lowland rain forest are Guinea and Ivory Coast. The southern parts of Togo and Bénin are considerably drier and have probably never been densely forested.

Compared with the South American tropical rain forest, the Guinean forest belt is poorer in species, although as many as 12,000 plant species do occur. However, during the last two decades radical ecological changes have been effected everywhere in this zone, leaving only relatively small islands of primary rain forest surrounded by a mosaic of secondary forests and thickets, palm and rubber plantations, and open agricultural land. This process has also affected wildlife. Some of the rain forest species, such as forest buffalo, red river hog, blue (Maxwell) and black duiker, bushbuck, leopard, civet cat, and other smaller carnivores, are quite adjustable to the development and remain to be widely distributed in the entire Guinean forest zone. Others, however, such as the forest elephant; pygmy hippo; giant forest hog; bongo; the bay-, zebra-, yellow-backed-, Jentink-, and Ogilby duikers, and most of the forest primates depend entirely on the rain forest ecosystem, and these are becoming more rare because the rain forest is being diminished by indiscriminate and destructive human influences.

This highlights the special importance of conservation action in this zone. Unfortunately, however, the economic and sociological pressures remain the greatest in this zone, mitigating against the establishment of national parks and equivalent reserves. Apart from relatively small conservation areas in Liberia and western Ghana, four national parks have been established in the Guinean forest zone in Ivory Coast and one biosphere reserve in Guinea, together comprising about 6,500 square kilometers (2,500 square miles). If one adds the rain forest conservation areas in Liberia and Ghana, a total of only 8,500 square kilometers (3,300 square miles), or roughly 2 percent of this zone, is legally protected.

By far the most important conservation area is the *Tai National Park* in the southwestern part of the Ivory Coast. Comprising 3,400 square kilometers (1,300 square miles) of largely primary rain forest, surrounded by an area of 1,390 square kilometers (537 square miles) that has game reserve status, it is the last remaining large block of Guinean lowland rain forest. It is located between the Sassandra and the Cavally rivers—the latter constitutes the border with Liberia—about 430 kilometers (270 miles) from the capital, Abidjan. It may be best visited from San Pedro, driving about 120 kilometers (75 miles) north to Guiroutou, or via Guiglo driving 100 kilometers (62 miles) south to Tai, both on the western side of the park. However, the access roads are poor and passable only during the dry season between December and April. There are no roads or tracks inside the park, and any penetration into the interior of the park has to be organized as camping tours on foot. Particularly rewarding is a hike from Guiroutou along the Hana River, a tributary of the Cavally, to Mount Niénokoué, a granite inselberg 623 meters (2,044 feet) high that overlooks the immense forest canopy. Whereas no accommodation facilities exist in Guiroutou, visitors may arrange through the Institute of Tropical Ecology in Abidjan to be accommodated at the Institute's Research Station at Tai.

The Tai National Park represents typical Guinean lowland rain forest, interspersed in the north with elements of moist semideciduous forest. It has a considerable floral wealth of 600–800 different tree species, and about 80 plant species in the park are endemic to the Sassandra area. The fauna comprises almost a thousand species of vertebrates, including almost all mammalian species that occur in the Guinean forest zone, of which eight are considered either "endangered," "vulnerable," or "rare" in terms of the IUCN's *Red Data Book*.[3] Tai is the last stronghold of the Guinean forest elephant and sustains viable populations of such rare species as the pygmy hippopotamus, jentink, zebra, Ogilby and Bay duiker as well as the more common forest duikers, bongo antelope, and giant forest hog. Chimpanzees, black-and-white, red and green colobus, and seven other species of primates are common, as are the melanistic forest leopard, the golden cat, and numerous viverids. Flying squirrels are observable, and the swampy parts and the periphery of the park contain large numbers of forest buffalo.

Although the park constitutes a biosphere reserve of Unesco's Man and the Biosphere Program and was included in the International Convention on World Cultural and Natural Heritage, its natural features are nevertheless seriously threatened by illegal gold washing, logging, and commercialized poaching.

Another extremely interesting conservation area in the Guinean zone is the more recently established *Azagny National Park*, located in Ivory Coast between the Bandama River, the Ebrié Lagoon, and the Atlantic coast, only about 120 kilometers (75 miles) west of the capital, Abidjan. It comprises a relatively small area of only 200 square kilometers (77 square miles) but is well controlled and easily accessible via Dabou. There is a well-equipped tourist camp in the eastern part of the park from which the swamp area may be visited by boat and tours on foot into the primary forest can be undertaken. The western and southern part of the park with mangroves, swamp forest, and coastal savanna, in which wildlife may be viewed from observation towers, is more easily accessible by boat from the Grand Lahou tourist camp.

The park has very diverse natural features. One-third of it is a swamp basin into which the adjoining forestland and palm plantations drain. The swampland is partly wooded, mainly with *Raphia* palm trees, and partly covered with a thick layer of floating vegetation, including many flowering herbs, grasses, and sedges. In the basin and at its northern edge there are numerous islands and peninsulas protruding that are covered with dense primary forest. The southwestern part of the park, however, is flat and comprises a mosaic of coastal savanna, littoral shrubland, and swamp forest. Accordingly, there are more than thirty distinctly different vegetational formations, including large pure stands of *Pandanus* palm trees, *Chrysobalanus* forest, thickets of *Achrostichium* and *Calamus*, mangroves, and also abandoned coffee and cacao plantations.

Wildlife is typically Guinean, including chimpanzees, colobus, and three other monkey species, pygmy hippos, water chevrotain, and blue, black, and yellow-backed duiker. The waters around the park are still frequented by the manatee. However, the main wildlife features are the forest elephants and buffalo, which can be viewed from the observation platforms or from the air as they feed in the open swamp and savanna areas. A nearby aeroclub organizes the popular air safaris.

Coastal and Montane Zones

Coastal and montane biomes of great scientific and conservation interest are located in the four biogeographical zones discussed above. The coastal biomes comprise coastal dunes, thickets, shrubs and savannas, swamplands, and mangrove forest. The montane biomes are characterized by moist semideciduous forest on the lower slopes and by montane savanna and tree ferns above 1,000 meters (3,300 feet) altitude. The ecological conditions vary greatly from area to area.

In Mauritania and Senegal five coastal national parks have been created, totaling an area of about 15,000 square kilometers (5,800 square miles), mainly for the conservation of bird life. Three other national parks, in the Casamance region of Senegal and in Ivory Coast, contain some coastal elements. Only one montane area has been granted conservation status, the Nimba Mountain massif at the intersection of Guinea, Liberia, and Ivory Coast. Other protected mountain areas, like the Ziama massif in Guinea and Mount Sanbgé and Mount Péko in Ivory Coast, are too low to have specific Afro-montane vegetation; rather they are representative of the Guinean forest and savanna zones.

A coastal conservation area of particular international importance is the *Banc d'Arguin National Park* in Mauritania, which comprises 11,730 square kilometers (4,530 square miles) of coastal waters interspersed with many islands and islets southwest of Nouadhibou, about 480 kilometers (270 miles) from the capital, Nouakchott. It has been set aside because of its significance as a place of rest and nesting for many tens of thousands of migratory birds, including large colonies of flamingos, herons, egrets, cormorants, and others. To better protect the coastal waters, a buffer zone of 3,100 square kilometers (1,200 square miles), the *Baie de Lévrier Fauna Reserve*, which also contains some Sahelian fauna, was established on the mainland facing the islands.

Djoudj National Park, located in the extreme northwest of Senegal, bordering Mauritania, assumes similar international importance mainly as a bird sanctuary. It comprises a 160-square-kilometer (62-square-mile) mosaic of Sahelian habitat within the vast delta area of the Senegal River.

The park provides a wintering site for West European migratory birds, mainly aquatic species. It is one of the first places with permanent fresh water immediately south of the Sahara. From September to April more than 2 million migrants, mainly ducks and waders, come to join the dense populations of resident breeding birds including thousands of white pelicans. The park is also inhabited by many Sahelian game species such as the red-fronted gazelle, Bohor reedbuck, and patas monkey; even the rare cheetah and serval have been recorded. The system of flooding channels also provides habitat for the West African manatee.

Unfortunately, the park has been invaded by pigs and donkeys that have become feral and are difficult to control. The damming of the Senegal River, with the resulting change of the flooding regime, also constitutes a grave threat to the park.

Another small coastal conservation area in Senegal, the *Langue de Barbarie National Park*, deserves special mention as perhaps the only site protected for the reproduction of marine turtles as well as seabirds. It comprises 20 square kilometers (8 square miles) of coastal dunes at the estuary of the Senegal River south of the city Saint-Louis.

The only montane conservation area in West Africa, the *Mount Nimba Nature Reserve*, was created in 1943 to protect a portion of the Nimba Mountain plateau. The plateau is located primarily in Guinea, but portions extend into the Ivory Coast and Liberia. It is home to French West Africa's highest peak, the 1,752-meter (5,748-foot) Mount Nimba. About 130 square kilometers (50 square miles) of the reserve are situated in Guinea and about 50 square kilometers (20 square miles) in Ivory Coast. The reserve can be comfortably visited from the Ivorian side via Danané and Yeale, where one can climb the peak in about 5 hours.

The Nimba Mountain massif rises from the Guinean forest zone, so lower slopes are covered with semideciduous, often degraded forest. Above 900 meters (3,000 feet) forest is confined to ravines, tree ferns are abundant, and there are dense, almost pure stands of *Parinari excelsa*, which is only sporadic in lowland

forests. The crest of the mountain massif is covered with a very specific sub-
montane savanna. Larger animal species are rather rare. Buffalo mount the
plateau at times in the rainy season, and duiker, chimpanzees, and other primate
species inhabit the lower forested slopes.

Because the flora and smaller fauna are of particular scientific interest, the
French colonial administration placed the reserve under the special control of
IFAN, which built a research station on the Guinean side. As a result, numerous
scientific studies were carried out in the reserve, rendering the Nimba Mountain
massif probably one of the scientifically best known West African montane
biomes. IFAN's involvement was terminated in 1960, and for a time protection
of the reserve was grossly neglected. More recently initiatives have been taken
by Unesco and the two governments concerned to reestablish scientific control.

ADMINISTRATION

Administrative Situation

All of the territories of the former AOF inherited an administrative structure
in which the water and forest service was responsible for the wildlife resource
without any special centralized administration of conservation areas. Wildlife
was traditionally considered to be a secondary forest product and administered
accordingly. In only a very few of the emerging new states were efforts made
to adjust the administrative structure and responsibilities to meet the challenge
of conservation. Outstanding in this respect was *Senegal*, where a network of
national parks and reserves was developed beginning in 1954. Responsibility
for these was vested in 1969 in a centralized national parks authority attached
directly to the presidency. The creation of this administrative structure has contributed significantly to the development and efficient management of national
parks and reserves comprising more than 5 percent of the country's surface.

In *Ivory Coast*, a separate national parks authority was created in 1973, upgraded to a Ministry of Nature Protection, and, unfortunately, disbanded in 1977.
Since then, the administration of national parks has become increasingly decentralized. Only the Azagny National Park still enjoys an autonomous status allowing development and efficient management. The territories and staff of all
the other parks and reserves, totaling some 6 percent of Ivory Coast's surface,
fall under the jurisdiction and financial responsibility of various, sometimes
multiple, local administrative authorities, rendering efficient management of
these areas very difficult if not impossible.

In *Burkina Faso* a Department of National Parks, Wildlife Reserves and
Hunting was created in 1976 and attached to the Ministry of Transport, Environment and Tourism, which obtained specific external aid to execute a survey
of its conservation areas. However, most important reserves have yet to be
upgraded to fully protected national parks, and some of the parks need to be

redescribed to include important adjacent areas. One wildlife area has the status of a game ranch.

In all of the other countries wildlife conservation still remains the responsibility of the water and forest services. In *Mauritania*, *Mali*, and *Guinea* these services are understaffed and underfunded. They have been unable to develop the previously existing protected areas or to create much-needed new ones. In *Niger*, *Bénin*, and *Togo* the water and forest services have more recently solicited external aid enabling them to consolidate and enlarge existing conservation areas, like the Pendjari and W du Niger national parks in Bénin and the Kéran and Fazao Mazfacassa national parks in Togo, and to propose additional areas like the Air Plateau in Niger.

Conservation Policies and Legislation

Since the territories of the former AOF achieved independence in 1960, a rather striking disparity has evolved between the administration of their conservation areas, which with the exception of Senegal is very inadequate, and the development of conservation policies, which is quite progressive. All countries have accepted progressive conservation principles, and most of them have become signatories to such international conventions as the Organization of African Unity's African Convention on Nature Conservation, the Convention on International Trade in Endangered Species of Flora and Fauna (CITES), and the Unesco World Heritage Convention. The Tai and Comoé national parks and Mount Nimba Reserve in Ivory Coast, and the Delta du Saloum, Niokolo-Koba, and Djoudj national parks in Senegal have been recognized by the convention as natural heritage sites of outstanding international importance and beauty. Most of the countries have promulgated new national parks and wildlife conservation legislation, and all have now banned tourist hunting. They are fully participating in international conservation programs, such as the Unesco Man and the Biosphere Program, and seven of the protected areas have become biosphere reserves. Since 1965 all countries are participating biennially in the FAO African Forestry Commission's Ad Hoc Working Group on Wildlife.

Some of the concerned countries, like Senegal, have accepted IUCN's World Conservation Strategy and have set up national conservation strategy committees. They have recognized the potential value of their conservation areas for tourist development and have included this aspect in their economic planning. They all look to East Africa in anticipation of similarly spectacular tourist development, without realizing that East African countries are only now reaping the benefits of half a century of costly and unselfish nature protection efforts that were not being made in West Africa.

Table 26.2 shows that, since independence, an impressive number of existing conservation areas have been upgraded to national parks; others have been newly created. Here, however, the disparity between policy and management is particularly evident: a large number of the national parks and reserves in French-speaking West Africa exist merely on paper, without any developed infrastructure. Thus, important national parks such as Tai in Ivory Coast and W in Bénin and Burkina Faso have remained almost totally inaccessible to visitors, and others like Marahoué in Ivory Coast and Arli in Burkina Faso are being increasingly infiltrated by settlers. All of these lack any form of protection or law enforcement. Only Senegal is a noteworthy exception; all of its parks and reserves are well demarcated, accessible, and developed for tourist and educational use.

Absent effective protection, the actual conservation status of the varied flora and fauna of West Africa is alarming. It is generally accepted that the environment and the fauna of West Africa as a whole are more degraded and in greater immediate danger than those of the eastern and southern parts of the continent. A number of reasons for this phenomenon have been articulated: the more heterogeneous historic development, the lack of awareness of the threat to the environment, the more or less uncontrolled possession of firearms, and particularly the lack of appropriate administrative structure and dedicated conservationists. As a result of these factors, the French-speaking countries of West Africa generally had a much worse starting point, lagging decades behind the achievements in East Africa. Unfortunately, this gap has not been closed at all in recent decades, and today there is a very real threat to many of the ecosystems and animal species of West Africa.

Even in the countries where conservation action was energetically undertaken after independence, the outcomes are sometimes negative. It is estimated that a strip 300 kilometers (186 miles) in width all along the Sahara has been lost to desertification with predictable consequences for fauna. About 90 percent of the Guinean rain forest belt has been lost to the encroachment of slash-and-burn agriculture and the development of large-scale industrial plantations. Despite awareness, international intervention, and legal action, the Tai National Park, the last large piece of this ecosystem, is about to be destroyed by gold prospectors and poachers. Even in the less densely populated Sudanian zone, population pressure and consequent invasion of the conservation areas threaten the survival of many game species. Despite the most intense policing efforts and the creation of a special protection force, Senegal is about to lose its last elephants to ruthless poaching.

Management Planning

Management of national parks and reserves requires thorough planning. Such planning presupposes knowledge of the respective area and therefore calls for prior inventory surveys. With this information in hand, it is essential to clearly define primary and secondary management goals for protected areas in the context of overall national development. Sometimes the zoning of different forms of land use, accompanied by clearly visible physical delimitation of the different zones, is necessary in order to regulate conflicts of land use. Infrastructures must be planned and developed and money budgeted in accordance with established and approved Management Master Plans defining objectives and zoning.

Despite the weakness of the administrative structures for national parks and reserves in most of the countries concerned, a great deal of good planning has been accomplished for almost all of the more important national parks, often through external assistance:

- in Banc d'Arguin National Park in Mauritania with WWF/IUCN assistance;
- in Niokolo Koba National Park in Senegal by a World Bank Team;
- in Boucle de Baoulé National Park in Mali through Dutch bilateral aid;
- in Comoé, Tai, and Azagny national parks in Ivory Coast through French bilateral aid and a German wildlife and national parks mission;
- in Pô and Arli national parks in Burkina Faso with U.N. Development Programme (UNDP)/FAO assistance;
- in Pendjari and W national parks in Bénin with UNDP/FAO and EEC assistance; and
- in Kéran and Fazao Malfakassa national parks in Togo with EEC assistance.

Infrastructure Development and Maintenance

Despite the described planning, actual management and development work has been implemented in very few of these national parks. In most of the countries, governments have not given a high enough priority to national parks development in their national budgets, so implementation of the plans has depended to a large extent on finding external finance. It is only recently that international donors like the World Bank and the European Economic Commission have started to recognize national parks development as a legitimate area of investment.

Even if investment aid is forthcoming, routine seasonal maintenance of the developed infrastructure remains the greater problem. This work is hampered by nonexistent or inefficient national parks administrations. As a result, only a few of the national parks and reserves listed in Table 26.2 have a permanently maintained infrastructure consisting of boundary delimitation, administrative headquarters with workshops and maintenance facilities, a network of permanent guards' posts, a system of all-weather roads and tracks, minimum tourist facilities, and interpretive exhibits. The more outstanding exceptions are:

- Niokolo Koba, Djoudj, Delta du Saloum, and Casamance national parks in Senegal;
- Azagny and Comoé national parks in Ivory Coast;
- Arli National Park in Burkina Faso;
- Pendjari National Park in Bénin; and
- W du Niger National Park in Niger.

Presently plans are being implemented by EEC to further develop the infrastructure of the Pendjari and W national parks in Bénin, and the World Bank intends to invest in the Comoé National Park in Ivory Coast. Both projects include the creation of special management units for infrastructure maintenance.

Protection and Law Enforcement

The effective protection of national parks and reserves depends on efficient, centralized administrative structures; well-maintained infrastructures; and sufficient park personnel, well trained, well equipped, and dedicated to conservation.

Unfortunately, these conditions exist together in only a very few of the West African national parks, making law enforcement the single greatest deficiency in national parks management. The lack of housing and equipment for guards and administrative personnel and the absence of marked boundaries and networks of all-season roads make physical protection in many of the national parks and reserves very difficult indeed.

Apart from the Senegalese national parks and the Azagny National Park in Ivory Coast, parks generally lack sufficient transportation, communication, and political support. They are fighting a losing battle against ever-increasing numbers of well-equipped and highly determined gangs of poachers. These not only kill game animals in large numbers, thus deterring tourist use of the parks, but also engage in regular and indiscriminate burning of habitat.

In contrast to the experience in eastern and southern Africa, law enforcement in the French-speaking West African territories has been hampered from the very beginning by the historical structure of conservation administration. Nowhere in French-speaking Africa are there national park administrative headquarters in, or at the periphery of, the parks with social amenities like shops, schools, football fields, and so on. Where headquarters exist at all, they are almost invariably located far from the parks' boundaries, sometimes more than 100 kilometers (62 miles) away in the nearest administrative center.

The absence or ineffectiveness of guards is a great problem. Even park access is not systematically controlled, rendering tourist use almost impossible. With a few exceptions, noted below, guards are based in villages at the periphery of the parks, and park interiors remain completely devoid of any law-enforcement personnel. In Senegal the guards live permanently inside the parks. In some of the parks of Bénin and Ivory Coast efforts are made to rotate guards temporarily into camps located in the interior of the parks as well as patrolling the parks from the periphery. However, field allowances are infrequently paid, and this has a deleterious effect on the motivation of park staff.

Parks in French-speaking West Africa are clearly suffering from their administrative past: there are no career possibilities in national parks per se, only in the forest services as a whole. A trained forest guard can be put to work in any of the services' areas of competence: forest management, wood industry, silviculture, freshwater fisheries—or wildlife and parks. A guard who chooses to specialize for idealistic reasons in wildlife conservation might be able to win training at the regional college for national parks personnel at Garoua, Cameroon, but his educational efforts will not be honored by grade promotion. Naturally, after a period of time, most personnel prefer to be posted to jobs that offer more social security, less physical hardship, and no risk of being killed or disabled by poachers, or they categorically demand special allowances for work in the parks.

Conservation personnel lack political support and are precluded from forming the emotional bonds associated with long-term service to a particular national park. Personnel are often deliberately transferred from one forestry responsibility to another, and a graduate of the Garoua school may find himself counting logs for export. International aid is uncoordinated and frequently competitive. High allowances are paid for work in some areas, creating discontent among those employed in other fields of the same service.

Apart from illegal hunting, most of the parks in the Sudanian zone suffer from livestock invasion with the concomitant risk of rinderpest, a highly fatal cattle disease that recently caused die-offs of buffalo in the Pendjari and W du Niger national parks in Bénin. This problem does not exist in the national parks and reserves of the moist Guinean zone where tsetse flies transmit trypanosomiasis, which precludes livestock husbandry. In the Guinean zone the major threat is timber exploitation coupled with gradual infiltration of the parks by slash-and-burn agricultural cultivators. These immigrants are often from the north and enjoy much stronger political support than the conservation authorities because their activities are generally considered to be an important contribution to gaining agricultural self-sufficiency. For example, large areas of the Mount Sangbé, Péko, Marahoué, and Tai national parks in Ivory Coast have been infiltrated by cultivators during the last decade.

Examples of successful resettlement of squatters and total reclamation of the park's territory are the Niokolo Koba, Djoudj, and Saloum national parks in Senegal and the Azagny National Park in Ivory Coast. For some time the former inhabitants were allowed to visit their previous habitations in the parks before they were permanently resettled in new, less remote areas.

Wildlife Management

Repeated aerial or ground census of game populations as a basis for wildlife management has been or is being carried out in only a few of the national parks and reserves of French-speaking West Africa, in the Niokolo Koba, Djoudj, and Saloum national parks in Senegal, Boucle de Baoulé National Park in Mali, the Comoé, Tai, and Azagny national parks in Ivory Coast, the Pô, Arli, and W du Niger national parks in Burkina Faso, and the Pendjari and W du Niger national parks in Bénin. Programs of routine aerial ecological monitoring of range, livestock, and wildlife, with computer analysis of correlations and trends, have been introduced only in eastern Senegal and northeastern Ivory Coast, including the large Comoé National Park. These programs were based on models in East Africa and developed in the framework of German bilateral aid in Ivory Coast and by a UNDP/FAO project in Senegal. However, the low level of law enforcement in most of the national parks and reserves makes it impossible to introduce control of burning of the range as one of the most important wildlife management measures. At the same time, the constant drain of game animals by illegal hunting excludes any overpopulation problems requiring regulatory measures as in the southern African parks.

In some parks attempts have been made to reintroduce extirpated species or to restock depleted game populations: giraffe and lions into the Niokolo Koba National Park, Dorcas and red-fronted gazelles, manatees and crocodiles into the Djoudj National Park, kob antelopes into the Casamance National Park in Senegal, and chimpanzees, pygmy hippos, and crocodiles into the Azagny National Park in Ivory Coast.

Use of Protected Areas

An understanding of modern conservation concepts and needs is now well developed in most of the countries of French-speaking West Africa. One approach is to put protected areas such as national parks and reserves to use for the benefit of man, and, in fact, the upgrading of former forest reserves into national parks in many of these countries implies such use. All of these countries have realized the enormous potential of national parks for tourism, although these parks may not offer the same spectacular game-viewing opportunities as in eastern and southern Africa. What is not sufficiently understood, however, is that tourist use of national parks requires considerable investment in infrastructural development and a relatively high level of management, conditions that presently exist in only a few of the national parks of French-speaking West Africa: the Niokolo Koba, Djoudj, and Delta du Saloum national parks in Senegal, the Comoé and Azagny national parks in Ivory Coast, the W National Park in Niger, and the Pendjari National Park in Bénin.

Except in Senegal, tourist access to most of the national parks and reserves varies from difficult to impossible, and camp facilities are rather primitive where they exist at all. Thus the parks remain largely unusable for tourism. Again, the reason lies mainly in the administrative situation: although tourist use of national parks is politically and economically desirable and officially encouraged, foresters in charge of parks are little interested in the enhancement of tourism, and tourist management of conservation areas remains totally alien to them.

In order to overcome this, Ivory Coast has recently considered leasing not only the tourist facilities but entire concession areas of the Azagny National Park to private enterprises. By means of these leases the government hopes to assure development and maintenance of the tourist infrastructure, continuous professional tourist management, and the guidance and control of visitor flow.

Recreational tourism is not the only legitimate use of national parks; equally important are the scientific and educational benefits that may be derived from these areas. Scientific research is perhaps the only use of conservation areas that was developed during colonial times. In this context one should mention the valuable association of the former IFAN with the Mount Nimba Reserve in Guinea and Ivory Coast and with other scientifically interesting areas, particularly in Senegal. Unfortunately, educational and conservation awareness programs are nearly nonexistent in the national parks and reserves of French-speaking West Africa. Again Senegal is the major exception, but recently also the Azagny National Park in Ivory Coast developed a successful public awareness and educational program financed and aided by the World Bank.

Conservation Perspectives

National parks development in French-speaking West Africa is of particular importance because of the diversity of West African biomes and their lack of effective conservation. At the same time it is evident that national parks management in this region is seriously constrained:

- In the northern zone increasing aridity and the advance of the Sahara poses almost insoluble problems; pressure of human population and of livestock on the last islands of natural vegetation becomes both politically and technically more and more uncontrollable.

- In the southern moist zone short-term economic considerations of maximum exploitation of the forest resources, and increased agricultural production to employ and feed the ever-increasing human population immigrating from the north, often have precedence over declared long-term conservation policies.

- Everywhere mounting pressure for material gain from wildlife resources in the form of meat and products results in commercially organized poaching of hitherto unknown intensity.

In the face of these constraints national parks will survive only if their management is quickly improved and modernized so that they can play their full and beneficial role in national economic and social development. This presupposes three major conditions:

1. The existing administrative structures must be reorganized so as to render national parks more autonomous and efficient. Conservation of flora and fauna in the framework of national parks systems must receive professional status, offering graduates interesting and attractive career opportunities outside the agricultural and forestry service.

2. Conservation education must be introduced and reinforced at all levels of schooling, and the awareness among policymakers and political leaders must be enhanced by means of all available media.

3. Conservation of natural resources and national parks development must be recognized by international and national donors of technical and financial aid as legitimate areas of engagement. There will be a continuing need to engage expatriate specialists in

national parks planning and wildlife conservation and to attract foreign investment to develop and maintain the necessary infrastructure in conservation areas. The conservation of the remaining large tracts of woodland savanna in the Sudanian zone is the most economic way of arresting desertification, and conservation of the immense genetic potential of tropical moist forests in situ is much more economical than any program to conserve gene pools in vitro.

Unless these three conditions are understood and fulfilled within the next decade, West Africa will lose many of its plant and animal species, and many of its remaining biomes will be irretrievably changed. Biological diversity may diminish to a point where even human survival is endangered.

NOTES

The authors and editor wish to thank François Goy for valuable information and assistance in the preparation of this chapter.

1. Robert Oliver, *The Gourma Elephants of Mali*, Consultant Report (Nairobi: UNEP, 1983).
2. Harald H. Roth and I. Douglas-Hamilton, "Distribution and Status of Elephants in West Africa," *Mammalia* (forthcoming).
3. Harald H. Roth and Guenter Merz, "Occurrence and Relative Abundance of Mammals in the Tai Rain Forest in Ivory Coast," [in German] *Säugetierkundliche Mitteilungen* 33 (1986): 171–93.

BIBLIOGRAPHY

General

Bigourdan, J., and R. Prunier. *The Wild Mammals of West Africa and Their Habitat* (in French). Paris: Lechevalier, 1937.
Blancou, L. "Destruction and Protection of the Fauna of French Equatorial and of French West Africa." *African Wildlife* 14 (1960): 241–44.
Bourgoin, P. *The Main Game Animals of Black French Africa* (in French). (Lorient), Editions et Imprimerie Britagne: 1949–1950.
Dekeyser, P. L. *The Mammals of French West Africa* (in French). Paris: IFAN, 1955.
IUCN. *Directory of Afrotropical Protected Areas*. Gland, Switzerland and Cambridge, England: IUCN, 1987.
MacKinnon, John, et al., eds. *Managing Protected Areas in the Tropics*. Gland, Switzerland: IUCN, 1986.

Mauritania

Verschuren, J. *Provisional Management Master Plan for the Banc d'Arguin National Park in the Islamic Republic of Mauritania*. Brussels: WWF/IUCN and Institut Royal des Sciences Naturelles de Belgique, 1984.

Senegal

Dupuy, A. R., and J. Verschuren. "Wildlife and Parks in Senegal." *Oryx* 14 (1977): 36–46.

Lariviere, J., and A. R. Dupuy. *Senegal: Her Parks, Her Animals* (in French). Paris: Editions Natan, 1978.

Verschuren, J. "Ecology of the Niokolo-Koba National Park in Senegal" (in French). *Bulletin de l'Institut Royal des Sciences Naturelles de Belgique* 55 (1983).

Guinea

Adam, J. G. *Description of the Flora and the Nimba Mountains (Ivory Coast, Guinea, Liberia)* (in French). Paris: Editions du Centre National de la Recherche Scientifique, 1981.

Gromier, E. *The Fauna of Guinea* (in French). Paris: Payot, 1936.

IFAN. "The Strict Nature Reserve of Nimba Mountain" (in French). *Mémoires de l'Institut Français d'Afrique Noire* 19 (1952), 53 (1958), 66 (1963).

Mali

Research on the Rational Utilization of Wildlife in the Sahel: Provisional Proposals for the Management of the Baoulé Zone (in French). Wageningen, Holland: Agricultural University Report, 1982.

Sayer, J. "Conservation of Large Mammals in the Republic of Mali." *Biological Conservation* 12 (1977): 245–62.

Ivory Coast

Roth, H. H., and R. Die Gbande. "Azagny—a New National Park in Ivory Coast." *Oryx* (in preparation).

Roth, H. H., et al. "Distribution and Status of the Large Mammal Species in Ivory Coast" (in French). *Mammalia* 48 (1984): 207–66, 50 (1986): 227–52, 51 (1987): 89–110.

Roth, H. H., W. Barthlott, M. Mühlenberg, and P. Röben. *Present Status of the Comoé and Tai National Parks, as well as the Azagny Reserve, and Propositions for Their Conservation and Development for Tourism* (in German and French). 4 vols. Königstein, Germany: FGU-Kronberg Consulting, 1979.

Burkina Faso

Bousquet, B. *Results of Aerial Inventory Surveys of Wildlife* (in French). FO:DP/UPV/78/008. Working Document no. 6. Rome: FAO, 1982.

Green, A. A. "Density Estimates of Larger Mammals of Arli National Park, Upper Volta." *Mammalia* 43 (1979): 71–84.

Inventory of Wildlife Resources and Economic Investigations into Their Utilization in Rural Zones. Upper Volta. Conclusions and Recommendations of the Project (in French). FO:DP/UPV/78/008. Final Report. Rome: FAO, 1983.

Spinage, C. A., and T. Souleymane. *Summary of Protected Wildlife Areas and Proposals*. FO:DP/UPV/82/008. Working Document no. 3. Rome: FAO, 1984.

Niger

Grettenberger, J. F. " 'W' National Park in Niger: A Case for Urgent Assistance." *Oryx* 18 (1984): 230–36.

Newby, J. "The Role of Protected Areas in Saving the Sahel." In *National Parks, Conservation and Development: The Role of Protected Areas in Sustaining Society*, edited by J. A. McNeely and K. R. Miller. Washington, D.C.: Smithsonian Institution Press, 1984.

Bénin

Development of National Parks. Bénin. Conclusions and Recommendations of the Project. FO:DP/DP/BEN/77/011. Final Report. Rome: FAO, 1982.

Roth, H. H., and W. Weimert. *Feasibility and Pre-Investment Study for the Establishment and Management of the Pendjari and W-National Parks, Benin*. Königstein, Germany: FGU-Kronberg Consulting, 1982.

Sayer, J., and A. A. Green. "The Distribution and Status of Large Mammals in Bénin." *Mammal Review* 14 (1984): 37–50.

Sayer, J., A. A. Green, and M. Peters. *Development of National Parks. Bénin. Management Master Plan for the Pendjari National Park* (in French). FO:DP/BEN/77/011. Working Document no. 1. Rome: FAO, 1979.

Szaniawski, A. *Development of National Parks. Bénin. Management Master Plan for the W-National Park* (in French). FO:DP/BEN/77/011. Working Document no. 3. Rome: FAO, 1982.

Togo

Duncan, P. *Feasibility Study for the Development of National Parks* (in French). England: Minster Agricultural Consultants, 1984.

Roure, G. *The Wild Animals of Togo* (in French). Rome: FAO/UNDP, 1967.

ZIMBABWE   27

Russell D. Taylor

This chapter outlines the history of wildlife conservation in Zimbabwe, the present system of protected areas, and the administrative framework within which they are managed. A basic concept of wildlife conservation in Zimbabwe is that custody of the wildlife resource is vested in the landholder, be it the state, the private landholder, or the communal land occupant. All derive benefits from the wildlife on their land. This feature, largely absent elsewhere in Africa where wildlife is the property of the state only, has important implications for the long-term security of national parks and other protected areas in Zimbabwe.

HISTORY

The history of nature conservation in Zimbabwe is best illustrated through the legislation developed for this purpose, which provides a useful insight into the country's conservation concepts since 1890. Major aspects of this legislation are covered in Table 27. 1.

The First Game Laws, 1890-1923

Between 1891 and 1923 the game laws were administered by the director of agriculture under authority delegated by the administrator of the British South Africa Company. Early conservation efforts were aimed at protecting large game and regulating hunting rights, seasons, and areas. Not until 1913 was any type of protection given to plant life. During this period there was some interest in national parks. In the Legislative Assembly on May 29, 1899, Dr. H. Sauer proposed the establishment of a national park. He suggested that an area of ground within the country should be reserved in the same manner as Yellowstone

Table 27.1
A History of Nature Conservation Legislation in Zimbabwe

Year	Act	Major Features
1891	Game Law Amendment Act	Certain mammal species listed for protection.
1899	Game Preservation Ordinance Act	Created 26 Administrative Ordinance districts, each listing which mammals are protected and which mammals could be hunted.
1906	Game Preservation Ordinance Amendment Act	Royal Game status conferred on certain species.
1913	Herbage Preservation Ordinance	Prevention of destruction to vegetation by fire; removal of trees at discretion of owner.
1927	Water Act	Prohibition of tree felling less than 100m from water's edge.
1929	Game & Fish Preservation Act	Designation of land for preservation of natural communities; lawful hunting methods prescribed; certain species declared vermin with rewards offered for their destruction; controls on fish exploitation.
1929	Nature Reserves Forest Produce Act	Controls on exploitation of indigenous and plantation timber.
1930	Tsetse Fly Act	Designation of hunting areas for complete elimination of game animals (tsetse fly hosts); cancellation of former restricted hunting areas.
1931-1935	Game & Fish Preservation Act Amendments	Proclamation of 9 game reserves, increased powers of law enforcement; introduction of prescribed management practices such as veld burning and vermin control.

Table 27.1 (continued)

Year	Act	Major Features
1935-1940	Game & Fish Preservation Act Amendments	Protection of certain amphibians and reptiles.
1941	Natural Resources Act	Protection of landscapes and scenery for their aesthetic appeal and scenic value; emphasis on protection of trees, grasses, and soils; conservation education.
1947-1949	Game & Fish Preservation Act Amendments	Game wardens appointed for law enforcement; first controls on utilization of certain areas by tourists; veld management regulations.
1949-1953	National Parks Act	Establishment of Government Department of National Parks, two types of nature reserve: (a) National Parks--mainly for outdoor recreation and protection of spectacular landscapes; (b) Game Reserves--specifically provided for the protection and viewing of wild animal life.
1954	Federal National Parks Act	Administration of all national parks in Rhodesia, Northern Rhodesia (Zambia) and Nyasaland (Malawi); 14 national parks in Rhodesia covering ca. 2 million ha of land.
1960	Wild Life Conservation Act	Establishment of government department designated as Game Department; personnel responsible for control of big game species in farming areas and tsetse fly zones.
1960	Fish Conservation Act	Further controls on fish exploitation.

495

Table 27.1 (continued)

Year	Act	Major Features
1964	National Parks Act	Amalgamation of National Parks and Game Departments; combined jurisdiction over 13 national parks, 8 game reserves, and 5 controlled hunting areas.
1972	Quelea Control Act	Provision for the control of quelea birds.
1973	Trapping of Animals Act	Improved controls on trapping methods.
1974	Bees Act	Controls on the exploitation of bees.
1975	Parks and Wild Life Act	Decentralization of authority to intensive conservation areas where the utilization of wildlife is under the control of landowners; certain plant species given status equivalent to that of Royal Game; redesignation of certain conservation areas for specific types of tourist utilization; jurisdiction over 67 conservation areas covering 11.8 percent of the total land area of Rhodesia.
1982	Parks and Wild Life Act Amendments	Jurisdiction over 65 protected areas covering 12.7 percent of the total land area of Zimbabwe.

Source: D.N.S. Tomlinson, "Nature Conservation in Rhodesia: A
   Review," Biological Conservation 18 (1980): 161-162.

National Park. Dr. Sauer's proposal failed because it affected the rights of the British South Africa Company. In 1902 the Matobo and Nyanga estates were bequeathed to the nation in the will of Cecil John Rhodes. Set aside as protected areas, they later became national parks.

Early Game Reserves and National Parks, 1923-1950

On the attainment of responsible government in 1923, the Colony of Southern Rhodesia assigned the game laws to the minister of agriculture and lands, who vested responsibility for their administration in the Forestry Department of his ministry. The importance of protecting catchment and alluvial areas against tree felling and cropping was first recognized in 1927 with the promulgation of the Water Act. The first officers of the government to be employed full-time on the preservation and control of wild animals were appointed in the Forestry Department in 1928. With the promulgation of the Game and Fish Preservation Act of 1929 this department acquired full responsibility for game and fish preservation until 1950.

The Game and Fish Preservation Act of 1929 provided the legal framework for establishment of the Wankie Game Reserve, the Victoria Falls Game Reserve, and the Urungwe Game Reserve, which included what are now Mana Pools National Park and the Chewore Safari Area. The act specified that the governor of the colony could by proclamation "define reserves within which it shall not be lawful, without special permission in writing of the Minister, to hunt any animal or such animals, as may be mentioned in such proclamation." Further, the governor could make regulations "providing for the protection and preservation of animals within any reserve established by proclamation . . . and for the appointment of wardens or rangers of such reserves, and for regulating the traffic through, and the carrying of arms in such reserves."

In 1938 the Game and Fish Preservation Act was amended to incorporate certain provisions of the International Convention of 1933 for the protection of the fauna and flora of Africa. The amendments enlarged the number of protected species and made more elaborate provision for the control of trade in wildlife trophies and products. Provisions of the 1933 International Convention that made reference to national parks were not incorporated into legislation until 1949, when the National Parks Act was promulgated.

Although amphibians and reptiles were included in the 1938 amendment, it was not until 1941 that legislation was passed to protect trees, grasses, and other soil products. Although special protection was given to commercially exploitable timber species in 1929, it was not until 1975 that rare or endangered plant species were given status equivalent to that of Royal Game.

By 1950, a Department of National Parks had been created under the minister of internal affairs, and Wankie Game Reserve, Robins Game Sanctuary, Kazuma Pan, and Chimanimani were established as national parks. The new Department of National Parks had a director and nine supporting staff, and the amount provided in the budget for running the department during its first year of operation amounted to £22,500.

The purpose of the first national parks was clearly declared in the National Parks Act of 1949:

Each of the areas defined in the Schedule to this Act is hereby constituted a National Park for the propagation, protection and preservation therein of wild animal life, vegetation and objects of geological, ethnological, historical or other scientific interest for the benefit, advantage and enjoyment of the inhabitants of the Colony.

Conservation and Pragmatism, 1950-1975

In February 1952, a game section was created in the Division of Agriculture and Lands, comprising one game officer, one clerk, and one vermin ranger, the annual budget being some £4,000. The primary function of this section was to destroy animals causing damage to stock, crops and property. In 1958-1959 recognition was given to the need for research into wild animals, birds, and fish, and the first three research officer posts were created.

During the Federation of Rhodesia and Nyasaland between 1953 and 1963, national parks in Southern Rhodesia became the responsibility of the federal government, while the game section was transferred to the Southern Rhodesia Department of Mines, Lands and Surveys. As a consequence, nature conservation was now being administered by two separate departments under two separate acts. The Department of National Parks was responsible for national parks under the terms of the 1949 National Parks Act. The Department of Wild Life Conservation, formerly the Southern Rhodesia Game Department, was responsible for wildlife matters elsewhere in the country, under the terms of the Wild Life Conservation Act of 1961, which had replaced the Game and Fish Preservation Act of 1929.

In 1964 a new National Parks Act was passed. Its language preserved the essential concepts of the 1949 statute establishing national parks: "for the propagation, protection, preservation, management and control therein of wild animal life, vegetation and objects of geological, ethnological, historical or other scientific interest for the benefit, advantage, enjoyment and recreation of the public." This concept of a national park strongly reflects that defined by the 1933 International Convention, which was also adopted by other African countries under British colonial influence.

It appears that administrative emphasis in the Department of National Parks was placed on public enjoyment, and most of the fourteen national parks proclaimed during the 1950s are now recreational parks or botanical gardens. For the rest of the country, the Wild Life Conservation Act provided for game reserves, private game reserves, nonhunting reserves, and controlled hunting areas.

With the dissolution of federation at the end of 1963, the two sister departments were merged into a single Department of National Parks and Wild Life Management, which was responsible for fourteen national parks, eight game reserves, and five controlled hunting areas. Nevertheless, the National Parks Act of 1964 continued in force alongside the Wild Life Conservation Act of 1961 until both were repealed and replaced by Parks and Wild Life Act of 1975.

An integral part of the country's development has been a continuing policy of using game elimination as a means of controlling tsetse fly (*Glossina* spp.). Many species of African large mammals are hosts of pathogenic trypanosomes, which are transmitted by the bite of an infective tsetse fly, causing sleeping sickness in humans and nagana in cattle. In Zimbabwe, this led to the Tsetse Fly Act of 1930 and subsequent large-scale hunting operations over vast tracts of land.

During the 1940s and 1950s some 30,000 square kilometers (11,500 square miles) of territory were almost totally cleared of tsetse fly at a cost of nearly 551,000 game animals destroyed in the course of these operations. There was such opposition to this shooting of wildlife that a Commission of Inquiry was appointed in 1954 to investigate other means of tsetse and trypanosomiasis control. These included the clearing of riverine vegetation, spraying, and tsetse fly blood meal analysis. By 1964, a clear pattern of host specificity had emerged, and selective hunting of a limited number of favored host species was introduced. Game elimination programs were resumed, however, following the rapid reinvasion of tsetse fly that had occurred after the cessation of hunting. Game and cattle fences, with hunting authorized in the corridors between them, became an integral part of control, as did the ground application of residual insecticides.

Two significant points emerge from the game elimination programs. First, wildlife populations generally demonstrated an exceptional ability to withstand prolonged hunting pressure and to repopulate previously hunted areas in a relatively short span of time. Second and perhaps more important throughout the history of the game laws and wildlife legislation of the country, there has been a provision for either the suspension of these laws or for the designation of areas in which game could be eliminated. For example, until 1960 controlled hunting areas were usually areas designated for selective game elimination to control tsetse fly.

The early development of Zimbabwe's legislation reflects a distinct lack of preservationism. This has been due not only to the game elimination programs, but also to the rapid economic development of game ranching on private land since 1959. Moreover, the Natural Resources Act of 1941 and its direct successors provide for public custody of the country's natural resources, such as soil, water, and vegetation, through the natural resources movement, headed by the Natural Resources Board. Consequently, in terms of this act, pressure can be brought to bear on public and private landowners to implement remedial action where accelerated soil erosion or overgrazing or both are evident. Invariably, this action requires a reduction of animal numbers, which in the case of wildlife is usually undertaken by cropping or culling operations. These practical necessities to destroy wild animals have had a strong influence on public and official sentiment and perhaps, in part, underlie the current view that wildlife and protected areas are renewable natural resources that can and should be used sympathetically in the long-term service of man, a philosophy that is embodied in the Parks and Wild Life Act of 1975.

A New Philosophy, 1975 to the Present

The Parks and Wild Life Act of 1975 took some years in drafting and built on the legal manipulations allowed by the 1961 act. It provided a radical departure from the framework of the past and brought considerable clarity to a confused scene. The preamble to the act states its objectives:

To provide for the establishment of national parks, botanical reserves, botanical gardens, sanctuaries, safari areas and recreational parks; to make provision for the preservation, conservation, propagation or control of the wildlife, fish and plants of Zimbabwe and the protection of her natural landscape and scenery, to confer privileges on owners or occupiers of alienated land as custodians of wildlife, fish and plants; to give certain powers to intensive conservation areas committees. . . .

The following important provisions were incorporated in the act:

1. It gave the landholder the responsibility for the wildlife resources on his property other than specially protected species of plants and animals, and in the case of people living in communal lands, it restored a similar right of use that had been denied to them since 1898.
2. It gave legal force to a diversity of conservation goals by making proper provision for conservation areas of differing types, including special conservation areas both inside and outside the nationally administered Parks and Wild Life Estate.
3. It extended the definition of wildlife to include all vertebrates and invertebrates, and so provided the basis for a genuine conservation of biological resources throughout the country rather than just the protection of game animals in reserves.
4. It made provision for the appointment of a statutory Parks and Wild Life Board that had clearly defined responsibilities to examine and advise the minister on policy in relation to each of the provisions of the act.
5. It made provision for landholders to invoke legislation to safeguard the wildlife resources on their land, and in particular it provided them with the right to benefit from those resources and thus the incentive to conserve and use them wisely.

The 1975 act defines the purposes for which the various types of protected area may be established. Under the act, national parks are established "to preserve and protect the natural landscape and scenery therein, and to preserve and protect wild life and plants and the natural ecological stability of wild life and plant communities therein; for the enjoyment, education and inspiration of the public."

While this contribution is concerned primarily with protected areas of which national parks have long been the cornerstone, rising human demands on nature require a new approach to traditional Western views of conservation. This perception is incorporated in Zimbabwe's present legislation, which provides an institutional framework with which to meet the pressures and threats protected areas face. Present conservation dilemmas in Africa are a consequence of alien concepts and behavior imposed upon local cultural traditions and economic realities. Unless the common rural man enjoys some sense of participation and tangible benefit from wildlife, there is little future for national parks.

PARKS AND RESERVES

The Parks and Wild Life Estate covers some 12.7 percent or nearly 50,000 square kilometers (19,000 square miles) of Zimbabwe (Figure 27.1), within which most higher plants and animals with an effective geographical range extending into Zimbabwe are protected. There are six classes of protected areas (Table 27.2) within the Parks and Wild Life Estate, comprising eleven national parks, fourteen botanical reserves, three botanical gardens, six sanctuaries, sixteen safari areas, and fifteen recreational parks. Figure 27.1 depicts these areas, and Tables 27.3–27.7 summarize their main characteristics and features. The criteria for classifying areas are based on types of permissible use, as defined by the Parks and Wild Life Act, and are further refined through park or area zonation. Together, the six classes of areas provide an integrated system of environmental biotic and abiotic protection for the enjoyment, education, inspiration, benefit, and recreation of the public.

Components of the Parks and Wild Life Estate

The purposes and permissible uses for which each of these protected areas has been set aside can be summarized as follows:

National Parks. Areas comprising large expanses of land, relatively untouched by human influence, and comprising diverse plant and animal communities. The primary objective is to preserve and protect the natural landscape and scenery and representative examples of all the major indigenous biotic communities that occur in Zimbabwe. National parks enjoy the highest conservation and protective status of any land in the country.

Botanical Reserves. Areas set aside to preserve and protect rare or endangered indigenous plants and/or plant communities growing naturally in the wild.

Botanical Gardens. Areas devoted to the propagation and cultivation of both indigenous and exotic plant species.

Sanctuaries. Areas set aside to afford special protection to all animals or particular species of animals that occur in unusual diversity, abundance, or rarity.

Safari Areas. Large protected areas with objectives similar to those of national parks but providing for outdoor recreational pursuits such as camping, hiking, sport hunting, fishing, photography, game viewing, and bird-watching.

Figure 27.1
The Parks and Wild Life Estate in Zimbabwe

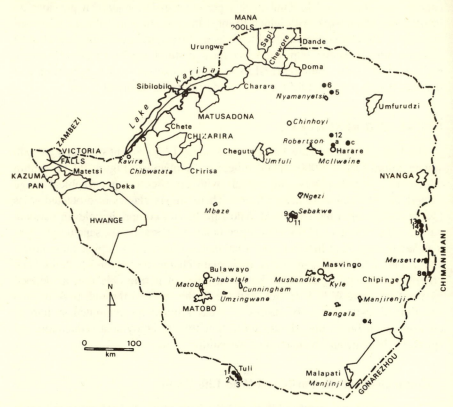

Note: National Parks, Sanctuaries, Safari Areas and Recreational
Parks are named as in Tables 27.3, 27.5, 27.6 and 27.7
respectively. Botanical Reserves are numbered 1 through 14 and
Botanical Gardens listed a through c as in Table 27.4.

Table 27.2
Components of the Parks and Wild Life Estate in Zimbabwe

PROTECTION STATUS	NUMBER	AREA (ha)	PROPORTION OF COUNTRY IN %
National Parks	11	2,703,960	6.9
Botanical Reserves	14	1,555	<0.1
Botanical Gardens	3	553	<0.1
Sanctuaries	6	18,620	<0.1
Safari Areas	16	1,897,300	4.9
Recreational Parks	15	357,085	<1.0
Total	65	4,979,173	12.7

Table 27.3
Main Characteristics of Zimbabwe's National Parks

NATIONAL PARK	AREA (ha)	NATURAL ATTRIBUTES								USE ZONING					VISITOR ACTIVITIES						DEVELOPMENT ACTIVITIES								
		Mountains	Scenery	Waterfalls	Important Catchments	Major Rivers	Lake Shore	Spectacular Wildlife	Historical Significance	Special Conservation Areas	Wilderness Areas	Wild Areas	Large Development Areas	Other Areas	Game Viewing by Car	Game Viewing on Foot	Game Viewing from Blinds	Driving - other	Hiking, Climbing, Walking	Angling	Major Administrative Center	Research Laboratory	Chalet Beds	Caravan Sites	Camp Sites	Hotel Beds	Exclusive Camps	Scheduled Air Service	Adjacent Hotel Beds
Chizarira	191,000	•	•		•			•			•	•	•		•	•			•		•	•			•		•		•
Gonarezhou	505,300	•	•					•			•	•	•		•	•			•		•	•			•		•		•
Matusadona	140,700		•		•	•					•	•	•		•	•			•		•	•			•				
Chimanimani	17,110	•	•								•	•	•						•		•	•							
Mana Pools	219,600					•		•					•		•	•			•		•	•			•		•		•
Kazuma Pan	31,300												•																
Hwange	1,465,100							•		•		•	•	•	•	•	•			•	•	•	•	•	•	•	•	•	•
Victoria Falls	2,340			•		•			•	•			•	•	•					•								•	•
Zambezi	56,010					•							•	•	•												•	•	•
Nyanga	33,000	•	•	•	•				•				•	•	•	•		•	•	•	•	•	•	•	•	•		•	•
Matobo	42,500	•	•		•			•	•				•	•	•	•		•	•	•	•	•	•	•	•	•	•	•	•

Source: G.F.T. Child, "Problems and Progress in Nature Conservation in Rhodesia," *Koedoe* Supplement (1977): 121.

503

Table 27.4
Botanical Reserves and Botanical Gardens in Zimbabwe

NAME	AREA (ha)	BOTANICAL IMPORTANCE AND SPECIAL FEATURES
Botanical Reserves		
1. Pioneer	38	Fuchsia tree, Schotia brachypetala
2. Tolo River	44	Monkey thorn tree, Acacia galpinii
3. South Camp	26	Nyala tree, Xanthocercis zambesiaca
4. Chisekera Hot Springs	95	Mangrove fern, Acrostichum aureum found nowhere else in Zimbabwe
5. Mwari Raffia Palm	34	Raffia palm, Raffia farinifera
6. Tingwa Raffia Palm	290	As above
7. Haroni	20	Rare, low altitude evergreen forest
8. Rusitu Forest	150	Evergreen forest species Rhino arborea and Coffea salvatrix found nowhere else in Zimbabwe
9. Sebakwe Acacia Karroo	60	Acacia karroo
10. Sebakwe Great Dike	165	Serpentine flora of the southern Great Dike, a geological anomaly
11. Sebakwe Mountain Acacia	53	Mountain "acacia" Brachystegia glaucescens
12. Mazowe A and B	46	Complete example of a Brachystegia woodland catena
13. Bunga Forest	495	Only example in Zimbabwe of medium altitude evergreen forest
14. Vumba	42	Medium altitude forest
Total	1,558	
Botanical Gardens		
a. National Botanic	67	Developed gardens of representative indigenous and exotic communities and National Herbarium
b. Vumba	200	Developed gardens with areas of natural forest
c. Ewanrigg	286	Developed gardens specializing in aloes and cycads
Total	553	

Recreational Parks. Areas within which the natural features are preserved and protected but which also have the potential for a wide range of outdoor recreational activities. They are often situated in close proximity to urban centers and include features such as large dams or lakes.

Zonation within Protected Areas

Protected areas in Zimbabwe may be divided into four types of zones:

Special Conservation Areas. These include biological reserves, refuges, witness stands, or areas reserved for research, where access is limited to that needed for scientific purposes.

Wilderness Areas. These are areas of such a size as to contain, as far as possible, the complete flora and fauna of that part of the protected area in which

Table 27.5
Sanctuaries in Zimbabwe

SANCTUARY	AREA (ha)	MAIN ATTRIBUTES
Manjinji	300	Bird (waterfowl) sanctuary on ox-bow lake in alluvial woodland
Melsetter Eland	1,800	Relict eland population, catchment protection, waterfalls
Mbaze Pan	40	Bird (waterfowl) sanctuary on ox-bow lake in alluvial woodland
Nyamanyetsi	2,480	Ungulate grazing research
Mushandike	12,900	Ungulate grazing research, natural resources training college
Tshabalala	1,100	Bird sanctuary
Total	18,620	

they are situated. Most are relatively large areas with minimal development. The public is permitted in low numbers, but visitors have considerable freedom of action.

Wild Areas. These are similar to wilderness areas but are serviced by roads, with designated stopping places, rustic buildings, camps, and viewing platforms, allowing reasonable public access. A greater density of visitors is permitted, but more restrictions are imposed than in wilderness areas.

Development Areas. These are established to provide administrative and research facilities, staff accommodation, and visitor amenities. Such areas are ideally situated at the extremities of the protected area so as not to encroach upon the wild and wilderness qualities of other zones.

World Heritage Status

Two protected areas in Zimbabwe qualify for consideration as natural World Heritage Sites and have been nominated for elevation to this status.

The first area encompasses Victoria Falls and the Zambezi River gorges immediately below these falls. This site is shared between Zimbabwe and Zambia, each with its own protected area, Victoria Falls and Mosi oa Tunya national parks respectively. The Victoria Falls are the largest and among the most beautiful waterfalls in the world. Here the Zambezi River plunges into a vertical chasm 100 meters (330 feet) deep before continuing through a series of rugged, spectacular gorges. Approximately 150 million years old, the Victoria Falls were first described to the Western world in 1855 by the missionary-explorer David Livingstone, reputedly the first European to see them.

The second area encompasses Mana Pools National Park and neighboring areas in the unflooded middle Zambezi Valley. This site is the foremost wildlife attraction in Zimbabwe with a unique and aesthetic combination of spectacular large mammals, escarpment, valley, and riparian woodlands and frontage on the Zambezi River. It is one of only two areas situated on a major African river that enjoy national park status.

Table 27.6
Safari Areas in Zimbabwe

SAFARI AREA	AREA (ha)	PRESENT USE AND FUTURE PLANS
Tuli	41,600	Hunting sold on individual tender basis to foreign and local participants
Chete	108,100	Long-term university research; hunting leased to safari company
Chipinge	26,100	Requires re-stocking for plains game hunting and other recreational opportunities
Malapati	15,400	Game-viewing wilderness area
Chirisa	171,300	Long-term wildlife research; hunting leased to safari company; requires zonation, protein production
Chegutu	44,500	Requires restocking for plains game hunting and other recreational opportunities
Sibilobilo	5,400	Large islands on Lake Kariba; require development for recreational opportunities
Charara	169,200	Hunting leased to safari companies; requires development for other recreational opportunities
Urungwe	289,400	Hunting sold on tender or auction or leased; Zambezi River frontage requires development
Doma	94,500	Hunting leased to Zimbabwean hunters association
Umfurudzi	76,000	Requires restocking for plains game hunting and other recreational opportunities
Dande	52,300	Hunting leased to safari company; requires development for protein production
Chewore	339,000	Hunting leased to safari companies; proposed elevation to national park
Sapi	118,000	Hunting sold on tender or auction; proposed elevation to national park
Deka	51,000	Limited hunting; presently leased to safari companies
Matetsi	295,000	Hunting concessions on lease to resident safari companies; proposed elevation to national park
Total	1,897,300	

Consideration may also be given to including Lake Kariba in this site. Harnessed in 1958 by a dam at Kariba Gorge to provide hydroelectric power, the Zambezi River rose to fill the Zambezi Valley along 300 kilometers (185 miles) of its length. The famous Operation Noah was internationally acclaimed when a handful of rangers headed by Rupert Fothergill rescued some 5,000 animals stranded on islands by the rising waters of the newly created Lake Kariba. Today, Matusadona National Park and the Charara and Chete safari areas are protected areas along the lakeshore. The Sibilobilo group of islands constitute a third safari area, and Lake Kariba itself is a recreational park.

Table 27.7
Recreational Parks in Zimbabwe

RECREATIONAL PARK	AREA (HA)	MAIN FEATURES AND VISITOR ACTIVITIES
Chibwatata Hot Springs	10	Geothermal springs for recreational use; rest camp nearby
Lake Kariba	287,200	Very large water body; sport angling and commercial fishing; game viewing, water sports, major tourist destination
Kavira Hot Springs	50	Geothermal springs; undeveloped
Ngezi	5,800	Medium-sized dam on Great Dike; some wildlife; quiet outdoor recreation
Umfuli	12,700	Rugged country on Umfuli River; highly suited to outdoor recreation; undeveloped
Lake Cunningham	4,172	Large dam with good recreational potential; undeveloped
Lake Robertson	11,200	As above, but with some minor recreational development
Chinhoyi Caves	120	Dolomite caves with very deep pools; campsite facilities
Manjirenji	3,400	Large dam with good recreational potential but so far undeveloped
Bangala	2,700	As above
Sebakwe	2,600	Medium sized dam on Great Dike especially suited to sailing; some angling and research
Robert McIlwaine	6,100	Large dam near Harare; adjacent game park; water sports; commercial fishing, ornithological research
Umzingwane	1,233	Medium sized dam near Bulawayo; some boating and angling; requires development
Kyle	16,900	Attractive dam, adjacent game park, water sports; commercial fishing; ungulate grazing research
Lake Matobo	2,900	Part of larger "Matobo complex," historic value; Boy Scout Movement; outdoor recreation
Total	357,085	

Ecosystem Conservation

In southern Africa, as indeed probably elsewhere on the continent, the most inadequately conserved biomes are those in which large and spectacular ungulate and carnivore species are absent or rare. The opposite is true of those systems for which vast areas have been set aside for conservation, and it is clear that community representation has rarely been an important reason for declaring protected areas. This situation reflects traditional concepts of wildlife conservation versus the current need to maintain biotic diversity and ecological processes. There is also an urgent requirement for protected areas to become an integral component of sustainable rural development, while continuing to provide

Figure 27.2
Relationship of Conserved Area to Total Area for Each of 25 Vegetation Types Occurring in Zimbabwe

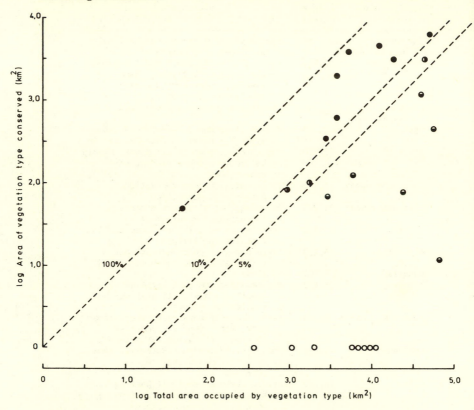

Note: Open circles represent vegetation types unrepresented in the conservation system. Half closed circles divided horizontally indicate that less than 5% of the area in which a type occurs is conserved. Half closed circles divided vertically indicate that 5 to 10% of the area in which a type occurs is conserved. Closed circles indicate that 10 to 100% of the area in which a type occurs is conserved. Logarithmic scales are used on each axis.

outdoor recreation and tourist destinations. To be effective in this regard, the protected area system of a country should provide adequate coverage so as to conserve representative samples of natural biomes and ecosystems.

Although the protected area coverage of 12.7 percent of Zimbabwe's land surface exceeds the 10 percent recommended internationally, there are clear disparities in the coverage extended to the twenty-five presently recognized main vegetation types or plant communities in the country. Figure 27.2 shows that seventeen of the twenty-five types occur within the national parks system. Two of the seventeen remain in doubt and require verification. An additional two types occur outside the national parks but within the Parks and Wild Life Estate as a whole. Eight community types have 10 percent or more of their total area protected within national parks. A further eleven types have between 5 and 10 percent of their area protected. Of the remaining fourteen types, eight are not protected within the national park system and six not at all.

The present vegetation classification of Zimbabwe is too broad, and a more refined survey and classification of the country's plant communities are urgently needed. This should be followed by a critical examination of the protection currently afforded to each community type. The highest priority for conservation should be assigned to plant communities that are least protected and most threatened.

The question of allocating conservation priorities to biotic communities is controversial. Because of subjective value judgments associated with representative sampling of community types, it has been suggested that emphasis should be placed on the selection of specific examples or areas for conservation priority. Within a broad representative framework, selection should be first, on the basis of rare, endemic, or threatened species, and second, on the basis of aesthetic values of community or landscape. This approach has recently become a focus for attention in Zimbabwe.

Threatened Species and Communities

The legal responsibilities to conserve all indigenous flora and fauna, as well as representatives of all biotic communities in Zimbabwe, are clearly established in terms of the Parks and Wild Life Act. Most large mammals whose continuous existence in Zimbabwe is at all tenuous are specially protected. The present list of nine species includes black rhinoceros (*Diceros bicornis*) and cheetah (*Acinonyx jubatus*), which are classified as vulnerable under the *IUCN Red Data Book*. Two other species listed as vulnerable by The International Union for the Conservation of Nature, leopard (*Panthera pardus*) and elephant (*Loxodonta africana*), are not threatened in Zimbabwe. The brown hyena (*Hyena brunnea*) and the wild dog (*Lycaon pictus*), which is probably the most endangered large mammal in the country, are listed as vulnerable by IUCN but receive no legal protection in Zimbabwe. Wild dogs range over large tracts of land and are not tolerated in stock-producing areas. Coupled with an early belief that their destruction would aid in the conservation of other species, this intolerance has reduced wild dog numbers drastically throughout the country.

The plight of the rhinoceros throughout its range is widely known and well documented. Zimbabwe has the last significant population of black rhinoceros surviving in the wild on the African continent, and this population has recently come under attack by international poaching gangs. An integrated and broad-based strategy that includes a field force of armed antipoaching units is currently being developed to combat this emergency.

The status of smaller mammals, some birds, and the amphibians and reptiles is not well established. However, one reptile, the python (*Python sebae*), and forty-three birds, including all the bustards, korhaans, cranes, flamingos, pelicans, storks, and vultures, are specially protected. The status of the country's invertebrate fauna is largely unknown, and this responsibility has been neglected to date.

A number of indigenous plants are specially protected and a tentative list of endangered, vulnerable, and rare species has been produced. The list includes eight threatened endemics, of which only four are legally protected. Many of the protected plants are uncommon, and their demand by plant dealers and collectors leads to the exploitation of wild populations. Aloes, orchids, and cycads are important examples.

Many plant species can be effectively protected only through protection of wild populations and their habitats. The provision of botanical reserves does meet this need for some species (Table 27.4). Of the fourteen botanical reserves in the country, six are within the Parks and Wild Life Estate. Three of the remaining eight protect particular species (Raffia palm and mangrove fern), and five protect particular plant communities, mainly evergreen forest.

Although the Parks and Wild Life Estate, and particularly national parks, provide for the conservation of many plant communities, in a number of cases these communities are under stress or are threatened by large herbivore populations and uncontrolled wildfires. For example, *Brachystegia* woodland communities in the Zambezi escarpment suffer from both the depredations of elephants and the effects of hot late season fires. Of equal or greater concern are those plant communities that have no legal basis for their protection. The protection of representative examples is of considerable urgency in the face of increasing human populations and diminishing resources.

ADMINISTRATION

Responsibilities and Objectives

The Department of National Parks and Wild Life Management is within the Ministry of Natural Resources and Tourism and derives its authority from several legal instruments, of which the Parks and Wild Life Act is the most important. The department is a scientifically based and ecologically oriented land-use agency with a specific responsibility, on behalf of the people of Zimbabwe, to ensure the proper conservation and use of the nation's wildlife resources. This includes administration and management of the Parks and Wild Life Estate and the servicing of the resource outside the estate.

The objectives of the department include the protection of landscape and scenery of special quality and the conservation of representative examples of natural ecosystems, biotic communities, and all organisms indigenous to Zimbabwe; the conservation and management of natural and seminatural areas for a range of outdoor recreational pursuits; and the conservation and appropriate use of Zimbabwe's wildlife resources for the long-term benefit, enjoyment, and inspiration of Zimbabweans and visitors to this country.

Departmental responsibilities and objectives are accomplished by

1. Protecting and managing the Parks and Wild Life Estate, which consists of all national parks, botanical reserves, botanical gardens, sanctuaries, safari areas, and recreational parks.

2. Research and development of appropriate management practices inside the estate.

3. Research, development, and encouragement of appropriate uses of the wildlife resource outside the estate for the benefit of rural landholders.

4. Promoting public awareness in all sectors of society as to the value of the Parks and Wild Life Estate and the wildlife resources of the country as a whole.

5. Providing the administrative machinery, including the training and development of staff, to support these functions.

6. Encouraging a rationalized and appropriate industry based on the wildlife resources of the country.

Administrative and Management Framework

The director of the department, his deputy, and three assistant directors—for administration, management, and research respectively—constitute the directorate. Three chief ecologists head branches of Terrestrial Ecology, Aquatic Ecology, and Interpretation, Training and Extension. The directorate advises the director on policy and major decisions, while the senior staff of the department, comprising the directorate, chief ecologists, and all provincial wardens and officers of equivalent authority, provide coordination within the overall structure of the department. Each branch has its own subsidiary commitment analysis supported by position charters indicating the responsibilities, authority, and accountability of the various posts.

In recognizing six classes of protected areas composing the Parks and Wild Life Estate, the Parks and Wild Life Act and the regulations flowing from it give a clear indication as to how each should be administered, managed, developed, and used. This direction is further refined by area policy documents, approved by the minister on the recommendation of the Parks and Wild Life Board, which interprets how the legislation is to be applied in each area. The administrative framework (Figure 27.3) that gives force to the act comprises essentially the minister, the Parks and Wild Life Board, and the director of the Department of National Parks and Wild Life Management. The key administrative devices include the following.

Policy Documents. A draft policy document is prepared for each protected area (or departmental function). This is debated by the Parks and Wild Life Board before submission to the minister for approval. Once approved, the policy document represents a ministerial directive to staff as to how the broad provisions

Figure 27.3
Legal and Administrative Framework for Wildlife Conservation in Zimbabwe

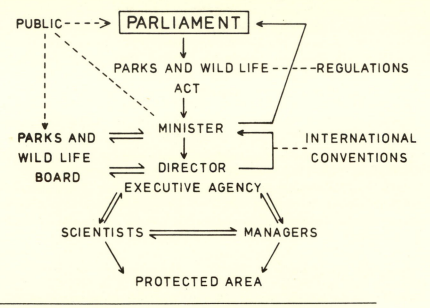

Source: D.H.M. Cumming, "The Decision-making Framework with
    Regard to the Culling of Large Mammals in Zimbabwe," in R.N.
    Owen-Smith (ed.), Management of Large Mammals in African
    Conservation Areas (Pretoria: Haum, 1983), p. 179.

of the act should be interpreted in each area. The policy document provides the
basis for long-term management, administrative, and development plans. Once
signed by the minister, it can be amended only by the same formal process.

Parks Plans. A park plan is developed from the policy document, again with
the close involvement of the Parks and Wild Life Board. Input to a planning
committee comes from provincial management and research staff of the department, under the chairmanship of the deputy director. Collation and preparation
of the park plan, which generally includes an explicit and detailed management
plan for the protected area in question, is undertaken by an ecologist specifically
appointed to the task.

Park plans are more flexible than the parent policy documents and can be
altered according to a defined procedure. In this way, the authority of Parliament
is decentralized, by formalized stages, to the park warden, who enjoys considerable autonomy within prescribed limits. This avoids the need for constant
referral to higher authority while preserving continuity of effort through time
and changes in personnel.

The Management Committee. Annually a committee—comprising members
of the directorate, chief warden, chief ecologist, and other staff members by

invitation—examines the recommendations for population reduction, capture, and translocation of large mammals. These recommendations are submitted either jointly or separately by management and research staff based in field stations. Recommendations are examined in relation to policy, evidence for overpopulation, and the resources available to carry out the tasks. Occasionally, when a contentious issue arises, the committee's deliberations may be extended to include a seminar or workshop with wider participation. This may or may not involve the presentation of formal papers.

Management Activities

In a national park the conservation of biological communities is defined by specified permissible limits to change with respect to soils, plants, and animals. As far as possible within these limits, the national park serves as a control or baseline area where interference with ecological processes should be minimal. However, it is accepted that it may be necessary to manage systems that show signs of imbalance. In the context of Africa, large herbivores, especially elephants, are capable of radical habitat modification, and their numbers may require periodic reduction in keeping within the specified limits to change. Although specific actions may be debatable, population reduction is often the only responsible course. Indeed, it is mandated by provisions of the Parks and Wild Life Act.

If a protected area is to be part of the region in which it occurs, management and development within the park may have to adjust to take into account constraints and requirements of the region it serves. In Zimbabwe, it has been accepted that protected areas cannot be isolated from their surrounding areas. Where human population densities around parks are low, a gradation of land uses involving buffer zones has been encouraged. Although managers subscribe to the principle of no exploitation in national parks, wildlife resources on the periphery of the protected area are subjected to a range of management treatments. These include safari hunting, sustained-yield cropping, and problem animal control where large mammals become incompatible with agricultural or pastoral activity.

Public Uses and Benefits

The maximum levels of development and visitor usage within a protected area or part thereof are laid down in policy. Recreational parks cater to relatively high numbers of visitors and thereby act as both an inducement for people to go to areas of higher quality and as a safeguard against the overuse and abuse of the latter. Consumptive uses such as recreational sport hunting or commercial fishing are strictly controlled and limited to certain classes of protected areas such as safari areas or recreational parks.

Although overt action in a park is determined purely by ecological considerations, products such as hides, meat, and trophies are sold on the open market to raise revenue or to local communities at a subsidized price in the interests of returning tangible benefits to these communities and softening the hard edge around the protected area. Benefits from management programs adjacent to protected areas and elsewhere are also returned to local inhabitants, who are being encouraged increasingly to participate in such programs.

Conclusion

In Zimbabwe, the wildlife management authority has set pragmatic goals that are both necessary and attainable under the prevailing circumstances and with the resources available to it. Although there is a level of ambiguity contained in the legal definitions of the country's protected areas, clear policy guidelines, based on the Parks and Wild Life Board's interpretation of the act, provide for long-term changes of substance, but help to avoid inappropriate, and perhaps irreversible, short-term decisions.

A full range of political, aesthetic, practical, and scientific interests within the Department of National Parks and Wild Life Management and the Ministry of Natural Resources and Tourism are involved in the administration and management of the wildlife resource. Consequently, decisions relating to such matters involve judgments based on sound technical information and aesthetic considerations. The Parks and Wild Life Board has clearly defined responsibilities to advise the minister on policy and to work closely with the director of the department on the generation and implementation of policy. Within the department, the administrative and decision-making framework has promoted effective links between scientific and management branches, facilitating the interplay of ideas between the two and open discussion of policy issues among the director, the Parks and Wild Life Board, and the minister.

BIBLIOGRAPHY

Child, G.F.T. "Problems and Progress in Nature Conservation in Zimbabwe." *Koedoe* Supplement (1977): 116–37.
————. "Protected Area Management in Zimbabwe." *Zimbabwe Science News* 17 (1983): 30–31.
Childes, S. L. "Wild Dogs: Victims of Ignorance." *Zimbabwe Wildlife* 41 (1985): 13–15.
Clarks, J. E., and R. H. V. Bell. "Representation of Biotic Communities in Protected Areas: A Malawian Case Study." *Biological Conservation* 35 (1986): 293-311.
Cockbill, G. F. "The History and Significance of Trypanosomiasis Problems in Rhodesia." *Proceedings and Transactions of the Rhodesia Scientific Association* 52 (1967): 7-15.
Cumming, D. H. M. "The Status of Threatened Large Mammal Species and of Plant Communities in Zimbabwe." Unpublished report to the Parks and Wild Life

Board. Branch of Terrestrial Ecology, Department of National Parks and Wild Life Management, Zimbabwe, January 1980.

———. "National Parks and Zimbabwe: Ideals, Concepts and Principles for the 1980's." Unpublished report to the Parks and Wild Life Board, Branch of Terrestrial Ecology, Department of National Parks and Wild Life Management, Zimbabwe, May 1981.

Dasmann, R. F. *African Game Ranching*. The Commonwealth and International Library of Science, Technology, Engineering and Liberal Studies. New York: Macmillan, 1964.

IUCN. *Proceedings of the Twenty-Second Working Session, Commission on National Parks and Protected Areas, Victoria Falls, Zimbabwe, 22–27 May 1983*. Gland, Switzerland: IUCN, 1984.

McNeely, J. A., and K. R. Miller, eds. *National Parks, Conservation and Development: The Role of Protected Areas in Sustaining Society*. Proceedings of the World Congress on National Parks, Bali, Indonesia, October 11-22, 1982. Washington, D.C.: Smithsonian Institution Press, 1984.

Owen-Smith, R. N., ed. *Management of Large Mammals in African Conservation Areas*. Pretoria: Haum, 1983.

Thomson, P. J. "The Role of Elephants, Fire and Other Agents in the Decline of a *Brachystegia boehmii* Woodland." *Journal of the Southern African Wildlife Management Association* 5 (1975): 11-18.

Tomlinson, D. N. S. "Nature Conservation in Rhodesia: A Review." *Biological Conservation* 18 (1980): 159-77.

Wild, H., and L. A. Grandvaux Barbosa. *Vegetation Map of the Flora Zambesiaca Area*. Salisbury: Collins, 1967.

Wild, H., and A. Fernandes, eds. *Vegetation Map of the Flora Zambesiaca Area, Supplement*. Salisbury: Collins, 1967.

INDEX

Page numbers set in **boldface** indicate the location of the main entry.

ABOUT THE EDITOR
AND CONTRIBUTORS

CRAIG W. ALLIN earned the B.A. degree at Grinnell College and the M.A. and Ph.D. at Princeton University. He is author of *The Politics of Wilderness Preservation* (1982) as well as articles on wilderness preservation and public lands management. He is presently Professor of Political Science at Cornell College, Mt. Vernon, Iowa.

HANS BIBELRIETHER was born in 1933 in Ezelheim, Germany, and was graduated as a forester. He has been responsible for the establishment and development of the first German National Park from the beginning and is today superintendent of the National Park Administration. He is General Secretary of the Federation of Nature and National Parks of Europe and a member of the IUCN Commission on National Parks and Protected Areas. He is the author of numerous articles and books on forest and nature conservation.

SUSAN CALAFATE BOYLE was born in Argentina. She earned her B.A. from the University of New Mexico, M.A. from the University of Arizona, and her Ph.D. from the University of Missouri, Columbia. She publishes in American social history and is with the Department of History at Colorado State University.

TERENCE P. BOYLE earned his B.S. and M.S. from the University of New Mexico and a Ph.D. in biological sciences from the University of Arizona. He has edited two books and written numerous articles in environmental sciences. He is a research ecologist with the National Park Service at Colorado State University, Fort Collins, Colorado.

G. WESLEY BURNETT is Professor of Recreation Resource Management at Clemson University, South Carolina. A geographer educated at Southern Methodist University and Oklahoma University, he is formerly Senior Lecturer and Chairman, Department of Geography, Kenyatta University, Nairobi. His research concerns the role of national parks in Third World development programs.

JAIME BUSTILLO-PON earned the Agronomist Degree at the Pan-American Agricultural School at El Zamorano, the B.S. in agriculture at Stephen F. Austin State University in Nacogdoches, Texas, and the M.S. in agronomy at the University of Florida, Gainesville. In Honduras he has worked with the National Planning Office, in the agricultural, forestry, and environment sectors. Until August 1986 he was the Executive Director of La Asociación Hondureña de Ecologia (Honduran Ecological Association), in Tegucigalpa, Honduras, a non-governmental, nonprofit environmental organization.

LUNG-SHENG CHANG earned the B.E degree at Cheng-Kung University and the M.C.P. degree at the University of Pennsylvania. He is author of *Major Issues in New Community Development in Taiwan*, published in 1973, as well as articles on wilderness preservation and national parks management. He is presently Director-General of the Construction and Planning Administration, Ministry of Interior.

JESÚS M. DELGADO was graduated as Agricultural Engineer in Brazil and earned the M.Sc. degree in Resource Policy and Planning at Cornell University in 1981. In the last six years he has worked as Assistant Professor of Park Management and Planning at the Universidad de los Llanos in Venezuela. Presently, he is studying the economic impacts of national parks in Brazil and Venezuela.

PATRICK J. DEVLIN is Senior Lecturer in Parks, Recreation and Tourism at Lincoln University College, Canterbury, New Zealand. His teaching and research interests are in resource management, visitor behavior, and park interpretation.

PAUL R. DINGWALL is a geomorphologist for the New Zealand Department of Conservation. He is a Vice-Chairman of the IUCN's Commission on National Parks and Protected Areas and Chairman of the New Zealand Committee for Unesco's Man and the Biosphere Program.

MARC J. DOUROJEANNI earned a degree in agronomy and forestry from the Universidad Nacional Agraria in Lima, Peru, and a doctorate in agricultural science from the Faculty of Agronomic Sciences of Gembloux, Belgium. Since 1964 Dr. Dourojeanni has served on the Forestry Faculty of the Universidad Nacional Agraria. He is the author of six books, including *The National Parks of Peru*, and some 200 scientific and technical papers. From 1973 to 1979 he was Peru's Director General of Forestry and Wildlife with responsibilities that included national parks and protected areas. He has held a variety of leadership positions with the IUCN and other international organizations and presently serves as Senior Environmental Officer for the World Bank.

ANDRÉ R. DUPUY, after graduating in Zoology in France, has devoted his entire lifetime to the creation and management of Game Reserves and National Parks in North and Northwest Africa. From 1967 to 1987 he served as Director of National Parks in Senegal and is now attached to the National Parks Administration of France.

PETER EATON has B.Sc. (Econ.) and M.Sc. (Econ.) degrees in Geography from London University and a Ph.D. from the Center for South East Asian Studies at Hull University. He worked for ten years in Sarawak, East Malaysia, and for twelve years in Papua New Guinea, where he was Associate Professor and Coordinator of Land Studies at at the University of Papua New Guinea. He is the author of a number of books, reports, and articles on rural development, land tenure, and conservation. His current appointment is to the Department of Public Policy and Administration, University of Brunei Darussalam.

HAROLD K. EIDSVIK, a native of British Columbia, is a forestry graduate of the University of British Columbia and holds an M.F. from the University of Michigan, where he is currently an Adjunct Professor in the School of Natural Resources. As Senior Policy Adviser to the Canadian Parks Service, he is also responsible for international conservation affairs. As chairman of the IUCN's Commission on National Parks and Protected Areas, he has visited and worked with park officials and nongovernmental organizations in more than sixty countries.

MICHAEL FROME is an environmental author and journalist and professor at Huxley College of Environmental Studies, Western Washington University.

OLAV GJÆREVOLL, D.Sc., is Professor of Botany at the University of Trondheim, Norway. He has been chairman of the National Council for Nature Conservation since 1961, is active in politics, and has been Lord Mayor of Trondheim, member of the *Storting* (Parliament), Minister of Social Affairs, and the first Minister of Environment in Norway.

BRYNMOR HUGH GREEN has B.Sc. and Ph.D. degrees in botany and plant ecology from the University of Nottingham. He has worked for the Nature Conservancy and served on councils of both state and voluntary conservation bodies. He is presently the Sir Cyril Kleinwort Professor of Countryside Management in the University of London at Wye College, Ashford, Kent.

WILLIAM D. HENWOOD earned the M.S. in resource planning from the University of Guelph in Ontario. He has been involved in parks planning in

Canada since 1974. Following a two-year study tour of national parks around the world, he has held positions as senior planner for marine parks and as policy analyst for the Canadian Parks Service. He is presently based in Vancouver, B.C., as the management planner for South Moresby National Park Reserve.

NORIYUKI ITO earned the B.A. in zoology, the B.A. and the M.A. in landscape architecture at Tokyo University. He has served as Deputy-Director of the Natural Parks Planning Division, Nature Conservation Bureau, Japan Environment Agency. He is presently Chief Researcher, Environmental Biology Division, National Institute for Environmental Studies, Japan Environment Agency.

SUSAN KAY JACOBSON earned the B.A. in biology from Brown University, the M.S. in zoology from the University of Florida, and the Ph.D. in forestry and environmental studies from Duke University. She has conducted research on parks and wildlife in East Africa, Costa Rica, and Malaysia. She is the author of a number of guidebooks and magazine and journal articles about national parks and environmental education in developing countries. She serves as research scientist in the Department of Wildlife and Range Sciences at the University of Florida, where she is coordinator of the Program for Studies in Tropical Conservation.

KOSTAS KASSIOUMIS earned a Diploma in Forestry from the University of Thessaloniki in Greece and a Ph.D. in planning forests and protected areas for recreation at Reading University in England. He is the head of the Section for the Forest Environment, National Parks, Forest Recreation, the governmental body with central responsibility for parks and recreation areas in Greece under the Forest Service of the Ministry of Agriculture.

FREDERICK I. B. KAYANJA earned the B.Sc., B. Vet. Med., and M.Sc. degrees at the University of London and the Ph.D. from the University of East Africa. He holds the MRCVS (U.K.). He has been Chairman of the Board of Trustees of Uganda National Parks since 1980. He is a Trustee of the East African Wildlife Society, Editor of the *African Journal of Ecology*, and Vice Chancellor of Mbarara University, Uganda.

P.H.C. "BING" LUCAS was formerly Director of National Parks and Reserves and later Director-General of Lands for New Zealand. He is now a conservation consultant and senior adviser to the IUCN's Commission on National Parks and Protected Areas.

J. GEOFFREY MOSLEY earned the B.A. (Hons.) and M.A. degrees at the University of Nottingham and the Ph.D. in geography at the Australian National University. He served as director of the Australian Conservation Foundation 1973 to 1986 and is the author of several books on conservation. He was a member of the IUCN Council from 1981 to 1988. Currently he is an evironmental consultant.

HELIODORO SÁNCHEZ PÁEZ earned the Forestry Engineer degree at the Universidad Distrital Francisco José de Caldas, Bogotá, Colombia, in 1966. He is coauthor of *Colombia Parques Nacionales* (1984), and author of several articles, reports, and plans about national parks and conservation in Colombia. He worked in national park management from 1968 to 1985 and has served as chief of the National Parks Division. He is presently a professional research specialist with INDERENA and serves on the editorial committee of its scientific research journal. He also serves as professor of soil conservation and national parks and wildlife at the Forestry School, Universidad Distrital Francisco José de Caldas.

PAUL C. PRITCHARD is president of the National Parks and Conservation Association, Washington, D.C.

LESLIE M. REID earned the B.S. degree in forestry at Michigan Technological University, the M.S. in park administration at Michigan State University, and the Ph.D. degree in conservation at the University of Michigan. He has served on national park and conservation boards, authored numerous publications on park administration and development, and has consulted on and studied national parks and tourism in over twenty countries. He served as head of the Department of Recreation and Parks at Texas A&M University (1965–1985), and presently is senior professor in that department.

ALAN H. ROBINSON is a national parks, conservation, and tourism planner with graduate education in zoology, marine biology, and oceanography. He is a long-term employee of United States National Park Service with assignments in the Virgin Islands, Florida, the western United States, and Alaska. He has authored park management plans and new area studies and advised internationally on marine parks and conservation. From 1979 to 1982 he led the Indonesia/FAO National Parks Project unit dealing with East Java, Bali, and the Lesser Sunda Islands.

W. A. RODGERS earned his B.Sc. and Ph.D. degrees at the University of Nairobi, Kenya, and his M.Sc. at the University of Aberdeen in Scotland. He served as a wildlife warden and biologist in the Tanzania Wildlife Division from 1965 to 1976 and then started a subdepartment of wildlife in the University of Dar-es-Salaam in Tanzania. In 1984 he joined the United Nations project at the Wildlife Institute of India, Dehra Dun.

HARALD H. ROTH earned doctoral degrees in both Veterinary and Biological Sciences at German universities. He has served as Assistant Director of National

Parks in Rhodesia, as Wildlife Officer of the FAO in Rome, as an ecological and wildlife consultant, and as National Parks Advisor to the Government of the Ivory Coast. Presently he is seconded to the Southern African Development Coordination Conference, based in Malaŵi, where he serves as Coordinator of Forestry, Fisheries and Wildlife. In 1968 he was appointed Honorary Professor of the Giessen University in Germany and has since published numerous scientific articles on wildlife conservation in Africa.

SAMAR SINGH joined the Indian Administrative Service in 1962. He has had intensive field experience and served as Secretary of the State Forest Department in Madhya Pradesh. Since 1980, he has served the Government of India as Joint Secretary in charge of Forests and Wildlife, Director of Wildlife Preservation, and Member Secretary of the Indian Board for Wildlife, which is headed by the Prime Minister. He is presently with the Ministry of Environment and Forests. He has also held international positions as Chairman of the CITES Standing Committee, IUCN Regional Councilor for East Asia, Vice-Chairman of IUCN's Commission for National Parks and Protected Areas for the Indo-Malayan Realm, and Whaling Commissioner for India. He is the author of *Conserving India's Natural Heritage* and the recipient of the Order of the Golden Ark.

GEORGE H. STANKEY received his B.S. and M.S. degrees at Oregon State University and his Ph.D. at Michigan State University, all in geography. He is a coauthor of *Wilderness Management*, published in 1978, and has written numerous articles on wilderness use and users. From 1968 to 1987 he served as Research Social Scientist in the Wilderness Management Research Unit at the U.S. Forest Service's Intermountain Research Station, Missoula, Montana. From 1987 to 1989 he served on a split appointment as a Social Science Consultant with the New South Wales National Parks and Wildlife Service and as a Visiting Principal Fellow in the Department of Leisure Studies, Kuring-gai College of Advanced Education in Sydney, Australia. He is presently affiliated with the College of Forestry at Oregon State University.

JACOBUS N. STEYN earned the B.A., M.A., and D.Phil. degrees in geography at the University of Stellenbosch, Republic of South Africa, and engaged in postdoctoral research at York University (Ontario, Canada) and at Texas A&M. He has authored 12 books, numerous journal articles, and government reports, and prepared portions of the Natural Outdoor Recreation Plan for South Africa. He served as Chairman of the Department of Geography at Pretoria University and presently is Vice-Rector, Cape Technikon, Cape Province, R.S.A.

EFFENDY A. SUMARDJA earned the doctorate in biology at Padjadjaran University, Bandung, Indonesia, and the M.Sc. in natural resources at the University of Michigan, Ann Arbor, Michigan. He has written many articles on nature conservation with particular reference to parks and wildlife in Indonesia. He is presently Subdirector of Conservation Education of the Indonesian Directorate of National Parks and Recreation Forests in the Directorate General of Forest Protection and Nature Conservation, Ministry of Forestry.

RUSSELL D. TAYLOR was born in Zimbabwe and holds the B.Sc. (Agri-culture), M.Sc., and D.Phil. degrees. He was first employed in 1971 as an agricultural extension officer before joining the Department of National Parks and Wild Life Management as a wildlife ecologist. For fourteen years he was based in Matusadona National Park on the southern shores of Lake Kariba, where he was engaged in applied research, park management, and land-use planning. He is presently with the Multispecies Animal Production Systems Project of the World Wide Fund for Nature in Harare, Zimbabwe.

SHIN WANG earned the Ph.D. degree in geology at Columbia University. He is author of *The Landform of Taiwan*, published in 1980, as well as articles on geomorphology and environmental conservation. He is presently professor of physical geography and remote sensing at National Taiwan University in Taipei.

ROLAND H. WAUER is recently retired from the National Park Service, where he served as a resource specialist, most recently at the Cooperative Extension Service, College of the Virgin Islands.

CARLOS A. WEBER is projects manager for the Chilean Forest Service's Protected Wildlands Program and also a professor of wildland management at the School of Forestry, University of Chile. He holds the degrees of Bachelor of Forest Engineering from the University of Chile and M.Sc. in Environmental Science from the State University of New York.

YURY YAZAN, doctor of biological science and professor of ecology, is the author of more than 200 publications on issues of population management of big animals, theory of protected areas, and criteria for selection of natural areas for different protective regimes. Since 1983 he has been Director of the All-Union Research Institute of Nature Conservation and Reserves, State Committee for Nature Conservation, and since 1984 Vice-President of the IUCN.